To Robert M. Nelson

from Elizabeth 201·

CW00799152

HISTORY OF
THE SECOND WORLD WAR
UNITED KINGDOM MILITARY SERIES
Edited by J. R. M. Butler

The authors of the Military Histories have been given full access to official documents. They and the editor are alone responsible for the statements made and the views expressed.

THE WAR AGAINST JAPAN

Volume I

CORRECTIONS

Page 1, line 2:
Delete 'despite the opposition of the Army which was largely pro-German'.

Page 1, line 4:
After 'conformity with' insert 'the general spirit of'.

Page 1, line 7:
After 'China' insert 'proper'.

Page 2, line 3:
After 'her' insert 'Shantung'.

Page 9, para. 4, last two lines:
Delete 'who thereupon resigned'.

Page 9, line 2 from bottom:
For 'would support' read 'supported'.

Page 10, para. 2, line 1:
For '30th September' read '24th October'.

Page 10, para. 3, line 6:
Delete 'These demands were ignored.'

Page 10, para. 3, line 7:
For 'four' read 'nine'.

Page 10, para. 3, penultimate line:
Delete 'outside the Settlement'.

Page 10, para. 4, line 1:
Delete 'officially'.

Page 11, line 2:
After '1932' add 'following the signature of an armistice agreement on the 5th'.

Page 12, para. 4, line 3:
For 'March' read 'February'.

Page 13, line 3 from bottom:
For 'her occupation of Jehol' read 'her penetration across the Wall into north China'.

Page 43, line 2 from bottom:
For 'League of Nations' read 'Assembly Hall'.

Page 44, lines 2 and 3:
Delete 'anxious to accelerate preparations for a southward advance'.

Page 44, para. 2, last line:
Insert 'a major' after 'for'.

Page 44, para. 3, lines 10–11:
Delete 'German pressure on the 'Vichy' Government of France and'.

Page 46, para. 2, lines 7–8:
For 'the Far East' read 'Asia'.

Page 46, para. 2, line 13:
For 'going to the aid of' read 'giving armed assistance to'.

Page 59, line 7 from bottom:
After 'pact' insert 'with Japan'.

Page 60, para. 3, line 4:
For 'were forced to accept' read 'accepted'.

Page 66, lines 7–8:
Delete 'and talked of dissolving the Tripartite Pact'.

Page 66, para. 2, line 7:
For 'Cabinet' read 'Supreme Command'.

Page 70, para. 3, line 7:
For 'The same day' read 'On the 29th'.

Page 71, para. 3, line 10:
For '29th' read '28th'.

Page 73, para. 3, line 1:
For 'differed considerably from the agreed version' read 'was disappointing to Mr. Churchill'.

Page 73, last line:
For '28th read '8th'.

Page 87, line 5 from bottom:
After 'that' insert 'public opinion in'.

Page 87, line 2 from bottom:
For 'would mean the collapse of morale in China' read 'would be a major blow to Chinese morale'.

LONDON: HER MAJESTY'S STATIONERY OFFICE: 1968

Dd.135590   K46.   4/68.

1. *Left to right:* Air Marshal Sir Robert Brooke-Popham, General Sir Archibald Wavell and Vice-Admiral Sir Geoffrey Layton.

THE WAR
AGAINST JAPAN

VOLUME I
The Loss of Singapore

BY

MAJOR–GENERAL S. WOODBURN KIRBY
C.B., C.M.G., C.I.E., O.B.E., M.C.

WITH

CAPTAIN C. T. ADDIS, D.S.O., R.N.
COLONEL J. F. MEIKLEJOHN, C.I.E.
COLONEL G. T. WARDS, C.M.G., O.B.E.
AIR VICE–MARSHALL N. L. DESOER, C.B.E.

This edition of The War Against Japan: Volume I
first published in 2004
by The Naval & Military Press Ltd

Published by
The Naval & Military Press Ltd
Unit 10 Ridgewood Industrial Park,
Uckfield, East Sussex,
TN22 5QE England
Tel: +44 (0) 1825 749494
Fax: +44 (0) 1825 765701
www.naval-military-press.com

The War Against Japan: Volume I first published in 1957.
© Crown copyright. Reprinted with the permission of
the Controller of HMSO and Queen's Printer for Scotland.

*In reprinting in facsimile from the original, any imperfections are inevitably reproduced
and the quality may fall short of modern type and cartographic standards.*

Printed and bound by Antony Rowe Ltd, Eastbourne

CONTENTS

Page

EDITOR'S PREFACE xiii

INTRODUCTION xvii

GLOSSARY OF MALAY WORDS xxi

LIST OF PUBLISHED SOURCES xxii

CHAPTER I. FAR EAST DEFENCE
POLICY, 1921–39 1

CHAPTER II. THE EFFECT OF WAR IN EUROPE
ON FAR EAST DEFENCE POLICY
(September 1939–August 1940) 23

CHAPTER III. THE DRIFT TOWARDS WAR IN
THE FAR EAST (July 1940–July 1941) . . 43

CHAPTER IV. THE MONTHS OF DECISION
(August–December 1941) 69

CHAPTER V. THE JAPANESE STRATEGIC PLANS 89

CHAPTER VI. OPENING MOVES IN THE PACIFIC 97

CHAPTER VII. HONG KONG BEFORE THE WAR 107

CHAPTER VIII. HONG KONG: THE FIGHTING
ON THE MAINLAND 119

CHAPTER IX. THE FALL OF HONG KONG . 127

CHAPTER X. MALAYA 1941 153

CHAPTER XI. THE INVASION OF SIAM AND
MALAYA 177

CHAPTER XII. THE FIRST WEEK OF DISASTER 201

CHAPTER XIII. THE INVASION OF BRITISH
BORNEO 221

Page

CHAPTER XIV. THE LOSS OF NORTHERN MALAYA 229

CHAPTER XV. REINFORCEMENTS FOR THE FAR EAST 251

CHAPTER XVI. ABDA COMMAND . . . 263

CHAPTER XVII. THE LOSS OF CENTRAL MALAYA 269

CHAPTER XVIII. THE ATTACK ON THE DUTCH BEGINS: CELEBES AND BORNEO . . 291

CHAPTER XIX. THE LOSS OF NORTHERN JOHORE 301

CHAPTER XX. THE WITHDRAWAL TO SINGAPORE ISLAND 327

CHAPTER XXI. THE GROWING THREAT TO JAVA AND SUMATRA 347

CHAPTER XXII. PRELUDE TO THE ASSAULT ON SINGAPORE ISLAND 359

CHAPTER XXIII. THE BATTLE FOR SINGAPORE ISLAND 375

CHAPTER XXIV. THE SURRENDER OF SINGAPORE 403

CHAPTER XXV. THE INVASION OF SOUTHERN SUMATRA AND THE LOSS OF BALI AND TIMOR 417

CHAPTER XXVI. THE FALL OF JAVA . . 431

CHAPTER XXVII. RETROSPECT 451

INDEX 553

APPENDICES

Page

APPENDIX 1. Table showing the Economic Importance of Malaya and the Netherlands East Indies to the Allied war effort 477

APPENDIX 2. The System of Government in Tokyo during the Years Preceding the Outbreak of War . . . 479

APPENDIX 3. The Japanese Oil Position 481

APPENDIX 4. The Directives to the Commander-in-Chief, Far East, and the Commander-in-Chief, Eastern Fleet . 484

APPENDIX 5. The Organization of the Japanese Navy, Army and Air Forces 490

APPENDIX 6. Japanese Order of Battle and Plan of Attack against Hong Kong 498

APPENDIX 7. The Organization of the British Navy, Army and Air Force in 1941 with Particular Reference to the Far East 501

APPENDIX 8. Some Particulars of British and Japanese Aircraft in use in the Far East Theatre during the Period covered by this volume 506

APPENDIX 9. Strength and Dispositions of the R.A.F. in Malaya, 7th December 1941 511

APPENDIX 10. Malaya Command, Order of Battle, 7th December 1941 . . . . . *facing page* 512

APPENDIX 11. Notes on the Indian Army . . . 513

APPENDIX 12. Notes on the Australian Imperial Forces . 516

APPENDIX 13. Notes on Local Forces in Malaya . . 517

APPENDIX 14. Disposition of Allied Naval Forces in the Eastern Theatre on 8th December 1941 . . . 518

APPENDIX 15. Order of Battle of Japanese *25th Army* on the 8th December 1941 521

Page

APPENDIX 16. Order of Battle of Japanese *3rd Air Division* and Naval Air Forces supporting *25th Army* . . . 524

APPENDIX 17. Order of the Day issued on the 8th December 1941 525

APPENDIX 18. Details of Japanese First Flights landed at Singora, Patani and Kota Bharu 526

APPENDIX 19. State of Training of Reinforcing Formations from India 528

APPENDIX 20. Directive to the Supreme Commander, ABDA Area, dated 3rd January 1942. . . . 529

APPENDIX 21. O̶r̶d̶e̶r̶ ̶o̶f̶ ̶B̶a̶t̶t̶l̶e̶,̶ ̶1̶8̶t̶h̶ ̶B̶r̶i̶t̶i̶s̶h̶ ̶D̶i̶v̶i̶s̶i̶o̶n̶ . . 534

Malaya Command, Skeleton Order of Battle, 8th February 1942.

APPENDIX 22. Japanese Naval Forces for the Invasion of the Netherlands East Indies 535

APPENDIX 23. Skeleton Order of Battle of Japanese *16th Army* 539

APPENDIX 24. Westforce Operation Instruction No. 4 dated 27th January 1942 541

APPENDIX 25. Order of Battle of Japanese *25th Army* for the Attack on Singapore Island 544

APPENDIX 26. Japanese Military Landing Craft used in Malaya: 8th December 1941–15th February 1942 . . 547

APPENDIX 27. Malaya Command Instruction No. 40 dated 10th February 1942 549

MAPS AND SKETCHES

Forest growth is only shown where it is considered necessary for the purpose of illustrating the text.

Natural jungle is shown in green on the coloured maps and in a neutral tint in black and white sketches. Plantations (mostly rubber) are indicated by the conventional symbol for trees, in black and white.

Conventional topographical symbols have been used on all maps. For economy in printing or for clarity, roads appear in black, red or brown.

Page

Strategic Map of the Pacific . . . . . *At end of book*

Map 1. Japanese strategic plans—1941 96

Sketch 1. The Philippines 102

Sketch 2. The Bismarck Archipelago 104

Map 2. Hong Kong and Leased Territories (with Canton area inset) 106

Sketch 3. Hong Kong, British Dispositions, December 1941 . 116

Map 3. Hong Kong—Mainland, 8th–13th December 1941 . 126

Map 4. Hong Kong Island 152

Map 5. Malaya 153

Sketch 4. Malaya, Location of Military Formations, Airfields and Air Force Units, 8th December 1941 172

Map 6. Kota Bharu 192

Map 7. British and Japanese naval movements, 4th to 10th December 1941 200

Map 8. Kedah 201

Map 9. The action at Jitra, 11th and 12th December 1941 . 208

Map 10. The action at Gurun, 14th and 15th December 1941 . 216

Map 11. British Borneo (Kuching area inset) 228

Map 12. Perak 229

Sketch 5. Grik Road 237

Map 13. The action at Kampar, 30th December 1941–2nd January 1942 248

ix

B

Page

Map 14. Selangor   269

Map 15. Kuantan   272

Map 16. The action at Slim River, 7th January 1942   .   .   280

Map 17. Netherlands East Indies (illustrating Japanese strategic
plan)   291

Sketch 6. Bakri   308

Sketch 7. The Bukit Pelandok defile   310

Map 18. Northern Johore (illustrating events from 14th to 24th
January 1942)   326

Sketch 8. Mersing and Endau   333

Map 19. Retreat down the trunk road in southern Johore,
27th–31st January 1942   336

Map 20. Southern Johore (illustrating events from 24th to 31st
January 1942)   346

Sketch 9. Amboina   349

Map 21. Singapore Island, Dispositions of the garrison—
February 1942   374

Map 22. The Assault on Singapore (illustrating the operations
on 8th and 9th February 1942)   384

Map 23. Operations on Singapore Island, 10th February 1942 .   392

Map 24. Operations on Singapore Island, 11th February 1942 .   400

Map 25. Singapore Town (illustrating fighting from 12th to 15th
February 1942)   416

Map 26. Palembang   430

Map 27. The Battle of the Java Sea, 27th February 1942 .   .   448

Map 28. Java   450

PHOTOGRAPHS

Most of the photographs in this volume are Crown copyright and are reproduced by courtesy of the Imperial War Museum and the Ministries concerned. For permission to reproduce Nos. 5, 8, 14, 16 and 17 the authors are indebted respectively to Major-General Maltby, the Federation of Malaya Information Services, the Australian War Memorial, Canberra, Lady Heath and Mrs. Pulford.

1. Air Marshal Sir Robert Brooke-Popham, General Sir Archibald Wavell, Vice-Admiral Sir Geoffrey Layton . . . . *Frontispiece*

2. Air Marshal Sir Robert Brooke-Popham, Rt. Hon. Alfred Duff Cooper, Rt. Hon. Sir Earle Page, Sir Archibald Clark-Kerr, Sir Shenton Thomas, Vice-Admiral Sir Geoffrey Layton . . *facing page* 80

3. The *Queen Mary* in the graving dock at the Naval Base, August 1940 80

4. Sir Mark Young 81

5. Major-General C. M. Maltby 81

6. Leased Territory Hong Kong looking north . . 120

7. North-eastern shores of Hong Kong Island looking west 121

8. Hill road in primary jungle . . .

9. Typical Malayan road in secondary jungle .

10. Rice fields . . . . . . *following*

11. A Rubber Estate . . . . . *page* 160

12. A Coconut Plantation . . . .

13. Typical view of east coast of Malaya .

14. Lieutenant-General A. E. Percival and Major-General H. G. Bennett . . . . . *facing page* 168

15. Lieutenant-General T. Yamashita 168

16. Lieutenant-General Sir Lewis Heath 169

17. Air Vice-Marshal C. W. H. Pulford 169

18. H.M.S. *Prince of Wales* 196

19. H.M.S. *Repulse* 196

20. Rear-Admiral A. F. E. Palliser and Admiral Sir Tom Phillips 197

21. The Kampar position 276

22. The Slim River position 277

23. The Bukit Pelandok defile looking west . . . 376

24. *5th Japanese Division's* point of attack on Singapore Island 376

25. *18th Japanese Division's* point of attack on Singapore Island 377

26. *Imperial Guards Division's* point of attack on Singapore Island 377

EDITOR'S PREFACE

THE PRESENT VOLUME is the first of a series on the War against Japan, forming part of the United Kingdom History of the Second World War on the military side. The history as a whole has been planned in accordance with a Government directive 'to provide a broad survey of events from an inter-Service point of view'; and the word 'military' is used throughout of all the three fighting Services.

In order to avoid detail unsuitable in a 'broad survey', the standpoint from which the campaigns have been viewed is that of the theatre commander, the treatment of discussions and decisions by the supreme authority at home being the province of the companion series of volumes on Grand Strategy. It must be admitted that this has involved considerable overlapping, but the overlapping may appear excusable if it saves the reader constant reference to other volumes. It must also be admitted that, at the lower level, 'a broad survey' has been broadly interpreted. The chapters dealing with the loss of Hong Kong and Malaya have gone into the fighting in considerable detail. This is due partly to the fact that in some cases the units concerned were small, while in other cases the nature of the ground made it necessary for formations to be broken up. It may also be pleaded that so unusual a story as the loss of two British colonies deserves a full treatment. There is the further consideration that the paucity of written records and the long captivity of so many of the men who survived the catastrophe have made the discovery of the facts particularly difficult, so that the funding of such information as was available seemed justified.

The writing of this volume has indeed been difficult, and though the authors have taken immense trouble to obtain and check all available evidence, written and oral, much still remains controversial. Recollections are unconsciously influenced by what one would like to think, and it is almost inevitable that great disasters should be followed by recriminations. In their final chapter the authors ask how it came about that British strength had so declined in the years between the two wars that 'Japan was able so swiftly to overrun the vast southern areas from the Philippines to the border of India and wrest from Britain, Hong Kong, Borneo, Malaya and Burma'. As they say, 'This is a military not a political history, and comment on the conduct of British foreign policy does not lie within its scope'. They are concerned however with the effect of political decisions on the military situation in the Far East, and they state their conclusion that the campaign in Malaya was lost before it began.

The story is complicated by the fact that, while our history is professedly that of the United Kingdom military effort, a large part of the troops engaged in Hong Kong and Malaya came from other countries of the Commonwealth. As a result of a visit to Australia General Kirby has been able in nearly every case to reach an agreed basis of fact with the Australian historians but naturally it has not always been possible to reach identical interpretations of the facts.

Outside the Commonwealth, the Americans, the Chinese and the Dutch were our allies in the war against Japan. Forces of one nation fought at times under a commander from another nation; even when that was not so, forces of the different nations often fought in pursuance of a single strategy, and it would be impossible to tell the story intelligibly or in proper balance without treating it as a whole. This has meant that in places it has been necessary to rely to greater or less extent on accounts written by Allied historians who hold the primary sources. General Kirby has throughout been in touch with Canadian, American and Dutch historians as well as with individual Dutch officers who took part in the defence of the Netherlands East Indies.

Where controversial points are many and important, as they are in this story, it is particularly desirable that authorities should be stated. But, as has been explained in prefaces to former volumes, it is not our practice to publish detailed references to documents which are not, and for many years are not likely to be, open to public inspection; such references are however printed in a confidential edition, which will presumably be available to students when the archives are opened. In the present case there are the further difficulties that many of the written records have been lost owing to the chances of war, and that much of the evidence on which the authors have reached their conclusions is oral and has been supplied in confidence. The authors admit frankly that the evidence is often incomplete; but they have felt justified in stating the conclusions drawn from what evidence is available to them; incomplete as it is, they have had opportunities of tapping sources which will not be available to future historians.

The writers of the military histories have greatly profited from the monographs, narratives, and summaries produced by the Service Departments, and we would express our thanks for constant assistance to Rear-Admiral R. M. Bellairs, Brigadier H. B. Latham and Mr. J. C. Nerney, and to their staffs. The maps have been prepared under the experienced direction of Colonel T. M. M. Penney of the Cabinet Office Historical Section. Several libraries have lent us books, and we acknowledge our indebtedness to their librarians. We are particularly grateful for help we have received from Vice-Admiral Sir Geoffrey Blake, Lieutenant-General Sir Henry Pownall, Air Chief Marshal Sir Guy Garrod, and Lieutenant-General Sir Ian Jacob who, as an advisory panel, have read and commented on our drafts. Finally we must express our thanks to Mr. A. B. Acheson of the Cabinet Office for all the assistance he has rendered us in matters of administration.

J. R. M. B.

INTRODUCTION

THIS DOES NOT ATTEMPT to be a comprehensive history of the war against Japan. Nor does it set out to be a complete British history. It is primarily concerned with the military effort of the United Kingdom of Great Britain and Northern Ireland in that war, using the word military in its broadest sense. The war effort of the rest of the British Commonwealth is however inseparable from that of the United Kingdom, for the British fought as one nation. Each of the nations of the Commonwealth is writing its own history and in order to prevent undue duplication we have adopted the following principle. Where forces of the Commonwealth fought side by side with those of the United Kingdom, their operations are given equal weight. Where they fought under American command as in the south-west Pacific, their story is told only in sufficient detail to enable the reader to grasp the nature and magnitude of the part played by the British Commonwealth of Nations.

After the first few months the United States assumed responsibility for the Pacific and from then on took the lion's share of the war. The British sphere became the Indian Ocean, and the greater part of these volumes is devoted to the history of operations in that area. In order to keep a proper perspective and so that the reader may follow the unfolding strategical plan which eventually brought about the defeat of Japan, the campaigns in the Pacific are described throughout these volumes in their proper chronological sequence but only in outline. The reader who wishes to study them in detail is referred to the American, Australian and New Zealand histories.

This is neither a navy, army nor air history. It is an inter-Service history, including where necessary the part played by the civil authorities in the various areas in which the war was fought. It is a broad survey written at the level of the High Command. Nevertheless, the actions of small units have had often to be described in some detail since, especially in the opening stages of the war, these had an important influence on the course of events.

This volume is the first of five which will cover the whole of the war period from 1941 to 1945. It tells of the first three months of unrelieved disasters in which the Allies vainly tried to stem the first flood of the Japanese advance. The loss of Burma properly belongs to this volume but, as Burma became part of the Indian Ocean theatre of war, it has been included in the second volume which covers the year of stabilization and recuperation, when India was built up as a base from which to launch a counter-offensive. Volume II ends with the announcement on the 25th August 1943 of the decision to form South-East Asia Command. Volume III will take the story up to July 1944 and describe the attacks and counter-attacks which resulted in the Japanese offensive from Burma being broken and their armies thrown back in confusion. Volumes IV and V carry the story through to the capitulation of Japan. They will deal with the counter-offensive which ended with the recovery of the greater part of Burma and the recapture of Rangoon. They will also include the operations of the British Pacific Fleet in the Pacific. They will end when all the Allied territories had been reoccupied and the large Japanese armies in the Southern Regions, still capable of resistance despite the fact that they were isolated from their home base, had been disarmed and placed under Allied control.

The war against Japan was fought not only over vast expanses of ocean at long distances from established bases, but in countries with few communications, subject to great heat, heavy rains and violent tropical storms. It was fought over high mountain ranges, through jungle and swamp and across wide fast-flowing rivers. Navies, armies and air forces are entirely dependent on the supplies which their lines of communication can deliver: administration therefore played a decisive part in every operation. For this reason the authors make no apology for the amount of space devoted to administrative matters throughout this history. The first volume is however an exception, for the collapse of the defence at the beginning of the war was so sudden and complete that administration had little effect on the outcome.

As is usual in defeat many of the battle records which would normally have been available to the historians were destroyed. Although fullest use has been made of such official war diaries and operational records as have survived, much of the story of the fighting in Volume I has had to be built up partly from diaries and narratives written from memory, often in prisoner of war camps, and partly from accounts written after the end of the war by men who throughout much of the campaign were half dazed with fatigue. It is not surprising therefore that narratives and reports covering the same period and the same events have been found to differ in times and even in dates. We have based our story upon the best evidence we have been able to obtain. We have also had difficulty in reconciling Allied and enemy figures of air losses. A careful study of our own and Japanese records has shown that air combat claims were frequently overestimated, especially when large numbers of aircraft were engaged. This is no reflection on the aircrews themselves or on those whose duty it was to analyse and assess the claims. Fighting usually took place at high altitudes and often above the clouds, which made the ultimate fate of an opponent difficult if not impossible to determine; and when formations were attacked more than one air gunner may have fired at and claimed the same aircraft.

We have tried to strike a balance between the various strategical and administrative factors which faced the High Command when formulating their plans, and the story of the actual fighting; and to point the lessons to be drawn from both success and failure. The necessity for fitting a large canvas into a small frame has inevitably resulted in the omission of much interesting detail, but we venture to hope that we have not entirely sacrificed the entertainment of the reader on the altar of conciseness.

This first volume is one of scarcely relieved gloom. It could hardly be otherwise, for it tells of an unbroken series of disasters and includes the greatest military defeat in British history. We have been given as part of our terms of reference the unenviable task of saying how and why these disasters occurred. Where in our opinion there were failures in leadership or mistakes made by those in responsible positions, we have not hesitated to say so. If in doing so we appear to have laid emphasis on what was done wrong rather than what was done right, it is in the belief that there is more to be learnt from failure than success. We would not have it thought however that we are not sensible of the courage and selfless devotion to duty of many of those who took part in these disastrous campaigns, and of the debt which is owed to them, and to the thousands of men and women of many races who gave their lives or suffered years of untold hardship in captivity.

The Editor in his Preface has already paid tribute to the historians, librarians and cartographers who are assisting in the preparation of the Military Histories as a series, but we should also like to thank those who have helped us with this volume in particular. We have had the advantage of using the staff histories written by Commander L. J. Pitcairn-Jones, R.N., and Major C. S. Goldingham, R.M., of the Admiralty Historical Section, the narratives written by Brigadier J. A. Blood and Captain W. Miles of the Cabinet Office Historical Section and accounts prepared by the Air Historical Branch of the Air Ministry. We are also indebted to Colonel A. M. L. Harrison whose excellent account of the operations of 11th Indian Division has proved invaluable. We are grateful to all those mentioned above and to Lieut.-General A. E. Percival, Brigadier I. Simson and to many others from the Services and civilian life for the ready help which they have constantly given us.

Our knowledge of the operations of the Commonwealth units has been greatly augmented and clarified by the assistance of Colonel C. P. Stacey of the Canadian Historical Section, of Mr. Gavin Long, the General Editor of the Australian War History, and of Mr. L. Wigmore, the author of the Australian volume covering the first four months of the Japanese offensive. Our main sources of information about the Australian operations are the reports and war diaries of the 8th Australian Division, a report and maps drafted by Lieut.-Colonel (later Brigadier) C. H. Kappe and other papers put at our disposal by Mr. Gavin Long. Interviews in Australia in 1953 with Lieut.-General H. G. Bennett, Brigadiers H. B. Taylor and D. S. Maxwell, Colonel J. H. Thyer and many other Australian officers who took part in events recorded in this volume have been most useful. We would like to express our thanks to the U.S. Japanese Research Division in Tokyo for supplying us with information from Japanese sources.

The personal recollections of many officers who took part in the operations described have proved to be invaluable where the contemporary records were inadequate or seemingly contradictory, as have been their comments on the various drafts of this volume. We wish to express our gratitude to them, more especially as in so doing they willingly revived memories of unhappy and painful experiences which they had hoped to forget. We are indebted to Brigadier M. R. Roberts for his advice and painstaking reading of the proofs. Miss M. M. Baird's and Miss M. Barton's careful research, advice and comments have been of the greatest value to us throughout. Miss C. Winter and Miss B. Wallen gave valuable secretarial assistance.

S. W. K.

C. T. A.

J. F. M.

G. T. W.

N. L. D.

GLOSSARY OF MALAY WORDS

Alor	river channel or pool
Bagan	landing place
Besar	large or big
Bukit (Bt)	hill
Kampong (Kg)	village
Kechil	small or little
Kota	fort
Kuala	mouth of a river
Padang	open space
Parit	ditch or drain
Paya	swamp
Pulau	island
Simpang	cross road
Sungei (S)	river
Tanjong (Tg)	cape
Tinggi	high
Ulu	upper reaches of a river

LIST OF PUBLISHED SOURCES

Despatch by Air Chief Marshal Sir Robert Brooke-Popham on operations
in the Far East from 17th October 1940 to 27th December 1941.
(Supplement to the *London Gazette* of 20/1/48, No. 38183)

Despatch by Lieut.-General A. E. Percival on operations of Malaya
Command from 8th December 1941 to 15th February 1942.
(Supplement to the *London Gazette* of 20/2/48, No. 38215)

Despatch by Air Vice Marshal Sir Paul Maltby on air operations during
the campaign in Malaya and the Netherlands East Indies from 8th
December 1941 to 12th March 1942.
(Supplement to the *London Gazette* of 20/2/48, No. 38216)

Despatch by Major-General C. M. Maltby on operations in Hong Kong
from 8th to 25th December 1941.
(Supplement to the *London Gazette* of 27/1/48, No. 38190)

Despatch by the Supreme Commander of the ABDA Area on operations
in the South-West Pacific, 15th January 1942 to 25th February 1942.
(H.M.S.O., 1948)

U.S. Congress, Report of the Joint Committee on the Investigation of the
Pearl Harbor Attack, 79th Congress, 2nd Session, Document No. 244.
(Washington, 1946)

FEIS, *The Road to Pearl Harbor* (Princeton, 1950)

MORISON, *The Rising Sun in the Pacific, 1931–April 1942* (O.U.P., 1948)
       History of U.S. Naval Operations in World War II. Volume III

BENNETT, *Why Singapore Fell* (Sydney, 1944)

STEWART, *History of the Argyll and Sutherland Highlanders 2nd Battalion*
(Nelson, 1947)

*'Defeat cries aloud for explanation;
whereas success, like charity, covers
a multitude of sins.'*

MAHAN

CHAPTER I

FAR EAST DEFENCE POLICY

1921–39

See Strategic Map and Map 5

WHEN the First World War broke out in Europe in 1914 Japan, despite the opposition of the Army which was largely pro-German, decided to act in support of Great Britain in conformity with the Anglo-Japanese Alliance.[1] She realized however that she now had an opportunity not only to enrich herself at the expense of Germany, but to gain, without the fear of active intervention by European powers, a footing in China which had for some time been her desire. She quickly captured the German concession at Tsingtao on the Shantung peninsula in China, and occupied German colonial possessions in the Marianas, Caroline and Marshall Islands in the Pacific Ocean.

In 1915, two months after the fall of Tsingtao, Japan made her notorious 'Twenty-one Demands' on China. This gave the world its first warning of Japan's dream of further expansion and of her determination to dominate China and thus the Far East both politically and commercially. Had China been forced by Japanese strength to accept all these demands, including the request that the Chinese Central Government should employ influential Japanese as advisers in political, financial and military affairs, Japan would have gained in one step a predominant position in that country. Both Britain and America however protested so strongly that she modified her demands, though she did wrest from China important concessions both in the Shantung peninsula and in southern Manchuria. These demands marked a new and ambitious stage in Japan's foreign policy, and at the same time a setback in her relations with Britain.

In 1917 she agreed to assist the Allied cause by providing badly needed convoy escorts in both the Mediterranean and the Indian Ocean, in return for an undertaking that Britain would support her at the peace conference in her claim for the former German rights

---

[1] The Anglo-Japanese Alliance, which cemented the friendship between the two nations and secured for Japan British neutrality and moral support during the Russo-Japanese war, was first signed in 1902. It was revised and renewed in 1905 and again in 1911 and, in its final form, bound either ally to go to the aid of the other in defence of its interests in the Far East and India, if attacked by any Power or Powers.

C

I

in the Shantung peninsula and for the cession of the German Pacific islands north of the Equator. Accordingly under the terms of the peace treaty with Germany, Japan was allowed to retain her concessions in China and was given the mandate, under the League of Nations, over the Marianas, Caroline and Marshall Islands, except Guam in the Marianas Group which remained an American possession. At the same time Australia was given the Mandate over northeast New Guinea and the islands in the Bismarck Archipelago, and New Zealand over the German Samoan Islands. The Mandate over Nauru was to be held jointly by the United Kingdom, Australia and New Zealand.

The elimination of the German Fleet and the growth of both the American and Japanese Navies during the course of the war had resulted in these nations becoming, after the British Commonwealth, the second and third strongest naval Powers. The centre of gravity of naval power thus tended to shift from the Atlantic and Mediterranean to the Pacific. This trend was of particular concern to the British Commonwealth, since it provided a potential threat to the security of the sea communications between Great Britain, India, Australia and New Zealand. It therefore became desirable that a British fleet should be stationed in the Far East. But at the end of the war, when it was assumed that no major war was likely for the next ten years, the British Government considered it neither necessary nor possible to maintain fleets of adequate strength in both the Western and Eastern hemispheres. It was accordingly decided that the British Fleet should be held in a central position in European waters, from which it could reinforce the Far East as and when required.

To implement this policy a naval base, having full facilities for maintaining a modern fleet and defended against likely forms of attack, was an essential. At the time there was no such base in the Far East. The only existing naval base was at Hong Kong, where the docking and repair facilities were insufficient and where only a limited scale of defence was possible. Furthermore as a base Hong Kong, situated as it was in close proximity to Japanese naval and air bases in Formosa and remote from the nearest source of British reinforcement, had become strategically unsound in the changed circumstances in the Pacific.

The Far Eastern situation was examined in 1921 by the Committee of Imperial Defence which came to the conclusion that there was no possibility of making Hong Kong sufficiently secure against attack. Thus it could no longer be considered an adequate base for British naval forces in the Far East. An alternative, more suitably located and with full facilities, was therefore required. After examining the claims of Sydney and Singapore the Committee recommended

Singapore as being strategically the best situated for the control of sea communications in the Indian Ocean and southern Pacific.

At that time there were only weak defences at the existing commercial port in Keppel Harbour, designed to meet attack by a squadron of cruisers and a raiding party of some two thousand men.[1] Singapore however seemed to be ideally placed for development into a large naval base, the defence of which did not at that time appear to offer any particular difficulties. The Cabinet on the 16th June 1921 approved in principle the recommendation of the Committee of Imperial Defence to establish an up-to-date naval base there. A few days later the Imperial Conference, then sitting in London, was informed of the Cabinet's decision.

In November 1921, the United States of America convened at Washington an International Conference and submitted proposals designed to contribute to the maintenance of the general peace and to reduce the burden of competition in armaments. As an outcome of these proposals a treaty between the British Commonwealth, the United States, France, Italy and Japan for the limitation of naval armaments was signed on the 6th February 1922. This treaty prescribed the permissible tonnage in capital ships as:

Great Britain . . .	525,000 tons
United States . . .	525,000 tons
Japan	315,000 tons
France	175,000 tons
Italy	175,000 tons

with somewhat similar ratios for aircraft carriers. The tonnage of ships built to replace those in these classes was limited to 35,000 and 27,000 respectively, and new ships of other classes (such as cruisers) to a maximum of 10,000 tons, with guns of a calibre not exceeding 8-inch.

Under Article XIX, Great Britain, the United States and Japan agreed to establish no new fortifications or naval bases in certain specified areas in the Pacific and to take no measures to increase existing facilities, though normal replacement of worn-out equipment would be permitted. The areas covered in the agreement were:

FOR GREAT BRITAIN
Hong Kong and any insular possessions east of the meridian of 110° E., except those adjacent to the coasts of Canada, Australia and New Zealand.

FOR THE UNITED STATES
The insular possessions in the Pacific, except those adjacent to the coasts of the U.S.A., Alaska (not including the Aleutian Islands), the Panama Canal zone and Hawaii (Pearl Harbour).

---

[1] See Map 21.

FOR JAPAN

The insular territories and possessions of Japan in the Pacific Ocean, to wit the Kurile, Bonin, Ryukyu Islands, Formosa and the Pescadores.[1]

The agreement also covered any insular territories or possessions in the Pacific Ocean which the three signatories might acquire in the future. The Marianas, Caroline, and Marshall Islands were not specifically mentioned in the treaty as they had been mandated to Japan and she was therefore responsible to the League of Nations for the maintenance of the 'status quo'.[2]

The underlying object of the Washington Naval Treaty, as far as the British Commonwealth and the United States were concerned, was firstly to prevent a naval armaments race in the Pacific, and secondly to prevent Japan, as far as was possible, from establishing advanced naval and air bases in the Pacific. It was hoped thus to curb her aggressive tendencies which had been so evident in 1915 at the time of the 'Twenty-one Demands'.

There was however another problem in the Pacific—the Anglo-Japanese Alliance—which called for a solution. It was evident in the changed strategical situation after the 1914–18 war that, whatever precautions were taken, a clash might occur between the United States and Japan through their conflicting interests in China and the western Pacific. In such circumstances the retention of the Anglo-Japanese Alliance would be harmful to Anglo-American relations, the overriding importance of which in the interests of world peace had been fully recognized on both sides of the Atlantic. The problem was to end it in such a way that Japan would not thereby lose face and to replace it by something which, while recognizing the post-war situation in the Pacific, would be acceptable to all concerned.

The Washington Naval Treaty was therefore followed by two further treaties: the Four-Power Treaty between the British Commonwealth, the United States, France and Japan, relating to their insular possessions and Dominions in the Pacific, and the Nine-Power Treaty relating to the integrity of China. In the former treaty the four Powers confirmed the 'status quo' in the Pacific; agreed, should any dispute arise between any of them out of their Pacific rights, to call a joint conference to resolve it; and also agreed to decide in concert on the measures to be taken in the event of any one of them being threatened by an outside Power. In the latter treaty, the nine signatory Powers agreed to respect the sovereignty, the rights and interests and the integrity of China.[3] Japan, as a signatory to this treaty, thus pledged herself to a policy of self-restraint towards China

---

[1] The Pescadores are a group of islands off the west coast of Formosa.

[2] Cmd No. 1627; 1922.

[3] Cmd No. 1627; 1922.

and at the same time relinquished her claim to the Shantung peninsula which she had occupied during the 1914–18 war.

The authors of this series of treaties and of the peace treaty felt no doubt that they had taken every step possible to preserve peace in the Pacific. Nevertheless, in the light of future events, it is interesting to note that two actions had been taken which were to have the opposite effect. The first was the granting to Japan, with her known expansionist tendencies, of the Mandate for the Pacific islands. These lay astride the American lines of communication to Guam and the Philippines and were clearly of great potential strategic value to Japan should she become involved in a war in the Pacific. From the Anglo-American point of view it was scarcely sound strategy to leave them in the hands of a possible enemy. It was however an inevitable consequence of the British agreement with Japan during the 1914–18 war.

The second was the abrogation of the Anglo-Japanese Alliance. Although this was done with the best intentions, it started the break-up of the friendship between Britain and Japan which had grown up over many years and through two wars—the Russo-Japanese war of 1904 and the First World War. Britain's influence in the past had carried great weight and her continued support and guidance might possibly have deterred Japan from taking the path which she eventually followed. Relations between the United States and Japan had not been cordial owing to American anti-Asian immigration policy and her opposition to Japanese post-war claims. Thus when Britain apparently abandoned her old ally in favour of the United States, whom Japan regarded with suspicion, the effect on the Japanese nation was profound.

The reader may wonder how it was that Japan, with her desire for expansion, accepted the Washington treaties and the consequent inferior naval status with such apparent meekness. After the discrediting of Prussian militarism which the Japanese Army leaders had used as their model, a wave of democratic sentiment which had affected the whole world struck a sympathetic chord in the hearts of the Japanese people. Thus by 1921, the year that the Washington Conference was called, a 'Liberal' Government, mainly civilian and commercial in character and bent on pursuing a policy of peace, was in power. The expansionist elements too no doubt saw the benefits which the post-war treaties had in fact conferred on their country. Neither Britain nor America could construct naval bases nearer to Japan than Singapore and Hawaii, while possession of the Pacific islands made the Japanese defensive perimeter extremely strong. Security for her communications in wartime with her new continental possessions and with China, for which purpose she had built up her Navy and had striven for so many years, was thereby assured.

Thus the policy of Japan for a considerable period was one which led the authors of the treaties to believe that they had provided a satisfactory solution to the Pacific problem.

During 1922 the siting of the proposed Naval Base at Singapore was considered. There were two possible sites—the existing commercial port in Keppel Harbour at the southernmost point of the island and in the Johore Strait on its northern side. The latter site, which was recommended by the Admiralty, was approved by the Cabinet in February 1923. The Imperial Conference held in London later that year reviewed the situation in the Pacific against the background provided by the Washington treaties, with special reference to the urgent need for a naval base at Singapore. The representatives of Australia, New Zealand and India naturally took particular interest in the project and pressed for work to be started without delay. Despite the fact that the amount of construction which could be undertaken was at that time limited by financial considerations, the Conference agreed that the scheme should proceed with as little delay as possible.

In 1924 however the first Labour Government came into power in the United Kingdom and decided that the Singapore project should be abandoned. This reversal in policy was due partly to financial reasons and partly to a fear that to proceed with the Base might, despite the treaties, lead to an armaments race—and the new government was anxious to encourage general disarmament. There was naturally considerable difference of opinion amongst the Dominions on this decision. Australia and New Zealand, as might be expected since they were most closely concerned, strongly opposed it, whereas Canada refrained from any comment and South Africa welcomed it as being a gesture in the interests of world peace.

The short-lived Labour Government was superseded towards the end of the year by the return of the Conservatives. One of their first actions was to authorize the continuance of work on the Naval Base, which they had originally approved in 1921. As a step towards this end, the Committee of Imperial Defence appointed a sub-committee, presided over by Lord Curzon, to re-examine the sites at Singapore which had been provisionally accepted in 1923, to consider the rate of construction of the Base and its defences, the future programme of development and the possible use of aircraft as an alternative weapon to the more usual fixed heavy coast defence batteries.

The Curzon Committee recommended that the site already approved in the Johore Strait should be developed into the Naval Base, for they considered that it would be freer from shipping and less exposed to attack from the sea than Keppel Harbour. The

Committee also accepted as suitable the proposed sites for an airfield and seaplane base nearby at Seletar.[1] The defence of the sites selected for the Naval and Air Bases against likely forms of attack was also fully examined. It was at that time the considered military opinion that the nature of the country would make an advance by enemy land forces through Johore exceptionally difficult. In any case, it was thought that the Japanese could not hope to capture the Base by landing an expeditionary force in Malaya some distance from it and by employing the traditional method of attack which they had adopted both at Port Arthur in the Russo-Japanese war and at Tsingtao in 1914. The Committee therefore accepted the premise that any attack on Singapore would be from the sea.

The suggestion that aircraft might take the place of fixed gun defences led however to a difference of opinion among the Chiefs of Staff, and started a controversy which lasted for ten years. This not only tended to delay the completion of the Singapore Base but also caused, in its repercussions, dissension between the Services which was not entirely cured till the test of war provided the answers to the various theoretical views.

The Air Ministry claimed that torpedo-bombers, protected by fighters and assisted by reconnaissance aircraft, could, as a supplement to medium and close gun defences, provide a cheaper and more efficient deterrent against an assaulting force protected by an enemy fleet than heavy gun batteries. They pointed out that an enemy force could be attacked far beyond the range of any heavy gun, and that, since aircraft were mobile, the squadrons required for the defence could be stationed elsewhere in peace and need only be moved to the Base when war became imminent, thereby ensuring the maximum economy in defence expenditure.

The Admiralty and War Office held the view that the heavy gun had in the past proved a deterrent against enemy warships and seaborne attack and, with improved technique in fire control, would continue to do so. They emphasized that heavy gun defences were permanent and therefore immediately ready for action in an emergency, whereas aircraft, which could be moved elsewhere to meet threats at other strategic points in the Commonwealth's extensive defence system, might not be available at the critical moment. Further, the torpedo-bombers had not at that date proved themselves reliable deterrents to naval attack.

After many months of indecision, the Committee of Imperial Defence recommended in 1926 that, as some four years would be necessary for the development of the air forces, the first stage of the Singapore defences should provide for the necessary close and

---

[1] See Map 21.

medium gun defences, plus three 15-inch heavy guns, and that the question of substituting aircraft for the remainder of the heavy guns should be re-examined later. In the meanwhile however action was to be taken to extend the air reinforcement route from Calcutta, where it then terminated, to Singapore.

A Committee, under Lieut.-General Sir Webb Gillman, was sent to Singapore by the War Office in 1927 to make recommendations for both the location and number of the fixed defence batteries and for the strength of the garrison. This Committee brought to light a divergence of views between the civil authorities in Singapore and the War Office on the need for developing the defences of the Naval Base, the Government of the Straits Settlements being unwilling to make land available for military purposes without first obtaining an assurance that no part of the cost would fall on the local civil community. The divergence of opinion delayed the preparation of the layout of the defences, cantonments and other military installations.

The Chiefs of Staff Committee, on receipt of the Gillman Report in March 1928, again reviewed the Singapore project. They recommended that the first stage of the defences for the Naval Base should be proceeded with and finished within five years, but that the second stage, which would complete the defences, should be postponed for the time being. They reiterated the view that a landing on the mainland in Johore with the object of an attack on Singapore Island would, owing to the nature of the ground to be crossed and the thick jungle, present such a difficult military operation that the possibility of an enemy attempting it on a large scale could be excluded. Thus the defences were designed primarily to resist a seaborne attack directed on the island of Singapore and its immediate vicinity.

In July 1928 the Cabinet asked the Committee of Imperial Defence to advise them on the general assumptions which should govern preparations for war, with particular reference to estimates of the Services. The Committee recommended that it should be assumed, for the purpose of framing estimates, that at any given date there would be no major war for ten years, and that this assumption should be reviewed annually.[1]

The second Labour Government, on taking office in 1929, decided that further efforts should be made to obtain international agreement to 'general' disarmament, despite the failure of the League of Nations to do so hitherto. In pursuance of this object a Naval Disarmament Conference was held in London in 1930. The British Government, confident that the signing of the Kellogg-Briand Pact in 1928 made war improbable in the foreseeable future, offered to

---

[1] This was a development of the assumption made by the Cabinet in 1919 that the British Commonwealth would not be engaged in any great war during the next ten years. See page 2.

reduce the number of cruisers deemed necessary for safety at the time of the Washington Treaty of 1922 and, as a gesture of good faith, suspended further work on the Singapore Base pending the result of the Conference.

The London Naval Treaty for the limitation and reduction of naval armaments was signed in April 1930 by the British Commonwealth, the United States, Japan, France and Italy who agreed not to exercise the right to construct capital ship replacements during the years 1931–36 inclusive (a fact which affected the original ratio of 5:5:3 favourably for Japan). They also agreed that the ratio of cruiser tonnage should be fixed at approximately 10:10:6½, while there should be parity between the three major naval Powers in both destroyers and submarines. A further meeting would be held by the Contracting Powers in 1935.[1]

The go-slow policy for Singapore was reaffirmed by the Government after the Naval Conference, and reluctantly accepted by the Imperial Conference held in the late autumn of that year. This further delay in the construction of the Singapore Base, and the signature of the London Naval Treaty, which reduced the potential naval strength of the British Commonwealth *vis-à-vis* Japan, caused grave concern in both Australia and New Zealand. Events however were shortly to prove that the British Government's hopes of peace, based on the Kellogg-Briand Pact of 1928, were false, and to result in a reversal of the standstill policy for Singapore.

Discontent at the enforced limitation of Japanese naval strength, together with the social unrest caused by the economic crisis which gripped the world at that time, gave those in Japan who advocated a forward expansionist policy the opportunity to regain power. Thus 1930 saw the beginning of the break up of the liberal forces which had been almost continuously in control since 1921.[2] The following year was to see the first signs of the rise to power of Hitler in Germany and the start of Japanese aggression in the Far East. Nevertheless the London Naval Treaty was ratified by the Japanese Government despite the opposition of the Chief of the Naval General Staff, who thereupon resigned.

On the 18th September 1931 the extremists, taking advantage of the fact that Japanese troops were stationed in southern Manchuria as guards for the Southern Manchurian Railway, which was owned and controlled by Japanese interests, staged an incident in such a way that national feeling in Japan would support their policy. A carefully arranged explosion—ostensibly the work of the Chinese—destroyed a

[1] Cmd. No. 3556; 1930.
[2] See page 5.

part of the railway track with the consequence that Japanese and Chinese troops came into conflict. This incident resulted in Japanese forces occupying Mukden and other strategic points and eventually the whole of Manchuria, a country in area larger than France and Germany combined. The Chinese Government at once appealed to the League of Nations and was supported by the United States of America, who also protested against the Japanese invasion of Manchuria.

On the 30th September 1931 the Council of the League of Nations called upon Japan to withdraw her invading forces. Japan not only failed to comply with this request but proceeded to create the puppet State of Manchukuo. This action was taken despite her obligations under the Nine-Power Treaty to respect the sovereignty, independence and territorial integrity of China, and her signature to the Kellogg-Briand Pact 'outlawing' war. The League of Nations appointed a commission to inquire into the situation. Its report confirmed the charge that 'Manchukuo' was nothing less than the artificial creation of the party in Japan in favour of aggression.

The Chinese in the meantime, partly as a reaction to the hostilities in Manchuria, had instituted a boycott of the Japanese, particularly in the International Settlement at Shanghai. The tension in that city rapidly mounted and, after a riot on the 18th January 1932, the Japanese demanded reparations and the suppression of all anti-Japanese associations. These demands were ignored. Japanese naval reinforcements were rushed to Shanghai, and four days later the demands were renewed in the form of an ultimatum. A state of emergency was thereupon declared throughout the International Settlement, and those Powers with military or volunteer forces in the city undertook the local defence of their respective sectors. In the afternoon of the fifth day the Chinese accepted the demands, but despite this a Japanese naval landing party, advancing that night to take up positions under the International Defence Scheme, attempted to dislodge Chinese troops outside the Settlement and fighting broke out.

In Japan, part of the Imperial Army was mobilized, officially for the protection of Japanese residents in China, and an expeditionary force consisting of one division and a brigade, later reinforced by another two divisions, sailed from Japan and landed a few miles north of Shanghai on the 7th February 1932. This force immediately began an offensive against Chinese troops in the vicinity of Shanghai, with the object of driving them inland. The British, American, French and Italian authorities in the Settlement combined to act as mediators between the opposing forces, but it was only after the Chinese army had been driven some twelve miles inland and away from Shanghai that negotiations for an armistice were successfully concluded. The Japanese troops were not withdrawn to Japan until the end of May 1932.

The international situation during this period had been critical. Any attempt by the League of Nations, by Great Britain, or by the United States to impose sanctions on Japan might well have provoked war. The Committee of Imperial Defence later received an unconfirmed report that the Japanese had a plan for an attack on Singapore by a force of one division, probably accompanied by light artillery, and that this force had been ready to embark at the time of the Shanghai crisis.

In the light of these disturbing events the Chiefs of Staff made a strong plea that the assumption that there would be no major war for ten years should be abandoned. The assumption had, they said, led to our defences being dangerously weak and they gave a warning that 'it would be the height of folly to perpetuate our defenceless state in the Far East'. This recommendation was accepted by the Committee of Imperial Defence in March 1932; the Cabinet expressed no dissent but said that this should not be taken to justify expanding expenditure by the Defence Services without regard to the very serious financial and economic situation.

The building up of the defences in the Far East could not however begin until the inter-Service controversy, which had arisen when the suggestion that aircraft might take the place of fixed defences had first been mooted, had been solved. In December 1931 a sub-committee of the Committee of Imperial Defence, presided over by Mr. Stanley Baldwin, had been set up to examine the question of coast defences and the security of defended ports throughout the Empire, with special reference to the employment of air forces in that particular role. Since Singapore was of such great importance the Committee, throughout its enquiry, tested the evidence before them by its bearing on the defence of that Base. The Service Ministries reiterated the views they had expressed in 1925–26. By this time however the improved performance of aircraft, and experience gained in torpedo and bombing technique, had proved that in suitable conditions aircraft could provide an effective defence against seaborne attack at a far greater range than that of the fixed gun. The arguments put forward therefore turned largely on the Air Ministry's previous claims of mobility.

The Air Ministry contended that, since air forces would be required to meet the growing menace of air attack and since, combined with light guns and local naval defences, they could provide an adequate deterrent to assault and bombardment, aircraft would provide a better insurance at less cost than heavy fixed gun defences, which in any case would need aircraft for observation.

The Admiralty and War Office, on the other hand, held that an overseas base must always be safe against surprise, whether by bombardment or by assault. They thought that Japan would be unlikely to give any warning of attack and might well strike when Britain was engaged elsewhere, and therefore they insisted that the defences at Singapore must be permanent.

The Baldwin Committee, having heard all the evidence available, recommended in May 1932 that coast defences should be organized on a basis of co-operation between the three Services, the gun retaining its place as the main deterrent against naval attack; and that air forces were to be considered as a valuable and essential addition to the fixed defences, as well as a means of attack. Accordingly air forces were to take part in all aspects of the defence of the Singapore Base, including fighter defence and offensive action against ships.

The recommendations of the Baldwin Committee were approved by the British Government which, in view of the situation in the Far East and elsewhere, decided to accelerate the first stage of the defence programme and the rate of construction of the Naval Base, to provide additional air force squadrons and to construct a second airfield.

The Shanghai Incident and the refusal of the Japanese to withdraw their army of occupation from Manchuria caused the Assembly of the League of Nations, in March 1933, to condemn Japan as an aggressor. The League however had no armed force at its disposal and Member States were not anxious to impose sanctions against Japan. Indeed British policy at that time was to avoid any action which might aggravate the strained relations that existed. Faced with this indictment, Japan gave notice of her intention to withdraw from the League of Nations.[1] She then moved southwards from Manchuria, and having occupied the province of Jehol, crossed the Great Wall into north China.

In the same year Germany withdrew from the League of Nations and from the Geneva Disarmament Conference, which subsequently failed. In these circumstances the Chiefs of Staff in their annual review in October 1933 told the Government that 'the accumulation of deficiencies resulting from the long continuance of the ten years rule is very heavy, and if we are to be ready for grave emergencies a steady increase in certain of our Estimates over a number of years is essential'. The following year (1934) Germany repudiated the military clauses of the Versailles Treaty and proclaimed her intention of

---

[1] This withdrawal became effective in 1935.

rearming. With Germany a potential aggressor and Japan already on the march Britain took the decision to rearm.

In December 1934 Japan, after due warning to the other signatories, denounced the Washington Treaty. She had a perfect right to do so under the terms of the treaty, but it meant that in two years' time no naval treaty with Japan would be in existence, for the London Naval Treaty of 1930 was due to expire in December 1936. It had been agreed at each of the conferences however that the contracting parties would hold another conference in 1935 to make new arrangements while the treaties were still valid. In preparation for this general naval conference Anglo-German talks were held in London. As a result a treaty was signed by the two countries in June 1935 giving Germany the right to build up to 35 per cent of the surface tonnage of the British Navy.[1] The treaty was claimed by the British Government of the day as a step towards the maintenance of peace and to the limitation of armaments, but it greatly affected the balance of naval power. It completely altered the strategic position in the Far East, for the rebirth of Germany's navy meant that, when her building programme was completed, the greater part of the British Fleet would have to be retained in home waters regardless of events in the Far East.

The position in Singapore at this time was that the first stage of the defences was due to be completed by 1936 or 1937 at the latest, but no work had yet begun on the second stage. In July 1935 however the British Government authorized work to begin on additional heavy gun emplacements and two more airfields, as part of the second stage. It was considered that, on the completion of the second stage, Singapore should be able to hold out against the estimated scale of attack until the arrival of a British fleet in eastern waters.

The general conference to frame a new treaty for the limitation of naval armaments opened in London at the end of 1935. The Japanese delegate stated that his Government insisted on parity in naval armaments and a common upper limit as a basis of the treaty. When this was unanimously rejected he withdrew from the conference. A treaty was ultimately signed in March 1936, by Britain, France and the United States laying down qualitative limits only and leaving the way open for eventual signature by Japan and Italy.[2] Japan however, after her withdrawal from the conference, at once put in hand an intensive building programme. If there had been any doubt previously, this, and her occupation of Jehol, made it clear that she aimed at achieving complete control over China and the suppression of Western influence in that country.

---

[1] Cmd. No. 4953; 1935.
[2] Cmd. No. 5136; 1936.

During the spring of 1936 the Dutch Government examined their defence measures in the Netherlands East Indies. Their own forces in the Far East were too weak to provide for adequate defence and, since they considered that the security of the Netherlands East Indies was of interest to Great Britain, they suggested that informal Anglo-Dutch conversations on defence should be held. Though agreeing that co-operation between the British and Dutch forces in the Far East was desirable, the British Government were not anxious to become committed to the defence of the Netherlands East Indies. The Committee of Imperial Defence, to whom the matter was referred, recommended in July that the Dutch should be encouraged to improve their defences, but that it would be unwise at that stage to consent to any proposals for a joint Anglo-Dutch Defence Scheme. Nevertheless confidential discussions took place between the Dutch authorities and the Air Ministry in London on technical matters, in the hope that the Dutch air forces in the Netherlands East Indies would be suitably equipped to play their part in a combined Anglo-Dutch air defence of the Far East.

At this time the only airfields in Malaya were those on the west coast required for the commercial air route from Calcutta to Singapore which passed down that coast. The need to extend the radius of British air forces based on Singapore, for reconnaissance and offensive operations against enemy seaborne forces approaching the coast from the Gulf of Siam and the South China Sea, resulted in a demand for new airfields both on the east coast of Malaya and on the northeastern frontier adjoining Siam. The Air Ministry therefore decided to construct over a period a group of three airfields near Kota Bharu in the State of Kelantan, one at Kuantan, and a landing ground at Kahang in eastern Johore.[1] It was clearly desirable to site these airfields as far forward as practicable so as to ensure not only that enemy convoys could be detected early, but also that more than one attack could be delivered on them before they reached the east coast of Malaya. The siting of these airfields was not however carried out in conjunction with the military authorities who would be responsible for their ground defence. As a result they were located in positions where their defence against an enemy who had succeeded in landing was well nigh impossible.

Further, since the existing defence scheme did not cater in any way for the defence of northern and eastern Malaya, their construction would eventually necessitate the revision of the defence scheme as a whole. At that time it was thought that Japanese sea communications were too long and vulnerable to allow of land-based aircraft being

---

[1] See Map 5.

established and maintained within range of Singapore. It was thus still assumed that any attack would be from the sea, and that air attack would have to be made by carrier-borne aircraft. Malaya Command was therefore reluctant to detach part of the small garrison to protect these new airfields in areas unsuited for defence.

It was however becoming apparent to both the army and air commanders in the Far East that the defence of the Naval Base at Singapore, on which attention had been concentrated for so long, did in fact involve the defence of the whole of the Malayan peninsula. As has already been stated, that problem had up to that time received little consideration; yet, bounded on the east by the South China Sea and on the west by the Strait of Malacca, Malaya had an extensive coastline open to seaborne attack. In 1937 therefore the General Officer Commanding, Malaya, (Major-General W. G. S. Dobbie) examined the defence problem from this new angle, and carried out exercises to test the feasibility of landings from the sea. As a consequence he reported to the War Office in October that, contrary to the views which had been previously held, landings on the east coast of Malaya were possible during the north-east monsoon (October to March). In his opinion an enemy landing during the monsoon was indeed probable since bad visibility at that time would seriously limit air reconnaissance.

During November of the same year he prepared an appreciation based on an invasion of Malaya from the Japanese point of view, assuming that a British fleet might not be able to reach Singapore in seventy days, the estimated period before relief.[1] This appreciation drew attention to the fact that before launching an attack the Japanese would be likely to establish advanced air bases in Siam, and pointed out the possibility of their making landings on the mainland. Among the landing places mentioned as possibilities were Singora and Patani in Siam and Kota Bharu in Malaya. It became clear that in such circumstances the security of the Naval Base was dependent on the defence of northern Malaya and Johore and that, to provide adequate land and air defence for these areas, some reinforcements would be required.

In July 1938 General Dobbie gave a warning that an enemy landing in Johore and an attack on Singapore from the north should be regarded as the greatest potential danger, that such an attack could be carried out during the north-east monsoon and that the jungle in Johore was not in most places impassable for infantry. As a result of this warning it was agreed by the Committee of Imperial Defence that the Indian battalion normally stationed at Taiping,

---

[1] See page 17.

which was due to return to India early in 1939 on relief by the newly-formed Malay Battalion, should remain in Malaya.

Since the fundamental task of the garrison at Singapore was to defend the Naval Base and not merely the island, General Dobbie considered that it should be prepared to fight well in front of the Base itself, namely on the beaches on the south of the island and in Johore. With this in mind he considered that, with the growing tension both in Europe and the Far East, those defences which could be erected in peace should be started. In December of that year he gave as his opinion that, owing to the physical features of the country in the vicinity of Singapore, the fortress area ought to be approximately a circle within a radius of twenty-one miles from the Base. Initial attacks might well be launched against the northern portion of this circle by enemy forces which had landed on the east coast of Johore. It was essential therefore to ensure that the southern flank of the fortress was sufficiently secure to allow at least a part of the general reserve to move into Johore. Owing to the overwhelming amount of construction work required, if and when an emergency arose, it would, he said, be wise to build in peace infantry machine-gun posts and obstacles not only on the southern beaches of the island but on beaches at specified places in Johore, and to provide adequate defences of the Johore river line about Kota Tinggi. The War Office accepted these proposals and allotted, in 1939, the sum of £60,000 to be used by General Dobbie as he thought best for these purposes. Of this sum about £23,000 was spent in building machine-gun emplacements and other defences in Johore.

Meanwhile political events both in Europe and in the Far East had been moving apace. In Europe Italy, incensed by the opposition of the League of Nations, and of Britain in particular, to her aggressive action in Abyssinia, began in 1936 to align herself with Germany, and the possibility that a hostile power might bestride the main Commonwealth line of communications to the east could not be ignored. The same year Hitler invaded the Rhineland; Britain and France failed to take any action and thus allowed him to consolidate his position. In Japan the era of liberal government finally came to an end. Several coups by the younger military officers against successive Cabinets had resulted in the formation in March 1936 of the Hirota Cabinet. The new Government was subservient to the Army and those who favoured an expansionist policy. Japan then opened conversations with Nazi Germany which culminated in November 1936 in the Anti-Comintern Pact. This Pact was nominally defensive but, by aligning herself with Germany in this way, Japan made her aggressive intentions once more clear to the world. She then began preparations to extend her influence in China during the following year, if necessary by force.

In 1937 the Chiefs of Staff prepared reviews of Imperial Defence and of the situation in the Far East for an Imperial Conference which was to take place later in the summer. Their review made it plain that in their opinion Japan ranked second to Germany as a possible enemy and Italy ranked third. They pointed out that in a war with Germany, even with France as an ally, a British fleet at least equal to the German Navy would have to be retained in home waters. The strength of the fleet which could be sent to the Far East would have to be governed by home requirements. In a situation in which Britain was faced with a war against Japan, Germany and Italy, with France as her only ally, they went on to affirm that the security of the United Kingdom and the security of Singapore would be the keystones on which the survival of the British Commonwealth of Nations depended. France could be relied upon to neutralize to some extent the Italian Fleet in the Mediterranean and to maintain command of the western Mediterranean. The British position in the eastern Mediterranean however would be precarious; but this weakness in the Mediterranean would not be nearly as serious as the surrender of British sea power in the Far East. That would enable Japan to undertake deliberate operations against Singapore which, in default of relief, might fall, leaving the coast of India, Australia and New Zealand and the sea routes to these Dominions open to attack. They urged, and the Committee of Imperial Defence agreed, that no consideration for the security of British interests in the Mediterranean should be allowed to interfere with the despatch of a fleet to the Far East. The period before relief for Singapore was estimated to be seventy days, though this did not allow for political or other circumstances delaying the despatch of the fleet.

The defence of Hong Kong was also discussed. The Chiefs of Staff accepted that the period before relief could not be less than ninety days, and agreed that, although it was not possible to assess the time that the garrison of four battalions could hold out, 'its powers of resistance would be materially increased if it were reinforced'. But even if a reinforced garrison were able to hold the colony, the port would be of little use, for it could be neutralized by powerful Japanese air forces operating from Formosa. There could be no question of evacuating or reducing the garrison on the eve of the outbreak of a war with Germany, for such an evacuation would entail a loss of prestige, and only by remaining in Hong Kong could Britain hope, in time of war, to encourage Chinese resistance to Japan. They considered therefore that Hong Kong should be regarded as an important though not vital outpost to be defended for as long as possible.

D

At the Imperial Conference the New Zealand delegates reiterated their wish for a British fleet in the Far East in peacetime. The British Government however adhered to their policy of maintaining the fleet in a central position in European waters. They thought that Japan would be unlikely to risk war with the British Commonwealth unless Britain were involved in warfare in Europe, and thus the retention of the fleet in European waters would tend to be a factor in the preservation of peace in the east.

On the 7th July 1937 Japanese and Chinese troops came into conflict near Peking in north China. This incident, which appeared to have been deliberately arranged by the Japanese Army, resulted in the outbreak of hostilities between the two nations. These military activities in China contravened the Nine-Power Treaty which Japan had signed in 1922. A conference under Article 7 of that Treaty was therefore held in Brussels in November 1937, to consider what peaceful means could be adopted to end the conflict. The Japanese refused to attend. The conference proposed a suspension of hostilities and offered mediation to bring about a settlement. Japan however took the view that the events in China were entirely her own affair. There was thus no prospect of bringing the war rapidly to an end.

Throughout the remainder of 1937 Japan staged incidents in China which involved British and American civilians. Though frequently of a minor nature in themselves, they were designed to undermine Western influence in China, even at the risk of war with Great Britain and the United States. The most flagrant of the incidents, which might have led to war, occurred on the 12th December 1937, when British and American gunboats and other craft in the Yangtze River were shelled by shore batteries and later bombed by Japanese aircraft, with the loss of the American gunboat *Panay* and two oil tankers. The Japanese stated officially that these attacks had been made in error. Although there was strong evidence to the contrary, Great Britain and the United States, anxious to avoid war, chose to accept this explanation.

In May 1938 Japan extended the war to south China and landed troops at Amoy, some 300 miles north-east of Hong Kong. In July the Chiefs of Staff once more reviewed the position in Hong Kong and reaffirmed their view that there could be no question of demilitarizing the colony in peace or war. It was possible however that the Japanese, widening their grip on south China, might close up to the mainland frontier before the outbreak of war and so, almost from the outset, bring the port under air and artillery bombardment. Since Hong Kong in such circumstances could no longer be considered a suitable base even for submarines and other small craft, the denial of the anchorage to the Japanese for as long as possible became the sole military reason for its defence. In October a Japanese expeditionary force landed at Bias Bay, only thirty-five miles north-east of Hong Kong, and advancing westwards occupied Canton by the 21st.[1] Hong Kong was thus cut off from the territories controlled by the Chinese National Government and the Japanese could at any time move up to the frontier on the mainland opposite to the island. In February 1939 the Japanese landed on Hainan Island some 300 miles south of Hong Kong. The isolation of the colony was almost complete.

In the autumn of 1938 events in Europe had reached a crisis. On the 15th September Hitler, under threat of war, had demanded from Czechoslovakia the cession of the Sudetenland to Germany. The integrity of Czechoslovakia had been guaranteed by France, and Britain was morally bound to join her in coming to the aid of that country. The British Fleet had been mobilized and war had been narrowly averted by the visit of the Prime Minister, Mr. Chamberlain, to Munich and the subsequent virtual agreement of the British Cabinet to Hitler's demands.

A new appreciation was completed by the Chiefs of Staff in February 1939, based as before on the assumption of a war against Germany, Italy and Japan. Although the general pattern differed little from the 1937 review, a change of policy as regards the despatch of a fleet to the Far East was apparent. The Chiefs of Staff accepted the fact that, since only a fleet could meet Japanese threats to Australia, New Zealand and India, a fleet would have to be sent, but said that its strength 'must depend on our resources and the state of the war in the European theatre'. While the Committee of Imperial Defence were discussing the appreciation, the situation in Europe was worsening. In March, German troops crossed the Czechoslovakian frontier, and in April Italy invaded Albania. Hitler denounced the Anglo-German Naval Agreement of 1935 and demanded Danzig.

On the 2nd May, the Committee of Imperial Defence considered the dispositions of British naval forces in the event of war with Germany, Italy and Japan simultaneously. Since the existing and potential naval strength had not been designed to engage three naval Powers simultaneously without grave risks, they came to the conclusion, 'that there are so many variable factors which cannot at present be assessed, that it is not possible to state definitely how soon after Japanese intervention a Fleet could be despatched to the Far East. Neither is it possible to enumerate precisely the size of the Fleet that we could afford to send'. This conclusion showed that the views expressed in 1937 no longer held good and that Japan and Italy had changed places in order of priority. Five days later a military and political pact between Germany and Italy was announced.

---

[1] See Inset, Map 2.

The question of the despatch of a fleet was again discussed in June when a crisis flared up in the Far East over the behaviour of the Japanese at Tientsin. The Admiralty made it quite clear that, if war did break out there, the fleet which could be sent could not include more than two capital ships without prejudicing British interests in the Mediterranean and home waters. The same month the Prime Minister of Australia (The Rt. Hon. J. A. Lyons) who was engaged on a review of the Commonwealth Defence Policy cabled London:

> '. . . I would appreciate, for the information of the present Government, whether assurance can be given that Australia is entitled to assume that in the event of war with Japan the United Kingdom Government would send a fleet to Singapore within appropriate time capable of containing [the] Japanese fleet to a degree sufficient to prevent a major act of aggression against Australia.'

The Prime Minister of the United Kingdom replied:

> 'In the event of war with Germany and Italy, should Japan join in against us, it would still be His Majesty's Government's full intention to despatch a fleet to Singapore. If we were fighting against such a combination, never envisaged in our earlier plans, the size of the fleet would necessarily be dependent on (a) the moment when Japan entered the war, and (b) what losses, if any, our opponents or ourselves had previously sustained. It would, however, be our intention to achieve three main objects: (i) the prevention of any major operation against Australia, New Zealand or India, (ii) to keep open our sea communications, (iii) to prevent the fall of Singapore.'

The Prime Minister added that he hoped that the assurance thus given would provide the necessary basis for Australian defence policy.

During Anglo-French staff talks which began in London in March the French agreed that, though the Royal Navy would play a vital part in the defeat of Italy, a fleet would have to go to the Far East some time, if Japan intervened. Its despatch would be a question of balancing risks when the time came. Arising from these talks an Anglo-French Conference was held in Singapore in June to discuss joint operations in the Far East. The conference placed on record its grave concern at the paucity of Allied naval and air forces in the Far East and recommended that, as it seemed impossible to station adequate naval forces there in peacetime, appreciably larger air forces formed the only practical solution. It also recommended that because of the precarious world situation, reinforcements amounting to two brigade groups should be sent to the Far East as soon as possible and that consideration should be given to the initiation of diplomatic action to deter Siam from complicity with Japan and, if possible, to obtain permission for the free passage of the troops of both nations through Siamese territory in the event of war.

In July 1939, the Committee of Imperial Defence, in view of the uncertainty over the arrival of a fleet in the Far East, decided to raise the period before relief for Singapore from seventy to ninety days, and ordered that the implications of stocking Malaya with reserves for the civil population and garrison for a period of six months should be investigated. They also decided that reinforcements should be sent to Singapore. In August, 12th Indian Infantry Brigade Group,[1] a mountain artillery regiment and two bomber squadrons arrived in Malaya from India. In September two bomber squadrons arrived from the United Kingdom.

At the outbreak of the war with Germany in September 1939 the position in the Far East may be summed up as follows:

By the end of August the Admiralty had begun to withdraw the major units of the China Squadron for the protection of convoys in the Indian Ocean and to reinforce the Home and Mediterranean Fleets. At Singapore and Hong Kong precautionary local defence measures were being taken as an insurance against a surprise attack by the Japanese. The Naval Base and coast defences at Singapore were in readiness but some engineering work on the five heavy 15-inch gun emplacements remained to be done. The defence of the island was entrusted to five regular battalions (three British, one Indian and one Malay) and two volunteer battalions, two heavy coast defence artillery regiments, three anti-aircraft artillery regiments, and four engineer fortress companies. At Penang the garrison included one Indian battalion, a volunteer battalion, a heavy coast defence battery and an engineer fortress company. The defence of northern Malaya was entrusted to the Federated Malay States Volunteers, and the defence of Johore to its State Forces. The 12th Infantry Brigade and 22nd Mountain Regiment were retained as a mobile reserve for the defence of Johore. There were six air force squadrons of fifty-eight first-line aircraft.[2]

In Hong Kong, the coast defences had been modernized. The local naval defences consisted of four destroyers (two of which were on

---

[1] For its composition see Appendix 10.

[2] 205 (Flying-boat) Squadron: four Singapores
  230 (Flying-boat) Squadron: six Sunderlands
   36 (Torpedo-bomber) Squadron: twelve Vildebeestes
 100 (Torpedo-bomber) Squadron: twelve Vildebeestes
   11 (Bomber) Squadron: twelve Blenheims
   39 (Bomber) Squadron: twelve Blenheims
   34 (Bomber) Squadron and
   62 (Bomber) Squadron, each of sixteen Blenheims,
      arrived from the United Kingdom on the 22nd September 1939.

loan from Singapore) and certain light craft, while the garrison included two British and two Indian infantry battalions, three heavy coast defence batteries, two anti-aircraft batteries, two mountain and two medium batteries and two fortress companies. There was a small station flight of communication aircraft; but no provision had been made for defence by fighter aircraft or for local air support of the garrison.

The attitude of the vast indigenous population in the British colonies in the Far East at this critical period was not unnaturally one of general indifference and apathy. The Chinese, Malay and Indian communities, other than a small minority with business interests, remained unconcerned and unaffected by world events. Following the opinion held at that time in London the general attitude of Government officials and the British and European civil communities was that war with Japan would be unlikely so long as there was a possibility that the United States would also be involved, since Japan would not be so unwise as to risk hostilities with Great Britain and the United States simultaneously. The British civil communities, consisting mainly of merchants and officials, were understandably influenced largely by business, economic and administrative considerations. Many had little conception of the critical situation facing the countries in which they served, and little had been done to enlighten them. There was at this time neither a proper civil defence organization nor an air raid precaution system in either Malaya, Singapore or Hong Kong.

At this time of international crisis, when for the second time in the century it seemed that 'the lamps were going out all over Europe', in the Far East as well they were beginning to burn low. The successful defence of British possessions throughout south-east Asia, let alone Hong Kong, against attack by a major power seemed doubtful. Everything depended on the despatch from European waters of a fleet; but there could be no guarantee that a fleet could be made available, or that if it were it would arrive in time and be of adequate strength. Meanwhile the defence of Hong Kong and Malaya and the security of the great Naval Base at Singapore had to be assured not by the sea, land and air forces considered to be necessary, but by such forces as could be spared.

CHAPTER II

THE EFFECT OF WAR IN EUROPE
ON FAR EAST DEFENCE POLICY
(September 1939–August 1940)

See Strategic Map and Map 5

THE OUTBREAK OF WAR in Europe at the beginning of September 1939 inevitably affected British interests in the Far East. So much depended upon how Japan would decide to act in view of her pact with Germany. The Japanese army of about a million men had been engaged in war with China for over two years and because of this conflict, which showed no sign of ending, it seemed improbable that she would wish to extend her commitments by entering a new war. Yet the steady progress of Japanese forces southwards in China could not be ignored. They already controlled almost all the China coast, and were advancing westwards from Canton towards the frontier of Indo-China.

Faced with a threat to her very existence Britain had no alternative but to seek to avoid war with Japan, while continuing to provide China with covert assistance. This policy was however made increasingly difficult by the need to wage economic warfare against Germany. The routine of control and search at ports and on the sea-routes from the Far East, necessitated by the belief that Japan was shipping abroad war material intended for Germany, imposed restrictions upon her which she resented and which were on occasions liable to result in 'incidents'. Therefore, any action Britain could take to avoid hurting Japanese susceptibilities, whether on the High Seas or elsewhere, was obviously desirable.

On the 5th September the Japanese Government requested that, to avoid incidents, the British, French and American garrisons and the river gunboats in China should be withdrawn. There were at that time some twenty British gunboats on the Yangtze and West Rivers, more than half of which were in areas controlled by the Japanese. With Japanese forces extending their occupation of southern China, it was thought prudent to withdraw these, and their dispersal began in October. The majority went to Singapore where they were subsequently refitted as minesweepers. The Chiefs of Staff advised that, since the presence of the three British battalions at Shanghai and

Tientsin might at any time lead to an incident, they should be withdrawn, but the British Government decided that for the time being they should remain. However, in December, the battalion at Tientsin was withdrawn and replaced by a company from Shanghai.

At sea the China Squadron which had already transferred ships to the East Indies Station,[1] was still further reduced by the withdrawal of a destroyer flotilla for duty in the Mediterranean and, later, the remaining ships of the cruiser squadron were replaced by old cruisers from the Reserve Fleet in the United Kingdom.

In November 1939, when Ministers from the Dominions and a representative from India came to London for a conference, the question of the despatch of a fleet to the Far East was once again discussed, in the light of the possibility that Italy might eventually take part in the war on the side of Germany. Mr. Churchill—then First Lord of the Admiralty—said that there could be no question of moving powerful naval forces to the Far East on the mere threat of a Japanese attack. British interests in the Mediterranean were very great but, if it came to a choice, they would take second place to the security of Australia and New Zealand. The United Kingdom could however subscribe to two principles, namely that she would neither allow Singapore to fall nor permit a serious attack on either Australia or New Zealand.[2]

In Malaya difficulties soon arose owing to the conflicting demands of economic and defence requirements. Malaya's industrial output was of the greatest importance to the British war effort for she produced 38% of the world's rubber and 58% of the world's tin. £93 million out of her total exports, valued at £131 million, went to foreign countries, mainly to the United States. Malaya was thus a treasure house for the accumulation of foreign currency, especially dollars.[3] It was not therefore surprising that with Britain in urgent need of both raw materials and dollars, the British Government raised the export quota for both tin and rubber, which prompted the Government in Malaya to give priority to the production of these commodities.[4]

At the end of 1939 it became clear to the Malayan Government

---

[1] See page 21.

[2] See J. R. M. Butler, *Grand Strategy*, Volume II (H.M.S.O., 1957), Chapter XIV.

[3] See Appendix 1.

[4] The export quotas for tin and rubber for the period 1939–41 were fixed by the authorities in London at:

				Tin	Rubber
1939	.	.	.	45%	58%
1940	.	.	.	120%	83%
1941	.	.	.	130%	105%

that they must make a start on building up a civil defence organization. The various civil defence services had to be staffed by volunteers drawn from all races in Malaya. These came forward in adequate numbers, but the backbone of each service had to be Europeans with a knowledge of the country. A large number of Europeans too had to be employed on essential Government services and few of these could be spared for other duties. At the same time the General Officer Commanding, Malaya, (Major-General L. V. Bond)[1] pressed for the introduction of compulsory service so that the strength of the Volunteer Forces could be increased and their efficiency improved by adequate military training. But most of the European staffs employed by business houses and in the production of rubber and tin were short-handed for, during the economic depression of the early thirties, they had been reduced in size and had not been brought back to their original strength when trade and economic conditions later improved. There was thus a general shortage of European manpower which was aggravated by the return of men to the United Kingdom to enlist. With what was available the Government had on the one hand to produce the maximum quantity of rubber and tin and on the other to keep the country running efficiently and staff both the Volunteer Forces and the newly organized civil defence services.

It was in these circumstances that Sir Shenton Thomas, Governor of the Straits Settlement, pointed out to the Colonial Office on the 27th January 1940 that in his discussions with General Bond he had found it increasingly difficult to decide the degree to which the claims of defence should be given preference over, or subordinated to, the economic contribution which Malaya was making to the prosecution of the war. He added, 'I conceive it to be our duty to give absolute priority to the claims of industry'. The Volunteer Forces, he said, had been organized on the assumption that Great Britain would be at war simultaneously with Germany and Japan, and that all trade and commerce in Malaya would be at a standstill. This situation had not however arisen. Britain was not at war with Japan and, though it would be foolhardy to assert that she would not be, there were signs that this had become less likely.

He therefore thought that the enforcement of conscription was inadvisable and, if applied, would affect most adversely the tin and rubber industries. At the same time he admitted that the organization of the Volunteer Forces was unsound, for many of its members would have to be exempted whatever happened, in case of attack, to undertake civil duties needed for the defence of the country. He expressed the opinion that the degree of readiness which could be

---

[1] Major-General Bond relieved General Dobbie on the 1st August 1939.

expected of the Volunteers would be little more than had been achieved at that time, and that the whole question would have to be re-examined at the end of the war.

In this despatch the Governor also reviewed the defences of Malaya. He thought that the success of any of the possible methods of attack open to the Japanese depended on their ability to overcome Allied naval and air defences. With the nearest Japanese base over 1,000 miles away, it appeared evident, he said, that they would have to establish an advanced base within striking distance of the Fortress before they could launch an attack. Such action could be opposed only by air forces. He therefore looked to the R.A.F., together with any submarines and other naval craft that might be available, for the defence of Malaya, and urged that the air forces in Malaya should be increased appreciably. Land forces, apart from anti-aircraft units, could possibly then be reduced and the problem of the Volunteer Forces would be lessened. Finally he pointed out that the paramount importance of a large increase in the R.A.F. had been placed on record in the report of the Anglo-French Conference in 1939,[1] and concluded by saying that he was convinced that the threat to peace in the Far East would be greatly reduced, and might even completely disappear, if this policy were adopted.

Similar views were held by the Air Officer Commanding, Far East (Air Vice-Marshal J. T. Babington), who, in a memorandum to the Air Ministry, stressed that, whilst in the past Far East defence policy had been based on the despatch of the main fleet to Singapore, such an assumption was no longer justified. The defence of the island was dependent upon the general defence of Malaya and should include provision against attack from Siam and Borneo. In the eyes of the military authorities the existing military garrison was too small to undertake any commitment outside the island of Singapore, except in an area on the mainland in Johore bounded by a line from Mersing to Kluang, and at Penang. Enemy landings could however be made at many places in Malaya, Siam and Borneo; if it were impossible for the army to dispute such landings, the defence of these threatened areas would have to be entrusted to the other two Services. Since naval forces might not be available for the Far East, such defence would inevitably devolve upon the air forces. He added that he was in no doubt that, should the Japanese gain a foothold in Malaya, the fate of Singapore would be sealed. Consequently, not only did the Air Officer Commanding recommend the strengthening of the air forces, but he went further: he suggested that the extension of the defences to include the whole of the Malay peninsula would free the land forces from a localized role, thus enabling them to

---

[1] See page 20.

support a defensive organization based primarily upon the use of air power.

The Governor's despatch was placed before the Oversea Defence Committee in London in March 1940. This permanent sub-committee of the Committee of Imperial Defence had under war conditions become a War Cabinet inter-Service Committee. Its chairman was the Under-Secretary of State for the Colonies and its membership, in addition to the Directors of Plans from the three Services, included representatives of the Foreign Office, Treasury, Colonial Office and Ministry of Home Security. It is of interest, in view of subsequent events, that when the Committee was discussing the despatch, the views of the Governor were supported by the Foreign Office which held that economic considerations should outweigh strategical requirements at Singapore. They based their opinion chiefly on the grounds that Japan had been at war for some three years and was in no position to embark upon adventure against distant British bases. There was moreover an internal crisis of the first magnitude in Japan. The Imperial Japanese Army was ranged against forces antagonistic to its policy, and was not strong enough to go to war with the British Empire. On that account the Foreign Office held that the threat to Singapore should be regarded as remote, and measures to guard against it should not be allowed to interfere with the economic effort of Malaya.

Against this the War Office took the view that, while no one could assess with certainty the chances of war with Japan, there could be no doubt they had been increased by the war in Europe. Any serious setback which the Allied forces might sustain in the course of the fighting in Europe might lead to rapid changes in the strategic situation in the Far East.

The Committee, having carefully considered the views expressed by the Governor, accepted that the security of Singapore was so vital to the safety of the British Commonwealth in the Far East that any matter relating to its fundamental defence policy was of the highest importance. Nevertheless, with the full scope of the general conflict not yet revealed, it was, they thought, out of the question to make any change in the existing policy. They pointed out that Britain was making every effort to expand her air forces to achieve superiority over Germany, and that only a minimum could be spared for areas where danger was not imminent. Preparations were already in hand to increase the air forces in the Middle East and in India, and these would form a strategical reserve for the Far East. Thus, whether or not there was any force in the Governor's argument that the air forces in Malaya should be greatly increased, there was in fact no immediate possibility of effecting such an increase or even of bringing the existing squadrons up to their wartime establishments; on the contrary, it might even prove necessary to withdraw squadrons from Malaya.[1] In these circumstances any extension in the near future of the responsibilities assigned to the air forces in Malaya was impracticable and, that being so, no purpose would be served in discussing the broad strategical issue. It was therefore more than ever necessary to ensure that the existing defences were as efficient as possible.

The Committee, while agreeing that the efficiency of the Volunteer Forces was much below that required under war conditions, recognized that the economic contribution of Malaya was of the first importance and should not be interrupted. They therefore suggested that some plan should be devised to improve the efficiency of the Volunteer Forces, without appreciably reducing the output or jeopardizing the marketing of rubber and tin. The Committee recommended that the Volunteer Forces should be reorganized so as to exclude if possible those men who could not be spared from their civil occupations for training, that a scheme should be evolved for training all volunteers in rotation, and that consideration should again be given to the possibility of introducing conscription.

The views expressed by the Oversea Defence Committee were received in Singapore early in April. The Governor, supported by both General Bond and Air Marshal Babington, felt that the Committee had not fully appreciated certain material aspects of the defence policy, and asked the Colonial Office for an opportunity to discuss the matter personally in London.[2] At the same time he submitted a memorandum on civilian manpower in Singapore and Malaya. In this he stressed that in an emergency, such as a threatened attack, the manpower available would not be sufficient to ensure the control and administration of essential services, such as measures for the preservation of internal order and security, and simultaneously permit the release of men for the Volunteers.

On the 13th April 1940 General Bond sent the War Office an appreciation of the defence of Malaya. This he had prepared in consultation with the Air Officer Commanding, and both the Governor and the Rear-Admiral, Malaya, were, he said, in general agreement with his conclusions. He pointed out that the Oversea Defence Committee had not taken into consideration certain new factors affecting the defence of the Naval Base which had arisen since 1939. The defence scheme had hitherto been based on the arrival of a British fleet at Singapore within 70 days of the outbreak of war, and the size of the garrison had been calculated on the basis of holding out for that period. In September 1939 however, the Chiefs of Staff had increased the period before relief to 180 days. This

---

[1] Two bomber squadrons were returned to India in the autumn of 1940.
[2] The Governor was about to proceed to London on eight months' home leave.

increased period entirely altered the defence problem. Not only was the strength of the garrison now inadequate, but there were no reserves to replace the heavy losses which would inevitably be suffered in prolonged fighting, and there was no defensive position which could be held indefinitely against largely superior forces.

Other factors too had completely altered the situation. The Japanese had gained considerable experience in their war in China and should be able to effect a landing at any time of the year at any of the ports on the east or west coasts of Malaya. Owing to their occupation of Hainan and southern China, it would be possible for them to assemble an expeditionary force, ostensibly for use in China, which in reality could be employed in a *coup de main* against Singapore or an attack on the coast of Malaya. Resistance had therefore to be organized for those areas in Malaya which could be considered as potential enemy bases. Further the Japanese southern advance had made it possible for their air force to establish advanced bases in Indo-China, from which air attacks on Singapore could be mounted, and, as they had already made considerable economic penetration into Siam, they would have no technical difficulty in moving land and air forces into the southern provinces of that country, thus threatening the northern frontier of Malaya.

In the changed circumstances the whole of Malaya would therefore have to be held. To enable this to be done the existing garrison would have to be considerably increased, and General Bond estimated that at a minimum, and excluding the Volunteer Forces which would only be fit for a purely static role, reinforcements amounting approximately to three divisions, three machine-gun and two tank battalions, backed by a twenty per cent pool of trained men would be necessary. Without such reinforcements the external defence of the area north of Johore could not be undertaken, and even the area immediately around the Naval Base would be inadequately defended. His estimate, he said, did not take into account the possibility of an advance into southern Siam; if this were contemplated two or more divisions would be required in addition to those he required for the defence of Malaya.

General Bond went on to say that, as the reinforcements which he estimated to be necessary were considerably in excess of what was likely to become available, some other and less difficult method of defence would have to be sought. Since a fleet would not be available for 180 days, the only solution, as already inferred in the Governor's despatch, rested on utilizing the R.A.F. to the fullest possible extent. He therefore suggested an alternative method of defence whereby the R.A.F. should be made absolutely responsible, if not for the detection and destruction of any expedition before it could reach the shores of Malaya, then at least for ensuring that the enemy could not maintain a base or operate any line of communication within striking distance of the airfields in Malaya.

The responsibility of the army would then be confined to the defence of Singapore, Penang and the northern area of Malaya (to safeguard the airfields at Kota Bharu, Alor Star and Sungei Patani and the food resources and rice growing areas); the beach defences at probable points of attack on the east coast such as Kota Bharu, Endau and Mersing; defence in depth, to prevent any penetration from the east or west coasts reaching the north and south communications; and the anti-aircraft defence of the Naval Base and of the airfields in Singapore and Malaya. If such a plan were adopted General Bond considered that the reinforcements he had hitherto thought necessary could be reduced to approximately four brigade groups, five unbrigaded battalions and a company of tanks.

The Oversea Defence Committee considered the Governor's memorandum on civilian manpower on the 16th May. They had before them General Bond's appreciation and noted that he had shown conclusively that Malaya would require a larger garrison. They agreed however that in view of the general war situation there was nothing in the way of land or air reinforcements which could be sent to the Far East. On this account therefore there was all the more reason for the training of the Volunteers to be put in hand at once. They saw no reason why conscription should not be introduced to facilitate the distribution of manpower. If the available manpower— and the British establishment of the Volunteer Forces was some 300 officers and 2,000 other ranks[1]—were properly distributed among the tasks which would have to be carried out, it should, they said, be possible to spare that number of men for the Volunteers as a whole at a time when, in all probability, much of the local industry would be at a standstill. If a scheme, such as the one previously recommended by the Committee, were enforced, Volunteers could be trained without the output and marketing of rubber and tin being affected.

The Committee noted that no action had apparently been taken in Malaya on their previous recommendations although the officer acting in place of Sir Shenton Thomas who was on leave in London, had been instructed early in May to implement them as far as possible. The views of the Committee were sent to Singapore by cable on the 18th May and, in forwarding them, the Colonial Office stated that the strategical situation in the Far East was being reviewed as a matter of urgency by the Chiefs of Staff.[2]

---

[1] See Appendix 13.
[2] Legislation to provide for compulsory service for male British subjects and British protected persons in the Federated Malay States, and for training of the Volunteer Forces was enacted on the 26th June 1940, and the enactments came into force the following day.

The difference of opinion between the army and the air force over the method of defending the Naval Base at Singapore, which had arisen in 1925 and on which the Baldwin Committee had given judgement in 1932, had persisted.[1] Despite the rulings of that Committee the two Services had tended to follow their own line of thought in connection with the defence of the Naval Base, without adequate liaison. The Air Ministry had adopted a policy of building airfields in northern Malaya and had sited them without reference to the War Office.[2] The latter had confined its activities to the building up of coast defences designed to defend the Naval Base against seaborne attack and had taken little interest in the defence of Malaya as a whole. There was insufficient consultation between the Services in Singapore.

In 1939, on the outbreak of the war in Europe, it so happened that the Air Officer Commanding, Far East, was one of those who held the view that the defence of Malaya was predominantly an air problem and consequently wished to hold the whole of the peninsula. The General Officer Commanding, Malaya, interpreted his task somewhat rigidly as the immediate defence of the Naval Base, which involved the defence of Singapore Island and Johore only. As a consequence, and in the absence of full and free exchange of information between them, and because of the support given by the Governor and the Defence Secretary to the views expressed by the Air Officer Commanding, the gulf between the Services tended to widen. Although General Bond in his appreciation of the 13th April took a broad view of the problem of the defence of Malaya and even suggested that the air forces should be given much greater responsibilities than heretofore, the friction between the two commanders remained. Thus, when General Bond and Air Marshal Babington realized in June 1940 that any reinforcements which could be spared for the Far East would be entirely inadequate, they found it impossible to come to any agreed plan as to how the existing resources should be employed.

General Bond, basing his scheme for defence on the possibility of the eventual arrival of the fleet as being the only military reason for defending Singapore, considered that the retention of the Naval Base was the primary and overriding consideration even if air attack destroyed its repair facilities. If the Base were to be secured against direct attack from the sea or from a landing within striking distance, no reduction in the initial deployment of the already inadequate garrison of the island or of the small mobile force available for operations in Johore could be accepted. The retention of Alor Star, he

---

[1] See pages 7 and 11–12.
[2] See pages 14–15.

agreed, was essential for the reception of air reinforcements, but he could only afford one regular battalion from Penang for its defence and this would leave the island practically undefended. He recognized the great importance of retaining the whole of Malaya, especially for the reception and deployment of air reinforcements, but in the circumstances could only provide Volunteers for its defence apart from the battalion for Alor Star. His defence scheme did not permit of the Base being able to resist land attack or survive blockade for more than two months, but he preferred this to the practical certainty that, if the garrison of Singapore Island were reduced, a direct attack would quickly succeed. Consequently General Bond proposed that almost the entire garrison of eight regular infantry battalions, together with the coast defence and anti-aircraft units, should be concentrated in Singapore and southern Johore, leaving only one infantry battalion and the Volunteers for the defence of airfields and for internal security on the mainland.

Air Marshal Babington took an entirely different view. He considered that the length of time for which Malaya and Singapore could hold out would be mainly determined by air action, and the controlling factor here would be the arrival of reinforcing squadrons from India and the security of the airfields from which they would operate. It would therefore be of the utmost importance that airfields on the mainland such as Alor Star, Kota Bharu and Kuantan should be guarded by land forces at least against small-scale attack. He pointed out that General Bond, in his appreciation of the 13th April, had himself suggested an alternative method of defence whereby increased responsibility would be placed on the air force. Yet, despite this, the General was not prepared to provide protection for airfields on the mainland, except for one infantry battalion for the Alor Star area.

The Acting Governor, finding that his two Service advisers could not agree on the defence policy to be adopted, decided that the conflict of opinion should be submitted to the Chiefs of Staff. He therefore forwarded their views to London saying that, while sympathizing with General Bond's desire to concentrate his forces in the south, he considered that this policy might well result in aircraft being unable to operate outside the Singapore area. In that event, he said, the air forces defending the Naval Base would be exposed to attack by land-based enemy aircraft and could not long survive. General Bond's plan would then be reduced to an attempt to hold Singapore with ground forces, the enemy being in command of the sea, established on the mainland and free to attack with land-based aircraft against which the aircraft remaining to the defence could offer only brief resistance. In these circumstances holding Singapore, even if possible, could mean no more than preventing the occupation of the island by the enemy. It could not mean the preservation of the Naval Base as more than an anchorage, and the loss of the Naval Base meant the loss of Malaya and its rubber. The Acting Governor concluded by saying that he did not venture to criticize the views of either General Bond or Air Marshal Babington, but he was convinced that the weaknesses of the defences disclosed were so vital that the only hope lay in the despatch of strong reinforcements.

At this stage in the discussion on the defence scheme for Malaya, disaster befell the Allied cause. The collapse of France and the evacuation of the British Expeditionary Force from Dunkirk, with the loss of practically all its equipment, which was at that time almost irreplaceable, brought the British Isles under threat of invasion. The disaster had however even more far-reaching consequences, for it entirely changed the balance of naval strength in the west. British policy in the event of war with Japan had relied on the ability of the French Fleet in the Mediterranean to contain the Italian Fleet, thus enabling a fleet to be sent to the Far East. The absence of the French Fleet now made it necessary to retain a British fleet in Mediterranean waters so as to prevent the Italian Fleet from operating in the Atlantic in co-operation with the Germans. This not only precluded the despatch of a fleet to the Far East and altered the whole conception of the strategy for that area, but made the defence of Malaya and Singapore by land and air forces of supreme importance.

In the light of these events the Chiefs of Staff, having informed Australia and New Zealand of the effect of the fall of France on their Far Eastern strategy, reviewed the situation in that area afresh and attempted to forecast the Japanese reaction. It was clear that the ultimate aim of Japan was to exclude Western influences from the Far East and to gain the sole control of the resources of that vast area. She could hardly be sure of attaining those aims unless she captured Singapore, which would always be a potential threat to her southward expansion so long as a British fleet remained in being in any part of the world. Her immediate aim, in accordance with the step-by-step policy which she had so far followed, seemed likely to be the exclusion of British influence from China and Hong Kong. The defeat of France however offered Japan an opportunity to extend her interests; but, until the effects within Europe became clearer, she might hesitate to risk an open breach with the British Commonwealth and the United States. Nevertheless, should she decide to do so, it seemed probable that her first move would be into Indo-China or even Siam, to be followed later on by an attack on the Netherlands East Indies, before she attempted a direct attack on Singapore.

E

They considered that penetration into Indo-China or Siam, or both, was Japan's most likely course of action. Though this would threaten Singapore and make the defence of Malaya and Burma more difficult, it did not, under existing conditions and with the resources available, justify war with Japan. In such an event the Chiefs of Staff recommended that counteraction should take the form of unobtrusive measures of an economic character designed to retard the Japanese advance southwards. But on the other hand, if the Japanese were to attack the Netherlands East Indies, Britain should offer the Dutch full military and economic support provided that they resisted.

They emphasized, though, the need to avoid a clash with Japan and indicated that a general settlement, including economic concessions to Japan, was desirable. But should some such settlement not be possible—and it was admitted that the prospects were far from favourable—they suggested that Britain should play for time, ceding nothing until compelled to do so, while building up her defences as quickly as possible. Meanwhile every endeavour should be made to obtain the full military co-operation of the Dutch.

It was evident, they said, that British strategy in the Far East had to rest, as heretofore, on the presence of an adequate fleet based on Singapore. Yet until Germany and Italy were defeated or their naval strengths drastically reduced, an adequate fleet for the Far East was clearly out of the question, and the problem to be solved was how to defend British possessions without a fleet at all—a formidable task. The object should be to limit the extent of the damage to those possessions and, at least, to retain a footing from which to launch a counter-blow when sufficient forces were available.

With this delicate position in mind the Chiefs of Staff decided that the British garrisons in north China were strategically useless and, *vis-à-vis* Japan, tactically in a hopeless position. They recommended that, despite the inevitable loss of prestige, they should be withdrawn for service elsewhere in the Far East. They reiterated their previous view that Hong Kong was not a vital interest and that the garrison could not withstand a Japanese attack for long. Even if it were possible to provide a strong British fleet for the Far East it would still be questionable whether Hong Kong could be held with the Japanese firmly established on the mainland of China. In any event it could not be used as an advanced naval base. Since therefore it could neither be relieved nor be expected to withstand a prolonged siege, it should be regarded merely as an outpost to be held as long as possible. Inevitably, there would be strong pressure to reinforce the garrison, but that would have to be firmly resisted. In fact, from the military point of view, the British position in the Far East would have been stronger without the unsatisfactory commitment of Hong Kong.

As regards Malaya, they considered that in the changed circumstances it would no longer be sufficient to concentrate upon the defence of Singapore. Instead it would be necessary to defend the whole of the Malay peninsula, which would mean reinforcing the army and air forces already stationed there. In the absence of a fleet it would be necessary to rely primarily on air power; but the provision of the air forces required would be considerably delayed, for it depended on the progress of the war in Europe and the Middle East, the rate of production in the British Commonwealth and the supply of aircraft from the United States. Until adequate air forces were available it would be necessary to increase the land forces in Malaya. Yet even these could not be found at that time from either British or Indian resources. Further, it would be essential, with the slender forces available, to concentrate on the defence of Malaya itself. Thus there would be no hope of defending British Borneo, and only very limited air forces could be spared to assist in the protection of trade in the Indian Ocean.

The Chiefs of Staff estimated that the air forces required to meet an attack across the northern frontier of Malaya from Indo-China or Siam and a seaborne attack on the coast of Malaya and Singapore Island, to deny the enemy the use of air bases in British Borneo, and to protect trade in the focal areas of the Indian Ocean would be twenty-two squadrons with a total of 336 first-line aircraft. Against this total there were available only eight squadrons equipped with eighty-eight first-line aircraft, mostly of an obsolete type.[1] They recommended that, as soon as possible, and certainly not later than the end of 1940, two squadrons of fighters and two of reconnaissance aircraft should be despatched to the Far East, and that the squadrons in Malaya should be re-equipped with modern aircraft and brought up to establishment. The increased air forces, up to the total of 336 aircraft required in the area, should be provided if possible by the end of 1941, and the airfields at Kuching, Miri, Mergui and Victoria Point should be prepared for demolition without delay.[2]

They reckoned that when the air force had been built up to the required strength of 336 first-line aircraft the minimum garrison required in Malaya would be six brigades. Until the air force had reached its full strength neither air reconnaissance nor striking forces would be adequate. The weakness of these forces would involve an increase in the existing military garrison by an amount which the General Officer Commanding, Malaya, had estimated as the equivalent of three divisions and attached troops.[3] Since it was impossible

---

[1] The total number of Dutch aircraft in the Netherlands East Indies was 144.
[2] For Miri see Map 11.
[3] See page 29.

for even one division from the United Kingdom or the Middle East to be spared, and India could not assist because of her many commitments, the Chiefs of Staff turned to Australia as the only source from which trained reinforcements could be provided; hence they recommended that the Government of Australia should be asked to provide, and equip as far as possible, the equivalent of one infantry division for Malaya. At the same time they considered that preparation should be made in Malaya to receive another division, in case one should become available at a later date.

They went on to recommend that reserves of food, both for the expected garrison and the civil population, should be built up in Malaya to the utmost practicable extent; that, as soon as the defence forces in Malaya had been strengthened, staff conversations should be opened in the Far East with the Dutch, to which representatives of Australia and New Zealand should be invited and at which a combined Anglo-Dutch defence plan should be considered; and finally that New Zealand should be invited to hold an infantry brigade in readiness for despatch to Fiji.

These recommendations were approved by the War Cabinet, and on the 28th August 1940 the Commanders of the three Services at Singapore were asked to prepare, in collaboration, a tactical appreciation based on the Chiefs of Staff's appreciation. This was to be divided into three parts depending on the land and air forces available at different times; firstly, the existing forces plus one division; secondly, the existing forces plus two divisions and four squadrons; and lastly, the full twenty-two squadrons (336 aircraft) and six brigades. But the tactical appreciation submitted should state what the three Commanders recommended as the final garrison for Malaya, on the assumption that the Japanese had established themselves in Indo-China and had use of the anchorage at Camranh Bay.

Meanwhile the Colonial Office had on the 2nd July replied to the Acting Governor of the Straits Settlements and had given instructions that the defences of Malaya should be placed in a state of readiness at five days warning. They also told him that the views expressed by General Bond and Air Marshal Babington were fully appreciated by the Chiefs of Staff, but that the difference of opinion between them appeared to be due principally to the lack of resources. It was hoped that this would be partially remedied by the arrival of one division and two squadrons of aircraft, which the Government of Australia had been asked to send as reinforcements.

We must, at this point, turn to events in India, for that country was to become the main base for the British forces engaged in the war in south-east Asia and the main provider of those forces. In 1938 the

Indian Government had expressed the desire that both the military and financial aspects of India's defence problem should be reconsidered, and that a new contract should be concluded between Britain and India in which the latter's financial limitations would be recognized.[1] Various committees were accordingly set up to report on the defence of India but, because of the political and financial implications involved, the Government decided to form a commission to report on the matter. The Chatfield Commission, which was sent to India in October 1938, came to the conclusion that the area of her defence against aggression should be regarded as covering not only her internal security and her North-West Frontier, but also sea communications in eastern waters and strategic points vital to the latter's security. It formulated the general principle that she should maintain adequate forces not only for local defence but to assist in ensuring security against external threats.

The Commission's report, together with the views of the Chiefs of Staff, was submitted to the Cabinet on the 28th June 1939. It proposed a new contract whereby India was to maintain a small navy for local defence; military formations and air units to provide for the requirements of her frontier defence, coast defence and internal security, with a general reserve in support, and in addition an external defence force consisting of Imperial Reserve formations and air squadrons on a higher scale of equipment, ready to proceed overseas in an emergency should the situation in India permit. All these naval and military forces were specified in detail but no agreement was reached on the size of the R.A.F. and Indian Air Force. It also proposed that Britain should agree to finance the provision of up-to-date equipment up to a total of £34⅓ million so that the Indian forces could be modernized and mechanized over a period of five years. The Cabinet approved the recommendations but took no decision on the size of the air forces; this was to wait till the Commander-in-Chief, India, visited Britain in the autumn of 1939 for discussions—a visit which never took place.

Before the outbreak of the war with Germany in September 1939, beyond this somewhat limited programme little attention had been paid by the authorities in Whitehall or in New Delhi to the part India might play either in a European war, or as a base for a Far Eastern war. Nevertheless India's munition factories and her reserves, especially of small arms ammunition, played an important part in helping Britain to survive during the difficult days of 1940.

In 1939, in anticipation of the acceptance of the scheme prepared by the Chatfield Commission, India had just begun the modernization and mechanization of her peacetime army, but little had

---

[1] The Government of India was spending £36½ million on defence out of a central budget of £64 million.

been done to modernize the R.A.F. squadrons, though a start had been made in raising the first Indian Air Force squadron and some flights for coastal defence. There were therefore only seven squadrons available in India[1] and these were with one exception equipped with obsolete aircraft and only fit to work with army formations on the North-West Frontier. Furthermore there were no bases from which an up-to-date air force could operate. The few airfields available were all located on the North-West Frontier and none had an all-weather runway of more than 1,100 yards in length.

In the late summer and autumn of that year India had sent overseas her Imperial Reserve formations, namely two infantry brigade groups to Egypt (these brigade groups plus a British brigade group formed 4th Indian Division) and one brigade group (12th) to Malaya.[2] After the outbreak of war in Europe India offered, subject to their replacement, to make one brigade group available for service in Burma and one in the Middle East. This offer was accepted. Early in 1940 she undertook to provide a complete division for service in the Middle East including the brigade already offered. For these purposes she recruited between September 1939 and May 1940 some 53,000 men on a voluntary basis. That this figure was not exceeded was due to the lack of accommodation, clothing and equipment and not to the lack of men. Men were available and anxious to serve in their tens of thousands.

The end of the 'phoney war' period and the disasters in France resulted in the British Government accepting an offer made by India to raise a field army of one armoured and five infantry divisions for operations on the Frontier or in Afghanistan. When making this offer, the Government of India said that they would agree to these divisions going overseas when trained, provided that the British Government would consent to finance replacement divisions and to provide the necessary equipment. The British Government accepted the offer of the five infantry divisions and thus India became committed to a further expansion scheme to replace them.

However she could proceed only one step at a time. Her expansion programme for 1940 provided for 31st Indian Armoured Division and 6th, 7th, 8th, 9th and 10th Indian Infantry Divisions, besides force, base and line of communication troops. The expansion was undertaken by a process of 'milking' existing units to provide a

---

[1] Air Forces in India, September 1939
     5 (Army Co-operation) Squadron R.A.F.: Wapiti
    20 (Army Co-operation) Squadron R.A.F.: Audax
    27 (Bomber) Squadron R.A.F.:   Wapiti
    28 (Army Co-operation) Squadron R.A.F.: Audax
    31 (Bomber Transport) Squadron R.A.F.: Valentia
    60 (Bomber) Squadron R.A.F.:   Blenheim I
     1 (Army Co-operation) Squadron I.A.F.: Audax

[2] See page 21.

trained nucleus for the new units—both the old and the new units being made up to strength with recruits. Since little artillery had been required for the internal security of the country under peacetime conditions, the expansion of this arm presented special difficulties and it was possible to provide from India's resources only one artillery regiment for each division. Similar difficulty arose over engineer, signal and maintenance units which needed technical personnel, not only difficult to find, but taking longer to train.

The provision of accommodation for the expanding army, a difficult problem in itself, was solved, but India could not equip the new formations from her own resources. She was entirely dependent on the United Kingdom for the majority of the weapons and technical equipment required for an up-to-date army, and the greater part of her stock of these had been sent overseas with the Imperial Reserve forces. They included anti-tank guns and rifles, mortars, light automatics, sub-machine guns, tanks, modern field artillery and anti-aircraft weapons. For her military vehicles India depended on imports from Canada and America, since the only large assembly plants were those owned by Fords and General Motors which together supplied most of the civilian trucks and cars in the country. The difficulty of obtaining dollars hampered this source of supply and the Indian Government were obliged, much against their will, to buy vehicles not necessarily suitable for the country, together with the necessary spare parts, and to train mechanics to handle and maintain types which were strange to them.

Despite these many handicaps great progress was made. In September 1940, 5th Indian Division (two brigade groups) was sent to the Sudan and 11th Indian Divisional Headquarters was sent to Malaya. By the end of the year some 120,000 additional men were under training and the 1941 expansion scheme had begun—a scheme which included the raising of a further five infantry divisions, viz. 14th, 17th, 19th, 20th and 34th, of which one (17th) was to be earmarked as a War Office Reserve Division.

India was not however to be allowed to expand her army in an orderly and efficient manner. The course of events in the Middle East and Iraq, and the requirements of the Far East in face of the growing threat of Japanese aggression, made it necessary to send the divisions raised under the 1940 programme overseas before they were fit to go. Two brigades (6th and 8th) were sent to Malaya in October–November 1940 and formed into 11th Indian Division; 9th Divisional Headquarters and 15th and 22nd Brigades to Malaya in March–April 1941; 6th, 8th and 10th Divisions to Iraq during the spring and summer of 1941; two brigades (13th and 16th) to Burma in the spring and autumn of 1941; and many divisional, corps and base units were sent to all theatres. This acceleration, unavoidable in the circumstances, had two unfortunate effects. Firstly, no Indian formation after the despatch of the brigades which formed 4th and 5th Indian Divisions left Indian shores fully trained and, secondly, the provision of the equipment for the formations going overseas so reduced the scale of equipment available for training that the preparation of the divisions raised under the 1941 expansion scheme was seriously delayed. This in turn had considerable repercussions on the conduct of the war, especially in the Far East.

It is now necessary to consider the problem of the air forces in India which, the reader will remember, had been left unsolved by the Chatfield Commission. Before the fall of France a flying training school and five coastal defence flights had been formed but little other progress had been made. By the end of 1940 however the two bomber squadrons had been re-equipped and, to increase the air striking force, one of the army co-operation squadrons was converted to a bomber role, but the only aircraft available for it were obsolete.[1]

The Japanese occupation of northern Indo-China in September 1940[2] and the consequent threat to the security of Siam, Malaya and Burma caused the Government of India to look to the air defence of their north-eastern as well as the north-western frontier. In March 1941, they drew up plans for an air force of considerable size which included four fighter squadrons for the Calcutta area. But so heavy were the demands in Europe and the Middle East on the limited production of aircraft that all the Chiefs of Staff could do was to authorize such measures as were possible from India's own resources. They did however agree to provide about one hundred Lysander aircraft to re-equip some of the army co-operation squadrons, and to supply some Glenn Martin bombers later.

In an endeavour to overcome the difficulty of obtaining aircraft from sources overseas, the Government of India sponsored the construction of an aircraft factory in southern India. The War Cabinet were not in favour of the proposal on the grounds that greater use could be made of the valuable raw materials for the construction of operational aircraft by the well-established factories in England. Nevertheless a civil firm backed by the Government of India proceeded with the project and tried to obtain the necessary machinery and materials from the United States. The factory was built towards the end of 1940 and it was planned that production of the first aircraft (training type) was to begin by May 1941, to be followed by light bombers in December. These plans however were not realized, mainly because of the difficulty of finding skilled technicians and

---

[1] 27 and 60 (B) Squadrons equipped with Blenheim I and 5 (AC) Squadron with Hawker Harts.

[2] See page 44.

mechanics in India. The factory was thereafter used for the overhaul and repair of flying-boats.

In February 1941 the growing danger in the Far East forced the Chiefs of Staff to ask India to place the two most modern of her squadrons at their disposal for use in that area. The Government agreed with great reluctance and 27 Squadron was sent to Singapore and 60 Squadron to Burma.

In June 1941 the Chiefs of Staff accepted, and the War Cabinet approved, a plan for the expansion of the air forces in India. Again little progress was made towards the realization of this plan, as events elsewhere drew all available aircraft to more active fronts, including the Russian, and those more nearly threatened by Japanese aggression.

The continued inability either to modernize or to expand the air forces in India during 1941 resulted in the aircraft and equipment of the existing squadrons becoming more and more obsolete, while their efficiency as an air striking force grew progressively less. Apart from the operational aspect this had an unfortunate effect on morale, for it was generally felt both by officers and airmen that they were a 'forgotten force' and, understandably, there was a general wish to be transferred to more active commands. Thus by the time war with Japan broke out the air forces in India were already ineffective.

While India was expanding her fighting forces, she did not neglect to organize her resources for the production of supplies of war material. Early in 1940 the War Cabinet accepted the principle that as far as possible the fighting forces in the Middle East should draw their supplies from east of the Mediterranean. India immediately placed the bulk of her expanding capacity for the production of clothing, tentage, and general ordnance stores at Britain's disposal, and was soon largely maintaining the Commonwealth troops in these in both the Middle and Far East. She made this offer in spite of her having received little in the way of arms and equipment from the United Kingdom, whose production could not keep pace with demand. This position was to some extent improved when an agreement was reached whereby ten per cent of the United Kingdom production was allotted to India to provide the nucleus for training the new formations.

The entry of Italy into the war and the consequent closing of the Mediterranean made it even more necessary for supplies to the Middle East and Far East garrisons to be found from sources east of Suez. On the initiative of India, a supply conference attended by representatives from New Zealand, Australia, Hong Kong, Malaya, Ceylon, South Africa, the Rhodesias and East Africa, was held in New Delhi in October 1940 to organize means of developing the production of these areas and to set up machinery to distribute the output in accordance with war requirements.

On the 9th January 1941, the War Cabinet approved in principle the recommendations of this conference. These were firstly, to set up an Eastern Group Supply Council, under the chairmanship of a representative of the British Government, to continue the work of the conference in planning and co-ordination, with power to purchase and hold stocks and to make allocations within the general strategical framework; secondly, to establish in India a Central Provision Office, military in character, responsible for supplying, apart from local resources, all the areas within the Group; and, thirdly, to divide the area into five sections, each under an Internal Provision Office, to meet internal needs from local resources as far as possible. The Eastern Group Supply Council and its Provision Offices started to function from the 31st March 1941.

The Conference had envisaged substantial additions to existing programmes of production for many major items of war supplies. These involved the construction of a number of new factories, particularly in South Africa and India. With this end in view a Ministry of Supply Commission carried out a survey in India, to ascertain her maximum productive capacity of the more important munitions of war and sanctioned the erection of seven new munition factories and additions to many of the existing ones.

Thus, during the period September 1939 to December 1941, India not only had vastly increased her army and sent invaluable military and air reinforcements to the Middle East, Iraq and Malaya, but had launched an immense programme of production of supplies and munitions. Without these great efforts on her part, as the reader will in due course see, the British Commonwealth would have been hard put to survive the blows that fate had in store.

CHAPTER III

THE DRIFT TOWARDS WAR IN THE FAR EAST

(July 1940–July 1941)

See Strategic Map and Map 5

DURING THE WINTER of the 'phoney war' in Europe, Japan had adopted a waiting policy while her armies went ever deeper into China in an effort to bring that 'Incident' to a satisfactory end.

On the 10th May 1940 Germany invaded the Netherlands and the Dutch Government were forced to move to London. The Japanese lost no time in taking advantage of the situation and, on the 15th May, demanded that the Governor-General of the Netherlands East Indies should give a definite assurance that specified large quantities of oil, rubber, tin, bauxite and other raw materials would be exported to Japan annually, in any circumstances that might arise in the future. On the 6th June the Dutch declined to give Japan any special privileges but, subject to a proper balance of trade being retained, agreed to meet any reasonable demands for the raw materials specified.

The collapse of France in June 1940 had far-reaching repercussions throughout the Far East and altered the whole political scene in Japan. Many of the moderates, and those who sympathized with Britain, felt that she would have to acknowledge defeat within a reasonable period. They saw in the fall of France and Holland, and in Britain's plight, a chance to make Japan master of the south-west Pacific, and thus they came into line with those who had throughout favoured a forward policy. On the 16th July the Army, which favoured a closer political and military relationship with Germany, forced the resignation of the Yonai Cabinet,[1] and on the 22nd July the Konoye Cabinet was formed. Mr. Matsuoka, who had curtly dismissed the British and American condemnation of the Japanese invasion of Manchuria in 1931 and who had later led the Japanese delegation out of the League of Nations at Geneva in 1933, became Foreign Minister; General Tojo became Army Minister; and several

---

[1] See Appendix 2 for the Japanese system of Government which enabled the Army to force the Cabinet to resign.

other members of the Government were selected from men already committed to an aggressive course, anxious to accelerate preparations for a southward advance, and thus in sympathy with the Army.

The new Cabinet, seeing in the military successes of the totalitarian Powers the failure of democratic methods and ideas, adopted a policy which Japan was to follow for the next twelve months and which eventually led her to war. This policy had two main objects: firstly, to hasten the end of the China Incident and, secondly, to solve the problem of control over the Southern Region by establishing a Greater East Asia Co-Prosperity Sphere without having to resort to war. In practice this meant a more vigorous approach to the Netherlands East Indies to obtain the oil and raw materials which Japan needed to build up her war potential; strong action against French Indo-China; all possible measures to prevent aid reaching China, including pressure on the remaining foreign concessions in that country; a military combination with the Axis Powers (Germany and Italy); and a readjustment of diplomatic relations with the Soviet Union, while maintaining a firm attitude towards the United States. At the same time the new Cabinet set out to suppress political parties within Japan,[1] to organize the country on totalitarian lines, and to prepare her for war as rapidly as possible.

On the 20th June, some time before the new Cabinet came into power, action along these lines had already begun and, in particular, pressure had been brought to bear on Britain for the closure of the Burma Road, the principal route for the supply of war materials to China,[2] and for the withdrawal of her garrisons in Shanghai and Tientsin. After the 22nd July 1940, no time was lost in taking full advantage of the confusion in Europe to press ahead with the new policy. On the 6th August Japan demanded from the Governor-General of Indo-China the right to control airfields and to move troops into the northern provinces of that country. Under German pressure on the 'Vichy' Government of France and Japanese threats to the Governor-General in Indo-China, the French gave in. On the 23rd September 1940 Japanese forces moved into the northern provinces.

Meanwhile the British were doing what they could to persuade the French authorities in Indo-China to throw in their lot with the British

---

[1] All political parties were amalgamated into an organization named the 'Imperial Rule Assistance Association'.
[2] The Burma Road ran from Lashio, the terminus of the railway from Rangoon, to the Chinese border near Wanting and thence via Kunming to Chungking. The war material was supplied mainly by America, some by the Soviet Union, and, before German occupation, by Belgium. A total of 21,965 metric tons were carried on the road during 1939.

Commonwealth. Admiral Sir Percy Noble, the Commander-in-Chief, China, negotiated with the civil authorities to ensure that the flow of shipping, carrying rice and other commodities from Saigon to Singapore and Hong Kong, would be maintained. He issued an invitation to Admiral Découx, the French Naval Commander, to transfer his squadron to Singapore. This was refused. Shortly afterwards, Admiral Découx succeeded General Catroux as Governor-General of French Indo-China. The Vichy régime then became firmly established and all hope of organizing a Free French movement, or of frustrating the activities of the Japanese in that country, had to be abandoned. Nevertheless negotiations were carried on by the Commander-in-Chief, China. These resulted in an agreement being signed in January 1941 which allowed some trade between the British possessions in the Far East and Indo-China to continue, and provided some restraint on anti-British propaganda.

With the British Commonwealth standing alone against the combined strength of Germany and Italy, with Great Britain in apparent danger of imminent invasion, and with the Japanese, in pursuance of their new policy, pressing for the closing of the Burma Road and the withdrawal of the remaining British garrisons in China, the Chiefs of Staff recommended that, on military grounds, war with Japan must be avoided. They suggested that the best way of doing so would be to reach a general settlement with the Japanese.

The British Government were doubtful whether by giving in to the Japanese demands a general settlement could be reached. After consulting the Dominion Governments, they decided that the Government of the United States should be told that, unless Britain received the clear assurance of American support, she would have to close the Burma Road. At the same time the British Ambassador in Tokyo was instructed to gain as much time as possible in exploring with the Japanese the reasons for this demand and the possibility of reaching a settlement without its full acceptance. In the last resort he was authorized to accede to it as imposed by *force majeure*.

The American assurance was not forthcoming, and the British Ambassador (Sir Robert Craigie) gave as his opinion that there was a real danger of Japanese entry into the war. The British Government considered they had no option but to suspend the passage of war material through Burma. They decided that the road would be closed for a provisional period of three months from the 18th July—a period covering the rainy season during which the traffic along the road would, in any case, be greatly diminished—on the understanding that during that time special efforts would be made to bring about a just and equitable peace in the Far East. Should these efforts fail the British Government would retain the right to allow transit trade to be resumed at the end of the three months period. They realized that in this case difficulties with the Japanese would certainly arise; but they hoped that either the general military position would have by that time improved or some settlement with Japan would have been reached. Early in August the Government decided that the British garrisons in China should be withdrawn.

Any prospect which might have existed of reaching an agreement with Japan vanished when, on the 27th September, four days after the entry of her troops into northern Indo-China, she signed the Tripartite Pact with Germany and Italy. By this agreement she recognized the leadership of Germany and Italy in the establishment of a new order in Europe, and the two European Powers recognized, in turn, her leadership in the establishment of a new order in the Far East. The three Powers agreed to assist one another by political, economic, and military means should one of them be attacked by any Power not involved in either the European war or in the China Incident. The object of this pact from the Japanese point of view was, firstly, to face America with the threat of a two-ocean war and thus to dissuade her from going to the aid of Britain and, secondly, to embarrass Britain in the Far East. At this time, through diplomatic channels, Japan was making every effort to improve her relationship with the Soviet Union.

The United States Government replied to the Pact on the 16th October by placing the export of all grades of iron and steel scrap under control. This, in effect, was tantamount to an embargo on the export of these materials to Japan. It forced Japan not only to draw on her stockpiles, but to divert men, material and machines to increase production of iron ore, coking coal and pig-iron plant in the areas she controlled. It thus, by making her more dependent on imports from China and Korea, imposed an additional drain on her already inadequate merchant fleet. At the same time the United States Government increased its material assistance to Britain, and gave a strong hint that British-American-Dutch conversations should be held at an early date. In view of this reaction, the Chiefs of Staff felt justified in proposing that the Dutch should be invited to join in conversations at Singapore. They recommended that Britain should assist the Dutch if the Netherlands East Indies were attacked, provided that some indication of American support was forthcoming; the British Government should not however tie themselves in advance to any definite course of action.

The Japanese Government had early in September sent a mission to the Netherlands East Indies,[1] primarily to obtain oil and thereby render Japan less dependent on American supply. The Dutch

---

[1] Mr. Kobayashi, with Cabinet rank, headed the mission. He was accompanied by a staff of twenty-four including one army, one air force and two naval officers.

welcomed the mission but flatly refused to discuss with it any political questions and insisted that the mission should discuss its requirements of oil and other materials with the companies concerned. Both Britain and America immediately brought diplomatic and commercial pressure to bear on the Dutch authorities. They urged that the companies should judge the Japanese propositions on a business basis, sell the Japanese only crude oil, in quantities not in excess of their normal commercial purchases, and withhold aviation spirit, the whole of which would be purchased by Britain. The mission uncompromisingly demanded not only three million tons of oil annually for five years—about forty per cent of the total Dutch production and some five times the amount of her normal annual purchases—but also large oil concessions in the Netherlands East Indies. The amounts asked for equalled approximately three-fifths of the normal Japanese annual supply and, if granted, would have been enough to enable her at a pinch to carry on without American supplies.[1]

The companies refused to meet these large demands and offered less than half and only a six months' contract. The Japanese Government, realizing that the armed forces would not be ready for a large scale war for many months and that the oil-wells and refineries might be destroyed in the event of war, but eager to obtain what oil they could, on the 12th November signed an agreement with the oil companies for the amounts offered. They thus had not only failed to obtain the oil and the oil concessions they sought, but had managed to achieve only a slight increase in the amount of other raw materials —rubber, tin and bauxite—which they had demanded.

By this time however the general strategical situation had changed. The Battle of Britain had been fought, the German air armada thrown back, and the coming of the autumn storms in the English Channel had brought to an end the possibility of a German seaborne invasion in 1940. In the Far East, the garrison of Malaya had been increased by the arrival from Shanghai in September of two British battalions and on the 12th October from India of 11th Indian Divisional Headquarters and one infantry brigade group, without artillery, to be followed by a second in November.[2] The British Government were thus emboldened to adopt a firmer policy towards Japan. They felt assured of American support in such a policy, for not only, as the reader has seen, had the United States Government reacted in no uncertain manner to the Tripartite Pact, but inquiries had been received from the United States Navy Department on the extent to which the Singapore Base would be at the disposal of the

---

[1] See Appendices 1 and 3.
[2] 11th Indian Division (Major-General D. M. Murray-Lyon); 6th Indian Infantry Brigade Group (Brigadier W. O. Lay); 8th Indian Infantry Brigade Group (Brigadier B. W. Key).

American Fleet. In these circumstances the British Government felt strong enough to reopen the Burma Road on the 18th October 1940, at the end of the stipulated period of three months.

On the 16th October 1940 the Commanders of the three Services at Singapore (Vice-Admiral Layton,[1] Lieut.-General Bond[2] and Air Vice-Marshal Babington) submitted their first joint tactical appreciation as requested by the Chiefs of Staff.[3] It was based on the assumption that, in the absence of a fleet, air power would be the principal weapon of defence of Malaya, and that the most probable form of attack would be by Japanese forces based in Siam, where heavy bomber aircraft would be within range of Singapore. They drew attention to the serious disadvantage imposed on the defence system by the decision not to make a Japanese entry into Siam a *casus belli*. This decision would result in the Japanese being able to mount an attack against the northern frontier of Malaya before counteraction was possible. Accordingly, they recommended that the Chiefs of Staff should consider seriously whether, if the Japanese entered Siam, an advance into the southern provinces of that country should be undertaken with a view to denying them the use of sea and air bases close to the Malayan frontier, and giving some protection to the chain of airfields along the air reinforcement route. Additional forces however would be required for such a purpose.

Their appreciation went on to define with some precision the role of the air forces. They were to repulse any enemy invasion force while it was still at sea and, if they failed in this, to shatter any of its attempts to land, and to attack advancing troops, landing grounds and bases. The army would undertake the close defence of the naval and air bases and the defeat of any Japanese forces which, despite naval or air action, might have succeeded in landing. The Commanders realized however that, until the air forces could be reinforced, the army would have to bear an added responsibility. After taking into account the reinforcements which might be expected during 1940, they recommended a minimum air strength which exceeded the Chiefs of Staff estimate by more than 200 aircraft—their final figure being some thirty-one squadrons totalling 566 first-line aircraft. They explained that in arriving at this total they had allowed for the probability of simultaneous attacks from Siam and a seaborne assault farther south.

They recommended that, when the air strength had reached the

---

[1] Vice-Admiral Sir Geoffrey Layton had relieved Admiral Sir Percy Noble on the 12th September 1940.
[2] Promoted Lieutenant-General on the 1st October 1940.
[3] See page 36.

contemplated figure of 566 first-line aircraft, the strength of the garrison in Malaya and Singapore could be reduced to twenty-three battalions; three more battalions would be required for the defence of British Borneo, Brunei and Sarawak, making a total of twenty-six battalions, eight more than the number proposed by the Chiefs of Staff.[1] They calculated their anti-aircraft requirements at 176 heavy and 100 light guns and 186 searchlights, and recommended that three flotillas of motor torpedo-boats should be provided to prevent enemy forces moving by sea along the coast of Malaya.

At the end of October 1940, on the suggestion of the Chiefs of Staff, the Commanders in the Far East called a defence conference, as a preliminary to the projected discussions with the Dutch. The conference was held at Singapore under the chairmanship of Admiral Layton, and those present were General Bond and Air Marshal Babington, representatives of Australia, New Zealand, India and Burma and a naval officer from the East Indies Station. The American Naval Attaché from Siam attended as an observer. Their task was to survey the defence problem in the Far East, in the light of the Chiefs of Staff's Far Eastern appreciation of August[2] and their own tactical appreciation for the defence of Malaya. The conference assumed that in the event of war with Japan the Dutch would probably participate, while the Americans would remain neutral, though their intervention was possible. The conference accepted that the primary consideration must be to ensure the security of Malaya against direct attack. They thought that, in view of the inadequacy of the naval forces in the Far East, the land and air forces actually available, including reinforcements already earmarked, were in both number and equipment far below what was necessary. They therefore recommended that this deficiency should be remedied without delay, and that the further co-operation of India, Australia and New Zealand should be sought immediately. They pointed out that the troops available for the defence of Burma were also inadequate and proposed that they should be brought up to a strength of at least five infantry brigades. They recommended further that the total of first-line aircraft proposed by the Far East Commanders' tactical appreciation should be increased to 582, by the addition of a fighter squadron to be located initially at Rangoon. Since it was of the utmost importance that the Japanese should be prevented from establishing naval and air bases within striking distance of vital interests in Malaya, Burma, the Netherlands East Indies, Australia and New Zealand, they urged that arrangements should be made to enable aircraft to be concentrated at any point in the Far East,

---

[1] In addition fourteen field batteries, five anti-tank batteries, a motor machine-gun battalion, three companies of light tanks and an armoured car company were required.
[2] See pages 33–36.

F

Australia or New Zealand. This, they said, involved advanced operational bases, with their ground organizations, whether adequate aircraft were available or not. They finally drew up an agenda as a basis for discussion with the Dutch authorities in the Netherlands East Indies, and a list of subjects for staff discussions with a United States delegation.

Meanwhile preparations were being made in Malaya to receive and deploy the air reinforcements expected by the end of the year. Since there had up to that date been no fighter aircraft in the Far East, there was no organization for their operational control, nor were there specialists to work the radio equipment. Thus much preparation had to be undertaken to ensure that the promised fighter squadrons could operate efficiently.

The efforts of the Commanders in the Far East to improve the state of their defences, and to ensure that their forces were deployed to the best advantage, still suffered from a lack of co-ordination due to the divergence of views between them. The Chiefs of Staff were well aware of this unsatisfactory state of affairs and also of the lack of any comprehensive scheme of defence covering Malaya, Burma and the Bay of Bengal. As a result, they recommended a unified system of command under a Commander-in-Chief, Far East. This recommendation was approved by the Prime Minister on the 13th October 1940; four days later Air Chief Marshal Sir Robert Brooke-Popham was appointed to fill the post. Sir Robert, after a distinguished career in the Royal Air Force, had retired in 1937 to become Governor of Kenya; but two years later, on the outbreak of war in Europe, he had been reinstated on the active list.

Under his command a General Headquarters, Far East, was formed on the 18th November 1940. It consisted of a small operational staff of seven officers, and was located at first at the Naval Base so as to be in close touch with the Naval Commander-in-Chief and the Combined Intelligence Bureau. It was not moved alongside the Army and Air Headquarters in Singapore till the middle of December 1941. The directive to the Commander-in-Chief, Far East, made him responsible for the operational control and the general direction of training of all British land and air forces in Malaya, British Borneo, Burma and Hong Kong; for the co-ordination of plans for the defence of those territories; and for the operations of the British air forces in Ceylon and the general reconnaissance squadrons which were to be employed in the Indian Ocean and the Bay of Bengal. The General Officers Commanding, Malaya, Burma and Hong Kong and the Air Officer Commanding, Far East, were all to be subordinate to him. On the other hand the control of naval operations was to remain directly under the Commander-in-Chief, China.

The Commander-in-Chief, Far East, was to deal primarily with matters of major military policy and strategy and was not to relieve his subordinate commanders of any of their administrative, financial or other normal functions. These officers were to continue to correspond with their respective Service Departments in the United Kingdom. He was required to co-operate with the naval Commanders-in-Chief, China and East Indies, as well as the Commander-in-Chief, India; and, on matters of routine, was authorized to communicate with the Defence Departments of Australia and New Zealand, although matters of major policy were to be referred to the Service Departments in the United Kingdom. He was to keep in touch with all His Majesty's representatives in the Far East and United States. He was normally to communicate with the Chiefs of Staff Committee, but would have the right to correspond with any individual Chief of Staff on matters particularly concerning his Service. The Combined Intelligence Bureau, which was to remain under the control of the Admiralty, would supply his headquarters with current intelligence. In practice the clause 'responsible for the operational control and the general direction of training' was later interpreted as 'responsible for the strategic control of the forces and for the co-ordination of plans for the defence of the territories included in the Command'. Two main principles were to guide his action: it was the British policy to avoid war with Japan, and the defence of the Far East would be based on air power until a fleet could be made available.[1]

The appointment of a Commander-in-Chief, Far East, although it was designed to solve the problem of co-ordinating the defence of that area, did little more than add another cog to an already somewhat complex machine. Since control of naval forces was excluded, there were two Commanders-in-Chief in Singapore, each responsible to a different authority in London. The Governors of the Straits Settlements, Hong Kong and Burma received their policy directives from the Colonial Office while, for the administration and financing of local defence, the General Officers Commanding, Malaya, Hong Kong and Burma, continued to be responsible to the War Office, and the Air Officer Commanding, Far East, to the Air Ministry. Thus, although it provided an organization in the Far East to co-ordinate defence plans with the Americans, Dutch and Free French and went some way towards ensuring co-operation between the three Services, the appointment left untouched the problem of co-ordinating, on the spot, the Services with the civil authorities in each Colony and the civil authorities themselves throughout the Far East.

The staff conversations with the Dutch, which had been authorized early in November 1940, were held at Singapore at the end of that

---

[1] See Appendix 4.

month, although the War Cabinet had not at that time decided whether the British would come to the assistance of the Dutch should they be attacked by Japan.[1] At this conference there was a frank exchange of military information, and the Dutch stated that they were prepared to co-operate without entering into political commitments. The conference decided that the only practicable form of co-operation was a scheme for mutual assistance and combined operations by the two air forces. It was therefore agreed that British aircraft might use bases in Sumatra, and similarly that Dutch aircraft would be free to operate in Malaya and north Borneo. Although no definite commitments were made, a tentative allotment of reconnaissance areas, embracing the immense region stretching from the Bay of Bengal to the Timor Sea, was agreed to. The conference suggested that the crossing of a line such as the parallel of 6° North between Malaya and Borneo by a formation of Japanese warships, or a convoy of merchant ships escorted by warships, should be deemed an act of war. The Dutch representatives pointed out that their army and air forces in the Netherlands East Indies were almost entirely dependent upon the British Commonwealth and the United States for their supply of armaments and ammunition, and that resistance would be limited by their shortages; they requested therefore, that every effort should be made to secure the delivery of material already ordered.

Recommendations resulting from these conversations were, in due course, approved both by the British Government and by the Dutch Government in London. They included provision for the exchange of liaison officers, the common use of an Anglo-Dutch code, joint facilities at certain airfields, and the delivery of armament and munitions to the Dutch but, in the circumstances, only at a low priority. At the same time, both Governments agreed to a plan for the control and supervision of Japanese nationals in British and Dutch territories and for bringing pressure on the Portuguese Government to prevent them giving further concessions to the Japanese in Portuguese Timor. The Chiefs of Staff were however not prepared to define in advance what action by the Japanese would constitute an act of war, for they considered that this could be decided only by the British Government at the time.

Sir Robert Brooke-Popham, on assuming his appointment as Commander-in-Chief, Far East, took the view that, as the problem in Malaya was one not of defending an isolated fortress but of ensuring that the Fleet could always use the Naval Base, the whole of the Malay peninsula would have to be held; to accomplish this the resisting power of the army would have to be combined with the

---

[1] The Dutch delegation was headed by Lieut.-General H. ter Poorten.

striking power of the air force. On the 7th December he sent the Chiefs of Staff his first appreciation of the situation in the Far East. He stressed that the British object was to prevent war, and that his policy should therefore be to convince Japan that British defence in the Far East was so strong that any act of aggression on her part against British territory would prove unsuccessful. His opinion was that, to prevent war, the threat of Japanese aggression would have to be countered by a policy of confidence and firmness, and not by appeasement, for the latter would be interpreted only as weakness. He advocated closer relations with China, the Netherlands East Indies and Siam. To encourage China to continue the fight, he proposed not only that closer liaison should be established with Chiang Kai-shek and that a mission should be prepared to go to Chungking should war break out, but also that communications between Burma and China should be developed and plans prepared for sending her air support. He recommended that British policy should aim at convincing Japan that an attack on the Netherlands East Indies would mean war with the British Commonwealth, and that an attack on British territory would entail active Dutch intervention. He said he was considering the military plan, mentioned in the joint tactical appreciation, whereby the southern part of the Isthmus of Kra would be occupied by British forces should the Japanese make an ostensibly peaceful penetration into Siam under the guise of giving protection. He felt that such action would not necessarily lead to war and would provide considerable strategic advantages; it would however necessitate a further strengthening of the garrison of Malaya. He ended his appreciation by saying that Anglo-American co-operation was the most potent single factor in restraining Japan from further aggression, and that every means should therefore be explored to encourage the United States to maintain their recent tendency of showing a firmer front to the Japanese, and to prepare joint measures of defence; a firm British policy would be a strong influence in this respect. He warned the Chiefs of Staff that the establishment of Japanese military forces in southern Indo-China or in Siam would seriously weaken the British position in the Far East.

It had been, up to that time, British policy to support Chiang Kai-shek, but not to the extent of becoming involved in war with Japan. The British Government, after the receipt of Sir Robert's appreciation, decided to enter into closer relations with China. Accordingly, Major-General L. E. Dennys was appointed Military Attaché at Chungking with the intention that, should war break out between Britain and Japan, he should be placed in charge of a military mission to organize aid for the Chinese.[1] This aid would include the preparation

---

[1] Major-General Dennys reached Chungking in January 1941. This mission became 204 Military Mission.

of airfield sites in China, the accumulation of stocks of fuel and bombs in anticipation of the arrival of British air forces, and the provision of facilities for guerrilla parties which were to be trained in Burma. The Chinese, for their part, undertook to provide troops to assist in the defence of Burma, should it be invaded by the Japanese. Moreover, if Hong Kong were attacked, they would launch an offensive towards Canton and the Japanese rear, to relieve pressure upon the Colony.

The Chiefs of Staff had, in the meantime, examined the joint tactical appreciation prepared by the three Service Commanders in Singapore and the report of the Singapore Defence Conference of October 1940.[1] On the 8th January 1941, after a further careful review of the strategic situation, they replied that they realized there was weakness in both land and air forces, particularly the latter, and were making every effort to remedy it, taking into account the demands of theatres which were already the scene of war. They agreed that the larger total estimate of 582 aircraft was the ideal, but considered, from experience gained in Great Britain, Malta and the Middle East, where Allied air forces had always been smaller than the enemy's, that their own estimate of 336 aircraft should give a fair degree of security. In any event, the target figure of 336 aircraft could not be reached before the end of 1941. Meanwhile, they would try to form five squadrons of fighters for the Far East during the year.

It seems not unlikely that this decision became known to the Japanese. Just a year later the Air Ministry received information from Singapore that a document recovered from a Japanese aircraft which had crashed in China showed their estimate of the British air forces in the Far East by the end of 1941 as 336 aircraft.

The Chiefs of Staff also agreed that they had underestimated the final strength of the army in Malaya assessed on the basis that the full air force target had been reached. They accepted the estimate of twenty-six battalions, including three for Borneo, given in the joint tactical appreciation. This figure, they said, could be reached by June 1941 when a second infantry division was due to arrive from India. They approved the recommended scale for anti-aircraft guns, and agreed to find light anti-aircraft regiments for the defence of those military formations which would be operating on the mainland. Equipment, including small arms, could be sent to Malaya only as it became available. They went on to say that they were unable to provide the reinforcements proposed for Burma; they would however find the equipment for four Burmese battalions which the Burma Government were in the process of raising, and would ask India Command to earmark a brigade group for Burma in an emergency.

---

[1] See pages 48–50.

Although the Chiefs of Staff had expressed their intention to send reinforcements to Singapore, the Prime Minister was himself reluctant to sanction any diversion of forces from the actual theatres of war. When the Chiefs of Staff met on the 13th January 1941, they had before them a minute from Mr. Churchill which read:

'I do not remember to have given my approval to these very large diversions of force. On the contrary, if my minutes are collected they will be seen to have an opposite tendency. The political situation in the Far East does not seem to require, and the strength of our Air Force by no means warrants, the maintenance of such large forces in the Far East at this time.'

The Chiefs of Staff explained that it was necessary to begin on the long-term air reinforcement plan for the Far East, and that modern flying-boats were needed to locate raiders in the Indian Ocean.

In continuation of the Singapore Defence Conference and the Anglo-Dutch staff conversations of November 1940, the Commander-in-Chief, Far East, called a conference on the 22nd February 1941, to produce a combined Anglo-Dutch-Australian plan for the defence of their common interests in the Far East. It resulted in what became known as the A.D.A. Agreement. The conference assumed that a Japanese invasion of Australia and New Zealand could be ruled out initially, that a simultaneous attack on Malaya and the Netherlands East Indies was improbable and that the most likely enemy action was an attack on Malaya from Indo-China and Siam.

The agreement contained a definite plan for mutual air reinforcement between Malaya, the Netherlands East Indies and Australia. The Dutch undertook to provide submarines to operate in the South China Sea, and the Australians to maintain army units and an air striking force at Darwin to reinforce the Dutch bases at Amboina and in Timor. It was agreed that on the arrival of Australian army units the Allied forces at Amboina would be under Dutch control, while the forces at Timor would come under Australian control. Since it was important to make the passage of the northern line of Dutch possessions as difficult as possible for the Japanese, it was agreed that the bases in north Borneo, north Celebes and Amboina were to be held. The Dutch therefore undertook to complete plans for the reinforcement of these bases. The agreement also covered proposals for the protection of sea communications by both naval forces and shore-based aircraft.

The conference stressed the importance of collective action against Japanese aggression, and the need for a clear understanding of what would constitute an act of war. Their countries' combined military strength could be fully developed only if the several Governments agreed to act together, should any one of them judge that the

Japanese had taken steps requiring military counteraction. They therefore specified certain moves by Japan which, in their opinion, would call for immediate and concerted counteraction by the Associated Powers. They defined the most important of these as: firstly, a direct act of war against territory or mandated territory of any of the Associated Powers; secondly, the movement of Japanese forces into any part of Siam to the west of 100° East or south of 10° North; thirdly, the movement of a large number of Japanese warships, or of a convoy of merchant ships escorted by warships, which from their positions and course were clearly directed upon the east coast of the Isthmus of Kra or the east coast of Malaya, or had crossed the parallel of 6° North between Malaya and the Philippines; and fourthly, an attack on the Philippines.

The Chiefs of Staff, while in general agreement with the reports of the conference, again emphasized that a decision to co-operate with the Dutch would remain a matter for the British Government at the time when Japanese aggression took place. On the other hand the Government of Australia considered that the conference had failed to formulate a co-ordinated naval plan, the absence of which was a serious handicap in the organization of Far Eastern defence measures. They requested that a further conference should be held at an early date to formulate one for the Far East and establish a broad outline of policy, with American co-operation.

The Commander-in-Chief, Far East, meanwhile had been giving much thought to the strategic position of Hong Kong in relation to the general defence of the Far East and had decided that it was more favourable than the Chiefs of Staff thought. His opinion was that, although Hong Kong should continue to be regarded as an outpost, it might yet be possible to relieve it during war with Japan. Accordingly he proposed that the garrison should be reinforced by two battalions making a total strength of six battalions. The Chiefs of Staff did not agree with this proposal and in framing their reply they had before them a minute from the Prime Minister which said:

> 'This is all wrong. If Japan goes to war with us, there is not the slightest chance of holding Hong Kong or relieving it. It is most unwise to increase the loss we shall suffer there. Instead of increasing the garrison it ought to be reduced to a symbolical scale. Any trouble arising there must be dealt with at the Peace Conference after the war. We must avoid frittering away our resources on untenable positions. Japan will think long before declaring war on the British Empire, and whether there are two or six battalions at Hong Kong will make no difference to her choice. I wish we had fewer troops there, but to move any would be noticeable and dangerous.'[1]

---

[1] W. S. Churchill, *The Second World War* (henceforth referred to as Churchill), Volume III (Cassell, 1950), page 157.

Sir Robert Brooke-Popham continued to press his case for a garrison of six battalions chiefly on the grounds that, with only four battalions, all would be in the front line with no reserve in hand. He was well aware that the security of Malaya was of the highest importance, but the arrival at Singapore early in February 1941 of 8th Australian Division[1] had, he said, greatly improved matters, so much so indeed that it was no longer a question of cutting our losses in Hong Kong but rather of ensuring its security, since it might be required for offensive action at a later stage. But his arguments had no effect upon the Chiefs of Staff. On the 7th February, they reaffirmed their decision not to reinforce Hong Kong. Further appeals by the Commander-in-Chief, Far East, met with no response; neither was he successful in obtaining replacements for the few obsolete aircraft there.

In March–April 1941 the Far East Command was further reinforced. The 9th Indian Division, consisting of two brigade groups less artillery, arrived from India.[2] It had been intended to send the whole division but the third brigade had to be diverted to Iraq to deal with the rebellion which broke out there in April.

At the end of April Air Vice-Marshal C. W. H. Pulford relieved Air Vice-Marshal Babington as Air Officer Commanding, Far East, and in the middle of May Lieut.-General A. E. Percival relieved Lieut.-General Bond as General Officer Commanding, Malaya.[3] These changes were important for these two men were destined to conduct the campaign in Malaya. At about the same time III Indian Corps was formed in Malaya under command of Lieut.-General Sir Lewis Heath who had led 5th Indian Division to victory at Keren in the Eritrean campaign.[4] He was made responsible for the defence of Malaya north of Johore and Malacca.

Much was to depend on the attitude of the United States towards Japanese aggression in the southern Pacific, and thus it will be of

---

[1] 8th Australian Division (Major-General H. G. Bennett) at this time consisted of Headquarters and 22nd Australian Brigade Group (Brigadier H. B. Taylor) only.

[2] 9th Indian Division (Major-General A. E. Barstow).
15th Indian Infantry Brigade (Brigadier K. A. Garrett).
22nd Indian Infantry Brigade (Brigadier G. W. A. Painter).

[3] General Percival had been Chief Staff Officer to General Dobbie from 1936 to 1938. Before returning to Malaya in 1941 he served as Brigadier General Staff at Aldershot Command and later at Headquarters of 1st Corps, B.E.F. Early in 1940 he commanded 43rd Division and then became an Assistant to the C.I.G.S. After the fall of France in the summer of 1940 until the spring of 1941 he commanded 44th Division which was employed in defending the coast of Great Britain.

[4] General Sir Lewis Heath had been an Instructor at the Senior Officers' School, Belgaum, from 1934 to 1936 and after that commanded successively an Indian Frontier brigade, the Deccan District in India and 5th Indian Division in the Middle East during the Eritrean campaign.

interest to trace the development of Anglo-American relations during this period. In November 1940 the British, Australian and Dutch Governments pressed for more positive American action to deter Japan. It was realized in Washington that there were only three practicable ways to restrain Japanese ambitions: by a show of military strength in the threatened area; by far greater assistance to China than had up to then been given; and by depriving Japan of the means of sustaining a long war. Any of these might lead to war. American opinion veered towards the last alternative since war materials might justifiably be required by herself and certainly by Britain.

At the beginning of December 1940 the British and American Chiefs of Staff agreed to hold staff conversations to work out how the forces opposing the Axis Powers and Japan could best be employed. About the same time the American Government put a hundred million dollars at the disposal of Chiang Kai-shek and promised him a supply of up-to-date fighter aircraft.[1] They told him that passports would be issued to those American citizens who were willing to serve in China as pilots or instructors—a decision which greatly assisted the development of the American Volunteer Group, destined to play such a prominent part in the defence of Burma.

The discussions of the British and American staffs at the end of January 1941 resulted in the production, in March, of a joint basic war plan known as A.B.C.1. The main elements of this plan were that, in the event of war involving both Powers, the primary strategic objective would be the defeat of Germany, the predominant Axis partner. The principal American war effort would therefore be directed towards the Atlantic Ocean and Europe. The United States would increase her naval forces in the Atlantic, and to a lesser extent in the Mediterranean, so that Britain could release the necessary forces to defend her territories in the Far East, where the forces of both Powers would be deployed to guard against Japanese intervention. In the event of such intervention, the strategy of both Powers in the Far East would be defensive. The American Pacific Fleet would however be used offensively in a manner best calculated to weaken Japanese economic power, and to divert Japanese strength away from the south-west Pacific.

These decisions, which were accepted in principle by the two Governments, meant that the American and British authorities had agreed upon their basic strategical plan to cover both the situation in which the United States, while supporting Britain, was not prepared to go to war, and that in which she became engaged in war with

---

[1] Britain at the same time made an additional contribution of £5 million to the Chinese Currency Stabilization Fund and a grant of export credits to China up to a maximum of £5 million.

either or both of the Axis Powers and Japan. The United States had however neither accepted an obligation to enter the war nor specified the circumstances in which they might do so. In pursuance of these plans, the American Navy had by the spring of 1941 started to operate a neutrality patrol over the western Atlantic. This trend towards the Atlantic made America less capable of any show of force in the Pacific and increased the importance of controlling those raw materials essential to Japan's economy and to her ability to wage a long war.

While the British and Dutch were building up their defences in the Far East and their accord with the United States, the Japanese were steadily pursuing their programme. They had four ends in view: to secure their Manchurian frontier with the Soviet Union, thus enabling them to move southwards without having to look over their shoulders; to obtain oil supplies and concessions from the Netherlands East Indies by means other than the use of force, thus making themselves less dependent on the United States; to obtain complete control of Indo-China, so as to be able to occupy, at an appropriate moment, Siamese territory as a base from which to mount an attack on Malaya, and to prevent the United States either from entering the war on the side of Britain or interfering with their own plans for their southward advance.

It was not enough to have signed the Tripartite Pact with Germany and Italy; some arrangement with the Soviet Union had to be reached, not only to protect the Manchurian frontier, but also to check any tendency on the part of the United States to interfere with their southward drive. Japanese foreign policy was therefore directed primarily to this end from November 1940 to April 1941. The diplomatic approach was initially made through Germany, but without success. Hitler was mainly interested in persuading Japan to commit herself to an attack on Singapore before he turned on the Soviet Union, as he had already planned to do, whereas Japanese statesmen looked for assurances from the Soviet Union before risking a war with Britain and possibly the United States.

A direct approach to the Soviet Union also met with difficulties for the Russians wanted a clear definition of what they were to receive in return and, until they could get one—from both Germany and Japan—they were not prepared to enter into any pact. An agreement was finally reached and on the 13th April Russia signed a neutrality pact with Japan, whereby the two countries agreed to maintain peaceful relations with each other and to respect each other's territory; should either be attacked by one or more Powers, the other would observe neutrality. Both parties, despite their different viewpoints, were satisfied with this pact—the Russians because it secured their eastern frontier in the event of a German invasion, and the Japanese because it secured their Manchurian frontier and freed them to carry on with their ambitions in the south. Nevertheless, so little did they trust each other that neither Power reduced the strength of its military forces on the common frontier.

Meanwhile a further attempt to obtain oil from the Netherlands East Indies had been made. Early in January 1941, the Japanese mission, headed this time by Mr. Yoshizawa (with Cabinet rank) returned to the attack. They asked, among other things, for the admission into the Netherlands East Indies of a greater number of their nationals; for permission to prospect for minerals and oil; for permission to maintain a fishing fleet in Dutch territorial waters, establish shore fishing stations and use their own ships for coastal traffic and for an unconditional promise that the Dutch would provide specific quantities of war materials. In fact their requests were a first instalment of their plan to acquire control of the economic life of the Indies.

The Dutch replied that they did not belong to any Japanese New Order in the Far East and firmly refused to agree to any such proposals. The Japanese, whose preparations for war had not by that time reached a sufficiently advanced stage, were forced to accept the position and by the end of February they reduced their demands to more modest and reasonable proportions.

This second failure with the Dutch spurred them on to bring to a successful conclusion their activities in Siam and Indo-China, where for political and geographical reasons resistance was likely to be much less. After the fall of France, the Siamese claimed from Indo-China those border provinces which had at one time formed part of their country. By January 1941 Siamese and French troops had clashed and Siam was threatening to invade Indo-China unless these provinces were returned to her. At this point, the Japanese offered to act as mediators in the dispute. Despite warnings from the United States that the acceptance of Japanese mediation was tantamount to 'taking a ride upon a tiger',[1] the Siamese Government on the 24th January, denying that the Japanese were seeking special favours, accepted their offer. On the 31st January, a cease-fire agreement was signed by both combatants and by Japanese representatives on board the Japanese cruiser *Natori* at Saigon.

The entrée having been thus obtained, a conference was held in Tokyo to discuss the best method of using this pathway to the national goal. It was decided that both Siam and Indo-China should be made, if necessary by force, to accept the settlement proposed; political, economic and military treaties should be concluded with

---

[1] Feis, *The Road to Pearl Harbour* (Princeton, 1950), page 151.

both countries; from Siam the rice crop would be demanded and from Indo-China the right to station troops and aircraft in the southern provinces, to use existing airfields and construct others near Saigon and to use the port at Camranh Bay. All these facilities were to be obtained, if possible, by April 1941.[1] On the 11th March the Vichy Government, facing the combined pressure of Germany and Japan, accepted the Japanese demands, including mediation by Japan in any future dispute arising between Indo-China and Siam; they undertook also not to enter into any political, economic, or military agreement directly or indirectly contrary to Japanese interests.

Finally, as a first step in their diplomatic approach to the United States, with whom the Navy were anxious to avoid a conflict, the Japanese Government appointed as Ambassador in Washington Admiral Nomura—an officer who was well known to be friendly with many Americans, and who had been Foreign Minister in the Abe Cabinet of 1939. He took up his post on the 11th February 1941.

Thus by mid-April 1941, Japan had set the stage for negotiations in Washington and secured her vulnerable northern flank. She had gained control over both Indo-China and Siam, the areas she needed for her contemplated attacks on British and Dutch possessions further south—attacks which would be launched as soon as her military forces were ready and a suitable opportunity offered.

When on the 13th April 1941 Japan signed the neutrality pact with Russia, she gave the world an indication of her intention to safeguard her position in the north as a preliminary to further action in China and the south. It was felt in London that there could be no more effective deterrent than a joint announcement that the British Commonwealth, the Netherlands East Indies, and the United States of America had prepared a combined strategic plan with which to meet any act of open Japanese aggression. There was unfortunately at that time no hope of obtaining such a declaration of American policy, for the United States Government were about to start discussions in Washington with the Japanese Ambassador, in an effort to find a solution to the Far Eastern problem. Nevertheless, although the United States were anxious not to countenance action of any kind which might prejudice the outcome of the talks, they agreed to discuss strategic plans for the Pacific and the Far East.

Accordingly, an inter-service conference of American, Dutch and British Commanders and their staffs was held at Singapore from the 22nd to 26th April 1941, under the presidency of the Commander-in-Chief, Far East. Australia, New Zealand, and India were all

---

[1] This date was however retarded as, until some agreement had been reached with Russia, the use of force could not be countenanced.

represented. The object of the conference was to reach agreement on a combined plan for the conduct of military operations in the Far East on the assumption that a state of war existed between the three Powers on the one hand, and Germany, Italy and Japan on the other. The terms of reference required that no political commitments were to be entered into, and that any agreement would be subject to ratification by the Governments concerned. This resulted in what became known as the A.D.B. Agreement.

The conference agreed that the object of the Associated Powers was to sustain a long-term economic pressure against Japan from their existing positions until offensive action could be undertaken. The delegates defined their important interests as the sea communications in the south-west Pacific and those of Singapore, and the security of Luzon in the Philippines since, so long as submarines and aircraft could operate from Luzon, enemy expeditions advancing on Malaya and the Netherlands East Indies could be outflanked. They realized that, though the Japanese, to secure their flank, would probably make an attack on Hong Kong and the Philippines simultaneously with an attack on Malaya and north Borneo, this latter move was unlikely till Japan had secured political and military domination of southern Indo-China. They assumed that an attack on Burma could not take place till after the occupation of Siam, and that attacks on Java, Sumatra, Australia and New Zealand could follow only after the success of the operations against Hong Kong, the Philippines and Malaya.

The conference based their recommendations mainly on the employment of naval forces. They accepted the fact that until the arrival of a battle fleet—to be known as the Eastern Fleet—the British would be forced to adopt a purely defensive policy. They proposed that the United States Asiatic Fleet should act from the flank against any Japanese movement southwards by sea, and should make use of Hong Kong as an advanced base, though they recognized that this fleet might be compelled to withdraw to Singapore, leaving only submarines, light craft and air forces for the defence of Luzon. They further proposed that the United States Pacific Fleet should operate against Japanese sea communications and the Mandated islands and endeavour to support British naval forces east of New Guinea and Australia. The Dutch military forces should mainly be retained for the defence of the Netherlands East Indies, but their naval and air forces should be available, to some extent, to reinforce the British. The Australians, who were prepared to provide troops, should reinforce the Dutch garrisons in Amboina and Dutch Timor. They agreed that plans were needed for offensive air operations based on Luzon and China against Japanese-occupied territory and Japan herself. They proposed that the United States should increase the volume of war supplies to Chiang Kai-shek, and supplement all British efforts to support the Chinese armies. Finally they reiterated that the specific moves by Japan which had been accepted at the A.D.A. Conference in February as calling for concerted action, should be confirmed, with the addition that a Japanese convoy clearly directed on the Philippines should be considered as a warlike move.

On the 27th April, immediately following this conference, British-Dutch conversations were held in Singapore to clear up outstanding points arising out of the Anglo-Dutch-Australian conversations of February 1941,[1] and to draw up plans for the disposition and employment of British and Dutch forces in the Far East. The American officers who had taken part in the A.D.B. Conference were present at these conversations as observers. Spheres of operational control of British and Dutch naval and air forces were agreed, and an outline plan for the employment of available naval and air forces was drawn up.

The Chiefs of Staff accepted in general the recommendations of the A.D.B. Conference. But they agreed neither to the proposal that Hong Kong should be regarded as an advanced base, for they still thought of it as more of a strategic liability than an asset, nor to the recommendation that the specified moves on the part of the Japanese would call for immediate counteraction, for they considered this out of the question until such time as the United States made it clear what their attitude would be should war break out.

The Americans on the other hand did not accept the A.D.B. report. They considered that it covered far too wide an area (Africa to New Zealand) and that there was a danger that the Commander-in-Chief, U.S. Asiatic Fleet, as principal naval officer directly under the Commander-in-Chief, British Eastern Fleet, might lose his identity and be ordered to operate in waters of no strategical significance to the United States, and that the dispositions allocated too small a portion of the British naval forces in the Netherlands East Indies to support the U.S. Asiatic Fleet. The conference and its report did not therefore bring about a joint plan for the Associated Powers in the event of war.

We must now once again turn to the activities of the Japanese Government and their plans for realizing the Greater East Asia Co-Prosperity Sphere. On 16th April, shortly after the signing of the Pact with the Soviet Union, the Japanese High Command held a conference at Imperial Headquarters to consider what could be done

---

[1] See pages 55–56.

to hasten the advance southwards. Attempts to gain economic and strategic control of the Netherlands East Indies by peaceful means had failed, and, although progress had been made in both Siam and Indo-China, the Japanese had not yet obtained use of the naval bases and airfields on the southern fringes of these countries from which they could mount an attack on Malaya. It seemed possible that Britain, the United States, and the Dutch had reached a military understanding, and the naval authorities thought that if an attack were made on Malaya the American Navy would be certain to intervene sooner or later. Admiral Yamamoto, the Commander-in-Chief, *Combined Fleet*, must have been thinking on the same lines, since in January 1941 he had started planning for a surprise attack on Pearl Harbour to destroy or neutralize the American Pacific Fleet.[1]

The conference resolved to proceed with the agreed programme of extending Japanese control over the Southern Region, but decided that no resort to arms should be made unless Great Britain, the United States and the Dutch threatened the existence of Japan either by embargoes or by encirclement. Realizing that the Services, particularly the Navy, were not ready to risk a long war and were doubtful of the success of a southward advance, the Japanese Government, while maintaining their policy towards China and the south which they had followed since June 1940,[2] decided to open discussions with the United States in Washington to find a peaceful solution. Nevertheless the Japanese Navy initiated part of their Naval Emergency War Programme, commandeered some 180,000 tons of shipping and organized the *11th Air Fleet*.

To this end the Japanese Ambassador in Washington presented, on the 11th May 1941, a scheme for a general settlement which included the following proposals: firstly, that the United States Government should request Chiang Kai-shek to negotiate peace with Japan and, if he refused, should discontinue assistance to the Chinese Government; secondly, that normal trade relations between Japan and the United States should be resumed; thirdly, that the United States should help Japan to acquire facilities for the exploitation of natural resources (including oil, rubber, tin and nickel) in the southwest Pacific. The scheme also contained an affirmation of Japan's adherence to the Tripartite Pact and of her obligation to come to the aid of Germany or Italy if either of them were attacked by a Power, other than the Soviet Union, not at that time engaged in the war in Europe or China.

It is of interest to note that, on the 16th April 1941, at a meeting in Washington with the Japanese Ambassador, the American Secretary

---

[1] United States Congress, *Report of Joint Committee on the Investigation of the Pearl Harbour Attack* (Washington, 1946), page 53.

[2] See pages 43–44.

of State had asked for a definite assurance that the Japanese Government were willing and had the power to abandon their doctrine of conquest by force, and were prepared to adopt four principles which America regarded as the proper basis of relations between nations. These four principles were:

(1) Respect for the territorial integrity and sovereignty of each and all nations.

(2) Non-interference in the internal affairs of other countries.

(3) Recognition of national equality, including the equality of commercial opportunity, and

(4) Maintenance of the *status quo* in the Pacific except where it might be altered by peaceful means.

The Secretary of State expressed America's willingness to consider any Japanese proposal consistent with these principles. It will be remarked that the proposals of 11th May paid absolutely no regard to any of the principles enunciated by the United States as a basis for negotiation.

Notwithstanding the narrow and one-sided character of the Japanese proposals, the American Government accepted them as a starting point from which to explore the possibility of working out a general settlement covering the entire Pacific area. Repeated conversations took place with Admiral Nomura in an effort to clarify certain points, particularly the peace conditions which Japan proposed to offer China. These were not clear-cut and included stipulations, disguised by innocuous-sounding formulae, whereby Japan would retain considerable control of that country.

Pressed by the Japanese for a reply, the American Government handed the Japanese Ambassador a tentative redraft of the proposals on the 21st June. This contained a formula by which Japan would not be committed to take action against the United States, should the latter be drawn in self-defence into the European war. It also made clear that the United States were not prepared to discontinue aid to the Chinese Government, and proposed that a further effort should be made to work out a solution of the questions of economic co-operation between China and Japan, and the stationing of Japanese troops in that country.

In the meantime, despite considerable pressure, the Netherlands East Indies had refused Japanese demands for increased supplies of oil and had deferred the question of concessions *sine die*. On the 17th June 1941 the talks were broken off and the Japanese delegation withdrew. Three days later, because of their own domestic scarcity, the United States Government placed a ban on exports of oil from the American eastern seaboard, except to the British Empire and the Western Hemisphere. On the 22nd June Germany invaded the Soviet Union.

G

These happenings caused acute differences of opinion in the Japanese Cabinet. The Foreign Minister, Matsuoka, held that Japan should co-operate with Germany and attack the Soviet Union, while still trying to avoid war with the United States. Should the latter enter the war, then Japan would have to fight her too. The Prime Minister, Konoye, on the other hand wanted to strike a bargain with the United States in return for neutrality in Europe, and talked of dissolving the Tripartite Pact. The Army, with large forces stalled in China, did not wish to get involved in the vast plains of Siberia. The Navy saw no hope of either glory or oil in a war with the Soviet Union, and realized that both Britain and the United States would take full advantage of such an opportunity to strengthen their defences in the south. All however realized that Germany's invasion of the Soviet Union had removed the restraining influence on their northern flank far more effectively than the neutrality pact, and had thus provided the longed-for opportunity for Japan to realize her dreams of empire in the Far East.

On the 25th June 1941 at a Liaison Conference it was decided that Japan should not, for the time being, join with Germany in the attack on the Soviet Union.[1] She should however adhere to the Tripartite Pact and secure control over the whole of Indo-China by taking immediate steps to obtain those military facilities which she required. The Vichy Government were to be asked for these privileges but, in case of refusal, the Cabinet resolved to take them by force and instructed the Services to prepare for swift action.

The German Government, on being informed of the relevant part of these decisions, protested angrily and brought considerable pressure to bear on the Japanese Foreign Minister. Matsuoka, who was in sympathy with German aims, failed however to convince his colleagues in the Cabinet, and on the 2nd July an Imperial Conference held in Tokyo in the presence of the Emperor confirmed the policy. The decisions of this Imperial Conference set in motion events which, almost exactly five months later, led to the outbreak of war. The Imperial Government declared its determination to follow a course which would result in the establishment of the Greater East Asia Co-Prosperity Sphere regardless of international developments. Their efforts to settle the China Incident would continue—efforts which would involve an advance into the Southern Region. Plans already formulated for Indo-China would be carried out regardless of the possibility of war with Britain and America. Japan's attitude to the German-Soviet war would be based on the Tripartite Pact, in the sense that she would not join in that war but proceed steadily with her military preparations, so that, should Russia be worsted, Japan

---

[1] See Appendix 2.

could then settle the Soviet question by force. This would guarantee the safety of her northern border, but she would take care that such measures would not seriously interfere with her basic military preparations for war with Britain and America. Japan would correlate diplomacy with these policies but, should the discussions in Washington fail and the United States enter the European war, she would act in accordance with the Tripartite Pact. Finally she would take immediate steps to place the nation on a war footing, and to draw up concrete plans to cover the programme adopted.[1]

These resolutions did not however finally commit the Japanese nation to war, for opinions were still divided on the ultimate wisdom of adopting a policy which might well lead to war with America. They were so worded that the diplomats were still free to negotiate a settlement of the Far Eastern problem—admittedly in accordance with Japanese ideas—although the Services had been given the 'all clear' to perfect their preparations for a major war. The die had not been cast but the moment to stand its hazard, as will be seen in the next chapter, could not long be delayed.

---

[1] These included extensive mobilization, the recall of Japanese merchant ships in the Atlantic, restrictions on travel, increased censorship of mails and communications in the homeland, and a press campaign preparing the nation for a possible war with the United States.

CHAPTER IV

THE MONTHS OF DECISION
(August–December 1941)

See Strategic Map and Map 5

THE RUPTURE of negotiations with the Netherlands East Indies on the 17th June 1941, and the German invasion of Russia five days later, left Japan undecided how to reply to the United States' Note of the 21st June. Although the Cabinet had determined on the 2nd July to occupy southern Indo-China regardless of American reaction, many members of the Government were desirous, provided Japanese leadership in their self-styled Greater East Asia Co-prosperity Sphere was accepted, to do everything possible to convince the United States and Britain that Japan desired peace and order in the Pacific. Even the Army wanted diplomatic conversations to be continued in Washington until the occupation of Indo-China had been completed and the outcome of the fighting in the Soviet Union was clearer.

Conferences were held on both the 10th and 12th July to consider the matter, and all, with the exception of Matsuoka with his anti-American outlook, agreed that it would be desirable to continue the conversations. Because of Matsuoka's opposition the Cabinet resigned on the 16th July, and Konoye re-formed his Cabinet two days later with Admiral Toyoda as Foreign Minister. Thereafter Konoye, Toyoda and Nomura made repeated and emphatic declarations of Japan's desire for peace and an equitable settlement in the Far East. No reply however was returned to the American Note and the discussions in Washington, as will be seen, did not begin again until August.

Meanwhile on the 12th July the Japanese Ambassador to Vichy had been instructed to tell Marshal Petain that, if he did not consent by the 20th July to the concessions which Japan required in Indo-China, Japanese forces would march in. As the Americans were now able to decipher Japanese diplomatic messages, these intentions had become known. It was realized that her occupation of southern Indo-China would virtually complete the encirclement of the Philippines and place Japanese armed forces within striking distance of areas and trade routes vital to Britain and America. The occupation would be an act directly menacing both Powers, and would create a situation in which it would no longer be a question of Britain and America merely avoiding the risk of war, but of their preventing the complete undermining of their security.

The American Government therefore decided that the stopping of trade with Japan had become an appropriate, warrantable, and necessary step as an open warning and as a measure of self-defence.[1] Accordingly, on the 10th July they informed the British Government that, if Japan went ahead in Indo-China, the United States would immediately impose both economic and financial embargoes. Four days later British and American representatives began discussions on how best to put these into effect.

On the 21st July the Vichy Government told Japan that they had no alternative but to submit to her demands. On the 24th President Roosevelt proposed to the Japanese Government that Indo-China should be regarded as a neutral country, though one from which Japan should be given the fullest opportunity to obtain raw materials and food, on the basis of her own stated requirements. This proposal was ignored. The same day negotiations were concluded with the Vichy Government for Japanese troops to march into southern Indo-China and by the end of the month they had occupied Camranh Bay and Saigon.

The American Government replied on the 26th July by freezing all Japanese assets in the United States, thus in effect bringing all trade transactions between the two countries under their own control.[2] Although the British Government did not wish to increase the risk of a Japanese attack in the Far East without a promise of American support, the Cabinet decided, after consulting the Dominions, to take similar action and immediately gave notice of the termination of the Anglo-Japanese, the Indian-Japanese and the Burma-Japanese commercial treaties. On the 27th July the Netherlands East Indies did likewise, though they realized they were taking a very grave risk, for they had no assurance of either British or American support in the event of a Japanese invasion.

The freezing of all Japanese assets caused the greatest consternation in Government and business circles in Tokyo, for they realized it meant the virtual cessation of all trade between Japan and the rest of the world. It was obvious that the commercial effects would speedily make themselves felt, for all business houses dealing in imports would have to close down, and factories and warehouses handling export goods would have to halt production. Heavy financial

---

[1] It is of interest to note that the Navy Department in Washington, on the 19th July, gave as their opinion that Japan was not likely to move beyond Indo-China in the near future unless an embargo were placed on oil, but that if such an embargo were authorized, the Japanese would make an early attack on both Malaya and the Netherlands East Indies.

[2] Lieut.-General D. MacArthur was appointed to command the United States Army Forces in the Far East on this date.

loss would quickly follow and there would be a consequent fall in the national revenues.

From a military point of view it was clear that production of war material would, within a few months, begin to decline unless the reserves of raw materials collected so painstakingly over the previous decade were brought into use, and even those would not arrest the decline for long. The most serious aspect of the embargo however lay in the fact that it cut off all outside oil supplies and Japan's own production provided for only some ten per cent of her normal requirements. Her reserves could only be made to last with the most rigid economy for some three years of peace or for a much shorter period in war. There was no adequate source of supply left that was not under hostile control.[1]

Much however depended on whether the freezing of the assets would be vigorously applied and whether sufficient raw materials—particularly oil—would reach her shores to enable her to carry on with her plans without drawing on her reserves. The Japanese realized that Britain and the United States would cut off all supplies which could be used for warlike purposes, but hoped that the Netherlands East Indies, weak and exposed as they were, would play a more cautious hand and continue to supply the quantities agreed upon during the protracted negotiations of the past year. On the 29th July the Dutch decided that special permits would be needed for all exports to Japan and warned the Japanese that all exports might be stopped unless matters improved. The Japanese now had to make up their minds whether to find a peaceful settlement in the Far East, which meant a considerable modification in the demands of their Note of the 11th May, or to go to war before the cessation of trade had destroyed their ability to do so with any prospect of success.

At the end of July a Liaison Conference was held to discuss the question. The Army would not countenance any arrangement with the United States and Britain which limited their freedom to move southwards or against the Soviet Union. The Navy, who were the custodians of the bulk of the oil reserves and who had always opposed war with the United States, pointed out that, if the embargo were maintained, these reserves would last for barely two years of war. They said it was a question of negotiation, collapse or war. They favoured negotiation and proposed that every possible step, including if necessary the abandonment of the Tripartite Pact, should be taken to avoid war with America. If all efforts failed, Japan should seize the initiative and resort to war rather than accept economic collapse.[2]

---

[1] See Appendix 3.
[2] It is noteworthy that this was the first time that the Japanese naval authorities had weakened in opposing a war which might involve the United States.

As a result of the conference Konoye decided once again to open discussions in Washington, and on the 6th August Admiral Nomura handed a Note to the Secretary of State which purported to be the long-delayed answer to the American Note of the 21st June. This demanded that the United States remove the restrictions she had imposed upon trade with Japan; suspend her defensive preparations in the Philippines; discontinue the supply of military equipment to the British and Dutch garrisons in the Far East, and aid to the Chinese Government. The United States were also to recognize Japan's special military position in Indo-China, and agree to her permanent preferential political and economic status in that country. In return the Japanese Government would not station troops in regions of the south-western Pacific other than in Indo-China, although they proposed to retain military establishments in that country for an indefinite period. These proposals were on the same general lines as those of the 11th May. They offered only one concession—that Japan would not advance farther south than Indo-China—and were in no way responsive to the American suggestions of the 21st June. This was pointed out to the Japanese Ambassador in Washington on the 8th August.

On the 9th August the Prime Minister and the President met at sea off Newfoundland, at what later became known as the Atlantic Conference, to discuss among other matters problems relating to the Far East.

Mr. Churchill proposed that the United States should not only give Japan a strong warning against any further encroachment in the south-west Pacific, but also give an assurance to both the British and Dutch Governments that she would come to their aid with armed support should either be attacked by the Japanese. The President, who was not able to give such assurances, said that, though the Japanese proposals of the 6th August were fundamentally unacceptable and he was under no illusion about their value or sincerity, it would be useful to discuss them if only for the sake of gaining even a month's time. He added that he intended to maintain fully the economic measures against Japan and to renew his proposals for the neutralization of both Siam and Indo-China when discussions re-opened. Finally, at the Prime Minister's request, he agreed to include in his next communication to the Japanese Ambassador in Washington a warning that any further encroachment by Japan would produce a situation in which the United States Government would be compelled to take counter measures, even though these might lead to war between the United States and Japan. The President also agreed to inform the Japanese that the American and

British Governments were acting in close accord, and the Prime Minister arranged to give a similar warning after his return to London.

On the 17th August the President received the Japanese Ambassador in Washington and, having made the suggestion that informal discussions should be resumed, gave him a warning which differed from the agreed version. It read,

> '... If the Japanese Government takes any further steps in pursuance of a policy or programme of military domination by force or threat of force of neighbouring countries, the Government of the United States will be compelled to take immediately any and all steps which it may deem necessary towards safeguarding the legitimate rights and interests of the United States and American nationals, and towards insuring the safety and security of the United States.'

The wording differed considerably from the agreed version in that it omitted the word 'war', made no reference to Great Britain, and laid much emphasis on the security of the United States. The Prime Minister had to alter the style of his pronouncement to accord with the modified warning. In a broadcast on the 24th August he said that Japanese expansionist activities could not be allowed to continue and that, should the efforts of the United States fail to bring about a peaceful settlement in the Far East, Great Britain would be at America's side if she became involved in a war with Japan.[1]

British policy at this time was determined by the overriding necessity of keeping in step with American policy. Thus from the inception of the embargo in July the British Government were content to leave the initiative in dealing with the Japanese to the United States. Both Governments were agreed on the importance of gaining time and of avoiding if possible any action which might result in war, but their methods differed. The British Government—and the Dutch too—realized that, if their policy remained in line with that of the United States, they could hope for American support if war broke out. The events described in the rest of this chapter, therefore, deal largely with the development of the negotiations between Japan and the United States. Britain watched and waited anxiously, while she built up her defences as best she could.

In an endeavour to find a way out of the *impasse* while diplomatic action was still possible, though the Army and Navy with an eye on the falling oil stocks might force the issue any day, Konoye on the 28th August suggested a meeting between himself and the President

---

[1] *The War Speeches of the Rt. Hon. Winston S. Churchill*, Volume II (Cassell, 1952), pages 61–62.

of the United States. 'I consider it,' he said, ' . . . of urgent necessity that the two heads of the Governments should meet . . . to explore the possibility of saving the situation.' While the statement which accompanied this suggestion contained many assurances of Japan's peaceful intentions, all the important ones were as usual qualified or conditional. The American reply on the 3rd September proposed that the meeting should be deferred, pending preliminary discussions of the fundamental and essential questions on which agreement was sought.

Thus September had been reached and Konoye had made no progress in the diplomatic field. Both the Army and the Navy demanded that, as settlement by diplomacy seemed unlikely, the issue should be faced and recourse made to arms before Japanese national power began to wane. The Cabinet and High Command after much discussion reached a compromise. All arrangements for war were to be perfected, and a time limit was to be set for diplomatic discussions.

This compromise was accepted at an Imperial Conference on the 6th September. It was decided then that: firstly, all war preparations would be proceeded with and completed by the end of October; secondly, every endeavour would be made through diplomatic channels to persuade the United States and Britain to agree to Japan's minimum demands, and thirdly, that if by early October there were no reasonable hope of these being met the decision to go to war at the most appropriate moment would be taken. There is no need to quote these minimum demands in full, for they were similar to those of the 6th August, except that the Japanese *quid pro quo* was changed to an undertaking not to use Indo-China as a base for southern operations,[1] and that, in the event of the United States becoming embroiled in the war in Europe, the interpretation and execution of the Tripartite Pact would be decided by Japan herself. They thus went very little way towards meeting the United States' proposals of the 21st June or towards recognizing the principles laid down on the 16th April.[2]

The Imperial High Command thereupon forced the issue, for time had become of vital importance. Not only did the passage of every day see a decline in the oil reserves, but it gave their opponents in the areas they coveted time to build up their strength. Time too affected their strategy. By the end of December the north-east monsoon would make the initial landings in Malaya and the Philippines hazardous and weather conditions in the north might endanger the success of the projected Pearl Harbour attack.[3] Moreover the possibility of a Russian attack in the north was always present, and Japan

---

[1] Operations against China were excepted.
[2] See pages 64–65.
[3] See page 64.

wished to complete the conquest of the southern area before the advent of spring opened up Manchuria for active operations. The period of indecision had come to an end. A time limit had been set, after which diplomacy would give way to armed force.

We must now go back in time and examine the British reactions to the Japanese occupation of southern Indo-China, and the preparations made to meet the new dangers threatening in the Far East. On the 11th August the Prime Minister had cabled from the Atlantic Conference that the President was shortly to present Japan with a note making it plain that any further encroachment on her part might lead to war. The following day the Chiefs of Staff had met to discuss steps to be taken in the immediate future to reinforce the Far East.

The long-term naval plan was to build up in the Indian Ocean a fleet of seven capital ships, one aircraft carrier, ten cruisers and about twenty-four destroyers. Under the most favourable circumstances this fleet could not be assembled before March 1942. As an interim measure the Chiefs of Staff proposed that one battleship from the Mediterranean should be sent east by mid-September and that four older battleships, then engaged on convoy work in the Atlantic, should follow by the end of the year. One aircraft carrier would be made available if possible, but no additional cruisers could be sent without prejudicing other operations.

On his return from the Atlantic Conference a difference of opinion arose between Mr. Churchill and the Admiralty over the quality and composition of the Eastern Fleet. He was in favour of placing in the triangle Aden, Singapore and Simonstown 'a formidable, fast high-class squadron', which would include at least one of the latest battleships.[1] The Admiralty on the other hand felt that none of the three latest battleships could be spared, as long as there was the possibility of the German battleship *Tirpitz* breaking out into the Atlantic. They proposed to use the four older battleships primarily as convoy escorts in the Indian Ocean, and to reinforce them early in the new year with two more battleships more nearly matching their speed, a battle cruiser and, in an emergency, an aircraft carrier.

Mr. Churchill found fault with these dispositions. He felt it wrong to maintain in the Indian Ocean a costly fleet of slow obsolescent ships which could neither fight a fleet action with the main Japanese force nor act as a deterrent to Japanese fast battleships used as raiders. He pointed out the value of a small number of fast modern ships, and drew an analogy between the influence of the *Tirpitz* upon

---

[1] Simonstown is the naval base near Capetown.

the Home Fleet and that of a small but powerful eastern squadron on Japanese dispositions.[1] The essential difference between the Prime Minister's views and those of the Admiralty was that he had in mind a potentially offensive force which by its presence would act as a deterrent to Japanese aggression, whereas the Admiralty wished to form a defensive force to protect shipping and convoys in the Indian Ocean. The two points of view conflicted and for a time no decision was taken.

Meanwhile in Washington the British and American staffs had been making further attempts to obtain a revised agreement on an outline plan for the employment of American, Dutch and British forces in the Far East area in the event of war, to replace the rejected A.D.B. report.[2] Bearing in mind the great importance that the American Chiefs of Staff attached to an A.D.B. agreement being kept closely in line with the proposals in the A.B.C.1 Agreement, they prepared by the 25th August a revised draft agreement, under the title of A.D.B.2. This met most of the objections which the American Chiefs of Staff had made to the previous paper, especially on the limitation of the area and the command of the naval forces.

Early in August 1941, the Commander-in-Chief, Far East, who had for months been considering the possibility of occupying part of the Isthmus of Kra sent the Chiefs of Staff details of a plan for an advance into the Singora–Patani area of Siam.[3] Singora was the only port of consequence on that part of the east coast and from it, he estimated, a force of three or four enemy divisions could be maintained; its geographical position alone would make its occupation by the Japanese very probable as the best and easiest way for them to build up a shore-based air threat to Malaya.

The plan, later given the code name 'Matador', was therefore to seize and hold the area with the object of denying to the enemy the use of the port of Singora, the adjacent airfields and the railway and road to the Malayan frontier. Sir Robert estimated that the scale of attack which might be expected against British forces once established in the Singora area would be an advance by one division from Bangkok, largely dependent on a single-line railway exposed to air attack, and a seaborne attack by up to two divisions anywhere on the coast north of Kota Bharu. It would therefore be necessary to hold not only the beaches near Singora but a defensive position north of the town. He considered that a minimum force of three brigade groups, supported by four bomber and two fighter squadrons, would be required

---

[1] Churchill, Volume III (Cassell, 1950), Appendix K.
[2] See pages 61–62.
[3] See page 53.

for the purpose. Such a force could not however be provided unless the Dutch honoured the A.D.B. Agreement and sent air reinforcements to Malaya, and until the arrival of an additional brigade group from India in September.

Meanwhile General Percival had formed his own estimate of the forces required for the defence of Malaya. He told the War Office on the 2nd August that he considered his minimum requirements were as follows: one division for the defence of the area Perlis–Kedah; two battalions for the defence of Penang; one division for the defence of the area Kelantan–Trengganu–Pahang; one division and certain corps troops, including a tank regiment, for III Corps reserve in northern Malaya; one division of two infantry brigades and a machine-gun battalion for the defence of Johore; one division and a tank regiment for the defence of Singapore Island and to provide reserves for southern Malaya, and one infantry brigade for Borneo—a total of forty-eight battalions to which the necessary field, anti-tank and mobile light anti-aircraft artillery, engineer and ancillary units would have to be added. He stated his anti-aircraft requirements to be two heavy anti-aircraft regiments for the field forces, and 212 heavy and 124 light anti-aircraft guns for the defence of the fortress itself. It will be noted that the main features of this demand were a complete division for the east coast in place of two infantry brigades, a division as a reserve for III Corps, two tank regiments, and an infantry brigade in place of one battalion for British Borneo.

On the 20th August Sir Robert, commenting on Percival's estimate, said that the Japanese plan for the capture of Singapore would include the establishment of airfields and landing grounds progressively nearer Singapore, while their long-range fighter squadrons based in southern Indo-China would support an invasion of southern Siam, from where most of Malaya would be exposed to air attack. He considered that an overland advance to capture the group of airfields in northern Malaya would probably follow, and that the airfields on the east coast were likely to become the objectives of seaborne expeditions. He pointed out that the Allied defences against such attacks were deplorably weak: the available naval strength was inadequate to dispute command of the sea, and the small air striking force, on which the defence organization rested, would soon be reduced by the normal attrition of war to a state which would greatly increase the possibility of successful enemy landings. The long stretches of beach on the east coast could not be properly defended, and it seemed likely that the Allied troops would find themselves fighting without adequate air support in the interior of a country in which the lack of road and railway communications would preclude the rapid movement of central reserves. Sir Robert therefore supported General Percival in his desire for an increase in the strength of the army so that forces would be sufficient both for the defence of the airfields on the east coast and for a full-scale 'Matador' operation. At the same time he once again stressed the need for increased air power with which to strike at enemy shipping.

On the 1st September the Chiefs of Staff asked Sir Robert if, with the forces available in the autumn, 'Matador' was in his opinion a practical proposition. A reconnaissance of the Singora area, undertaken meanwhile by British officers in plain clothes, had disclosed that the size of the force required to defend the area would depend on whether the operation was undertaken in the dry or wet season. During the former, four brigade groups would be needed, but during the latter three would suffice. He therefore replied that sufficient forces would be available provided that 'Matador' was not undertaken before the 1st October.

On the 17th September, the Chiefs of Staff told Sir Robert that as their policy was to avoid war with Japan they did not intend to enter Siam before its violation by the Japanese. Nevertheless they agreed that the occupation of Singora would be most desirable as a defensive measure, and enquired what would be the minimum period of warning needed to implement the operation. They accepted General Percival's estimate of the land forces required for the defence of Malaya, but in the existing circumstances were unable to meet his requirements in the foreseeable future. They pointed out that as naval and air strength increased so would the need for land forces diminish, and that material increases in both were likely to occur before his requirements could be met. The strength of the forces would therefore have to be kept constantly under review. In reply to their enquiry, Sir Robert informed them that 'Matador' could begin thirty-six hours after the receipt of the order to implement it reached his headquarters.

Meanwhile the British Ambassador to China had suggested, at the end of June 1941, that a policy and programme of co-ordinated civil activities for the whole of the Far East should be worked out, in case communications between the various civil authorities in that area and London were interrupted. He proposed the setting up of an appropriate civil administration, headed by someone of sufficient standing to command the confidence of all concerned, to carry out any agreed policy and programme in detail. This suggestion would have overcome some of the weaknesses in the system which had been introduced with the appointment of a Commander-in-Chief, Far East, and would have provided a system of co-ordination of all civil activities in the Far East instead of in London.[1]

---

[1] See page 51.

The War Cabinet agreed to investigate these proposals and sent out Mr. Duff Cooper (Chancellor of the Duchy of Lancaster). His terms of reference, issued on the 18th July 1941, were that he was to examine the existing arrangements for consultation and communication between the various British authorities in that area—military, administrative and political—and report how these could be made more effective. He arrived in Singapore on the 9th September and spent the following seven weeks consulting with the local authorities, military and civil, the British Ambassador to China and the Minister in Siam and in visiting the Netherlands East Indies, Burma and India.

On the 29th September he called a conference at Singapore. The Commander-in-Chief, Far East, the Commander-in-Chief, China (Vice-Admiral Sir Geoffrey Layton), the Governor of the Straits Settlements (Sir Shenton Thomas), the British Ambassador to China (Sir Archibald Clark-Kerr), Sir Earle Page (Special Australian Envoy to the British War Cabinet), and the British Minister at Bangkok (Sir Josiah Crosby) attended. The conference were emphatically of the opinion that the only deterrent to further Japanese aggression would be the presence of a British fleet based on Singapore, since, in the absence of a fleet, Japan would be able to strike when she chose. Realizing the difficulties involved in providing a fleet of adequate strength, the conference emphasized the propaganda value of even one or two battleships at Singapore; urged the issue by the British, American and Dutch Governments of an agreed announcement that a combined plan of action existed for use in the event of any Japanese movement against their territories in the Far East; and appealed for closer liaison with the Soviet forces in the Far East.

The general tone of the conference was however optimistic, for it was believed—as events proved, quite erroneously—that Japan was concentrating considerable forces for war against Russia, and it seemed safe to assume that she must be well aware of the danger of becoming involved in war simultaneously with the British Commonwealth, the United States of America and the Dutch. Moreover it seemed unlikely that the Japanese would attempt a landing on the east coast of Malaya during the north-east monsoon, which was due to break in the following month. The conference therefore doubted if Japan were contemplating war in the south—at any rate for some months.

On the 29th October Mr. Duff Cooper submitted his report. In this he recommended that a Commissioner-General for the Far East should be appointed, with a small staff and permanent headquarters at Singapore, who would prepare the way for the establishment of a Council of War should that become necessary. The Commissioner-General would assume responsibility for certain diplomatic and political activities hitherto performed by the Commanders-in-Chief,

Far East, and China; would keep the War Cabinet informed of Far Eastern affairs and keep civil and military officials in the Far East in touch with the policy of the War Cabinet. He would in fact provide the missing piece in the machinery for co-ordination between all the authorities concerned in the defence of the Far East. This report reached London on the 24th November and was under consideration at the time war broke out.

Meanwhile in August 1941 the replacement of Air Chief Marshal Sir Robert Brooke-Popham as Commander-in-Chief, Far East, by a younger officer with up-to-date experience of war had been proposed. It was not till the 1st November that the Prime Minister agreed to this and Lieut.-General Sir Henry Pownall, who had been Chief of Staff to the Commander of the British Expeditionary Force in France, was selected to succeed Sir Robert. General Pownall's departure was however delayed, for at this juncture it was suggested to the Chiefs of Staff that the system of command in the Far East might be altered to agree with that of the Middle East, where there was a joint command by three commanders, one from each Service.[1] On being asked for his opinion Sir Robert strongly recommended that the existing system should remain. On the 25th November the Chiefs of Staff agreed that no change should be made in the system. When war with Japan broke out the Chiefs of Staff decided that it would be inadvisable after all to make a change in command in the Far East, pointing out that in any case the conduct of operations lay in the hands of the Service Commanders. As a result of pressure from Mr. Duff Cooper they changed their minds on this point and General Pownall was directed to take over command as soon as possible.

By the end of September the garrison in Malaya had been further strengthened. Two infantry brigades and one regiment of field artillery had arrived at the end of August and early September.[2] A reconnaissance regiment for III Corps was expected to arrive in October,[3] and three field artillery regiments and one anti-tank regiment in November.[4]

Despite the previous failure of the Commander-in-Chief, Far East, to persuade the Chiefs of Staff to provide reinforcements for Hong

---

[1] There was at this time a Resident Minister in the Middle East.

[2] 27th Australian Brigade Group (Brigadier D. S. Maxwell) on the 15th August and 28th Indian Infantry Brigade Group (Brigadier W. St. J. Carpendale) on the 3rd September.

[3] 3rd Cavalry. This unit had only recently been mechanized and neither the drivers nor the mechanics were fully proficient. Its armoured cars were not available so it was equipped with 15 cwt. trucks in lieu.

[4] 5th, 88th and 137th Field Regiments, and 80th Anti-Tank Regiment.

2. *Left to right:* Air Marshal Sir Robert Brooke-Popham, Rt. Hon. Alfred Duff Cooper, Rt. Hon. Sir Earle Page, Sir Archibald Clark-Kerr, Sir Shenton Thomas and Vice-Admiral Sir Geoffrey Layton.

3. The *Queen Mary* in the graving dock at the Naval Base, August 1940.

4. Sir Mark Young.

5. Major-General
C. M. Maltby.

Kong,[1] this colony was now to be strengthened by the addition of two battalions to the garrison. Major-General A. E. Grasett, after handing over his command in Hong Kong to Major-General C. M. Maltby on the 20th July, returned to England by way of Canada. He was himself a Canadian, and while in Ottawa he told the Chief of the Canadian General Staff that the addition of two or more battalions to the garrison would make Hong Kong strong enough to withstand a Japanese attack for a prolonged period.[2]

On arrival in England he submitted an optimistic report on Hong Kong to the Chiefs of Staff. He expressed the opinion that, despite the almost total lack of aircraft and the weakness of anti-aircraft artillery, a small reinforcement would not only prove to have a great moral effect on the garrison, but would also show Japan and China that, in spite of her commitments elsewhere, Britain intended to fight it out at Hong Kong. He suggested that, in view of her interests in the Pacific, Canada might be prepared to provide one or two battalions.

The Chiefs of Staff approved the suggestion and recommended its acceptance to the Prime Minister. They observed that the Commander-in-Chief, Far East, had asked repeatedly for more infantry for Hong Kong and, as diplomatic relations with Japan appeared to be easier and the Malayan defences were in better shape, the additional battalions now likely to be forthcoming from a hitherto unconsidered source could be spared; they were thus ready to reverse their previous policy concerning the reinforcement of the garrison. They added that if the worst should happen this reinforcement would undoubtedly enable the garrison to conduct a more worthy and more prolonged defence of the island. The Prime Minister agreed and the request was passed to the Canadian Government on the 19th September.

In his telegram to Ottawa, the Secretary of State for the Dominions said that the approved policy had been to regard Hong Kong merely as an outpost to be held for as long as possible in the event of war. Now however the position in the Far East had changed. The defences in Malaya had improved, and there were some signs of weakening in Japan's attitude towards the United States. In these circumstances a small reinforcement of Hong Kong would be justified. One or two additional battalions would increase the strength of the garrison out of all proportion to the numbers involved, and would provide a strong stimulus both to the garrison and to the colony; it would moreover have a great moral effect on the whole of the Far East and would reassure Chiang Kai-shek of the reality of the British intention to hold Hong Kong. This telegram, on which the Canadian

---

[1] See page 56.
[2] Duff, *Report on the Canadian Expeditionary Forces to the Crown Colony of Hong Kong* (Ottawa, 1942), pages 13–14.

H

Government based their decision, was interpreted by them to mean that the 'outpost' policy had been abandoned. But when, on learning that Hong Kong was to be reinforced, the Commander-in-Chief, Far East, asked for clarification on this point, the Chiefs of Staff replied that the original policy remained unaltered—that Hong Kong was still regarded as an outpost.

The Canadian Government agreed to send a brigade head-quarters, two battalions and some ancillary units. The Canadian Chief of the General Staff, who did not wish to disrupt 4th and 6th Canadian Divisions then under training in Canada, decided to select two battalions out of nine listed as 'not recommended for operational consideration' either because of insufficient training or because they required refresher training. The Royal Rifles of Canada, who had just been relieved from garrison duties in St. John's, Newfoundland, and the Winnipeg Grenadiers, who had been carrying out similar duties in the West Indies, were eventually chosen. These two battalions were brought up to establishment, provided with first reinforcements, equipped for active service and embarked for Hong Kong on the 27th October.[1]

During September discussions were held in Washington on the proposals put forward by the Japanese Government as a result of the Imperial Conference on the 6th.[2] On the 27th the Japanese Ambassador submitted a complete redraft which embodied little change in the basic demands. In the meantime the Japanese High Command, who held the view that there was no hope of satisfactorily concluding negotiations with the United States, stressed the danger of being caught by American delaying tactics, and demanded on the 24th September that the Japanese Government should make a decision on peace or war by the 15th October.

On the 2nd October the United States gave their answer. It expressed disappointment at the narrow character of Japan's reply and the vague presentation of her proposals regarding China and of her relationship with the Axis Powers. It repeated that the Government of the United States welcomed the suggestion for a meeting between the heads of the two countries, but renewed consideration would first have to be given to those fundamental principles on which alone proper relations between the two countries could be built.[3]

The negotiations had reached a deadlock. America demanded a change of heart in Japan, but the Japanese considered there was nothing they could change. They knew that their highest instrument

---

[1] Duff, pages 19–42.
[2] See page 74.
[3] See page 65.

of Government—the Cabinet—lacked the political power to carry through the necessary radical changes in the national policy, and they realized that the United States could attain their ends with little difficulty by extending their existing economic controls. They felt that America was deliberately dragging on the discussions. Konoye himself and his Foreign Minister however thought that diplomacy might still provide an answer. The Navy—uncertain of the outcome—did not want to go to war, but was of two minds as it watched its oil reserves diminishing. The Army, influenced by the time factor, would not agree to any further delay and insisted that the third resolution in the programme decided upon on the 6th September should be carried out.

Konoye, reluctant to drag his country into a war which might end in her defeat, decided that he could not be responsible for implementing the decisions of the 6th September. He therefore resigned on the 16th October. Two days later General Tojo—the Minister for War in Konoye's Cabinet—formed a new Japanese Government, retaining the portfolios of Minister of War and Home Minister, and replaced the Foreign Minister—Admiral Toyoda—by Mr. Togo. The period of diplomacy had ended. The period of action had begun.

The new Japanese Cabinet discussed the position with the Service Chiefs, and by the end of October it was clear that neither Service was prepared to accept any delay. The Army and Navy pointed out that diplomacy had failed and would continue to fail since the United States would not understand why Japan had to have control in China. They said that, rather than await extinction, it would be better to fight while there was a reasonable hope of victory. An Imperial Conference was held on the 5th November at which a programme giving an 'Outline for the Execution of National Policy' was accepted. It was agreed that the military forces were to be ready for war by the 1st December; that the 25th November should be fixed as a deadline for the final decision to go to war, should no accord by then have been reached with the United States; and that two last proposals, Plan 'A' and Plan 'B', should be placed before the American Government.

Plan 'A' was a restatement of the Japanese terms. These were: acceptance of economic equality in China; the retention of Japanese troops for some twenty-five years in north China, Mongolia and Hainan; withdrawal of all other Japanese troops in China within two years of the restoration of peace between the two countries; withdrawal of Japanese forces in Indo-China when a just peace had been brought about in China. A more conciliatory attitude was taken on the Tripartite Pact, but in such vague terms as to be largely without meaning. The United States were in return to force Chiang Kai-shek to make peace with Japan, by withdrawing their support should he fail to accept Japan's terms.

An alternative Plan B was included in case of American refusal to accept Plan 'A'. It did not meet any of the American proposals of the 21st June or recognize the American fundamental principles, and was to be submitted only if Plan 'A' were not accepted. Plan 'B' proposed a *modus vivendi* by which Japan and the United States and the other Powers involved could carry on without war, while remaining in fundamental disagreement. It read:

'1. Both the Governments of Japan and the United States undertake not to make any armed advance into any of the regions in the South-eastern Asia and the Southern Pacific area excepting the part of French Indo-China where the Japanese troops are stationed at present.

2. The Japanese Government undertakes to withdraw its troops now stationed in French Indo-China upon either the restoration of peace between Japan and China or the establishment of an equitable peace in the Pacific area.

In the meantime the Government of Japan declares that it is prepared to remove its troops now stationed in the southern part of French Indo-China to the northern part of the said territory upon the conclusion of the present arrangement which shall later be embodied in the final agreement.

3. The Governments of Japan and the United States shall co-operate with a view to securing the acquisition of those goods and commodities which the two countries need in Netherlands East Indies.

4. The Governments of Japan and the United States mutually undertake to restore their commercial relations to those prevailing prior to the freezing of the assets.

The Government of the United States shall supply Japan a required quantity of oil.

5. The Government of the United States undertakes to refrain from such measures and actions as will be prejudicial to the endeavours for the restoration of general peace between Japan and China.'

The Conference also decided to send a diplomat, Mr. Kurusu, with the rank of ambassador to assist Nomura in Washington. At the same time Nomura was told that American agreement to Plan 'A' or 'B' must be obtained by the 25th November.

The fall of the Konoye Government on the 16th October, and the probability that it would be replaced by a new Government likely to be under the influence of extreme elements, once again focused the attention of the authorities in London on the Far East. On the 17th the Prime Minister instructed the Admiralty to consider the proposal to send one capital ship and an aircraft carrier to join the *Repulse* at Singapore as quickly as possible. His views and arguments for sending an aircraft carrier and one of the latest battleships had not changed. He felt that the despatch of such ships would have considerable effect in the Far East and that as a result of the sinking of the German battleship *Bismarck* in May they could be spared from home waters.

The Admiralty still wished to retain all three of the latest battle-ships in Atlantic waters, for they had to consider not only the *Tirpitz* but also the German battle-cruisers *Scharnhorst* and *Gneisenau*, whose condition was uncertain. In their opinion the Japanese would not be deterred by the presence of one fast battleship, for Japan could easily afford to send four modern ships to protect any force moving south. But the presence of six British battleships at Singapore (even though four were obsolescent) would force the Japanese to detach the greater part of their fleet, and thus uncover Japan to the American Navy, of whose co-operation in the event of a Japanese attack the Admiralty felt assured.

Mr. Churchill was unconvinced. He did not foresee an attack in force on Malaya. He thought the main danger lay in Japanese attacks on the trade routes by fast battleships, against which the four old battleships would be impotent. The only thing which would induce caution in Japan was a fast striking force whose presence would be even more effective before war actually began. He would like to see the *Prince of Wales* sent at once and the situation reviewed when the *Nelson* became available. The Foreign Office supported his view and drew attention to the tremendous political effect of a really modern ship. The Admiralty agreed that the report of the arrival of the *Prince of Wales* at Capetown would have great value, and compromised by suggesting that she should sail forthwith for that port, and that a decision on her ultimate destination could be taken when she arrived. This suggestion was adopted by the Defence Committee on the 20th. Nevertheless on the 21st October an Admiralty signal informed all the authorities concerned that the *Prince of Wales* would shortly leave for Singapore.

The battleship sailed from home waters, flying the flag of Acting Admiral Sir Tom Phillips, the Commander-in-Chief designate of the Far Eastern Fleet. The *Repulse* meanwhile, had arrived at Durban on the 3rd October and had sailed for Ceylon. The new aircraft carrier *Indomitable*, earmarked for the Far East, ran aground in the entrance to Kingston harbour, Jamaica, on the 3rd November and had to be docked. No other aircraft carrier could be spared.

By October the attempt to obtain an agreed plan for the employ-ment of the British, American and Dutch forces in the Far East had received a further set-back when the United States Navy Department intimated that they were not prepared to accept the draft A.D.B.2. Agreement.[1] Their chief criticism of it was that, because of British naval weakness in the Far East, an effective combined operational plan appeared impossible.

In November a new approach was made, based on the Anglo-American staff conversations of January–March 1941 which had culminated in the production of the A.B.C.1 Agreement. By the end of the month the British and American staffs had agreed on the procedure for producing a detailed joint plan in the Far East. Follow-ing a preliminary British conference in Singapore, a conference was to be held in Manila between Admiral Phillips (Commander-in-Chief, Eastern Fleet) and Admiral T. C. Hart (Commander-in-Chief, U.S. Asiatic Fleet) to decide on the broad outline for joint naval operations which later could be developed into joint operational plans. The preliminary British conference was to begin at Singapore on the 8th December 1941, after the return of Admiral Phillips from his courtesy visit to Manila on the 4th December.

In the meantime the Commander-in-Chief, China, (Admiral Layton) had prepared a joint operational plan known as 'Plenaps' for the British and Dutch forces in the Far East on the basis of the British and Dutch conversations of 27th April 1941.[2] This included plans for the American forces in the Far East based on the draft A.D.B.2 proposals with the proviso that, if the United States did not become a belligerent, 'Plenaps' would apply to the British and Dutch forces only. Thus despite efforts spread over nine months, and with the situation growing ever more threatening, the critical month of December was reached with no agreed combined plan in the Far East. When war broke out the British and Dutch forces operated in accordance with 'Plenaps'. The American forces in the Far East were directed to conduct operations in accordance with the A.B.C.1 Agreement and to co-operate with the British and Dutch as much as possible, without prejudicing their primary mission of defending the Philippines.

The United States Government, well aware that Japanese diplomacy was working to a pre-determined date, were presented with Plan 'A' on the 7th November, and asked to give an immediate reply. On the 15th the Japanese Ambassador was informed that the American

---

[1] See page 76.
[2] See page 63.

Government—and in this the British Government concurred—took exception to receiving representations suggestive of an ultimatum. Plan 'A' was therefore dropped.

On the 18th November Nomura and Kurusu suggested a Japanese withdrawal from southern Indo-China in exchange for a relaxation of economic pressure on Japan—a return to the position prevailing up to the 26th July—as a possible way to tide over the abnormal situation. The United States Government indicated that this proposal might be worth discussion. The Japanese Government, to whom their Ambassadors had also made the suggestion, replied immediately that they would accept nothing but Plan 'B' *in toto* and informed them that the deadline had been extended to the 29th—the positively final date. Plan 'B' was presented in Washington on the 20th November. No mention however was made of the dead-line being the 29th.

The United States Government knew that this was Japan's final word. They knew also that, though it contained a provision by which Japan would move her forces from southern to northern Indo-China, there was no limit to the numbers which might be stationed there and that no withdrawal would take place until peace had been restored. There was nothing to prevent fresh Japanese aggression in any part of eastern Asia north of Indo-China, nor any pledge by Japan to pursue a peaceful course. Finally the Plan still left Japan a full member of the Tripartite Pact, and hence a potential enemy of both Great Britain and the United States.

America had therefore to decide whether she should continue to insist on Japan giving up her determination to conquer and control the south-west Pacific, or give way herself on the fundamental principles for which she stood. The final Japanese proposals were quite unacceptable. The only honourable course was to refuse the proposals and face a war in the Pacific.

The United States Government decided in the first instance to present a reasonable counter-proposal for a *modus vivendi*, including a modification of the 'freezing' and export restrictions whereby trade, compatible with normal Japanese civilian needs, could be resumed between the two countries. Such a counter-proposal was prepared and submitted to Great Britain, Australia, the Netherlands and China for consideration. On the night of the 24th/25th November the British Ambassador in Washington informed the United States Government that, if they considered it desirable to put forward a counter-proposal, they would have British support.

It was soon clear however that the United States would not agree to the supply of any oil to Japan, even in the very limited quantities needed for normal civil requirements, and that agreement to the counter-proposal would mean the collapse of morale in China and the complete loss of American prestige in that country. There was also doubt whether the Japanese Government would for one moment consider the proposal. In these circumstances the United States Government abandoned the idea. On the 26th November Nomura and Kurusu were told that Plan 'B' was unacceptable and at the same time were handed a Note containing proposals for a comprehensive settlement between the two countries. But inasmuch as points 3 and 4 called for the evacuation of all Japanese military, naval and air forces from China and Indo-China and the abandonment of the Nanking Régime, it was clear that there was no likelihood that the Japanese Government would accept such drastic terms, even though their tentative character was stressed. The Note was studied at a Liaison Conference in Tokyo on the 27th November when all were agreed that it was unacceptable. At an Imperial Conference held on the 1st December Tojo said that Japanese claims could not be obtained by diplomatic means and, since it was no longer possible from the point of view of either military strategy or the national power to allow the present situation to continue, recourse would be made to war. No one demurred and thus the final decision was taken. On the following day all Japanese naval and military commanders were told that war would begin on the 8th December.

CHAPTER V

THE JAPANESE STRATEGIC
PLANS

See Map 1

IN ORDER to achieve her national object—to set up a Greater
East Asia Co-Prosperity Sphere and become the dominant Power
in the southern Pacific—Japan had to become self-sufficient in
oil, rubber, tin, bauxite and other essential raw materials. This
entailed not only the settlement of the China Incident but the capture and exploitation of Malaya, Borneo, Java and Sumatra, areas
rich in these commodities. This meant war with the British Commonwealth, the Netherlands East Indies and, sooner or later, the United
States of America. It was the problem of how best to capture this
vast area from powerful opponents, and to keep possession of it, that
the naval and military staffs of the Japanese *Imperial General Headquarters* had to solve in 1941.

Up to that year Japanese staff exercises had been largely theoretical and confined to consideration of war with either Russia, America
or Britain separately. The preparation of plans for an advance into
the Southern Region, involving war with the British, Dutch and
Americans, began in the early part of 1941 but it was not until the
end of July, when Japanese assets were frozen by the three Powers
in reply to the occupation of southern Indo-China, that *Imperial
General Headquarters* started planning on the assumption that war
would begin before the end of the year.

The problem before the planning staffs was a complex one. Japan's
industrial potential and her economic resources were such that she
had if possible to avoid a long war. Her merchant fleet, on which as
an island Power she was dependent, was barely adequate for her
peacetime needs. Her industrial capacity, although greatly expanded
during the previous five years, was still far short of that of each of her
two main prospective enemies. Expansion of her industrial potential
had increased her dependence on foreign markets for strategic raw
materials, and practically all these had been closed to her by the
embargo on her overseas trade. Her imports of oil had ceased altogether and by autumn she would be drawing on her stockpiles even
for domestic purposes.[1] Japanese plans had therefore to ensure the

---
[1] See page 71 and Appendix 3.

capture of the oil-producing centres in Borneo, Sumatra and Java as soon as possible and, to reduce the chances of destruction of plant, the principle of surprise had to be exploited to the full. Thus economic rather than strategical considerations dictated to a large extent the areas to be occupied and the points of attack.

To secure the line of communications to the south and to eliminate bases from which counter-attacks could be launched, the British and Americans had to be expelled from Singapore and the Philippines. To prevent its intervention during the critical opening months of the war, the U.S. Pacific Fleet had to be destroyed, or at least crippled. Siam, as a stepping stone to Malaya and Burma, had to be occupied at an early stage.

Weather conditions in the widely separated areas had an important influence on the planning. War had to start in December before the north-east monsoon in the South China Sea and the winter gales in the north Pacific reached their full force, and the occupation of the southern areas had to be completed during the Manchurian winter, when Japan's northern flank would be comparatively safe from attack by her traditional enemy Russia.

Nevertheless, so long as Russian divisions remained on the border, large military and air forces had to be kept in Manchuria. These, with the forces required to settle the China Incident, limited the number of divisions and aircraft available for the Southern Operation. Thus only eleven out of a total of fifty-one divisions and some 700 out of 1,500 first-line army aircraft, augmented by about 480 land-based naval aircraft of the *11th Air Fleet*, could be allotted for the conquest of the vast Southern Region. Since the High Command considered a local margin of ground and air superiority of at least two to one necessary for success, plans had to allow for the employment of the same formations in successive operations.

The sequence in which the various southern territories should be invaded was therefore the first problem to be settled. Four possible alternatives were considered:

(1) To capture the Netherlands East Indies first and then to attack Malaya and the Philippines.

(2) To advance in a clockwise direction, attacking the Philippines, Borneo, Java, Sumatra and finally Malaya.

(3) To carry out the advance in the reverse order to (2) above.

(4) To attack the Philippines and Malaya simultaneously, and then advance southwards to capture the Netherlands East Indies from the east and the west.

The invasion of Burma would automatically follow the occupation of Malaya.

The first alternative was discarded as strategically unsound. Although it offered the best chance of an immediate supply of oil, it left powerful British and American bases on the southward line of communications, and gave time for them to be reinforced. The Japanese Navy favoured the second, which provided a secure line of communications, and made concentration of forces comparatively easy, but the Army feared that by the time Sumatra and Malaya were attacked, their defences would have been so strengthened that the attack would fail. The Army therefore favoured the third alternative. They pointed out that, by leaving the Philippines unmolested, there was a slender chance that the entry of America into the war might be delayed. The Navy, having already envisaged a surprise attack on Pearl Harbour,[1] and convinced that America was certain to enter the war, held that Japan could not afford to have a powerful American fleet in being, and what might become an impregnable fortress astride the most vulnerable part of their southward communications.

After considerable discussion, the two Services agreed by the middle of August upon the last alternative, which exploited in full the principle of surprise and gave a reasonable measure of economy in the employment of forces, since formations used in the initial attacks on Hong Kong, the Philippines and Malaya could later be used for the invasion of Sumatra, Java and Burma. Since both Services felt that the proposed attack on the Philippines would bring the United States into the war, they included in the plan a carrier-borne air attack on Pearl Harbour. Finally they decided that Burma should be occupied because of its strategical value as a key point on the north-western flank of the Southern Offensive Zone, and the importance of its oil and rice to Japanese economy.

The latter part of August and September was spent by the two Services in preparing detailed plans based on these decisions, in examining their practicability by means of exercises without troops and in allotting forces to the various tasks. The final plan for war with the British Commonwealth, the United States and the Netherlands East Indies was agreed upon by both Services on the 20th October. It was divided into three periods:

First period. The attack on the American Pacific Fleet at Hawaii; the seizure of the Southern Region; and the capture of the strategic areas required for the formation of a strong defensive perimeter round the Japanese mainland and the newly-acquired territories. The perimeter to be established ran from the Kuriles, through Wake Island, the Marshall and Gilbert Islands, the Bismarck Archipelago, New Guinea, Timor, Java, Sumatra and Malaya to Burma and the Indian border.

---

[1] See page 64.

Second period. The consolidation and strengthening of the perimeter.

Third period. The interception and destruction of any forces attempting to penetrate the defensive ring or threaten vital areas within it, and action to destroy their enemies' will to fight.

It will be noted that the Japanese plan envisaged no all-out victory over Britain and the United States. Japan gambled on the hope that, having seized the territories which would give her economic independence, she could ring them with a circle of steel against which her enemies would dissipate their forces until compelled to accept the *fait accompli.* The operational plans for each area, drawn up as they were to meet the conditions peculiar to that area, differed in form. They were all however based on the principle of eliminating the defenders' air power before the landing of invasion forces.[1]

The first period—the offensive period—was divided into phases; the plans for which had to be worked out in great detail and carefully co-ordinated, for the success of each phase depended on the previous one:

First Phase. War was to open with six operations taking place almost simultaneously. These were to be:

(a) A surprise attack on Pearl Harbour with the object of destroying or neutralizing the American Pacific Fleet; the occupation of Siam to secure a land base for operations against Malaya and Burma, and to cut British communications to Malaya; landings in northern Malaya and on the Isthmus of Kra, as the first step towards the capture of the Singapore Base;[2] air attacks on Luzon with the object of destroying American air power in the Philippines; attacks on Guam and Wake to sever American communications with the Philippines, and on the Gilbert Islands; and the invasion of Hong Kong to eliminate this British outpost. These initial attacks were to be synchronized as far as possible in order to obtain the advantage of surprise on all fronts.

(b) The air attacks on the Philippines were to be followed up by the invasion of both Luzon and Mindanao Islands in order to occupy Manila and Davao. The island of Jolo in the Sulu Sea was also to be occupied, for together with Davao it was the base from which the second phase operations to capture the Netherlands East Indies would be launched. The landings in Malaya were to be followed by the invasion of British

---

[1] Since the British air bases in Malaya lay outside the range of Japanese fighters based in southern Indo-China, and British naval forces based on Singapore constituted a menace to assault forces making their landing, it was decided to abandon this general principle in the case of Malaya and to make the initial landings simultaneously with the start of the air offensive, relying on surprise to overcome the disadvantages of this procedure.

[2] For Isthmus of Kra see Map 5.

Borneo in order to seize the oil-producing centres in that area and to protect the line of communications to Malaya.

Second Phase. Operations to secure the south-eastern corner of the perimeter in the Bismarck Archipelago; the occupation of the whole of Malaya and the capture of the Naval Base; the capture of airfields in south Burma; and all preliminary operations necessary to secure air bases for the final attack on Java. These preliminary operations were to take the form of a three-pronged advance, to be made through the South China Sea, the Strait of Makassar and the Molucca Passage in order to capture strategic points in southern Sumatra, Dutch Borneo, Celebes and the islands of Amboina and Timor.

Third Phase. The capture of Java by simultaneous attacks on the eastern and western ends of the island; the occupation of northern Sumatra and the invasion of Burma. On completion of this phase, the second period of consolidation and strengthening of the perimeter was to begin. This included the completion of the operations in Burma and the occupation of the Andaman and Nicobar Islands in the Indian Ocean.

Imperial General Headquarters estimated that, in the absence of serious interference by the Allied navies, the first period would be completed in accordance with the following timetable

Philippines	50 days
Malaya	100 ,,
Netherlands East Indies . . .	150 ,,

The plan was finally approved on the 5th November, and operation orders allotting formations and units to the various tasks were issued the following day. The attack on the Southern Region was to be made by *Southern Army* under the command of General Count Terauchi. This comprised:

14th Army:
16th and *48th Divisions, 65th Independent Brigade* and *5th Air Division* for the invasion of the Philippines.

15th Army:
33rd Division and *55th Division* (less one infantry regiment) for the invasion of Siam and Burma.

25th Army:
Imperial Guards, 5th, 18th and *56th Divisions* and *3rd Air Division* for the invasion of Malaya.

16th Army:
2nd Division, 48th Division (after completion of its task with *14th Army*), *38th Division* (after completion of its task with *23rd Army*) and *56th Regimental Group* for the invasion of the Netherlands East Indies.

Reserve:

    21st Division and *21st Independent Mixed Brigade* (and for the internal security of Indo-China).

The *Southern Army* was to be transported and covered by the naval *Southern Force*, under Vice-Admiral Kondo, composed of:

    2nd Division of *3rd Battle Squadron*
    4th Carrier Squadron (light carriers)
    4th, 5th, 7th and *16th Cruiser Squadrons*
    2nd, 3rd, 4th and *5th Destroyer Flotillas*
    11th Air Fleet

The detailed allotment of formations to tasks is given below. In making the allotment *Imperial General Headquarters* chose the most highly-trained divisions and the fastest transports for the Malayan operation, for they regarded Singapore as the key to victory in the south and the greatest obstacle to be overcome.

Distribution of Japanese Naval and Military Forces at the outbreak of War

Task	Army	Navy	Remarks
A. GENERAL			
1. Protection of Japan	Five divisions: *1st Air Division*	*Northern Force**	
2. Korea	Two divisions		
3. Manchuria	*Kwantung Army* of thirteen divisions and *2nd Air Division*		
4. China (North, Central and South)	*1st, 11th, 12th, 13th* and *23rd Armies* totalling twenty-two divisions, and *1st Air Brigade*	*China Area Fleet*	
B. PACIFIC OPERATIONS			
5. Surprise attack on Pearl Harbour		*Striking Force** (Vice-Admiral Nagumo)	Left rendezvous on 26th November for attack 8th December
6. General naval cover		*Main Body** (Admiral Yamamoto)	
7. Capture of Guam, Wake, islands in Gilbert Group, Bismarcks and New Guinea	*South Sea Detachment: 55th Regimental Group,* naval landing detachments	*South Sea Force** *24th Air Flotilla*	This group consisted of *144th Infantry Regiment* of *55th Division* together with supporting units
8. Invasion of Hong Kong	*38th Division* plus one infantry regiment and additional artillery, under command of *23rd Army*	*China Area Fleet*	

Task	Army	Navy	Remarks
C. SOUTHERN OPERATIONS			
Controlled by:	*Southern Army* (General Count Terauchi)	*Southern Force** (Vice-Admiral Kondo)	Headquarters at Saigon
9. Philippines invasion	*14th Army: 16th* and *48th Divisions, 65th Independent Brigade, 56th Regimental Group, 5th Air Division*	Elements of *Southern Force** and *11th Air Fleet* (less *22nd Air Flotilla*)	*14th Army* was based on Ryukyu Islands, Formosa and Palau
10. Occupation of Siam, airfields in Isthmus of Kra and Tenasserim coast† and the invasion of southern Burma	*15th Army: 33rd Division, 55th Division* (less one infantry regiment)		*15th Army* was based on Indo-China. *5th Air Division* was transferred in support of this army after the fall of Manila. *33rd Division* left Nanking on 13th December and arrived in Siam on 10th January
11. Invasion of Malaya, Singapore and British Borneo and, after the fall of Singapore, northern Sumatra	*25th Army: Imperial Guards Division, 5th, 18th* and *56th Divisions, 3rd Air Division*	Elements of *Southern Force** and *22nd Air Flotilla*	*25th Army* was based on Indo-China, Hainan Island and Canton. *56th Division* remained in Japan and was moved on 16th February to join *15th Army* in Burma. The operations in British Borneo were under direct control of *Southern Army*
12. Occupation of Dutch Borneo, Celebes, Amboina, Timor, southern Sumatra and the invasion of Java	*16th Army: 2nd, 38th* (a) and *48th Divisions* (b), *56th Regimental Group* (c), naval landing detachments, airborne troops	Elements of *Southern Force** and *11th Air Fleet* (less *22nd Air Flotilla*) reinforced by aircraft carriers which had formed part of the *Striking Force*	*16th Army* was based initially on Formosa and Palau Island. (a) After the capture of Hong Kong. (b) After the capture of Manila. (c) After the capture of Davao and Jolo. For sub-allotment of the naval and military formations to the various tasks in Phases 2 and 3 see Appendices 22 and 23
13. Southern Army reserve and internal security of Indo-China	*21st Division, 21st Independent Mixed Brigade*		Part of *21st Division* left Tsingtao for the Philippines on 20th January. *21st Independent Mixed Brigade* was in Indo-China on the outbreak of war

Note *For details of composition of these naval task forces see Appendix 5.

†The Tenasserim coast stretches from Victoria Point to Rangoon (see Strategic Map).

On the 7th November all forces were warned that the approximate date for the beginning of the war would be the 8th December (East Longitude Time). On the 15th November Headquarters *Southern Army* issued orders to prepare for the southern attack, and a week later the commanders of the various invasion armies issued their own operation orders. On the 21st November all naval task forces were ordered to their rendezvous positions. On the 1st December all forces were told that a decision to enter into a state of war had been made, and on the following day the date to begin hostilities was confirmed as the 8th December (East Longitude Time). The choice of date was governed by the tactical requirements of the Pearl Harbour attack. It was selected primarily with regard to the phase of the moon, and the need for darkness to give concealment to the force during the final run-in to the aircraft launching point. The 10th December would have been the best day but the 8th was chosen because it was a Sunday, when the entire American Pacific Fleet would normally be in harbour.

The planned times of the initial attacks were:

	Greenwich Mean Time	Local Time	Japanese Time
Pearl Harbour	6.25 p.m./7th	7.55 a.m./7th	3.25 a.m./8th
Malayan Landing	5.15 p.m./7th	12.45 a.m./8th	2.15 a.m./8th
Hong Kong (approx.)	11.30 p.m./7th	8.00 a.m./8th	8.30 a.m./8th
Singora Landing	7.00 p.m./7th	2.30 a.m./8th	4.00 a.m./8th

Note: In Malaya the moon rose at 9 p.m. local time.

Map 1
Japanese Strategic
Plans 1941

Legend
First Phase.............................
Second Phase..........................
Third Phase............................
■ Army HQ   ⊞ Regimental Group
⊏ Division   ✚ Air Division
▷ Brigade

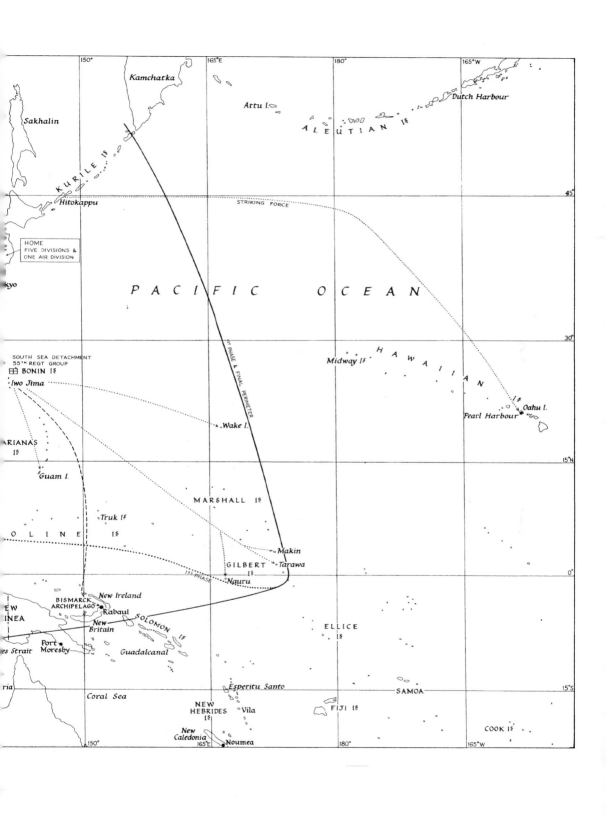

150° 165°E 180° 165°W

Kamchatka

Sakhalin

Attu I.

Dutch Harbour

A L E U T I A N I$

K
U
R
I
L
E I$

Hitokappu STRIKING FORCE   45°

HOME
FIVE DIVISIONS &
ONE AIR DIVISION

kyo

P A C I F I C O C E A N

30°

SOUTH SEA DETACHMENT
55TH REGT GROUP

⊞ BONIN I$

Midway I$ H
A
W
A
I
I
A
N

Iwo Jima

I$
Oahu I.
Pearl Harbour

1ST PHASE & FINAL PERIMETER

.*Wake I.*

RIANAS
I$

15°N

Guam I.

MARSHALL I$

O L I N E I$

Truk I$

Makin

GILBERT *Tarawa*
I$

1ST PHASE *Nauru* 0°

New Ireland

BISMARCK
ARCHIPELAGO *Rabaul*

EW
INEA *New* SOLOMON
 Britain I$

ELLICE
I$

Port
Moresby

Guadalcanal

es Strait

Esperitu Santo SAMOA 15°S

ria Coral Sea NEW *Vila* FIJI I$
  HEBRIDES
  I$

New
Caledonia COOK I$

•*Noumea*

150° 165°E 180° 165°W

CHAPTER VI

OPENING MOVES IN THE PACIFIC

See Map 1

THIS VOLUME is mainly concerned with telling the story of the British effort in the war. Before describing in detail the events resulting in the loss of Hong Kong, Malaya and the Netherlands East Indies in which British and Commonwealth troops were involved, it is necessary to recount shortly the initial Japanese attacks in the Pacific. This chapter will therefore be devoted to the operations at Hawaii, in the Philippines and the Pacific islands.

THE PEARL HARBOUR ATTACK

Preliminary study of the Pearl Harbour attack by a staff of selected officers had begun as early as January 1941. It was tried out in war games in Tokyo early in September and became the subject of controversy between senior officers. It was not finally approved until the conference of the 5th November. The operational plan was based on the assumption that the main body of the Pacific Fleet would be at anchor in Pearl Harbour on the day chosen; that carrier forces could be put within striking distance of the harbour without undue risk of detection and that, by making use of tactical surprise, a powerful air strike could cripple the land-based aircraft at Hawaii as well as the Pacific Fleet, and so allow the carrier force to withdraw without being counter-attacked.

Three possible routes of approach were considered; a northern course (which was the one used), a central course heading eastwards and then down the line of the Hawaiian Islands, and a southern route through the Marshall Islands. Two requirements dictated the choice: the achievement of surprise and the ability to refuel. On the central and southern route, calmer weather could be expected for refuelling but the chances of detection by reconnaissance aircraft from Wake, Midway and other American-held islands were rated high. The northern route was selected as being furthest from the normal shipping track, and as giving the best chance of avoiding American reconnaissance flights. The Japanese Naval Command hoped that the problem of refuelling at sea, which was not then the commonplace it is today, could be overcome by training and decided that at the worst the destroyers could be left behind and the force proceed unscreened. The chosen route ran from Hitokappu, a lonely snowbound island in the Kuriles, passing between the Aleutian Islands and Midway outside the range of American air patrols, to a point two hundred miles north of Pearl Harbour. The time of take-off of the first strike was to be as near daybreak as possible, to get maximum light for the attack. Sunrise at Hawaii on the 7th December (West Longitude Time) was at 6.26 a.m., but full daylight at Pearl Harbour came later, when the sun had cleared the mountains to the east.

Vice-Admiral Nagumo, Commander-in-Chief, *1st Air Fleet*, was given command of the operation. Four fleet carriers and two light fleet carriers, screened by a flotilla of destroyers, formed the air striking force. They were to be supported by two fast battleships and the *8th Cruiser Squadron* (two 8-inch cruisers), accompanied by eight tankers. Three submarines were to move well ahead of the force to give warning of approaching ships. Submarines of the *6th Fleet* were to arrive in Hawaiian waters the day before the attack, to reconnoitre and report. After the attack, they were to destroy any ships trying to escape. Five of them carried midget submarines which were to be launched in the approaches and enter the harbour immediately after the air strike.

Specific training by the carriers and their air groups started in September, for which a miniature replica of Pearl Harbour was built on an unfrequented island. Special attention was paid to the exercise of dropping aerial torpedoes in shallow water and it was found that special fins fitted to them prevented 'porpoising'.

The carrier force assembled in Hitokappu Bay on the 22nd November and sailed four days later on its 3,000 mile voyage to Hawaii. Admiral Nagumo reached the flying-off position shortly before 6 a.m. on the 7th December (West Longitude Time) without having been detected, and at once launched the first wave of forty torpedo-bombers, fifty high-level bombers and forty dive-bombers escorted by fifty fighters. By 7.15 a.m. a total of 360 aircraft had been flown off.

At Pearl Harbour no special precautions were being taken other than a radar search from 4 a.m. to 7 a.m. and an alert against sabotage. Aircraft were at four hours' notice. On board the ships in harbour, the watch on deck was returning cleaning gear, the watch below was awaiting the hoisting of colours. Less than two-thirds of the officers had returned on board from night leave. There were no naval shore anti-aircraft batteries, but the eight battleships, eight cruisers and twenty-nine destroyers mounted 780 anti-aircraft guns among them. One anti-aircraft gun in four was manned but none of the main or secondary armaments.

The raiders approached at a height of 9,000 feet above a dense cloud layer. They were detected at 7 a.m. by a mobile army radar unit at a distance of 132 miles, but were thought to be friendly and no action was taken. The first wave arrived over the island of Oahu about 7.40 a.m. and fifteen minutes later the first bombs fell. Surprise, the essence of the Japanese plans, was complete and there was very little air opposition. At the airfield which received the first attack, most of the aircraft were parked wing tip to wing tip; in the harbour the battleships were secured singly or in pairs in 'Battleship Row'. Provided with accurate charts on which the exact position of each ship was clearly marked, Japanese pilots were able to select their targets with ease and hit with accuracy. Hardly had the first wave finished its attack, when the second came in to complete the holocaust. By 9.45 a.m. all was over, and the last enemy aircraft had disappeared from sight.

The success of the attack must have exceeded the wildest dreams of even Admiral Yamamoto himself, the originator of the plan. In less than two hours all eight battleships of the United States Pacific Fleet had been sunk or put out of action, with three light cruisers, three destroyers and a number of auxiliaries; 188 aircraft were destroyed and thirty naval aircraft damaged; 2,403 men of the United States Navy, Marine Corps, Army and civilians were killed and 1,178 wounded. Japanese losses in the actual attack were no more than twenty-nine aircraft. All five midget submarines, only one of which is known to have penetrated the harbour, were sunk. It was a catastrophic blow to the Americans. There was however one ray of light in the darkness: three fleet carriers had escaped attack. The *Enterprise* and *Lexington* were at sea on the day of the attack, the former some 400 miles south-east of Midway and the latter on passage from Wake to Pearl Harbour; the *Saratoga* and the battleship *Colorado* were on the west coast of America.

The Japanese carriers, after flying on their aircraft, withdrew on a north-westerly course for a thousand miles before turning west for home. Admiral Nagumo had planned an attack on Midway Island on his return journey but strong winds and heavy seas made it impracticable. All American efforts to locate Admiral Nagumo's force during and after the raid failed. The two task forces at sea were ordered to search for it but, perhaps fortunately, were unable to make contact.

The failure of the Japanese to seek out and destroy the American carriers was to cost them dear. Six months later, with their battle fleet still out of action, the American Navy, by making skilful use of the mobility of its carriers, inflicted on the Japanese Fleet at Midway

a defeat from which it never fully recovered. Their failure to destroy
the naval base at Pearl Harbour was perhaps in the long run even
more costly. Had their bombers chosen as their primary targets the
harbour installations, the workshops, the dry dock and the oil storage,
they would have delayed the American counter-attack across the
Pacific for even longer than did the damage to the ships, for the
American Fleet had no other base in the Pacific.

THE INVASION OF THE PHILIPPINES

Coincidentally, or within a few hours of the raid on Pearl Harbour,
the planned attacks were made on Hong Kong,[1] Malaya,[2] and the
Philippines.[3] In the Philippines the first aim of the Japanese was to
destroy General MacArthur's Far Eastern Air Force and gain command of the air, before they landed their invasion forces. Here again
surprise was the keynote of the plan. The number of islands and the
vast extent of coastlines of the Philippine archipelago made tactical
surprise comparatively easy. Landings to seize air strips for use by
short-range army aircraft were planned at a number of widely
separated points. Three, mounted in Formosa, were to be made on
Luzon and one, mounted in Palau, on Mindanao. The main landing
was to be in Lingayen Bay.

Lieut.-General Homma was placed in command of *14th Army* which
was to carry out the invasion. It consisted of *16th* and *48th Divisions*.
During November *16th Division* was concentrated in one of the
northern islands of the Ryukyu group and *48th Division* in Formosa;
detachments were in the Pescadores and Palau.

Although the Japanese expected little opposition from the weak
American Asiatic Fleet, a powerful fleet was placed under the command of Vice-Admiral Takahashi, Commander-in-Chief, *3rd Fleet*.
He divided his ships into two forces—a northern force based on
Formosa to support the northern and western landings, and a
southern force based on Palau for the landings in the south and
east. Units of the *2nd Fleet* under Admiral Kondo, after covering the
Malayan landings, were to give distant cover during the main landings in Lingayen Bay.

The problem of launching the initial air attack on American-
held airfields in central Luzon presented considerable difficulties.
Japanese army aircraft had not the range to reach these airfields,
and the aircraft carriers were needed at Pearl Harbour. Reliance
for the long-range attack had therefore to be placed on land-based
naval bombers. The *21st* and *23rd Air Flotillas* of Vice-Admiral

---

[1] See Chapters VII, VIII and IX.
[2] See Chapter X *et seq.*
[3] See Sketch 1.

Tsukahara's *11th Air Fleet* were stationed in Formosa, with a small detachment at Palau, to undertake the main strike. The *5th (Army) Air Division* was also located in Formosa, for use against the nearer airfields in northern Luzon.

The strikes were planned to take place at daylight (6.30 a.m.) on the 8th December. This was some three hours after the raid on Pearl Harbour, but the two attacks could not be exactly synchronized for it was dark in Formosa and Luzon when the sun rose in Hawaii. But when dawn broke on the morning of the 8th thick fog covered the Formosan airfields. The Japanese were filled with dismay. They felt certain that the Americans, warned by the attack on Pearl Harbour, would withdraw their aircraft further south out of range of the bombers. Despite the fog however, small flights of army bombers left Formosa shortly after daybreak and at about 9.30 a.m. bombed airfields in northern Luzon. At dawn, too, a force of 500 men was landed on Batan Island (off the north coast of Luzon) to develop an airfield for the close support of the main invasion force.[1] In the south, where the weather was clearer, the fighters from the light fleet carrier *Ryujo* attacked a seaplane tender in Davao gulf at dawn.

Later in the morning the fog lifted and the 192 naval bombers, which had been waiting on the Formosan airfields, took off for the main strike. They arrived over the airfield in the Manila area shortly before 1 p.m. to find to their amazement practically all the American squadrons on the ground. Their bombs wrought havoc among the closely packed aircraft. By the close of day, half the heavy bombers and one-third of the fighters of the American Far Eastern Air Force had been destroyed, and many of the remainder heavily damaged.[2]

The following day was comparatively quiet, for fog again closed down, but on the 10th the attacks were renewed on the airfield and on the naval yard at Cavite, which was practically wiped out. By the evening of the 10th all remaining American heavy bombers had been withdrawn to the south; reconnaissance aircraft, with half their strength lost, followed four days later; the few remaining fighter aircraft were thereafter used primarily for reconnaissance, leaving the Japanese in complete control of the air over the Philippines.

The invasion of the Philippines began on the 10th December, two days after the first air attack, with preliminary landings at Aparri and at Vigan in northern Luzon, and on the following day at Legaspi in the south-east of the island. The main landings were made at Lingayen Bay, where *48th Division* was landed on the 22nd December, and at Lamon Bay on the east coast opposite Manila, where *16th Division* was landed on the 24th December. The capital was thus

---

[1] Owing to the success of the main air attack, this airfield was not used.
[2] The Americans had few serviceable airfields in the Philippines, nor, despite having been warned, were they at that time alive to the need for dispersion on the ground.

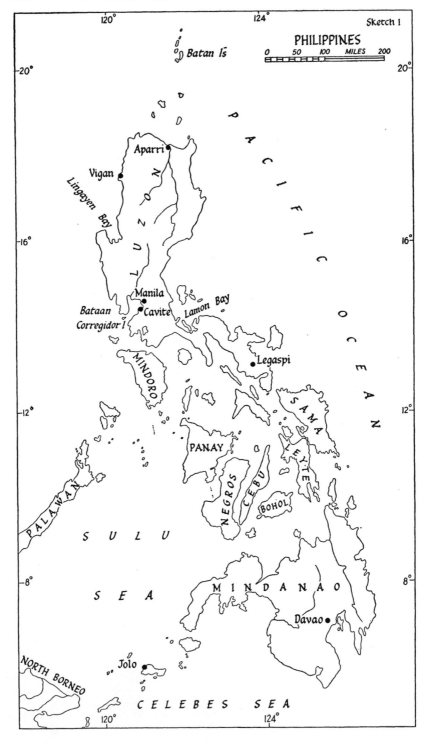

Sketch 1

PHILIPPINES

0   50   100   MILES   200

threatened from both north and south and General MacArthur, declaring it an open town, withdrew the garrison. Fighting a skilful delaying action, he retreated into the mountains and jungles of the Bataan peninsula. The Japanese occupied Manila on the 3rd January 1942.

This, from the Japanese point of view, virtually ended the campaign in Luzon. Completely isolated, the American forces could exert no further influence on the course of events. Desperate fighting took place locally, but the issue was never in doubt and on the 9th April Bataan was forced to surrender. The island fortress of Corregidor to which the remnants of the defenders finally withdrew—by then the last American stronghold in the Philippines—held out for another month. On the 6th May it, too, was overwhelmed.

Meanwhile in the southern Philippines the Japanese had attacked Mindanao, which they wanted as their base for their invasion of the Netherlands East Indies. On the 20th December a strong Japanese force from Palau was landed against slight opposition at Davao. The port was attacked three days later by six Dutch flying-boats from Celebes and north-west New Guinea; a tanker and shore installations were damaged.

A part of the force from Davao was then sent to the island of Jolo in the Sulu Sea, halfway between Mindanao and Borneo, and occupied it on the 25th December. Within a very few days the *21st* and *23rd Air Flotillas* moved their headquarters from Formosa to Davao and Jolo respectively; Vice-Admiral Takahashi's fleet assembled in Davao Harbour and, early in the New Year, transports laden with troops were sailing in convoy from there for the invasion of the Netherlands East Indies.

OPERATIONS IN THE PACIFIC ISLANDS[1]

While the Japanese main thrusts in Malaya and the Philippines were in progress, Vice-Admiral Inouye, with the Japanese *4th Fleet* based on Truk in the Caroline Islands, the *South Sea Detachment* and the *24th Air Flotilla*, was engaged in forging the eastern half of the ring to encircle the newly-won territories.[2] After two days' bombardment by aircraft, Guam was taken by a naval landing force on the 10th December. On the same day a small force sent from the Marshall Islands occupied Makin Island in the Gilberts and began the construction of a seaplane base. A token force of 200 men was landed at Tarawa in the same group but was withdrawn on the arrival at Makin of flying-boats which were used to patrol the area. Wake

---

[1] See Sketch 2.
[2] The *South Sea Detachment* consisted of *55th Regimental Group* comprising *144th Infantry Regiment* supported by artillery and engineer units.

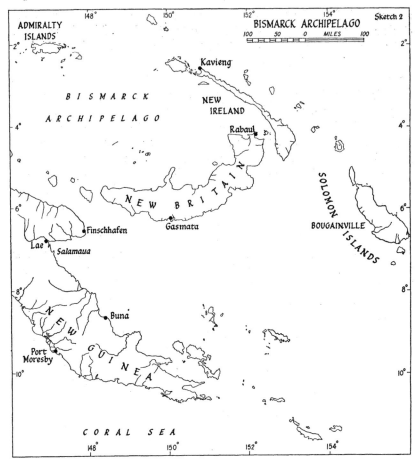

Island fell on the 23rd. By the end of the month all the outlying islands west of the 180th meridian and north of the Equator were under Japanese control.

The only serious resistance encountered was at Wake where a small garrison of American marines put up a stout defence. They repelled the first Japanese assault on the 11th December, sinking two destroyers. On the 22nd the Japanese returned to the attack with overwhelming reinforcements including two carriers and two heavy cruisers from Admiral Nagumo's *1st Air Fleet* (then on its way back to Japan from Pearl Harbour) and some of the special naval landing force troops which had occupied Guam. On the following day the garrison was forced to surrender. An American force, which on the arrival at Hawaii of the carrier *Saratoga* from San Diego had sailed to relieve the island, was therefore recalled.

Early in January 1942, aircraft from Truk began a series of bombing attacks on the Bismarcks and on the 23rd, under cover of the

4th Fleet supported by carriers of the *1st Fleet*, the *South Sea Detachment* seized Rabaul driving out without difficulty the small Australian garrison. Kavieng in the adjacent island of New Ireland was taken on the following day. The two ports were quickly organized as forward air bases thus freeing the carriers for the support of operations in the Netherlands East Indies. Gasmata two hundred miles south-west of Rabaul on the south coast of New Britain was occupied on the 9th February, but it was not until a month later that the Japanese moved across to New Guinea and occupied Lae and Salamaua. Thus by the middle of March 1942 Admiral Inouye had practically completed his task of closing the ring in the east. How the Japanese, encouraged by the ease of their early victories, decided to expand the defensive perimeter they had originally planned, lies outside the scope of this volume and will be dealt with in its proper chronological setting in Volume II.

Map 2

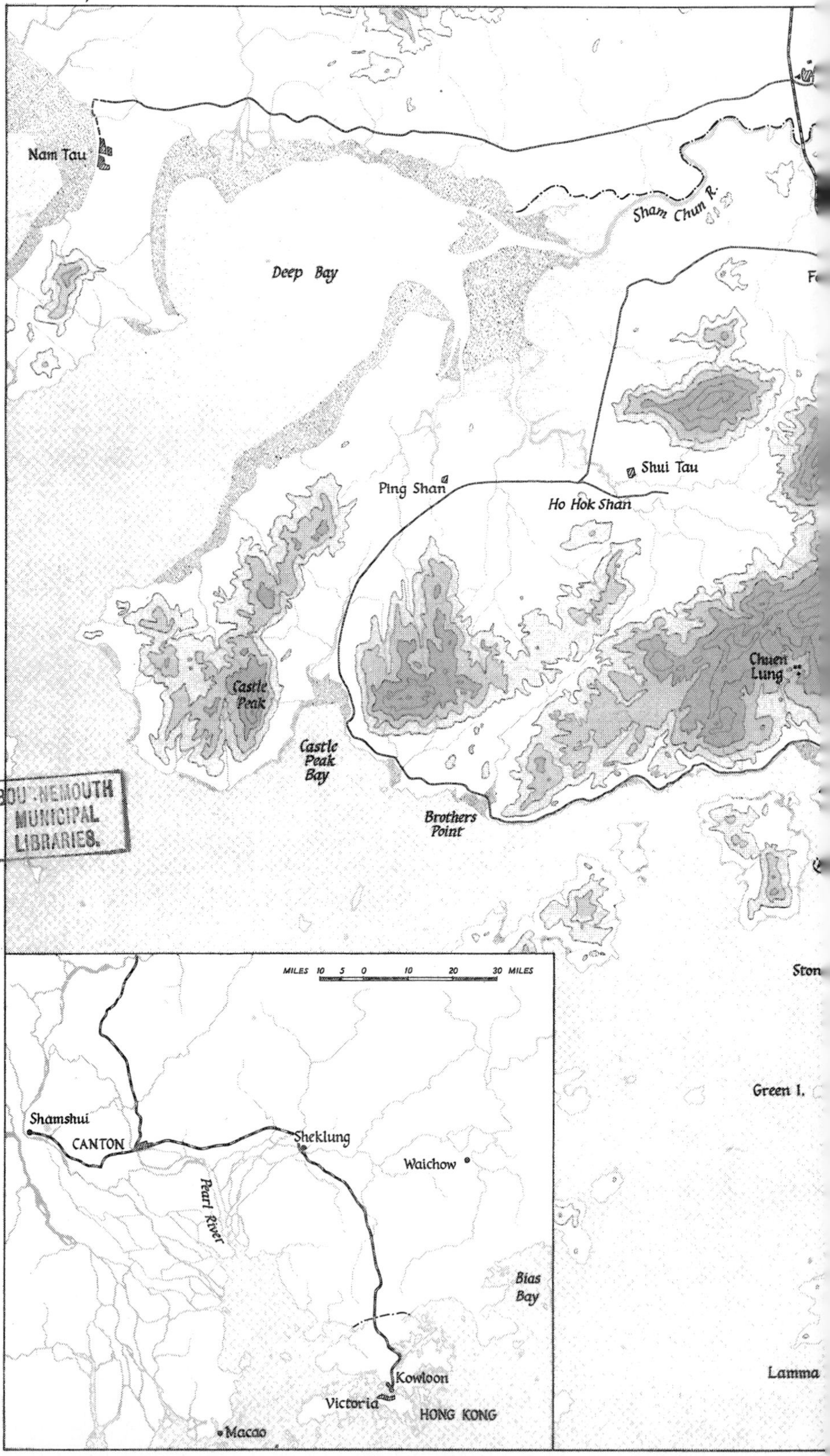

Nam Tau

Sham Chun R.

Deep Bay

Shui Tau

Ping Shan

Ho Hok Shan

Chuen Lung

Castle Peak

Castle Peak Bay

Brothers Point

BOURNEMOUTH MUNICIPAL LIBRARIES.

Ston

Green I.

MILES 10 5 0   10   20   30 MILES

Shamshui

CANTON

Sheklung

Waichow

Pearl River

Bias Bay

Lamma

Kowloon

Victoria

HONG KONG

Macao

HONG KONG
&
LEASED TERRITORIES

MILES 1   0   1   2   3   4 MILES

Mir's Bay

Tai Po

Tolo Harbour

Grassy
Hill

Tide Cove

lee
voir

Needle
Hill

Shing Mun R.

Buffalo
Hill

Smuggler's Ridge

olden
Hill

Filter
Beds

Customs
Pass

Port Shelter

Kai Tak

KOWLOON   Kowloon
Bay

Ma Lau
Tong

Yau Ma Ti

Whampoa

Hai Wan

High
Junk

Devils
Peak

VICTORIA

Causeway
Bay

Tai Koo

Lei U Mun

he Peak

Aberdeen

Wong Nei Chong

Big Wave
Bay

ma Channel

Deep Water Bay

Cape D'Aguilar

Stanley
Peninsula

METRES
300
200
100
SEA LEVEL

CHAPTER VII

HONG KONG BEFORE THE WAR

See Map 2 and Sketch 3

THE ISLAND OF HONG KONG, eighty miles south-east of Canton, was first occupied by the British in 1841 and was formally ceded by China in the following year. It gives its name to the Crown Colony, which includes a considerable tract on the Chinese mainland—the Kowloon peninsula—ceded in 1860, and the Leased Territories acquired on a ninety-nine years lease in 1898. In the fine harbour enclosed between the north shore of the island and Kowloon, British enterprise had developed one of the great international ports of the world, which had become the main distribution centre for south China.

The island has an area of about twenty-nine square miles. The ground rises picturesquely and steeply from the sea in an irregular cluster of hills—partly treeclad, partly barren—which culminates in The Peak 1,800 feet above sea level. The nearest point on the mainland lies opposite the north-east corner of the island across the narrow but deep Lei U Mun, which is a quarter of a mile wide. The port of Victoria stands on a flat narrow strip of land along the western part of the northern shore; it extends for about five miles, occupying nearly the whole of the southern side of Hong Kong harbour between Causeway Bay and Belcher Bay. In contrast to the small shops and crowded tenements of the Chinese quarter, Victoria has a university, a cathedral and many fine public buildings as well as those owned by banks and commercial houses. The coastline is indented by numerous bays, the largest being on the southern side. There is good anchorage throughout the channel between the island and the mainland, the best being in Victoria harbour.

An excellent motor road, following the levels near the shore, encircles the island, with branch roads to Stanley Peninsula, Cape D'Aguilar and Big Wave Bay. Another road traverses the centre of the island from north to south, crossing over the main ridge at Wong Nei Chong Gap. Apart from these roads there are only steep and narrow tracks incapable of taking motor transport.

The Leased Territories stretch from Kowloon to the general line of the Sham Chun River, about seventeen miles to the north, and with the adjacent islands cover some 400 square miles. The Kowloon peninsula, with its wharves, docks and other installations forming part of the great port, is in striking contrast to the comparatively open rugged country of the Leased Territories which lies beyond it. The western part of this region centres on the Tai Mo Shan massif, rising to 3,000 feet and encircled by a good road from Kowloon. Except for an area of swamp and irrigated land lying south-west of the Sham Chun River, the greater part of the Leased Territories consists of a jumbled mass of steep hills whose lower slopes are mostly covered with pine and bamboo forest, giving place near the summit to light scrub and long grass. Kowloon is connected with Canton and the Chinese railway system by a single track standard gauge railway line, which follows the eastern portion of the circular road as far as Fan Ling, passing through a number of tunnels and cuttings and over many bridges. The approaches to Kowloon from the north are barred by Golden Hill and Smugglers Ridge, but these features are dominated in their turn by Tai Mo Shan and Needle Hill. South-east of Kowloon Bay, Devils Peak (700 feet) gives observation over Lei U Mun and the north-eastern part of the island. In the naval dockyard and Tai Koo shipyard on the north side of the island there are dock and repair facilities for naval and commercial vessels. On the other side of the anchorage lie the Kowloon commercial docks. Nevertheless in 1941 no dock capable of accommodating a capital ship existed.

The inhabitants of the Colony are predominantly Chinese, the majority being British subjects by birth; but after 1937, when Japan began to wage open war on China, there was a great influx of refugees.[1] By December 1941 the population of the island, chiefly concentrated in Victoria, was nearly 800,000, while the people who lived afloat in junks and sampans were reckoned at 154,000. Kowloon, and the small scattered communities in the Leased Territories, accounted for another 775,000 so that, when the Japanese attacked, the Colony, apart from the garrison, contained nearly one and three quarter million people.

The climate of Hong Kong is sub-tropical with summer and winter monsoons; the rainfall is erratic. The temperature reaches its maximum between May and October, when it often exceeds 90°F. The winter months—December and January—are relatively cold and dry, though there is normally no completely dry season. A marked feature of the climate is the humidity, which accentuates the effects of both high and low temperatures.

The water supply of the Colony has always been a problem, for the variable rainfall often leads to water shortages, usually during the winter months. Under normal conditions the island depended on the mainland for more than half its water. The rest was obtained

---

[1] In 1935, out of a population of 966,341 only 21,370 were non-Chinese.

from reservoirs on the island fed by concrete channels sited to collect the surface water. The supply constituted a serious weakness in the defence of the island for both sources were clearly vulnerable. The channels leading to the reservoirs formed additional tracks through the hills which were used to good effect by the Japanese.

The Hong Kong defence scheme was based upon the decision taken in 1938 that the harbour must be denied to the Japanese;[1] it was afterwards modified by the pronouncement of the Chiefs of Staff in August 1940 that, in the event of war with Japan, Hong Kong should be regarded as an outpost to be held as long as possible.[2] With the limited force then available the defence of the island could be conducted only in and from the island; but time would be required to clear the harbour, destroy installations on the mainland, and remove supplies and equipment. As these measures could not be undertaken until war began, the defence scheme provided for delaying action in the Leased Territories against a possible Japanese advance.

With only two British and two Indian battalions available however, General Grasett considered it impossible to spare more than one for the mainland. Thus there was no question of covering by fire any obstacles created by demolitions; neither could a defensive position be occupied for any length of time. The task of the battalion allotted to the mainland was solely to protect the operations of demolition parties and then to slow down the forward troops of the invader without becoming closely engaged. He estimated that all the troops might have to be withdrawn to the island after forty-eight hours; and during this very short period the destruction of the installations on the Kowloon side of the harbour had to be carried out and the final preparations made for the defence of the island itself.

The coastal armament of the island, designed primarily for defence against a seaborne attack, consisted of twenty-nine guns.[3] Many of these however were able to bring fire to bear upon the mainland and were ready to engage at call a number of selected targets. They had a limited amount of ammunition suitable for this purpose.

The naval forces comprised the local defence vessels under the command of Commodore A. C. Collinson, R.N.—the destroyer *Thracian*, the 2nd Motor Torpedo-boat Flotilla (eight boats), four gunboats and some armed patrol vessels. Two destroyers, *Thanet* and *Scout*, were at Hong Kong when war broke out. These however were ordered to Singapore and sailed at 7.30 p.m. on 8th December. A boom defended Lei U Mun and mine-fields covered the outer approaches to the harbour.

The coastline of the island offered many possible landing places.

---

[1] See page 18.
[2] See page 34.
[3] Eight 9·2-inch, fifteen 6-inch (including three on Stonecutters Island), two 4·7-inch, and four 4-inch, manned by 8th and 12th Coast Regiments.

The system of beach defence aimed at leaving none of these points unguarded. It was based on machine-guns in camouflaged pillboxes (reinforced later by a number of 18-pounder guns) covering wire obstacles and land mines. Beach lights were installed and the defence of the island against landings was to be on the beaches. The island's perimeter was divided into four sectors. An Indian battalion was to hold the north-east and south-east sectors; a British battalion the south-west sector; and the north-west sector was to be held by the fourth battalion on withdrawal from the mainland. The 1st Middlesex Regiment—a machine-gun battalion—was to man the pillboxes round the coast.

The British air forces were negligible. At Kai Tak airfield on the mainland, and the adjoining seaplane station on Kowloon Bay, were three obsolete Vildebeeste torpedo-bombers and two Walrus amphibians. Together they formed a station flight primarily for target towing purposes. This total lack of air-power was rendered even more serious by the grave shortage of anti-aircraft artillery.

The lack of aircraft and anti-aircraft guns did not by any means constitute the only gap in the defences: security measures, that is to say counter-espionage, were markedly unsatisfactory. Britain was at peace with Japan, and in Hong Kong the Japanese consular staff can have had little difficulty in making a full and accurate survey of the whole defensive system, including the detailed dispositions of troops when manning exercises were carried out. The special branch of the Hong Kong police was weak, and the civil administration was slow to arrest or deport suspicious characters, some of whom were known to be enemy agents. The normal unrestricted movement of all and sundry between the island and the mainland facilitated the activities of enemy agents, who passed unnoticed in the guise of Chinese coolies or traders.

The case of Colonel Suzuki, a Japanese 'language officer', illustrates well the attitude taken over the question of security.[1] He lived in Hong Kong and, when the British military authorities pointed out that he made no attempt to take English lessons, the Japanese Consul-General admitted that the Colonel was really an intelligence officer who had his contacts with Chungking and southern China. The question of issuing an expulsion order was referred to the Foreign Office, who thought however that, since Japan might regard this as an affront, it would be better to wait until Suzuki went on leave. If and when the question of his return arose, action could then be taken to prevent it. Thus Colonel Suzuki eventually departed for Japan at his own convenience.

The Air Raid Precautions organization had enrolled 12,000 people,

---

[1] Great Britain and Japan had, for many years, exchanged officers who took up residence in order to learn the language.

mostly Chinese, before the war began. Tunnels were driven into the granite hills behind Victoria; some of the more solidly built houses were strengthened, but the bulk of the city population could depend for safety only on dispersal outside Victoria. In the light of after events it is apparent that these arrangements left much to be desired, but General Maltby has pointed out that at that time few had any experience of the precautions needed. To make adequate arrangements would have caused severe economic dislocation and entailed very considerable financial outlay—and this applied not only to Air Raid Precautions but to other defence measures. The truth is that few people really believed that Japan would go to war; it is not surprising therefore that unpopular and expensive decisions, which would have involved the dislocation of trade, the occupation of land, major construction or demolitions and the purchase of special equipment, were postponed until it was too late. For similar reasons the machine-gun defences of the island were sited in specially constructed pillboxes rather than in reconstructed houses, despite the disadvantages that such defences would be known to the enemy and that they would be hard to camouflage.

The authorities reckoned that, even if the mainland supplies were cut, the island with its catchment areas, reservoirs, filter beds, pumping stations and large mains would have sufficient water if strictly rationed. Sea water could be used to fight fires. But all depended on keeping the island system intact; and unfortunately the water mains were rarely buried to a depth of more than six inches, and some were fully exposed.

In February 1940 the home authorities decided that food reserves for 130 days should be held for the garrison. They asked the Governor to provide foodstuffs—chiefly rice from Burma—for the civil population on the same scale, and supplies for not far short of this period were in fact accumulated; no mean achievement in view of the size of the population and of existing shipping facilities. In January 1941 the period before relief was extended from 90 to 130 days for all reserves, to bring them into line with food.

After the fall of France in 1940, the Japanese redistributed their forces in south China in such a way that the Colony was effectually cut off from land communication with the territory held by the Chung-king Government. An invasion of the Leased Territories when the time was ripe was thereby made easier. At the same time the local Chinese agents reported rumours that the Japanese-sponsored 'National Peace and Regeneration Army' of Wang Ching-wei contemplated an attack upon Hong Kong.[1]

---

[1] Wang Ching-wei had seceded from Chiang Kai-shek's national government in Chungking in 1938. The Japanese had made him head of the 'puppet' government in Nanking in March 1940.

These reports, coupled with Japanese activities so near to the frontier, naturally resulted in certain defensive precautions being taken on the mainland: charges were placed at the chief demolition sites; the frontier railway bridge over the Sham Chun River was made impassable; and the bridges carrying the Canton road were demolished.

Although the Foreign Office thought that the evacuation of European and Indian women and children from Hong Kong might be regarded by the Japanese as a 'panic measure' and thus encourage their aggressive policy, this wise decision was taken in July 1940. No less than 1,646 service families and over 1,800 wives and children of European civilians were eventually sent away.

The withdrawal of British troops from north China, begun in August 1940, was recognized by the Generalissimo as an inevitable measure,[1] but his anxiety that Hong Kong should be defended became more and more evident. Pending the arrival in the Colony of a mission under Admiral Chan Chak, Chinese officers approached General Grasett with proposals for arming the Chinese population and for concerted British action with Chiang Kai-shek's armies, one of which was south-west of Canton and another seventy miles east of Canton in the area of Waichow. Since War Office instructions were to preserve cordial relations with the Chinese without making any promises or plans, he made no response. Early in August the Japanese had an estimated total of 3,000 troops along the frontier, but reports of troop movements by road and river to and from Canton were inconclusive. What was quite definite was that the Japanese were displaying particular interest in naval dispositions at Hong Kong.

Since the local intelligence services had proved to be unreliable General Grasett sent his own intelligence officers to Chungking in 1940 and arranged for reports on Japanese troop movements in the Canton area to be sent to him. At the same time an air raid warning network with Chinese operators was established on the mainland.

On the 20th July 1941, Major-General C. M. Maltby succeeded Major-General Grasett. He took over at a critical time, for the Japanese had been engaged since the 6th June in activities which were undoubtedly meant to undermine British prestige and, possibly provoke some reprisal which might lead to war. A number of Hong Kong junks had been sunk and their crews subjected to brutal treatment, and at the same time the Japanese had occupied islands in the vicinity of the Colony. As ever, British policy was conciliatory and, after representations had been made by the Ambassador in Tokyo, these matters were allowed to lapse. On the 10th September 1941 Sir Mark Young succeeded Sir Geoffrey Northcote as Governor and Commander-in-Chief, Hong Kong.

---

[1] See page 46.

Towards the end of the month reports were received of a considerable concentration of Japanese artillery in the Nam Tau–Sham Chun River area. The Japanese forces seemed however at this time to be fully occupied by operations further north in Hunan; the capture of Changsha, its capital, was announced on 29th September.[1] It may be noted here that it was actually not until the 6th November that General Hata, Commander-in-Chief of the Japanese armies in China, received orders to prepare a plan for the capture of Hong Kong.

When General Maltby assumed command in July 1941 the four regular battalions composing the normal infantry garrison of Hong Kong were 2nd Royal Scots, 1st Middlesex, 5/7th Rajput and 2/14th Punjab. To provide more infantry, he gained permission to raise a battalion of Chinese; but recruiting did not begin until October, too late for the unit to be formed by the time the war began. The mobile artillery of the garrison comprised two mountain and three medium batteries of the Hong Kong and Singapore Royal Artillery.[2] These batteries were much below strength and therefore included a number of locally enlisted Chinese. Chinese civilians were employed as drivers in transport and other units.

Early in October the Chiefs of Staff told General Maltby that in November he would receive a reinforcement of two Canadian battalions: the Royal Rifles of Canada and the Winnipeg Grenadiers, together with a brigade headquarters and signal section under the command of Brigadier J. K. Lawson.[3] The two battalions had recently completed a tour of garrison duty, one in Newfoundland and the other in the West Indies, and both had been reinforced at the last moment, the Royal Rifles receiving 154 other ranks and the Grenadiers 12 officers and 282 other ranks. Neither battalion had had the opportunity for the type of intensive tactical training so vital to success in battle. Indeed it was understood both in London and Ottawa that they were intended for garrison duty only. The carriers and lorries, on which the force depended for its mobility, were not shipped with the troops and never reached Hong Kong.[4]

Immediately Maltby knew that the reinforcements were assured he revised his defence scheme. Three battalions would still remain in the island defences, but on the mainland three battalions could now

---

[1] See Strategic Map.

[2] The H.K. and S.R.A. was a regular unit raised to man certain coastal, anti-aircraft and mobile artillery units in Hong Kong and Singapore. Officers and some N.C.Os. were British and there were Indian Viceroy's Commissioned Officers. Other ranks were Indians recruited in India by special arrangement with G.H.Q., India, and some Chinese locally enlisted. The mobile batteries in Hong Kong were all H.K. and S.R.A. Each mountain battery had the unusual composition of two troops, one of which was a four gun 3·7 howitzer troop on pack, the other a four gun 4·5 howitzer troop on wheels. The medium batteries consisted of four 6-inch howitzers.

[3] See pages 81–82.

[4] Duff, pages 50–61.

K

be deployed instead of one. He considered that these units, in a good defensive position and supported by part of the mobile artillery would be capable of offering serious resistance.[1] The withdrawal to the island could now be delayed for much longer than the forty-eight hours previously considered as the maximum.

There was no question of checking a Japanese invasion at the frontier. As a defensive position the Sham Chun, navigable by small craft drawing four feet of water as far up as the Canton railway bridge, had too extended a front and all the disadvantages of a river line. Since the size of the force available necessitated the shortest possible front being held, it was perhaps inevitable that the choice should fall upon the mainland position already sited and worked upon, but abandoned when the 1938 defence scheme came into force. This was the so-called Gindrinkers Line which ran from Gindrinkers Bay on the west, north of Golden Hill and Smugglers Ridge to Tide Cove, along the southern edge of the cove and thence south-eastwards through the hills to Port Shelter. The position was about eleven miles long and needed much work and material to place it in a tolerable state of defence. As it was barely three miles from Kowloon this line had to be held until all was ready for withdrawal to the island. Lack of depth precluded a second position. Another disadvantage was that, to the northward, the Tai Mo Shan massif and Needle Hill—only a mile away—overlooked much of the area. The position was considered to be particularly vulnerable in two places: the low ground at Gindrinkers Bay and, on the other flank, at Customs Pass, where a drive through southwards would sever the Devils Peak peninsula from the rest of the mainland defended area. The key to the position lay in the Golden Hill–Smugglers Ridge area, which guarded the direct approaches to Kowloon.

The garrison was divided into the Mainland Brigade (Brigadier C. Wallis) and the Island Brigade (Brigadier Lawson).[2] The Mainland Brigade consisted of 2nd Royal Scots, 2/14th Punjab and 5/7th Rajput, supported by 2nd Mountain Battery, the 3·7-inch howitzer troop of 1st Mountain Battery and 25th Medium Battery, all H.K. and S.R.A. The three mountain battery troops were in close support of forward battalions; the medium battery was superimposed on the whole front. The three static 6-inch howitzers and two 60-pounders on Stonecutters Island could fire on some mainland targets. This made a total of twenty-one guns; thus, bearing in mind the extent of the front to be covered, the nature of the country, and the total absence of any air support, it will be seen that both the strength and mobility of the artillery left much to be desired. The Island Brigade

---

[1] Previously, the deployment of artillery on the mainland had been regarded as too hazardous, for guns would have been difficult to withdraw in the very short time available.

[2] For dispositions of the troops see Sketch 3.

consisted of the Royal Rifles of Canada, the Winnipeg Grenadiers and the Middlesex supported by the 4·5-inch howitzer troop of 1st Mountain Battery, the 3rd and 4th Medium Batteries and the 18-pounder beach defence guns. The arrival of the Canadian contingent had brought the combatant strength of the Hong Kong garrison up to nearly 12,000 men.

General Maltby had held a series of manning exercises in August and September, and a small covering force which was to act as a frontier screen had also been practised in its role. In October the troops went into training camps until the Canadians arrived in mid-November. The three battalions of the Mainland Brigade were then moved into their respective sectors of the Gindrinkers Line and began work on the defences. It had not been considered advisable for these troops to occupy their new positions before the arrival of the Canadians, since to do so might have indicated that reinforcements were expected. Commanding officers were however taken into General Maltby's confidence, and all the necessary preliminaries carried out (reconnaissance, calculation of tasks, estimate of materials required, etc.). The Royal Scots were unfortunately in an area much infested by mosquitoes and malaria took a considerable toll of both officers and men. Although the invalids recovered quickly, the work of digging and wiring undoubtedly reduced the fighting efficiency of many of them who were hardly past the convalescent stage.

Such was the length of the defensive position that not only was there a gap between the right of the Royal Scots (which rested on the Shing Mun Redoubt) and the left of 2/14th Punjab, but there was only one company of the Rajputs as a reserve under the hand of the brigade commander.[1] Sir Robert Brooke-Popham gave it as his opinion in his despatch that at least two divisions would have been required to hold the Gindrinkers Line properly. General Maltby's object, however, in holding this extended position was to delay the enemy and deny the line of observation which the Kowloon hills provided, until such time as the enemy launched a full-scale attack.

The defence suffered from two grave disabilities; firstly the lack of mules and pack equipment for the carriage of mortars, a most serious deficiency in view of the broken and hilly nature of the country; and secondly, the shortage of mortar ammunition. So little was available that preliminary firing practice with these weapons could seldom be carried out.

Since the obsolescent British aircraft would be no match for the enemy fighters, General Maltby directed that none was to take off, unless torpedo-bombers should have a chance at dusk or dawn to attack a capital ship or heavy cruiser. There is no need to emphasize

---

[1] See Map 3.

how greatly the position was prejudiced from the start by the lack of air defence.

Under the defence scheme the Royal Navy was responsible for transporting the troops from the mainland when the withdrawal to the island took place. The navy was also responsible for the demolition, during the withdrawal, of naval stores at Kowloon and all installations on Stonecutters Island. It had also to complete the transfer to Aberdeen of coal, oil fuel and other essential stores from the main dockyard, before the north shore could come under fire from the mainland. Since preparations could hardly begin before the actual opening of hostilities but yet had to be complete by the time the order to withdraw was issued, this was by no means an easy task. It was considered that the Aberdeen docks could easily suffice for the maintenance and repair of the small naval force remaining at Hong Kong.

In the early days of November Japanese military activities above the normal were reported in the Canton–Pearl River area, and the defence lines around Canton were said to have been drawn in as though an attack were expected. On the 10th November an agent calculated that eighteen tanks and fifty-two armoured cars, besides a quantity of mechanical transport, had arrived near the frontier. At the request of the War Office General Maltby forwarded on the 29th an estimate of enemy forces in the Canton–Pearl River area, where he placed the Japanese *18th, 48th* and *104th Divisions*, with one medium brigade (regiment) of artillery and one tank battalion. He said that there was no lack of landing craft, but the numbers were unknown, and no movement had been reported near the frontier. Actually at this time the Japanese *23rd Army* in the Canton area comprised *18th, 38th, 51st* and *104th Divisions* with one mixed brigade, and artillery much in excess of the medium brigade which General Maltby had reported.

Information on the quality of the Japanese forces was no better than the information about their dispositions. They were reported to be inexpert at night operations and addicted to stereotyped methods and plans and their automatic weapons were thought to be neither so numerous nor up to date as the British. Although their combined operations in China had been well planned and well equipped, their undoubted success was weighed against the poor quality of the Chinese resistance. The Japanese air force, judged by European standards, was believed to be inferior, its bombing poor, and night flying little practised. Soon after their arrival, Canadian officers attended a lecture by a British officer who told them that opposite the frontier the Japanese had only 5,000 ill-equipped troops with very little artillery; that they were not used to night fighting; and that their aircraft were for the most part obsolete, the pilots myopic and thus

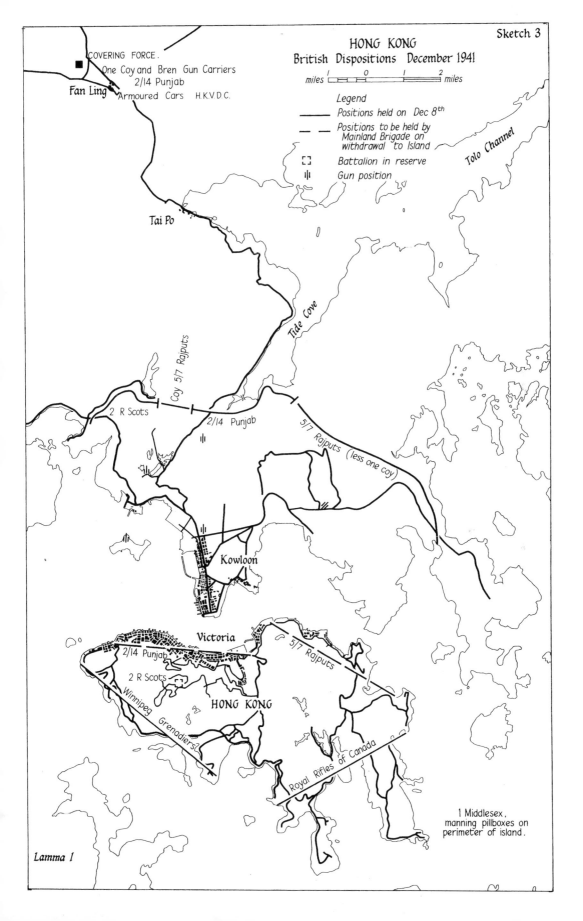

Sketch 3

HONG KONG
British Dispositions December 1941

miles 1 0 1 2 miles

Legend
——— Positions held on Dec 8th
– – – Positions to be held by
        Mainland Brigade on
        withdrawal to Island
⊏⊐ Battalion in reserve
╷╵╷ Gun position

COVERING FORCE.
One Coy and Bren Gun Carriers
2/14 Punjab
Armoured Cars H.K.V.D.C.

Fan Ling

Tolo Channel

Tai Po

Tide Cove

Coy 5/7 Rajputs

2 R Scots

2/14 Punjab

5/7 Rajputs (less one coy)

Kowloon

Victoria

5/7 Rajputs

2/14 Punjab

2 R Scots

HONG KONG

Winnipeg Grenadiers?

Royal Rifles of Canada

1 Middlesex,
manning pillboxes on
perimeter of island.

Lamma I

unable to carry out dive-bombing. Among the troops, and in certain civilian circles, it was freely said that the island was impregnable—a light-hearted and rather foolish assumption which was difficult to contradict without damage to morale.

There were indications towards the end of November of an early Japanese offensive, and certain precautionary measures were put into effect. The harbour was closed at night; British and Allied ocean-going steamers were diverted to Singapore; notices were published advising all not engaged in defence services to leave the Colony; vital points were closely guarded and emergency coast-watching organizations set in operation. By the 2nd December all troops had been placed at short notice; the frontier training camps had been cleared, except those occupied by the Volunteers who could mobilize at six hours warning; the Lei U Mun strait had been closed by booms; and navigation lights at the harbour approaches had been extinguished.

There was however considerable doubt about Japanese intentions, for on the 3rd December it seemed that Japanese troops were withdrawing from the frontier region. On the 4th, General Maltby, from information received, reckoned that the Japanese forces in south China were insufficient for a major attack upon the Colony. But within forty-eight hours there had been three violations of British territory by Japanese aircraft, presumably on reconnaissance. On the evening of the 6th three Japanese divisions were reported to have arrived on the previous day within eight miles of the frontier. Despite this fact and other indications General Maltby was not yet convinced that war was imminent. On the 7th he told the War Office that in his opinion reports that ten to twenty thousand troops were expected to arrive in the Nam Tau–Sham Chun Hu area for an attack on the Colony were certainly exaggerated and had the appearance of being deliberately fostered by the Japanese who, to judge from their defensive preparations around Canton and in the frontier area, appeared distinctly nervous of being attacked. He considered that they were disseminating these reports to cover up their numerical weakness in south China, although some reinforcement of the skeleton Japanese forces in the frontier zone was extremely likely in future. In fact the enemy had four divisions in the Canton area alone, which can hardly be regarded as 'numerical weakness'. In Formosa which strategically is part of south China there were three divisions. There were in addition two Japanese divisions in French Indo-China and one in Hainan Island. These were not likely to be diverted to Hong Kong, but, excluding those in French Indo-China, the enemy still had four divisions within easy reach of Hong Kong and three others within call. The reports of ten to twenty thousand troops expected in the Nam Tau–Sham Chun Hu area, which General Maltby considered exaggerated, were surprisingly accurate since *38th Division*, with attached troops, was on this date, the 7th, about to attack the Colony.

Nevertheless General Maltby, despite his over-optimistic views, was taking no risks. The Volunteers were recalled from their training camps near the frontier on the 5th December, and the anti-aircraft defences of the island were in a state of immediate readiness from the night of the 6th. The 7th was a day of great activity. On the mainland, supporting artillery was deployed, and was ready for action by 7 a.m. A company of the Hong Kong Volunteer Defence Corps at Kai Tak airfield was prepared to deal with possible parachute landings. The Canadian battalions were ferried across to the island from Kowloon and completed the manning of their positions by 5 p.m. In accordance with naval orders, twenty-six merchant ships in Hong Kong harbour cleared for Singapore by noon on the 7th, and eight more left within the next twelve hours. The Gap Rock Lighthouse about thirty miles S.S.W. of Hong Kong was dismantled.

Life in the city of Victoria went on as usual. Ferry traffic across the harbour to Kowloon continued. The newspapers on the 7th December announced the personal plea for the preservation of peace sent by President Roosevelt to the Emperor of Japan on the previous day. In the evening the cinemas displayed notices recalling all service men to their stations, but the majority of the people had no idea that the storm was about to break.

CHAPTER VIII

HONG KONG: THE FIGHTING
ON THE MAINLAND

See Maps 2, 3 and 4

IN THE EARLY MORNING of the 8th December General Maltby's intelligence staff heard Tokyo warn all Japanese nationals on the wireless that war was imminent. At 5 a.m. Naval Headquarters in Hong Kong received a signal from Singapore reporting a Japanese attempt to land on the coast of Malaya. By 6.45 a.m. the whole Hong Kong garrison was standing to arms.

As dawn broke,[1] reports began to come in of Japanese troop movements along the Sham Chun River, which formed the frontier line. At 6.50 a.m. the first demolition charges were fired, and by 7.30 a.m. all road and railway bridges on the frontier had been destroyed. Japanese bridging parties however immediately started to work south and south-west of Sham Chun Hu.

The first air attack was delivered at 8 a.m. A force of thirty-six bombers, with fighter escort, swooped down upon the Kai Tak airfield and seaplane moorings. All five Royal Air Force and eight civilian aircraft were destroyed and the airfield badly damaged. Meanwhile the Japanese had begun to cross the river on a broad front. The advance was made in two groups; the western group, under command of Major-General Ito, comprised *230th* and *228th Infantry Regiments* and included three mountain artillery battalions; *229th* Regiment formed the eastern group.[2] The Japanese plan was to throw the weight of their attack on the western end of the Gindrinkers Line, between Jubilee Reservoir and Gindrinkers Bay. Their western group was therefore the stronger. After reaching Shui Yau, the group, with the exception of one battalion of *230th Regiment* which was to act as flank guard on the Castle Peak road, was directed to advance south-east through the hills towards Chuen Lung. The main body of *229th Regiment* was directed on Tai Mo Shan and Tai Po. The regiment was ordered to find a detachment which was to cross Tide Cove and make contact with the eastern end of the defences while the main body continued its advance due south.

---

[1] Sunrise was just before 7 a.m.
[2] The Japanese order of battle and plan will be found in Appendix 6.

The Japanese worked forward steadily throughout the day in small columns led by local guides, using tracks across the hills and supported by the fire of light artillery. The British covering force withdrew slowly before them, finally taking up a position for the night on Grassy Hill.

The transfer of craft and stores from naval establishments on the mainland to Aberdeen began—a task not made easier by the great influx of Chinese craft, which had crowded for shelter into Aberdeen harbour as soon as the air raids started. Mines were laid in Port Shelter and south of the islands. A Japanese cruiser, a few destroyers and patrol vessels were observed to seaward, out of range.

By dawn on the 9th December the covering troops on the mainland had retired, under increasing pressure, to a position between Needle Hill and Grassy Hill, not far in front of the Gindrinkers Line. Here they remained all day, denying reconnaissance of the main position to the Japanese. The unguarded gap in the line south-east of the Shing Mun Redoubt (on the right of the Royal Scots) offered too favourable an opportunity for a Japanese night advance and forced Brigadier Wallis to sacrifice his only reserve (a company of the Rajputs) to fill it.

During the afternoon Maltby told the Commodore that the Japanese advance into the Leased Territories was swifter than he had expected, and requested that the removal of naval stores and ammunition from Kowloon and Stonecutters Island should be accelerated. Work on the north shore boom defences had to be suspended since the Chinese boats' crews refused to continue. At dusk Brigadier Wallis withdrew the covering troops—who, in Maltby's words, had 'fulfilled their role admirably'—to a position in rear of the Punjabis. The enemy were by now also reported on the front of the Rajputs and were approaching Buffalo Hill from the direction of Tide Cove.

General Dennys (204 Mission) reported during the day from Chungking that, on the previous day, Generalissimo Chiang Kai-shek had issued orders for three armies under General Yu Han-mo to attack westwards towards the general line of the Canton–Kowloon railway, with the ultimate object of joining up with the Hong Kong garrison.[1] Another group of three armies was to attack Canton, to contain Japanese reinforcements.[2] The Chinese stated they could start these operations on the 1st January, but would prefer a postponement till the 10th. Maltby however did not place much reliance on this offer of assistance.

---

[1] A Chinese army (normally three divisions) was equivalent in fire-power to about one British division.

[2] The Japanese had disposed their *51st* and *104th Divisions* to be ready for any such moves by the Chinese.

6. Leased Territory, Hong Kong, looking north.

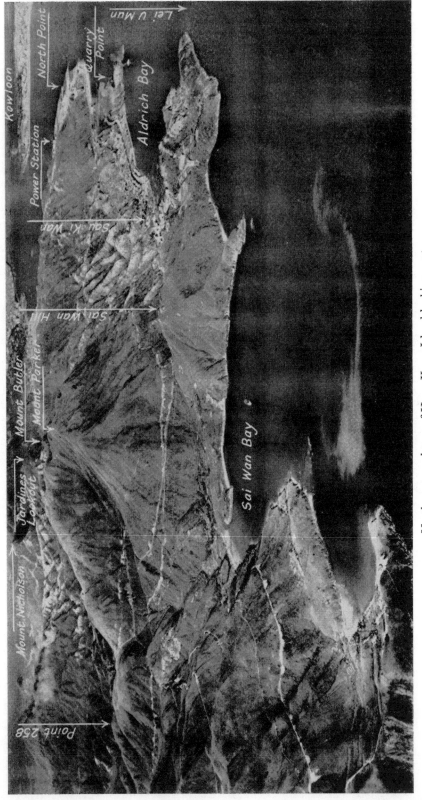

7. North-eastern shores of Hong Kong Island looking west.

During the night of the 9th/10th an incident occurred which prejudiced the defence of the whole of the left sector of the Gindrinkers Line, and led to an earlier evacuation of the mainland than had been anticipated. About 200 yards south of Jubilee Reservoir, sited on the north-western end of Smugglers Ridge, was the Shing Mun Redoubt which was of considerable tactical importance since it dominated other defended localities further west and contained a forward artillery observation post.[1] A platoon of the Royal Scots provided the garrison for the redoubt, but had in addition the task of patrolling by night west of the Jubilee Reservoir and to the south-east. The headquarters of the company to which this platoon belonged was located in the artillery observation post on the higher ground at the southern end of the redoubt. Shortly before midnight the company commander reported that the Japanese had broken into the redoubt and were being counter-attacked. About two hours later he made another report in which he said that, although the enemy were in great strength, he hoped he could hold out in the observation post until dawn. Shortly afterwards the telephone line went dead. Immediate counteraction was limited to bursts of concentrated artillery fire on the Shing Mun Redoubt and River and on the approaches thereto. Wallis decided that no counter-attack could be delivered before daybreak since the nearest troops were nearly a mile away, the ground precipitous and broken, and the exact situation round the redoubt obscure. A company of the Winnipeg Grenadiers was however immediately sent over from the island to provide a reserve for the mainland.

The Japanese version is that, although the redoubt lay in the area allotted to *230th Regiment*, Colonel Doi, commanding *228th Regiment*, considered after a reconnaissance during the late afternoon of the 9th that, until it was captured, an attack on the remainder of Smugglers Ridge was not possible. He therefore decided to assault it without delay and ordered *III/228th Battalion* to launch a surprise attack with *II/228th Battalion* in support. The advance began at about 10 p.m. and the two leading companies, wearing rubber-soled canvas shoes, cleared gaps in the wire and assaulted the position at about 11 p.m. Grenades were dropped down the ventilating shafts of the tunnels at the northern end of the redoubt and the troops stormed their way into the underground defences where fierce fighting at close quarters ensued for at least an hour. The Japanese admit meeting stubborn resistance in other parts of the redoubt and it was not till nearly 2 a.m. that the whole of it was in their hands.

Colonel Doi then informed his divisional headquarters by wireless of his successful action. He was immediately told to withdraw his

---

[1] It consisted of five pillboxes linked by fire trenches and tunnels surrounded by barbed wire and covered some twelve acres of rocky hillside.

troops, but refused to do so. It was only at noon on the 10th, when he was able to speak on the telephone to his divisional commander, that he received official permission for his troops to remain in the captured position. Nevertheless he was then told that he should make no further attacks on this front, and during the morning of the 11th the Chief of Staff of *38th Division* carried out an investigation into Colonel Doi's unauthorized action.

Before dawn on the 10th Wallis urged the commanding officer of the Royal Scots to counter-attack at first light to recover the redoubt, and undertook to support such an attack with the Rajput company on the right flank, most of the mainland artillery and some of the island guns. The battalion commander was however reluctant to undertake the proposed operation; he considered the task beyond the capacity of his reserve company (which owing to sickness was less than half its normal strength), for the enemy was strongly entrenched and the ground both difficult and exposed. Wallis did not override him and order the attack to be carried out because, as he informed Maltby, 'it seemed useless to force a battalion commander to execute a plan in which he had no confidence'.

At 7.45 a.m., after an artillery bombardment, the Japanese launched an attack in company strength from the redoubt against the Rajput company which, it will be remembered, had been moved across to fill the gap in the defences on the right of the Royal Scots. This attack was repulsed after close fighting which lasted over an hour. During the afternoon Wallis, mindful of his lack of reserves, withdrew the Royal Scots to a position running south-west of Golden Hill down to Gindrinkers Bay, thereby considerably shortening the line to be held. This movement was completed by 8.30 p.m. that evening.

At 12.40 p.m. the first enemy aircraft to be brought down by anti-aircraft fire crashed in Tide Cove. The gunboat *Cicala*, supporting the left flank from Castle Peak Bay, was repeatedly bombed during the afternoon and received a direct hit which made dockyard repair necessary. She was relieved by the *Tern*, which at once came under the fire of medium artillery from the direction of Ping Shan. During the day enemy artillery began a systematic bombardment of the Gindrinkers Line, although the Japanese infantry made little attempt to close.

The loss of the Shing Mun Redoubt led Maltby to doubt whether the Gindrinkers Line, as adjusted, could be held against serious attack and at 10 a.m. on the 10th therefore, he warned the Commodore that it might be necessary to evacuate the mainland that very day. The latter protested at such short notice. It was therefore decided to make every effort to hold on for another twenty-four hours, but that preparations for withdrawal were to be completed at the earliest possible moment. Accordingly at Stonecutters Island, which was under dive-bombing as well as artillery attack, final measures were taken for the destruction of the wireless station and the magazines, and preparations were made for dismantling the dockyards at Whampoa and Tai Koo. During the afternoon Maltby ordered the R.A.F. to destroy any remaining aircraft at Kai Tak, obstruct the airfield and concentrate all personnel at Aberdeen, where they would come under naval command.

Since the great press of Chinese junks in Hong Kong harbour formed a serious obstacle to the passage of vessels engaged on evacuation duties, steps were taken to remove them. The Harbour Master succeeded in collecting about 15,000 junks and sampans in the Yau Ma Ti typhoon anchorage on the Kowloon side, and bottled them up by sinking three river steamers across the entrance, but despite this collection, many craft remained obstructing the bays of the mainland and the island.

Brigadier Wallis held a conference at 8 a.m. on the 11th to explain the plan for the withdrawal which, he said, he did not expect to take place for at least a week. An hour later however he learnt that soon after dawn the Japanese, under cover of a heavy mortar barrage, had attacked the two left-hand companies of the Royal Scots in their new positions, which consisted of shallow and widely dispersed weapon pits, ill-provided with wire obstacles. Severe and often hand-to-hand fighting had then occurred. Both sides suffered heavy casualties but finally the two companies, whose commanders had been killed, were forced to withdraw on to their reserve company. The battalion, less the company on Golden Hill, finally stabilized the position at a point astride the road half a mile north of Lai Chi Kok. The Japanese made no further attempt to advance down the main road, but swung left-handed against the remaining company of the battalion which held the steep reverse slope of Golden Hill. Light automatic and rifle fire caught the Japanese as they came over the crest and, though they persisted in their efforts for over two hours, they were finally forced back after fierce hand-to-hand fighting.

The stout resistance of the Royal Scots had discouraged the enemy from exploiting to the full what might have been a break-through. The news of the fighting which filtered back caused Maltby to send his chief staff officer to the mainland to control what appeared to be a critical situation. This officer organized a lay-back position in rear of the Royal Scots, using a detachment of the H.K.V.D.C. and the company of the Winnipeg Grenadiers which had been sent across from the island the previous night. Although in the event this position was never attacked, the Canadians came under shell fire, and thus the 11th December became the first day of action for Canadian infantry in the Second World War.

From dawn on the 11th the Punjabis in the centre of the line were shelled persistently and it was apparent that the Japanese had deployed more than the normal allotment of divisional artillery. The presence of the enemy south of Golden Hill directly threatened Kowloon and rendered the position of the troops holding the centre and right of the Gindrinkers Line most precarious. By 11 a.m. Maltby was convinced that, if he were to get the Mainland Brigade away more or less intact, the withdrawal must begin at once. The Governor was informed accordingly and orders were issued at noon that day.

The withdrawal plan provided for the occupation by the Rajputs (less a company) with one troop of 3·7-inch howitzers in support of a covering position across the Devils Peak peninsula known as the Ma Lau Tong Line. The Punjabis, retiring south-eastwards, were to pass through, and cross to the island by Lei U Mun, while the Royal Scots and nearly all the artillery were to embark on the western side of Kowloon. This method of withdrawal was by no means the most direct, but it avoided the risk of troops becoming entangled in the labyrinth of Kowloon, where much demolition work remained to be carried out. Moreover Devils Peak, since it commanded the narrow strait and the north-eastern part of the island, could obviously only be relinquished in the final stages of the evacuation.

The Kowloon denial scheme was carried out during the afternoon. The oil supplies were destroyed, the Kowloon dockyards demolished, the coast batteries on Stonecutters Island blown up, all British and Allied merchant vessels scuttled and, in an excess of zeal, a Swedish vessel as well. The naval arrangements for the evacuation were however upset by the desertion of many of the Chinese crews manning the ferries, who had to be replaced by naval ratings. Nevertheless by 3.15 p.m. all ferries were in position. The evacuation of guns, heavy equipment and transport went on throughout the rest of the day, despite some interference by enemy artillery.

The Royal Scots from the western flank began to embark about 7.30 p.m. The Canadians followed, the Punjabis taking over the protection of the left flank south of Golden Hill. Both units were safely transferred to Victoria by midnight. In Kowloon, where blackout was complete after the destruction of the power station, looting broke out. The retirement of the Punjabis began soon after dark and was completed by the morning of the 12th. The Rajputs had not far to move to their allotted positions at Ma Lau Tong and their withdrawal was effected without incident. Some stores and equipment had to be abandoned for, owing to the necessity of having to withdraw all three battalions simultaneously, insufficient transport was available. Nevertheless, all the artillery and armoured cars, together with most of the motor transport, were safely withdrawn.

At 4 a.m. on the 12th Wallis reported that the Rajputs were in position. By 3 p.m. the Japanese had established contact and some two hours later attacked in strength. The Rajputs, covered by artillery on the island and the supporting 3·7-inch howitzers, repelled this assault with ease, inflicting heavy casualties. It is noteworthy that, on this occasion, the Japanese put in their infantry without the support of either artillery or mortar fire, apparently expecting, in the fading light, to achieve surprise.

At 9 p.m. that night Maltby decided that it would be wiser to give up the Ma Lau Tong position and withdraw to the Hai Wan area. There the flanks would be less exposed to waterborne attacks and, being narrower, the front could be held with fewer troops and supporting weapons. Accordingly, one company of the Rajputs and the howitzers were at once evacuated to the island through the Hai Wan position, which was held by the rest of that battalion. Then at 3.30 a.m. on the 13th, the question arose whether it would not be better to evacuate the mainland.

As Devils Peak overlooked much of the north-eastern end of the island, Wallis was reluctant to give it up; moreover, he thought that a hasty evacuation might end in disaster. On the other hand, a prolonged resistance at the tip of Devils Peak peninsula was hardly feasible, and Maltby wanted to ensure that the Rajput battalion, intact, would be able to occupy its allotted position in the island defences. Apart from tactical considerations, the question of maintenance would have presented grave difficulties; all the mule lighters had been sunk by enemy action, most of the crews of the so-called War Department Fleet had deserted, and all that remained was the old and slow *Victoria*, manned by Royal Army Service Corps officers. It was decided therefore to complete the evacuation of the mainland without delay, even though the operation could not be finished before daylight. At dawn all the island guns which could be brought to bear gave covering fire. Fortunately neither Japanese aircraft nor artillery attacked the points of embarkation or the landing places on the island side.

This final evacuation was carried out mainly by motor torpedo-boats and the *Thracian*, though not without difficulty and damage to the ships because of the low tide. A hundred and twenty mules had to be left behind for lack of suitable lighters, a loss subsequently keenly felt, and much ammunition was abandoned; but there were few casualties.

While these events were taking place on the mainland, the island was subjected to frequent air attacks and artillery bombardment. At

10 a.m. on the 11th the Japanese began to land on Lamma Island and were engaged by two of the coastal batteries. Then followed an attempted crossing, in sampans, to Aberdeen Island, which was frustrated by machine-gun fire;[1] later, coastal batteries shelled a concentration of junks off Lamma which presaged a second attempt to cross the East Lamma Channel. On the 12th, with the control of the mainland in his hands, the enemy concentrated his fire on artillery positions and on the beach defences along the whole of the north coast of the island.

The civil population as a whole continued to behave well, despite their dismay at seeing troops arriving from the mainland, but in Victoria subversive elements were circulating alarmist reports and in some quarters indulging in looting and violence. The police kept control, but these disturbances made the distribution of rice and other commodities to the civil population more difficult. Chinese employed upon various military and civil works and duties continued to desert.

That night, it was decided to move several tons of dynamite from Green Island across to Hong Kong. The time of departure of the vessel carrying this dangerous cargo was fixed in concert with the military authorities. All pillbox detachments along the north shore were warned. A later message, putting the time forward two hours, may have caused some misunderstanding; but it was undoubtedly overstrained nerves which caused fire to be opened on the craft as she neared the vehicular ferry route across the harbour. The dynamite blew up, killing all on board. The heavy explosion caused widespread alarm, and persistent reports, all false, that the Japanese were landing were current throughout the night. The loss of the explosives was serious and the resulting shortage stultified the plan to localize fires by the creation of fire-lanes.

The actual withdrawal from the mainland may be accounted a success. It might have been so pressed by superior ground forces, and so harassed by air attacks (against which there was little defence), as to cause disaster. In spite of the short notice given to staff, troops, the navy and the civil authorities, it had been accomplished with no loss of artillery and little sacrifice of equipment. This was partly due to the Japanese rigidity of mind, for there is no doubt that the withdrawal took them by surprise. The enemy had expected to have to launch a set piece attack, and had planned accordingly. Confronted by an unforeseen situation, he could not react in time to take full advantage of it. It is nevertheless true that, judged by hopes and expectations, the withdrawal was premature. The defence of the mainland had lasted only five days.

---

[1] See Map 4.

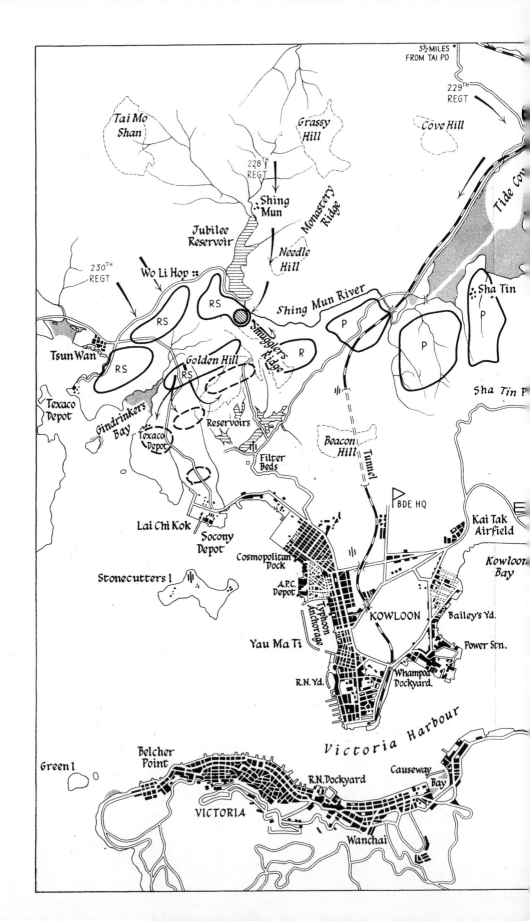

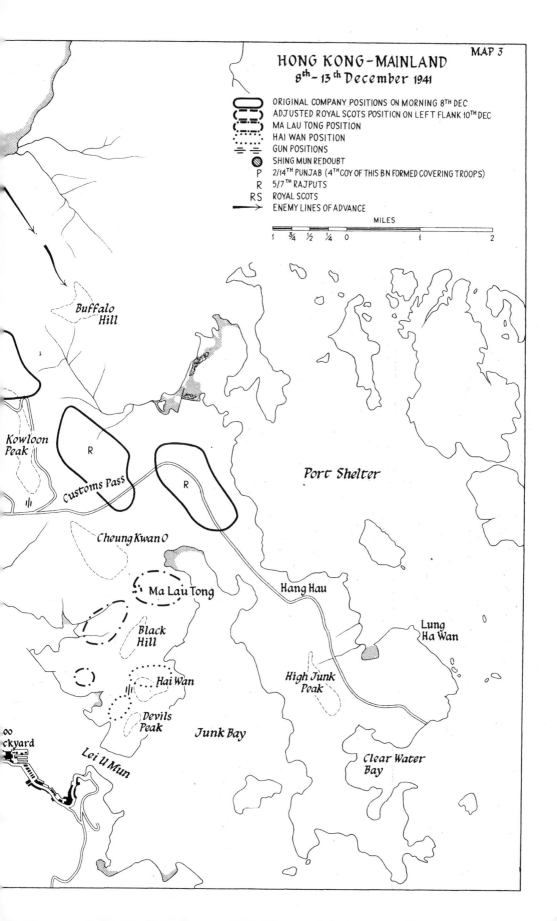

MAP 3

HONG KONG – MAINLAND
8th – 13th December 1941

	ORIGINAL COMPANY POSITIONS ON MORNING 8TH DEC
	ADJUSTED ROYAL SCOTS POSITION ON LEFT FLANK 10TH DEC
	MA LAU TONG POSITION
	HAI WAN POSITION
	GUN POSITIONS
	SHING MUN REDOUBT
P	2/14TH PUNJAB (4TH COY OF THIS BN FORMED COVERING TROOPS)
R	5/7TH RAJPUTS
RS	ROYAL SCOTS
	ENEMY LINES OF ADVANCE

MILES

1 ¾ ½ ¼ 0 1 2

Buffalo Hill

Kowloon Peak

R

Customs Pass

R

Port Shelter

Cheung Kwan O

Ma Lau Tong

Hang Hau

Lung Ha Wan

Black Hill

Hai Wan

High Junk Peak

Devils Peak

Junk Bay

oo ckyard

Lei U Mun

Clear Water Bay

CHAPTER IX

THE FALL OF HONG KONG

See Map 4

AT 9 a.m. on the 13th December a launch, flying a white flag, crossed the harbour. It bore a staff officer with a letter from Lieut.-General T. Sakai, commanding the Japanese *23rd* (*South China*) *Army*, summoning the Governor to surrender under threat of severe aerial and artillery bombardment. The summons was refused.

General Sakai's letter proved to be no idle threat: enemy artillery fire directed on the coastal batteries and Victoria increased as the day wore on and continued on the 14th. The bombardment set the battery at Belcher Point ablaze, caused serious fires in the city, none of which could be controlled, and damaged water mains beyond repair. Disorders occurred in the crowded quarters of Victoria: Chinese civilian transport drivers deserted and fifth column Chinese, under cover of darkness, unsuccessfully attacked an important anti-aircraft gun position.

In general the Chinese population remained subdued and orderly, unmoved by propaganda leaflets dropped by enemy aircraft. Cases of armed banditry however did occur in the air raid shelter tunnels. These were effectively dealt with by the Chungking Government secret societies, which had been ignored in time of peace, but whose assistance was now sought and freely given.

Without either air reconnaissance or radar to give warning of impending attack, General Maltby felt he had to defend the whole of the perimeter of the island. Although he now had every reason to expect attack from the mainland, he dared not weaken the beach defences looking seaward, since the Japanese might combine an assault from the sea with one across the harbour.

The island was divided into two brigade commands—East and West—the dividing line running roughly north and south through the centre of the island. East Brigade (Brigadier Wallis) was disposed with 5/7th Rajput on the north shore waterfront from Pak Sha Wan to Causeway Bay.[1] Two companies of 1st Middlesex occupied the pillboxes from Sai Wan Bay to West Bay.[2] The Royal Rifles of

---

[1] Two companies were in the shore defences and two in local reserve, one south of Tai Koo and one at Tai Hang Village.
[2] 1st Middlesex was directly under Fortress Headquarters for defence purposes, but the detachments manning pillboxes came under the operational command of the battalions in whose areas they were located.

Canada manned the southern seaward defences from the D'Aguilar Peak area, north through Obelisk Hill and thence southwards to Stone Hill and Stanley Village, with a reserve company further north covering the Lye Mun Gap. Two companies of the H.K.V.D.C. were in reserve. The mobile artillery (four 6-inch, four 4·5-inch, and three 3.7-inch howitzers) was deployed in support of the north-east sector, where an enemy landing was thought to be most likely. The beach defences, on either side of the isthmus at Stanley and Tai Tam Bay, were each strengthened by two 18-pounders; and there were also five anti-aircraft guns in the area.

West Brigade (Brigadier Lawson) was disposed with 2/14th Punjab on the north shore waterfront from Causeway Bay to Belcher Point.[1] The Winnipeg Grenadiers manned the seaward defences of the south-west coast with three companies; their fourth providing the brigade reserve at Wong Nei Chong Gap. The 1st Middlesex (less two companies) occupied the pillbox defences in the West Brigade area and a defended locality on Leighton Hill. The Fortress reserve consisted of 2nd Royal Scots near Wanchai Gap, and four companies of the H.K.V.D.C. near The Peak. Anti-aircraft guns were located at Wong Nei Chong Gap, Wanchai Gap and in the Aberdeen area.

At dawn on the 15th December the Japanese began a systematic artillery and air bombardment, supplemented by mortar fire, which continued almost without respite and with ever-growing intensity for the next four days. The shelling not only caused widespread military and other damage but prevented artillery ammunition, urgently required by the defenders, being drawn from the Lye Mun Magazine. Air attacks directed against the coast defences and Aberdeen dockyard were particularly destructive. The *Thracian*, docked for repairs, was so badly damaged that she had to be beached on Round Island. Other vessels, including two motor torpedo-boats, were also hit and naval casualties were heavy.

At about 9 a.m. on the 15th the enemy made a bold attempt to cross the Lei U Mun channel, using rubber boats and improvised rafts but were detected and repulsed with considerable loss. At 9.30 a.m. on the 17th, Japanese bombers attacked Victoria and military targets throughout the island. A short sharp artillery bombardment of the whole central district of Victoria followed. Two launches flying the white flag then crossed the harbour; they brought Japanese staff officers with a second summons to surrender, signed by Lieut.-General Sakai and Vice-Admiral Niimi. Sir Mark Young replied:

'The Governor and Commander-in-Chief, Hong Kong, declines most absolutely to enter into any negotiations for the surrender of

---

[1] This battalion also provided protection for Government House and Fortress Headquarters.

Hong Kong and he takes this opportunity of notifying Lieut.-
General Takaishi Sakai and Vice-Admiral Masaichi Niimi that he
is not prepared to receive any further communications from them
on the subject.'

General Maltby considered that this summons—since the envoys
seemed rather taken aback at the Governor's refusal—might indicate,
apart from a general intention to undermine the morale of the
defenders, the enemy's desire to obtain quick and cheap victory without having to attack across the harbour. The Japanese might, he
thought, also be influenced by Chinese action, or threatened action,
in their rear.

As the day progressed the Japanese were seen to be collecting
barges, ferry-boats and other craft in Kowloon Bay. These and the
Japanese guns near Devils Peak and the mortars on the Kowloon
waterfront, were brought under fire. At sea an enemy cruiser with
some destroyers and patrol vessels was visible. The only British naval
vessels now remaining afloat were the gunboat *Cicala* stationed at
Belcher Point, where the battery was out of action, the gunboat *Robin*
and the depleted motor torpedo-boat flotilla.

That evening Wallis described the situation on the north shore as
'not very bright'; many pillboxes had been destroyed, searchlights
hit and machine-guns damaged by the constant bombardment,
whilst it proved almost impossible to keep communications in repair.
The Japanese, he thought, might attempt to land anywhere between
Sai Wan and Causeway Bay or across from the High Junk to the
Sheko Peninsula.[1] Even as he spoke Japanese shelling set on fire the
large paint factory near Braemar Point, compelling the hasty removal
of the nearby 18-pounders in the beach defences. That night Aberdeen
was shelled from the sea, and the local naval headquarters hit.

On the 18th Japanese air raids increased in intensity. The oil tanks
at North Point were set on fire, and an important searchlight in the
vicinity had to be abandoned owing to the heat. The central district
of the city was heavily bombed, and all roads and paths leading from
it were blocked by the exodus of the panic-stricken Chinese. It was
significant that late in the afternoon the enemy changed his point of
attack from the Tai Tam Gap, Lye Mun Gap and Stanley Fort areas
to the observation posts on Sai Wan Hill, which were dive-bombed
and shelled until destroyed. A heavy artillery and mortar bombardment of the whole Lye Mun peninsula opened just before dark, and
a little later the enemy put down another concentration on Sai Wan
Hill. British guns fired with good effect on troops seen moving down
the Devils Peak peninsula.

It had become obvious that the Japanese would attempt to cross

---

[1] See Map 2.

L

the harbour after darkness fell that night. The conditions were ideal: the tide would be at the full about 9 p.m. and the moon did not rise till after midnight. Along the waterfront hung a pall of smoke from the burning oil tanks and paint factory, and the great heat from the fire at Sau Ki Wan rubber works threatened to disorganize the nearby defences. Only four of the sixteen beach lights in the Rajput sector were then in working order, and it was impossible to keep in repair the signal lines to the pillboxes and other forward defences. The whole north-east front was so shrouded in smoke that enemy approach would be easy; the troops were therefore on the alert and knew there must be no withdrawal.

The Japanese plan for the attack on the island was for the three infantry regiments of *38th Division* to land simultaneously on the night of the 18th/19th on the north-east coast between Pak Sha Wan and North Point. Once the troops were established ashore, an advance was to be made westward towards Victoria; the *230th* on the right, the *228th* in the centre and the *229th* on the left. It was expected that by daylight on the 19th the centre and left regiments would be in position immediately east of The Peak, almost isolating the city. All did not go according to plan however, though the actual landings were accomplished without much difficulty.

At 8 p.m. on the 18th the Aldrich Bay defences were heavily shelled. Soon afterwards the Rajputs received reports from Tai Koo docks that ferry steamers were approaching with small craft in tow. Then came reports of landings at Quarry Point, Braemar Point and later at North Point, where fifth columnists had cut the beach defence wire. The Rajputs were presented with good targets and their 3-inch mortar fire did considerable damage at close range. But neither this, nor artillery concentrations, checked the Japanese advance for long. Six battalions attacking in two flights were ashore before midnight, two from each regiment (the third being in divisional reserve). Lieut.-General Sano, the divisional commander, landed near Tai Koo dockyard at 1 a.m. on the 19th.

The *III/229th Battalion* moved towards Mount Parker from Aldrich Bay; *II/229th Battalion* advanced southward on Sai Wan Hill and Lye Mun Gap; and *228th Regiment* from Braemar Point advanced south on Mount Butler. The *230th Regiment*, crossing from Kowloon, under heavy machine-gun fire from Causeway Bay, came ashore near North Point. It assembled south of the reservoir and then advanced towards Jardines Lookout and Wong Nei Chong Gap.

The whole weight of the Japanese attack had fallen on the Rajputs, who suffered severely, losing most of their officers, British and Indian. Aided by fifth columnists, the enemy by a swift advance seized Sai

Wan Hill; but a Rajput detachment was not ejected from Tai Koo until midnight. It then fell back to Sanatorium Gap.

Brigadier Wallis (East Brigade) ordered an immediate counter-attack to recapture Sai Wan Hill and fort, but, in the darkness and confusion, this was not easy, particularly with inexperienced troops. The reserve company of the Royal Rifles went forward about midnight, supported by the fire of two 6-inch howitzers sited just north of the Gap. The attackers reached the wall of the fort but failed to scale it in face of heavy fire, and at 1.30 a.m. were withdrawn to the south of Lye Mun Gap, the 6-inch howitzers being abandoned. The Brigadier now faced a critical situation, for the Lye Mun peninsula, including the Lye Mun Gap, had been lost and he did not know what was happening on his left. With a view to strengthening this flank he sent, in succession, three platoons of the Royal Rifles to occupy and hold Mount Parker. The enemy had however forestalled them, and the attack was not pressed home.

As soon as Brigadier Lawson (West Brigade) heard of the landings, he formed three platoons from the Winnipeg Grenadiers Headquarters and ordered them forward to occupy Mount Butler, Jardines Lookout, and the road junction near the Filter Beds respectively. The first reached its objective but, attacked by superior numbers, was forced back next morning. The second found that the enemy was already holding Mount Butler and withdrew under heavy fire; the third held the road junction throughout the night despite heavy fire from Jardines Lookout. Realizing that the vital Wong Nei Chong Gap, from which radiated routes to all parts of the island, might be difficult to hold owing to the loss of Jardines Lookout, Lawson at about 2.30 a.m. ordered the company of the Winnipeg Grenadiers, which was holding the Brick Hill–Deep Water Bay area in the south, to counter-attack Jardines Lookout, with Mount Butler as the final objective.

Meanwhile Maltby had taken steps to reinforce the Gap itself. A senior officer of the Royal Engineers was directed to organize a force of seventy British and seventy Chinese engineers for use in this area, and a company of 2/14th Punjab was directed to occupy the Mound, due west of Jardines Lookout. The General also appealed to the Commodore for naval help and was informed that over two hundred men were being assembled at Naval Headquarters, Aberdeen, for action when required. These too were ordered to report to West Brigade Headquarters at the Gap.

By dawn on the 19th December the Japanese *229th Regiment* had occupied Lye Mun Gap and Mount Parker, the *228th* Mount Butler and the *230th* Jardines Lookout. The defence held Tai Tam Gap and a general line from Wong Nei Chong Gap to Causeway Bay. Wallis had in hand near Tai Tam Gap the Royal Rifles, two companies of the Middlesex, two companies of H.K.V.D.C. and such artillery personnel as he had been able to collect. Lawson held Wong Nei Chong Gap with West Brigade reserve (a company of the Winnipeg Grenadiers) and the crews of a light anti-aircraft battery; the Filter Beds with a Grenadier platoon; the Mound with a company of the Punjabis; and from Caroline Hill to the sea with the survivors of the Rajputs and elements of the Middlesex. Small bodies of troops were still holding out in isolated positions near the Power Station, Tai Hang Village and on the slopes of Jardines Lookout.

About 9.30 a.m. Wallis conferred with Maltby on the telephone. Maltby pointed out that, in order to prevent the enemy cutting the defence in two, East Brigade must stabilize the position Tai Tam Gap–Gauge Basin–Wong Nei Chong Gap. The Brigadier explained that his troops were scattered, and in no condition to repel a determined thrust southward by a force reckoned already to number two battalions, well supplied with mortars, and almost certain to be reinforced. He suggested that he should withdraw his whole force to the Stone Hill–Stanley Village area, reorganize, and launch a properly co-ordinated counter-attack with the least possible delay to retake Mount Parker and Mount Butler. To this Maltby agreed.

The withdrawal was not however to take place without loss. The British officer in command of the 4·5-inch howitzers had been killed, and the order to 'get out of action' was misunderstood by the Indian officer, who put his guns out of action by destroying them. The anti-aircraft guns at Gauge Basin, which could not be withdrawn, were also lost. The Indian gunners, who were under automatic and mortar fire, removed the sights and breechblocks and withdrew. The loss of the howitzers was to have a serious effect on the fortunes of East Brigade.

Later in the day Wallis informed Fortress Command that he was unable to counter-attack before dawn on the 20th. A defensive position had first to be organized; the troops required rest; and, in any case, a night advance over unreconnoitred country was inadvisable. By midnight the brigade defensive dispositions had been completed, the front extending from the inlet south-west of Red Hill, through Sugar Loaf and Stanley Mound, to Repulse Bay. East Brigade was not in touch with the enemy during the day, for, after the two battalions of *229th Regiment* had captured Mount Parker and Sai Wan Hill, their orders were to advance 'south and west' through Wong Nei Chong Gap. The regiment concentrated at Gauge Basin and advanced to Stanley Gap leaving one company on Point 258. At 6 p.m. scouts reported heavy fighting in the vicinity of Wong Nei Chong Gap, and Colonel Tanaka, the regimental commander, decided to move south-west towards Violet Hill so as to 'strike the coast road and then to follow its course westward'. By dawn on the 20th, *229th Regiment* had occupied Violet Hill, Middle Spur and Point 143, and had reached the grounds of the Repulse Bay Hotel.

Meanwhile the enemy, using every type of craft, continued to ferry troops and equipment across the harbour. Few guns could be brought to bear to hamper these movements and, in any case, there were now no observation posts; but during the morning of the 19th the Commodore sent in a motor torpedo-boat attack. The first two boats, tearing into the harbour from the west at their maximum speed of thirty knots, sank two landing craft and made good their withdrawal; the second pair met with heavy shell fire and low level air attack, and one was lost. Further attacks were cancelled, but a single boat dashed into Kowloon Bay without orders and was promptly sunk. Nevertheless the gallant effort made by the flotilla was not entirely wasted: many enemy small craft were capsized by the wash of the boats, and their occupants drowned.[1]

North Point was held until the late afternoon of the 19th, when its defenders were forced to surrender, but the Power Station held out until the following day. This was a truly epic defence. The garrison was made up of a party of the Middlesex—all wounded men—who had taken refuge there, and a detachment of the H.K.V.D.C. known as the 'Hughesiliers', after Colonel A. W. Hughes who raised them. They numbered four officers and sixty-six men, mostly prominent business men (all over 55 years of age); two officers and six men were Free French. These men were veterans—most of them had fought in the First World War, some also in the South African War or, in the case of the Free French, in Spain. This mixed garrison, although surrounded, put up a spirited defence all through the night, refusing all calls to surrender. On the morning of the 19th the Hughesiliers tried to cut their way out, but were all killed or captured. The party of the Middlesex elected to fight it out where they were, and did so, until they too were overwhelmed.

Let us now return to the struggle of West Brigade on the 19th around Wong Nei Chong Gap. The company of the Winnipeg Grenadiers, advancing with orders to occupy Jardines Lookout and penetrate to Mount Butler, moved west through the Gap immediately before dawn. What happened on Jardines Lookout is uncertain, but the leading wave won the crest of Mount Butler at the point of the bayonet, and held it with great gallantry for several hours. All the officers were either killed or wounded and the Grenadiers were forced off the hill. The depleted company then found itself surrounded and attacked with grenades from all sides. Company Sergeant-Major

---

[1] The flotilla was manned by the R.N.V.R.

J. R. Osborn caught and threw back at the Japanese their own unexploded grenades. Finally one fell where he could not retrieve it in time and, throwing himself on it, he gave his life for his comrades.[1] Eventually the survivors were forced to surrender.

The *228th Regiment*, which had already suffered severely from machine-gun and artillery fire, was seriously delayed by this gallant action and it was not until nightfall on the 19th, after overrunning some anti-aircraft guns near Stanley Gap, that it advanced on Wong Nei Chong Gap and made contact with *230th Regiment*. The latter, having captured Jardines Lookout, advanced south-west on Mount Nicholson and Wong Nei Chong Gap, overwhelming two platoons of West Brigade reserve; the remainder of the company, holding a group of shelters immediately north-east of the Gap which commanded the road, withstood all efforts to eject them from their position.

At 7.30 a.m. on the 19th, Maltby had ordered a company of his reserve (Royal Scots) to be sent forward in motor vehicles to counter-attack and secure the Gap. This attack, pressed with great resolution, eventually reached a point astride the road within 100 yards of the Gap, but under the withering fire of rifles and automatics could make no further progress. The company suffered severely, all the officers being killed. Meanwhile part of the naval detachment from Aberdeen, moving towards the Gap from the south along the main road in trucks, was ambushed at about 9.45 a.m. and sustained heavy loss; the survivors were forced to take cover at Postbridge, a house on the main road south of the Gap.

Further misfortune followed. At 10 a.m. Lawson telephoned from West Brigade headquarters to say that the enemy was firing into his shelters at pointblank range, and that he was 'going outside to fight it out'. He did so and was killed, as were nearly all the members of his own headquarters, those of the artillery supporting his brigade, and some men of the Royal Scots who had fought their way through in an attempt to relieve brigade headquarters. The remnants of West Brigade reserve however still held out east of the Gap road, which it kept under fire.

At about 1.30 p.m. Maltby decided that the time had come to launch a general counter-attack. Accordingly, he ordered two companies of the Punjabis from Victoria to advance eastward from Leighton Hill in order to enable the remnants of the Rajputs, still fighting near Tai Hang Village, to disengage. At the same time he ordered the Royal Scots and Winnipeg Grenadiers, supported by eight field guns, to make a general advance at 3 p.m. The first objective was to be the general line Middle Spur–the reservoir east

---

[1] Company Sergeant-Major Osborn received the posthumous award of the Victoria Cross for his gallant conduct in this action.

of Wong Nei Chong Gap–Sir Cecil's Ride, joining up on the left with the two companies of Punjabis, who were to push on towards North Point.

The main attack started with a composite company of the Grenadiers moving forward along the southern slopes of Mount Nicholson, followed by the Royal Scots astride the mount itself. The Canadian company, meeting strong resistance, was held up just short of the Police Station at the Gap. The Royal Scots, advancing north and south of Mount Nicholson, were met with devastating fire and despite repeated attacks on the Police Station could gain no ground. Further north the Punjabi companies became involved in confused fighting about Tai Hang Village and were also forced back with considerable loss; they were eventually withdrawn into reserve at Victoria.

The day ended with neither side in control of the Gap. The Japanese held Jardines Lookout and Stanley Gap and were astride the road at the Police Station at the Gap itself. The defenders held the eastern slopes of Mount Nicholson and the main road immediately north and south of the Gap, with the Grenadiers and the Royal Scots intermingled. Further north a Punjabi company held the Mound, and the remnants of the Rajputs and some Middlesex Leighton Hill; Middlesex machine-gun posts on the western side of Causeway Bay still remained in action.

Just before dark a machine-gun platoon of the H.K.V.D.C. which had been gallantly holding out on the slopes of Jardines Lookout was finally overwhelmed. It was the dogged resistance of small detachments such as this, coupled with the numerous though unco-ordinated counter-attacks, which had temporarily brought the enemy advance to a stand-still even though the objectives were not attained. The opportunity for a co-ordinated counter-offensive by the defence had thus been created. Maltby had however neither fresh troops nor adequate artillery to support them and thus the moment passed.

During the night a number of unco-ordinated attempts were made from the north, south and west to recapture the Police Station and gain control of the Gap. In the darkness and general confusion these all failed to achieve their object, though more than one almost succeeded, and the night fighting resulted in no change in the positions held the previous night. The defending troops were however exhausted, units were intermingled and a pause for reorganization was badly needed.

The counter-attack of East Brigade planned for the 20th did not begin till 8 a.m. Wallis advanced along the main Repulse Bay road and the catchment channel on the western slopes of Violet Hill with the Gap as his objective, using the Royal Rifles supported by all the meagre artillery left him (one 18-pounder and two 3·7-inch howitzers). By 10 a.m. the advance had reached the Repulse Bay Hotel, where a number of women and children had taken refuge, defended by a subaltern of the Middlesex and a mixed party of sailors, soldiers and airmen. The Canadians quickly cleared the Japanese out of the hotel outbuildings and garages, which they had occupied during the night, killing an officer and twenty-five men.

Attempts to advance further were however held up by bursts of fire from the direction of Middle Spur, Point 269 and Violet Hill, which the Japanese appeared to be holding in considerable force. It is hardly surprising that East Brigade's counter-attack, after making slow progress, was eventually halted altogether immediately north and north-west of the Repulse Bay Hotel, for with the equivalent of one weak battalion, untrained for mobile warfare, and with practically no artillery, it was endeavouring to dislodge from a strong position a numerically superior and experienced enemy supported by mortars and guns.

About 5 p.m. Stanley Mound came under mortar fire and Japanese infantry was reported on Point 362. As night fell and heavy rain set in, with his forward troops in danger of being cut off, Brigadier Wallis withdrew his brigade to its former positions in the Stone Hill–Stanley Mound area, leaving a company at the Repulse Bay Hotel which Maltby had directed must be 'held at all costs'. He then reported to Fortress Headquarters that he had not sufficient strength to force his way through the enemy holding Violet Hill and Middle Spur and proposed that, in order to regain contact with West Brigade, he should attack on the 21st between Tai Tam Gap and Gauge Basin, a route hitherto deemed impracticable, for he believed the enemy was not so strong in that area. The plan, desperate though it appeared, was approved.[1]

The enemy occupation of Point 143 caused Fortress Headquarters on the 20th to reinforce the Aberdeen area with a weak company of the Punjabis from Victoria, with orders to clear the road from Aberdeen to Repulse Bay Hotel. The Punjabis however were unable to make any progress but, assisted by a platoon of the Grenadiers from Aberdeen Island and a party of thirty-five naval ratings, they succeeded in organizing a hastily improvised defensive position which included Brick Hill, Bennets Hill and the Magazine at Little Hong Kong. The *Cicala* in Deep Water Bay gave covering fire throughout the day despite repeated air attacks. The Japanese, involved in the struggle around Repulse Bay Hotel, made no attempt to advance further westwards during the day.

Early on the 20th Maltby appointed Colonel H. B. Rose (Com-

---

[1] The country was difficult with several narrow defiles, and in its later stages the advance would be taken in flank by fire from Mount Butler and Jardines Lookout.

mandant of the H.K.V.D.C.) to command West Brigade in succession to Brigadier Lawson and ordered him to drive the enemy from the Wong Nei Chong Gap and from the high ground beyond. Rose decided to attack early the following morning with a fresh company of the Grenadiers, about 100 strong, withdrawn from the western coastal defences. Meanwhile he reorganized the Royal Scots and Grenadiers, who had become intermingled in the night's fighting; the Canadians withdrawing to a position facing south-east at Middle Gap, and the Royal Scots to one along the northern slopes of Mount Nicholson from Middle Gap past the Filter Beds to the main road north of Wong Nei Chong Gap. Mount Nicholson itself was thus left unoccupied.

About midday the Japanese from Jardines Lookout attacked the Punjabis holding the Mound. The Indians held their own, but a company of the Royal Scots sent up to cover their right suffered heavy losses. The Japanese admit that little progress was achieved on the 20th; they spent the day in reorganization, their plans having been upset by 'the strong British resistance'. They planned to launch a fresh attack on the 21st with both the *230th* and *228th Regiments*, supported by the divisional artillery reinforced by 150-mm. howitzers and mortars, the objective being Leighton Hill and Mount Nicholson. But on the afternoon of the 20th Mount Nicholson was covered in mist and Colonel Doi (*228th Regiment*) decided to take advantage of this. At 5 p.m. he occupied the crest without meeting any opposition. Meanwhile the Grenadiers, preparatory to the dawn attack, had been ordered to occupy a forward position astride Mount Nicholson. While moving there they came under heavy fire from Doi's men on the hill and had to be withdrawn to Middle Gap, where they spent the night exposed to pouring rain and a cold wind —a cheerless prelude to a dawn attack.

As the 20th December drew to its close, the strain on the troops, who had had little or no respite under conditions of considerable hardship, was beginning to be apparent. But there was heartening news: Admiral Chan, head of the Chungking Mission in Hong Kong, reported that 60,000 Chinese were concentrating on the frontier of the Leased Territories and were about to attack the Japanese. This report, coming from such a source, was regarded as authentic and the troops were told they need look forward to 'only a few more days of strain'. Alas, the hopes raised proved to be false.

The 21st was for East Brigade another day of disappointment and frustration.[1] Wallis had intended to attack through Tai Tam Gap

---

[1] The term 'brigade' is misleading: this force now consisted of only three companies Royal Rifles, two companies H.K.V.D.C., a small detachment of the Middlesex, and two 3-inch mortar detachments.

with the Royal Rifles and strike at the enemy's flank and rear, but his leading troops were soon held up by strong enemy forces holding Red Hill and Bridge Hill. Nevertheless by the afternoon they had gained a footing on both Bridge Hill and Notting Hill, some troops even reaching the crossroads at the southern end of the reservoir. There the attack was halted. Wallis knew that his troops were nearly at the end of their tether; he had no reserves; his losses had been heavy, particularly in officers; the Canadians on Bridge Hill were being enfiladed by mortar fire from Point 362; all the 3-inch mortar ammunition was expended; there was no transport to carry up food and night was coming on. Reluctantly he decided on withdrawal. The Japanese had brought up *I/229th Battalion* from their reserve to relieve the company which Colonel Tanaka had left at Point 258 and to guard the flank of *229th Regiment*. It was this force which East Brigade had encountered. But though the attack had failed, it caused the enemy further to reinforce this area with a second battalion (*I/230th*) from Kowloon.

While East Brigade's attack was in progress, Maltby decided to make another attempt to reach the Wong Nei Chong Gap from the Repulse Bay Hotel area. At 1 p.m. he instructed Wallis to send all the men he could make available to the hotel in carriers, with orders to break through to the Gap from the south. An artillery officer (Major C. R. Templer), then in action with East Brigade, was brought back to command a hastily assembled party of about forty men, comprising Canadians, coast defence gunners and Volunteers. In two carriers and a number of trucks, this small force arrived at the hotel about 5 p.m. Leaving the Volunteers to garrison the hotel, Templer added the company of the Royal Rifles (which was already there) to his command and, mounting them in lorries, pushed on up the road. Almost at once the two carriers and an ammunition truck were knocked out by fire at close range, but the rest of the force drove on. Three trucks eventually reached the last bend in the road south of the Gap. Here Templer organized an attack on the Police Station, but his two Bren guns jammed, and without covering fire success became impossible. As it was getting dark a withdrawal to the hotel was ordered; despite the enemy's fire it was successfully accomplished.

It is evident that the fighting which took place in the Repulse Bay area during this period, though tactically unsuccessful from the British point of view, not only considerably delayed the Japanese advance on Victoria but caused them serious loss. Colonel Tanaka (*229th Regiment*) has said that he remained for three whole days on a hill about 500 yards north-west of the Repulse Bay Hotel. The *III/229th* battalion commander said that his unit suffered heavy casualties in the vicinity of Repulse Bay.

In West Brigade area early on the 21st December the Grenadier company launched its attack on Wong Nei Chong Gap. It was met by devastating fire from Mount Nicholson; half the company including all the officers, were killed or wounded and the survivors were forced to withdraw to Middle Gap. Here they came under heavy shell fire, and the withdrawal was continued to Wanchai Gap. Meanwhile the Punjabis on the Mound, augmented by a platoon of the Royal Scots, held on until the afternoon when, almost overwhelmed, they were forced to retire to the Filter Beds. The line from Leighton Hill to the sea still held. During the day all that remained of the Grenadiers (approximately 100 men) were collected and reorganized. They were then sent to establish a position on Mount Cameron, which they held for the rest of the day under continual artillery and mortar fire.

Although *228th Regiment* had occupied Mount Nicholson and the *230th* had secured the Mound, the Japanese Divisional Infantry Commander (Major-General Ito), dissatisfied with the progress made on the northern flank on the 21st, continued to urge the latter regiment to make greater efforts to press on. At dawn on the 21st, enemy attempts to occupy Brick Hill were repulsed by a detachment of the Middlesex. The *Cicala*, firing from Deep Water Bay, engaged and silenced enemy guns in action near Wong Nei Chong Gap until Japanese aircraft finally succeeded in sinking this gallant little ship. This reduced the naval strength to two small gunboats and five motor torpedo-boats. The *Robin*, firing from Aberdeen harbour, silenced an enemy battery at Middle Spur. There were no guns however capable of subduing the continual enemy bombardment of the Aberdeen area.

Meanwhile, in a final effort to occupy Point 143 and join hands with the defenders of the Repulse Bay Hotel, Maltby ordered West Brigade to send a senior officer of the Punjabis to take control in the Aberdeen area. The commanding officer elected to go himself. To his two remaining officers and twenty-five other ranks he added an equal number of naval ratings, and made a desperate attempt to reach Point 143. In a gallant but vain effort to breast the wet, slippery slopes under a withering fire the commanding officer was killed; only eight of the Punjabis survived, all of them wounded; and the naval contingent also lost heavily. This failure ended the attempt to break through to Repulse Bay.

The 22nd saw the end of the defence of the Repulse Bay Hotel. The enemy gradually closed in under heavy supporting fire until the area held by the company of the Royal Rifles, together with other small detachments, was limited to the hotel itself. All plans to rescue the women and children in the hotel had to be abandoned, as they were unfit to walk and no transport could get through to them. It was considered that the surest way to save their lives was for them to remain where they were and surrender. The garrison was then ordered to withdraw to Stanley Peninsula. They tried to get away after dark in small groups, but only a few got through. The company commander with about thirty men held the hotel until the following night, and then made a dramatic escape by boat to the wreck of the *Thracian* off Round Island. They eventually reached Telegraph Bay only to find the garrison had surrendered.

Brigadier Wallis had in the meantime set about organizing three defence zones, the forward one of which included Stone Hill and Stanley Mound. Each of these positions was to be held as long as possible so as to rob the enemy of an easy and early success. There was little hope of achieving more than this. By this time, too, the supply of water had become an anxiety, as the Tai Tam pumping station was no longer working.

From daylight onwards the whole of the forward area had been under observed artillery and mortar fire; in the afternoon the Japanese attacked and there was hard fighting. They captured the extreme right of the position, which rested on the sea, but were thrown out by a counter-attack by a detachment of the Middlesex. The H.K.V.D.C. on Stone Hill and the Royal Rifles on Stanley Mound were subjected to intense mortar fire, and after repelling three attacks made with grenade and bayonet, were forced to abandon the crest of the hills and withdraw to the reverse slopes. Owing to the absence of reserves an immediate counter-attack to regain the lost ground could not be launched, but the Brigadier ordered an attack for the 23rd.

On the western side of the island, at first light on the 22nd the Japanese were holding Brick Hill and Point 143, Mount Nicholson, the Mound and the Tai Hang road to the sea at the eastern end of Causeway Bay. West Brigade held the machine-gun post between Brick Hill and Point 143, and Little Hong Kong Magazine, with small garrisons. The remnants of the Grenadiers held Mount Cameron, and the Royal Scots the road between the Filter Beds and Wanchai Gap facing Middle Gap and the northern slopes of Mount Nicholson. The Punjabis (thirty-five strong) held the Filter Beds, and two weak platoons of the Rajputs, with some Middlesex, from Leighton Hill to the western side of Causeway Bay.

A small detachment of the Grenadiers, the remnants of a company which had been in the Gap area when West Brigade Headquarters was overrun on the 19th December, were still gallantly holding out on the 21st though completely surrounded.[1] Early on the 22nd, with only thirty-seven men left—all wounded—and with no food, water or ammunition, this little garrison was forced to surrender. Maltby

[1] See page 134.

in his despatch paid a special tribute to its brave and prolonged resistance, which had cost the enemy dear. The Japanese account, referring to the defence put up by this Canadian company, says: 'The enemy fire from those positions was so heavy that not only was the advance checked but our troops were thrown into confusion.'

During the day the Japanese, rather surprisingly, made no major attack, but their air raids and mortar fire became heavier and more effective. On the western slopes of Mount Cameron, close to the summit, the remnants of the Grenadiers clung precariously to their position: to air attack and artillery and mortar fire they could reply only with small arms, and in the rocky ground they could not dig in. Artillery support was almost negligible and as the day wore on the Japanese bombardment grew still heavier. Further north the Punjabis had to be pulled back from the Filter Beds to the south-western corner of the Racecourse in order to prevent a gap developing in the defences between them and the Royal Scots. As a result the Rajputs had to withdraw their right flank to the south-eastern corner of the Racecourse and occupy Mount Parrish with such reserves as they could muster.

As darkness fell on the 22nd, an artillery and mortar barrage, the heaviest yet, fell on the Grenadiers still holding Mount Cameron. At 10 p.m. *II/228th Battalion* reinforced by an additional company delivered a fierce attack. It pierced the flank and fought its way along the position, using captured mortars and light automatics with deadly effect. In the darkness and confusion the defenders were forced down the hillside and retreated through Magazine Gap in small groups. At 1.30 a.m. Rose (commanding West Brigade) reported to Maltby that Mount Cameron was lost and the troops were falling back in disorder. Since this endangered the position further south, the small mixed detachment holding Bennets Hill was told to withdraw to Aberdeen, an order which was subsequently cancelled.[1] The Japanese however, despite their success, made no attempt to establish themselves on the western slopes of Mount Cameron.

Early on the 23rd, East Brigade delivered a counter-attack to recover Stone Hill and Stanley Mound. The Royal Rifles, supported by the few remaining guns and the machine-guns of the Middlesex, re-gained both positions but had not sufficient men to hold them; soon after 10 a.m. under heavy artillery and mortar bombardment they were again driven back. Their commanding officer advocated a

---

[1] The composition of this force—and there were others like it—illustrates the straits to which the defence had now been reduced. It comprised 34 Canadians (all that was left of a company of the Winnipeg Grenadiers), 14 airmen, 10 sailors and 43 Dockyard Defence Corps (the last reserves from Naval Headquarters at Aberdeen).

retirement to the more level ground near Stanley Village, where he thought his tired men could fight to better advantage. To this Wallis agreed. Because of the heavy losses suffered by *I/229th Battalion* during the fighting on the 22nd and 23rd, the enemy did not immediately follow up the withdrawal. Thus the defence had the opportunity, albeit under heavy fire, to organize a new defensive zone in depth from Stanley Mound southwards.

In West Brigade area, at dawn on the 23rd a detachment of Royal Marines was sent forward in lorries from the dockyard and reached the northern slopes of Mount Cameron, making contact with the Royal Scots who were still in position on the road facing the north-western slopes of Mount Nicholson. Two companies of the H.K.V.D.C. were in reserve near Magazine Gap; and a Royal Engineer detachment was holding Mount Kellett, north of Aberdeen.

At 9 a.m. the enemy attacked the Royal Scots, only to be driven off. No more infantry assaults developed, the Japanese contenting themselves with low-level air attacks. Later in the day the Royal Scots were withdrawn to a line facing the north-western slopes of Mount Cameron covering Wanchai Gap, in touch with the Punjabis at the south-western end of the Racecourse. By evening the reorganized remnants of the Grenadiers were in position south of them, covering the reservoirs between Wanchai Gap and Bennets Hill. The garrison at Little Hong Kong continued to hold out and it was still possible during the hours of darkness to draw ammunition from the magazine.

Nearer the harbour, the day had also been an anxious one. From 8 a.m. onwards the Rajputs, at the southern end of Leighton Hill, had beaten off several attacks until, running short of ammunition, they were obliged to withdraw to the northern and western edges of the Racecourse. The Middlesex however still clung to their position on Leighton Hill. The Japanese were able nevertheless to infiltrate in small groups through their thinly-held line amongst the streets and houses, and eventually forced them to make a slight withdrawal to get clear of the debris of their destroyed defences. On this day the Japanese brought up *III/230th Battalion*, their last reserve, and allotted it to its own regiment for the final break through to Victoria, planned for the 24th.

Early on the 24th, Wallis discussed the situation with the commanding officer and senior officers of the Royal Rifles, who were all firmly convinced that their men could do no more and that further resistance was useless. For five days and nights this battalion had borne the brunt of attack and counter-attack; the men had had little or no rest, and had gone for long intervals without food. Incompletely trained, they had bought their knowledge of warfare at a heavy price, their hardships and casualties being all the greater because of their total lack of battle experience. The Brigadier decided that the Canadians should be relieved by composite units under Middlesex and Volunteer officers and withdrawn into reserve at Stanley Fort.

It was not until noon that the Japanese, supported by artillery, mortars and armoured cars, assaulted the right flank near the coast. The attack failed, but the bombardment continued and was supplemented by a series of air attacks. Meanwhile the shortage of water became more serious, for bombing had cut the mains; the tanks at Stanley Fort had been hit by shell fire and all reserve water had been lost.

On the western side of the island, dawn on the 24th showed that most of Mount Cameron was in enemy hands, although the Royal Scots, now only 175 strong, held the north-western slopes and Wanchai Gap. Artillery and mortar fire was incessant and there were continual low-level air attacks. The Japanese made only one attack in this area, just south of Wanchai Gap, at 9.30 a.m., which was repulsed by the Grenadiers after heavy fighting.

In the northern sector the Middlesex on Leighton Hill were shelled, mortared and bombed throughout the morning. At about 3.30 p.m. they were attacked frontally and from both flanks and, with the houses all round them on fire, were forced off the position; but not before the 57th Foot—the famous Die Hards of Albuhera— had, once again, justified their title. The Rajputs and Middlesex then held a line from Mount Parrish across the north-western corner of the Racecourse and thence to the coast. The Japanese did not follow up, but their intensive mortar fire knocked out all the remaining Middlesex machine-guns. Otherwise the *228th* and *230th Regiments* remained comparatively inactive on the 24th, for the general attack upon the defences barring the way to Victoria, originally ordered for that day, had been postponed till the morrow.

During the night of the 24th/25th there was heavy fighting at Stanley, where *I/229th Battalion* reinforced by *I/230th Battalion* from Kowloon delivered a most determined attack upon the neck of the peninsula. Despite heavy losses from machine-gun fire, the enemy pressed the assault home on a wide front and overran the whole forward position, the defenders—Middlesex, Volunteers, prison warders—fighting to the end. At 3.30 a.m. automatic fire and showers of hand grenades opened the enemy attack on the next line of defence; coastal pillboxes were reduced by flame-throwers. Wallis was once again obliged to call upon the Royal Rifles, and the enemy for the time being was stopped.

As a last effort a company of the Royal Rifles launched a counter-attack on the enemy positions at 1.30 p.m. on the 25th. The attack failed, the company being almost completely wiped out.

Throughout the night the Japanese bombarded the centre of the city, the naval dockyard and Fortress Headquarters. Shortly after midnight a battalion of *229th Regiment* attacked south of Wanchai Gap, and the right flank of the Grenadiers was forced to give ground. The summit of Bennets Hill was lost but regained before dawn.[1]

Early on Christmas morning Major C..M. Manners and Mr. A. H. L. Shields, who had been captured, arrived at Fortress Command Headquarters.[2] They had been sent by General Sakai to describe, from their own observation, the enemy's immense superiority in men and armament and thus convince the Governor of the futility of further resistance. The General said that his troops would stand fast until noon. The Defence Council, summoned by the Governor, nevertheless agreed that this opportunity to surrender should be ignored: Maltby, indeed, was occupied with plans for a fresh counter-attack, while the Commodore, who had no ships left except the *Robin* and some motor torpedo-boats, said that he was prepared to defend the dockyard to the last.

The enemy did not however observe his own informal armistice. There were widespread air attacks; incendiary bombs set the hillside on fire and destroyed signal cables. At about 2.30 p.m. Maltby was informed that Mount Parrish was lost, that the remnants of the Royal Scots were holding the high ground north-west of Wanchai Gap, that Magazine Gap could not hold out much longer, that the positions near the north shore seemed about to disintegrate, that only eight of the mobile guns remained in action and ammunition was running low.[3] He then telephoned the Commodore, who said he could hold on for another two hours, but agreed that the end had come.

At 3.15 p.m. Maltby told the Governor that in his opinion there was no possibility of further effective resistance. After consultation with two civilian members of his Defence Council and further discussion with his naval and military commanders, the Governor authorized Maltby to arrange for a cease-fire. That evening at the Peninsula Hotel, Kowloon, Sir Mark Young, Governor and Commander-in-Chief of Hong Kong, formally surrendered the Crown Colony without conditions to Lieut.-General Sakai, Japanese *23rd Army* Commander.

---

[1] After the end of the fighting at Repulse Bay on the 22nd, *229th Regiment* had re-formed and had been directed to advance on to Victoria on the left of *228th Regiment*.

[2] The former, a retired artillery officer, was manager of Kowloon Dockyard; the latter was a member of the Hong Kong Executive Council.

[3] Wanchai Gap was held to the end.

Meanwhile on Stanley Peninsula Wallis was in process of reorganizing the defence, in anticipation of a Japanese night attack, when a car displaying a white flag appeared from the Japanese lines. It carried two British officers, bringing verbal orders from Maltby for the Stanley force to surrender. Wallis found this hard to believe. In his view, surrender was 'unwarranted by the local situation'. Although the water supply was damaged beyond repair and he had now no artillery or mortars fit for action and very few grenades, he was determined to continue the struggle. He demanded confirmation in writing and sent his brigade major back in the car to obtain it. This officer returned after midnight with orders in writing and at 2.30 a.m. on the 26th, after warning the troops, Wallis ordered the white flag to be hoisted and himself went across to the Japanese lines.

This account of the Hong Kong campaign would not be complete without reference to the escape of the Chungking Mission. Admiral Chan Chak and his staff had been given a guarantee that they would not fall into Japanese hands. Accordingly the motor torpedo-boat flotilla had been told to embark them at Aberdeen after dark on the 24th and take them to Mir's Bay.[1]

The Admiral and his officers duly arrived at Aberdeen but, finding no trace of the boats, took over the most suitable civilian motor launch in the harbour. After filling the tanks from a local petrol store they set off to attempt the passage to Mir's Bay. Unfortunately they took the Aberdeen channel and thus came under Japanese fire from Brick Hill. The Admiral, who was without his artificial leg, received a bullet in the wrist, and others of his party were killed or wounded. The survivors, including the Admiral, abandoned the launch and swam to the southern end of Aberdeen Island. Here they appeared to be stranded, but a reconnaissance discovered the flotilla lying to the westward of the island, awaiting their arrival. In sorry plight the survivors of the party embarked, and the motor torpedo-boats under cover of darkness sailed to Mir's Bay. There they scuttled the boats and set out for the interior, led through the Japanese-occupied territory by a Chinese guerrilla leader. They eventually reached Chungking, from where the crews of the motor torpedo-boats were flown to Rangoon on the 14th February 1942.

News of the loss of Hong Kong after only eighteen days' fighting came as a shock. The War Cabinet and the Chiefs of Staff had not, of course, expected Hong Kong, which could neither be reinforced

---

[1] See Map 2.

M

nor relieved, to survive attack upon a major scale; nevertheless, it had been ordered to hold out 'as long as possible', and it may be asked whether resistance could not have been prolonged.

The Japanese assault on the Colony, well planned in every particular, was based upon accurate and detailed knowledge of the defences, troop dispositions and communications both on the mainland and on the island. This the enemy owed to his efficient intelligence service, which had been in action for many years before the war and which took full advantage of the inadequacy of the British security measures.[1] The first point to bear in mind, therefore, is that the defence was handicapped from the very outset by the superiority of the Japanese local intelligence system.

Japanese tactics presented no novel features. In attack, great reliance was placed on the initiative and aggressive spirit of the infantry—hardy soldiers, well trained in night work and in hill fighting, and well practised in the use of ground. Lightly equipped and wearing rubber-soled shoes, they moved swiftly and silently, blending boldness with cunning. Although the men leading the attacks upon the Shing Mun Redoubt and on the island were thought at the time to be special storm troops, they were in fact an ordinary Japanese division (*38th*), a formation which had been blooded during the China Incident. The Japanese did not greatly outnumber the British garrison in infantry, but they had an overwhelming superiority in artillery and complete control of the air. The *38th Division* was a homogeneous force of highly trained troops with battle experience, whereas the British forces consisted mainly of units employed overlong on garrison duties, indifferently equipped, lacking experience of warfare and even of battle training, and hastily formed into extempore formations.

As regards infantry weapons, the enemy's machine-guns were well supplied with armour-piercing ammunition, which proved devastatingly effective against the steel shutters of concrete pillboxes and shelters. Light mortars came into action well forward and without delay; these weapons, with their ammunition, were transported over the roughest tracks, by local Chinese impressed as carriers. The enemy's heavy mortars, too, wrought great havoc. The facts regarding the British mortars have already been mentioned: their arrival on the eve of battle afforded no time for training, and pack transport was woefully short. The Japanese artillery, greatly augmented beyond the normal divisional allotment, was well handled and the defence was heavily out-gunned.

One reason why resistance came to an end earlier than had been expected was the disappointing failure of demolitions on the mainland

---

[1] See page 110.

to impose any serious delay on the enemy's advance. The Japanese engineers did excellent work. This was first seen by the speed with which they bridged the Sham Chun River on the 8th December. Preparations for demolitions could hardly have been kept entirely secret; but the enemy certainly possessed exact information of the quantities and types of material required for repairs and the points where such materials would be needed.

It was not only in the engineering field that meticulous attention had been devoted by the enemy to the requirements of the Hong Kong campaign: their signals, transport and all ancillary services were well equipped and organized for the special tasks which lay ahead. On the other hand, the defence was largely dependent for transport on untrained and undisciplined Chinese civilians who proved unreliable, while in the hills the serious shortage of pack mules reduced mobility.

The performance of the Japanese air force came as a revelation, even allowing for the fact that the bombers needed no fighter escort and encountered no very formidable anti-aircraft ground defence. Under these conditions general air reconnaissance and observation for the artillery could go on almost undisturbed and Japanese troops ran no risk in using ground signals to indicate their positions to aircraft patrols. Expert as the enemy proved to be at high-level bombing, the skill and boldness displayed by his pilots in low-level attacks were equally remarkable. Indeed the garrison, nourished as they had been on pre-war disparaging reports on the Japanese air force, firmly believed that Germans must be leading the sorties.

From the outset a dominant factor was the British inability to dispute the Japanese command of the air and, it must be added, of the sea. The absence of air power meant that there was no means of preventing the activities—reconnaissance, observation, high and low-level attacks—of some eighty aircraft based on Canton. The lack of sea power meant that the island was always exposed to seaborne assault, and this ever present threat greatly influenced the defensive dispositions. The light forces of the Royal Navy were insufficient, and not of the type to undertake patrols to seaward. The gunboats which so gallantly supported the troops on shore were under constant air attack and paid the penalty. Motor torpedo-boats operated in difficult conditions for which their armament was ill-suited.

To a great extent, the duration of the resistance depended upon the length of time the enemy could be held at bay in the Leased Territories. But it is idle, since the troops were not available, to speculate whether, if at the outset of the campaign a stronger covering force had been detailed, the delay imposed on the Japanese initial advance might not have been considerably prolonged. Three battalions were not enough to carry out an effective delaying action

on the mainland; they were even inadequate to man the Gindrinkers
Line, for there was no reserve. Nor was it possible to reinforce the
mainland without unduly weakening the defences of the island, thereby exposing it to the ever present threat of invasion from the sea.

Granted then that the enemy could not be delayed forward of the
Gindrinkers Line, why, it may be asked, did the troops not stay and
fight it out on their prepared position, instead of withdrawing before
the enemy was ready to assault in earnest? The withdrawal, indeed,
appears to have taken the Japanese by surprise. But the loss of the
Shing Mun Redoubt and the misfortune which then befell the left
flank exposed the junction of the Castle Peak and Tai Po roads, thus
(as recorded in General Maltby's despatch) 'seriously endangering
the withdrawal of all the troops based on the Tai Po road'. Although
the left flank had been strengthened by bringing up a company of the
Winnipeg Grenadiers, Maltby's chief staff officer reported back that
the situation in the area was still precarious. He therefore recommended withdrawal that night, and all the evidence indicates that
any postponement of the evacuation might well have led to disaster.

When the assault on the island began, the Japanese, using special
flat-bottomed craft, had no difficulty in establishing themselves
on shore. Undoubtedly the enemy was favoured by the dark night
and exceptionally high tide, and by the heavy clouds of smoke
from the burning oil-tanks and paint factory which hid them
from the defenders. With some justification the defences along
the north shore had been criticized because the pillboxes were
built too high above ground; the machine-guns were not laid on lines
which gave effective cross-fire, and the whole system lacked depth.
One must not however underestimate the difficulty of converting for
purposes of defence a waterfront crowded with sheds, dockyards,
industrial establishments and public installations. To requisition pro-
perties of this nature in time of peace in the face of opposition from
vested interests, was not an easy matter for the administration.

Once ashore the Japanese avoided the centres of resistance which
held out, and advanced inland by all routes leading to commanding
ground. The defence suffered a great disadvantage in that no strongly
fortified localities existed on which to rally when the enemy broke
through the beach defences on the north-eastern shore: the need to
guard the whole perimeter of the island caused a wide dispersal of
force, and prevented the interior being highly organized for defence.

Here, without incurring the charge of being wise after the event,
it may be permissible to offer two main criticisms of the conduct of
the defence. East Brigade's withdrawal, on the morning of the
19th December, southwards to the Stanley Mound–Stone Hill area
appears to have been a major tactical error. By retiring in a south-
westerly direction towards Violet Hill–Deep Water Bay, it would

have maintained contact with West Brigade. By withdrawing to the south it allowed the enemy to penetrate unopposed between the two brigades, thereby splitting the defence in two, with all the disastrous consequences which that entailed.[1]

The second criticism concerns the actual defence dispositions. In view of the obvious Japanese preparations for a crossing in the north on the night of the 18th/19th, should not the risk have been taken of concentrating at least some of the troops from the southern defences to hold the vital Wong Nei Chong Gap, and to provide an adequate force for immediate counter-attack, particularly in the gravely menaced north-eastern sector? It is of course true that the enemy could have launched an invasion from the sea against the south of the island concurrently with his crossing in the north, but when confronted by two dangers—one obvious and imminent, and the other only potential—it is perhaps wise to secure oneself against the former and to ignore the latter, accepting the risk involved. Be that as it may, the failure to concentrate adequate reserves in the vicinity of the Wong Nei Chong Gap resulted in the enemy being able to reach this vital point without encountering serious resistance.[2]

Once the enemy had established himself ashore, persistent counter-attack was the only policy if the Japanese were not to win the island merely by landing on it. The delay of twenty-four hours which occurred in appointing a commander for West Brigade, owing to no report of Brigadier Lawson's death reaching Fortress Head-quarters on the 19th December, resulted in the lack of any co-ordinating authority in the fighting zone during this critical period and probably affected the whole course of the operations. The general advance ordered by Maltby in this sector on the afternoon of the 19th, and the various piecemeal attacks in company strength made during the night of the 19th/20th, all failed to reach their objectives. Had a brigade commander been on the spot, a properly co-ordinated assault might have achieved some success.

Throughout the fighting on the island, counter-attacks had usually to be launched by mixed detachments which had been hurriedly assembled and had received orders at such short notice that there was little opportunity for reconnaissance; uncertain communications and the difficult nature of the ground hindered co-ordinated effort, and the ever-dwindling mobile artillery was too weak to give adequate support. Under these conditions the objectives were seldom won and,

---

[1] General Maltby wanted Brigadier Wallis to fall back to the line Tai Tam Gap–Wong Nei Chong Gap and so link up with West Brigade, but in view of Brigadier Wallis's representations he reluctantly agreed to a withdrawal to the Stanley area (see page 208).

[2] General Maltby, in accepting this criticism, points out that he had no 'eyes' seawards —no reconnaissance aircraft and no naval patrols. Had he known that no enemy landing from the south could be made for at least twenty-four hours, he would have effected the necessary concentrations.

if won, seldom retained. There was however no lack of good and gallant leadership. Though disaster befell some detachments, men of the British, Canadian and Indian battalions fought well, in circumstances which were always discouraging and were soon recognized to be hopeless. Gunners, sappers and airmen, and men of many races and all services, fought as infantry and acquitted themselves with credit. The Volunteers, in Maltby's words, 'proved themselves stubborn and gallant soldiers'. The scope of this story does not permit of full justice being done to their exploits, but 'Z' Force merits special mention. This was a band of local Volunteers, trained beforehand for work behind the enemy's lines, whose final achievement was to blow up, on the night of the surrender, a park of Japanese munition lorries near Kowloon.[1] The men of the Royal Marines and the naval ratings once again showed themselves to be redoubtable fighters on land; and the Royal Navy had its own tasks and responsibilities which were all faithfully discharged.

The number of battle casualties sustained by the British forces up to the capitulation on the 25th December is not easy to determine, but the approximate total seems to have been 4,440.[2] The fighting and the capitulation together involved the loss of 11,848 combatants.

The official figures of the Japanese casualties, which appear to have been heaviest round the Wong Nei Chong Gap, and at Stanley on the 24th and 25th December, are: killed 675, wounded 2,079; total 2,754. The commander of *230th Regiment* states that he had lost 800 men by the night of the 20th and gives his total casualties as 1,000. The *229th* is said to have lost 600. No figures are available for the *228th*, but if they be averaged at 800 the total loss of infantry of *38th Division* amounts to 2,400. This is only an estimate, but since the infantry would be the chief sufferers it tends to support the official total of 2,754 for all arms. There is however other evidence, which though unofficial cannot be altogether ignored, suggesting that the Japanese casualties may have been higher.

These casualty figures are not unimportant in view of the Prime Minister's message to the Governor, on the 21st December, directing that 'the enemy should be compelled to expend the utmost life and equipment'. This message ended with the words, 'Every day that you are able to maintain your resistance you help the Allied cause all over the world, and by a prolonged resistance you and your men can win the lasting honour which we are sure will be your due'. Commenting on this telegram in Volume III of *The Second World War*, Mr. Churchill wrote: 'These orders were obeyed in spirit and

[1] Mackenzie, *Eastern Epic*, Volume I (Chatto & Windus, 1951), page 216.
[2] This may be an underestimate: Colonel Simson, the Director of Medical Services, estimated that his hospitals on the island had treated about 4,000 wounded, which indicates that the total casualties must have considerably exceeded 4,400.

to the letter . . . Under their resolute Governor, Sir Mark Young, the colony had fought a good fight. They had won indeed the "lasting honour" which is their due.'[1] All the evidence examined in preparing this story of the struggle for Hong Kong shows that the high tribute to the sense of duty and gallantry of all concerned was well merited.

[1] Churchill, Volume III (Cassell, 1950), page 563.

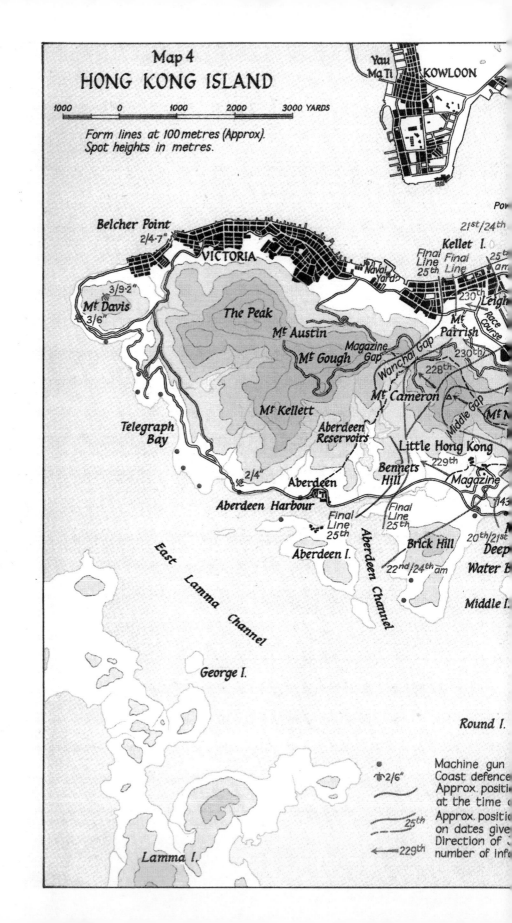

Map 4
HONG KONG ISLAND

1000   0   1000   2000   3000 YARDS

Form lines at 100 metres (Approx).
Spot heights in metres.

Yau Ma Ti   KOWLOON

Belcher Point
2/4·7"

VICTORIA

Naval Yard?

Mt Davis
3/9·2"
3/6"

The Peak

Mt Austin

Mt Gough

Magazine Gap

Wanchai Gap

Mt Parrish

230th

Race Course

Leigh

Mt Kellett

Telegraph Bay

Aberdeen Reservoirs

Mt Cameron

228th

230th

Middle Gap

Mt N

Little Hong Kong

229th

Bennets Hill

Magazine

2/4

Aberdeen

Final Line 25th

Aberdeen Harbour

Final Line 25th

Aberdeen Channel

Brick Hill

143

20th/21st

Deep Water B

Aberdeen I.

22nd/24th am

Middle I.

East Lamma Channel

George I.

Round I.

Machine gun
Coast defence
Approx. positi
at the time
Approx. positi
on dates give
Direction of
number of infe

2/6"

25th

229th

Lamma I.

21st/24th

Kellet I.

Final Line 25th   Final Line 25th

25th
am

230th

Po

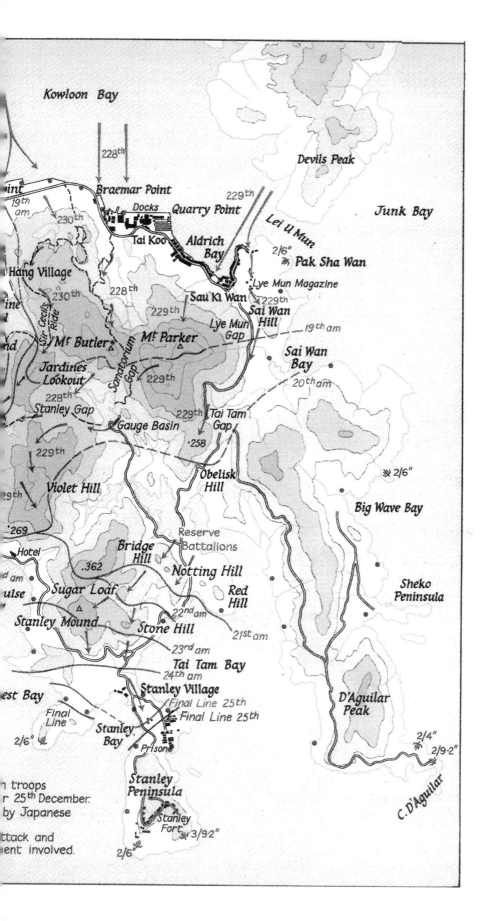

Kowloon Bay

Devils Peak

Junk Bay

228th

...int
19th
am

230th

Braemar Point

Docks

Quarry Point

229th

Lei U Mun

Tai Koo

Aldrich
Bay

2/6"

Pak Sha Wan

...Hang Village

...ine

228th

229th

Sau Ki Wan

Lye Mun Magazine

Sir Cecil's Ride

230th

Lye Mun
Gap

229th
Sai Wan
Hill

19th am

Mt Butler

Mt Parker

△

Jardines
Lookout

Sanatorium Gap

229th

Sai Wan
Bay

20th am

228th
Stanley Gap

229th

Tai Tam
Gap

Gauge Basin

•258

229th

.269

Violet Hill

...9th

Obelisk
Hill

Big Wave Bay

2/6"

...Hotel

...d am

...ulse

Reserve
Battalions

Bridge
Hill

.362

Notting Hill

Sugar Loaf

△

Red
Hill

Sheko
Peninsula

Stanley Mound

Stone Hill

22nd am

21st am

23rd am

Tai Tam Bay

24th am

...est Bay

Stanley Village

Final
Line

Final Line 25th

Final Line 25th

2/6"

Stanley
Bay

Prison

D'Aguilar
Peak

2/4"

2/9·2"

...n troops
...r 25th December.
...by Japanese

Stanley
Peninsula

Stanley
Fort

3/9·2"

C. D'Aguilar

...ttack and
...ent involved.

2/6"

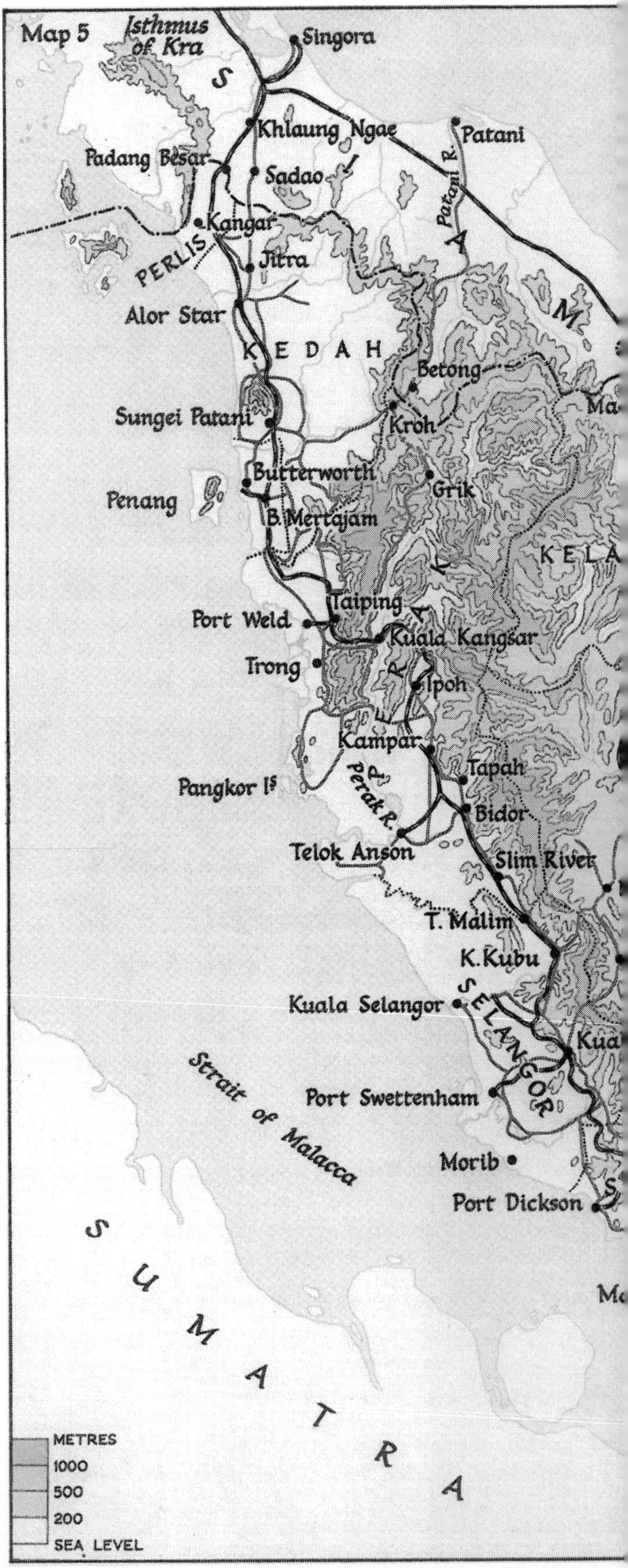

Map 5

Isthmus of Kra

Singora

S

Khlaung Ngae

Patani

Padang Besar

Sadao

Patani R.

Kangar

A

Jitra

M

PERLIS

Alor Star

KEDAH

Betong

Ma

Sungei Patani

Kroh

Butterworth

Grik

Penang

B. Mertajam

KELA

Taiping

Port Weld

Kuala Kangsar

Trong

Ipoh

Kampar

Tapah

Pangkor Is

Perak R.

Bidor

Telok Anson

Slim River

T. Malim

K. Kubu

Kuala Selangor

SELANGOR

Kua

Strait of Malacca

Port Swettenham

Morib

Port Dickson

S

SUMATRA

METRES
1000
500
200
SEA LEVEL

MALAYA

MILES 20 10 0   20   40   60   80 MILES

Kota Bharu

Redang I.

Gong Kedah

Kuala Krai

N

T
R
E
N
G
G
A
N
U

Kuala Trengganu

Kuala Dungun

uala Lipis

Jerantut

Kuantan

ong

Maran

S. Pahang

P
A
H
A
N
G

pur

GRI

Bahau

mban

Gemas

Endau

LAN

Segamat

Tampin

CACCA

Mt Ophir

Labis

Mersing

Kahang

Jemaluang

Muar

Kluang

JOHORE

Batu Pahat

Ayer
Hitam

Rengam

Kota Tinggi

Johore Bahru

SINGAPORE

CHAPTER X

MALAYA, 1941

See Strategic Map, Maps 5 and 8 and Sketch 4

THE MALAY PENINSULA, lying between the Strait of Malacca on the west and the South China Sea on the east, is about as large as England and Wales. It is approximately 400 miles long from north to south, and varies in width from about 200 miles at its widest part to sixty miles at its narrowest. On the north it joins the Isthmus of Kra. The island of Singapore lies at its southern extremity, separated from the mainland by the narrow Strait of Johore.

A jungle-covered mountain range runs down the centre of the peninsula, rising to just over 7,000 feet in the north and dropping to some 3,000 feet at its southern end. It is flanked on either side by coastal plains, fringed on the west coast by mud flats and mangrove swamps, and on the east by broad curving sandy beaches, except at the mouths of rivers, where there are also areas of mangrove. These plains are intersected by innumerable streams which rise in the central range. They combine to form a number of swift rivers which flow into the sea at regular intervals, and are obstacles to free north and south movement. The heavy rainfall and the dense tropical vegetation choke the streams and cause bad drainage; thus, in the vicinity of all the rivers, there are usually large areas of jungle swamps. In these swamps all kinds of thorned and closely intertwined jungle creepers often make passage through them impossible.

More than half the total inland area of Malaya is covered with dense primeval jungle ranging from trees 150–200 feet in height down to a thick undergrowth of bamboo, tropical creepers, tree-ferns and herbaceous plants. On the western plain and in Johore the jungle had been cleared and the land cultivated, often to a considerable distance on either side of the road and railway; the eastern plain in 1941 was largely undeveloped. The cultivation consists mainly of coconut and oil palms (near the coast), rice-fields (especially in the north), rubber plantations, pineapple plantations (especially in the south), tapioca and vegetables. Many areas are devoted to tin mining. Where however cultivation has been abandoned, either a secondary jungle of indescribable density grows up, impassable unless a passage is cut through it, or 'lalang'—a form of elephant grass— which reaches a height of five to six feet.

153

Rainfall throughout the year is heavy, varying from 50 inches in the driest regions to as much as 260 inches in the central mountains. Malaya is affected annually by two monsoons: from June to September by the south-west and from November to March by the north-east. The former affects the west coast and the Strait of Malacca but is usually relatively light in force, owing to the shelter afforded by the mountains of northern Sumatra. The latter however, sweeping across the South China Sea, reaches gale force at times and sets up a swell, with consequent fairly heavy surf along the more exposed stretches of the east coast of Malaya. Violent tropical thunderstorms occur frequently, usually in the late afternoon and often for much of the night, especially during the south-west monsoon; associated with these are heavy cumulo-nimbus clouds, which increase during the day and often stretch in an unbroken mass from as low as 300 feet above the ground to heights of twenty or even thirty thousand feet. They constituted to the aircraft of those days a hazardous and virtually impenetrable barrier, for it was seldom possible to fly over them and, in mountainous country, dangerous to fly under them. On land, the heavy rainfall during the period of the north-east monsoon results in much of the low-lying ground, particularly in the eastern coastal belt, becoming so water-logged that movement off the roads or railways, other than on foot, is usually impracticable for several months of the year. Partly for this reason the western coastal belt is more developed and more populated than the eastern. The climate is typically equatorial, hot and humid, the average temperature being about 80 degrees in the shade; but although enervating, it is not unhealthy.

Singapore is connected with Bangkok by a single line metre gauge railway, which passes through the western coastal plain of Malaya, with branches to the main ports: Malacca, Port Dickson, Port Swettenham, Kuala Selangor, Telok Anson, Port Weld, and Prai (near Butterworth) for Penang Island. It enters Siam at Padang Besar and then follows the eastern coast of the Isthmus of Kra to Bangkok with a short branch serving Singora. A branch line leaving the main line at Gemas serves Pahang and Kelantan. It passes through Kuala Lipis and Kuala Krai and, after crossing the frontier into Siam just west of Kota Bharu, rejoins the main line south-west of Singora.

The road system of Malaya is extensive, especially in Singapore Island, Johore, and in the western coastal plain through which runs the main trunk road from Singapore to Siam. This road has feeders to all important inland centres and ports, and there are, in addition, many minor roads serving rubber estates and tin mining areas. On the eastern side of Malaya the roads are few. In the south there are roads from Johore Bahru and from Kluang to Mersing and Endau.

Further north, the east coast can be reached from Kuala Lumpur or Kuala Kubu across the central range to Raub and Kuantan. In addition, in the north-west there are roads from Sungei Patani and Kuala Kangsar to Kroh and thence a road across the frontier to the east coast of Siam at Patani. These, being the only connecting links between the eastern and western coastal plains, were of considerable strategic importance.

The peoples of Malaya are of many races. The bulk of the large Asian population consists of Malays and Chinese in about equal numbers. The Malays are indigenous to the peninsula. They are predominantly small cultivators and fishermen living on their own small holdings. There is however a small highly educated Malay aristocracy which provides the governing class. The Malays, as the result of centuries of an enervating tropical climate and the debilitating effects of malaria, are a gentle, dignified but somewhat easygoing race, content to live a simple life and accept the edicts of their rulers with good grace. In December 1941 there were estimated to be just over two million Malays in the country—about 43 per cent of the total population.

The Chinese also numbered about two million. More commercial in their interests, they had been attracted to Malaya by trade, and had drawn an endless stream of immigrants from China. Unlike the Malays, the Chinese tended to concentrate in the towns and larger villages and, in due course, came to control a large part of the commerce of Malaya. They were not however a united community politically or racially. About one third of their total number had been born in Malaya; the majority, having come from China and intending to return there, were not specially interested in the administration of Malaya nor, before the war, were they prepared to take an active part in the defence of the country, despite the fact that their homeland (China) had been invaded by the Japanese. Nevertheless after the outbreak of war the various Chinese political parties sank their differences and on Christmas Day 1941, representatives of all parties approached the Governor. They placed themselves unreservedly at his disposal, saying that the defeat of Japan was their only interest. Sir Shenton Thomas accepted their offer and they undertook to organize themselves to supply labour, to undertake watch and ward as required and to deal with propaganda within the Chinese community. The offer in fact produced very little, for the Chinese representatives made demands for terms of service and amenities which, in the circumstances, could not possibly be met. The problem of settling terms of service which would persuade men to work in those areas liable to be bombed, was one of great difficulty and, as will be seen, it was to be many weeks before suitable action was taken to find a solution to this problem, by which time it was too late.

The majority of the Indian population in Malaya were Tamil labourers from the Madras Presidency who returned home on an average after three years. They worked on rubber estates, on the railways and in the Public Works Department. The more educated Indians had adopted some professional career or were engaged in trade, while many Punjabis and Sikhs and some Pathans were enrolled in the Malay Police Force. There were also about 48,000 Anglo-Indians in Malaya who were employed generally in some clerical capacity.

The European population, of which 20 per cent were non-British and 42 per cent women and children, numbered in 1939 about 18,000. This had been reduced to approximately 9,000 by December 1941, but, despite the increasing danger of war, many women and children had not been evacuated. Almost the whole of the British civilian community was employed in Government service or engaged in the professions, commerce, planting, or mining. There was no racial discrimination in Malaya, and the relations between the various communities were generally cordial; the Asians of different races, however, mixed more freely with Europeans than with one another. It can be said that pre-war Malaya was a happy, prosperous and loyal land, with a comparatively high standard of living produced by the industry of private civilian enterprise and sound government extending over many years. Nevertheless it was not united by the bonds of common citizenship, nor was there any national spirit to which in an emergency an appeal could be made for 'the defence of the homeland'.

The Japanese in Malaya, though few in number, were a source of considerable anxiety to the civil and military authorities. In the larger towns there was a small number of Japanese business men; and Japanese nationals provided the majority of the barbers and photographers throughout Malaya. In country districts they owned a number of rubber estates, often adjacent to points of strategic importance. They owned iron mines in Kelantan, at Kuala Dungun in Trengganu, near Endau in Johore, and at Batu Pahat. They were allowed to operate a direct service of freight ships from Malaya to Japan. They thus had an intimate knowledge of the coasts. In addition, the fact that a number of executives on the rubber estates and in the iron mines were Service or ex-Service men enabled them to organize an efficient espionage system throughout the country. They were therefore aware of all defence works constructed. As the possibility of war became increasingly evident, arrangements were made to intern all Japanese nationals on the outbreak of hostilities; but until December 1941, in accordance with the British policy of avoiding discrimination against foreigners, nothing was done to restrict their movements or activities.

The constitution of the Civil Government in Malaya was complicated, cumbersome and markedly unsuited to war conditions. The division of the country into a number of independent states was, in itself, a contributory factor. In 1941 Malaya comprised, firstly, the Straits Settlements which included Singapore, Malacca and Penang with Province Wellesley; these formed a Crown Colony. Secondly, there were the Federated Malay States of Perak, Selangor, Negri Sembilan and Pahang. On matters of general policy concerning Malaya these were administered by a Federal Government at Kuala Lumpur, but in other respects they were self-governing states under their own rulers, assisted by British Residents. Thirdly, there were the Unfederated Malay States of Johore, Trengganu, Kelantan, Kedah and Perlis, each governed by its own Sultan with the help of a British Adviser, which had all been incorporated in the British Empire by separate treaties. Over all these was the Governor of the Straits Settlements who, to ensure co-ordination, was also High Commissioner for both the Federated and Unfederated States. In practice, such an arrangement implied that on most subjects the Governor and High Commissioner had to deal with no less than eleven separate bodies, all of which had to be in agreement before measures affecting Malaya as a whole could be introduced.

The co-ordination of the Services and the civil authorities in matters affecting the defence of the Federated Malay States and the Straits Settlements had in peacetime been secured by means of a Defence Committee, the secretary of which was provided by the Services. In October 1939 this committee was replaced by a War Committee which met under the chairmanship of the Governor and Commander-in-Chief,[1] and was empowered to discuss questions affecting the Services and the civil defence departments, but had no executive functions. The Services were represented by their respective heads, and the civil government by the Secretary of Defence, Malaya, who was the secretary of the Committee; he was also head of a Defence Secretariat, which was linked with all existing departments of government and such additional departments as had to be created to control civil defence activities. He thus became the channel through which all demands from the Services reached the civil authorities, and upon him depended not only the co-ordination of the defence effort of the colony with that of the Services, but also the executive action taken by government departments on recommendations made by the War Committee.

The Secretary of Defence was empowered to deal direct with the British Resident or Adviser in each of the Malay States on defence matters, and an agreement had been reached with each Sultan

---

[1] It was customary for the Governor of a British Colony to be given the title of Commander-in-Chief but it had no practical significance.

whereby the Resident or Adviser could use his own initiative in making a decision on behalf of the State, knowing that covering authority or, if necessary, legislative action would follow. This system was designed to, and did largely, overcome the cumbersome nature of the constitution, and enabled decisions on defence matters taken by the War Committee to be translated quickly into action throughout Malaya.

Before the outbreak of war in Europe, the possibility that Malaya might some day be subject to sustained heavy air attacks seemed so remote that, although a start had been made and orders placed for certain material, no organization for civil defence had been established nor had any protection been provided for the civil population in the towns.[1] At the end of 1939 however the government began actively to organize civil defence in the Straits Settlements. An Air Raid Precautions Headquarters was set up and certain passive defence measures were introduced in Singapore and Penang. A corps of air raid wardens, medical and fire auxiliary services, and a local defence corps, on the lines of the Home Guard, were organized. These were manned chiefly by Asian voluntary workers, who came forward in adequate numbers, supervised by a skeleton European staff.

At the same time arrangements were made to install air raid sirens and to construct shelters. In Singapore however it was considered that the construction of shelters on anything approaching an adequate scale would be exceptionally difficult, for the water level of the island was so near the surface that digging of underground shelters, or even trenches, was often impracticable. Sufficient open spaces in which to construct above ground the large numbers of shelters needed did not exist. Plans were therefore made and put into effect to provide hutted accommodation outside the town, to which some of the civil population could move in the event of air raids, though it was not intended to enforce evacuation. In the hot and humid climate the introduction of an effective blackout system, which would not deprive houses of ventilation, was found to be impossible. A scheme was therefore adopted by which lighting could be restricted and a blackout enforced by cutting off current throughout the area on an actual warning of the approach of enemy aircraft.

An observer corps to form part of the civil air raid warning system was also raised. This corps was originally placed under the command of the General Officer Commanding, Malaya, but was later transferred to the control of Air Headquarters, Far East. The lack of an adequate telephone system and the absence of road communications in many parts of the country made it impossible to establish and maintain a continuous chain of observer posts. Thus, though in 1941

---

[1] The pre-war scale of attack had been laid down by the Oversea Defence Committee as 'occasional medium attacks by aircraft from carriers'.

the warning system was strengthened by a radar unit at Mersing in direct communication with the Fighter Control Operations Room in Singapore, and though in the vicinity of Singapore Island there were three radar stations in operation and others under construction, there were serious gaps in the cover afforded by the observer system.

The organization of civil defence developed in practice very slowly and did not initially cater for the Malay States, the defence of which was not considered till after the fall of France and the entry of the Japanese into Indo-China. The fact that the Federated Malay States were excluded led the ex-Service Association, Malaya, the Federated Malay States Chamber of Mines and the United Planters Association of Malaya, in October 1940, to express their dissatisfaction with the Government's failure to take adequate measures for the defence and safety of the civil population of the Malay States and the security of the tin and rubber industries, which were essential to the war effort. They recommended that an officer of the fighting Services should be placed in control of security and civil defence measures for the duration of the war.

The Acting Governor passed their views to the Colonial Office expressing resentment at the criticism. He said that he was strongly opposed to the military taking over civil defence, for he felt such a change would cause so much friction and ill-feeling that progress with defence measures would be seriously handicapped. The Secretary of State for the Colonies expressed neither resentment at nor disapproval of the proposals. He approved the Acting Governor's suggestion to inform selected leaders of the civil community that it was proposed to extend the civil defences to include the whole of Malaya. He said that they should be encouraged to make practical suggestions for improving both civil defence measures and the efficiency of the Volunteer Forces, and that the Colonial Office would not be averse to the appointment of a military officer to command the civil defence organization. Although no change was made in the organization of the civil defence, it was then extended to cover all Malaya.

The organization of the civil defence service was only one of the measures which had to be taken in preparation for war. The building-up of adequate food reserves was of equal importance for, in Malaya, Europeans and Asians alike depended upon imports for the basic ingredients of their national diets. The extension of the period before relief from three to six months meant doubling the existing stocks.[1]

A Food Controller had been appointed before the outbreak of the war in Europe and a department to control stocks and prices set up.

[1] See page 28.

The main problem was the provision of rice, which was the staple food of the greater part of the population. Some 80,000 tons were consumed each month, of which 53,000 had to be imported. The storage of milled rice for a sufficiently long period was not considered possible until experiments proved later that it could be preserved by a coating of powdered lime. In consequence the original stocks were of padi (unmilled rice). These were stored close to the existing mills, which were for the most part in the rice-producing areas in the north and west of the peninsula. Thus the largest stocks, apart from those in Singapore, were in Perlis, in Kedah (in particular at Alor Star) and at Telok Anson.

The inadvisability of this concentration of vital food reserves in the most vulnerable parts of the peninsula was pointed out by both the navy and the army in July 1940. The War Committee was unable however to reach a compromise between the civil authorities' wish to avoid excessive and possibly unnecessary expenditure and the military view that the stocks should be spread over Malaya, if possible *pro rata* to the density of the population. In these circumstances General Bond and Admiral Layton referred the matter to London. As a result the civil authorities were asked in October 1940 to reconsider their policy in consultation with the local Service authorities. Shortly afterwards the transfer of stocks from Kedah and Perlis to new centres further south began. By December 1941 six months' supply of all essential food-stuffs was available in Malaya, though much of the 325,000 tons of rice in reserve was still locked up in the north and consequently fell into enemy hands in the first fortnight of the campaign.

From the military point of view, the full scale of reserve stocks of food, petrol, ammunition, medical supplies and most engineer stores for the forces was available to cover the estimated period before relief of 180 days. These stocks had been dispersed throughout the country. For the movement of troops and supplies the Services relied on the Federated Malay States railway system, augmented by military mechanized transport convoys. Since, with the exception of the east coast, the road system was good and most of the military units were equipped with mechanical transport, it was considered that these transportation services would be adequate. Responsibility for handling all shipping rested with the Singapore Harbour Board.

Despite repeated warnings from the Services during the years preceding the war, the effect of air raids on native labour employed on essential services had not been fully realized. The question of the conscription of labour had been considered but had been rejected as unworkable because of the administrative difficulty involved. Malaya Command had then made efforts to obtain some agreement on the control of labour in the event of war, but, although frequent

9. Typical Malayan road in secondary jungle.

8. Hill road in primary jungle.

10. Rice fields.

12. A Coconut plantation.

11. A Rubber Estate.

13. Typical view of east coast of Malaya.

discussions had taken place and schemes had been prepared, no definite action had been taken and the problem had been left unsolved.

General Bond had foreseen the need for organized military labour to work essential services at a time when civil labour might be difficult to get. At the end of 1940 he asked India Command for two labour companies, since coolie labour in Malaya was scarce and expensive owing to rubber and tin mining operations in the north. These were provided, but a further request was refused by the War Office, who suggested that, in view of the large resources of local labour, Malaya Command should make arrangements for its immediate use when the necessity arose. In April 1941 the Command obtained War Office permission to raise locally up to six labour companies on mobilization.

The Labour Controller in Singapore however advised against this on the ground that their formation would be detrimental to the production of rubber and tin and the completion of civil defence projects. He pointed out that local labour would be difficult to recruit for service in military units, for they would be required to leave their homes. By June General Percival realized that the most he could raise locally would be one Chinese company. Faced with this situation he appealed for additional Indian labour companies, but India was unable to send more companies as her output was being fully absorbed by the Middle East and Iraq.

By September Percival found that even the Chinese company would not be forthcoming, for the War Office had fixed the rate of pay at 45 cents a day which was below the lowest rate for unskilled female labour. For some time they refused to increase this rate despite the fact that the Malayan authorities, who were in a position to know the local situation, had proposed a scheme whereby coolies were paid $1.10 a day plus free rations and accommodation.[1] In the circumstances it is scarcely surprising that considerable recruiting efforts produced such poor results. Percival had perforce to turn to Hong Kong where there was a surplus of labour. In October the War Office gave him permission to raise companies there, but a further delay occurred when it became clear that to recruit reliable English-speaking Chinese platoon commanders a high rate of pay ($2.75 a day) would be necessary. On the 19th November he was authorized to offer $2 a day, but the decision came too late and the rate was too low. As a result the only formed labour units available in Malaya on the outbreak of war were the two Indian companies supplied in 1940.

Thus by December 1941, despite continued efforts by the military authorities in Malaya, no scheme existed for either the conscription or the control of local labour in wartime. General Sir Archibald

---

[1] A Straits Settlement (Malayan) dollar was worth 2s. 4d.

N

Wavell, in his report on the loss of Malaya, gave as his opinion that had there been available even 5,000 labourers, organized under vernacular-speaking British officers, much of the chaos in December 1941 and January 1942 might have been avoided.

The air forces in Malaya, on the outbreak of war with Japan, consisted of formations and units drawn from the United Kingdom, Australia and New Zealand.[1] All were placed for operations and administration under Air Command, Far East, (Air Vice-Marshal Pulford), whose headquarters was in Singapore.[2] Headquarters, Air Command, was linked for operations with Headquarters, Malaya Command, by a Combined Army/Air Operations Centre.

There were four fighter squadrons for operations by day, whose primary responsibility was the air defence of the Singapore area, and there was one night fighter squadron. There were also two light bomber squadrons, two general reconnaissance squadrons, two torpedo-bomber squadrons and one flying-boat squadron, together with maintenance and administrative units.[3]

The standard of training and operational efficiency varied in different units. The four fighter squadrons for day operations were equipped with American Buffalo aircraft, which had arrived only that year. Not all of the pilots of these aircraft had received sufficient training, and on the 8th December 1941 only three squadrons were considered operationally trained. The night fighter squadron was equipped with Blenheim I aircraft which were old and in poor condition; the two torpedo-bomber squadrons, whose aircrews were highly trained and experienced, were equipped with Vildebeeste aircraft, declared obsolete in 1940 and overdue for replacement by more modern types. The two light bomber squadrons equipped with Blenheim I and IV aircraft, and the two general reconnaissance squadrons with Hudson II, constituted so small a force for their respective roles that all four squadrons had to be trained for oversea reconnaissance and all types of bombing by day and by night. Except for the Buffalo fighters, there was a serious shortage of reserve aircraft, and few of the squadrons were complete to their authorized establishment. On the outbreak of war there were only 158 first line aircraft available for operations in Malaya, and many of these were obsolete or obsolescent. The total in the Far East Command did not exceed 180, against the target figure of 336 modern aircraft which the Chiefs of Staff considered to be the minimum and the 566 asked

[1] For the organization of the R.A.F. see Appendix 7.
[2] For particulars and comparative characteristics of British and Japanese aircraft in 1941, see Appendix 8.
[3] The strength and dispositions of the R.A.F. in Malaya on the 8th December 1941, and the location of airfields and landing grounds, are shown in Appendix 9 and on Sketch 4.

for by the Service Commanders on the spot; figures which took into account only first-line aircraft.[1] Including essential reserves, the total deficiency in the Command was 415 aircraft.

Great difficulties had been experienced in finding staffs for head-quarters of formations and stations. There were few regular officers with staff experience left, for many had been transferred elsewhere because of the war in Europe. Officers to fill vacancies in the greatly expanded Headquarters, Air Command, and at new airfields had been found largely from Australia and New Zealand, and they mostly had little Service experience. During the latter half of 1941 the number of airmen in the Command had been doubled by the arrival, in anticipation of the completion of the air force expansion programme, of partly trained reinforcements direct from the United Kingdom. Thus in December there was a surplus of air force personnel in Malaya.

The failure to send to Malaya the aircraft required for the planned air force expansion resulted in the land forces, designed to be ancillary to the air forces, having to meet the full force of the Japanese on-slaught with only negligible air support.

The army garrison of Malaya on the outbreak of war with Japan consisted of thirty-one British, Australian, Indian and Malay battalions (the equivalent of about three and a half divisions). These were organized into three divisions (9th and 11th Indian and 8th Australian) each of two brigades, with a quota of supporting artillery and other divisional units, two reserve brigade groups, two fortress brigades for Singapore Island and a battalion as garrison for Penang.[2] There were in addition the fixed coastal defence and anti-aircraft batteries for the defence of Singapore, some airfield defence battalions and the local volunteer units. There were no armoured forces. There was one battalion in Sarawak which also formed part of Malaya Command.[3]

The total strength of the regular and volunteer forces in Malaya, including all the administrative units required to operate the base and the lines of communication, was approximately 88,600. Of this total there were 19,600 British, 15,200 Australian, 37,000 Indian and some 16,800 locally enlisted Asians. The garrison was well below both General Bond's and General Percival's estimates of the forces required until the full air strength had been reached.[4] The main deficiencies were seventeen infantry battalions and two tank regiments.

---

[1] See pages 35 and 48.
[2] For the organization of the British Army in 1941 see Appendix 7.
[3] The organization of the garrison and the names of the formation commanders are given in detail in Appendix 10. Its distribution on the 8th December 1941 is shown on Sketch 4.
[4] See pages 28–30 and 77.

The jungles, mangrove swamps and thickly treed areas of cultivation presented a peculiar and difficult problem to those responsible for the defence of Malaya. Visibility, except in pineapple plantations, rice-fields and tin mining areas, is very limited; thus the use of long-range weapons and the application of effective supporting fire for the infantry was very difficult. The opportunity for ambush lies almost everywhere. In jungle there are no fields of fire, tactical features tend to lose significance and roads and tracks become of great importance. All-round protection is essential, and movement, although nearly always possible, is severely restricted; static defence spells defeat. In rubber, movement is easier but the interminable lines of evenly spaced trees and the limited view make it difficult for troops to keep direction. Both in jungle and in rubber plantations control becomes difficult, the tempo of fighting is very different from that in more open country, emergencies crop up suddenly and unexpectedly and in consequence the action of junior commanders has a far greater influence on the general scheme of operations than would normally be the case. Errors of tactics, judgement and decision on their part may easily decide the result of an action. In such close country the infantry becomes the dominant arm. In open country any mistakes on the part of the infantry can often be offset by the use of armour or by increased fire support, but in Malaya this was not possible, and success depended therefore on the quality and training of the infantry.

To troops unused to it, the jungle is apt to be terrifying and to produce physical and emotional stresses which have to be felt to be appreciated; rubber too, with its gloom, dampness and sound-deadening effect, gives them a feeling of isolation and tends to lower their morale. The only antidote to jungle fear, or to the depressing effect of rubber, is to give troops the opportunity of learning sufficient jungle lore to enable them to regard the jungle as a friend rather than an enemy, or at least as a neutral, and to teach them how to operate efficiently in the restricted visibility of the rubber plantations. If troops are to acquit themselves well in this type of country not only must they undergo very intensive training, but it must be designed to acclimatize them to the conditions in which they will have to live and fight, to teach them to withstand the heat and the frequent downpours of rain, to show them how to overcome the obstacles which swamps and rivers present, and how to move off the roads through jungle and rubber alike, to develop junior leadership and to produce and practise tactics suitable to the terrain.

The greater part of the formations and units of III Corps and of the Command Reserve had been furnished by India. To meet requirements in the Middle East, Iraq and Malaya, as well as to provide for home defence, the Indian Army had by 1941 already expanded to at least four times its peace strength. This expansion had led perforce to an extensive withdrawal of regular and experienced officers and men from existing units so as to provide a nucleus for newly-formed units —a process known as 'milking'. Indian Army units in Malaya were consequently milked even after their arrival, and as a result were composed largely of young soldiers, many of them fresh from their recruit training. There was also a great shortage of experienced leaders.

The junior leaders in an Indian Army battalion were Indian commissioned and non-commissioned officers and the British officers were consequently fewer than in British battalions. The rapid expansion of the Indian Army had exceeded the supply of efficient junior Indian leaders, while the junior British officers were usually wartime-commissioned officers with little training, unable to speak the language of their men and unfamiliar with their mentality and outlook. The efficiency of such Indian units, unless fully trained, rested almost entirely on the small handful of regular British and Indian officers. Should these become casualties the efficiency of an Indian unit tended to drop rapidly.[1]

The British infantry battalions in Malaya had been on garrison duties in India and the Far East for a long period. They had had therefore little opportunity of training in mobile warfare with field formations, and had had to send some of their more experienced officers and N.C.Os. to Britain and the Middle East without replacement, with a consequent reduction in their efficiency. Both British and Indian units were moreover without an adequately large pool of trained reinforcements accustomed to the climatic conditions in Malaya. Thus, as there was no reserve division to relieve battle-weary formations, it was clear that as soon as fighting began the strength and efficiency of the garrison would suffer a rapid decline, for battle casualties could not be replaced.

Throughout the Command, headquarters staffs suffered from a lack of trained and experienced officers, for between 1939 and 1941 the War Office had withdrawn many of the best officers to the Middle East and elsewhere and had usually ordered that they should be replaced by promotion from those who remained. This policy was short-sighted, for not only did it gradually diminish the efficiency of the staff in the Command, but it resulted in the lessons learnt in the campaigns in France and in the Middle East not being fully appreciated in Malaya. A factor which seriously handicapped the selection of officers to fill staff appointments for which they were best suited was the considerable differences in the rates of pay between officers

---

[1] See Appendix 11: Notes on the Indian Army.

serving with the British formations such as Headquarters, Malaya Command, and Indian formations such as Headquarters, III Indian Corps.

Training always plays a primary role in the outcome of all contests, not least in war. In Malaya it was of particular importance owing to the poor standard of training of the troops on their arrival in the country, the constant withdrawal of trained men and the need to fit them for the peculiar conditions they were likely to meet. Since the great majority of the troops forming the garrison had been recruited from parts of the world where the country was open, 'or from towns and cities, they had first of all to be taught how to live in jungle and rubber.

The Headquarters staff of Malaya Command had been designed for the control of a small garrison and, although it had been expanded after the outbreak of war in Europe, the organization had not been adjusted to enable it to cope efficiently with the changed and increased load placed upon it. There was no separate training branch of the staff. Training became one of the functions of the organizational (staff duties) branch, already overburdened because of the wide variations of race and organization of the forces forming the garrison. As a result the higher direction of training tended to be pushed into the background. This partly accounted for the fact that no detailed study of the available information regarding the training and tactics of the Japanese army was made at Command level, despite the fact that Japan was the only possible enemy and that the danger of war in the Far East had greatly increased as a result of the outbreak of war in Europe.

The Military Attachés in Tokyo had for many years sent accurate reports to the War Office showing that the Japanese Army was a most efficient force. Yet Malaya Command consistently underrated the efficiency and skill of the Japanese. It may have been the fact that they appeared unable to subdue the poorly-equipped Chinese forces that led to the belief, widespread throughout the Far East, that their armed forces were inefficient.

That two views of Japanese military prowess existed is seen in the fact that in 1940 Army Headquarters, Australia, and Malaya Command held almost opposite views on this vital matter. The 8th Australian Division, before it left its homeland, had been issued with training pamphlets which gave warning that the Japanese were ruthless, had a high standard of armament and technical training, great physical endurance, few bodily requirements compared with British troops, a talent for misleading their opponents, a large potential fifth column in Malaya, and ample experience of landing operations. This pamphlet stated that Japanese troops could move across country at great speed and could be self-supporting for several days; that, as the thick country did not favour static defence, offensive action should be taken against the enemy wherever he was met; and that there was a need for training all ranks in moving through jungle, since the difference between trained and untrained troops in that type of country was immense. On their arrival in Malaya the first training instruction issued to the Australians echoed the necessity for making the troops jungle-minded and asserted that the enemy was unaccustomed to surprise and reacted badly to it. It stated that the enemy would not be jungle trained, was weak in unit training and that the initiative of the junior commanders was poor. The fact that the skill of the potential enemy was greatly underestimated resulted in the general need for very intensive and specialized training not being fully grasped.

The fact that most of the units and formations forming the garrison of Malaya were found by the rapidly expanding Indian Army made it difficult to ensure that a proper standard of training was reached. The repeated milking of units to find the nucleus for new units in India, which periodically forced commanders to begin their training programmes all over again, seriously handicapped progressive training. Formation training was handicapped by the piecemeal arrival of newly formed and semi-trained formations from India and by the late arrival of field and anti-tank artillery and specialist units. For example, III Corps had no proper signal organization and had to rely throughout the campaign almost entirely on civil communications.

Another factor which affected training was the lack of sufficient civilian labour. This forced Malaya Command to use troops on the construction of beach defences and other defensive positions to the detriment of training. It may well be asked why it was necessary for defences to be constructed by the troops themselves instead of by civil labour supervised by the army. The reason is that, as priority was accorded to the production of rubber and tin, the Services could obtain only labour surplus to civil requirement and that only through contractors for specific contracts. Priority had also to be given to the construction of airfields, since the air force was to be the primary defence weapon. The building of hutted camps to accommodate army and air force reinforcing formations and units had to be the next in order of precedence. These and the normal maintenance requirements of the country absorbed such labour as was available; the troops had therefore to construct their own defences or go without.

As a result of these many difficulties and the failure to realize that special methods were needed to prepare for a war with the highly trained Japanese, the standard of training of the troops was far below that of their opponents both as individuals and formations. The

Japanese forces earmarked for the invasion of Malaya had been trained for that special task. Their tactics were based on surprise attacks straight along the roads with the object of breaking through defensive positions, led by tanks followed by infantry in motor vehicles. When such an attack was brought to a standstill, both minor and major outflanking moves were immediately set in motion to get behind the forces holding up the armoured column and cut their communications. To these tactics, the partly trained British forces, without armour and with inadequate anti-tank weapons, which they had not had time to learn to use effectively, had no reply. They might have made a better showing had there been a properly co-ordinated and objective training doctrine sponsored by Malaya Command based on a carefully considered assessment of Japanese tactics. But local commanders had to train their troops, as opportunity offered, according to their own ideas, and in the case of 9th and 11th Divisions, opportunities were scarce owing to their many commitments, their dispersion and the fact that their role was not clearly defined.

The training of 8th Australian Division and 12th Indian Brigade was on a different level from that of the majority of the garrison, for they were not so widely dispersed, there was no doubt as to their role and they were able to train as formations. The Australian division had had the advantage of training with its ancillary units,[1] had not been milked as had the British and Indian units, and had much greater freedom to develop its own tactical doctrines. By December 1941, 22nd Australian Brigade had been in Malaya nearly eleven months and had undergone considerable training in the new conditions. As a result this brigade was probably better fitted for mobile warfare in both jungle and cultivated country than most of the other formations in the garrison. The 27th Australian Brigade had trained strenuously along lines similar to those of 22nd Brigade, but, having arrived only in August 1941, had not had as long in which to become accustomed to Malayan conditions.[2]

The Volunteer Forces were inadequately armed and their state of training was such that they were not fit to take part in mobile warfare. They had been embodied for training for short periods in the latter half of 1940. Again in February–March 1941 about half of them had been called up for further training. It had been the intention to call up the remainder later in the year but owing to strikes among native labour, which, it was contended, were due to the absence on training of European and other overseers, the civil authorities, in order to maintain the maximum output of rubber

---

[1] The Australian artillery regiments arrived in Malaya equipped with 18-pounders, 4·5-inch howitzers and 3-inch mortars. They did not receive their 25-pounders till shortly after the outbreak of war.

[2] See Appendix 12: Notes on the Australian Imperial Forces.

14. *Left to right:*
Lieut.-General A. E. Percival and
Major-General H. G. Bennett.

15. Lieut.-General T. Yamashita.

16. Lieut.-General
Sir Lewis Heath.

17. Air Vice-Marshal
C. W. H. Pulford.

and tin, decided to postpone the balance of the training to a later date. It never took place.[1]

General Percival was in no way free to dispose his troops to the best advantage for the defence of the Naval Base, since, in the absence of a fleet, the air force had become nominally the principal weapon for the defence of Malaya, and the security of the airfields, and particularly the two groups of airfields near the frontier on the east and west coasts, had become of paramount importance. He could reasonably assume that the enemy's first objectives would be the groups of airfields in Kedah and Kelantan, and that the Japanese would therefore land at Singora and Patani with a view to an advance down the western coastal plain, and at Kota Bharu. He could not however discount the possibility of a landing to capture the airfield at Kuantan and a subsequent advance westwards towards the western plain, or at Mersing with a view to attacking Singapore from the 'north, or even on Singapore Island itself. Neither could he discount the possibility of simultaneous attacks at several of these places. When considering how best to dispose his forces he was handicapped not only by having to be prepared to advance into Siam but by being forced to disperse his meagre resources to defend a number of widely separated areas. The Japanese on the other hand, holding the initiative, could always concentrate at the selected point of attack.

In these circumstances Percival entrusted III Corps with the defence of northern Malaya and with preparations for operation 'Matador', giving General Heath 9th and 11th Divisions and 28th Brigade; made 8th Australian Division responsible for the defence of Johore; retained two infantry brigades as a garrison at Singapore Island; and kept 12th Brigade in reserve at Port Dickson and Singapore.

Heath also had his hands tied. The security of airfields in exposed positions not only compelled the dispersion of his comparatively small force over a very wide area, but also committed the troops to areas unsuited, both strategically and tactically, to a defensive battle. But for the presence of the airfields in Kelantan he could have ignored a landing in north-east Malaya, for this flank was secured by the vast jungle areas of central Malaya, penetrated only by a single line railway which could have been put out of action without difficulty. Similarly, had it not been for the airfield at Kuantan, he could with small forces have prevented the enemy from making use of the east-west road from Kuantan to Raub. However, as these airfields offered the enemy ready-made bases for the air forces supporting the invasion, they had to be defended. He was therefore forced to disperse

---

[1] See Appendix 13: Notes on Local Forces in Malaya.

9th Indian Division in tactically isolated detachments for the static defence of this large area. The 8th Brigade, reinforced by a battalion from 22nd Brigade, was located at Kota Bharu, where it was dependent for its communications on a single line railway, and 22nd Brigade (less one battalion) at Kuantan.

On the western plain he was compelled, by the existence of two alternative plans—an advance into Siam or the defence of the airfields at Alor Star and Sungei Patani—to locate the bulk of his forces near the north-west frontier, an area which was unsuited to the fighting of a defensive battle, where they could easily be outflanked by an enemy force landing at Patani and advancing along the Kroh road. The two possible roles, which were in no way compatible, immensely increased his difficulties. 'Matador' involved a very rapid advance by road and rail through a neutral country, from which at least token resistance might be expected, to seize Singora and hold it against land or seaborne attack. Not only had the troops to be specially trained to fit them for the topographical conditions at Singora, which differed considerably from those in northern Malaya, but their whole organization had to be adjusted to meet the peculiar needs of the operation. Quantities of stores for the rapid preparation of a defensive position would have to accompany the troops, and also large quantities of bridging material to strengthen weak bridges and to repair those which the Siamese might destroy, for delays could not be accepted. So much detailed administrative planning by the staffs of III Corps and 11th Division was necessary if 'Matador' were to become a feasible proposition, that preparation for the alternative defensive role was consequently relegated to the background.

The 11th Indian Division was disposed with 6th and 15th Brigades in north Kedah and General Murray-Lyon was instructed to be ready either to move forward to Singora or to occupy a defensive position near Jitra, eighteen miles from the frontier, covering the Alor Star airfield. To defend the approach along the Patani–Kroh road an improvised column (Krohcol) consisting of one battalion from Kroh and one from Penang was to be formed in the event of war. Whichever role was given to 11th Division, Krohcol was to move forward to defend a position known as the Ledge, thirty miles north of the Siamese frontier. General Heath kept 28th Brigade in corps reserve centrally placed at Ipoh.

To assist the army in Malaya to carry out its various defensive tasks beach defences had been erected on Singapore Island and at Mersing, Kuantan and Kota Bharu; defensive positions were in preparation at Jitra and Kroh and it was proposed that one should eventually be constructed at Gurun.[1] Except for the beach defences

---

[1] See Map 8.

on the island and the few machine-gun emplacements covering Kota Tinggi, which had been constructed in 1939, these defences had been mainly built by the troops who were to man them.[1] Although experience in Europe had shown the danger of deep thrusts by armoured formations supported by aircraft, and the Japanese were known to be skilled in adapting themselves to Western methods, no preparations other than the construction of an anti-tank ditch at Jitra had been made to meet this form of attack. Behind the beach defences and the positions at Jitra and Kroh, there were no lay-back defensive positions nor were there any anti-tank obstacles astride the main roads where they passed through the defiles in which the country abounded.

The coastal defences on the mainland consisted of machine-gun emplacements covering the beaches, which were also protected by barbed wire and under-water obstacles. Because of the length of the beaches to be covered there was no second line of posts to afford the necessary depth, and many of the emplacements, especially those south of Kota Bharu, were dummies. The Jitra position consisted of defended localities and concrete machine-gun emplacements protected by barbed wire. It was covered by an anti-tank ditch, which when war broke out was still in the process of construction by the Kedah Public Works Department, and, west of the railway, by a vast expanse of swamp. The position three miles west of Kroh, designed for occupation by two battalions, consisted of a number of defended localities astride the road itself.

The naval forces available for the defence of the Malay barrier consisted of the British Eastern Fleet,[2] the Dutch naval forces under the command of Vice-Admiral C. E. L. Helfrich, R.N.N. based on the Netherlands East Indies, and the United States Asiatic Fleet under the command of Admiral Hart based on the Philippines.[3]

On the 3rd December, the day after the *Prince of Wales* and *Repulse* with their attendant destroyers berthed at Singapore, Admiral Phillips, who had arrived by air from Colombo three days earlier, assumed command of the Eastern Fleet. Admiral Layton remained temporarily in command of the shore establishments and the China Station, so that Rear-Admiral, Malaya (Rear-Admiral E. J. Spooner), who was directly responsible for the Naval Base and for the local naval defences, and the Commodore, Hong Kong, (Commodore Collinson) remained under his orders. On the 8th, on orders from

---

[1] See page 16.
[2] For the organization of the Royal Navy in 1941 see Appendix 7.
[3] For details of the composition of the British, Dutch and American naval forces for the defence of the Malay barrier see Appendix 14.

the Admiralty, the command of the China Station was merged with that of the Eastern Fleet and all British naval forces in the Far East came under the command of Admiral Phillips.

The series of conferences held during 1941 at Singapore and Washington had done something to unify these scattered forces. Operational planning had been based on the assumption that the British Commander-in-Chief, China, and later the Commander-in-Chief, Eastern Fleet, would exercise strategic direction of all naval forces in the eastern theatre. It had been assumed by both the British and Dutch admirals that, if Manila became untenable, the United States Asiatic Fleet would fall back on Singapore to assist in the defence of the Malay barrier. But by the beginning of December no combined plan had been officially agreed upon, and when war broke out co-ordination of the Allied navies was on a basis of mutual co-operation only.

The occupation of southern Indo-China by the Japanese during July 1941 had greatly increased the threat to Malaya, for Camranh Bay provided them with the advanced naval base which they required for an assault on Malaya, Saigon offered a convenient assembly centre for assaulting formations, and airfields were available or could be constructed within fighter range of both the Isthmus of Kra and the Malayan coast. The Commander-in-Chief, Far East, considered at the time that it would take the Japanese some months to make their preparations at Camranh Bay and to carry out the construction of essential airfields. He found it difficult at this stage to judge whether the occupation of southern Indo-China was a strategic move intended as an asset for future negotiations, a final move before the occupation of Siam or the final step before an invasion of Malaya.

During October however information began to come in of landing craft being constructed at Shanghai, of Japanese troops being trained in jungle warfare in Hainan, of shipping being collected in Japanese controlled ports and of the construction of airfields in southern Indo-China. Although these were clear indications of preparations, they gave no certainty of an early assault on Malaya. It would only be the movement of naval units and shipping and the arrival of long-range fighter or bomber aircraft in Indo-China which would clarify Japanese intentions. Despite the knowledge that the Japanese were making preparations in Indo-China, Sir Robert still held to his opinion, which was in line with that held in the United Kingdom, that they did not contemplate an immediate war with Great Britain but were preparing to support Germany by an attack on Russia.

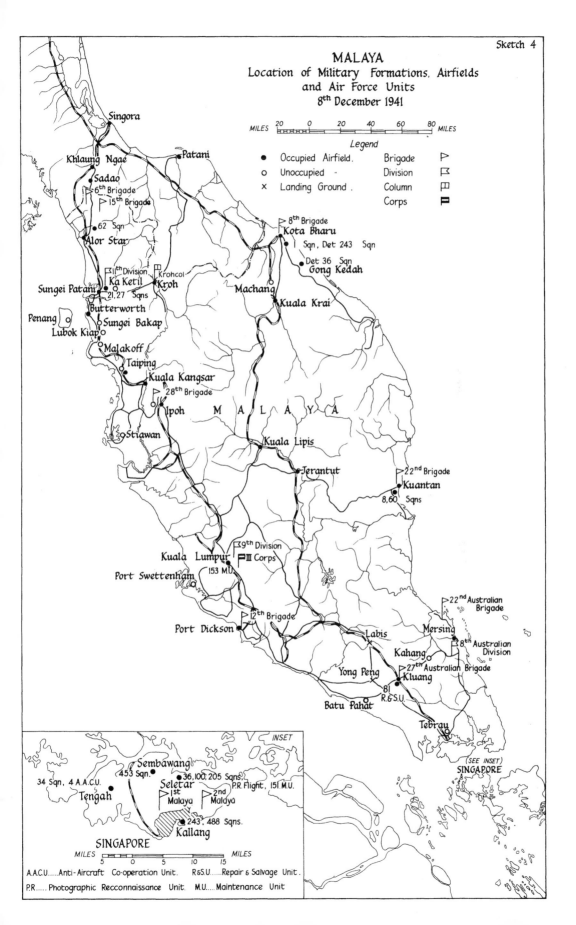

Sketch 4

MALAYA
Location of Military Formations, Airfields and Air Force Units
8th December 1941

MILES 20 0 20 40 60 80 MILES

Legend

● Occupied Airfield.	Brigade	▷
○ Unoccupied "	Division	
× Landing Ground.	Column	
	Corps	▬▬

Singora

Patani

Khlaung Ngae

Sadao

6th Brigade
15th Brigade

62 Sqn

Alor Star

8th Brigade
Kota Bharu
Sqn, Det 243 Sqn

Det 36 Sqn
Gong Kedah

11th Division Krohcol
Ka Ketil Kroh
Sungei Patani
21, 27 Sqns
Butterworth
Penang Sungei Bakap
Lubok Kiap
Malakoff
Taiping
Kuala Kangsar
28th Brigade
Ipoh

Machang

Kuala Krai

M A L A Y A

Stiawan

Kuala Lipis

Jerantut

22nd Brigade
Kuantan
8, 60 Sqns

9th Division
III Corps
Kuala Lumpur
153 M.U.
Port Swettenham

22nd Australian
Brigade

12th Brigade
Port Dickson

Mersing

Labis
Kahang
8th Australian
Division

Yong Peng 27th Australian Brigade
Kluang
81
R.&S.U.
Batu Pahat

Tebrau

(SEE INSET)
SINGAPORE

INSET

Sembawang
453 Sqn.
34 Sqn, 4 A.A.C.U.
Seletar 36, 100, 205 Sqns,
P.R. Flight, 151 M.U.
Tengah 1st Malaya 2nd Malaya

243, 488 Sqns.
Kallang

SINGAPORE

MILES 5 0 5 10 15 MILES

A.A.C.U.......Anti-Aircraft Co-operation Unit. R&S.U.......Repair & Salvage Unit.

P.R.......Photographic Recconnaissance Unit. M.U.......Maintenance Unit

During November reports came in that enemy shipping was gradually moving southwards, that landing craft at Shanghai had been embarked, that a convoy had arrived at Hainan and that shipping had increased at both Saigon and Camranh Bay. At the same time additional aircraft were reported in Indo-China. Faced with these indications Sir Robert began to give careful attention to the implications of launching operation 'Matador'.[1] On the 21st November he had reminded the Chiefs of Staff that the ability to forestall the Japanese at Singora was essential to the success of 'Matador', and asked whether it was not possible to define the circumstances in which permission to launch the operation would be given. The next day he gave orders for military precautions to be taken in Malaya. These included the move of some air force units to their battle stations, and instructions to General Percival to be ready to launch 'Matador' and to bring the troops on the east coast of Malaya to the second degree of readiness.

On the 25th the Chiefs of Staff told Sir Robert that it was not possible for the British Government to commit itself in advance to any particular action. They instructed him however that, as soon as any situation arose which in his opinion was likely to lead to 'Matador', he should make preparations to launch the operation without delay should he be ordered to do so. The War Cabinet's decision should reach Singapore within thirty-six hours of the receipt of a report that the Japanese were on the move.

Sir Robert reminded the Chiefs of Staff on the 27th that as 'Matador' was an operation to forestall an invasion of southern Siam it had to be ordered in time. If the Japanese intended to land in the Isthmus of Kra at the same time as they invaded northern Siam, there would not be a moment to lose, since their troops could start disembarking at Singora within thirty-three hours of sailing from Saigon. Thus, even if they were to defer sailing until they had violated Siamese territory, their troops could arrive at Singora within the thirty-six hours taken up by the deliberations on Government level. The same day Sir Robert was told that the United States Consul at Hanoi had reported two days earlier that the Japanese were expected to attack the Isthmus of Kra and northern Malaya on about the 1st December without previous warning.

On the 28th the Admiralty ordered Admiral Phillips, who had arrived at Colombo in the *Prince of Wales*, to fly to Singapore and thence to Manila to co-ordinate plans with Dominion, Dutch and American admirals. The same day Admiral Layton asked the Dutch for submarines to undertake reconnaissance off the coast of Siam near Singora; Sir Robert asked the Americans in the Philippines to

---

[1] See pages 76–78.

undertake the reconnaissance of the area Manila–Camranh Bay[1] and arrangements were made for the air forces in Malaya to reconnoitre a sector with a radius of 180 miles from Kota Bharu, but which through lack of aircraft excluded the Gulf of Siam.

At the same time Sir Robert told the Chiefs of Staff that the great increase of Japanese naval, army and air forces in the South China Sea and in southern Indo-China indicated an early attack on Siam. He reminded them of the vital importance of his being able to undertake 'Matador' without delay if required, and explained that, as southern Siam was largely waterlogged in December, the tactical advantage lay with whoever was first on the ground. He therefore requested permission to undertake 'Matador' should reconnaissance report escorted Japanese convoys approaching the coast of Siam.

On the 29th, Sir Robert was told that the United States negotiations with Japan might break down at any moment and that Japanese offensive action against the Philippines, Siam (including the Isthmus of Kra) or possibly Borneo, might be expected at any time. In view of the imminent threat of war, III Corps was at once placed at twenty-four hours' notice and warned to be prepared for 'Matador'. Since the whole object of this operation was to forestall the Japanese at Singora, the troops taking part had to be prepared to start without delay after the order to move. They were therefore ordered by III Corps to be at six hours' notice.

The same day the Chiefs of Staff considered Sir Robert's request of the 28th. They agreed with his views, but considered that the presence of escorted Japanese ships off the Siamese coast would not itself constitute an attack on Siam. Consequently they took the view that to move into the Isthmus of Kra on this pretext alone would be to place the British Commonwealth in the position of being the first to violate the neutrality of Siam, and of running the risk of becoming involved in war with Japan. So they informed Sir Robert that they were not prepared to agree to his request, unless they could first obtain an assurance that America would immediately join in the fight.

On the 1st December Sir Robert was told that the American-Japanese negotiations had broken down but might apparently be resumed, that Japan under the pressure of extremists was likely to take prompt action and that the United States Government had been asked for an assurance of armed support if action were taken to forestall the Japanese on the Isthmus of Kra. As a result of this information the Volunteers were mobilized and the whole garrison brought to the second degree of readiness.

On the 2nd, Sir Robert received information that the pro-Japanese members of the Siamese Cabinet had proposed to Tokyo that, in

[1] They were forbidden by instructions from Washington to undertake reconnaissance of Camranh Bay and Palau.

order to make Britain appear to be the aggressor against Siam,
Japanese forces should land at Kota Bharu whereupon British forces
might be expected to cross the frontier. Siam could then declare war
on Britain. On the 4th, Sir Robert told the Chiefs of Staff that, in circumstances such as these, he considered the need of avoiding war
with Japan would no longer apply. An attack at Kota Bharu would
only be a step in the operations against Malaya. It was possible that
Singora would be the next step although it was more likely that both
would be taken simultaneously. Should however the Japanese attack
be made only at Kota Bharu the military arguments in favour of
'Matador' still held good. He therefore requested the authority to
order 'Matador' should such circumstances arise.

On the 5th, the Chiefs of Staff informed Sir Robert that American
assurance of armed support had at last been vouchsafed, conditional
on the Japanese attacking British territory, or the Netherlands East
Indies, or on 'Matador' being undertaken either to forestall a Japanese
landing on the Isthmus of Kra or as a reply to a violation of any other
part of Siamese territory. Accordingly with the approval of the War
Cabinet they told him that he could order 'Matador' without
reference to Whitehall, should the Japanese violate any part of
Siam, or if there were good information that a Japanese expedition
was advancing with the apparent intention of landing on the Isthmus
of Kra. They also told him that in the event of a Japanese attack on
the Netherlands East Indies he could put into operation plans already
agreed with the Dutch.

Thus at the eleventh hour the Chiefs of Staff gave Sir Robert the
permission, for which he had been asking, to launch 'Matador'
without reference to London. They had however worded their
instructions in such a way that the chances of its succeeding were
greatly reduced, for it would be too late to take action by the time
that he could be sure that a Japanese expedition was making for the
Isthmus of Kra. This was to have serious consequences.

CHAPTER XI

THE INVASION OF SIAM
AND MALAYA

See Maps 1, 5, 6, 7 and 8

THE Japanese Imperial General Headquarters had detailed *25th Army* (Lieut.-General Yamashita) to undertake the invasion and occupation of Malaya. This army was composed initially of *5th* and *18th Divisions, Imperial Guards Division* and *56th Division*.[1]

The first of these was stationed before the outbreak of war in Hainan, the second in south China, and both were experienced formations which for the previous four years had taken part in numerous operations including landings. The *Imperial Guards Division* was in Indo-China and *56th Division*, a new formation, was in Japan. This latter division, in the event, did not fight in Malaya and was later employed for the invasion of Burma.

General Yamashita planned that *5th Division* (less *21st Infantry Regiment*) would act as the spearhead of the invasion and effect the main landings at Singora and Patani;[2] *56th Infantry Regiment* of *18th Division* would make a subsidiary landing at Kota Bharu. These landings were to take place simultaneously during the night of 7th/8th December 1941.

The *5th Division* was ordered to advance southwards across the Siam–Malaya border; the main body, *9th Infantry Brigade* (*11th* and *41st Infantry Regiments*), using the Singora–Alor Star road, and *42nd Infantry Regiment* the Patani–Kroh road. The division's objectives were given as, firstly, the line of the Perak River and the capture of the group of British airfields in Kedah and, secondly, Kuala Lumpur. It was expected that the advance from the Perak River to Kuala Lumpur would begin on approximately the 23rd December. The *56th Infantry Regiment*, making the subsidiary landing, was ordered to capture the airfields at Kota Bharu and Gong Kedah and the landing ground at Machang, and then to move south by the coastal route towards Kuantan.

---

[1] See Appendix 15: Order of Battle *25th Army*.
[2] It was planned that *21st Infantry Regiment* (the fourth regiment of *5th Division*) would arrive at Singora on the 27th December.

The main body of *Imperial Guards Division* was to be lent during the initial stages to *15th Army*, which was entrusted with the invasion of Siam and the advance into Burma. The *Imperial Guards Division* was to move overland from the Indo-Chinese border to occupy Bangkok, the main Siamese airfields and key points on the railway in that country. One battalion was, however, to land at Bangkok on the morning of the 8th December to overawe the Siamese Government, before the arrival of the rest of the division. After the occupation of Siam, the *Imperial Guards Division* was to revert to *25th Army*. The *4th Guards Regiment*, with supporting arms, was to move by rail down the Isthmus of Kra and follow up the advance of *5th Division*, concentrating in the Taiping–Ipoh area by the 23rd December. The rest of the division, when relieved by *55th Division* in Siam, was also to move south and concentrate in central Malaya as soon as possible after the 23rd.

It was planned that *18th Division*, less *56th Infantry Regiment* (which was to land at Kota Bharu) and less *35th Infantry Brigade Headquarters* and *124th Infantry Regiment* (which were to invade British Borneo),[1] was to land at Singora and Patani early in January together with the rest of *25th Army*. This division was then, as events dictated, either to take part in the attack on Singapore or to prepare for the invasion of northern Sumatra. The *56th Division* was to stand by in Japan in readiness to make a landing, if necessary, in the Endau–Mersing area to assist *5th* and *Imperial Guards Divisions* in overcoming resistance in Johore.

To secure southern Siam between Bangkok and Singora, protect the rear of *5th Division*, gain control of airfields in that area, and provide for the security of the Siam–Malaya railway, *143rd Regiment* of *55th Division* of *15th Army* was to move with the first flight of *5th Division* and land at Nakhorn, Bandon, Jumbhorn, and Prachuab.[2] Elements of this regiment were, as soon as possible after landing, to advance across the border into southern Burma and, by capturing Victoria Point, cut the British air reinforcement route to Malaya.

In the event of the British forces advancing into southern Siam before the war started, part of *5th Division* was to help *143rd Infantry Regiment* to capture Nakhorn and the group of airfields in that area and the main landing at Singora was to be postponed until air superiority over the British air forces in northern Malaya had been gained.

The first flight of *5th Division* embarked at Samah (Hainan Island) in nineteen transports. The convoy sailed at 5.30 a.m. on the 4th December, escorted by one light cruiser (*Sendai*) and three divisions of destroyers. The *143rd Regiment* sailed in convoy from Saigon at 1.50 p.m. on the 5th, in seven transports escorted by one

---

[1] See Chapter XIII.
[2] See Map 7.

light cruiser (*Kashii*). Vice-Admiral Ozawa, flying his flag in the cruiser *Chokai*, was in command of the whole operation. Close cover was provided by the *7th Cruiser Squadron* (Rear-Admiral Kurita) of four 8-inch cruisers, screened by a division of destroyers, and distant cover by Vice-Admiral Kondo (*Southern Force*) with a force consisting of two battleships, two cruisers and some destroyers.

Both convoys were to be at a rendezvous in the Gulf of Siam (9° 25′ North, 102° 20′ East) at about 9 a.m. on the 7th December. The convoys were routed close to the coast so as to be under land-based air cover and to keep out of range of British reconnaissance aircraft for as long as possible. The rendezvous was selected to give credence to the rumours, spread in Indo-China and elsewhere, that the convoys were proceeding to Siam. From the rendezvous the various detachments were to proceed at maximum speed direct to their objectives. The seven transports carrying *143rd Regiment* were to move separately to their destinations in the Isthmus of Kra, under the general escort of one destroyer and a sloop. The convoy carrying *5th Division* was to divide into two parts: sixteen transports going to the Singora–Patani area and three to Kota Bharu, each supported by a light cruiser and a division of destroyers. Three seaplane carriers were to accompany the convoys and provide anti-submarine patrols for the Singora and Patani anchorages. The remainder of *5th Division*, with the necessary base and line of communications troops, was to follow in two flights, timed to arrive at Singora on the 16th and 27th December respectively.

The operation was to be covered by *3rd Air Division* (Lieut.-General Sugawara) of the Japanese Army Air Force, which was to complete its concentration on airfields in southern Indo-China by the 5th December.[1] This air division, assisted where necessary by detachments from the *11th Air Fleet*, was to cover the move of the convoys into the Gulf of Siam, attack British airfields in the Kota Bharu, Alor Star, and Sungei Patani areas with a view to gaining air superiority in northern Malaya, and to occupy and operate from the airfields in southern Siam and northern Malaya captured by *5th Division*. They were also to attack British communications and to bomb Singapore and other strategic points.

The Anglo-Dutch seaward reconnaissance plan had been put into effect on the 3rd December. The British reconnaissance area stretched from Kota Bharu to Cape Cambodia, thence south-east to the Anamba Islands and westwards to Kuantan, but as recorded earlier did not include the Gulf of Siam. The Dutch were responsible for the area immediately to the south, including Borneo.

---

[1] See Appendix 16.

Shortly after midday on the 6th December a Hudson of 1 (G.R.) Squadron, operating from Kota Bharu at the extreme limit of its range, reported Japanese convoys with naval escort some eighty miles south-east of Cape Cambodia. There were three sighting reports: the first, of three transports with a cruiser as escort steering approximately north-west seen at 12.12 p.m.;[1] the second, of twenty-two transports seen considerably further east with a heavy escort of cruisers and destroyers steering west; the third, similar to the second, but the position given was slightly to the south and it appeared that there were two similar convoys sailing on parallel courses.[2] The sightings were fortunate for not only did the frequent tropical rain-storms and low clouds of the north-east monsoon seriously reduce visibility, but the position and course of the leading convoy indicated that the ships would soon be in the Gulf of Siam and thus outside the reconnaissance area. The same day information was received that Japanese convoys had left both Camranh Bay and Saigon, and that Siamese frontier guards had started erecting road blocks on the trunk road to Singora and on the Kroh–Patani road. It was clear that the Japanese were on the move, but where were they bound—Bangkok, Singora, the coast of Malaya, or all three?

Sir Robert Brooke-Popham, after consultation with Admiral Layton and Admiral Palliser (Chief of Staff to Admiral Phillips),[3] came to the conclusion that the Japanese would in all probability assemble in Kau Rong bay so that they would be under close air cover by daylight and, if bound for Singora, would make the final approach under the cover of darkness. It was considered therefore that, after rounding Cape Cambodia, the rearward convoys would probably turn north-west following the leading four ships and that all the convoys would proceed to Kau Rong Bay from where they could equally well move on Kota Bharu, Singora or Bangkok.

Bearing in mind the policy of avoiding war with Japan if possible —a policy which had been reaffirmed by the Chiefs of Staff as recently as the 29th November—and the situation in the United States where the diplomatic talks were still going on, Sir Robert decided that he would not be justified in ordering 'Matador' on this information. Nevertheless that afternoon, as a precautionary measure, he ordered that all the forces in Malaya should be brought to the highest degree of readiness. General Percival was at III Corps Headquarters when the news of the sightings was telephoned to him about 3.15 p.m. He immediately ordered General Heath to assume the first degree of readiness and, anticipating that 'Matador' might be ordered,

---

[1] This was the convoy carrying *143rd Infantry Regiment*.
[2] The second and third sightings were in fact the same convoy which was carrying the first flight of *5th Division*.
[3] Admiral Phillips was at this time in Manila on a visit to Admiral Hart, the Commander-in-Chief, United States Asiatic Fleet.

instructed him to arrange that 11th Division would be ready to move at short notice. At the same time he arranged for the railway trains required for the operation to be held in readiness at the entraining stations.

Meanwhile air reconnaissance had been intensified in an endeavour to re-establish contact with the convoys. Owing to the very bad weather over the South China Sea throughout the 6th and the night of the 6th/7th, and to the fact that the enemy convoys had turned north-west into the Gulf of Siam towards their rendezvous, thus passing out of the reconnaissance area, no further information of the enemy movements was forthcoming. On the 7th the search for the Japanese ships was extended, since it was considered that they might be concentrating in the vicinity of Kau Rong. Early that morning a Catalina flying boat was sent especially to reconnoitre that area, but nothing was heard from it and it failed to return. During the afternoon, however, two merchant vessels were seen steering west and south in the Gulf of Siam. At 5.30 p.m., some thirty hours after the first sighting of the convoys, a merchant vessel and Japanese cruiser were sighted about 110 miles north of Kota Bharu steaming towards Singora. One hour later, in very bad visibility, four Japanese war-ships, which were thought to be destroyers, were sighted about sixty miles north of Patani steaming south parallel with the coast. All this information reached Headquarters, Far East Command, about 9 p.m. that night.

During the day Sir Robert had received a telegram from the British Minister in Bangkok, sent after an interview with the Siamese Minister for Foreign Affairs, which urged in the strongest terms that British forces should not be allowed to occupy one inch of Siamese territory unless or until the Japanese had struck the first blow. The Minister went on to say that Siam was with Britain in opposition to Japan, but that it would be otherwise, and that irreparable harm would be done, if Britain were the first to violate Siamese territory.

Late that evening Sir Robert held a conference with Admiral Phillips (who had just returned from Manila) to decide, in the light of the latest information and the telegram from Bangkok, what action he should take. The conditions for reconnaissance had been very bad and there was no real certainty that the ships seen that day were part of an expedition. There was the possibility (particularly in view of the information received on the 2nd) that the movements of the ships seen were part of a deliberate attempt to induce a British violation of Siamese neutrality. It was evident that, if the convoys already reported were part of an invasion force bound for Singora, they could arrive there about midnight on the 7th/8th. Since 'Matador' needed at least a twenty-four hours start before the expected time of a Japanese landing, it was clear that the opportunity to forestall it had passed. The object of 'Matador' had always been to forestall the enemy; no provision had therefore been made in the plan for an encounter battle near Singora. These factors and the fear that the launching of 'Matador' might, if the Japanese ships were not heading for Singora, result in Britain being the first to violate Siamese territory—a fear which had been increased by the British Minister's telegram—led the Commander-in-Chief to decide for the second time not to order the operation.

Since there was no certainty that the convoys were bound for Singora and the opportunity to forestall the Japanese there might still exist, Sir Robert, no doubt mindful of the view he had expressed in his telegram of the 4th, to which no reply had so far been received, asked for a dawn air reconnaissance of the Singora area before finally deciding to order 'Matador' or the alternative plan. At 11.20 p.m. however Heath was warned to be prepared to put 'Matador' into operation at dawn on the 8th.

The conference had barely ended when events in north-east Malaya disposed of any doubts about Japanese intentions. Shortly after midnight on the 7th/8th December the troops of 8th Brigade defending the beaches north-east of Kota Bharu reported three transports anchoring off the beaches and added, shortly afterwards, that the beach defences were being shelled. About 1 a.m. Wing Commander C. H. Noble, commanding the airfield at Kota Bharu, in a telephone message to Air Headquarters at Singapore confirmed the presence of the ships and reported artillery fire.[1] To clear up the situation, Air Vice-Marshal Pulford ordered him to send out an air reconnaissance, but before this could be done definite information was received from 8th Brigade (Brigadier Key) that Japanese troops had begun to land. Thereupon Air Headquarters ordered all available aircraft at Kota Bharu to attack, and at the same time made arrangements for further attacks to be delivered by torpedo-bombers and other aircraft from first light onwards. After the heavy rain of the previous evening the weather at Kota Bharu was clearing and by this time the moon had risen. Though the airfield at Kota Bharu was partly waterlogged, Hudson aircraft were despatched to attack the Japanese ships and troops landing from them. Under fire from artillery and under attack from the air, all the three transports were damaged (one was set on fire and sank the next day) as were some landing-craft on passage to the beaches.[2]

While these events in north-east Malaya were absorbing the attention of Far East Command, the main Japanese forces had reached

---

[1] There is a conflict of evidence as to the exact time at which the first landing was actually made. It is probable that it was close to the planned time of 12.45 a.m. (See page 96.)

[2] *Awajisan Maru* sunk; *Sakura Maru* damaged; *Ayato Maru* damaged.

Singora and Patani at about 2.20 a.m. and by about 4 a.m. had started to land against virtually no opposition.

The civilian population on Singapore Island, unaware of these momentous events, was to receive a rude awakening. At 3.30 a.m. the Fighter Control Operations Room at Singapore reported the approach from the north-east of unidentified aircraft at a distance of some 140 miles from the island. Warning was at once passed to all Service establishments and formations on the island, and the anti-aircraft gun defences were brought to instant readiness. It was not possible for similar warning to be given to the civil defence authorities, as the headquarters of the Air Raid Precautions organization was not manned. The civil air defence scheme could not therefore be put into effect, in spite of the fact that more than thirty minutes elapsed from the time of the first radar reports before the enemy aircraft arrived over Singapore.

Some seventeen Japanese naval bombers, operating from southern Indo-China, carried out the raid; it was directed mainly against Tengah and Seletar airfields, where most of the bombs fell without causing much damage,[1] but some fell in a congested area in the centre of the town, causing some two hundred casualties among the Asian population. Singapore was fully illuminated when the raid took place; there was no attempt at any blackout and the street lamps were not extinguished until after the all-clear had been given at 4.40 a.m. Although the Japanese air crews may have been astonished to find the town a blaze of lights, it is unlikely that it helped them to locate their targets, since the attacks were carried out in brilliant tropical moonlight in which the whole of the island would be clearly visible. Night fighters were standing by at immediate readiness, but in order to avoid confusing the defence, which had not been sufficiently practised in the control of aircraft, searchlights and guns at night, they were not allowed to take off. The defence was therefore restricted to the anti-aircraft batteries. No enemy aircraft were destroyed. Understandably, this first air raid on Singapore had a profound effect upon civilians. It was their first intimation that war had begun, and took them completely by surprise. It must have been an unpleasant shock to those members of the European community who had shared the often expressed official view that war with Japan was unlikely.

At 6.30 a.m. on the 8th December, the Commander-in-Chief, Far East, issued an Order of the Day which he and the Commander-in-Chief, China, had drawn up in May 1941.[2] It had been necessary to prepare the Order at that early date to allow time for its translation into the different languages used throughout the Far East, and

---

[1] See Inset, Sketch 4.
[2] See Appendix 17.

distribution within the Command for issue on the first day of war. The wording of this Order of the Day showed how much the official view of the situation on the outbreak of war was out of touch with reality.

Meanwhile Pulford, after consultation with Percival, had issued orders for an all-out attack to be launched, as soon as it was daylight against the enemy ships lying off Kota Bharu. When the squadrons arrived over the area however they found little to attack, since the Japanese transports had by then been withdrawn northwards. Accordingly they landed at forward airfields in Kedah and Kelantan States to refuel and rearm.

At about 7.30 a.m. the Japanese air forces began intensive attacks in order to eliminate, in the shortest possible time, all air opposition in northern Malaya. Operating at first from forward airfields specially prepared in southern Indo-China and, later in the day, from the airfields at Singora and Patani, they carried out a series of damaging raids against the British air force. Their aim was to destroy aircraft on the ground and then put the airfields and buildings temporarily out of action so as to deny them to any British aircraft which were already airborne or had escaped the ground attacks. From the outset they met with success, for their initial attacks took place at the very moment when most of the British bomber aircraft were refuelling after the abortive early morning operations against the landings at Kota Bharu. Throughout the day, they systematically developed their offensive against all the main airfields in northern Malaya.

A decision as to the action of III Corps had been deferred until an air reconnaissance at dawn on the 8th had shown whether or not the Japanese had landed at Singora during the night. At 8 a.m. on the 8th the Commander-in-Chief, Far East, received a reply from London to his request of the 4th. This gave him the authority to violate Siamese neutrality by launching 'Matador', should he so wish, subject to the Japanese first having landed at Kota Bharu. He was thus free to order Krohcol to enter Siam and seize the Ledge position, and, since this operation was to take place whichever role was given to 11th Division, he could have ordered the column to move without any further delay. When Malaya Command, having received a copy of the telegram, telephoned Far East Headquarters asking for instructions, the answer was 'Do not act', presumably because Sir Robert had decided to await the arrival of the recon-naissance aircraft, shortly due back from Singora before taking any decision.

At 9.15 a.m. a badly damaged British photographic reconnaissance aircraft landed at Kota Bharu with the news that troops were landing from a large concentration of ships at Singora and Patani. The receipt of this information in Singapore about 9.45 a.m. not only showed Sir Robert that his decision not to launch 'Matador' was justified, but enabled him to tell Percival that 11th Division should be ordered to adopt the alternative defensive plan. By the time however that the news had reached Singapore, Percival had gone to attend a routine meeting of the Legislative Assembly and it was not till about 11 a.m. that he returned to his headquarters, and was given permission to send troops into Siam. At 11.30 a.m. he gave orders that III Corps should occupy the Jitra position, send a delaying column into Siam along the trunk road and launch Krohcol to occupy the Ledge position on the Patani road. For some reason which cannot be ascertained, the gist of these orders was not passed immediately to III Corps on the telephone and it was not till shortly after 1 p.m. that Heath received them. To make quite certain that he was free to enter Siam he spoke on the telephone to Percival at about 1.10 p.m. At 1.30 p.m. he ordered 11th Division to adopt the alternative plan, and at the same time gave instructions that the selected position at Gurun should be prepared for defence as soon as possible.

Meanwhile, 11th Division, which since the afternoon of the 6th had been standing by at short notice in incessant rain, was still impatiently awaiting orders to undertake 'Matador'. Repeated telephonic requests to III Corps during the morning had brought no decision. When at 1.30 p.m. General Murray-Lyon was ordered to adopt the defensive plan and was told that 28th Brigade was to come under his command,[1] 'Matador', for which the division had been keyed up for so long, was by implication abandoned. In theory it should have been equally prepared for either alternative, but in practice this was not possible, for the transport arrangements for a rapid advance to Singora and the need for speed in launching the operation were such that the normal organization of the formations taking part had to be adjusted for their particular tasks.[2] The adoption of the defensive therefore caused delay, for the division had to revert to its normal organization at the same time as it occupied the Jitra position.

The hesitation on the part of the Commander-in-Chief, Far East, to launch 'Matador' is understandable in view of his uncertainty as to the Japanese intentions, the importance placed on Britain not being the first to violate Siamese territory and the absence of an answer to his telegram of the 4th December. The reasons why he kept 11th Division standing by for 'Matador' until he had received the result of a dawn air reconnaissance, although he had decided on

---

[1] This brigade entrained at Ipoh at 5 p.m. on the 8th and reached Alor Star early on the 9th.

[2] Of the six battalions in the two brigades, two were standing by alongside the trains at Anak Bukit (six miles south of the Jitra position) ready for the advance into Siam; two were in their camps with their trucks loaded ready to move by road and two were deployed near the frontier.

the evening of the 7th not to order the operation, are obscure. Everything pointed to the fact that the Japanese plan was to land on the Isthmus of Kra. The delay may have been due to his doubt whether the military arguments in favour of 'Matador' still held good if the Japanese attacked Kota Bharu only. To Sir Robert, with the telegram of the 2nd in mind, the possibility that the Japanese would attack at Kota Bharu only would not perhaps have seemed wholly ruled out. This, coupled with the fact that he gravely overestimated the mobility of army formations, resulted in his hesitating at a moment when a rapid decision was necessary. When at 8 a.m. on the 8th he received a cable from London which gave him authority to move into Siam if the Japanese landed at Kota Bharu, he might at least have set Krohcol in motion. It is possible that he did not fully realize the importance of speed in relation to this particular operation which demanded an advance of thirty miles through Siamese territory before the Ledge position could be reached. It was not till the news that the Japanese had actually landed at Singora was received in Singapore at 9.45 a.m. on the 8th that he finally dismissed 'Matador' as impracticable, and realized that III Corps must be committed to its alternative defensive role. The enemy already had a flying start of some six hours and there was a risk that there would be insufficient time for the defence to take up positions before contact was made.[1] The need for a quick decision was not apparently realized at Headquarters, Malaya Command, for several hours were allowed to pass before 11th Division received its orders. The enemy was thus given a start of some ten hours over III Corps; this was to prove disastrous.

Krohcol (Lieut.-Colonel H. D. Moorhead) crossed the frontier into Siam at about 3 p.m. on the 8th, and was immediately faced by road blocks and manned by some 300 Siamese armed constabulary.[2] It had been hoped that the Siamese would not oppose the entry of British troops; their action in doing so delayed the advance of the column which, by dusk that evening, was only about three miles beyond the border. After a night of sniping, the advance continued on the 9th in the face of further opposition from the armed constabulary. All opposition however ceased suddenly at 3 p.m., and Betong was occupied that evening.

The next morning (10th) the column moved forward in trucks to a

---

[1] From approximately 4 a.m. till 9.45 a.m.

[2] As Krohcol was not fully assembled, 3/16th Punjab began the advance alone. The column was later reinforced by 5/14th Punjab (less one company) and 10th Mountain Battery from Penang, and one troop 273rd Anti-Tank Battery from Jitra.

point six miles short of the Ledge position, from where it continued the advance on foot. Before it had covered the next mile, the advanced guard came under fire from enemy troops and an encounter battle developed. Heavy fighting ensued, but the enemy, who was in considerable strength and supported by light tanks, checked the advance. By nightfall on the 10th, 3/16th Punjab, with two companies cut off, was forced to take up a defensive position some twenty-five miles beyond the frontier, after destroying a road bridge to provide a tank obstacle.[1] Meanwhile, 5/14th Punjab (less one company) and 10th Mountain Battery had arrived at Kroh. Moorhead ordered them to take up a defensive position in support nine miles north of Betong.

The delay in launching Krohcol across the frontier, and the cautious fashion in which the unexpected Siamese resistance was dealt with, enabled the enemy to forestall Krohcol on the only really good defensive position north of Kroh. Credit must however be given to the enemy who, in the space of some sixty hours, had landed men and equipment, and covered some seventy-five miles over roads which were none too good, thus winning the race for the point on the route—the Ledge position—vital to 11th Division's line of communications.

During the afternoon of the 11th, 3/16th Punjab repelled repeated strong attacks along the road, but casualties began to mount, and Moorhead, who had correctly estimated the enemy strength as three battalions, realized that an early withdrawal was his only course of action. He explained the position to Murray-Lyon and was given permission to withdraw at his discretion. Accordingly he made preparations to pull back early next morning. At dawn on the 12th the enemy renewed his attacks astride the road, and in addition attempted to by-pass the defences by working south along the right bank of the Patani River. Moorhead then ordered the withdrawal to begin at 9 a.m., but at 8.30 a.m. a further enemy attack supported by artillery upset his plan and it was only with great difficulty and further heavy casualties that he managed to disengage. During the afternoon 3/16th Punjab, reduced to about half its original strength, passed through 5/14th Punjab in position north-east of Betong and that evening reached the prepared defensive position on the Baling road three miles west of Kroh. Moorhead gave 5/14th Punjab orders to act as covering troops and to delay the enemy for as long as possible without becoming too much involved.

Simultaneously with the despatch of Krohcol, a small mechanized force[2] advanced into Siam from north Kedah to harass and delay the

---

[1] One company was lost, the other rejoined next day.
[2] The force consisted of two companies and the carrier platoon of 1/8th Punjab, a section of 273rd Anti-Tank Battery and two sections 17th Field Company.

advance of the Japanese forces from Singora. An armoured train was also sent into Siam from Padang Besar on the frontier of Perlis. By dusk on the 9th, the mechanized force halted at Sadao, ten miles north of the frontier on the Jitra–Singora road. At about 9 p.m. a Japanese column, headed by tanks and moving in close formation with full headlights, was seen approaching. The leading enemy tanks and a convoy of some thirty motor vehicles behind them were engaged and brought to a standstill; but the Japanese infantry quickly debussed and started an enveloping movement. Thereupon, the mechanized force withdrew southwards towards the frontier, destroying road bridges as it went. It passed through 1/14th Punjab[1] (who had been detailed both to provide the covering troops on the frontier and to hold an outpost position three and a half miles north of Jitra) and rejoined 11th Division. Meanwhile, the armoured train had reached Khlaung Ngae where the engineer detachment was successful in destroying the large railway bridge. The train then withdrew through a covering detachment provided by 6th Brigade[2] at Padang Besar.

To revert to the events at Kota Bharu: although the Japanese convoy and escorts had arrived without incident at the selected anchorage some two miles off the beach, the actual landing of troops and equipment proved to be more difficult. A fairly heavy swell was still running, in spite of the wind having dropped to little more than a light breeze, with the result that lowering landing-craft and loading them when alongside was not easy. Several capsized and some of their occupants were lost. Nevertheless the landing, made without close supporting fire, was eventually carried out between Sabak and Badang. It was made in three separate flights, with an interval of about one hour between each, the same landing-craft being used for each flight.[3] The troops of the first flight suffered loss from artillery fire, and had difficulty in dealing with the determined defence offered by 3/17th Dogras and with the heavily wired and mined defences. Yet by 3.45 a.m., after severe fighting and with considerable losses on both sides, they succeeded in capturing two strong points, one on either side of Kuala Pa'amat in the centre of the Dogras' defences The second and third flights, though attacked by aircraft from Kota Bharu during their approach to the beaches and suffering casualties,

---

[1] Supported by 4th Mountain Battery and a section of 2nd Anti-Tank Battery and 23rd Field Company.
[2] Two companies 2/16th Punjab supported by 7th Mountain Battery, one section of 273rd Anti-Tank Battery and 3rd Field Company.
[3] See Map 6 and Appendix 26.

also landed successfully. Since the Japanese landings clearly represented a serious threat to the airfield at Kota Bharu barely two miles inland, Brigadier Key at 2 a.m. moved 2/12th Frontier Force Regiment and 73rd Field Battery to Kota Bharu to protect it.

At dawn on the 8th December, the Dogras were still holding their beach defences—except at Kuala Pa'amat—but the Japanese were gradually extending their foothold ashore. Key therefore ordered 1/13th Frontier Force Rifles to counter-attack eastwards along the beaches from Badang, and 2/12th F.F. Regiment (less one company) to attack westwards from Sabak, to join hands and destroy the enemy troops who had landed. The 73rd Field Battery and 21st Mountain Battery were to support from a position near the airfield. Owing however to the difficulties of the country, with its innumerable creeks and rivers, both these attacks failed to achieve their object. Further efforts later in the morning also failed and the situation in the beach area remained very confused. During the morning 4/19th Hyderabad, from the Command Reserve (12th Brigade), was allotted to 9th Division and sent by rail to Kuala Krai.

The airfield was bombed and machine-gunned at frequent intervals throughout the day, with consequent casualties and damage to aircraft. At about 4 p.m. a rumour began to spread on the airfield that enemy troops had broken through and reached the perimeter defences. This was not in fact the case, but the passage of stray bullets probably gave credence to it and resulted in some unauthorized person giving instructions that the denial scheme was to be put into effect. The airfield buildings were set on fire and the station staff began to evacuate the airfield. A joint reconnaissance by the brigadier and the wing commander proved that the rumour was false, but the damage was done, and by 6.15 p.m. the station and squadron maintenance staff had left in local transport for the railhead at Kuala Krai. Although they had set fire to the operations room and to most of the stores, they had failed to destroy the stocks of bombs and petrol or to make the runways unfit for use.

Shortly after 4 p.m. Air Headquarters had been informed that the airfield was being attacked by ground forces, and Air Marshal Pulford had immediately ordered all serviceable aircraft to be withdrawn to Kuantan. In view of the general air situation, and since raids on airfields in Kelantan had caused much damage to aircraft on the ground, his decision was justified, but the hurried evacuation of the airfield at Kota Bharu was premature and not warranted by the ground situation. At about 7 p.m. enemy transports again appeared off the beaches. Key already had permission from General Barstow (9th Division) to withdraw if it became necessary. At about 8 p.m., the airfield having been abandoned, he decided that a withdrawal from the northern beaches to a position covering Kota Bharu should begin at midnight, and that 2/10th Baluch should start with-drawing towards Peringat at the same time.

At about 10 p.m. 73rd Field Battery, firing at point-blank range, set fire to the petrol stores. Shortly afterwards enemy forces reached the airfield. Nevertheless the anti-aircraft guns, the field battery and over two hundred vehicles were able to make an orderly withdrawal, without loss, through Kota Bharu. The three forward battalions, involved in intricate country, in darkness and heavy rain, confused by the many streams and swamps and by encounters with small parties of the enemy, found the withdrawal much more difficult. By dawn, somewhat disorganized and very tired, all three were in their allotted positions. They were however to be given little respite.

At 6.30 a.m. on the 9th the enemy, supported by mortars, attacked the right flank of the new position in considerable strength and began to infiltrate through and round it. Key, after a personal recon-naissance, realized that the new line was not suited for prolonged defence and that his troops were too extended. Since all European women and children, the Sultan of Kelantan and his household, and many others had already left Kota Bharu, he had no further need to cover the town. He therefore decided to withdraw southwards by stages. By the afternoon 8th Brigade was on the general line Peringat–Mulong, and 4/19th Hyderabad, which had arrived that morning, in a supporting position at Ketereh. Late that evening Key withdrew his brigade through the Hyderabads to Chondong.

During the 10th there was little action, but many small parties which had been lost or cut off rejoined their units, bringing the strength of the battalions up to some 600 men each. In view of reports of further enemy landings at Kuala Besut received during the after-noon and of the resulting threat to his line of communications, Key abandoned the airfields at Gong Kedah and Machang—neither of which, in the existing circumstances, was of any use to the R.A.F.—and concentrated his brigade immediately south of Machang, where it could better protect its communications. This withdrawal was completed during the 11th December without interference from the enemy. Demolitions were carried out effectively on both road and railway; at both airfields, buildings and petrol stores were fired but the runways were left intact.

Barstow had, in the meantime, submitted to Heath a proposal that 8th Brigade should be withdrawn to the Kuala Lipis area. He pointed out that its primary task had been the defence of the airfields in north Kelantan. All three of these had already been abandoned, and the brigade was left facing an enemy of approximately equal strength, but at the end of a very precarious line of communications consisting of a single line railway from Kuala Krai southwards, which might easily be cut by bombing or sabotage. Though Heath agreed, Percival was not prepared to authorize the proposed withdrawal until he had consulted the Commander-in-Chief, Far East, and the Governor. Heath then decided to press his point of view in person and during the night 11th/12th took the train to Singapore, having arranged to fly back, if possible, to his advanced headquarters at Bukit Mertajam on the afternoon of the 12th. As it turned out his absence from the front at this critical juncture was inopportune.

Units of the Japanese *3rd Air Division* had meanwhile been quick to establish advanced air bases in the Singora area, from which they began to operate large numbers of fighter and light bomber aircraft. Air Marshal Pulford, who fully realized the offensive capabilities of the enemy fighters, decided to use his much depleted bomber force for daylight attacks on Singora. On the 9th December he launched the first raid with six Blenheims from Tengah, routed to pass over Butterworth where they were to have been joined by a fighter escort.[1] The fighters at Butterworth were however fully engaged on standing patrols over the airfield and in providing close support for the army. The Blenheims, deprived of the little protection they might otherwise have been given, flew on to Singora unescorted and on approaching their objective encountered heavy anti-aircraft fire and were intercepted by not less than thirty fighters. They succeeded in bombing a group of fighters on the airfield despite having to take violent evasive action, but three were shot down.

A second raid, planned for later that day, did not take place, for, as a composite force of the remaining Blenheims of 34 and 62 Squadrons was about to take off, the Japanese made a combined bombing and low-level attack on Butterworth airfield. All the Blenheims were damaged or destroyed with the exception of the leading one which had taken off a few seconds before the attack began. Instead of abandoning what was to have been a raid in formation, the pilot (Squadron Leader A. S. K. Scarf) flew on to Singora alone. Despite opposition from a large number of fighters he carried out his bombing attack successfully, but was mortally wounded. Although a running fight continued until the Malayan frontier was reached he was able, before losing consciousness, to make a successful forced landing near Alor Star without injury to his crew.[2]

The intensity of the Japanese air attacks against the forward air-fields in northern Malaya throughout the 8th December had disastrous consequences. There was no effective organization for the

---

[1] See Sketch 4.
[2] Squadron Leader Scarf received the posthumous award of the Victoria Cross for his outstanding gallantry in this action.

fighter defence in the forward areas and the limited light anti-aircraft defences afforded little protection.[1] The warning system was inadequate and squadrons were often caught on the ground refuelling and rearming. At the beginning of the day, the total number of operational aircraft based on airfields in northern Malaya was 110; at the end of it only fifty were fit for operations. As a means of defence and as support for land operations in the forward areas, the British air effort had almost ceased within twenty-four hours of the opening of hostilities. This result had been achieved, with relatively slight loss to themselves, by some 530 aircraft of the Japanese naval and army air forces, operating from airfields in southern Indo-China and southern Siam.

The Commanders-in-Chief, Far East, and Eastern Fleet, believing that the outcome of the fighting in northern Malaya would depend largely on air superiority, telegraphed to the Chiefs of Staff on the 8th December emphasizing the urgent need for reinforcements and, in particular, for two squadrons of long-range bombers and two squadrons of night fighters. They explained that, in the event of the Japanese gaining air superiority, the situation would be very difficult. At the time of the despatch of this message the full extent of the air losses was not known. In fact the Japanese had already gained air superiority.

On the 9th, in accordance with the mutual reinforcement plan, four Dutch submarines and the cruiser *Java* were placed under British orders. The same day three Dutch bomber squadrons and one fighter squadron arrived in Singapore Island.[2] Their aircrews however had not been trained in night flying and, as the operation of bombers by day was not considered feasible until effective fighter cover could be provided, there was no alternative but to return the squadrons, one at a time, to complete their training in the Netherlands East Indies.

Meanwhile Air Marshal Pulford, bearing in mind the serious losses of aircraft which had occurred on forward airfields in northern Malaya, decided early on the 9th to reduce the congestion at Kuantan by withdrawing all but two squadrons to Singapore Island. About midday the Japanese air force attacked the airfield, which was without any anti-aircraft gun defences, and destroyed seven aircraft. Orders were then issued for the withdrawal of the remaining squadrons and from then on the airfield was used only as an advanced landing ground for refuelling.

---

[1] The scale of anti-aircraft artillery for airfields decided upon before the war was to be eight heavy and eight light guns to each airfield; but this was altered after the outbreak of war to four heavy and twelve light guns. In practice, however, owing to lack of resources even this scale was never approached.
[2] Twenty-two Glenn Martins and nine Buffaloes.

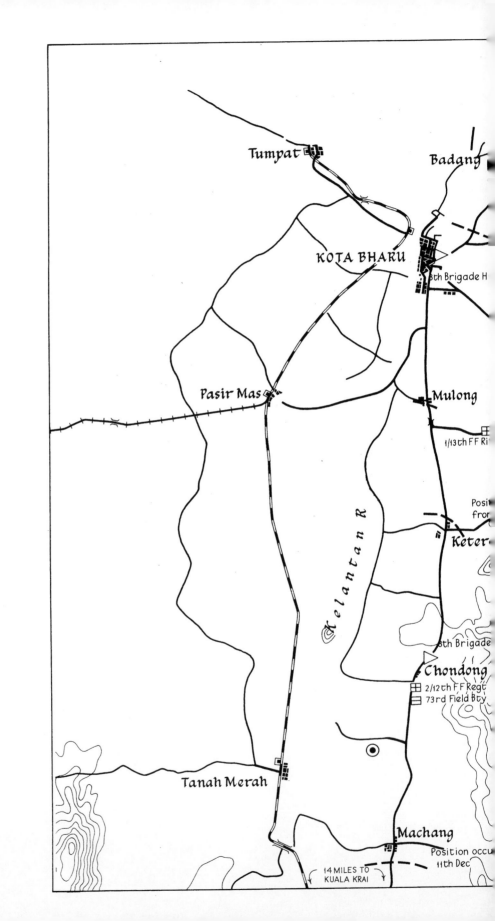

Tumpat

Badang

KOTA BHARU

8th Brigade H

Pasir Mas

Mulong

1/13th FF Ri

Posi
fror

Keter

Kelantan R

8th Brigade

Chondong

2/12th FF Regt
73rd Field Bty

Tanah Merah

Machang

Position occu
11th Dec

14 MILES TO
KUALA KRAI

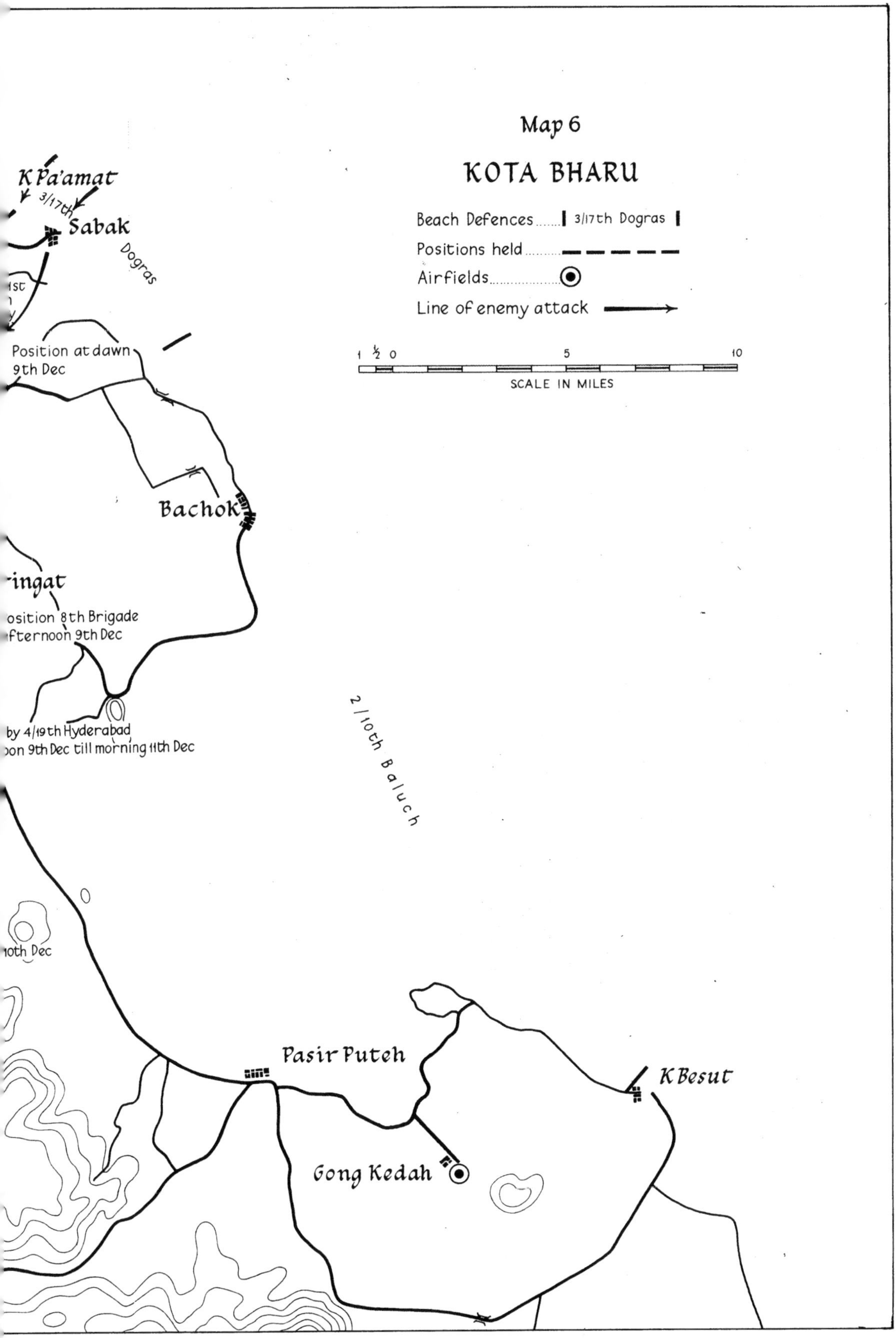

Map 6

KOTA BHARU

Beach Defences......| 3/17th Dogras |
Positions held........ ▬ ▬ ▬ ▬ ▬
Airfields.................◉
Line of enemy attack ━━━➤

|←½→|0━━━━━━━━5━━━━━━━━10
SCALE IN MILES

K Pa'amat
3/17th
Sabak
Dogras
1st

Position at dawn
9th Dec

Bachok

ingat

osition 8th Brigade
fternoon 9th Dec

by 4/19th Hyderabad
oon 9th Dec till morning 11th Dec

oth Dec

2/10th Baluch

Pasir Puteh

K Besut

Gong Kedah

Later that afternoon a Hudson of 8 (GR) Squadron reported a merchant vessel of about 3,000 tons steaming south some seventy-five miles to the north of Kuantan and a group of ten covered barges a similar distance to the south. This apparently reliable sighting report was passed to III Corps and that evening 22nd Brigade (Brigadier Painter) was told that ships towing barges had been observed moving in the direction of Kuantan. Painter warned 2/18th Royal Garhwal Rifles holding the beaches to be on the alert. Not long after dark the battalion reported enemy craft approaching the beaches on its left flank near the mouth of the Sungei Balok.[1] Later similar reports were received from both the centre and right of the battalion's front, accompanied by calls for artillery fire. These calls were answered. Painter reported these events to 9th Division saying that he expected an attack at dawn. Malaya Command was informed about 10 p.m. that a landing was believed to be taking place. Six Vildebeestes and three Hudsons were at once ordered to attack any enemy ships off Kuantan before dawn on the 10th. The Vildebeestes arrived on the scene at 4 a.m. to find only three small boats in the area, which they bombed. The Hudsons, arriving later, found no targets. At dawn no shipping was visible and it became evident that the reports received during the night were false. Enemy patrols may have tried to land, for several small boats, containing some enemy equipment and riddled with bullets, were found four days later stranded on the beaches south of Kuantan. Local Malay fishermen gave as their opinion that these craft had been abandoned near the mouth of the Sungei Balok and had drifted south with the prevailing current to the beaches south of Kuantan. These false reports of a landing were however to have a profound effect on the movement of the British naval forces.

Admiral Phillips called a meeting on board the *Prince of Wales* at 12.30 p.m. on the 8th which was attended by his Chief of Staff (Rear-Admiral A. F. E. Palliser), the Captain of the Fleet (Captain L. H. Bell), the Captains of the *Prince of Wales* (Captain J. C. Leach) and *Repulse* (Captain W. G. Tennant) and staff officers. Phillips told the meeting that his information was that the Japanese were landing at Singora and Kota Bharu and that the transports were being covered by at least one battleship of the *Kongo* class, three heavy and two light cruisers and twenty destroyers. He had little information of the strength, disposition or efficiency of the Japanese air forces in the Indo-China area. He thought that given fighter support and surprise the *Prince of Wales* and *Repulse* would have a good chance of 'smashing the Japanese forces' at Singora and Kota Bharu and he proposed to

---

[1] See Map 15.

P

attack them at dawn on the 10th. All were unanimous that it was impossible for the Navy to remain inactive in this grave emergency and that his plan for a sudden raid, though hazardous, was acceptable. Earlier that morning Admiral Phillips had discussed the question of fighter support with Air Marshal Pulford and had asked for reconnaissance to about 120 miles north of the force during daylight on the 9th, reconnaissance to Singora and beyond from first light on the 10th and fighter protection near Singora at daylight on the 10th. Pulford could give no assurance that he could meet this request until he had further news of the situation in the north.

Force 'Z' consisting of the *Prince of Wales* and *Repulse*, the destroyers *Electra, Express, Vampire* and *Tenedos* left Singapore at 5.35 p.m. on the 8th December. Just before sailing, the Admiral was informed that the provision of fighter protection off Singora on the 10th was doubtful. Course was shaped to the eastward of the Anamba Islands in order to avoid possible minefields.[1] At 1.25 a.m. on the 9th the Commander-in-Chief received a signal from Admiral Palliser, who had remained ashore, which confirmed that the reconnaissance asked for on the 9th would be provided, that it was hoped to carry out a dawn reconnaissance of the coast near Singora on the 10th, but that fighter protection on the 10th would not be possible. It added that the Japanese had large bomber forces based on southern Indo-China and possibly also in Siam, that Kota Bharu airfield had been evacuated and it appeared that 'grip' on the northern airfields was being lost. Although one of the two conditions postulated by Admiral Phillips—fighter support—could not be fulfilled, he decided nevertheless to proceed with his plans provided he was not sighted by aircraft during the 9th, and at 4 a.m. he altered course to the northward.

Shortly after daylight on the 9th an unconfirmed report of a momentary sighting of an enemy aircraft was received from the *Vampire*, but as low cloud and frequent rainstorms favoured evasion the report was disregarded. That evening however the weather cleared and three aircraft were sighted from the *Prince of Wales*. The second of Admiral Phillips' conditions—surprise—had thus gone: the ships would be expected, their targets might well have been withdrawn and a heavy scale of air attack was probable. In these circumstances the Admiral considered that the risk of continuing with the operation was unjustifiable and, having taken steps to shake off the shadowers, at 8.15 p.m. he reluctantly turned and set course at high speed for Singapore.

During the evening a signal from Admiral Palliser gave warning of the possible presence of two aircraft carriers off Saigon and of enemy bombers 'in force and undisturbed' in south Indo-China. It

---

[1] See Map 7.

also told him that all the northern airfields were becoming untenable and that the concentration of all air effort on the defence of Singapore was under consideration. It was followed just before midnight by another signal from Palliser informing him that an enemy landing had been reported at Kuantan. It seemed to the Admiral improbable that the enemy would expect his force, last seen steering to the north-wards in the latitude of Singora, to be as far south as Kuantan by daylight. Kuantan, which he considered to be of military importance, was not far off the return track to Singapore and was 400 miles from the Japanese airfields in Indo-China. On these grounds the Admiral thought surprise possible and the risk justified and at 12.52 a.m. on the 10th he altered course for Kuantan.

He had however underrated Japanese efficiency. The enemy had long been aware of the presence of the *Prince of Wales* and *Repulse* at Singapore—their arrival had been broadcast to the whole world—and had taken elaborate precautions against any interference by the two ships. The *22nd Air Flotilla* reinforced by aircraft from the *21st* and based on airfields in the neighbourhood of Saigon had been specially trained in bombing and torpedo attacks, and its pilots were the pick of the Naval Air Arm. On the morning of the 8th the battle-ships *Kongo* and *Haruna* and two heavy cruisers with a screen of destroyers under the Commander-in-Chief, Vice-Admiral Kondo, were off the coast of Indo-China south of Pulau Condore providing distant cover for the landings. The convoys were escorted by three destroyer divisions and covered by Rear-Admiral Kurita's *7th Cruiser Squadron* (four heavy cruisers) with a number of destroyers. Mines had been laid in the passage between the Anambas and Pulau Tioman on the 6th, and twelve submarines were on patrol off the coast between Singapore and Kota Bharu. At about 1.40 p.m. on the 9th, unbeknown to Admiral Phillips, the most easterly submarine in the patrol line had sighted his force and reported its position, course and speed. Admiral Kondo had at once ordered the *7th Cruiser Squadron* to fly off its aircraft to locate and shadow the British ships and to meet his battle squadron at a rendezvous fifty miles south of Pulau Condore. This junction having been effected at 2.30 a.m. on the 10th, the combined force had taken a southerly course so as to be in a position to intercept the British force that day.

The *22nd Air Flotilla* at Saigon was preparing for a raid on Singa-pore when the report was received. They at once exchanged their bombs for torpedoes and at dusk the aircraft took off for a night attack on Force 'Z'. They were unable however to find the British ships and returned to their base shortly before midnight, but the cruisers' aircraft had sighted the *Prince of Wales* and *Repulse* just before dusk, on a northerly course, and it is probable that these were the aircraft seen by the *Prince of Wales* on the evening of the 9th.

A second submarine in the patrol line sighted Force 'Z' at about 2.10 a.m. on the 10th steering a southerly course and fired five torpedoes, all of which missed their mark. On receiving this new position Admiral Kondo, realizing that his ships had no hope of interception, turned the fleet back to the northward and ordered the *22nd Air Flotilla* to attack at dawn. Twelve reconnaissance aircraft left the Saigon airfield while it was still dark on a sector search of the area in which Force 'Z' had last been reported. They were followed just before dawn by a striking force of eighty-five aircraft (thirty-four high-level bombers and fifty-one torpedo-bombers) organized in flights. Having made their rendezvous the flights flew independently down the 105th Meridian until almost in sight of Singapore without seeing the British ships, and then turned back to the north. At about 10.20 a.m. one of the reconnaissance aircraft sighted the *Prince of Wales* and *Repulse* and directed the striking force to its quarry.

Meanwhile Force 'Z', unaware of the hornets' nest which had been stirred up, had been steaming southward at 25 knots and at dawn on the 10th was sixty miles east-north-east of Kuantan. As it grew light an enemy reconnaissance plane was reported by the *Repulse*. The ships however held their course to the westward. The two heavy ships flew off their aircraft for reconnaissance and anti-submarine patrol, and at 8 a.m. the force arrived off Kuantan. Nothing of the enemy could be seen and the *Express* which was sent in to reconnoitre the harbour reported 'complete peace'. The Commander-in-Chief then decided to go back to examine a small ship and a number of junks and barges which he had passed at extreme range an hour before reaching Kuantan. Course was accordingly altered to the northward and then to the eastward. Shortly after 10 a.m. reports of hostile aircraft were received from the *Tenedos* then being bombed 140 miles to the south-east.[1] At 10.20 a.m. a shadowing aircraft was sighted by the *Prince of Wales* and the first degree of readiness was assumed. Shortly afterwards, enemy aircraft coming in from the south-west were picked up by the *Repulse*'s radar and at 11 a.m. nine aircraft were sighted approaching from the starboard bow at a height of about 10,000 feet. At 11.13 a.m. all ships within range opened fire. Without losing formation the enemy concentrated a high level bombing attack on the *Repulse*. The attack was carried out with great accuracy: bombs fell on either side of the ship and one hit her amidships but failed to pierce the armoured deck.

Twenty minutes later (11.44 a.m.) nine torpedo-bombers attacked from the port bow. The *Repulse* turned to starboard and successfully combed the tracks. The *Prince of Wales* altered to port and was

---

[1] The *Tenedos* had been detached to Singapore at 6.35 p.m. on the 9th as she was short of fuel. Apparently the report that she was being bombed was never received on shore.

18. H.M.S. *Prince of Wales*.

19. H.M.S. *Repulse*.

Their last voyage.
Leaving Johore Strait, 8th December 1941.

20. *Left to right:* Rear-Admiral A. F. E. Palliser and Admiral Sir Tom Phillips.

struck by two torpedoes simultaneously on the port quarter. The effects were disastrous. Both port propeller shafts stopped, the steering gear failed and from that moment the ship was never again under complete control. Within a few minutes she had taken a list of about 13 degrees to port and her speed had dropped to 15 knots. All her secondary armament with the exception of one gun was put out of action.

At 11.50 a.m., uncertain what signals if any had been made by the Flagship, Captain Tennant made an emergency report by wireless 'enemy aircraft bombing'. Shortly afterwards the *Repulse* was attacked almost simultaneously by torpedo and high-level bombers, but by skilful use of the helm Captain Tennant avoided damage in both attacks. At 12.10 p.m. the *Prince of Wales* hoisted the signal 'Not under control' and Captain Tennant, whose ship during the last attack had separated from the Flagship, closed her to ask if he could be of any assistance. He also asked the Commander-in-Chief if his wireless were still in action in case he wished to make any reports, but received no reply. While the ships were in close formation, nine aircraft were sighted low down on the horizon on the starboard bow of the *Repulse*. When about three miles distant they split into two groups. Six aircraft attacked the *Prince of Wales* from starboard. The ship, incapable of rapid manoeuvre, was hit by three torpedoes which reduced her speed to 8 knots. The *Repulse* had turned to starboard to comb the tracks, when the remaining three aircraft which appeared to be making for the *Prince of Wales* suddenly turned and fired a salvo at her, hitting her with one torpedo on the port side. She stood up to the attack well however and continued to manoeuvre at 25 knots; but not for long. Within a few minutes she was attacked by torpedo-bombers which seemed to come in from all directions. The ship was hit by four torpedoes, the first of which jammed the rudder and put the ship out of control. Captain Tennant, realizing that his ship was doomed, gave the order for everyone to come on deck and to cast loose the life-saving floats. The end of the *Repulse* is best told in her Captain's own words:

'Men were now pouring up on deck. They had all been warned twenty-four hours before to carry or wear their life-saving apparatus. When the ship had a thirty degree list to port I looked over the starboard side of the bridge and saw the commander and two or three hundred men collecting on the starboard side. I never saw the slightest sign of panic or ill discipline. I told them from the bridge how well they had fought the ship and wished them good luck. The ship hung for at least a minute and a half to two minutes with a list of about 60 or 70 degrees to port and then rolled over at 12.33 p.m.'

Forty-two out of sixty-nine officers (including Captain Tennant) were picked up by the *Vampire* and *Electra* and 754 out of 1,240 ratings. The work of rescue was not interfered with by the enemy.

Meanwhile the *Prince of Wales* had been heading north at 8 knots with her quarter deck almost awash. Just after the *Repulse* sank, nine high-level bombers attacked from ahead. They scored only one hit, but by this time it was obvious that the ship was sinking. The *Express* went alongside to take off the wounded and men no longer required to fight the ship. By 1.10 p.m. the *Prince of Wales* was settling fast with a heavy list to port and the Captain gave the order to abandon ship. At 1.20 p.m. she heeled over sharply, capsized and sank. Ninety officers out of 110 and 1,195 ratings out of 1,502 were rescued but neither Admiral Phillips nor Captain Leach was among them.

The reason why Admiral Phillips did not report his position when he knew he was being shadowed at 10.20 a.m. on the 10th cannot be explained. While still making for Singora, he had passed a signal to the *Tenedos*, when he detached her on the evening of the 9th, giving an anticipated position of Force 'Z' at dawn on the 11th, with orders that it should be sent by wireless at 8 a.m. on the 10th. This was the only signal he passed to Singapore. The first intimation that he had changed his plan and was off Kuantan was received in the war room at about 11.30 a.m. on the 10th from the pilot of the *Prince of Wales*'s aircraft after landing at Penang. Captain Tennant's emergency signal was the first and only news to reach Singapore that the ships were being attacked. It was handed to the operations room at Air Head-quarters at 12.19 p.m. and seven minutes later eleven Buffaloes of 453 Squadron, which had been specially detailed to stand by at Semba-wang to give air protection to the fleet, took off for the scene of the tragedy to arrive only as the *Prince of Wales* sank. They found the sea covered with men and wreckage. In the distance a flight of Japanese bombers jettisoned their bombs and disappeared over the horizon.

One ray of light emerges from the darkness of the tragedy—the con-duct of the crews of the two ships. The pilot of the first Buffalo to arrive on the scene, in a report to Admiral Layton, paid them high tribute.

> 'It was obvious,' he said, 'that the three destroyers were going to take hours to pick up those hundreds of men clinging to bits of wreckage and swimming round in the filthy, oily water. Above all this the threat of another bombing and machine-gun attack was imminent. Every one of those men must have realized that. Yet as I flew round every man waved and put up his thumb as I flew over him. After an hour lack of petrol forced me to leave, but during that hour I had seen many men in dire danger waving, cheering and joking, as if they were holiday makers at Brighton waving at a low-flying aircraft. It shook me, for here was some-thing above human nature.'

Admiral Layton had already embarked in a liner for passage home when the news of the disaster reached the Admiralty. He was at once recalled and ordered to assume temporary command of the Eastern Fleet.

The news of the victory was naturally received in Japan with jubilation. Her people had good reason to rejoice. Their naval aircraft, four hundred miles from their base, had sunk two capital ships at sea, a feat which no other air force had yet accomplished in the history of war, and this for the trifling loss of three aircraft. Within just over forty-eight hours they had annihilated the American and British Fleets in the Pacific and had gained undisputed command of the sea in the Far East. The loss of the two great ships cast a gloom over the whole of the English-speaking world. In Malaya, where for years the people had been led to believe that once the fleet arrived all would be well, the shock was profound. That evening, at the request of the Commander-in-Chief, Far East, Mr. Duff Cooper made a broadcast speech to the Services and people of Malaya, in which he emphasized that the loss of the two ships was not to lead to despondency but rather to a determination to fight all the harder and so avenge their loss. But the knowledge that the sea around them was in enemy control and that for them there could be no 'Dunkirk' must have, subconsciously, at any rate, affected the troops. Faith in their leaders, who appeared to have misjudged the enemy, was shaken. The catastrophe led to a belief in the invincibility of Japanese air power, a belief which was given strength by the ease with which the enemy outmatched the obsolescent Allied aircraft. It created the myth of Japanese superiority in all three Services, which took a long time to die.

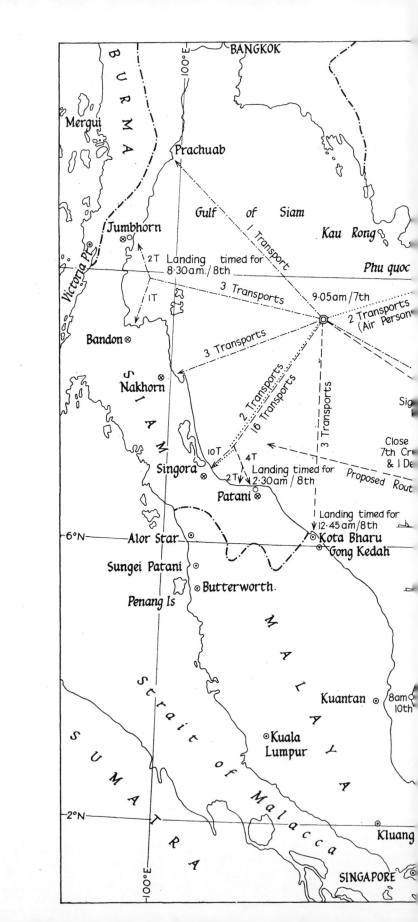

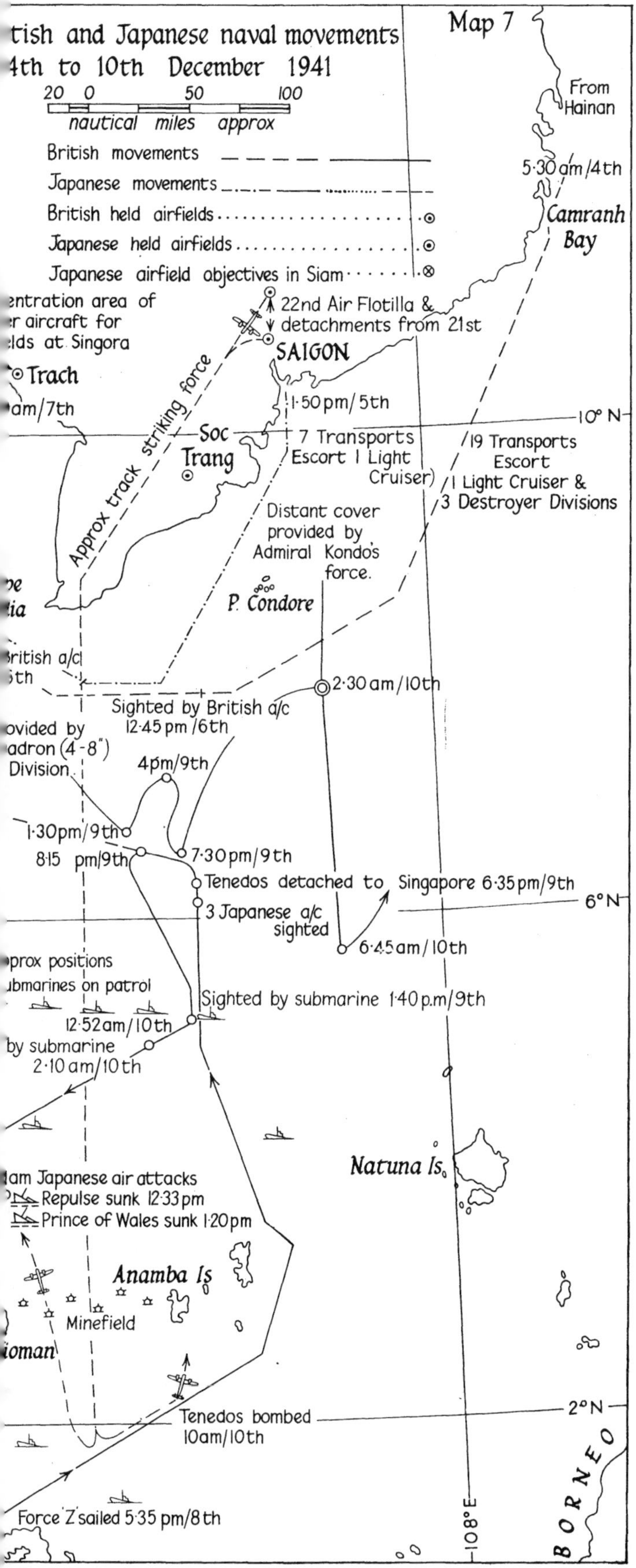

Map 7

British and Japanese naval movements
4th to 10th December 1941

20 0   50   100

nautical miles approx

British movements   – – – – –
Japanese movements – ·· – ·· – ——— ············· – – –
British held airfields ···················· ·⊙
Japanese held airfields ················ ·⊙
Japanese airfield objectives in Siam ····· ·⊗

...entration area of
...r aircraft for
...lds at Singora

·⊙ Trach

...am/7th

From
Hainan

5·30 am/4th

Camranh
Bay

22nd Air Flotilla &
detachments from 21st

SAIGON

1·50 pm/5th

Soc
Trang ⊙

7 Transports
Escort 1 Light
Cruiser

19 Transports
Escort
1 Light Cruiser &
3 Destroyer Divisions

10° N

Distant cover
provided by
Admiral Kondo's
force.

P. Condore

...e
...ia

...ritish a/c
...5th

Approx track striking force

2·30 am/10th

Sighted by British a/c
12·45 pm/6th

...ovided by
...adron (4-8")
...Division

4pm/9th

1·30pm/9th
8·15 pm/9th

7·30 pm/9th

Tenedos detached to Singapore 6·35 pm/9th

3 Japanese a/c
sighted

6° N

6·45 am/10th

...prox positions
...ubmarines on patrol

Sighted by submarine 1·40 p.m/9th

12·52 am/10th

...by submarine
2·10 am/10th

...am Japanese air attacks
Repulse sunk 12·33 pm
Prince of Wales sunk 1·20 pm

Natuna Is.

Anamba Is

Minefield

...oman

2° N

Tenedos bombed
10am/10th

108° E

BORNEO

Force 'Z' sailed 5·35 pm/8th

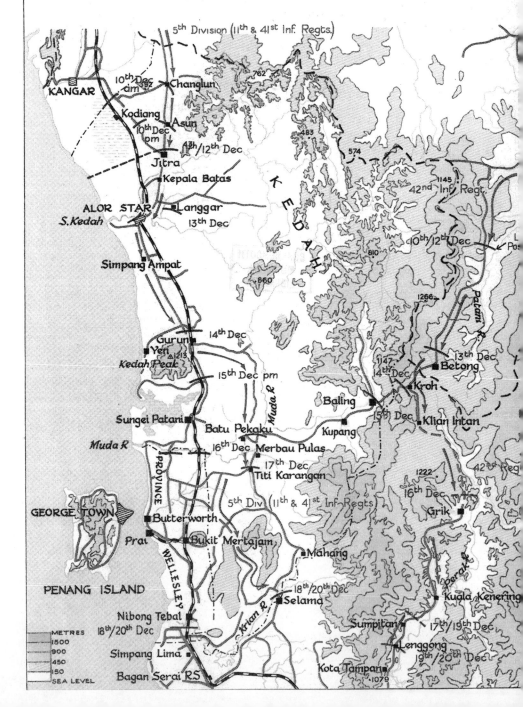

Map 8

KEDAH

0   5   10   15   20   25
Scale of Miles approx.

British in Red
Japanese in Blue

CHAPTER XII

THE FIRST WEEK OF DISASTER

See Maps 5, 8, 9 and 10

THE JAPANESE air offensive directed against the forward airfields in northern Malaya met with such success that, within the first forty-eight hours, Air Command, Far East, was compelled to withdraw squadrons from Alor Star and Sungei Patani, as well as from Kota Bharu, Machang and Gong Kedah. By the evening of the 9th December the combined British fighter and bomber force, then concentrated at the Butterworth air base, was unable to muster more than ten serviceable aircraft, whereas the Japanese by that time were operating some hundred and fifty from their forward airfields in the Singora–Patani area.

The withdrawal of aircraft from airfields exposed to air attacks, against which little defence was possible, had been essential to avoid the destruction of the few still remaining. The withdrawal of the ground staffs, which followed, was however premature and disorderly. With the exception of Kota Bharu, no airfield was at the time within range of Japanese land forces. Nevertheless some airfields, notably at Sungei Patani on the 8th and at Kuantan on the 10th, were hurriedly abandoned, stocks of petrol, oil and stores being left to the enemy. At Alor Star, where the denial scheme was put into effect on the 10th, the pall of smoke and the sound of explosions behind them caused much alarm amongst the forward troops. Orders were therefore issued that, if the air force had to evacuate an airfield in future, no fires were to be started and petrol and oil were to be allowed to run to waste. Demolitions which required the use of explosives were to be undertaken by the army.

Throughout the 11th and 12th there was little air support on either side for the troops engaged in the battle. The Japanese *3rd Air Division* was occupied in establishing advanced units in southern Siam, and in maintaining its offensive so as to drive the British air forces from northern Malaya and ensure that the Japanese troops advancing southwards would be free from air attacks. Headquarters Air Command, Far East, at the same time, was making hurried preparations to use airfields in central and southern Malaya, for which the administrative and maintenance arrangements had to be improvised.

The general air policy at this time was to give priority to the defence of the Naval Base and of convoys bringing reinforcements, and thus all fighter aircraft were based on Singapore. In view however of the complete lack of air defence in northern Malaya, Air Marshal Pulford decided on the 12th, as an emergency measure, to send 453(F) Squadron to Butterworth to support III Corps, although fighter aircraft could only be detached to that area at the expense of the defence of the Naval Base.

A solitary Buffalo aircraft, operating from Butterworth, undertook long-range photographic reconnaissance and provided valuable information, but little use could be made of it. The report of one hundred Japanese aircraft concentrated on the airfield near Bangkok served only to emphasize the meagre resources of the British air forces. Despite the attractive target offered by the enemy aircraft crowded on the airfield at Singora and elsewhere, the only attack that could be made on enemy airfields was one on the 12th by three Blenheim bombers from Singapore on Singora, and this caused little damage. Thereafter Pulford decided that, owing to the impossibility of providing fighter protection, all bombing attacks by day would have to be abandoned.

On the 10th December Mr. Duff Cooper was appointed Resident Minister for Far Eastern Affairs with Cabinet rank. His terms of reference were to assist the successful conduct of operations in the Far East by:

(a) relieving the Commanders-in-Chief, as far as possible, of the extraneous responsibilities with which they had up to that time been burdened;

(b) giving them broad political guidance;

(c) settling emergency matters on the spot, when time did not permit reference to Whitehall;

(d) while expenditure remained the responsibility of the appropriate Minister in London, and departmental representatives on the spot were to work under existing delegated powers, the Resident Minister was authorized, at his own discretion, to give overriding authority to departmental officers to incur expenditure when he was satisfied that urgent action was necessary and that there was no time to refer to Whitehall. (The proviso was added that such action would rarely be necessary where large financial commitments were involved.)

The terms of reference included however a paragraph that the appointment of a Resident Minister was not in any way to impair the existing responsibilities of the Commanders-in-Chief or His Majesty's representatives in the Far East, or their official relationships with their respective departments in London, with which they were to continue to correspond direct.

The Resident Minister was also to preside over a War Council. The members of this body were the Governor of the Straits Settlements and High Commissioner, Malaya, the Commander-in-Chief, Far East, the Commander-in-Chief, Eastern Fleet, the General Officer Commanding, Malaya, the Air Officer Commanding, Far East, Mr. V. G. Bowden (representing the Australian Government), and later Sir George Sansom who was responsible for propaganda and press control. In addition Major-General Bennett, commanding the Australian Imperial Forces, was at liberty to attend meetings if and when he wished to do so. The War Council held its first meeting that evening and thereafter met every morning. Although it was designed to be a consultative and co-ordinating body for the war effort throughout the Far East, in practice, as the war progressed, its attention was concentrated mainly on events in Malaya.

The first flight of the Japanese *5th Division* and its attached units had completed its concentration in the Singora–Patani area by the evening of the 8th December.[1] On landing, the Japanese had met with only half-hearted resistance from Siamese constabulary, which had been quickly overcome. Thereafter the attitude of the local population towards the Japanese troops was not unfriendly and, in fact, some assistance was given in administrative matters.

The *5th Division's* orders were to advance rapidly southwards to the line of the Perak River, as the first stage in the conquest of Malaya. It began its drive southwards from the assembly area without delay, using the two roads, Singora to Alor Star, and Patani to Kroh. The *9th Infantry Brigade (11th and 41st Infantry Regiments)*, supported by a tank battalion and a battalion of field artillery, moved down the Alor Star road with orders to engage and destroy the British forces known to be at Jitra.[2] The *42nd Infantry Regiment*, with two companies of light tanks and a battery of field artillery, moved by the Kroh road, with the object of breaking through any opposition and cutting the communications of any British forces north of the Perak River

The 11th Division had meanwhile moved from its assembly areas for 'Matador' into its defensive position astride the road junction at Jitra, where the road to Kangar branched from the main trunk road to Siam. This, the only possible tactical position for the defence of the area, would not have been used but for the necessity to protect the airfield at Alor Star and the group of airfields further south. It had been only partly prepared before the outbreak of war. Work on

[1] See Appendix 18.
[2] See Map 8.

the defences had been undertaken by the troops themselves, at a time
when they were also engaged in preparation and training for operation 'Matador' which understandably had priority. The work therefore was delayed and, although much had been done, it was far from
complete. To make matters worse, when the troops came to occupy
the position, they found that most of the defensive localities already
prepared had become waterlogged with the heavy rain which had
been incessant for two days. Moreover some of the stores required for
the defences were held by the division in readiness for its advance
into Siam. Thus, when the alternative defensive plan was adopted,
the troops moving into position had to erect barbed wire, lay anti-
tank mines and provide signal communications. There was no time
to do more than lay field telephone cables on the soaking ground,
with the result that signal communications within the division often
proved ineffective.

The position was to be held by two brigades forward (15th on the
right, 6th on the left), and one brigade (28th) in reserve.[1] The
15th Brigade, with 2/9th Jat on the right and 1st Leicestershire on
the left, held a front of some 6,000 yards from the jungle-clad hills on
the right flank, through the flooded rice fields and then through the
rubber estates astride the main road to Manggoi. The 6th Brigade,
with 2nd East Surrey on the right and 2/16th Punjab on the left,
extended the position for some 18,000 yards to the sea coast; with the
exception of the sector given to 2nd East Surrey and a belt of cultivated country on either side of the main railway line, the greater part
of this wide front consisted of swamp. Artillery support was provided
by 155th Field Regiment of two batteries, 22nd Mountain Regiment (less two batteries), and 80th Anti-Tank Regiment (less one
battery).

Early on the morning of the 10th, the Japanese crossed the frontier
and made contact with forward detachments of 1/14th Punjab, the
third battalion of 15th Brigade, which was providing both the
covering and outpost troops of this sector.[2] The Punjabis withdrew
slowly southwards. Meanwhile, to give sufficient time for 15th and
6th Brigades to prepare and occupy their allotted sectors, General
Murray-Lyon instructed Brigadier Garrett (15th Brigade) to delay
the enemy north of Jitra till dawn on the 12th, and gave him
2/1st Gurkha Rifles (less one company) from 28th Brigade to assist
him. Garrett ordered this unit to take over the outpost position at
Asun, and concentrated the whole of the Punjabis forward.[3]

By the evening of the 10th the Punjabis were occupying a defensive

---

[1] See Map 9.
[2] The advanced guard of *5th Division* consisted of: *5th Reconnaissance Regiment, II/41st
Battalion*, one mountain artillery battery, one tank company and one engineer platoon.
[3] 4th Mountain Battery (two Breda guns of which were given an anti-tank role), and
one section 2nd Anti-Tank Battery were under command.

position at Changlun.[1] At about 8 a.m. on the 11th, enemy infantry attacked and, in the fighting, the defence lost some ground and the two Breda anti-tank guns. Since the role of the battalion was to delay the enemy without becoming too involved, Garrett had decided to withdraw it during the afternoon through the outpost position at Asun, but at 3 p.m. Murray-Lyon ordered him to occupy an intermediate position near Nangka, some two miles north of the outpost position, and to hold it overnight. The Punjabis were moving to this position in heavy rain and in poor visibility when at 4.30 p.m. a Japanese mechanized force, led by medium tanks followed by lorried infantry, suddenly attacked the rear of the column. Firing indiscriminately ahead and to both sides, the tanks broke through the rearguard and drove through the column, overrunning the section of 2nd Anti-Tank Battery which was limbered up and not in action. They caused utter consternation among the Indian troops, most of whom had never before seen a tank.

The enemy column then rushed the bridge in front of the outpost position before it could be blown up, and was brought to a halt only when the leading tank was hit and disabled by anti-tank rifle fire. This blocked the road well within the outpost position held by the Gurkhas. In a gallant but unsuccessful attempt to blow the bridge the officer commanding 23rd Field Company S. & M. lost his life. The Punjabis were thrown into confusion by this attack and forced off the road. Only some 200 men, including the Brigadier, succeeded in rejoining the division the following day. Small parties made their way back later but, for the time being, the battalion could not be regarded as a fighting unit.

Taking advantage of the confusion, the Japanese infantry attacked the Gurkhas frontally and from the flanks, managed to clear the road and allowed the tanks to resume their advance. They quickly broke through the outpost position, overwhelming most of the forward troops and isolating battalion headquarters. All attempts to withdraw the battalion in an orderly fashion failed; small parties however succeeded in fighting their way out, and others found their way back to 15th Brigade next day.

On the left flank of the divisional front the covering troops of 6th Brigade were withdrawn to Kodiang on the 10th. The withdrawal of British forces from the State of Perlis resulted in a protest by the Sultan, on the ground that failure to provide protection for the State in time of war was a violation of the treaty obligations undertaken by Great Britain. On the 11th both the covering and outpost troops of 6th Brigade were ordered to withdraw within the main Jitra position. While the column was on the move after dark

---

[1] See Map 8.

the officer responsible for the demolition of the road bridge over the stream at Manggoi, thinking the approaching column was the enemy, blew the bridge on his own initiative. As there was no suitable material to hand with which to repair it in the time available, all the transport and some of the carriers of the column, together with seven anti-tank and four mountain guns, had to be abandoned.

The disaster to 1/14th Punjab and 2/1st Gurkha Rifles, followed by the loss of this artillery, was a severe blow, for it not only further lowered the morale of 11th Division but affected the tactical conduct of the subsequent fighting on the Kedah front. The immediate effect was that General Murray-Lyon ordered Brigadier Carpendale (28th Brigade) to assume command of 15th Brigade in place of Garrett who was missing, and placed a further battalion of 28th Brigade (2/2nd Gurkha Rifles) under the orders of 15th Brigade so as to provide it with a reserve. This left him with only one battalion in 28th Brigade; and this he had already disposed for the protection of the Alor Star–Sungei Patani area. Thus he had no divisional reserve.

Early in the evening of the 11th, enemy infantry came into contact with 2/9th Jats and began to feel for the right flank. At about 8.30 p.m. Japanese tanks with their headlights on drove southwards down the main road towards the centre of the position. They overran a forward patrol of 1st Leicestershire before the two leading tanks were hit by 215th Anti-Tank Battery and brought to a standstill in front of the main position. During the night the Jats were heavily sniped, and inaccurate reports were sent back to brigade head-quarters that the enemy had occupied Bukit Jantan and Bukit Alur. These reports caused Carpendale to come to the conclusion that there was a distinct danger of the Japanese enveloping his right flank, and without reference to his divisional commander he asked Brigadier Lay (6th Brigade) for assistance. Lay responded by placing two companies of his reserve battalion (1/8th Punjab) and, later, two companies of 2/16th Punjab at his disposal. Carpendale then ordered his reserve battalion (2/2nd Gurkha Rifles) to occupy a position on the line of the Sungei Bata from the bridge on the trunk road east-wards, with one company of 1/8th Punjab on its right, and sent the two companies of 2/16th Punjab to Kelubi to strengthen the rear of his right flank. These moves were completed before dawn. He ordered the second company of 1/8th Punjab to hold the line of the Sungei Jitra east of the main road, in rear of the left of the Jats, but recalled it before it reached its position.

At 3 a.m. on the 12th the Japanese rushed the block on the trunk road and penetrated into the area held by the right forward company of the Leicesters; immediate counter-attack failed and it was not till dawn that a further counter-attack supported by carriers drove them out. At about 6 a.m., in heavy rain, an enemy infantry company supported by fire from tanks launched a frontal attack east of the road at the junction of 1st Leicestershire and 2/9th Jats, which penetrated some distance between the two battalions and overran a forward artillery observation post. Another immediate counter-attack failed but the enemy made no attempt to exploit his success. Considering it essential to drive the enemy out of this area, Carpendale once again called on Lay for assistance. He was given the headquarters and the remaining two companies of 1/8th Punjab, and ordered them to launch a deliberate counter-attack supported by artillery to regain the lost ground. Moving to the attack, part of the battalion passed close to the headquarters of the Jats who, mistaking it for the enemy, opened fire. This unfortunate incident caused a delay which resulted in the loss of the planned artillery support, and when at 10 a.m. the attack was eventually launched it failed with heavy loss, the commanding officer being killed.

Early on the morning of the 12th, Murray-Lyon learnt of these events from his forward brigades. At 9 a.m. he went forward to 15th Brigade Headquarters and, from the information available there, he concluded that an enveloping movement round the right flank was in progress. Owing to the loss of the two battalions on the 11th and Carpendale's action in committing, without his authority, all the reserves of 6th Brigade during the night, he had no reserves available with which to influence the battle. His troops were tired and dispirited, and the fact that Krohcol, in face of superior enemy forces supported by tanks, was being forced to withdraw made him anxious about his communications. It had been impressed on him that, as his division was the only one with which northern Malaya could be defended, he was to take no risks. In the circumstances he decided to ask for permission to withdraw from Jitra and occupy the previously selected defensive position at Gurun, some thirty miles further south. His request was referred through Headquarters III Corps to Malaya Command, since General Heath was at the time at Singapore. General Percival thought that, apart from tactical considerations, such an early and long withdrawal would have a demoralizing effect both on the troops and on the civil population. His views were endorsed by the Far East War Council, and Murray-Lyon was told that, pending further orders, the battle was to be fought out at Jitra.

About noon the commander of the Japanese *9th Infantry Brigade* (Major-General Kawamura) visited his forward area and ordered *41st Infantry Regiment* to relieve the advanced guard and deliver a night attack on the eastern side of the road, while *11th Infantry Regiment* attacked simultaneously on the western side. Shortly afterwards, however, the enemy advanced guard launched a further attack in battalion strength immediately east of the main road. After

extremely fierce fighting the Japanese drove a wedge into the centre
of 15th Brigade's position, overrunning the left forward company of
the Jats and forcing the company immediately behind it to withdraw
to the south-east. They then attacked the right of the Leicesters and
by 2.30 p.m. had made contact with 2/2nd Gurkha Rifles on the line
of the Sungei Bata. Both these battalions, although there was a gap
of about a mile between them, held firm, and a counter-attack by the
carrier platoon from 2nd East Surrey, sent across from 6th Brigade,
temporarily checked the enemy's attempt to envelop the Leicesters'
right. By 3 p.m. all was quiet.

Murray-Lyon visited 15th Brigade Headquarters early in the
afternoon and found Carpendale full of confidence and convinced
that the Japanese had shot their bolt for the day. As the flanks of
both the Jats and the Leicesters were by now dangerously exposed,
he had planned that during the evening the former should withdraw
to fill the gap between Kelubi and the right of the Punjabis on the
Sungei Bata, and the latter should concentrate west of the trunk road
and north of the river from where they could counter-attack eastwards next morning. He had suggested to Lay that the East Surreys
might also counter-attack on the left (northern) flank of the Leicesters.
Murray-Lyon approved this plan, except for the proposed use of the
East Surreys, for he required them as a divisional reserve and for
other tasks. He then went to 6th Brigade Headquarters. There he
ordered Lay to move the two companies of the East Surreys nearest
to the railway by train to Kepala Batas to protect the bridges over
the Sungei Kedah and, as soon as the Leicesters had linked up with
2/2nd Gurkhas, to withdraw the remainder of the battalion into
reserve at the Alor Star airfield.

Carpendale abandoned his plan for concentrating the Leicesters for
a counter-attack and, deciding to give them a defensive task instead,
ordered them at about 3.15 p.m. to withdraw to a line from Rimba
along the Sungei Jitra to within half a mile of the trunk road and
thence due south through Padang to the Sungei Bata. The Leicesters,
who felt secure in their existing defences and who had suffered only
thirty casualties, protested, pointing out that the new line had no
depth, ran through rice-fields and was unreconnoitred. Carpendale
however insisted that the withdrawal should take place. It began at
4 p.m. and was completed with great difficulty and some confusion
by 7.30 p.m. The only means of communication that the battalion
then had with its companies and with brigade headquarters was by
runners to whom the country was unknown. The Jats withdrew as
planned except for the right forward company to which no orders
were sent, owing to false reports that it had been overrun.

When at about 6 p.m., on his way back to his headquarters,
Murray-Lyon reached the trunk road south of Tanjong Pau, he

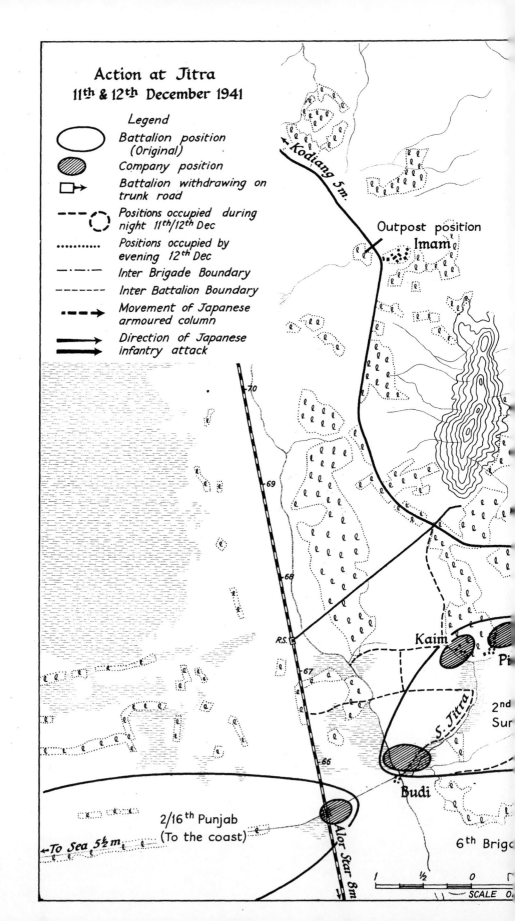

Action at Jitra
11th & 12th December 1941

Legend

⬭ Battalion position (Original)

⬭ (shaded) Company position

⬕→ Battalion withdrawing on trunk road

--◯ Positions occupied during night 11th/12th Dec

·········· Positions occupied by evening 12th Dec

—·—·— Inter Brigade Boundary

— — — Inter Battalion Boundary

▪▪▪▶ Movement of Japanese armoured column

▬▬▶ Direction of Japanese infantry attack

←Kodiang 5m.

Outpost position
Imam

70

69

68

R.S.

67

66

Kaim

Pi

2nd
Sur

S. Jitra

Budi

2/16th Punjab
(To the coast)

←To Sea 5½m.

Alor Star 8m.

6th Brig

1   ½   0

SCALE 0

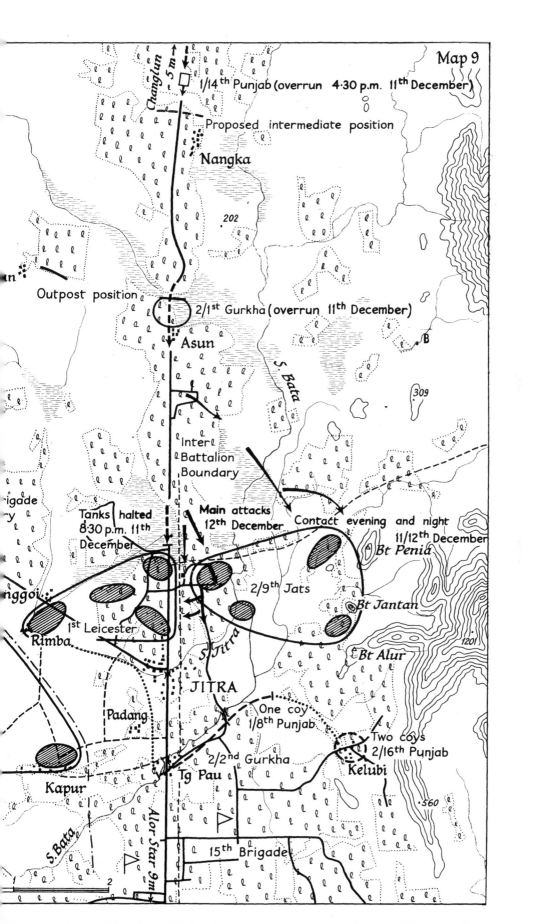

Map 9

Changlun 5 m

1/14th Punjab (overrun 4·30 p.m. 11th December)

Proposed intermediate position

Nangka

202

Outpost position

2/1st Gurkha (overrun 11th December)

Asun

B

S. Bata

309

Inter
Battalion
Boundary

Main attacks
12th December

Contact evening and night
11/12th December

Tanks halted
8·30 p.m. 11th
December

Bt Penia

nggoi

2/9th Jats

Bt Jantan

1st Leicester

1201

Rimba

S. Jitra

Bt Alur

JITRA

One coy
1/8th Punjab

Padang

Two coys
2/16th Punjab

2/2nd Gurkha

Kelubi

Tg Pau

·560

Kapur

Alor Star 9m

S. Bata

15th Brigade

1   2

found a scene of panic amongst the transport, caused by false reports that tanks had crossed the Sungei Bata. Back at his own headquarters at 6.30 p.m. reports awaited him that the Leicesters had been attacked as they were withdrawing, that the Jats had been overrun and that the enemy was attacking 2/16th Punjab at Kelubi—all of which were untrue—and that 3/16th Punjab (Krohcol) had reached Kroh with its strength reduced to three hundred and fifty.

Realizing that there was a distinct danger to his communications, since Krohcol was unlikely to halt the enemy in the Kroh–Baling area for more than two to three days, Murray-Lyon appreciated that he could not delay for long a withdrawal well to the south. He also realized that the enemy with the support of tanks might destroy his tired and disorganized division next day, unless he could get it behind a tank obstacle. He therefore decided that a withdrawal during the night behind the Sungei Kedah had become essential, and at 7.30 p.m., again asked for permission to fall back to the position covering Gurun. His request was passed by III Corps to Headquarters Malaya Command, where General Heath was still with General Percival.[1]

Heath, after consultation with Percival, sent the following message to Murray-Lyon through III Corps Headquarters:

> 'It is decided that your task is to fight for the security of north Kedah. It is estimated that you are only opposed by one Japanese division. Consider best solution may be to hold up the advance of enemy tanks on good obstacles and dispose your forces to obtain considerable depth on both roads and to obtain scope for your superior artillery. Reserves for employment in the divisional area are being expedited.'

In passing this message to 11th Division by telephone, III Corps Headquarters gave Murray-Lyon discretion to withdraw from the Jitra position and informed him that Krohcol would cease to be under his command from midnight 12th/13th December.

At 10 p.m. Murray-Lyon issued orders for 11th Division to withdraw to the south bank of the Sungei Kedah at Alor Star, starting at midnight. The disengagement and withdrawal from Jitra on the night of 12th/13th, on a single road, in exceedingly bad weather, and over a distance of fifteen miles was a most difficult operation for young and insufficiently trained troops, who were extremely tired and whose morale had been severely shaken. Units were widely scattered, the area was ill-served by communications and, though the enemy did not follow up closely, the withdrawal proved disastrous. Some units

---

[1] General Heath could not be flown back to his headquarters and had to await a night train to the north. See page 191.

Q

did not receive the order and were still in position the following morning;[1] these got away next day in small parties, but with the loss of most of their equipment. There were no roads to the west of the position. Many units, fearing congestion on the trunk road and the possibility of meeting enemy tanks, decided to make their way across country. Some units made their way along the railway to Alor Star; others made for the coast hoping to be able to move south by boat and rejoin their division later; some were ship-wrecked; one small party eventually reached northern Sumatra. Much equipment was lost; guns and motor vehicles became bogged in the mud and had to be abandoned.

Shortly after midnight the Japanese made an attempt to rush the bridge over the Sungei Bata but were repulsed by 2/2nd Gurkha Rifles. At 2 a.m. on the 13th the bridge was destroyed and the battalion withdrew through a rearguard formed by 2/9th Gurkha Rifles. The rearguard, after a sharp action, withdrew at 4.30 a.m. Contact with the enemy was temporarily broken.

The action at Jitra was a major disaster for the British forces in Malaya. The main body of the enemy *5th Division* was never employed. A Japanese advanced guard of a strength equivalent to two battalions supported by a company of tanks had, with comparatively few casualties, defeated 11th Division and driven it from its prepared defensive position in some thirty-six hours. The British losses were severe: 15th Brigade was reduced to about a quarter of its strength, 6th Brigade was seriously depleted, and in 28th Brigade two battalions had some 100 casualties each, while the third battalion (2/1st Gurkha Rifles) was reduced to one company. The losses in guns, equipment and transport were heavy. The loss of morale was more serious. With insufficient reserves of men and equipment to replace losses and with no reserve formation at hand to relieve it, the division was to be hard put to it to recover its cohesion.

What were the causes of this disaster? The fact that the 'Matador' operation was one of two alternative plans to be adopted on the outbreak of war was undoubtedly a primary cause. Preparations for this operation had reduced the time that 11th Division had been able to give to the construction of the Jitra position, with the result that when that position had to be occupied it was far from complete; they had also interfered with the training of the troops for a defensive battle; and they prevented commanders from giving their full attention to the study of the defence of Kedah. The subsequent indecision as to which of the two alternative roles 11th Division was to adopt

---

[1] Two companies 1st Leicestershire, one company 2/9th Jats, and a detachment 2/1st Gurkha Rifles.

presented the enemy with many hours' start, and in so doing, caused General Murray-Lyon to reinforce his covering and outpost troops, and to ask them to delay the enemy for longer than was reasonable in the circumstances. Despite the fact that the initial clashes at Sadao had shown that the Japanese had tanks, two battalions were committed without adequate anti-tank support to a long delaying action north of the Asun swamp, the only possible tank obstacle covering the Jitra position. The few anti-tank guns failed to stop the tanks and the demolition of the one vital bridge was unsuccessful. Two battalions, a mountain battery and some anti-tank guns were lost, and with them the major part of the divisional reserve.

The long period of indecision as to the role which the division was to adopt, besides giving the enemy several hours start, had had a psychological effect on the troops and added to the disadvantages under which they went into battle. They had partly prepared a defensive position when they were told to prepare for an offensive operation. When the moment for action arrived, they were standing by ready to advance to forestall the enemy at Singora. The unexplained delay which followed made them restive. Then came the order to occupy their defensive positions. They marched there in the pouring rain to find their defences waterlogged, and had to start again to put them in order. It is small wonder they were dispirited.

Even in the best circumstances they were not in a fit condition to meet a first-class enemy on equal terms. Due mainly to the constant calls to return trained men to India to facilitate the raising of new units, and to the standard of the recruits received in exchange, the basic training of the units forming the division was inadequate. Brigade and divisional training had not been possible owing to the late arrival of artillery and signal units. In consequence commanders and their staffs had not had sufficient practice in handling their formations in the field. It should thus cause no surprise that, when battle was joined, these two factors resulted in demolitions failing or being ordered prematurely, and in inaccurate reports of enemy movements being sent back which led to commanders making false appreciations of the situation and to the faulty use of reserves.

The Japanese speed of movement, their ability to overcome obstacles and their bold use of tanks, came as a complete surprise. Against partly-trained troops without armour or air support, ill-provided with anti-tank weapons and already off their balance as a result of the period of indecision, the sudden onslaught proved decisive. The enemy thus came into contact with 11th Division at Jitra before it was fully ready, and Murray-Lyon was left without a reserve.

The deployment of 11th Division at Jitra led to defeat in detail. It was only on the two roads, less than 3,000 yards apart on the selected alignment, that the enemy could bring his strength to bear with any weight and speed. But, instead of the defence being organized in depth astride these roads near their junction, 11th Division, in an attempt to guard every subsidiary line of approach, was spread over a front of seven miles with half a battalion detached on the coast. Because of the poor lateral communications and this wide dispersion, when the Japanese attack fell on the right-hand brigade, the remainder of the division could take no part in the action. During the night of the 11th/12th all local reserves of the two forward brigades were committed to action without the knowledge of the divisional commander. On the morning of the 12th, Murray-Lyon without a divisional reserve, was powerless to sway the course of the action. Thus when the Japanese advanced guard made a deep penetration into one battalion area, there was no means at hand to eject them; the prepared positions were abandoned and confusion reigned.

Even before the penetration Murray-Lyon was faced with a difficult decision. Since he was unable to counter-attack, he had to decide whether to withdraw while he could, or attempt to hold the position against further and heavier enemy attacks which might break through and destroy his division. It must not be forgotten that he was also responsible for the critical operations of Krohcol, which he was expected to control from a distance of more than a hundred miles with unreliable communications.[1] Before the Japanese invasion he had frequently urged that he should be relieved of this responsibility. His requests had been refused and he was therefore unable to give his undivided attention to the confused battle which developed at Jitra. In the circumstances, his inevitable anxiety over Krohcol was bound to affect the decision he had to make. He had in addition been told that, as his division provided the only defence for northern Malaya, he was not to risk heavy losses. The situation at Jitra on the morning of the 12th was such that the destruction of the division was a possibility: he therefore decided that his best course of action was to withdraw. But, as the enemy's rapid progress on the Kroh road threatened his lines of communication, he asked permission to withdraw his division thirty miles to the position at Gurun which had been reconnoitred but not prepared, instead of to the Sungei Kedah which offered an excellent tank obstacle. He was told however to fight it out at Jitra. But by evening the situation was so much worse that a withdrawal was inevitable and once again he asked for permission to go back to Gurun. This was granted, but by this time there was considerable disorganization among the forward troops and there was little time for orders to reach them. He had to decide between two hazardous alternatives—to risk an unreconnoitred withdrawal at night under extremely difficult conditions,

[1] The civil telegraph and telephone systems provided the sole means of communication between the two forces.

or to hold on till dawn and withdraw in daylight. The latter would give the enemy time to launch a dawn attack on unprepared positions lacking anti-tank defences and located in front of a river line, and, since he had by that time complete local air superiority, would offer opportunities of causing heavy casualties to the withdrawing troops and transport, especially at the bridges over the Sungei Kedah. It was a difficult decision for any commander to make. Murray-Lyon chose to withdraw under cover of darkness. With the knowledge we now have of the Japanese plan for a night attack astride the trunk road by two regiments, it is clear that the course which he took was the lesser of two evils.

In response to Murray-Lyon's repeated requests, Heath took over direct command of Krohcol and the responsibility for the vitally important Kroh–Baling road at midnight on the 12th/13th December.[1] At the same time Percival placed 12th Brigade (less 4/19th Hyderabad already in Kelantan)[2] at the disposal of III Corps and arranged to move it by rail to Ipoh. The leading battalion—2nd Argyll and Sutherland Highlanders (Lieut.-Colonel I. McA. Stewart)—was due at 4 p.m. on the 13th, and Brigade Headquarters and 5/2nd Punjab twenty-four hours later.

The threat to 11th Division resulting from the Japanese advance along the Patani–Kroh road continued to grow. Following up his successes of the 12th, the enemy quickly made contact with 5/14th Punjab during the night of the 12th/13th. To avoid becoming too heavily engaged this battalion withdrew about noon on the 13th to Betong, from where, after destroying the road bridge, it moved to join 3/16th Punjab in the defensive position west of Kroh. This withdrawal uncovered the road running south from the village of Kroh through Grik to link with the main west coast road at Kuala Kangsar. North of Grik, it was little more than a narrow unmetalled track fit for use by light motor vehicles in dry weather. Nevertheless, as the Japanese infantry could use it, it represented a serious threat to the line of communication serving III Corps. On the afternoon of the 13th Heath therefore sent one company of 2nd Argyll and Sutherland Highlanders with some armoured cars to Grik to secure this route. He moved the remainder of the battalion to Baling with orders to take up a defensive position in support of Krohcol by 4 p.m. the following day.

On the 14th he placed Krohcol under the command of Brigadier Paris (12th Brigade) and ordered him to protect the right flank of 11th Division's communications against any enemy advance along

---

[1] See Map 8.
[2] See page 189.

the Kroh–Baling road. Brigadier Paris thereupon sent 5/2nd Punjab
to Merbau Pulas to protect his left flank and instructed Krohcol to
withdraw during the night of the 14th/15th through the Argylls who,
in accordance with their previous instructions, were in the process of
occupying a position covering Baling.

On the Kedah front 11th Division had succeeded in withdrawing
south of the Sungei Kedah by 9 a.m. on the 13th December. The
6th Brigade held a line astride the railway and road at Simpang
Ampat, covered by rearguards found by 28th Brigade, at Alor Star
on the Sungei Kedah, and at Langgar on the right flank; 15th
Brigade was in reserve. There the division paused to reorganize its
scattered units. There was however considerable confusion south of
the river as large numbers of stragglers, many without arms, made
their way back from Jitra to rejoin their units. This confusion was not
lessened by the presence of Japanese snipers who, wearing Malay
dress, had infiltrated into the area.

The road and railway bridges at Alor Star had not been prepared
for demolition, though the charges had been stored alongside them.
These charges were hastily laid during the night of the 12th/13th
December. Early next morning Murray-Lyon and his senior Royal
Engineer officer, Lieut.-Colonel J. F. D. Steedman, were at the
bridge awaiting the arrival of the last of the retreating troops, when
two Japanese motor cyclists reached it. These having been disposed
of, the General gave the order to blow the bridges. The demolition
of the road bridge was successful, but the railway bridge though
damaged, failed to fall.[1] At this moment the armoured train arrived
from the north and, to complete the destruction of the bridge, was
ordered to steam across it. To everyone's amazement the driverless
train jumped the severed rails, and disappeared to the south. It
reached Taiping before coming to a standstill. Shortly afterwards the
Japanese closed up to the river and during the day made a determined effort to force a crossing. Although at one moment they gained
a foothold on the south bank, a counter-attack by 2/9th Gurkha
Rifles drove them back across the river.

It was obvious by this time that many of the British and Indian
troops were in no condition to withstand an attack in strength.
Murray-Lyon accordingly ordered the withdrawal to continue to the
reconnoitred but unprepared position at Gurun, some twenty miles
further south. This was carried out throughout the night of the
13th/14th along a road jammed with traffic and in heavy rain.

---

[1] Eight carriers of the 2nd East Surreys were cut off when the bridge was demolished.

Owing to orders going astray 6th Brigade's retirement started very late and its rear battalion (1/8th Punjab), weary and hungry, did not reach Gurun till midday on the 14th.

The Gurun position lay astride the main road and railway, about three miles north of Gurun, between the jungle-covered slopes of Kedah Peak rising to 4,000 feet on the west, and the jungle area two miles further east on the far side of the railway.[1] It had been selected before the outbreak of war and the intention had been that, when required, civilian labour would prepare it for defence. The necessary labour was found, but there was not time to make use of it and during the confusion of the retreat it dispersed. In consequence when the troops, who had been fighting or on the move for a week, arrived in the area they had once again to set about this arduous task. They had very little time, for the Japanese advanced far more quickly than had been expected.

The 11th Division plan for the occupation of the new position placed 6th Brigade on the left covering the railway and trunk road, with 28th Brigade on its right and the depleted 15th Brigade, about 600 strong, in reserve.[2] The 88th Field Regiment, with an extra battery and three anti-tank batteries, provided the support for both brigades; observation was however restricted and the forward localities had only a limited field of fire.

The last of the troops had hardly reached their allotted positions when opposing patrols met near the crossroads. At 2 p.m. about a dozen lorries carrying infantry, preceded by three tanks, came down the road. The presence of tanks came as a great surprise, for it had been expected that the damage to the bridges over the Kedah and other rivers would keep them out of the battle for several days. The tanks were engaged by an anti-tank battery; one was hit and the others withdrew. By 4 p.m. the enemy infantry, which had been steadily reinforced, had succeeded in penetrating the position held by 1/8th Punjab whose morale was by this time shaky, and some retrograde movement began. Brigadier Lay immediately organized a counter-attack with the slender resources available; leading it forward himself, he restored the position around Milestone 20 and gave new spirit to his tired troops. The crossroads however remained in enemy hands.

During the afternoon of the 14th, Heath visited Murray-Lyon at his headquarters some four miles south of Gurun. The latter urged that the time had come to concentrate in order to avoid defeat in detail and explained that his troops were quite unfit for a series of

---

[1] See Map 10.
[2] Brigadier Garrett had resumed command of 15th Brigade and Brigadier Carpendale had reverted to the command of 28th Brigade.

dog-fights at frequent intervals. He submitted that any further withdrawals should be by long bounds, in lorries or even by rail, to the
area selected for concentration, which should be well to the south, for
he felt that the enemy would advance down the Grik road without
delay and threaten his communications. Heath agreed with his views
but emphasized the importance of delaying the enemy's advance by
every possible means, and said that the immediate role of 11th Division was to hold the Japanese at Gurun. He told Murray-Lyon that
12th Brigade had been placed under the command of III Corps and
that he proposed to use it to defend the Kroh and Grik roads. He
expressed the opinion that the Japanese were unlikely to threaten
the lines of communication at Kuala Kangsar for some time, but
that, when they did, III Corps would be forced to withdraw across
the Perak River. That evening Heath told Percival on the telephone
that, if 11th Division were to be reconstituted, it would be wrong to
fight at Gurun; the plan should be to go right back to the Perak
River, the enemy's advance being delayed by demolitions and a
temporary stand on the Muda River in order to give time for Penang
to be evacuated. Percival replied that III Corps was to continue to
cover Penang and was not to withdraw further than the line of the
Muda River without his permission.

At Gurun, in an effort to drive the enemy north of the crossroads,
Lay had planned a counter-attack by one company of 2nd East
Surrey for first light on the 15th. He was forestalled however by the
Japanese who, after a heavy and accurate mortar bombardment,
attacked at about 1.30 a.m. straight down the road and, besides
breaking through the right of 1/8th Punjab, infiltrated deeply into
6th Brigade's area. Not only was Headquarters 2nd East Surrey
overwhelmed, the commanding officer and five other officers being
killed, but also 6th Brigade Headquarters, the whole of which was
lost with the exception of Brigadier Lay who was absent from his
headquarters at the time.

Meanwhile the commanding officer of the Punjabis, thinking that
the enemy had overrun the forward companies of 2nd East Surreys
on his right flank and that he was completely isolated, withdrew
what remained of his battalion and a company of the East Surreys
westwards to Yen, with the object of rejoining the division by the
coast road. This action left the trunk road and the whole position
west of it completely undefended, but Brigadier Carpendale (28th
Brigade) took prompt action and managed to hold the enemy
around Gurun using troops from his own and 15th Brigades.

When Murray-Lyon visited his forward brigades early on the
morning of the 15th, he realized that the tactical situation was
extremely dangerous, and ordered an immediate withdrawal to a
position some seven miles south of Gurun, which was already held by

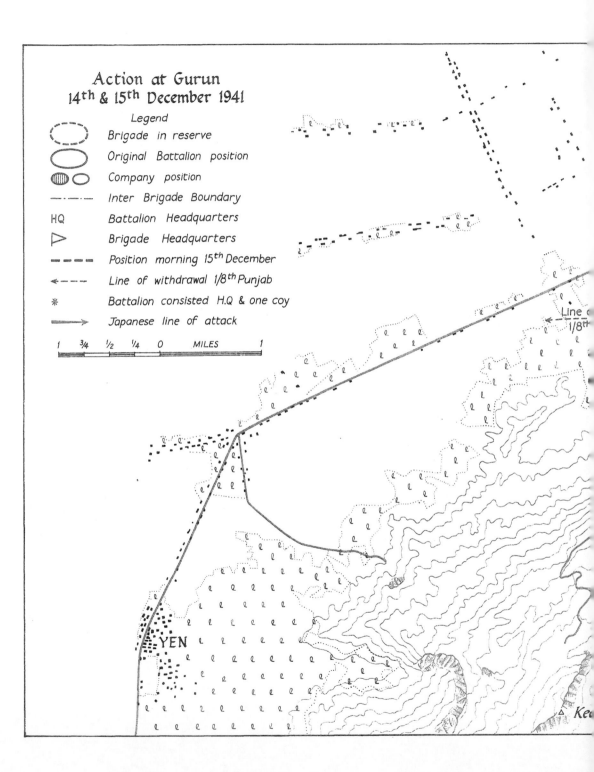

Action at Gurun
14th & 15th December 1941

Legend

Brigade in reserve
Original Battalion position
Company position
Inter Brigade Boundary
HQ   Battalion Headquarters
▷   Brigade Headquarters
Position morning 15th December
Line of withdrawal 1/8th Punjab
*   Battalion consisted H.Q & one coy
Japanese line of attack

1   ¾   ½   ¼   0   MILES   1

Line o
1/8th

YEN

Ked

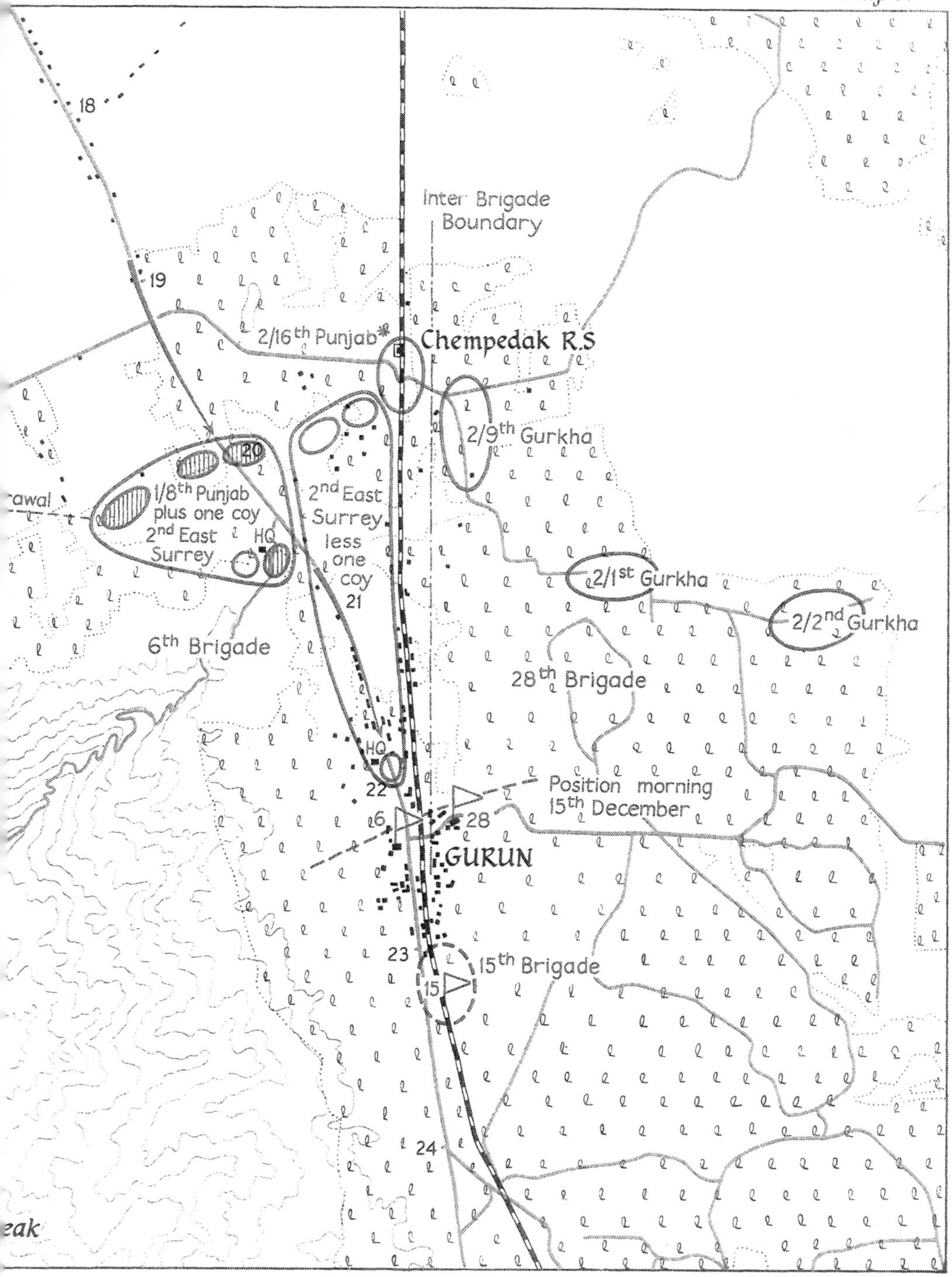

Map 10

18

19

Inter Brigade
Boundary

2/16th Punjab ⚓ **Chempedak R.S**

2/9th Gurkha

awal

1/8th Punjab
plus one coy
2nd East
Surrey

2nd East
Surrey
less
one
coy
21

HQ

2/1st Gurkha

2/2nd Gurkha

6th Brigade

28th Brigade

HQ
22

Position morning
15th December

6
28

GURUN

23

15th Brigade

15

24

eak

1st Independent Company and a squadron of 3rd Cavalry.[1] As further information came in, he realized that 28th Brigade was the only formation in his command which could be relied upon. He decided therefore to withdraw his division behind the Muda River during the night of the 15th/16th.

The enemy, who had suffered considerably from artillery fire while attempting to penetrate southwards between 28th Brigade and Kedah Peak, did not follow up closely, and 11th Division, having sustained further losses in men, equipment and transport owing to premature demolitions, was south of the Muda River by the morning of the 16th.

The policy for the future employment of 8th Brigade had been discussed by Percival and Heath at Malaya Command Headquarters on the 12th December. In view of the fact that the enemy's main thrust appeared to be on the west coast, Percival had decided that the Kelantan force should be withdrawn by rail. The Commander-in-Chief, Far East, in giving his approval, emphasized that the enemy must be prevented from using the railway. Orders for the withdrawal were issued and the removal of surplus stores began at once.

The enemy attacked the Machang position on both the 12th and 13th but was driven back after heavy fighting.[2] Thereafter the withdrawal to the railhead at Kuala Krai continued without much interference. All surplus stores and equipment having been moved by the 15th, the withdrawal of 8th Brigade started with the despatch of 4/19th Hyderabad to rejoin 12th Brigade on the west coast. The bridges just south of the town were destroyed and the railhead was evacuated on the 19th. By the 22nd the withdrawal from Kelantan had been completed. Brigadier Key, who had conducted this difficult operation with skill, disposed his brigade in the area Kuala Lipis–Jerantut. Although losses of vehicles, machine guns, mortars and anti-tank rifles had been heavy and its strength had been reduced by 553 all ranks, killed, wounded and missing, 8th Brigade remained a fighting formation.

---

[1] The 1st Independent Company was a self-contained unit, formed in April 1941, with headquarters and one British and three Indian platoons. It was intended for harassing and guerilla tactics behind the enemy lines, but in the circumstances of the campaign it was never used for that role.

The 3rd Cavalry took delivery of sixteen Marmon-Harrington armoured cars at Singapore in December 1941. These vehicles were new, not run in, and were without machine-gun fittings, spares and tools. During the journey to III Corps area, the inexperienced drivers and mechanics either ditched or rendered unserviceable thirteen of them.

[2] See Map 6.

The rapid withdrawals in Kedah produced a threat to the security of Penang, which was of military importance on account of its port facilities, fixed defences and stocks of ammunition and stores, and as the terminus of ocean cables connecting Malaya with India and Ceylon. The intention had been to defend the island and secure the anchorage by detaching two infantry battalions, with supporting troops, from the forces on the mainland, but, after the action at Jitra and the withdrawal from Kroh, there could be no question of transferring any troops to the island.

On the 11th December Penang experienced its first air raid. Forty-one Japanese bombers escorted by fighters bombed George Town, the only town on the island, and caused many casualties among the civilian Asian population, most of which had gathered in the streets to watch. The raid was repeated the following day, but on a smaller scale, and there were fewer casualties. Both of these raids were unopposed, for at that time no fighter aircraft were available in northern Malaya, and there were no anti-aircraft defences on the island. On the 13th however 453(F) Squadron from Singapore Island arrived at Butterworth airfield, on the mainland opposite Penang Island, for the direct support of III Corps. When the Japanese made a further raid on Penang, using a force of twenty-six bombers without fighter escort, they were engaged by eight Buffaloes and lost five aircraft for only one Buffalo shot down.

These air raids on Penang caused extensive damage to buildings and dock installations. Half the town was set on fire and a breakdown in the municipal services resulted; although about half of the Penang A.R.P. Corps and members of the Medical Auxiliary Service remained at their posts, most of the police deserted and the entire labour force disappeared. After consultation between the Resident Counsellor and the Fortress Commander (Brigadier C. A. Lyon) it was decided to evacuate all European women and children, together with the sick and wounded from the Military Hospital. These were transferred to the mainland by the night of the 13th. Evacuation of Asian civilians was not considered feasible, since there was no possibility of providing transport for large numbers.

On the 14th the War Council, to whom General Percival had referred the question of the defence of Penang, decided that the retention of the island depended entirely upon the outcome of the fighting on the mainland, and that it would be unwise to divide the available forces in an effort to hold both. If it proved impossible to halt the enemy's advance on the mainland, the Council decided to remove the garrison and as many essential stores as possible from the island by sea. They appreciated the effect on morale of evacuating Penang but decided that, in view of the military situation, it would have to be accepted. General Heath, in whose area of responsibility Penang lay, was instructed to this effect.

By the time these decisions had been taken conditions in Penang had become worse and the civil authorities gave warning of the probable outbreak of cholera and typhoid. On the 15th, with 11th Division preparing to withdraw to the south bank of the Muda River, Heath issued orders for the evacuation of the island, which was to be completed by the night of the 16th/17th. Most of the combatant troops had already been moved to the mainland, and only a very small garrison remained. Brigadier Lyon had but a short time in which to put the denial scheme into effect. The fixed defences, most of the stocks of ammunition, and much of the petrol and oil were destroyed. The power station, the civil airport buildings and installations were also destroyed, as well as much equipment and machinery in civil establishments. But time was lacking to complete the work, and two omissions in particular had unfortunate results. The first was the failure to destroy the broadcasting station, which was later used by the Japanese for spreading anti-British propaganda throughout the Far East. The second was the failure to remove or scuttle all ships and craft in the harbour. The Japanese, when they entered Penang, found twenty-four self-propelled craft and many large junks and barges, all of which had been deserted by their crews; these were later of inestimable value to them for seaborne operations on the west coast of the mainland. When this failure was realized an attempt was made to mine the southern channel from the harbour, and to despatch a special demolition party to ensure destruction of the craft, but both these efforts proved ineffective.

The shipping required to evacuate the garrison to Singapore had to be found locally and was limited to four small coastal vessels. The evacuation—which included all Europeans, except a few who elected to stay behind—was none the less completed by midnight on the 17th/18th. About 500 Asians of the Straits Settlements Volunteers, with their arms and equipment, chose to remain on the island to protect their families. The Resident Counsellor had been informed on the 16th that, in the event of any further withdrawal of civilians being necessary, there was to be no distinction of race. There was however insufficient shipping to evacuate large numbers of Asians, nor was it considered desirable to add to the large population of Singapore. It was also thought that their welfare and conditions generally would probably be better if they remained in their own homes on the island.

CHAPTER XIII

THE INVASION OF BRITISH BORNEO

See Map 11

WHILE THE EVENTS described in the three previous chapters were taking place in Malaya, war spread to British Borneo. This region formed part of Malaya Command and therefore came directly under General Percival's control.

The island of Borneo is a land of primeval jungle. The coasts are fringed with mangrove and swamp, and over nine-tenths of the interior is covered with thick evergreen forests. In 1941 the population was small—that of the whole island was estimated at less than three million—and there were less than a dozen settlements large enough to be called towns. There were few roads and only one short railway; communication was by the many waterways or by narrow jungle paths. Much of the interior was unexplored, or very inadequately known. It was rich in oil and other raw materials.

The island was partly Dutch and partly British. British Borneo lay along its northern seaboard and comprised the two states of British North Borneo and Sarawak, the small protected State of Brunei, and the Crown Colony of Labuan Island.

Borneo occupies a position of great strategic importance in the south-west Pacific. It lies across the main sea routes from the north to Malaya and Sumatra on the one hand, and Celebes and Java on the other. Strongly held, it could have been one of the main bastions in the defence of the Malay barrier, but neither the Dutch nor the British had the necessary resources to defend it. The available forces had to be concentrated further south for the defence of Singapore and Java, and all that could be spared for Borneo and the outlying Dutch islands were small detachments at important points which it was hoped might prove a deterrent to attack.

To gain control of the oilfields, to guard the flank of their advance on Malaya and to facilitate their eventual attack on Sumatra and western Java, the Japanese decided, as a subsidiary operation to their Malayan campaign, to seize British Borneo.[1] This operation was launched by *Southern Army* eight days after the initial attack on Malaya.

---

[1] See Chapter V.

The oilfields in British Borneo lay in two groups: one at Miri close to the northern boundary of Sarawak, and the other thirty-two miles north, at Seria in the State of Brunei. The crude oil was pumped from both fields to a refinery at Lutong on the coast, from which loading lines ran out to sea. Landings were possible all along the thirty miles of beach between Miri and Lutong and there was, with the forces available, no possibility of defending the oilfields against determined attacks. Plans had therefore been made for the destruction of the oil installations, and in December 1940 a company of 2/15th Punjab was sent to Miri for the protection of the demolition parties. In August 1941 a partial denial scheme, which reduced the output of oil by seventy per cent, was put into effect. It was decided that no attempt should be made to defend British North Borneo, Brunei or Labuan, and the Governor of North Borneo was informed that the Volunteers and police were to be used solely for the maintenance of internal security.

It was however decided to defend Kuching because of its airfield, and because its occupation by the enemy would give access to the important Dutch airfield at Singkawang II, sixty miles to the south-west and only some 350 miles from Singapore. In May 1941, therefore, the rest of 2/15th Punjab was sent there to provide a garrison. Lieut.-Colonel C. M. Lane who commanded the battalion was placed in charge of all forces in Sarawak, which included the native Volunteer Corps, Coastal Marine Service, the armed police and a body of native troops known as the Sarawak Rangers. The whole force was called 'Sarfor'.

The country between Kuching and the sea is roadless, but is intersected by a number of winding waterways which flow through mangrove swamps to the sea. There are two main approaches to the town: the first by the Sarawak River, which is navigable by vessels up to sixteen foot draught; and the second by the Santubong River, which will take vessels up to twelve foot draught. The roads from Kuching run east to Pending, north-west to Matang, and south to Serian a distance of forty miles from Kuching. The airfield lay seven miles south of the town on the Serian road. At the airfield a road branched off to the west; after crossing the Sarawak River at Batu Kitang, where there was a vehicular ferry, it terminated at Krokong fifteen miles short of the Dutch frontier.

The original plan of defence of Kuching had been to attempt to hold the enemy north of the town and to engage him with mobile forces during his advance to the airfield. In September 1941 however, at a conference with the Dutch, it was decided that the town could not be defended against the weight of attack which was to be expected, and the plan was reluctantly changed to one of static defence of the airfield.

Orders for the demolition of the refinery at Lutong and the denial of the oilwells reached the officer commanding at Miri on the morning of the 8th December, and by the evening of the same day the task was completed. On the following day the landing ground there was made unfit for use, and on the 13th the Punjabis and the oil officials left by sea for Kuching.

The destruction of the oilfields had been completed none too soon. On the afternoon of the 13th the Japanese *35th Infantry Brigade Headquarters* and *124th Infantry Regiment* augmented by the *Yokosuka 2nd Special Naval Landing Force* left Camranh Bay in ten transports with a strong naval escort.[1]

The convoy crossed the South China Sea without being sighted, and shortly before midnight on the 15th anchored off Miri, one ship being detached to Seria. Landing began at once; although heavy weather hampered boat work, both forces were ashore by daylight and, meeting no opposition, occupied the oilfields and air strip.

News of the landing did not reach Air Headquarters, Far East, until 9 p.m. on the 16th. Reconnaissance aircraft from Singkawang II were ordered to investigate at daylight on the 17th. Dutch naval aircraft attacked the ships at anchor later that day and again on the 18th, but without effect. On the 19th Dutch army aircraft from Singkawang II bombed the convoy and sank a destroyer. Kuching realized that its turn was soon to come and work went on day and night to complete the airfield defences. This work was delayed on the 19th by a raid on the town by fifteen Japanese bombers which set fire to a large petrol store but otherwise did little material damage. A large part of the native population however fled from the town, and labour, which had been difficult to obtain before, became almost unprocurable.

On the 22nd December the main body (two battalions) of the Japanese invasion force re-embarked at Miri and left for Kuching, leaving one battalion to secure all British Borneo outside Sarawak. This detached battalion occupied Labuan on the 1st January 1942 and Jesselton on the 8th. On the 17th two infantry companies landed at Sandakan, the seat of government of British North Borneo. On the morning of the 19th January the Governor surrendered the State and, refusing to carry on the administration under Japanese control, was interned with his staff.

The convoy which left Miri on the 22nd December was sighted and reported to Air Headquarters, Far East, by Dutch reconnaissance aircraft on the morning of the 23rd, when it was about 150 miles from Kuching. At 11.40 that morning twenty-four Japanese aircraft bombed Singkawang II airfield, so damaging the runways that a

---

[1] See Appendices 15 and 23.

Dutch striking force which had been ordered to attack the convoy was unable to take off with a bomb load. Despite the critical situation the Dutch authorities urged the transfer of their aircraft to Sumatra. Air Headquarters, Far East, agreed and during the afternoon of the 24th the aircraft were flown to Palembang.[1]

The convoy did not however escape unscathed. On the evening of the 23rd a Dutch submarine sank two enemy ships and damaged two others, and the following night another Dutch submarine sank a destroyer, but was herself sunk on her way back to Sourabaya. Five Blenheims of 34(B) Squadron from Singapore, at almost extreme range, bombed the ships at anchor the same evening, but did little damage. The convoy was seen at 6 p.m. on the 23rd approaching the mouth of the Santubong River. Two hours later Colonel Lane received orders from Singapore to destroy the airfield. It was too late to change back to mobile defence and, as there seemed to him no point in attempting to defend a useless airfield, he asked General Percival for permission to withdraw as soon as possible into Dutch north-west Borneo.

While awaiting a reply Lane concentrated his battalion at the airfield, with forward detachments in the Pending area east of the town and on the roads to the north of it, 18-pounder gun and 3-inch mortar detachments covering the river approaches, and a Punjabi gunboat platoon, working with the Sarawak Rangers and the Coastal Marine Service, patrolling north of Kuching.

As day broke on the morning of the 24th December the Japanese convoy was seen at anchor off the mouth of the Santubong River, and at 9 a.m. twenty enemy landing craft were observed approaching the shore. The small Punjabi gunboat platoon, hopelessly outnumbered, withdrew up the river without loss. At 11 a.m. the landing craft as they neared the town were engaged by the gun and mortar detachments, who sank four before themselves being surrounded and killed. During the afternoon three more craft were sunk by gunfire, but the remainder were able to land their troops on both sides of the river, and by 4.30 p.m. the town was in Japanese hands.

Meanwhile Lane had been instructed by Percival to hold the Japanese for as long as possible and then act in the best interests of west Borneo as a whole. Since the capture of the town threatened to cut off the forward troops, Lane ordered them to withdraw to the airfield. The Japanese followed up and before dark made contact with the airfield defences. Throughout the night sporadic firing went on as they felt their way round the perimeter. As Christmas Day dawned, firing temporarily ceased and advantage was taken of the lull to send the hospital detachment with the women and children on

---

[1] See Map 17.

ahead into Dutch Borneo. During the morning the Japanese encircling movement continued, and a company was sent to hold the ferry crossing at Batu Kitang so as to keep the road clear for escape.

A general withdrawal into Dutch Borneo was ordered to start at dusk, but heavy firing was heard to the north of Batu Kitang shortly after noon and, fearing that his line of retreat would be cut, Lane decided on immediate withdrawal. The enemy, soon aware of his intention, launched a full-scale attack on the two Punjabi companies forming the rearguard. Of these two companies only one platoon succeeded in rejoining the main body. The remainder, totalling four British officers and some 230 Indian troops, were cut off and either killed or captured. The rest of the battalion reached Batu Kitang without loss to find the village deserted and the ferry unattended. They had great difficulty in crossing the river, but by dark all except the covering force were over. Most of the transport had to be left behind. Renewed Japanese attacks threatened to cut off the covering force, but it managed to make good its escape to the southward, and after a march of about sixty miles through dense jungle with little food or water rejoined the battalion at Singkawang II airfield on the 31st.

The main body made its way to Krokong. There the road ended, and the remaining vehicles and heavy equipment had to be abandoned. There, too, the Sarawak State Forces, in view of their agreement to serve only in Sarawak, were released to return to their homes. From the 26th 'Sarfor' ceased to exist as a combined Indian and State Force, and the Punjabis, much reduced in strength, carried on alone. On the morning of the 27th the column crossed the border into Dutch Borneo and two days later arrived at Singkawang II airfield where there was a garrison of 750 Dutch troops. The women and children were sent on by road to Pontianak on the coast, whence they escaped by ship on the 25th January, only four days before the Japanese occupied the town. Lane placed his battalion under Dutch command for the defence of the airfield and the surrounding area. There followed a breathing space while the Japanese prepared for their next advance, though clashes took place between patrols near the border.

It was realized at Headquarters, Malaya Command, that the Punjabis would be urgently in need of food and ammunition. On the 30th December air reconnaissance confirmed that the airfield was unfit for use. Thereupon Air Headquarters made arrangements for supplies to be dropped and the following day three Blenheims from Singapore, modified to carry containers, successfully dropped 900 pounds of supplies on the airfield.

The Japanese planned to attack the airfield from the north, and also from the west by a force landed on the coast. This attack was

R

held up by bad weather for nearly a week, but on the 24th January
five companies advanced along the road from the Dutch border, and
by the 25th had reached a village two and a half miles north-east of
the airfield. Having destroyed the stores and barracks, the defenders
launched an attack on the 26th which was repulsed. That evening a
counter-attack succeeded in turning their flank and early on the
27th the order was given to evacuate the airfield. During the withdrawal two Punjabi platoons were surrounded but, refusing to surrender, they fought on under their Indian officer until late in the
afternoon. It was only when their ammunition was expended and the
enemy was attacking in overwhelming numbers that the gallant little
party laid down its arms. Japanese reports have since given their
casualties at the hands of these two platoons as between 400 and
500 killed or wounded. Of the seventy Punjabis engaged only three
escaped. The remainder were never seen again; there is evidence to
show that they were brutally put to death by the infuriated Japanese.
On the evening of the 27th January the remnants of the Punjabis
crossed the Sungei Sambas and took up a position on the high ground
at Ledo, fifteen miles south-west of the airfield.

Meanwhile three Japanese companies had left Kuching in small
craft during the night of the 25th and by daybreak on the 27th had
landed at Pemangkat due west of the airfield. Striking north-east and
south and meeting with little opposition, they quickly captured the
coastal villages and moved towards Bengkajang, thus threatening to
surround the Allied force at Ledo.

On the 29th, after a series of rearguard actions, the Punjabis withdrew to Ngabang and two days later to Nangapinoh. By this time
further resistance was useless, and on the 4th February the Punjabis
with Dutch agreement set out in two columns for Sampit and Pangkalanboeoen on the south coast in the hope of finding ships to take them
to Java.

Of the adventures of the two columns on their long journey
through the almost unexplored jungles and swamps of southern
Borneo much might be written. Travelling by forest track and by
raft and boat on treacherous rivers, short of food and clothing, and
constantly exposed to tropical heat and rain they finally reached the
coast. The western column which took the shorter route reached
Pangkalanboeoen on the 24th February; there, finding escape impossible, it joined the local Dutch garrison for the defence of the landing
ground. The eastern column arrived at Sampit on the 6th March
only to find that the Japanese had landed at the mouth of the river
on the previous day.

The news of the surrender in Java reached Pangkalanboeoen on the
8th March. This was followed the next day by a Japanese broadcast
calling on all Allied forces in the Netherlands East Indies to lay down

their arms. The broadcast was accompanied by a threat of reprisals if resistance continued. Retreat into the jungle-covered mountains· was considered, but the bitter experience of the past few weeks had made it clear that troops could not long survive the trying climatic conditions. The order to surrender was therefore given on the afternoon of the 9th. In the ten weeks since leaving Kuching 2/15th Punjab had fought many actions, inflicting heavy casualties on the enemy, and had travelled under most adverse conditions over 800 miles through extremely difficult country. They had carried with them their light automatics, rifles and ammunition. As General Percival has said, it was 'a feat of endurance which assuredly will rank high in the annals of warfare. . . . It says much for the morale of this fine battalion that it remained a formed and disciplined body to the end.'[1]

---

[1] Percival, *The War in Malaya* (Eyre and Spottiswoode, 1949), page 173.

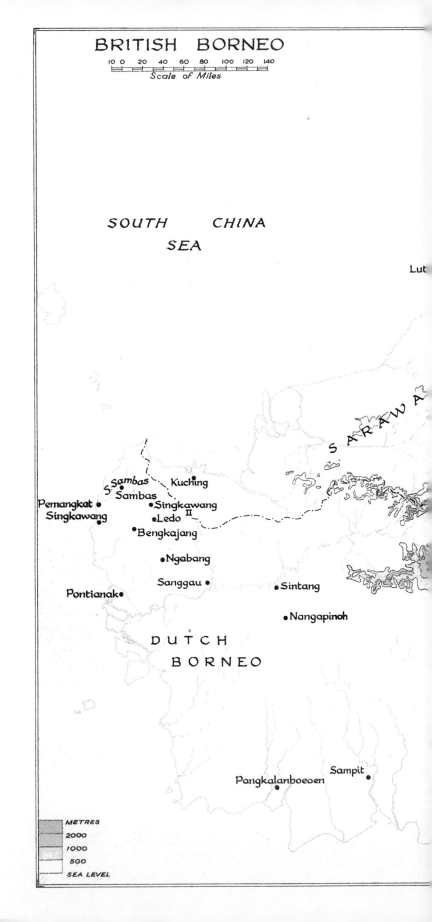

BRITISH BORNEO

10 0   20   40   60   80   100 120 140
Scale of Miles

SOUTH   CHINA
        SEA

Lut

SARAWA

S.Sambas   Kuching
S.Sambas
Pemangkat •   •Sambas
Singkawang   •Singkawang
            •Ledo   II
            •Bengkajang

            •Ngabang
        Sanggau •   •Sintang
Pontianak•
                    •Nangapinoh

    D U T C H
        B O R N E O

                        Sampit
            Pangkalanboeoen •   •

METRES
2000
1000
500
SEA LEVEL

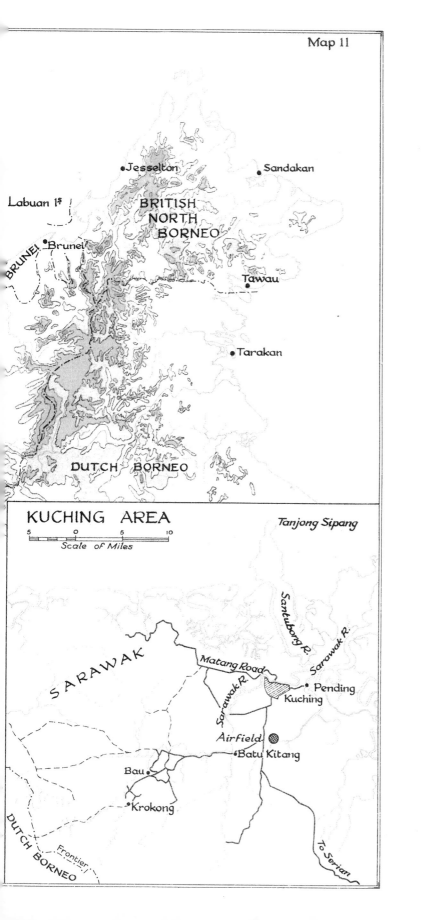

Map 11

•Jesselton   •Sandakan

Labuan I⁵

BRITISH
NORTH
BORNEO

BRUNEI •Brunei

•Tawau

•Tarakan

DUTCH   BORNEO

KUCHING   AREA

5   0   5   10
Scale of Miles

Tanjong Sipang

SARAWAK

Santuborg R.

Matang Road

Sarawak R.

Sarawak R.

•Pending

Kuching

Airfield

•Batu Kitang

Bau•

•Krokong

DUTCH
BORNEO

Frontier

To Serian

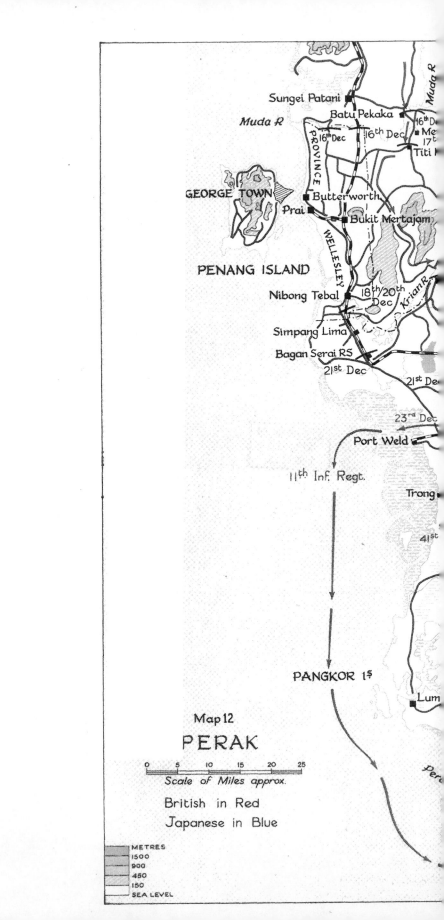

Sungei Patani

Batu Pekaka

16th De

Muda R

PROVINCE

16th Dec

16th Dec

Me

17t

Titi

GEORGE TOWN

Butterworth

Prai

Bukit Mertajam

WELLESLEY

PENANG ISLAND

Nibong Tebal

18th/20th
Dec

Krian R

Simpang Lima

Bagan Serai RS

21st Dec

21st De

23rd Dec

Port Weld

11th Inf. Regt.

Trong

41st

PANGKOR I^s

Lum

Per

Map 12

PERAK

0   5   10   15   20   25
Scale of Miles approx.

British in Red

Japanese in Blue

METRES
1500
900
450
150
SEA LEVEL

CHAPTER XIV

THE LOSS OF NORTHERN
MALAYA

See Maps 12, 13 and 14 and Sketch 5

ON THE MORNING of the 16th December General
Heath, after meeting General Murray-Lyon at his headquarters, decided to withdraw 11th Division to the line of
the Krian River some thirty miles further south. His reasons for this
decision were that the division, as a result of the actions at Jitra and
Gurun, was in no shape to offer battle without a respite; that an
advance by the enemy column (which was supported by armour)
from Patani westward through Baling would outflank the positions
on the Muda River, and it was unlikely that such a move could be
held in check by 12th Brigade; and lastly that, since the country
between the Muda and Krian Rivers was suitable for armour, it was
necessary to get behind the Krian River, which, with its extensive
swamps, was a good tank obstacle. Heath therefore ordered 6th and
15th Brigades to Taiping to rest and refit and 28th Brigade, supported by 88th Field Regiment and two anti-tank batteries, to move
back to Simpang Lima by road and rail to occupy, on the 17th, a
position covered by the Krian River, from the road and railway
bridge at Nibong Tebal westwards to the sea. Krohcol was disbanded.
The 3/16th Punjab, supported by 10th Mountain Battery, was
ordered to cover the right flank by holding the river crossing at
Selama, and 5/14th Punjab to withdraw to Taiping. To cover the
withdrawal from the Muda River, 12th Brigade was ordered to fight
a rearguard action along the Titi Karangan–Selama road and then,
having passed through 3/16th Punjab, to join 11th Division at
Taiping. Nearer the coast a small force[1] under Lieut.-Colonel
Holme, R.A., was organized to destroy the bridges and to hold the
south bank of the Muda River for as long as necessary.

Realizing that the withdrawal of 11th Division behind the Muda
River would lay his brigade open to attack from the north-west as
well as from the east, Brigadier Paris had already concentrated his
forces. On the 15th he had ordered 5/2nd Punjab to hold the bridge

---

[1] This force consisted of 137th Field Regiment, one section 22nd Mountain Regiment,
one troop 80th Anti-Tank Regiment, 1st Independent Company, one company 1st
Leicestershire, one squadron 3rd Cavalry and an armoured train.

over the Muda River at Batu Pekaka, and had withdrawn the Argylls, with whom the enemy had not made contact, to Kupang. On the 16th he moved the latter battalion to Titi Karangan. The same afternoon the Japanese, who had advanced from Gurun by the inland road instead of direct on Sungei Patani, attempted to rush the Batu Pekaka bridge which had been only partly demolished. This attempt, made by infantry disguised in native dress and led by a European in plain clothes, failed and the bridge was destroyed.

Early on the 17th, Paris withdrew 5/2nd Punjab from Batu Pekaka, but the Japanese followed up closely and by 10 a.m. had made contact with the Argylls, who had orders to hold Titi Karangan till noon. A spirited action followed, but at 11.30 a.m., just as he had decided to launch a counter-attack, Stewart received permission to withdraw. By midnight 12th Brigade reached Selama and came under command of 11th Division. By dawn on the 18th the whole force was south of the Krian River.

There was at that time considerable anxiety lest the Japanese should attempt further landings on the east coast. A large convoy had been reported steaming south-west from the direction of Saigon, and it was thought that it might be making for Kuantan or Mersing. Most of the bomber force was held in readiness at Singapore to attack the convoy as it approached the coast, and extensive seaward reconnaissances were undertaken daily both from Singapore and Borneo, but the report remained unconfirmed. The convoy was in fact the forty-one transports carrying the second flight of *25th Army* to Singora and Patani, which reached its destination without loss on the 16th.

The small force of infantry and armoured cars,[1] which had been guarding the Kroh–Kuala Kangsar road, was attacked on the 16th just north of Grik and compelled to fall back towards Kuala Kenering and on the following day to Sumpitan. The possibility that the enemy might use the road through Grik to reach Kuala Kangsar, despite its unsuitability for wheeled transport, had not been overlooked and plans had been made to prepare the road for demolition, but the speed of the Japanese advance southwards through Grik came as an unpleasant surprise and prevented the charges being laid. The Japanese *42nd Infantry Regiment*, instead of moving westward through Baling, had on arrival at Kroh turned south towards Grik in an endeavour to reach the main road at Kuala Kangsar and thereby cut the line of communications to 11th Division, but, because of the heavy rain and the poor road surface, it had been forced to leave its light tank battalion behind.

---

[1] One company 2nd Argylls plus a detachment of their armoured cars. See page 213.

Heath realized the gravity of this threat and saw that, unless the progress of the Japanese column could be checked, a further withdrawal to the Perak River would become inevitable. He had already sent 1st Independent Company to Lenggong to reinforce the small force of Argylls, but such was the strength and speed of the enemy advance that he decided, late on the 17th, to take 12th Brigade under his own command and move it direct to Kuala Kangsar to stop the enemy advance along the Grik road. Since the line of the Perak River, which runs from north to south, was unsatisfactory for prolonged defence, he foresaw that he might eventually be forced to withdraw as far south as Kampar where he felt he would be in a better position to halt the Japanese advance.

Meanwhile General Percival had been considering his strategy in the light of events at Jitra and Gurun. His task was the defence of the Naval Base. From the information at his disposal he estimated that the Japanese had one division on the trunk road, one on the Patani–Kroh–Grik road and one on the east coast in Kelantan, with reserves in Indo-China. To meet the enemy attacks he had the equivalent of one division on the west coast and two brigade groups on the east coast. The former was exhausted by almost continuous fighting and by day and night movements, and its morale though not broken was approaching breaking point. In Johore he had 8th Australian Division (two brigade groups) and in Singapore Island the garrison troops; but, as the enemy had undisputed command of the sea and was therefore free to make a seaborne attack on Singapore or eastern Johore at will, he considered that he could not take the risk of moving these to the northern front without replacement. He contemplated moving part of the Australian division to relieve 11th Division, but discarded the idea since he considered it was undesirable to break up the Australian self-contained organization. Moreover a relief would take a long time and would temporarily leave the Johore defences held by troops to whom the ground was unfamiliar.

He was well aware that the fate of Malaya and the Naval Base depended upon the safe and timely arrival of the reinforcements which he knew would be sent, but which he also knew could not possibly begin to arrive before the first half of January. As the convoys bringing reinforcements approached Singapore they would be exposed to the danger of air attack. This danger would be enhanced if the Japanese had the use of airfields in central Malaya and could give close fighter support to their bombers. He therefore had to keep the Japanese as far north as possible in order to prevent them capturing airfields from which they could threaten the arrival of convoys.

He knew that the Japanese air force was consolidating and extending the air superiority already gained and would shortly be in a position to give close support to their advancing formations. The

Allied air forces, which, including the Dutch reinforcements, were now reduced to about a hundred aircraft, had to be kept for general reconnaissance, the defence of the Base and the protection of convoys. There were no aircraft therefore for offensive action or for intervention in the land fighting. Nor was there hope of reinforcement for some time, since the enemy had already cut the established air route from India, and the alternative route by way of Sabang off the coast of northern Sumatra could be used only by long-range bombers. Fighters would have to come by sea or fly from Australia by way of the Netherlands East Indies. It was clear therefore that the build-up of Allied air strength would be extremely slow and that the army, with only a meagre and diminishing scale of air support, would have to hold the enemy practically unaided. Percival considered he had no alternative but to ask the weary troops of III Corps, without adequate air support or tanks and faced with superior enemy forces well supported by both, to hold the enemy as far north as possible until reinforcements reached Singapore and were ready for action.

It was clear that Perak was more suitable for delaying action than were the states further south, with their extensive network of roads. Since these states were centres of the tin mining and rubber industries, he decided that every effort should be made to hold the enemy in Perak. The Perak River however ran parallel with and not at right angles to the main north-south communications. This fact combined with the nearness of the coastline, which in the absence of adequate naval forces could not be protected, militated against the adoption of delaying tactics in an area otherwise eminently suitable.

By the 17th, Percival had come to the conclusion that his policy should be to withdraw III Corps behind the Perak River where, while avoiding becoming inextricably committed, it should prevent the enemy from crossing the river for as long as possible. That evening, in view of the situation on the Grik road, he authorized Heath to withdraw III Corps behind the Perak River when he considered it to be absolutely necessary.

During the night of the 17th/18th he travelled north to Ipoh and on the 18th, after a reconnaissance of the Perak River area, a visit to some of the forward units and discussion with Heath, he issued the following orders: III Corps was to continue to impose the maximum delay on the enemy west of the Perak River, withdrawing across the river only when it became necessary to do so; the corps was immediately to select and prepare positions between Ipoh and Tanjong Malim which, with demolitions along the line of communication, would impose the maximum delay on the enemy with the minimum expenditure of force;[1] 9th Division was to be used to continue to deny

[1] See Map 14 for Tanjong Malim.

the airfield at Kuantan and protect 11th Division and its communications from attack from the east; the Perak Flotilla, consisting of the destroyer *Scout* and some light craft (originally formed to stop enemy landings in northern Sumatra) was to deal with any attempt to move by sea down the west coast between the mouths of the Krian and Perak Rivers; a seaborne raiding force, to be known as 'Roseforce', was to disrupt enemy communications west of the Perak River;[1] priority in the supply of labour was to be given to the air force for the maintenance of new air strips in southern Johore and on Singapore Island; and lastly, 11th Division was to be reorganized to include 12th Brigade, and the depleted 6th and 15th Brigades were to be amalgamated to form a composite brigade known as 15th Brigade.

On the 18th December an Allied conference, attended by British, American, Dutch, Australian and New Zealand representatives, was held at Singapore, under the chairmanship of Mr. Duff Cooper, to make recommendations for common Allied action. The conference reported to the Chiefs of Staff that the situation in Malaya was very serious and gave an estimate of the reinforcements which should be sent as quickly as possible. These included four fighter and four bomber squadrons, one infantry division and one brigade group, reinforcements for 9th and 11th Indian Divisions, three light and two heavy anti-aircraft regiments, an anti-tank regiment, fifty light tanks and a supply of small arms and artillery ammunition. The report contained a warning that the Japanese had reserve divisions available for use in Malaya, and that to meet this added threat further large reinforcements would probably be necessary. Owing to the importance of gaining time for the safe arrival of both army and air reinforcements, the conference recommended that the strategy for Malaya should be to hold the Japanese as far north as possible, so as to prevent them from using the airfields in central or southern Malaya from which they would be able to threaten the arrival of convoys at Singapore. The conference thus endorsed the strategy which Percival had already adopted. They also recommended that a combined naval striking force should be built up round Rear-Admiral W. A. Glassford's American Task Force, for the defence of the Netherlands East Indies, and that it should be maintained in the Strait of Makassar and the Celebes Sea.

The same day Mr. Duff Cooper sent a letter by air to the Prime Minister in which he attempted to portray the situation in Singapore. He said that he was becoming dissatisfied with the civil defence

---

[1] The force, consisting of fifty Australians, was to be based on Port Swettenham, where a flotilla of lightly armed craft had been organized by the Royal Navy.

preparations and that some senior civilian officials did not appear to be able to adjust themselves to war conditions. He indicated that it might later be necessary to make some changes.

On the 31st December he expressed his apprehensions to the War Council. He said that, although the security of Singapore depended upon the arrival of reinforcements, a breakdown in the civil defence organization, an organization which in his opinion was unsound, might well nullify the efforts of the armed forces defending the town. He pointed out that a certain lack of confidence existed among the civil population in the measures being taken for its defence, and that the best way of restoring public confidence was to take a new line or some drastic step which would make civilians feel that at least something was being done. The almost dictatorial powers exercised by the Singapore Harbour Board within the confines of the area under its jurisdiction were a lesson on how important problems could be tackled to ensure the greatest rapidity in the execution of important work. He therefore considered that the time had come when one man should be appointed who would have control, unhampered by petty restrictions and applications to committees. He proposed that Brigadier I. Simson, Chief Engineer, Malaya Command, who had had recent experience of air raids and similar difficulties in the United Kingdom, should be appointed Director General of Civil Defence. The Council unanimously decided that Brigadier Simson should be appointed with plenary powers under the War Council through the Governor. It was also decided that the Colonial Secretary should report this to the Governor on his return from Kuala Lumpur that afternoon and that the proposed terms of reference for the Director General which Mr. Duff Cooper read out should be discussed the following day.

In anticipation of the Council's approval Mr. Duff Cooper informed Brigadier Simson that he was appointed Director General and handed him terms of reference which gave him plenary powers for Singapore Island and Johore and informed him that all executive departments of the Government would be under his control in matters affecting civil defence. He sent a copy of this to the Governor.

The Minutes of the War Council meeting on the following day record 'The Governor will issue a statement which briefly is to the effect that Brigadier Simson would be responsible to the Governor (who would appoint him), who would report in turn to the War Council.' The communiqué as issued made no mention of plenary powers nor of any authority in the State of Johore; it merely substituted Brigadier Simson for the Colonial Secretary as the head of the existing civil defence organization. Simson therefore had no special powers to enable him to compel Government departments and civilian organizations to take such action as he considered necessary and, further, his activities were confined to Singapore Island only. Mr. Duff Cooper's plan to appoint one man who would have unhampered control did not materialize.

The selection of the senior Royal Engineer Officer in Malaya for the appointment of D.G.C.D., at a time when it was possible that Singapore might be invested and when all the available engineer effort should have been concentrated on the construction of defences, seems in retrospect to have been a mistake. Indeed, Brigadier Simson, who from the moment of his arrival in Malaya had advocated the construction of considerably more field and anti-tank defence works than had been authorized, accepted the appointment only under pressure. Not only did he consider his task as Chief Engineer to be the more important, but in his opinion it was too late to reorganize effectively the civil defences, especially in a cosmopolitan area already under bombardment. Nevertheless he did what he could, and it was largely due to his efforts and to the devotion to duty of the members of the various units that, when put to the test, the civil defence services functioned as well as they did.

In Perak a long stand on the Krian River was not considered possible, for, although a large area in the centre was protected by swamps, the front was too extended and the thick vegetation on the river banks provided the enemy with covered approaches. Thus, when on the 20th the enemy reached Selama, 3/16th Punjab (which had sustained heavy losses in the fighting on the Kroh front) was given permission to withdraw at discretion. By evening, the enemy began to outflank the Punjabis and Moorhead decided to fall back towards Ulu Sapetang during the night. Thereupon 28th Brigade, which had been instructed to conform, after destroying the river bridges and arranging for the Perak Public Works Department to flood the trunk road between Nibong Tebal and Bagan Serai, withdrew through Bagan Serai to the vicinity of Ulu Sapetang. The stand on the Krian River line had ended.

Meanwhile early on the 19th Brigadier Paris (12th Brigade) had sent the Argylls, with one troop of a field battery, to join their detached company and 1st Independent Company on the Grik road with orders to prevent the enemy from moving southwards towards Kuala Kangsar for as long as possible. To protect Stewart's communications he also sent one company of 5/2nd Punjab to Kota Tampan where the Perak River ran close to the road. During the day there was severe fighting north of Sumpitan and by evening the Argylls and 1st Independent Company had been forced back to Lenggong.

On the 20th the Japanese made a frontal attack on the Argylls and, in an effort to cut them off, moved down the river on rafts to Kota Tampan.[1] The Punjabi company drove them off after some fierce fighting, but it became clear during the afternoon that neither Lenggong nor Kota Tampan could be held. That evening the whole force withdrew to a position at Milestone 55 south of the causeway, which it then demolished. Meanwhile, to prevent further enemy attempts to use the river and outflank the defence, Paris ordered 5/2nd Punjab to occupy the road on the western shore of Chenderoh Lake in depth and send a detachment to the Power Station. The Punjabis reached their positions late that evening.

During the morning of the 21st, Heath placed 12th Brigade and all troops west of the Perak River under command of 11th Division from midnight 21st/22nd. On receipt of these orders Murray-Lyon went forward to Kati to discuss the situation with Paris. He found that Paris intended to withdraw the Argylls that evening through the Punjabis to Kati and to order 4/19th Hyderabad—just arrived from Kelantan—to watch the tracks across the Sungei Plus which led directly to the trunk road at Sungei Siput. In view of the ease with which the Japanese could outflank 12th Brigade's position on the Grik road by crossing the lake and threatening his main line of communications at Sungei Siput, Murray-Lyon decided that the withdrawal of 11th Division behind the Perak River could not long be delayed. That night he withdrew 28th Brigade to the Lawin area, sent 3rd Cavalry to delay any outflanking advance on the road west of the river which led to Blanja and ordered 2/1st Gurkha Rifles, supported by a mountain battery and a troop of anti-tank guns, to hold a bridgehead over the river at Blanja.

Early on the 22nd he again visited 12th Brigade, to find that during the night the Punjabis had withdrawn to the Milestone 48–Kampong Sauk area. The day had passed quietly, but, feeling that the absence of pressure was ominous and that the enemy might be moving directly on Sungei Siput, Murray-Lyon paid the brigade another visit late in the afternoon and then decided to withdraw behind the Perak River during the night. He ordered 12th Brigade to Sungei Siput, and 28th Brigade, as soon as 12th Brigade had cleared the road junction at Lawin, to cross the Iskandar Bridge and move to Siputeh in support of the Blanja bridgehead. With the exception of the bridgehead detachment at Blanja, all troops of 11th Division were behind the Perak River by dawn on the 23rd, and the Iskandar and Enggor Bridges had been destroyed. That night the pontoon bridge at Blanja was sunk and the bridgehead detachment withdrawn.

The withdrawal across the Perak River led to a short pause in the

---

[1] See Sketch 5.

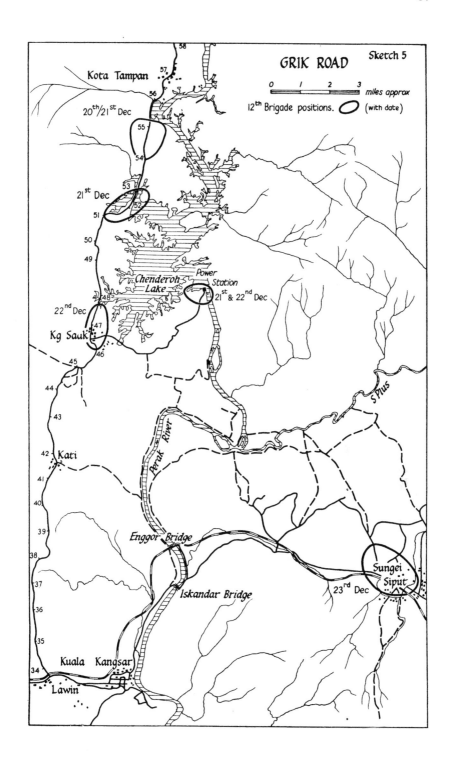

GRIK ROAD   Sketch 5

Kota Tampan

0 1 2 3 *miles approx*
12th Brigade positions. (with date)

20th/21st Dec

21st Dec

Chenderoh Lake

Power Station
21st & 22nd Dec

22nd Dec

Kg Sauk

Kati

Perak River

S Plus

Enggor Bridge

Iskandar Bridge

Sungei Siput
23rd Dec

Kuala Kangsar

Lawin

operations. General Yamashita expected that the crossing would have to be forced in the face of considerable opposition, for the river was a first-class tank obstacle and he thought the British could not afford to give it up without a struggle. He therefore concentrated *4th Guards Regiment*, which had arrived in the Taiping area from Siam on the 23rd,[1] at Kuala Kangsar and *5th Division* in the Blanja area. In order that the bridges could be repaired and tanks and artillery taken across the river in preparation for a further southward advance, he ordered the former to gain a footing on the east bank opposite Kuala Kangsar.

General Heath considered that the lateral road from Kuala Kangsar to Blanja on the right bank of the river, which was not duplicated on the left bank, would enable the enemy to move rapidly to any point he chose for a crossing with little fear of being forestalled. This fact, and the possible danger to his right flank from the column on the Grik road, made him decide that he could not afford to dispute the crossing at Kuala Kangsar. He therefore ordered 11th Division to the general line Sungei Siput–Siputeh and told Murray-Lyon to make use of the short pause in the operations, which would occur while the enemy crossed the river, to rest and reorganize his weary troops. Since the Allied air forces were too weak to make any serious effort to interfere with the crossing and subsequent bridging operations, the Japanese to their astonishment were able, without opposition, to cross the biggest obstacle they had yet met.

During III Corps' withdrawal from the Muda to the Perak River the Japanese air force had held firmly to its policy of denying to the British the use of the airfields in northern Malaya, and had begun intensive bombing of the Ipoh airfield. Such was its effect that by the 19th all aircraft in support of III Corps were driven back to Kuala Lumpur, where the airfield was rapidly becoming an advanced base at which men, equipment and stores from airfields already abandoned were concentrated.

Plans for the evacuation of airfields in north-west Malaya had included the demolition of buildings, the cratering of runways and the destruction of stores, fuel and ammunition that could not be removed. The efforts to carry these out were only partly successful, for in the short time available it was difficult to damage the runways effectively, and in the confusion of the withdrawal misunderstandings between the Services resulted in stocks of high octane petrol being left intact.[2] Furthermore the enemy occupation of the airfields

---

[1] See page 178.
[2] Between 100,000 and 200,000 gallons of 90 octane petrol were left at the Sungei Patani airfield.

followed so rapidly that in most instances there had not been time for the heavy rains to affect the cratered runways, and, by using the large stocks of road metal which had been accumulated for maintenance at each airfield and which could neither be removed nor destroyed, the Japanese had little difficulty in repairing them. There was also abundant native labour which they could impress for such work. In consequence, as early as the 20th the Japanese were using the captured airfields in the north-west of Malaya. Photographic reconnaissance disclosed more than fifty aircraft at Sungei Patani, most of which were fighters. An attempt by Blenheim bombers from Singapore to attack them at first light on the 21st failed owing to bad weather.

The Japanese then began increasingly heavy attacks on the airfield at Kuala Lumpur which was defended by six 3·7-inch, four 3-inch and eight Bofors anti-aircraft guns, and where 453(F) Squadron (fifteen Buffaloes) was stationed with the dual role of providing tactical reconnaissance for III Corps and fighter defence for the Kuala Lumpur area. On the 21st and 22nd the squadron engaged enemy fighters and bombers attacking the airfield, and many individual air combats took place. The Australian pilots fought courageously against an equally determined and better equipped enemy in superior numbers. By the evening of the 22nd only three Buffaloes were left fit for action. It was not possible to assess the enemy casualties with any accuracy, but it was clear that they represented only a very small percentage of the Japanese strength, whereas the British losses were proportionately serious.

Such heavy losses could be replaced only by weakening further the air defence of Singapore itself. Since it had been agreed that fighter squadrons in Malaya should be retained for the protection of the Base and of convoys bringing reinforcements, Air Vice-Marshal Pulford ordered what remained of 453(F) Squadron to return to Singapore and, with the concurrence of the Commander-in-Chief, Far East, gave instructions for the evacuation of Kuala Lumpur airfield to begin early on the 23rd.

The possibility that it might become necessary for air operations to be based on Sumatra had been considered by Headquarters, Air Command, even in the pre-war planning period. There were many objections to this, in particular the lack of communications and the difficulty of distributing the necessary large stocks of aviation fuel and stores. The issue was however forced by the speed of the Japanese advance which threatened the airfields in central Malaya, and the need to find room for the expected air reinforcements for which adequate dispersion was not possible on the airfields still available. It was therefore decided on the 27th December to make arrangements for basing bomber aircraft in Sumatra and to establish a nucleus bomber group there. A few days later Dutch fighter aircraft were flown from Singapore to Palembang where they were given the task of protecting convoys bringing reinforcements through the Sunda and Banka Straits.[1]

The enforced withdrawal of the British air forces from northern Malaya was a direct result not only of the overwhelming strength of the Japanese air force but of the superiority of its aircraft. Although inadequate maintenance facilities and the absence of effective warning systems had placed squadrons using the northern airfields at a disadvantage, the superior performance of the Japanese Zero fighter compared with the Buffalo was the decisive factor.[2] Up to the outbreak of war a totally wrong assessment of the calibre and general efficiency of the Japanese Army Air Force had persisted. Despite the fact that the Japanese had gained combat experience in air operations in China and had had the benefit of the services of German technicians for a long period before December 1941, it had always been assumed that the Japanese Army Air Force would be found to be much less efficient than the air forces of the European Powers.

Until June 1941, Headquarters, Air Command, Far East, had no air intelligence organization and had to rely upon the Combined Intelligence Bureau, primarily a naval organization under the control of the Commander-in-Chief, China. This had neither the staff nor the means to satisfy air intelligence requirements in addition to those of the navy and the army. An attempt to improve the organization was begun in July 1941, but had not been completed when the war started. Nevertheless, despite the absence of a proper organization, technical data on the Zero fighter were available at Headquarters, Air Command. This had been passed to the Air Ministry, but unfortunately not to the air crews of squadrons in the Far East Command who, had they received it, might have been able to adopt fighter tactics to meet the Zero on more equal terms.[3]

After the evacuation of the air force from Kuala Lumpur the fighter squadrons were reorganized. A composite fighter squadron

---

[1] See Strategic Map.

[2] See Appendix 8.

[3] (a) At a meeting of the Chiefs of Staff on the 25th April 1941, the Vice-Chief of the Naval Staff advocated the despatch of Hurricane fighters to Malaya. The Vice-Chief of the Air Staff thereupon stated that Buffalo fighters would be more than a match for the Japanese aircraft which were not of the latest type.

(b) In May 1941 a Japanese Zero fighter was shot down in China. Details of the armament and tankage reached Singapore and were passed to the Air Ministry on the 26th July 1941, as well as to Headquarters, Air Command, Far East. Later, the Air Attaché, Chungking, forwarded estimated performance figures which subsequently proved reasonably accurate. On the 29th September 1941, the Combined Intelligence Bureau transmitted this data to the same two authorities. Faulty organization at Headquarters, Air Command, whose establishment did not include an intelligence staff, resulted in this valuable report remaining unsifted from the general mass of intelligence information, and in no action being taken upon it.

was formed whose primary role was to co-operate with III Corps, using Kuala Lumpur as an advanced landing ground. At the same time efforts were made to improve the performance of the Buffalo aircraft engaged in the defence of Singapore, by changing their armament and reducing their ammunition and petrol loads.[1] Although some improvement resulted, this fighter was still no match for the Japanese Zero.

Extensive reconnaissance patrols were flown daily over the South China Sea and the Strait of Malacca to detect the approach of enemy convoys towards Mersing and Kuantan on the east coast and any attempt by the Japanese to use coastal craft to move down the coasts of the Malayan peninsula in support of their land advances. Dutch aircraft co-operated by covering the coast of northern Sumatra from Sabang to Medan to a distance of fifty miles out to sea, for enemy landings in that area would threaten the air reinforcement route from India.[2] No convoys were however sighted, and the results of the coastal reconnaissance were generally negative owing to the ease with which small vessels could take cover by day in the many creeks and mangrove swamps lining the coast.

At the same time the solitary photographic reconnaissance Buffalo made long flights northwards and brought back valuable information. On the 26th December thirty-four transport and supply ships were observed off Singora, while on the 27th no less than 120 aircraft were reported at Sungei Patani. That night a striking force of six Blenheim bombers of 34 (B) Squadron from Singapore bombed the airfield at Sungei Patani, causing numerous fires and a large explosion, and returned without loss. Subsequent photographic reconnaissance confirmed that twelve fighters were destroyed or damaged and three bombers damaged by this attack. The target was attacked again on the following night and more fires and damage were caused, but on this occasion one Blenheim failed to return. These night bombing raids involved flying long distances over jungle-clad country and, at times, through violent tropical thunderstorms. The British, Australian and New Zealand air crews who made these hazardous flights with determination and skill were worthy of the highest praise.

On the 23rd December Lieut.-General Sir Henry Pownall arrived in Singapore and four days later took over command in the Far East from Air Chief Marshal Sir Robert Brooke-Popham.[3] The new Commander-in-Chief's directive differed in some respects from that

---

[1] The all-up weight of the Buffaloes was reduced by approximately 1,000 lb.
[2] See Strategic Map.
[3] See page 80.

S

given to his predecessor. He was to be jointly responsible with the Commander-in-Chief, Eastern Fleet, for the conduct of British strategy in the Far East, but it was not intended that he should assume operational control, or the administrative and financial responsibilities and the normal day-to-day functions exercised by the General Officers Commanding Hong Kong, Malaya, Burma and the Air Officer Commanding, Far East.[1]

On the 24th December Brigadier Paris, an officer with considerable experience of bush warfare, replaced General Murray-Lyon in command of 11th Division and, since all the original brigade commanders were in hospital, new brigadiers were appointed.[2]

Heath had selected two main positions suitable for defence south of Ipoh, the first at Kampar, some twenty miles to the south, and the second north of Tanjong Malim to cover the important road junction at Kuala Kubu, with three intermediate positions at Tapah, Bidor and in the Slim River area.[3] He had decided that the reconstituted 15th Brigade should occupy the Kampar position,[4] while 12th and 28th Brigades fought delaying actions on the main road north and south of Ipoh and on the Blanja front respectively. In accordance with this plan 15th Brigade, now rested and partly re-equipped, had moved to the Kampar position on the 23rd and had begun preparing its defences. On the same day Heath had sent a message to Percival asking that steps should be taken to construct a series of defensive positions south of Kampar on which his troops could retire, for he was unable both to fight the Japanese and to prepare rearward positions. Percival arranged in the following week that surplus officers from the Public Works Department should be organized into works groups in selected areas under the State Engineers. He informed both Heath and Bennett of these arrangements on the 29th and said that the State Engineers would report to them for orders, the object being to prepare a series of obstacles, especially anti-tank obstacles, in great depth on probable lines of enemy advance. Since III Corps staff was too much occupied to give time to the construction of such defences well in rear of the fighting line and the P.W.D. officers could not provide sufficient labour, this effort produced little result. Had the organization of all defence works in rear areas been placed under the Chief Engineer, Malaya Command, with instructions to provide permanent anti-tank obstacles in selected defiles, something useful might have been accomplished.

---

[1] See Appendix 4.

[2] 15th Indian Infantry Brigade, Lieut.-Colonel Moorhead (3/16th Punjab). 12th Indian Infantry Brigade, Lieut.-Colonel Stewart (2nd Argyll & Sutherland Highlanders). 28th Indian Infantry Brigade, Lieut.-Colonel Selby (2/9th Gurkha Rifles).

[3] See page 232.

[4] After reorganization 15th Brigade was composed of the British Battalion (made up from 1st Leicestershire and 2nd East Surrey) the composite Jat/Punjab Battalion, 1/14th Punjab, 2/16th Punjab and 3/16th Punjab.

The Japanese crossed the Perak River unopposed and by morning on the 26th had concentrated *4th Guards Regiment* east of it with orders to advance on Ipoh. General Yamashita believed that the fighting spirit of the British troops had been so reduced that III Corps would offer serious resistance only at long intervals, and would rely almost entirely on the destruction of bridges and communications to delay his advance. He appreciated correctly that III Corps would plan to hold a series of defensive positions along the stretch of country between Kampar and Kuala Kubu, which constituted a defile, for the single road and railway offered little opportunity for outflanking movement except by the coast. He hoped however that the speed and momentum of his advance would prevent prolonged resistance in the defile. He therefore decided that, after the capture of Ipoh, *5th Division* was to advance rapidly southwards on the trunk road with Kuala Lumpur as its objective, while *4th Guards Regiment* was to be kept in reserve with the idea that it might be used when *5th Division* had reached Kuala Kubu, to carry out a rapid outflanking movement, by way of Bentong, to cut the British retreat route south of Kuala Lumpur.

Brigadier Stewart (12th Brigade) had meanwhile disposed his battalions in depth on the trunk road north of Ipoh covering Chemor, supported by 137th Field Regiment, and had selected positions to the south in case he was forced to withdraw. On the afternoon of the 26th, after two days of minor patrol activity, the Japanese *4th Guards Regiment* attacked. Fierce fighting followed and continued the next day, during which the enemy, at heavy cost, gained only some three miles of ground. The 12th Brigade sustained about 200 casualties, including a company of 4/19th Hyderabad which was surrounded and almost annihilated.

General Paris, whose instructions were to delay the enemy north of Kampar but to keep his division intact for the subsequent role of holding the Kampar position, was by this time deeply concerned about the fatigue of the troops of 12th Brigade who had been in contact with the enemy almost continuously for twelve days. An eye-witness described the condition of the men as follows:

> 'The troops were very tired. Constant enemy air attacks pre-
> vented them from obtaining any sleep by day. By night they
> either had to move, obtaining such sleep as was possible in
> crowded lorries, or had to work on preparing yet another
> defensive position. The resultant physical strain of day and night
> fighting, of nightly moves or work, and the consequent lack of
> sleep was cumulative and finally reached the limit of endurance.
> Officers and men moved like automata and often could not
> grasp the simplest order.'

Paris felt that further attacks by fresh enemy troops might make the withdrawal of the brigade extremely hazardous. Moreover, enemy

activity at Blanja threatened to involve 28th Brigade, which he wished
to be fresh for the defence of Kampar. He therefore ordered both
brigades to withdraw south of Ipoh during the night of the 27th/28th.
The 28th Brigade was to move to Sahum on the right flank of the
Kampar position and 12th Brigade to covering positions in depth
along the main road from Gopeng to Dipang.

He had hoped that a respite of at least three days would be gained
by the withdrawal of 12th Brigade from the Chemor area. This hope
was short-lived. The Japanese followed up quickly and made contact
at Gopeng during the afternoon of the 28th. The subsequent action,
which lasted throughout the night and continued on the 29th, was
nearly disastrous. Subjected to dive-bombing and the heaviest
artillery bombardment yet experienced, the troops were by midday
forced back to within three miles of Dipang. In these circumstances
Paris ordered 28th Brigade to establish a two-company bridgehead
covering the bridge across the Sungei Kampar at Dipang and gave
Stewart permission to withdraw through Dipang at 7 p.m.

At 3 p.m. the Japanese, supported by about eight tanks, launched
a strong attack on the tired Argylls who for the second time that
day were in an unprepared position without any effective anti-tank
support, since owing to a misunderstanding of orders 2nd Anti-Tank
Battery had failed to take up its allotted position. The tanks failed to
break through, but the Argylls were forced back on to 5/2nd Punjab.
The rearward impetus was stopped only by the resource of Lieut.-
Colonel C. C. Deakin, commanding the Punjabi battalion, who
somehow contrived to establish a check position about three-quarters
of a mile north of Dipang, covered by a troop of 2nd Anti-Tank
Battery hurriedly brought into action.

At about 6.15 p.m. 12th Brigade, which for the past fortnight had
so doggedly borne the brunt of the attacks by the greater part of the
Japanese *5th Division*, withdrew through the bridgehead troops[1] and
then moved to Bidor where it was hoped that it would have time to
rest and reorganize.

At the Dipang bridge, disaster was narrowly averted. The bridge
had been prepared for demolition, but on the morning of the 29th for
reasons unknown 28th Brigade had ordered 23rd Field Company to
withdraw the charges. This order was carried out and the field
company then moved to undertake work elsewhere. During the day,
as 12th Brigade withdrew on to Dipang, the officer commanding
3rd Field Company (under command of 12th Brigade) discovered
that the bridge was not prepared for demolition. He was told to have
it ready in half an hour. After some delay the explosives removed
from the bridge that morning were found, but by that time it was

---

[1] One company 2/9th Gurkha Rifles and one company 2/2nd Gurkha Rifles.

raining heavily and a stream of traffic was pouring southwards across the bridge. There was no time to fix or tamp the charges thoroughly and the primers were wet. When the order to blow the bridge was given as the last troops cleared it, the charges failed to explode and the bridgehead had to be reoccupied in face of the advancing enemy and new charges and circuits fixed. Owing to the danger of the bridge being rushed, it was then decided to blow any section as it was ready, but it was only at the third blow that one end of the bridge was dropped into the river and an adequate obstacle provided.

General Percival had hoped that the whole of the Perak Flotilla could be based on Port Swettenham,[1] but, a few days after it had been formed, part had to be diverted to counter any enemy movement across the Strait of Malacca towards northern Sumatra. The remainder of the flotilla was used, on the 28th December, to transport 'Roseforce' to undertake a raid against the enemy line of communication, west of the Perak River.[2] Although some of the motor vessels broke down, thus reducing the strength of the party, a landing was made on the coast near Trong and some motor transport on the coastal road and staff cars carrying senior Japanese officers were ambushed and destroyed. On completion of its task, the raiding party returned to Port Swettenham. The success of this minor operation encouraged the hope of developing and repeating it; but two days later H.M.S. *Kudat*, the base depot ship for the flotilla, was bombed and sunk at Port Swettenham. A serious loss was also sustained when five fast motor boats, on their way north to reinforce the flotilla, were attacked by enemy aircraft and sunk or driven ashore. These losses could not be made up and thus no further operations of this nature could be undertaken.

The Kampar position, where General Heath hoped to halt the Japanese advance, lay either side of a steep jungle-clad hill (known as Bujang Melaka) which covered an area nine miles long and six miles wide, stretching southwards from Dipang between the trunk road and the Sahum road.[3] To the north and west lay an extensive open tin mining area, broken only on the extreme south-west by the Cicely Rubber Estate, giving, with the exception of the rubber area, a field of fire for small arms extending to 1,200 yards or even more. Artillery observation was good except to the east of the hill. The position could be turned only from Telok Anson by troops transported either by sea or down the Perak River.

---

[1] See page 233.
[2] See footnote, page 233
[3] See Map 13.

The 15th Brigade, with 88th Field Regiment and 273rd Anti-Tank Battery under command, was disposed in considerable depth astride the trunk road at Kampar village. The 28th Brigade, supported by 155th Field Regiment and one troop of 215th Anti-Tank Battery, was in depth astride the Sahum road, and was initially given the dual role of protecting the road itself and striking at the enemy's communications, once he was committed to the attack on Kampar village. To meet any threat from Telok Anson by enemy formations moving by sea or down the river, Paris had placed 12th Brigade, with 137th Field Regiment and two troops of 215th Anti-Tank Battery in support, at Bidor and ordered 1st Independent Company and 3rd Cavalry to guard the approaches to Telok Anson. He retained 5/14th Punjab, a mountain battery and an anti-tank battery at Temoh in divisional reserve.

The Japanese lost no time in making contact with the Kampar position and on the 30th their patrols were observed to the east of the Sahum road. This, and the fact that he had that day been ordered to send 2/1st Gurkha Rifles to Temoh to increase the divisional reserve, induced Brigadier Selby to withdraw 2/9th Gurkha Rifles from its exposed outpost position to replace the 2/1st. On the 31st, air reconnaissance reported small convoys of boats off Pangkor Island. During the afternoon a patrol of 1st Independent Company, watching the approaches to the mouth of the Perak River, observed enemy troops both at Lumut and a few miles east of Simpang Ampat. The same day strong Japanese patrols were reported in the Cicely Estate south-west of the Kampar position. Paris therefore decided to move his reserve during the night from Temoh to the Kampar–Changkat Jong road so as to be ready to counter-attack if, as seemed probable, the Japanese attacked his left flank.[1] In this he was wise for, as is now known, the Japanese plan was for *9th Infantry Brigade* to attack at Kampar, using *41st Infantry Regiment* astride the road while the *42nd* undertook an encircling movement to envelop the British left flank. The *42nd Regiment* however had great difficulty in crossing the swamps on either side of the Sungei Kampar and after a slow and arduous three days' march arrived exhausted in its allotted position too late to play any effective part in the battle.

At 7 a.m. on New Year's Day 1942, after half an hour of intensive bombardment, the Japanese launched a strong attack down the trunk road on the British Battalion holding Kampar. The attack was held, except on the extreme right of the position, where the enemy managed to make a lodgement on Thompsons Ridge. Severe fighting continued throughout the day, but by nightfall, although the

---

[1] 5/14th Punjab, 2/1st Gurkha Rifles and 7th Mountain Battery.

British Battalion was still holding its own, the Japanese held the northern edge of Thompsons Ridge. On the Sahum road the day was quiet and it seemed that the Japanese had abandoned that line of advance. In view of the growing threat to his lines of communication along the Bernam River, which was navigable for a long distance inland, Paris decided during the day to reduce the force holding the road and ordered 28th Brigade to send 2/2nd Gurkha Rifles to the Slim River area.

Meanwhile at about 9 a.m. a patrol of 1st Independent Company had seen a tug and four barges grounded on a sandbank at the mouth of the Perak River. This information was passed to Headquarters III Corps in the hope that naval and air action could be taken. By the time that bomber aircraft arrived however, the tug had been re-floated and moved elsewhere. In the evening a flotilla of seven small steamers, each towing several barges and landing craft, was reported off the mouth of the Bernam River and at about 7.30 p.m., one and a half battalions of the Japanese *11th Infantry Regiment*, which had embarked at Port Weld, began landing at Utan Melintang. Driving back a patrol of 3rd Cavalry, the enemy had by 8 p.m. gained possession of the village and of the crossroads about half a mile further north. Paris immediately ordered 12th Brigade, with 137th Field Regiment in support, to hold the approaches from Telok Anson to Bidor and Tapah.

In view of the threat to his communications which had developed during the day, Paris asked permission to be allowed to withdraw from Kampar at his discretion. Heath referred this request to Percival, who was with him at Kuala Lumpur reconsidering his strategic plans after having recently visited both 9th and 11th Divisions to see for himself the state of the troops. It was still necessary to hold the enemy for as long as possible in central Malaya,[1] and Percival therefore hoped that control of the Kuantan airfield could be retained until about the 10th January, after which he could withdraw 9th Division west of Jerantut.[2] This meant that 11th Division would have to keep the enemy north of Kuala Kubu until the 15th. Since the division had a depth of some seventy miles in which to manœuvre and the road south of Kampar passed through a defile, he felt this should be possible. He therefore agreed to 11th Division's withdrawal from Kampar on the understanding that III Corps held the enemy north of Kuala Kubu till the 15th, although if any further threats developed on the west coast this date might have to be advanced.

At dawn on the 2nd the Japanese renewed their attack astride the trunk road and made repeated attempts to gain possession of

[1] See page 231.
[2] See Map 5.

Thompsons Ridge. By midday they had succeeded in penetrating as far south as Green Ridge. An immediate counter-attack failed to eject them, but later in the afternoon an attack by the Gujar and Sikh company of the Jat/Punjab Battalion, led with great gallantry and carried out with the utmost determination, succeeded in retaking the ridge at the cost of heavy casualties. The British Battalion had withstood repeated and relentless attacks for two days. Its staunch defence under the leadership of Lieut.-Colonel C. E. Morrison fully accorded with the fine traditions of the Leicestershire and East Surrey Regiments, from whose battalions it had been so recently formed. But although for the time being the situation had been restored, it was soon evident that the Japanese were assembling for further attacks and Brigadier Moorhead informed Paris that he could not hold out indefinitely.

The decisive factor however was the course of events on the west coast. The Japanese force which had landed at Utan Melintang was reinforced on the 2nd by *III/4th Guards Battalion*, which had moved down the Perak River in small boats and had begun to land at 7 a.m. at Telok Anson, where it became involved in street fighting with 1st Independent Company. The 12th Brigade meanwhile had taken up positions in depth, with 2nd Argylls some four miles to the east of Telok Anson and the rest of the brigade behind them. At 9 a.m. 1st Independent Company and 3rd Cavalry were withdrawn through them to Degong. This brigade had no easy task, for the enemy was able to move not only along the road but up the rivers which were tidal and navigable for many miles inland, and many small craft were available. By 2 p.m. the leading enemy troops were once again in contact with 2nd Argylls, who withdrew slowly, and by nightfall 12th Brigade was holding a position on the road some seven miles east of Telok Anson.

General Paris decided that he would have to pull out of the Kampar position that night. In the evening he ordered 28th Brigade to take up a position from which the enemy could be held north of Tapah till dusk on the 3rd, 12th Brigade to deny Ayer Kuning to the enemy until midnight on the 3rd/4th, and 15th Brigade to begin its withdrawal from Kampar at 9 p.m. and cover the road junction at Bidor until both the other brigades had cleared it. The 15th Brigade was able to disengage without much difficulty, and throughout the 3rd the enemy was held at Tapah and Ayer Kuning. During the night of the 3rd/4th January both 28th and 12th Brigades withdrew according to plan through 15th Brigade at Bidor to the Slim River area. The 15th Brigade then withdrew to Sungkai.

Apart from the air reconnaissance on both coasts of the peninsula, little direct air support was available for III Corps throughout this critical period. By contrast, the Japanese air force was constantly

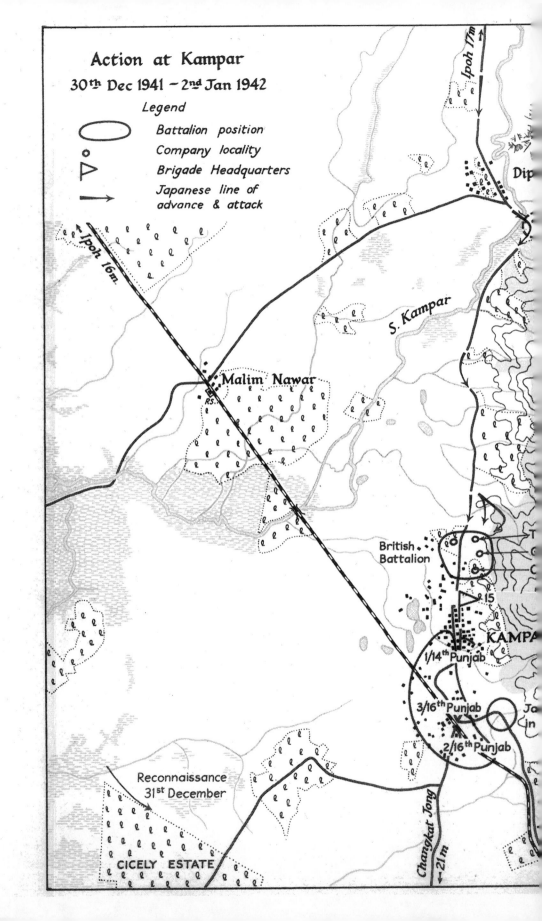

Action at Kampar
30th Dec 1941 – 2nd Jan 1942

Legend

Battalion position
Company locality
Brigade Headquarters
Japanese line of advance & attack

Ipoh 17m.

Dip

S. Kampar

Ipoh 16m.

Malim Nawar

R.S.

British Battalion

15

KAMPA

1/14th Punjab

3/16th Punjab

2/16th Punjab

Ja
In

Reconnaissance
31st December

Changkat Jong

21m.

CICELY ESTATE

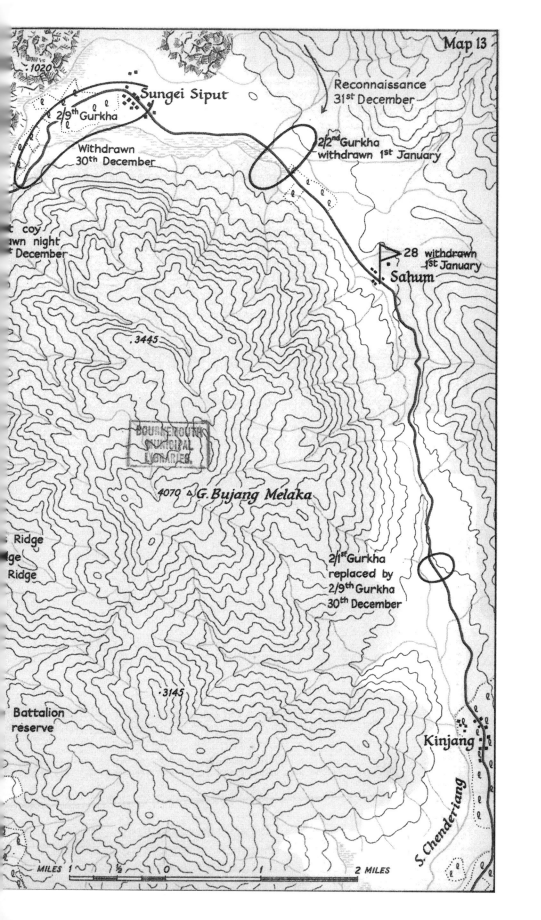

Map 13

Reconnaissance
31st December

Sungei Siput

2/9ᵗʰ Gurkha

2/2ⁿᵈ Gurkha
withdrawn 1ˢᵗ January

Withdrawn
30th December

t coy
wn night
December

28 withdrawn
1ˢᵗ January

Sahum

.3445

BOURNEMOUTH
MUNICIPAL
LIBRARIES.

4070 △ G. Bujang Melaka

Ridge
ge
Ridge

2/1ˢᵗ Gurkha
replaced by
2/9ᵗʰ Gurkha
30ᵗʰ December

.3145

Battalion
reserve

Kinjang

S. Chenderiang

MILES 1   ½   0   1   2 MILES

attacking forward troops and communications. The casualties and damage they inflicted were insignificant, but their unopposed bombing and machine-gunning undoubtedly affected the morale of both British and Indian troops. Allied air resources were quite inadequate to meet their many commitments. Priority had been given to assuring the arrival, free from enemy air attack, of the all-important convoys bringing reinforcements, and throughout the action at Kampar the whole of the Allied fighter force had been concentrated on that task. On the 3rd January, under cover of fighter aircraft and guarded against submarines by air reconnaissance, the first reinforcement convoy, carrying 45th Indian Infantry Brigade, reached Singapore safely.

CHAPTER XV

REINFORCEMENTS FOR THE
FAR EAST

See Strategic Map

BEFORE WAR SPREAD to the Far East, the defence of
Britain and the Middle East had been given precedence over
those areas where war, though growing ever more probable,
was not yet certain. As a result in December 1941 the garrisons
in Malaya and Hong Kong fell far short of the strength necessary for
their security.

India was little better off. Although in the previous two years of
war her army had been expanded to over a million men, it was short
of equipment and had suffered from the defects inherent in rapid
expansion. Trained officers and men had been taken from existing
formations to give body to new ones, and the level of efficiency of the
whole had fallen in consequence. As soon as her formations had been
raised and trained they had been sent overseas. In all, some 200,000
men had gone to the Middle East, Iraq and Persia, Burma and
Malaya.[1] It was quite clear therefore that the forces in the Far East
at the outbreak of war with Japan could not contend unaided with
the strength that the enemy could bring against them.

It was against this background that the Chiefs of Staff met to see
what naval, military and air reinforcements they could find for the
new theatre of war from the limited resources at their disposal.
From the naval point of view, the importance of the Indian Ocean
was second only to that of the Atlantic. On its security rested the
ability to supply the armies in the Middle East, to give aid to Russia
through Persia, to reinforce India, Burma and Malaya and to come
to the help if need be of Australia and New Zealand. Its defence was
therefore vital, but in the new situation it was threatened by naval
forces far greater than any which could be spared to meet them.

The sinking of the *Prince of Wales* and *Repulse* had removed the
only remaining force of capital ships which, after the destruction of
the United States Pacific Fleet at Pearl Harbour, could have
seriously interfered with the operations of the Japanese Navy. The

---

[1] See page 39.

enemy had thus obtained, in the first three days of the war, complete naval superiority from India to the Pacific. There was nothing in Far Eastern waters capable of challenging that superiority. The American, British and Dutch squadrons in the south-west Pacific could muster between them no more than nine cruisers and some twenty-three destroyers, most of them over-age. Their main strength was in submarines. In Australian waters there were five cruisers and three destroyers. What was left of the United States Pacific Fleet after the holocaust at Pearl Harbour was several thousand miles away on the other side of the Pacific. In the Indian Ocean there was the small aircraft carrier *Hermes*, and a few cruisers engaged on convoy work. The aircraft carrier *Indomitable*, which had been refitting in the United States, was due to arrive at Capetown about the 1st January.

Admiral Layton, who had been appointed Commander-in-Chief of the Eastern Fleet after the loss of Admiral Phillips, told the Admiralty on the 11th December that in his opinion the correct strategy in the Far East was to maintain sea communications, inflict the maximum damage by air and submarine on the enemy, and, by holding as much of Malaya as possible, retain the use of Singapore as a base for the Eastern Fleet. For these tasks he asked for all the submarines, minesweepers, destroyers and aircraft that could be spared.

The Chiefs of Staff, though approving this strategy, held out no hope of immediate reinforcements. Minesweepers from the Red Sea had already been transferred to the Commander-in-Chief, East Indies; all available cruisers were already under Admiral Layton's command; no destroyers could be spared from other theatres, which were already desperately short of these craft, and no submarines could be moved from the Mediterranean until the battle then raging in Libya was over. Four of the older battleships were however being sent and one had already arrived in the Indian Ocean. The reconstitution of the Eastern Fleet, based initially in the Indian Ocean, remained the Chiefs of Staff's long-term policy. They hoped to bring this fleet up to a strength of five modern capital ships, four old battleships and three or four carriers, but owing to losses and war damage this strength could not be attained before April 1942 at the earliest. Thus for the time being Admiral Layton had to do the best he could with the very limited resources at his disposal.

The provision of army and air reinforcements was not quite so difficult, for the Japanese entry into the war coincided with a short breathing space in the war against Germany. The unexpected Russian victories along the Don and in the Crimea had temporarily diminished the threat of a German thrust through the Caucasus to Iraq and Persia, and the success of General Sir Claude Auchinleck's

Libyan campaign had eased the situation in the Middle East. Reinforcements previously earmarked for these theatres could therefore be spared for the new theatre of war.

The Chiefs of Staff decided not to draw on military units and equipment already in the Middle East and Iraq, since to weaken the west in order to strengthen the east would have been robbing Peter to pay Paul and might well have resulted in a repetition of the reverses suffered in Libya when military forces were sent to the aid of Greece. It happened that 18th British Division, two anti-tank and two anti-aircraft artillery regiments were in convoys rounding the Cape on their way to the Middle East, and could easily be diverted to the Far East. They therefore decided on the 11th December that this division, and one anti-tank regiment,[1] would be put at the disposal of General Sir Archibald Wavell, who had become Commander-in-Chief, India, in July 1941; that the other anti-tank regiment and both anti-aircraft regiments should be sent to India for subsequent delivery to Malaya;[2] that 17th Indian Division, due to concentrate for training in Iraq by mid-February 1942, would remain in India to be used as Wavell thought fit; and that the control of Burma would be transferred to India Command, a move which successive Commanders-in-Chief, India, had long advocated.

The Chiefs of Staff had already received on the 8th December a telegram sent jointly by the Commander-in-Chief, Far East, and the Commander-in-Chief, Eastern Fleet, stating that the outcome of the battle in northern Malaya might well turn on the number of aircraft available and emphasizing the need for the maximum air reinforcements as early as possible. They fully appreciated the urgent need for more aircraft and decided to despatch all they could spare from the European battle to India, which was to become the concentration area and base for all air reinforcements for the Far East.

The first reinforcements were flown from Australia and the Middle East. On the 19th December, Australian air crews left Singapore by air for Darwin to collect eight Hudson II aircraft, which they delivered safely four days later. Between the 12th and 14th December twelve Blenheim IV aircraft were sent from Egypt by the air reinforcement route to Singapore, and six more followed later.[3]

---

[1] 82nd Anti-Tank Regiment (Officers and men only).
[2] 85th Anti-Tank Regiment (48 guns), 6th Heavy Anti-Aircraft Regiment (16 guns), and 35th Light Anti-Aircraft Regiment (24 guns).
[3] Air reinforcement route to the Far East: United Kingdom–Gibraltar–Malta–Egypt–Habbaniya (Iraq)–Basrah–Sharjah–Karachi–Allahabad–Calcutta–Mingaladon (Rangoon)–Victoria Point–Singapore. By December 1941, the air route was only partly developed and the problem of ferrying was considerable. It was calculated that delivery flights from the United Kingdom would involve some sixty hours flying time, mostly in the mornings, over a period of fifteen to twenty-one days. Normally, five or six aircraft would make up each formation, for which essential facilities would have to be provided.

On the 12th December the Japanese air force had attacked the airfield at Victoria Point in southern Burma. The airfield was evacuated the following day and occupied by the Japanese on the 15th. Thereafter the normal air reinforcement route along the west coast of Malaya was unusable and Sabang, off the coast of Sumatra, had to be used in place of Victoria Point. Since the new stages covered distances beyond the range of fighters, all reinforcement of such aircraft had to be sent by sea. On the 17th a Hurricane wing, loaded in a convoy then at the Cape, was diverted to Singapore. In this convoy there were fifty-one Hurricanes in crates, with twenty-four pilots, a wing headquarters and the ground staffs for four fighter squadrons. It was arranged that on arrival at Durban on the 18th the fifty-one aircraft, with the pilots and ground staff for one squadron, would be transhipped and go direct to Singapore. The wing headquarters and ground staff for the remaining three squadrons would go to Bombay where they would be placed at the disposal of the Commander-in-Chief, India. To equip these squadrons with aircraft in India, the *Athene* was ordered from Gibraltar to Takoradi (West Africa) to embark forty Hurricanes, deliver them to Bombay, and then proceed to Port Sudan for a further forty.[1]

In the United Kingdom, arrangements were made for thirty-six light bombers (Hudson III) to be flown to the Far East, while a further sixteen were earmarked as special reinforcements. The first of these left on the 29th December, and by the 6th January twenty-three Hudsons were *en route*. Since they would be unlikely to reach Malaya much before the end of January, the Chiefs of Staff urged that American four-engined bombers, which they understood had arrived in Australia, should be flown without delay to Malaya or the Netherlands East Indies.[2]

On the 12th December the Prime Minister cabled General Wavell:

'You must now look east. Burma is placed under your command. You must resist the Japanese advance towards Burma and India and try to cut their communications down the Malay peninsula. We are diverting 18th Division now rounding [the] Cape, to Bombay, together with four fighter squadrons of R.A.F., now *en route* for the Caucasus, Caspian theatre. We are also sending you a special hamper of anti-aircraft and anti-tank guns, some of which are already *en route*. You should retain 17th Indian Division for defence against the Japanese. Marry these forces as you think best and work them into the Eastern fighting front to the highest advantage . . . I hope these new dispositions, arising

---

[1] In the event, H.M.S. *Athene* was diverted to Batavia after embarking forty Hurricanes at Takoradi.

[2] No four-engined bombers had in fact arrived in Australia.

from the vast changes in the world situation of the last four days, will commend themselves to you. I shall endeavour to feed you with armour, aircraft and white personnel to the utmost possible, having regard to the great strain we are under.'[1]

On the 13th the Chiefs of Staff's detailed decisions were sent to Wavell and he was asked for his proposals for reinforcing Burma. He replied that, as Burma was not from the administrative point of view capable of maintaining even one brigade group of British troops at that time, and since Indian troops were more suitable for that theatre of operations, 18th Division should be disembarked at Bombay and its destination settled later. In the meantime he was sending 45th Infantry Brigade Group (17th Indian Division) to Burma. It was to sail from Bombay on the 22nd December.

In reply to the Prime Minister's telegram Wavell said that the state of communications in Burma prevented any immediate action on land to cut the Japanese communications to the Malay peninsula. He felt that the main requirements were air and land reinforcements for Malaya, and some action to reduce the weight of air attack on that area. The bombing of airfields and harbours in southern Siam and enemy shipping in the Gulf of Siam might accomplish this, but he had no bombers left in either India or Burma. 'When may we expect Blenheims?' he asked. 'Unless they can arrive very soon it may be too late.'

Within a very few days of the Japanese entry into the war a flow of reinforcements to the Far East had started, but it was to be weeks, even months, before they could arrive and even longer before they could play an effective part in the defence of the threatened areas. It should be noted that, with the exception of fighter aircraft, the flow was directed towards India and Burma rather than to Malaya, for at that time it was hoped that the existing garrison of Malaya would be able to check the Japanese advance, provided that its deficiencies in aircraft were quickly made good. These hopes were soon to be rudely shattered.

The reverses in Malaya and the heavy losses suffered by 11th Division in the Kedah fighting resulted in the Commander-in-Chief, Far East, asking on the 16th for the immediate despatch from India of one brigade group and reinforcements for 9th and 11th Divisions. On the same day General Wavell, who had been kept fully in touch with the Malayan situation, offered one or two infantry brigade groups from 17th Indian Division if the need in Malaya really were urgent. Sir Robert, in replying to this offer, said that he would like two brigade groups, but since the time factor was all important he would rather have the reinforcements for the two Indian divisions

---

[1] Churchill, Volume III (Cassell, 1950), page 564.

with only one of the brigade groups, if they could be sent more quickly. He gave warning that 18th British Division would also be required for Malaya.

The reaction of the Chiefs of Staff to these requests was immediate: they asked Wavell to divert 45th Infantry Brigade from Burma to Singapore, to despatch the reinforcements for 9th and 11th Divisions as quickly as possible and to consider following these up by the second brigade he had tentatively offered. Wavell agreed to 45th Brigade being diverted and said that he was loading a second brigade group (44th) for Burma about the 1st January which could be sent to Malaya, though he was unwilling to agree to this at that moment. He had no objection however to 53rd Brigade Group of 18th Division, which he understood was loaded in one ship, proceeding direct to Malaya. As many reinforcements as he could find would embark about the 8th January.

The proposed diversion of 53rd Brigade Group gave rise to new difficulties. The brigade was in the American transport *Mount Vernon*, sailing in convoy with the remainder of 18th Division. This convoy was due at Bombay about the 31st December, and the divisional equipment and stores during the following week. If the *Mount Vernon* remained with the convoy, it was thought necessary that she should stay at least a week at Bombay so that the troops, who had been cooped up on board for nearly two months, would be able to stretch their legs ashore before going on to Malaya. This would mean that she would not leave Bombay before the 10th January and could not therefore arrive at Singapore before the 24th at the earliest. The alternative was that the *Mount Vernon* should go to Mombasa to refuel, and then join, at sea, a convoy which was leaving Durban on the 24th December direct for Singapore with reinforcements. This would give the troops only two or three days ashore at Mombasa and meant that they would arrive at Singapore without their transport or guns and with the minimum of equipment. The brigade would however arrive nearly a fortnight earlier.

The first course was obviously preferable, but at the urgent request of General Percival the Chiefs of Staff decided on the 23rd December that, despite the inherent disadvantages, the *Mount Vernon* should go direct to Singapore, subject to American approval. Two days later this was given.

By the 23rd it was evident that the enemy was concentrating on Malaya before turning to attack Burma; consequently the second formation from India (44th Indian Infantry Brigade) was ordered to embark for Singapore as soon after the 1st January as an escort could be provided. At the same time the Australian Cabinet offered to send a machine-gun battalion, one of the only two A.I.F. battalions in Australia at that time, and 1,900 reinforcements for 8th Australian

Division; this offer was gratefully accepted and arrangements were put in hand to move them without delay to Singapore.

By the 25th the following reinforcements were under orders for Malaya; 45th Indian Brigade; 53rd British Brigade Group, together with one anti-tank and two anti-aircraft regiments and the crated Hurricanes; 44th Indian Brigade; reinforcements for the two Indian divisions; an Australian machine-gun battalion; and reinforcements for 8th Australian Division.

The problem still unsolved was that of providing sufficient aircraft. Fighter aircraft had to be transported by sea, and the nearest at that time were at Durban 5,000 miles away. Bomber aircraft could be flown to Malaya, but they could be found only from a distance and the air reinforcement route was insufficiently developed. Thus many aircraft which started out failed to reach their destination and those that did arrived in small numbers, without ground staffs and not as complete units. They had to be thrown into action before their air-crews were acclimatized or trained for local conditions. Out of the eighteen bombers despatched from the Middle East, only seven Blenheims had reached Singapore by the 25th December; the others had either crashed or made forced landings on the way. The crated Hurricanes, due on the 8th January, would not be available for some time as they had to be erected and tested before they could be of any operational value.

More aircraft were still needed. On the 26th December the Prime Minister cabled to General Auchinleck that he had a hard request to make. Everything had been concentrated on the war in the Middle East with the result that the Far East was now desperately short of aircraft and equipment. He suggested that, without compromising the Libyan offensive, Auchinleck should be able to spare at once for Malaya four Hurricane fighter squadrons, and an armoured brigade equipped with American tanks. He pointed out that the ability to bring in reinforcements depended on having sufficient aircraft at Singapore to protect the sea approaches. Only air power at Singapore and Johore, he said, could keep the door open, and if the door was shut the fortress would fall.

Auchinleck made a generous response to the request. The aircraft were immediately made available and the *Indomitable* was ordered, on arrival at Durban on the 31st December, to proceed to Port Sudan to embark forty-eight Hurricanes with forty-eight pilots. She was then to sail eastwards, escorted by three Australian destroyers taken from the Mediterranean, to fly off her aircraft to Sumatra or Java and thence to Singapore. He made arrangements for the despatch of fifty light tanks, half of which were to be manned by 3rd Hussars and the other half by an Indian squadron, and prepared an armoured brigade, consisting of a brigade headquarters and two regiments

T

equipped with American light cruiser tanks.[1] In addition, he offered to send one Australian infantry brigade group, provided he could be assured of replacements before April 1942. He was however asked for still further sacrifices. On the 29th the Chiefs of Staff decided that two anti-aircraft regiments[2] together with the ground staff of a wing headquarters and three R.A.F. squadrons, due to arrive at Durban on the 8th January on their way to Suez, should go direct to Singapore.

As the threat to Singapore increased, Australia's growing anxiety for her safety was expressed in a series of telegrams from her Prime Minister to Mr. Churchill. The Commonwealth Commissioner in Singapore, Mr. Bowden, had on the 26th December painted a gloomy picture to the Australian Government. He thought that the measures taken for reinforcement were, from a practical standpoint, little more than gestures. In his view, the only thing that could save Singapore would be the immediate despatch from the Middle East of powerful reinforcements in the form of large numbers of the latest fighter aircraft, with ample operationally-trained crews. Military reinforcements should not be in brigades but in divisions.

Meanwhile General Bennett had telegraphed to Army Headquarters, Australia on both the 18th and 23rd saying that, if the situation were to be saved, it was essential that an Australian division from the Middle East should be sent to Malaya by the fastest possible means.

A report on the 29th from the Commander-in-Chief, Far East, was no less disquieting. It appeared to him that the enemy was seeking a decision in the Philippines, the successful outcome of which would release large forces for operations further south. An attack on Rangoon, if only to hamper the Chinese war effort, was probable. The security of Sumatra was essential for the defence of the convoy route through the Sunda and the Banka Straits, and full Dutch co-operation was clearly needed; to obtain this, it was necessary to hold Java. Hence the protracted defence of Singapore called for the defence of southern Malaya, Sumatra and Java. The army reinforcements now planned could do little more than relieve tired troops, guard against landings on the west coast of Malaya and increase slightly the ground and anti-aircraft protection for the airfields in Sumatra. The fighter reinforcements would give a welcome temporary relief but their strength could not be maintained. He could not give a precise estimate of all the reinforcements required but confirmed on the 1st January that the whole of 18th Division would be wanted in Malaya and that at least one other division should follow at once.

---

[1] This afterwards became known as 7th Armoured Brigade.
[2] 21st Light Anti-Aircraft Regiment and 77th Heavy Anti-Aircraft Regiment.

The diversion of formations allotted to India and Burma brought a protest from Wavell on the 29th. He was very much disturbed, he said, at the manner in which formations and units promised him for the defence of Burma and India had been diverted wholesale elsewhere. Since he had assumed responsibility for the defence of Ceylon and Burma, his reserves had been weakened rather than strengthened. He pointed out that immediately after the outbreak of war with Japan he had been promised by the Prime Minister 18th British Division and a 'special hamper' of anti-aircraft and anti-tank guns, and had been told that he could retain 17th Indian Division for the defence of Burma and India. But one brigade of the former division and two brigades of the latter together with various regiments of anti-aircraft artillery had all been sent to Malaya, leaving him only Headquarters 17th Division with one brigade group and one semi-trained brigade for the immediate reinforcement of Burma. Further, two East African brigades, which had been previously offered to him and which he required for the defence of Ceylon, would not be arriving before the end of February because of shipping and other difficulties. He asked that the remainder of 18th Division should be left in India and added, 'If I am to carry out my tasks it is essential that there should be increased quotas of equipment to India instead of diversions'.

It was cold comfort however that Wavell received from the Chiefs of Staff. They replied on the 30th that, while they fully sympathized with his views, the situation had changed considerably since the Prime Minister's offer had been made and had become much more critical than had at that time seemed likely. They considered that the Japanese would probably make the capture of the Philippines and Malaya their main objects before turning their attention to Burma. In the circumstances they had no option but to use the meagre resources available to meet the more immediate danger.

The policy of reinforcements for the Far East had been under constant review by the Chiefs of Staff ever since the outbreak of war with Japan. On the 1st January they formulated their decisions, which were accepted by the War Cabinet and cabled to the commanders concerned. The governing considerations were that the security of Singapore and the sea communications in the Indian Ocean were second only to the security of the United Kingdom and the sea communications thereto; that the defeat of Germany must remain the primary object, and thus no more forces could be diverted to the Far East than were absolutely necessary to hold the Japanese; and that the Libyan offensive should be exploited to the greatest possible extent, with the proviso that it must not prevent the despatch of essential reinforcements to the Far East. With these considerations as a background, the reinforcements allotted to the Far East were to be two divisions and one armoured brigade for Malaya, two divisions for the Netherlands East Indies and two divisions and one light tank squadron for Burma. At the same time, the Chiefs of Staff fixed the target strength for the air forces at eight light bomber squadrons, eight fighter squadrons and two torpedo-bomber squadrons for Malaya; and six light bomber squadrons and six fighter squadrons for Burma. No air target for the Netherlands East Indies was fixed, as the only channel of supply was from the United States by way of Australia, but the importance of re-equipping, maintaining and expanding the Dutch air forces was stressed to the American authorities in Washington, who were asked to assist.

The political and strategical importance of holding the Naval Base, which by the end of December was seriously threatened, had caused the Chiefs of Staff to abandon the original idea of counter-action from Burma and concentrate everything on the defence of Singapore. They were in fact forced into bolstering up what was already a lost cause. The initiative lay with the enemy, and his early successes had enabled him to draw all the available reinforcements which Britain could spare from the war in Europe and the Middle East to the point where they could most easily be destroyed.

The remainder of 18th Division then at Bombay was ordered to go at once to Malaya; Middle East Command was ordered to despatch 7th Armoured Brigade and, with the approval of the Australian Government, to prepare 1st Australian Corps, composed of 6th and 7th Australian Divisions, for despatch to the Netherlands East Indies. These formations, with those already on their way, provided for practically all the estimated requirements of both Malaya and the Netherlands East Indies. India Command was faced with the difficult problem of finding the troops for Burma. Two brigades from 17th Indian Division and the whole of 18th Division, originally allotted to India, had been diverted to Singapore. Wavell was thus left with only one brigade of 17th Division, and, though in theory two new Indian divisions would be coming forward during the early part of 1942,[1] any large reinforcements from India required during January or February could only be semi-trained, partially equipped and hastily assembled formations.

Although the decision had been taken to send these reinforcements to Malaya and the Netherlands East Indies, it was many weeks before they could arrive. The 45th Indian Brigade was due on the 3rd January and its equipment on the 6th; 53rd British Brigade Group (without transport and guns), with the additional Hurricanes and artillery regiments, on the 13th; 44th Indian Brigade, 2/4th Australian Machine-Gun Battalion and the reinforcements for 8th

---

[1] 14th and 19th Indian Divisions.

ASSESSMENT OF REINFORCEMENTS 261

Australian Division about the 25th; the remainder of 18th Division
at the end of January and the reinforcements for 9th and 11th Indian
Divisions on the 5th February. The 7th Armoured Brigade could not
leave Suez until the end of January. As the move of the Australian
Corps involved the shipment of 60,000 men and 8,000 vehicles three
separate convoys were needed, the first of which could not leave
before the first week in February.

The reinforcements sent to Malaya were not nearly as strong as
they appeared to be on paper. The troops India had sent overseas
before December 1941 had had perforce to leave her shores ill-
equipped and semi-trained, and had had to undergo several months
of formation training after they had received their full equipment on
arrival in the theatre of war to which they had been sent. The 44th
and 45th Brigades were no exception, but they were all India had to
offer. The 18th Division had been destined for the Middle East where
it had been intended that it should complete its training. It was not
therefore tactically loaded and would arrive at the end of a long and
tedious voyage without transport, supporting arms, or adequate
maintenance facilities. It would not be an efficient fighting formation
ready for action for some time. The troops would be soft after several
weeks at sea in crowded transports; and they had had no training in
jungle warfare.

The only reinforcing formations which were fully trained and had
experience of war, and which could therefore be expected to overcome the difficulties of climate and terrain, were the Australian Corps
and 7th Armoured Brigade, but these were the last to move and thus,
unless the situation changed for the better, might well arrive too late.
The difficulties of finding shipping and the need for speed however
led the Chiefs of Staff to select those formations which were immediately available and nearest to the scene of operations, regardless
of their fighting value.

The defence plan for Malaya rested largely on the strength and
efficiency of the air forces available in the country and on the speed
with which they could be reinforced. The theory on which so
much of the pre-war planning had been based—that the mobility
of aircraft would always enable them to reach rapidly any threatened
point along prepared air reinforcement routes—proved in practice
to be unsound.[1] Although the air forces were fully engaged in
Europe and the Middle East, large numbers of aircraft were found
for the Far East during December 1941–January 1942, but with the
Japanese astride the air reinforcement route from India at Victoria
Point in southern Burma, the problem was how to get the short-
range fighters to Malaya in time. They could only be shipped direct

[1] See pages 7 and 11-12.

to Singapore or to Java to be erected on arrival, flown off aircraft carriers, or shipped to Australia and then erected and flown to Java by way of Timor and Bali. All this required time and depended on whether the rapidly diminishing naval and air strength available on the spot could keep the lines of communication to Singapore through the Sunda Strait, and to Java from Australia, open long enough to enable Allied air strength to be built up.

The lack of transport aircraft to convey the necessary servicing parties and technical spares led to inadequate maintenance facilities both on the reinforcement routes and at their destination. In conjunction with the weight of enemy air attacks on airfields this prevented the reinforcing aircraft from operating efficiently when they did arrive. Thus, despite all efforts to reinforce them, the air forces in the Far East continued to be a wasting asset and air superiority could not be gained.

CHAPTER XVI

ABDA COMMAND

See Strategic Map

FIVE DAYS after the outbreak of war with Japan Mr. Churchill and the Chiefs of Staff left for the United States of America in H.M.S. *Duke of York* to attend a conference in Washington.[1] At this conference, which was given the code name 'Arcadia', agreement was reached on a number of matters of vital import to the war in both hemispheres. Among the chief of these were the decisions to defeat Germany before Japan, to support China and keep her in the war, and to maintain in the Eastern theatre only the forces necessary to hold vital areas from which an Anglo-American offensive could eventually be staged.

The area in which the greatest danger lay was far from the American coast. At one of the early meetings Mr. Churchill said he thought there was little likelihood that even the Japanese would attempt an invasion of the North American continent, although the west coast might be 'insulted from time to time'. The main problem in the Japanese war was over on the other side of the Pacific, where it was feared that the enemy, already established in Indo-China, Malaya and the Philippines, would drive southwards through the Netherlands East Indies to Australia and westwards through Burma to India.

The new theatre of operations covered the huge confused area from Formosa to Australia, and from New Guinea to the Bay of Bengal. In it no less than five Commanders-in-Chief, representing five different countries, held command.[2] The outlook of each of these was inevitably coloured by national interest. All were aware of the importance of holding the Malay barrier, formed by the Malay peninsula, Sumatra, Java and the chain of Dutch islands stretching east to New Guinea; but for the British the predominant interest was the security of Singapore and the eastern entrance to the Indian Ocean. For the Americans, who knew that they could not hope to retain the Philippines, the chief concern was to hold Australia

---

[1] Field Marshal Sir John Dill went in place of General Sir Alan Brooke who had relieved him as C.I.G.S. on the 1st December.

[2] Philippines (Lieut.-General D. MacArthur), Malaya (Lieut.-General Sir Henry Pownall), Australia (General Sir Thomas Blamey), Netherlands East Indies (Jhr. Doctor A. W. L. Tjarda van Starkenborgh Stachouwer), India (General Sir Archibald Wavell). India was also responsible for the defence of Burma.

and bases on the lines of communication between it and the United States so that forces could be built up for the eventual reconquest of the Pacific. The Australians naturally held similar views and for the Dutch their East Indian possessions were all important. Apart from their wealth, the islands had a sentimental value for them akin to that of the British for the Dominions. The Japanese on the other hand had no such conflicting loyalties and enjoyed the advantage of being a homogeneous force acting on interior lines. These conflicting interests had obviously to be reconciled to ensure the best use being made of the exiguous forces available.

The problem of an overall direction of the forces in the Far East was first discussed by the Chiefs of Staff at a conference at the White House on Christmas Day 1941. General Marshall, the Chief of Staff of the United States Army, expressed his personal view that there should be complete unity of command over all naval, military and air forces, and said 'he would go to the limit' in bringing this about. He did not advocate the placing of individual detachments of United States forces under the command of a particular British service, but held that national forces should be used as far as possible in homogeneous bodies under their own commander. There should however, he insisted, be one supreme authority and, although it would be impossible to choose a Supreme Commander with full technical knowledge of all three Services, a man of good judgement should be able to exercise strategical direction of all forces within his jurisdiction. He proposed that a directive should be drawn up which gave this commander sufficient latitude, and yet prevented him doing anything contrary to the national interests of the countries involved.

Mr. Churchill was not at all sure that unity of command in the Far East would be a valuable or desirable arrangement. Certain strategic points in the Pacific had to be held and the commander in each locality ought to be quite clear what he had to do. The difficulty, he thought, was the application of the available resources to each area. This could be settled only by the Governments concerned. After considerable discussion with the Chiefs of Staff and with the President, Mr. Churchill was finally convinced of the soundness of General Marshall's proposal. It was therefore decided that a new command should be formed covering all the various theatres of operation in the Far East as distinct from the Pacific. It would be known as the ABDA area—the initials standing for American, British, Dutch and Australian.

The President then proposed that General Wavell should be appointed Supreme Commander of this new area. The British Chiefs of Staff were apprehensive of the effect on American public opinion if disasters occurred—and there seemed every likelihood of them occurring—under the command of a British officer. The Prime

Minister however, appreciating the high confidence shown by the President in General Wavell, insisted that the British ought not to shirk the responsibility offered them. He therefore on the 29th December sent a telegram to the General offering him the post.

It was an unenviable command, which many a man might well have hesitated to assume, a command which offered little chance of success and seemed likely to end in defeat and even disaster. General Wavell, being the man he was, accepted without demur,[1] but he asked that no announcement should be made until he had at least received instructions and had had time to study them.

The machinery for control of the various British and American operations was also considered at the conference. The outcome of the deliberations was the decision to form the Combined Chiefs of Staff Committee composed of the United States Chiefs of Staff and of high-ranking representatives of the British Chiefs of Staff, stationed permanently in Washington. These representatives were in constant touch with London, and thus were able to express the views of the British Chiefs of Staff to their United States colleagues on every problem as it arose. Acting under the authority of the Prime Minister and the President, the Combined Chiefs of Staff Committee eventually became responsible for the complete co-ordination of the war efforts of the two countries.

The question of what territories should be included in the ABDA area caused difficulty. The Americans, who attached much importance to the maintenance of Chinese resistance and stressed the need for giving every encouragement to China, were insistent on the inclusion of Burma. They argued that the entry to the Burma Road, by which alone support to China could be given, was through Rangoon. Burma thus provided a link between the ABDA area and China and a base for possible future operations against Siam and Indo-China.

The British took the view that Burma should remain under India Command to which it had just been transferred. They pointed out that it was dependent on India for administration, reinforcements and supplies, and Rangoon, its only port, lay in the Indian Ocean outside the ABDA area. After much discussion it was agreed that Burma, as the only supply route to China, should be included for operational purposes in the ABDA area while remaining under India for administration. The British Chiefs of Staff in coming to this decision were largely influenced by the overriding importance of retaining Chiang Kai-shek's approval and support. To meet the wishes of the Americans, Siam and Indo-China were excluded, for

---

[1] His comment was 'I have heard of men having to hold the baby but this is twins'.

the American Government had already suggested to Chiang Kai-shek that these two countries should form part of the China theatre.

In the draft directive to General Wavell, prepared jointly by the British and American planning committees, Australia and New Zealand had been excluded from the ABDA area, the boundary being placed north of the coast of Australia. This brought a protest from the Australian Government on the ground that Australia and New Zealand might well fall between two stools and receive insufficient support from either the Americans or from ABDA Command. They feared that they would be left with entirely inadequate naval, military and air forces and that the vital line of sea and air communication between the United States and Australia 'upon which the defence of the Western Pacific areas mainly depended, would be endangered'.

This problem was finally resolved by Admiral King, Chief of United States Naval Operations, who proposed that a new area, to be known as the 'Anzac' area, should be set up to include the eastern coast of Australia and the whole of New Zealand. In this area a naval force would operate under the strategical direction of the Commander-in-Chief of the United States Navy, exercised through one or more American flag officers assisted by one or more flag officers appointed by Australia and New Zealand or by one of these Dominions. Its main function would be to cover the eastern and north-eastern approaches to the two countries in co-operation with the air forces in the area.

The problem of China was inevitably linked with the delimitation of the ABDA area. It was obvious that no part of the Chinese republic could be placed under Anglo-American command. The Americans however were afraid that China might throw in her hand and felt that it was vital, in view of her great potential strength, to give all the encouragement possible to keep her in the field. They believed that Americans would be more readily welcomed in China than the British, and at a meeting on the 10th January proposed that they should themselves control communications from Rangoon to China and command any United States and Chinese air forces operating in Burma. General Marshall admitted that these were exceptional proposals, but thought they were warranted by the exceptional conditions in that area.

The British Chiefs of Staff were strongly opposed to a divided command in Burma or to American control of communications used by British troops. A compromise was finally reached by which a United States Army officer, accredited to General Chiang Kai-shek, would command all United States forces in China and any Chinese forces assigned to him. If any of these forces had to operate in Burma, they would come under the command of the Supreme Commander of the ABDA area. The United States officer appointed would represent his Government on any international war council in China and would supervise and control American air supply services to that country. He would control and maintain the Burma Road and, with the consent of the British, arrange if necessary for additional bases in Burma and India to support the Chinese war effort. The appointment was offered to Major-General J. W. Stilwell on the 23rd January 1942, and three weeks later he left to take up his new and important duties.

Agreement was eventually reached on the area to be covered by ABDA Command and was precisely defined in a directive sent to General Wavell on the 3rd January.[1] In general terms it covered Burma, the Andaman and Nicobar Islands, Malaya, the Netherlands East Indies, the Philippines, and Christmas and Cocos Islands. It did not include Australia, China, Indo-China or Siam.

At the instance of General Wavell certain modifications were introduced later. The southern boundary of ABDA area had been defined in the directive as the northern coast of Australia from the meridian 143° east, westwards to the meridian 114° east, thence north-westwards to latitude 15° south, longitude 92° east. This left the Supreme Commander's responsibility for the defence of Darwin in doubt, and his first telegram after taking over command asked what was intended. He thought that Darwin should be within his sphere of responsibility since its defence depended on the control of the Timor Sea which was already in the ABDA area. The matter was referred to the Australian Government who agreed that the responsibility should be laid on General Wavell not only for the defence of Darwin but also for any sections of the north-west coast of Australia needed to exercise that defence. The Combined Chiefs of Staff accepted Wavell's view and on the 24th January extended the southern limit of the ABDA area to include the mainland of Australia, northwards from a line running from Onslow on the west coast to the south-east corner of the Gulf of Carpentaria.

General Wavell received his directive on the 4th January, and the announcement of his appointment as Supreme Commander of the South-West Pacific area was made on the same day. It was followed by a telegram in which the urgency attached by the President and the Prime Minister to the assumption of his new responsibilities was emphasized. General Wavell assumed command of ABDA area on the 15th January 1942. General Pownall, at that time Commander-in-Chief, Far East, became his Chief of Staff; and Headquarters, Far East, was abolished. The announcement that Generalissimo Chiang Kai-shek had accepted Supreme Command of Allied land and air

---

[1] See Appendix 20.

forces in the China theatre was made at the same time as that of Wavell's appointment.

ABDA Command was an organization hastily created to meet a desperate emergency. It was of necessity understaffed and its forces were entirely inadequate for the tasks placed upon it. In the short six weeks of its existence it did not have a chance to fulfil its proper functions. Before forces could be assembled to defend the vast area it embraced, it was overwhelmed by the tide of the Japanese advance. Nevertheless it served one useful purpose. It was the first unified command of the war and provided a pattern, however rudimentary, on which the combined Allied commands in North Africa, South-East Asia and Western Europe were later modelled.

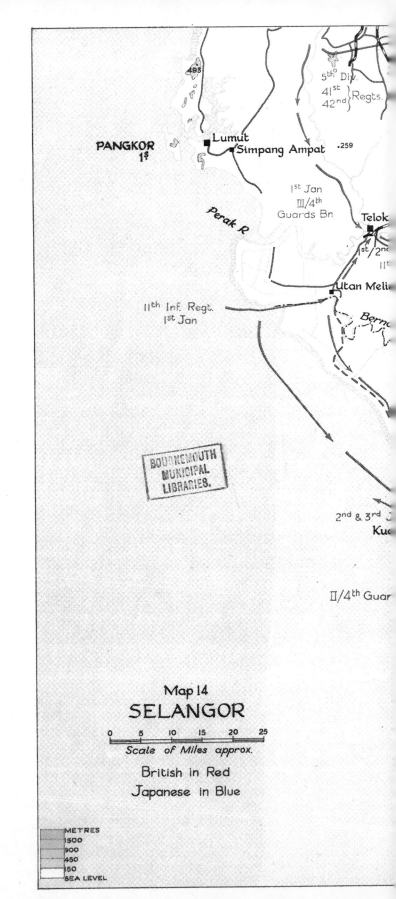

PANGKOR
1$

493

Lumut
Simpang Ampat

·259

5th Div.
41st
42nd } Regts.

Perak R.

1st Jan
III/4th
Guards Bn

Telok

1st/2nd

11th

Utan Meli

11th Inf. Regt.
1st Jan

Bern

BOURNEMOUTH
MUNICIPAL
LIBRARIES.

2nd & 3rd
Kua

II/4th Guar

Map 14
SELANGOR

0   5   10   15   20   25
Scale of Miles approx.

British in Red

Japanese in Blue

METRES
1500
900
450
150
SEA LEVEL

CHAPTER XVII

THE LOSS OF CENTRAL
MALAYA

See Maps 5, 14, 15 and 16

WHILE THE EVENTS described in Chapter XIV were taking place, 9th Indian Division, with 8th Indian Brigade in the Kuala Lipis–Jerantut area and 22nd Indian Brigade (to which its third battalion had been returned) at Kuantan,[1] was not in contact with the enemy.

On the east coast General Yamashita had planned that two battalions of *55th Infantry Regiment* should make a surprise landing at Kuantan about the 28th December in order to capture the airfield. On the 23rd however he postponed the operation, since he considered that the power of the British air forces in Johore and Singapore had not yet been sufficiently reduced. Meanwhile *56th Infantry Regiment*, after occupying Kuala Krai on the 19th, had moved along the coast and had made contact with patrols of 22nd Indian Brigade north of Kuantan on the 23rd. As it appeared probable that Kuantan could be captured by an overland attack and the hazards of an opposed landing avoided, Yamashita cancelled the seaborne operation. The *55th Infantry Regiment* was then landed at Kota Bharu on the 30th and ordered to follow the *56th* down the coast towards Kuantan.

The 22nd Brigade (Brigadier Painter) had the task of defending the Kuantan airfield. It was disposed astride the river, over which there was only a single ferry, in readiness to meet a seaborne attack as well as an enemy advance from the north.[2] The 2/18th Royal Garhwal Rifles, with a company of 2/12th Frontier Force Regiment under command, held the beach defences stretching eleven miles northward from Kuantan and 5/11th Sikhs the line of the river itself. The 2/12th (less one company) was in reserve near Gambang some fifteen miles westwards on the Jerantut road, where it could guard the approaches from the upper reaches of the Sungei Pahang. The brigade was supported by 5th Field Regiment (less one battery) and a battery of 88th Field Regiment. Some of the guns were located east of the river. The airfield lay west of the river close to the main road some nine miles from the coast.

---

[1] See page 170.
[2] See Map 5.

Throughout the withdrawal on the west coast General Heath had in mind that, by making use of the lateral east-west road Jerantut–Raub–Kuala Kubu, 9th Division might be used at the right moment to make a counterstroke against the Japanese left flank. He was therefore particularly anxious that 22nd Brigade should not be jeopardized by attempting to defend the Kuantan airfield which by that time was of little value to the R.A.F. On the 27th he suggested to General Barstow (9th Division) that the brigade (except for outposts and reconnaissance troops) should be withdrawn behind the Kuantan River as soon as a threat developed from the north.

At a conference at Kuantan on the following day Brigadier Painter told Barstow that it would be difficult to deny the airfield unless his main strength was deployed east of the river, and that there was a danger in making a last minute change of plan. To this view Barstow agreed, provided that the amount of transport retained between the river and the coast was reduced to a minimum. The only change therefore made in the brigade's dispositions was the move of the reserve company of the Garhwalis to cover the Jabor valley on the threatened northern flank.

On the 29th however Heath wrote to Barstow saying,

'General Percival is in entire agreement with me that the preservation of the entity of 22nd Brigade is of greater importance than the imposition of two or three days' delay upon the enemy advance to Kuantan airfield[1] . . . I therefore still adhere to the view that, from the strategical aspect, it is definitely wrong to risk the loss of a large number of vehicles and the mutilation of one-third of the force by attempting to fight the enemy east of the river. I therefore wish you to issue an instruction to the Commander 22nd Brigade to redispose his brigade in accordance with the view expressed above.'

Barstow immediately issued orders to this effect and wrote to Painter saying,

'The preservation of the future fighting efficiency of your brigade under existing circumstances is of greater importance than imposing a delay of a few more days in the denial of the airfield to the enemy.'

On the 30th therefore, Painter ordered the Garhwalis to withdraw to an outpost position covering the river line, and all guns and transport to cross by the ferry that night. During the day however the Japanese attacked in strength down the Jabor valley and overran the Garhwalis' left flank. In the subsequent confused fighting two companies were cut off, and the battalion was driven back to the east

---

[1] General Percival affirms that Heath must have misunderstood him, for his policy throughout was to give first priority to denying the enemy the use of Kuantan airfield. See pages 232–233 and 247.

bank of the river where a weak line of outposts was organized by nightfall. Throughout the day the enemy air force had made repeated attempts to put the ferry out of action. But Painter had taken the wise precaution of dividing it into two and, although one half was sunk, all the guns and transport were able to cross the river on the other during the night.

On the morning of the 31st Painter informed Barstow that, in view of his orders not to risk his force, he proposed to withdraw towards Maran on the night of the 31st December/1st January. In reply he received an order which read:

> 'It is of the utmost importance that your brigade with its valu-
> able material should not be jeopardized. Within the limitations
> that the above imposes, you will ensure that every advantage is
> taken to hold the enemy and deal him such blows as opportunity
> offers. The question of denial of ground particularly applies to the
> Kuantan airfield. It is highly desirable that this should continue
> to be denied to the enemy. Reinforcements are shortly expected
> in Malaya and their safe arrival might be hampered if enemy
> fighters had the use of the airfield.'

Accordingly Painter moved the 2/12th to defend the airfield peri-meter and ordered the hard-pressed Garhwalis to withdraw west of the river during the night of the 31st December/1st January. The Garhwalis, by then only some 300 strong, crossed the river with great difficulty that night and were moved to the airfield. The ferry was then destroyed. But on the 1st January Painter's instructions were again altered and he was told that for strategical reasons it was of the utmost importance to deny the use of the airfield to the enemy for as long as possible, and particularly for a period of five days from the 1st.

The Japanese wasted no time and on the 1st and 2nd crossed the river, fordable by infantry anywhere in its upper reaches, and infil-trated steadily towards the airfield. It soon became clear therefore that 22nd Brigade would be unable to hold the airfield for the speci-fied time without becoming heavily engaged. However the decision to withdraw 11th Division from Kampar during the night of the 2nd/3rd once again altered the situation.[1] It had now become im-perative for 9th Division to concentrate without delay in the Kuala Lipis–Jerantut–Raub area in preparation for a withdrawal from Pahang. On the 2nd, since the Kuantan airfield could not in any case be held for much longer, Heath ordered it to be abandoned, and 22nd Brigade withdrawn to Jerantut.

Buildings and installations at the airfield were accordingly demo-lished and preparations made to withdraw the brigade on the even-ing of the 3rd. At about 8 p.m. that day, while the final withdrawal

---

[1] See page 247.

was in progress, the Japanese, who had been closing in all day, attacked the 2/12th (less two companies), which was acting as rearguard, just as it was about to leave the airfield and, getting in behind it, formed road blocks between it and the main body of the brigade. Very fierce fighting at close range ensued. Eventually Lieut.-Colonel A. E. Cumming and forty men fought their way back through two road blocks.[1] The paramount necessity to preserve the brigade as an organized formation prevented any attempt being made to rescue the remainder, some of whom rejoined later in small parties. The next day the retirement continued through Maran and by the night of the 6th/7th, 22nd Brigade, reduced to two-thirds of its original strength, crossed the Jerantut ferry and moved to the Raub area.

The reader will remember that the threat to its communications from enemy landings in the Telok Anson area had forced 11th Division to withdraw from Kampar, although it had withstood attacks in great strength from the north for two days, and that by the 4th January the division was disposed in the Sungkai–Slim River area.[2] In view of the imminent arrival of the convoys bringing reinforcing formations, Percival had told Heath that for strategical reasons it was of the utmost importance to deny the enemy the use of the airfields at Kuala Lumpur and Port Swettenham until at least the 14th January, and after that for as long as possible. He had urged him to take every opportunity of imposing delay by attacking the enemy's flanks and rear. Heath knew that Japanese landings in the vicinity of Kuala Selangor and Port Swettenham, which were now more than probable, might well force him to make a rapid withdrawal south of Kuala Lumpur, and had decided to take steps to guard against such a contingency while delaying the enemy's advance on the trunk road as long as he could, without becoming involved in a major action.

With this end in view he had, on the 1st January, already transferred 3rd Cavalry (less one squadron) from 11th Division, and 3/17th Dogras and 73rd Field Battery from 8th Brigade, and placed them under command of Brigadier R. G. Moir (Line of Communications Command), with orders to prevent enemy landings at Kuala Selangor. He had decided that the best delaying position on the trunk road was some two miles north of Tanjong Malim,[3] and had given instructions that civilian labour should be used to prepare the position. On the night of the 4th/5th he instructed Paris to move

---

[1] Lieut.-Colonel Cumming, commanding 2/12th Frontier Force Regiment, was awarded the Victoria Cross for his part in this action.
[2] See Map 14.
[3] See page 242

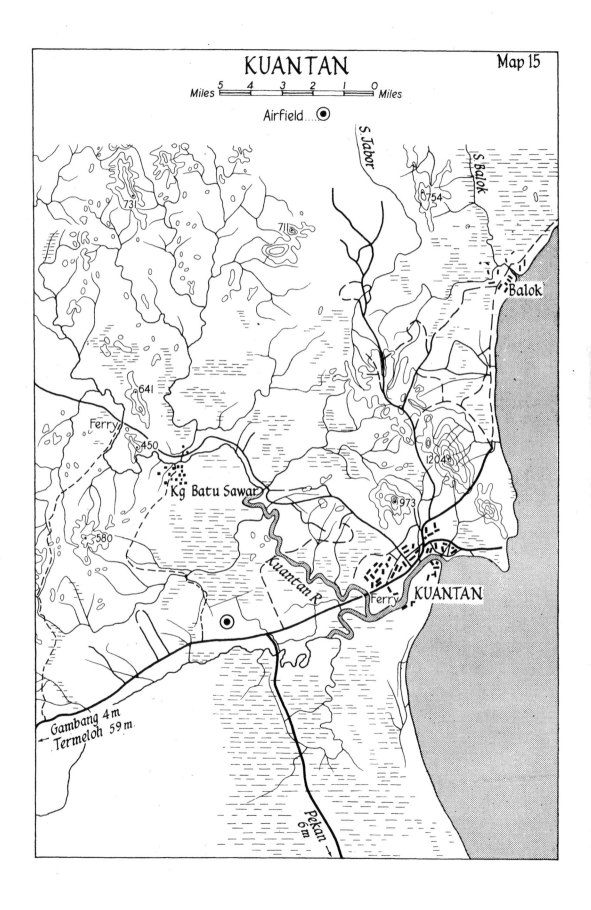

KUANTAN

Map 15

Miles 5 4 3 2 1 0 Miles

Airfield....◉

S. Jabor

S. Balok

754

Balok

731

711

641

Ferry

450

1204

Kg Batu Sawar

973

580

Kuantan R.

Ferry

KUANTAN

◉

← Gambang 4 m
Termeloh 59 m

Pekan 6 m

15th Brigade (less 3/16th Punjab) from Sungkai to Tanjong Malim, 3/16th Punjab to Rawang, and to dispose the rest of 11th Division to hold an intermediate position in the Trolak–Slim River area covering the river crossings. He hoped that these dispositions would prevent the enemy from making contact with the main position at Tanjong Malim for at least four days.

Meanwhile, having driven the British forces from Kampar and Telok Anson, General Yamashita altered his plans. He decided to advance down the trunk road and along the coast and to make a seaborne landing behind the British forces. He ordered *5th Division*, reinforced by a tank battalion, to advance down the trunk road direct on Kuala Lumpur, while *III/11th Battalion* followed by *4th Guards Regiment* continued its progress down the coast by land and sea so as to secure Kuala Selangor and Port Swettenham, from where an advance on Kuala Lumpur could be made from the west. The *5th Division* ordered *42nd Infantry Regiment* supported by the tank battalion to pursue the retreating British forces along the trunk road, *11th Infantry Regiment* (less *III/11th Battalion*) to follow close behind ready to pass through as soon as the British forces had been defeated north of Kuala Lumpur, and retained *41st Infantry Regiment* in reserve.

The first brush between the opposing forces in this new phase was at Kuala Selangor where on both the 2nd and 3rd January enemy attempts to land were frustrated by artillery fire. These attempts made Heath send the Jat/Punjab Battalion from 15th Brigade, then at Sungkai, and 1st Independent Company to reinforce Brigadier Moir's force.[1] On the 4th one squadron from 3rd Cavalry, with a company of the Jat/Punjab Battalion under command, met the enemy moving southwards along the coastal track some eight miles north of Kuala Selangor. The Japanese in battalion strength drove them back and, reaching the north bank of the Sungei Selangor that evening, turned eastwards towards the bridges over the river in the Batang Berjuntai area, twelve miles inland. By the morning of the 5th they made contact with 1st Independent Company, reinforced by 'Roseforce', which was occupying a position covering these important bridges, only eleven miles from Rawang on the direct line of communications northwards to 11th Division.

This threat to his left flank forced Heath to move 15th Brigade from Tanjong Malim to Rawang on the 5th.[2] Brigadier Moir was then relieved of the operational responsibility which events had thrust upon him, and Brigadier Moorhead took command of the whole of

---

[1] Brigadier Moir's force then consisted of 3rd Cavalry (less one squadron) 3/17th Dogras, Jat/Punjab Battalion, 1st Independent Company, 88th Field Regiment, 73rd Field Battery, 272nd Anti-Tank Battery, 'Roseforce', two F.M.S.V.F. battalions, and a light battery and armoured car squadron (F.M.S.V.F.).

[2] Consisting of the British Battalion, 1/14th Punjab, 3/16th Punjab and 2/16th Punjab.

U

the coastal area including Kuala Selangor, Batang Berjuntai, Rawang and Kapar. On assuming command Moorhead ordered 3/17th Dogra to counter-attack north of Batang Berjuntai. This attack, which took place during the night 5th/6th, drove the enemy from the road junction north of the river. Next morning however, owing to the presence of Japanese further east, Moorhead withdrew behind the river and destroyed the bridges. For the time being the position in the coastal area was stabilized on the line of the Sungei Selangor.

Headquarters, Malaya Command, had meanwhile asked Rear-Admiral, Malaya, to do all he could to prevent further Japanese landings on the west coast. But the Perak Flotilla which had been formed for this purpose had now been reduced to only two motor launches and, in the face of the constant enemy air attacks against shipping in the Strait of Malacca, had no other defence than evasion.[1] In consequence, inshore patrols along the west coast could operate only by night and were powerless to interfere with the enemy's activities.

The 11th Division had meanwhile occupied the intermediate delaying position covering the Slim River crossings. General Paris had divided this position in depth into two sectors: the Trolak sector, extending for seven and a half miles from a point on the Trolak road, three and a half miles north of Trolak, to a point one mile north of Kampong Slim; and the Slim River sector, which included Slim River Station and Kampong Slim, stretching eastwards some seven miles to the Slim River Bridge.[2] The 12th Brigade (Brigadier Stewart) reinforced by one squadron 3rd Cavalry and 5/14th Punjab, with 137th Field Regiment, 3rd Field Company and one troop 215th Anti-Tank Battery under command, was allotted to the Trolak sector, and 28th Brigade (Brigadier Selby), with 155th Field Regiment, 23rd Field Company and one troop of 215th Anti-Tank Battery under command, to the Slim River sector. The 80th Anti-Tank Regiment, less the portion of 215th Anti-Tank Battery allotted to the forward brigades, was in reserve near 11th Divisional Headquarters at Tanjong Malim. All bridges and many culverts were prepared for demolition under arrangements made by divisional headquarters.

From its forward edge at about Milestone 60 for some two and a half miles the Trolak sector, in which the road and railway ran parallel to each other some 400 yards apart, was flanked by unusually dense jungle. So thick was the undergrowth that it was thought the

[1] See page 233.
[2] See Map 16.

Japanese would be unable to adopt outflanking tactics and would be compelled to attack down the road and railway. With the exception of the road itself this part of the sector was considered to be tank proof. The remainder of the Trolak sector ran through rubber estates, except for a strip of jungle between the road and the railway. The country bordering the road throughout the Slim River sector was covered almost entirely by rubber.

Brigadier Stewart disposed 12th Brigade in considerable depth on both the road and the railway. The 5/2nd Punjab held the main defences on both these approaches between Milestones 61 and 62, with the Argylls behind them guarding the exits from the jungle so as to check any possible enveloping movement through it. The Hyderabads held an outpost position about Milestone 60. To provide additional depth 5/14th Punjab was to be ready at short notice to occupy a check position at Milestone 65, but was kept back at Kampong Slim to get some much-needed rest. The troop of anti-tank guns and all the mines were allotted to 5/2nd Punjab, and movable concrete obstacles to the outpost battalion.[1] As there was little scope for field artillery in a normal role, only one battery of 137th Field Regiment was deployed; the other two were parked in the Cluny Rubber Estate between Kampong Slim and the Slim River Bridge. The 28th Brigade had reconnoitred positions on the road and railway near Kampong Slim and in the Cluny Estate but these had not been occupied, for General Paris considered that the troops should get as much rest as possible in bivouac at Kampong Slim. The brigade was however in readiness to occupy them at short notice.

The 12th Brigade moved into its sector early on the 4th January and spent the following two days preparing it for defence. Much of the work had to be carried out at night since during daylight Japanese aircraft bombed and machine-gunned the stretches of jungle bordering the road and railway, even when there were no visible targets. These indiscriminate attacks caused only slight damage and comparatively few casualties, but the demoralizing effect on troops badly in need of rest was considerable. Colonel Deakin (5/2nd Punjab) describes the condition of his men at the time:

> 'The battalion was dead tired; most of all the Commanders, whose responsibilities prevented them from snatching even a little fitful sleep. The battalion had withdrawn 176 miles in three weeks and had had only three days' rest. It had suffered 250 casualties of which a high proportion had been killed. The spirit of the men was low and the battalion had lost 50 per cent of its fighting efficiency.'

---

[1] The 12th Brigade had only twenty-four anti-tank mines. The 11th Division held a further 1,400 but these were not sent forward.

He added:

> 'During the 5th January, I found a most lethargic lot of men who
> seemed to want to do nothing but sit in slit trenches. They said
> they could not sleep because of the continued enemy air attacks.
> In fact, they were thoroughly depressed. There was no move-
> ment on the road and the deadly ground silence emphasized by
> the blanketing effect of the jungle was getting on the men's
> nerves. It was broken again and again by the roar of engines
> overhead. The airmen could not see the troops but knew they
> were there and continually attacked the road and railway areas
> in which the defences were sited. The jungle gave the men a blind
> feeling.'

This description of 5/2nd Punjab applied in general to the whole of
12th Brigade. Nevertheless by the morning of the 6th, defended
localities had been dug and wired and the few available tank
obstacles placed in position.

On the 5th, enemy infantry (estimated at two companies) advanced
down the railway. They were met by fire from 4/19th Hyderabad at
close range and withdrew, leaving some sixty dead. Next day the
Japanese began to move around the Hyderabads' flanks and that
evening Stewart warned the battalion to be prepared to withdraw
from the outpost position early on the 7th, so as to give greater depth
to the defence. During the afternoon Paris had decided to give 28th
Brigade one more night's rest, but ordered it to occupy its positions
by midday on the 7th. Late on the 6th, Chinese refugees making their
way south from Kampar reported having seen large numbers of tanks
on the trunk road. This information reached 11th Division and 12th
Brigade, but not 28th Brigade.

Shortly after midnight on the 6th/7th enemy infantry engaged the
Hyderabads on both the main road and the railway. At about
3.30 a.m., in brilliant moonlight and under cover of shelling, a
column of tanks, with infantry in lorries distributed between them,
attacked straight down the trunk road. The infantry, covered by fire
from tanks and artillery, succeeded in clearing the first of the road
blocks and in overrunning the Hyderabads' forward company. The
column then drove rapidly down the road. Later, enemy infantry
and tanks attacking down the railway and moving along a disused
loop road, forced the remainder of the Hyderabads to withdraw along
the railway line.

Meanwhile the column on the trunk road drove on till at about
4.30 a.m. the leading tank struck a mine in a cutting in front of the
Punjabis' foremost defended locality, just north of Milestone 61. For
the moment the on-rushing column was checked, and fierce fighting
at close quarters ensued in which three tanks were destroyed. Within
the area held by the Punjabis there were two loop roads, disused and

21. The Kampar position.

Milestone 61

Milestone 62

Trolak

Check Position

22. The Slim River position.

overgrown but still fit for traffic, which had been left open as a temporary measure for use by the transport of the outpost battalion.[1] The Japanese were not slow to discover the first of these loops and their tanks were thus able to surround and overwhelm the defenders. The column then went on down the road and, quickly overrunning the next defended locality at Milestone $61\frac{1}{2}$ which had no anti-tank defence, was halted only when the leading tank struck a mine at about 5.30 a.m. in front of the Punjabis' reserve company just north of Milestone 62.

Colonel Deakin described the ensuing action as follows:

'The din which followed baffles description. The tanks were head to tail, engines roaring, crews screaming, machine-guns spitting tracer, and mortars and cannon firing all out. The platoon astride the cutting threw grenades, and one tank had its track smashed by an anti-tank rifle. The two anti-tank guns fired two rounds, one of which scored a bull, and then retired to the Argylls' area. One more tank wrecked itself on the mines.'

The reserve company and battalion headquarters of the Punjabis held the main weight of the attack for about an hour, with their numbers steadily diminishing. The enemy however discovered the second disused loop on the road and by about 6.30 a.m. had surrounded the defenders. The column then moved on southwards.

Having counted thirty tanks and hearing others approaching, the survivors of the Punjabis then attempted to make their way through the dense jungle towards the Slim River Bridge. The delay of two hours which had been gained by their gallant defence should have given those behind a chance to organize anti-tank measures in depth had communications been working. But all telephone lines in the forward area had been cut by 5 a.m. and Stewart knew only that the enemy, after having broken through 4/19th Hyderabad, had been halted by the leading company of 5/2nd Punjab. He ordered Deakin to hold on, even should tanks break right through his position, 2nd Argylls to construct road blocks covering Trolak, and 5/14th Punjab to move forward and occupy its check position at Milestone 65.

The Argylls thereupon hastily put one block where the trunk road entered the rubber estate area, and another covering the bridge at Trolak. It was now daylight. At about 6.30 a.m. four medium tanks reached the first of these improvised road blocks and quickly swept it aside. They went straight on down the road and at about 7 a.m. reached the second road block at Trolak, where they were temporarily checked by the Argylls' armoured cars with their pitiably

---

[1] These small loops are not shown on Map 16 illustrating this action. At some time previous to December 1941, the original trace of the trunk road had been adjusted to straighten out the worst bends. This left short loops of unused road in fair condition. There were three such loops in the position: one about 700 yards south of Milestone 60, a second just north of Milestone 61 and a third about Milestone 62.

278 THE LOSS OF CENTRAL MALAYA

inadequate anti-tank rifles. Two of the armoured cars were knocked out and the tanks overran the road block. By way of further misfortune the demolition of the bridge at Trolak failed. There was little that the Highlanders could do but watch helplessly as enemy tanks drove southwards. By about 8.30 a.m. their right forward company which had not been involved in the fighting, and the remnants of the company which had been overrun on the road, had concentrated at the Trolak bridge. When more enemy tanks and infantry arrived at about 9 a.m. this party destroyed the remaining armoured cars and carriers and set off through the jungle in an attempt to reach the Slim River Bridge. Meanwhile the company defending the railway, assailed on both flanks, retired along the line towards Kampong Slim.

A considerable part of the equipment of 11th Divisional Signals had been lost during the retreat and apart from wireless, which in Malaya was subject to many interruptions, the only means of communication between divisional and brigade headquarters was by the telegraph line along the railway and by despatch riders. The former had been cut by the blowing-up of the railway bridge over the Slim River and remained out of action throughout the battle, so it was not until 6.30 a.m., by which time the two forward battalions had been overrun, that Paris (whose headquarters was at Tanjong Malim) received any information from 12th Brigade; even then it was merely that 'there had been some sort of break-through'. He immediately ordered 28th Brigade to occupy its position. Brigadier Selby, after having issued his orders for deployment at 7 a.m., went forward to see Stewart at his headquarters on the estate road. The latter, who was by that time quite out of touch with events owing largely to his headquarters being on a side road, told Selby at about 7.20 a.m. that although the situation was serious it was not critical. He thought however that he would probably have to withdraw his brigade about noon. By this time Stewart was in touch only with the company of the Argylls on the estate road and the remnants of the Hyderabads who had joined them. At 9 a.m. he ordered this detachment to delay the enemy's advance down the estate road and then withdrew his headquarters to Kampong Slim. The detachment was eventually surrounded and all were killed or captured.

To revert to events on the trunk road: the Japanese tanks, having broken through the Trolak sector, drove southwards without infantry support and at about 7.30 a.m. ran headlong into 5/14th Punjab about one mile north of Kampong Slim. This battalion was moving up the road to occupy the check position as ordered. The leading company was scattered, and the next company left with only twenty unwounded men. The two rear companies, moving on both sides of the road among the rubber trees, escaped with a few casualties and established a position covering the road from which they were later driven by other enemy tanks and infantry. So sudden had been the Japanese break-through that the only troop of anti-tank guns under command of 28th Brigade, which had been sent forward to help the Punjabis hold the check position, was overrun on the road before it could come into action.

Further south 2/9th Gurkhas was moving into position near Kampong Slim when at about 8 a.m. the leading tanks drove past. The battalion remained steady and, expecting that an infantry attack would quickly follow, hastily occupied its battle positions. A few minutes later the leading tanks overtook 2/1st Gurkha Rifles moving eastwards in column of route along the road to take up its allotted positions in Cluny Estate. Caught in close order and taken completely by surprise, the battalion was quickly overrun, and scattered. Thus of 28th Brigade, only 2/2nd Gurkha Rifles was able to occupy its position covering the railway without encountering the enemy armour. The tanks then surprised the two batteries of 137th Field Regiment parked beside the road in the Cluny Estate. They paused on the road for a few moments to rake the batteries with gun and machine-gun fire and then swept on towards the vital Slim River Bridge, which they reached at about 8.40 a.m.

At the bridge there was only a troop of 16th Light Anti-Aircraft Battery H.K.S.R.A. equipped with Bofors guns, and a demolition party of sappers. Warned of the approach of tanks by a party of signallers in a truck, the officer in command set his sights 'at near' and prepared to open fire with the two guns which could bear on the road. Several tanks were engaged at a range of 100 yards, but the light shells merely bounced off the armour leaving the tanks unscathed. The unprotected gun detachments were soon driven off their guns with heavy casualties.

The tank column crossed the bridge, which was still intact, leaving one tank to guard it, and continued its advance for another two miles until at about 9.30 a.m. it met 155th Field Regiment which was moving north to take up its position in support of 28th Brigade. The appearance of tanks nineteen miles south of the front line caught this fine regiment unawares, but it was master of the occasion. Although the tanks overran the regimental headquarters, one detachment managed to get its 4.5-inch howitzer into action and, despite being under heavy fire, hit and stopped the leading tank at a range of about thirty yards. This finally halted the enemy armour which in six hours had destroyed one brigade and part of another. The tanks patrolled for a short distance south of the river during the remainder of the day but, harassed by hastily formed tank-hunting parties, withdrew later in the afternoon to the bridge which was kept under fire by 155th Field Regiment.

To try to find out what was happening, for all communications had failed, General Paris had sent Colonel A. M. L. Harrison, his senior staff officer, forward by car at 7.45 a.m.[1] Just before he reached the Slim River Bridge, Harrison met 350th Field Battery moving south to occupy a position at Tanjong Malim. Hearing from it that the enemy had broken through 4/19th Hyderabad he drove on, but as he approached Milestone 73 he was suddenly confronted by enemy tanks. His orderly was wounded and the car smashed. He himself managed to escape and, taking cover among the trees by the side of the road, watched the tanks driving past. He realized that the bridge would be captured intact, but was unable to warn anybody. Eventually, by bicycle and on foot, passing the remains of the two field batteries which had been destroyed and abandoned, and the scene of the disaster to 2/1st Gurkhas, he reached 28th Brigade Headquarters where he learnt the full extent of the catastrophe.

It was not until about 8.30 a.m. that Paris received definite information that tanks had broken through the Trolak sector, and nearly 10 a.m. before he heard that they had been halted some two miles south of the Slim River Bridge and so became aware of the disasters of the morning. He immediately ordered an anti-tank battery to block the road north of Tanjong Malim, warned all troops in that area to be prepared to meet tanks, and informed III Corps of the position. General Heath immediately ordered 2/16th Punjab from 15th Brigade, then at Rawang, to return to Tanjong Malim.

Meanwhile by about 11 a.m., 28th Brigade had established its headquarters, with that of 12th Brigade, on a hill near the road east of Kampong Slim. The situation, as known to them at that time, was that all four battalions of 12th Brigade and 2/1st Gurkha Rifles of 28th Brigade had been dispersed or were lost. Brigadier Selby decided to hold the Kampong Slim area until dusk with his two remaining battalions and any stragglers he could collect, and then withdraw down the railway track to Tanjong Malim. The withdrawal proved most difficult. Enemy infantry, which had been arriving in the area in increasing numbers during the afternoon, engaged 2/9th Gurkha Rifles and followed it up as it closed in towards the railway. The railway bridge across the Slim River had already been destroyed, but 3rd Field Company was able to construct a plank bridge across the gap; at dusk, after the remaining transport had been destroyed, the withdrawal across the river began. There was considerable congestion as the troops crossed the improvised plank walk and many of 2/2nd Gurkhas who attempted to swim the river were swept away by the strong current; others lost their way in the darkness. Eventually the survivors of 28th Brigade completed their twelve mile trek along

---

[1] 28th Brigade Headquarters' wireless had been destroyed by a direct hit from an enemy tank.

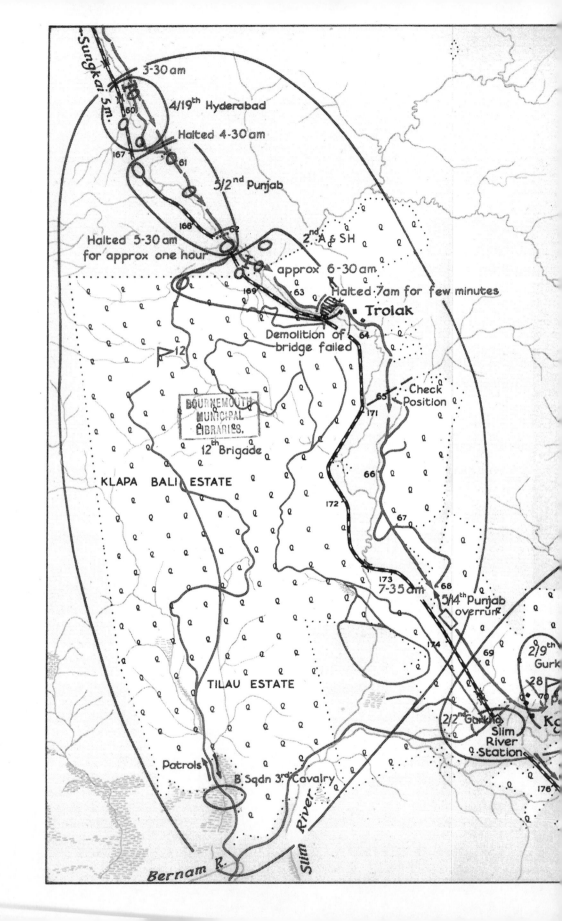

Sungkai 5m.

3-30 am

4/19th Hyderabad

Halted 4-30 am

160

167

61

5/2nd Punjab

168

162

Halted 5-30 am
for approx one hour

169

163

2nd A & SH

approx 6-30 am

Halted 7am for few minutes

Trolak

64

Demolition of
bridge failed

12

Check
Position

65

171

BOURNEMOUTH
MUNICIPAL
LIBRARIES.

12th Brigade

66

KLAPA BALI ESTATE

172

67

173

7-35 am

68

5/4th Punjab
overrun

174

69

2/9th
Gurk

28

70

TILAU ESTATE

2/2nd Gurkha

Ko

Slim
River
Station

Patrols

B Sqdn 3rd Cavalry

Slim River

176

Bernam R.

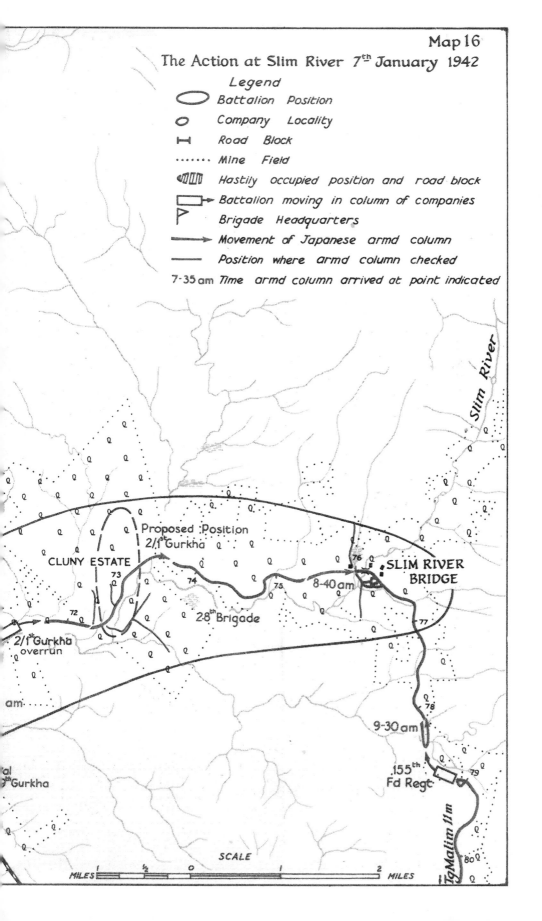

Map 16

The Action at Slim River 7ᵗʰ January 1942

Legend

⬭ Battalion Position
○ Company Locality
⊢⊣ Road Block
...... Mine Field
◖▯▯▯ Hastily occupied position and road block
▭▭► Battalion moving in column of companies
⚐ Brigade Headquarters
━━► Movement of Japanese armd column
━━ Position where armd column checked
7-35 am Time armd column arrived at point indicated

Slim River

Proposed Position
2/1ˢᵗ Gurkha

CLUNY ESTATE

73

72

2/1ˢᵗ Gurkha
overrun

am

al
¹ˢᵗ Gurkha

74

75

28ᵗʰ Brigade

76

8-40 am

SLIM RIVER
BRIDGE

77

78

9-30 am

155ᵗʰ
Fd Regt

79

80

Tg Malim 11 m

SCALE

MILES ▭▭▭▭▭▭ MILES
1 ½ 0 1 2

the railway, and succeeded in reaching Tanjong Malim at about 3 a.m. on the 8th. In the day's fighting 12th Brigade had virtually ceased to exist and 28th Brigade had been reduced to a third of its original strength:[1] all the transport of both brigades had been lost as well as the guns and equipment of two field batteries and two troops of anti-tank guns.

The spearhead of the Japanese attack had been one tank company, one infantry battalion of *42nd Infantry Regiment* in motor transport, and some engineers. The rest of the tank battalion and the remaining two infantry battalions had been held in reserve. In the event of the spearhead being held up 'by stubborn resistance', these battalions were to co-operate by encircling both flanks so as to get behind the British formations, cut their line of retreat and attack them in the rear. The Japanese state that during their southward drive only the leading tanks were directly engaged; the remaining tanks of the company had given support by firing upon the British and Indian troops on either side of the road.

The action at Slim River was a major disaster. It resulted in the early abandonment of central Malaya and gravely prejudiced the chances of holding northern Johore long enough to enable the reinforcing formations, then on their way to Singapore, to arm and prepare for battle. For some time to come, 11th Division ceased to be an effective fighting force.

The immediate causes of the disaster were the failure to make full use of the anti-tank weapons available and, possibly, too great a reliance on the delaying value of demolitions. The division had an anti-tank regiment and some 1,400 anti-tank mines, yet 12th Brigade, acting as rearguard, had only the meagre allotment of one troop of anti-tank guns, twenty-four anti-tank mines and a few concrete obstacles. Further, although the brigade had under its command a field regiment, which because of the nature of the country could not be used to support the forward infantry, no attempt was made to employ it in an anti-tank role. Communications were bad; brigade headquarters was well off the main road and, as a result, lost touch with the situation at a critical stage. It is evident that the bold thrust down the main road by Japanese armour achieved complete surprise although it was not the first time such tactics had been used.

---

[1] The approximate strength of the seven battalions of 12th and 28th Brigades on the 8th January was:

4/19th Hyderabad	3 officers and 110 men
5/2nd Punjab	1 officer and 80 men
2nd Argyll and Sutherland Highlanders	4 officers and 90 men
5/14th Punjab	6 officers and 129 men
2/2nd Gurkha Rifles	400 all ranks
2/9th Gurkha Rifles	350 all ranks
2/1st Gurkha Rifles	Nil

While these events were in progress, General Percival had been reconsidering his plans for the future. On the 4th, General Bennett told him that he would like to be allowed to exercise control of all troops in Johore should III Corps have to fall back into that State, but, if this were impossible, he would prefer 8th Australian Division to be responsible for western and III Corps for eastern Johore. Percival considered that the fusion of the corps and the A.I.F. would lead to command and administrative difficulties, and that the transfer of the whole of the Australian division from east to west was not a practicable proposition in the middle of active operations. He did not therefore accept Bennett's suggestion.

The following day Percival held a conference at Segamat at which both Heath and Bennett were present. It was considered that, although every day's delay was of advantage, any serious attempt to stem the enemy's advance between Kuala Lumpur and Gemas would be most unwise: not only did the well-developed road systems in Selangor, Negri Sembilan and Malacca give the Japanese the opportunity to use their armour to outflank and destroy 11th Division, but, as they were free to land anywhere on the Malacca coast, they might be able to occupy the bottleneck at Tampin through which all but one of the roads to Johore passed.[1] Further, 11th Division was becoming less and less capable of holding the enemy unaided, and a withdrawal behind the Tampin bottleneck would enable 9th Indian and 8th Australian Divisions to intervene effectively in the battle. Percival therefore decided that 45th Brigade, then at Malacca, would be placed under command of III Corps which was to deny the airfields at Kuala Lumpur and Port Swettenham till the 14th January and after that for as long as possible. When it was forced to withdraw, the main line of resistance would be the line Mersing–Segamat–Muar. The III Corps would then be responsible for the defence of western Johore and 8th Australian Division for eastern Johore. Heath thereupon instructed 11th Division to undertake 'an orderly withdrawal, while effecting the maximum delay and casualties on the enemy' and gave Paris the following tentative withdrawal programme: 10th January, north of Kuala Kubu; 14th January, Ulu Yam; 16th January, Serendah; 21st January, Seremban–Port Dickson; and 24th January, Tampin.

On the 7th, while the fighting at Slim River was taking place, Percival prepared a further appreciation and plan. His policy, to oppose the enemy on the mainland in order to cover the arrival of reinforcements, remained unchanged. Provided the enemy could be held till the middle of February, he planned to relieve the Australian division in Johore by 18th Division (he expected all three brigades

---

[1] See Map 5.

to have arrived by the end of January) and to use the Australians as a striking force. He foresaw that III Corps might be forced back to northern Johore by the 24th January and that if this occurred there would be a critical period between then and the middle of February. Thus a flexible plan was required which could be adjusted as the situation developed. The basis of this plan was that one Australian brigade group should be left for the defence of the east coast of Johore, while the other should be made available for offensive operations in the Segamat area on the general line Batu Anam–Muar.[1] This latter brigade would have to be replaced by other troops. Percival proposed therefore that, after 53rd Brigade of 18th Division had arrived at Singapore, one battalion from Fortress Command would relieve the Australian battalion at Kota Tinggi and one battalion from III Corps would replace the two Australian battalions on the Kluang–Kahang road. If these moves took place, Bennett was to continue to command in eastern Johore and Heath in western Johore. Bennett, who had telegraphed on the 6th to Army Headquarters, Australia, urging that the 'purely defensive attitude should be replaced by strong counter-attack methods', agreed to 27th Australian Brigade coming under Heath's orders, despite the fact that he had in the same telegram wrongly attributed the recent withdrawals to the lack of fighting spirit in commanders and especially the corps commander.

On the very day of the disaster at Slim River, however, General Wavell arrived in Singapore on his way to Java to take up his appointment as Supreme Commander, ABDA Command. He had already decided that, in order to halt the Japanese southward advance, he would have to secure the line of naval and air bases from Darwin through Timor, Java and southern Sumatra to Singapore.[2] He had realized from the first that if that line were to be held it would be a race against time, and that much would depend upon the ability of the troops in Malaya to delay the Japanese north of Johore until sufficient reinforcements could arrive. If the Japanese could be delayed there till the end of January, 18th British Division could reinforce the defence. There was then the possibility that the Australian corps could be landed at Singapore and undertake a counter-offensive northwards, and the Indian formations in Malaya be used to reinforce the Netherlands East Indies. The main object of his visit was to see for himself the state of the troops, to discuss with their commanders the possibility of holding the Japanese advance and to estimate the time factors involved.

Having been apprised of the situation and of Percival's intentions, Wavell went north on the 8th to discuss the problem with both

[1] See Map 18.
[2] See Strategic Map.

Heath and Bennett and visit some of the troops of 11th Division. He formed the opinion that the units forming III Corps, which had been fighting and retreating continuously for a month under the most trying conditions, would be of little further fighting value unless they had a rest, and that, as the country south of Kuala Lumpur was not suitable for a delaying action, they would disintegrate altogether if the policy of gradual withdrawal were continued. Before returning to Singapore, Wavell instructed Heath to cover Kuala Lumpur for as long as possible without awaiting full-scale enemy attack, making the fullest use of demolitions to delay the enemy. He also told him that he proposed to withdraw III Corps to Johore at an early date to rest and refit.

That evening the Supreme Commander, without any further discussion, gave Percival the following general plan for the defence of southern Malaya:

- (a) III Indian Corps, after delaying the enemy north of Kuala Lumpur for as long as possible, was to be withdrawn by rail and road into Johore, leaving only sufficient mobile rearguards to cover demolition schemes.
- (b) 8th Australian Division (less one brigade group which was to remain in the Mersing area) was to move immediately to the north-west frontier of Johore, and prepare to fight a defensive battle on the general line Segamat–Mount Ophir–mouth of the Muar River. The brigade group remaining in the Mersing area was to be moved to the same general line as soon as it could be relieved by troops from Singapore Island, but this could not be carried out till after the arrival of 53rd Infantry Brigade.
- (c) 9th Indian Division, made up from the freshest troops of III Indian Corps, and 45th Indian Infantry Brigade from Malacca, were to be placed under command of 8th Australian Division and used in the southern portion of the position as indicated.
- (d) III Indian Corps after withdrawal was to take over responsibility for the east and west coasts of Johore south of the line Mersing–Kluang–Batu Pahat, thus leaving General Bennett free to fight a battle in north-western Johore. The III Indian Corps was to reorganize 11th Indian Division, and organize a general reserve from reinforcements as they arrived.

Wavell has said that he realized that his plan had certain disadvantages and dangers. It allowed the enemy to advance with little opposition through Selangor, Negri Sembilan and Malacca, but III Corps was no longer fit to fight for these states which, with their well-developed road systems, were unsuitable for delaying tactics. It involved taking a calculated risk by weakening the defences of the east coast to strengthen the immediately threatened west and replacing the Australian troops on the east coast of Johore by troops with no knowledge of the ground. It was, he said, 'a time problem between the rate of Japanese advance and the arrival of reinforcements', and he felt that in the circumstances he had provided the best general solution to this problem. Finally, finding that, although reconnaissance had begun, no defences had been constructed or even planned in detail on the north side of Singapore Island, he ordered these to be put in hand at once in case a withdrawal to the island became necessary.

Next morning, after a discussion with Bennett, Percival issued the following orders: 8th Australian Division (less one brigade) was to concentrate in the vicinity of Segamat; 45th Indian Infantry Brigade immediately and 9th Indian Division on entering Johore, were to come under command of 8th Australian Division; III Corps was to withdraw to Johore, covered by demolitions, and pass through 8th Australian Division which would then take over operational control of northern Johore; and on completion of the withdrawal III Corps was to take over operational responsibility for southern Johore up to and including the line Endau–Kluang–Batu Pahat. He also ordered 8th Australian Division to be relieved of the responsibility for the Kota Tinggi area by an Indian battalion from Fortress Command, and of the responsibility for the protection of the airfields at Kluang and Kahang by a brigade group found by III Corps.

On the 10th, a conference was held at Segamat to arrange details of the handover between III Corps and the Australians; Percival, Heath and Bennett were present. It was then decided that the force under Bennett's command was to be called 'Westforce' and consist of 8th Australian Division (less 22nd Australian Brigade Group), 9th Indian Division (8th and 22nd Indian Brigades) and 45th Indian Brigade; that 9th Indian Division was to be reinforced by 2nd Loyals, less one company, from Singapore; and that the main line of resistance to be held by 'Westforce' was to be the general line Batu Anam–Muar. The III Corps was to take command of 22nd Australian Brigade Group in the Mersing area and be responsible for the defence of Johore from the line of the lateral road Endau–Kluang–Batu Pahat southwards;[1] 11th Indian Division (15th and 28th Brigades) was to be rested and reorganized in Johore, and 12th Brigade was to go to Singapore Island to re-form and re-equip.

While the British commanders were planning the defence of Johore, the Japanese were bringing forward reinforcements and preparing plans to expedite its capture. The *21st Infantry Regiment* of *5th Division* and a large number of administrative units reached Singora on the 8th with the loss of only one transport, which caught fire. The *5th Guards Regiment* closely followed by the Guards divisional troops, who had been relieved of their task in Siam, reached Ipoh on

---

[1] General Bennett telegraphed Army Headquarters, Australia, on the 11th saying, 'Consider situation justifies separation but badly need 22nd Brigade to help me'.

the 10th. At the same time *Southern Army* made preparations to land the rest of *18th Division* (*114th Infantry Regiment*, the remaining battalion of *55th Infantry Regiment* and the divisional troops) at Endau towards the end of January, with the object of shortening the long lines of communications from Singora and threatening the British line of retreat from northern Johore. The landing was to be carried out simultaneously with the capture of the Anambas, which the Navy required as an advanced base.

Throughout the first fortnight of January the enemy air force repeatedly attacked 11th Division and communications in III Corps area. These attacks caused few casualties and little material damage, but affected the morale of the troops and were thus a contributory cause of the disasters sustained by the corps. The Japanese used bombers only, and these in small formations, sometimes of only three or four aircraft. In this respect there appears to have been no effective higher direction of enemy air operations in central Malaya, for aircrews were left to choose their own targets. Thus, though the troops could not have realized it at the time, the sporadic bombing they endured had much of a 'hit and miss' element in it. General Wavell said in a telegram to India Command, 'had the Japanese used their air superiority effectively there would have been complete disaster'. Fortunately they failed to do so.

Although the small British and Dutch air forces were unable to intervene effectively in central Malaya, they were far from idle. The railway yards and shipping at Singora were bombed on the 7th and attacks were made against the airfields held by the enemy at Ipoh, Sungei Patani, and Kuantan. Photographic reconnaissances were carried out in both Malaya and British Borneo, while reconnaissance of the sea approaches to northern Sumatra and the east coast of Malaya continued daily.

During the second week in January the Japanese, in an attempt to destroy the air defences, began to intensify their daylight raids on Singapore Island. The loss of observer corps post on the mainland as the Japanese advanced, and inadequate radar cover meant that the period of warning of approaching enemy raids was frequently insufficient, as at least thirty minutes were needed to enable the Buffaloes to reach the height of 24,000 feet at which the enemy often flew. The air defence was thus handicapped by the short warning received as well as by the poor performance of the Buffaloes compared with the Zero fighters. The anti-aircraft defence too could play only a limited part. There were sufficient light anti-aircraft guns to give protection against all low-level attacks, but the majority of enemy raids were flown at heights of over 20,000 feet. At that height they were above the effective range of the 3-inch guns, which formed one-third of the heavy anti-aircraft defences. Only the 3·7-inch guns, of which there were not more than forty for the defence of the many targets on the island, could engage aircraft at such altitudes.

On the 12th, Japanese bombers escorted by fighters made three daylight raids on Tengah airfield without doing any serious damage. The defence had a fighter force of one Dutch and four British Buffalo squadrons, which could muster some fifty-six serviceable aircraft daily. These squadrons intercepted all three raids and in the course of the day's fighting destroyed six Japanese fighters for the loss of five Buffaloes.

On the 13th, the arrival at Singapore of the second reinforcement convoy, including several large American liners, presented an additional target. The approach of the ships was covered by low cloud and heavy rain and, although a force of approximately eighty enemy bombers with escorting fighters made a raid on Singapore, it failed to sight the ships. Twenty fighters succeeded in intercepting this raid but three were lost. So bad was the weather that the enemy aircraft dropped their bombs in salvos from the clouds with the result that many fell into the sea and on waste ground, only a few falling in the town. These caused some 200 civilian casualties.

The convoy was thus unmolested; the ships were unloaded as quickly as possible and left Singapore without delay. The reinforcements landed were 53rd British Infantry Brigade Group of 18th British Division,[1] 6th Heavy and 35th Light British Anti-Aircraft Regiments and 85th British Anti-Tank Regiment. In addition, the fifty-one Hurricane aircraft in crates were landed together with twenty-four fighter pilots. Most of the Hurricanes were at once dispersed to previously selected concealed positions, where they were quickly erected and moved to adjacent airfields for air tests. Great hopes were placed upon them as a means of regaining air superiority over central Malaya.

In Selangor 15th Brigade, which on the 8th had reverted to the command of 11th Division, was already committed to the coastal area.[2] The remnants of 12th Brigade and 28th Brigade (now reinforced by 2/16th Punjab) were the only troops available to dispute the enemy's advance on the trunk road, and they were in no condition to fight. Heath had no alternative but to withdraw out of contact and try to gain a little respite for his battered forces. On the 8th therefore he instructed 11th Division to hold Kuala Lumpur till midnight on

---

[1] See Appendix 21.
[2] See pages 273–274.

the 10th/11th and then to fall back thirty-two miles to the area of Seremban.

Paris organized the defence of the area north and west of Kuala Lumpur into three sectors: the trunk road sector covered by 28th Brigade, which he reinforced with 3/17th Dogras (less two companies); the central sector, which was to include the Batang Berjuntai–Rawang road, covered by 15th Brigade reinforced by 5/11th Sikhs (originally part of 22nd Brigade); and the coastal sector, which was taken from 15th Brigade's command and once more placed under Brigadier Moir, covered by the Jat/Punjab Battalion and 3rd Cavalry. He decided that the key points Rawang, Sungei Buloh, and Klang would have to be held till 4 p.m. on the 10th. Subsequently either 28th or 15th Brigade, as circumstances dictated, was to hold Kuala Lumpur, and Brigadier Moir's force Batu Tiga, until midnight on the 10th/11th. Arrangements were made for all troops to be moved back by motor transport. On the trunk road and in the central sector 28th and 15th Brigades managed, despite very severe enemy pressure, to frustrate repeated attempts to break through and were eventually able to break contact and withdraw as planned.[1]

In the coastal sector *4th Guards Regiment* was ordered to seize Klang, near Port Swettenham, by moving *II/4th Guards Battalion* by sea while the main body of the regiment, crossing the river at Kuala Selangor, moved southwards along the coast road. During the night of the 9th/10th the Japanese crossed the Sungei Selangor unopposed, and by noon on the 10th their advanced guard was attacking the position covering the bridge over the river at Klang, held by a small force composed of the Jat/Punjab Battalion, 3rd Cavalry and 73rd Field Battery under command of Lieut.-Colonel C. K. Tester. Very heavy rainstorms may have delayed the arrival of their main body, for the attack was not pressed. At 4.30 p.m. Tester disengaged and began to fall back with the intention of fighting a delaying action back to Batu Tiga. The enemy quickly followed up and sharp fighting broke out during the night in which Tester's force lost heavily. Eventually at 1 a.m. on the 11th, reduced to some 200 all ranks, it reached Batu Tiga. Here the survivors were embussed and moved through Kajang to the south.

The Japanese battalion which was to attack Klang from the sea arrived off the mouth of the river considerably in advance of the force moving down the coast road. As the attack on Klang could not be synchronized, the battalion was ordered to land near Port Swettenham on the afternoon of the 10th and move inland towards Kajang on the main road south of Kuala Lumpur, in an attempt to cut off

[1] In these actions the headquarters and two companies 3/17th Dogra (28th Brigade) and the whole of 1/14th Punjab (15th Brigade) were overrun and lost.

11th Division. It reached Kajang the following evening, a few hours after the last of the division had passed through on its way southwards.

The Japanese troops entered Kuala Lumpur at 8 p.m. on the 11th, when they took over the civil administration and quickly enforced law and order. The following day Headquarters *5th Division* was established in the town. With the capture of the capital of the Federated Malay States the first phase of the *25th Army* plan for the conquest of Malaya was completed.

The evacuation of Kuala Lumpur, the main base for III Corps and the air forces operating initially in northern Malaya, involved the loss of large quantities of military stores. Much of the reserve stocks of ordnance equipment and supplies had been moved back to Singapore by rail or road, but the unexpectedly quick collapse of the front at Slim River had prevented the completion of the task. Whenever possible bulky stores which could not be moved were destroyed. Petrol and oil stocks at Kuala Lumpur and Port Swettenham were run to waste or fired, buildings on the airfield at Kuala Lumpur demolished and runways cratered. Nevertheless much of value fell into enemy hands.

The withdrawal of III Corps continued, undisturbed by the enemy. The 11th Division held successive rearguard positions on the 11th and 12th, and on the 13th reached Tampin. On the night of the 13th/14th it withdrew through 'Westforce' to the Kluang–Rengam area. The 9th Division conformed, 8th Brigade reaching Batu Anam on the 11th by rail and the rest of the division Tampin on the 12th. On the 13th it came under command of 'Westforce' and occupied the positions allotted to it for the defence of northern Johore.

x

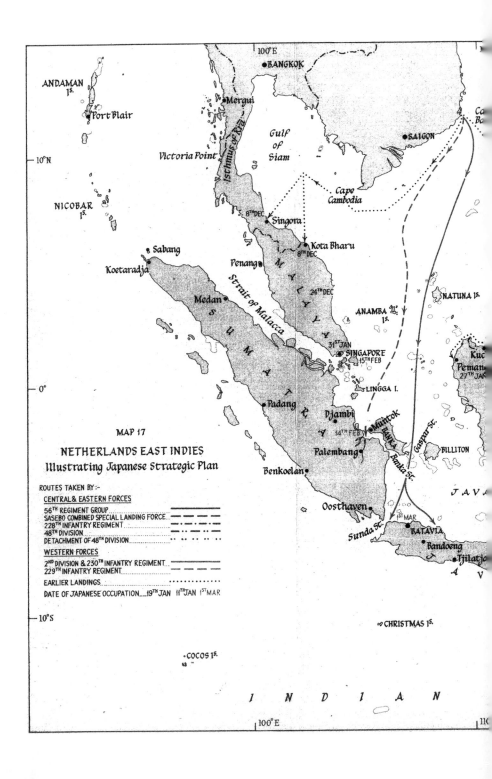

MAP 17

NETHERLANDS EAST INDIES
Illustrating Japanese Strategic Plan

ROUTES TAKEN BY:-

CENTRAL & EASTERN FORCES

56TH REGIMENT GROUP
SASEBO COMBINED SPECIAL LANDING FORCE
228TH INFANTRY REGIMENT
48TH DIVISION
DETACHMENT OF 48TH DIVISION

WESTERN FORCES

2ND DIVISION & 230TH INFANTRY REGIMENT
229TH INFANTRY REGIMENT

EARLIER LANDINGS

DATE OF JAPANESE OCCUPATION.....19TH JAN   11TH JAN   1ST MAR

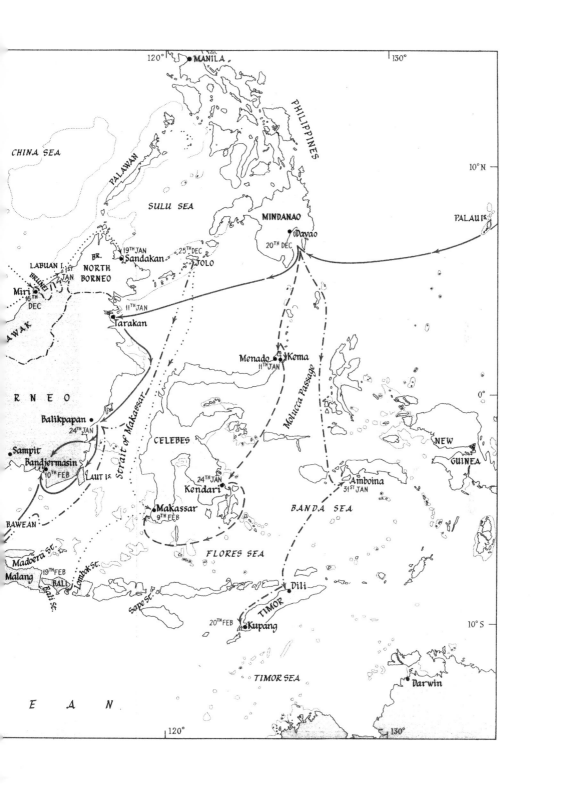

CHINA SEA

120°

●MANILA

130°

PALAWAN

PHILIPPINES

10°N

PALAU IS.

SULU SEA

MINDANAO

19TH JAN
●Sandakan

25TH DEC
●JOLO

●Davao
20TH DEC

LABUAN I.
1ST
JAN

BR.
NORTH
BORNEO

Menado ●Kema
11TH JAN

Miri●
16TH
DEC

BRUNEI

11TH JAN
●Tarakan

Molucca Passage

AWAK

0°

R N E O

Balikpapan●
24TH JAN

Strait of Makassar

CELEBES

NEW
GUINEA

●Sampit
●Bandjermasin
10TH FEB

LAUT IS.

24TH JAN
●Kendari

Amboina
31ST JAN

●Makassar
9TH FEB

BANDA SEA

BAWEAN●

FLORES SEA

Madoera St.
Malang●
BALI
19TH FEB

Bali St.

Lombok St.

Sape St.

●Dili

TIMOR

20TH FEB ●Kupang

10°S

E   A   N

120°

TIMOR SEA

●Darwin

130°

CHAPTER XVIII

THE ATTACK ON THE DUTCH
BEGINS: CELEBES AND BORNEO

See Map 17

JAPANESE PROGRESS IN MALAYA had been more rapid than *Imperial General Headquarters* had expected and at the end of December, with British Borneo, Davao and Jolo in their hands they felt they were in a position to begin their drive on the Netherlands East Indies.

Their plan was for a three-pronged advance: a *Western Force* based on Camranh Bay to invade southern Sumatra (Palembang) as soon as the fall of Singapore was assured; a *Central Force* to move down the Strait of Makassar from Davao to occupy in succession the oilfields at Tarakan and Balikpapan and then Bandjermasin in Dutch Borneo; and an *Eastern Force* to take, again in succession, Menado in north Celebes and Kendari and Makassar in south Celebes. This force was also to capture Amboina in order to protect the left flank of the advance, and Timor so as to cut the air route between Australia and Java. The movements of the *Central* and *Eastern Forces* were to be synchronized to provide mutual support. On completion of this programme all three forces were to combine for the invasion of Java; the *Western Force* landing near Batavia and the *Central* and *Eastern Forces* near Sourabaya.

Vice-Admiral Kondo, Commander-in-Chief, *2nd Fleet*, was in supreme command of all southern naval operations, and with his battle fleet provided distant cover throughout the campaign.[1] Vice-Admiral Ozawa commanded the *Western Force* and Vice-Admiral Takahashi the *Central* and *Eastern Forces*.[2] All land forces were under the command of Lieut.-General Imamura, commanding *16th Army*, with headquarters at Saigon. Air cover was provided by the *21st* and *23rd Air Flotillas* of Vice-Admiral Tsukahara's *11th Air Fleet*, the small aircraft carrier *Ryujo* and four seaplane tenders. Large aircraft carriers were employed for some of the operations such as the attack on Amboina.

Menado, at the north-east corner of Celebes, was selected as the first objective for the *Eastern Force*, and the oil port on Tarakan

---

[1] See page 100.
[2] For details of the composition of the three forces and *16th Army* see Appendices 22 and 23.

Island off Borneo for the *Central Force*. The *21st* and *23rd Air Flotillas* moved to Davao and Jolo respectively during the first week in January. The southward advance began on the 7th January when *56th (Sakaguchi) Regimental Group* and the *Kure 2nd Special Naval Landing Force* left Davao for Tarakan Island. Naval escort and cover were provided by the *Central Force*, and air cover by the *23rd Air Flotilla*. The convoy was sighted and attacked during its approach by three American heavy bombers from Java. Visibility was bad, bombs were dropped from a great height and the ships suffered no damage. Three American submarines ordered to intercept arrived too late.

The smoke of the convoy was seen and reported by coastguards on Tarakan Island during the afternoon of the 10th, and without waiting for orders, the Dutch commander of the garrison at once destroyed the oilfield. As the ships came over the horizon, clouds of smoke rising from the island warned the Japanese that their hopes of capturing the oilfields intact had gone.

The convoy anchored some ten miles east of the island. At about midnight the landing craft were sent in, and by dawn landings had been made on the north and south coasts. Having delayed the enemy's advance long enough to enable the destruction of the oilfields to be completed, the Dutch garrison of 1,300 men surrendered on the morning of the 12th. The transports were attacked on the 12th and 13th by Dutch army aircraft from Samarinda II, an airfield 100 miles inland from Balikpapan, but with little effect. Four days later aircraft of the *23rd Air Flotilla* were able to use the airfield, and by the 25th the headquarters of the flotilla was established on the island.

Two days after the departure of the *Central Force* for Tarakan, the *Sasebo Combined Special Naval Landing Force* left Davao for Menado. Naval escort and cover were provided by Admiral Takahashi's *Eastern Force*, and air cover by the *21st Air Flotilla*. Allied aircraft from Amboina attacked the transports at anchor, but without success, and before dawn on the 11th the Japanese landed on the beaches at Menado, and at Kema on the opposite side of the peninsula.

These landings were closely followed by an airborne attack on the airfield just south of Menado. Shortly after 10 a.m. twenty-eight transport aircraft from Davao dropped 334 paratroops of the *Yokosuka 1st Special Naval Landing Force* on the airfield. This was the first time that such troops had been used by the Japanese, and the operation, so they state, left much to be desired. There was a strong wind blowing and the aircraft made their drops from too great a height, with the result that the troops arrived on the ground widely scattered and separated from their equipment. It had the effect however of causing confusion among the garrison of approximately 1,500 men, only one quarter of whom were regular troops, and of diverting forces which might have been used in defence of the beaches. On the 12th a second drop was made by a further 185 paratroops, and by the evening the Japanese had control of the whole area. The airfield was quickly repaired and by the 24th was occupied by units of the *21st Air Flotilla*. Thus by the 12th January the Japanese had gained control of the northern approaches to the Strait of Makassar and the Molucca Passage, had extended the range of their aircraft some 300 miles further south and had effectually prevented the Allies from reinforcing the Philippines with aircraft other than long-range bombers.

During his visit to Singapore early in January, General Wavell had closed the headquarters of the Commander-in-Chief, Far East, and when he flew on to Batavia he took General Pownall and Major-General I. S. O. Playfair with him to assume their appointments at ABDA Headquarters. On arrival at Batavia he met the senior members of his staff and discussed the organization and location of the new headquarters. This he decided to set up at Lembang, in the foothills some ten miles north of Bandoeng. He assumed responsibility for the whole of the ABDA area on the 15th.

To facilitate control of land and air forces the vast area was divided into a number of subsidiary areas, each under a commander responsible to the Supreme Commander. No definite delimitation of these areas was necessary as far as land forces were concerned, because the respective commands had been in existence long enough for their boundaries to be generally recognized. One exception to this was the Darwin sub-area, which was established from midnight on the 7th/8th February. Here a mixture of Australian, Netherlands East Indies and American units made it necessary to define more closely the boundaries of the area. The southern boundary coincided with that of the ABDA area and, outside Australia, included the island of Timor and the islands in the ABDA area east of Celebes and south of latitude 5° north.[1]

Lieut.-General H. ter Poorten was placed in control of the land forces branch of ABDA Staff and retained command of the troops in Java; Major-General Playfair acted as ter Poorten's deputy and Chief of Staff. The Army Commanders in the sub-areas were: Burma, Lieut.-General T. J. Hutton; Malaya, Lieut.-General A. E. Percival; Philippine Islands, Lieut.-General D. MacArthur, U.S. Army; and Darwin sub-area, Major-General D. V. J. Blake, A.I.F.

Air Marshal Sir Richard Peirse, with Major-General L. H. Brereton, United States Army Air Force, as his deputy, became the Supreme Commander's Chief of the Air Staff and exercised command

[1] See Strategic Map.

of all the Allied air forces in the ABDA area.[1] The area was divided
into five sub-commands: Norgroup (Burma), Wesgroup (Malaya,
Sumatra as far south as, and including, Palembang, and western
Borneo), Cengroup (western Java and Sumatra south of Palembang),
Easgroup (eastern Java and the islands to the east as far as the Flores
Sea, the Celebes, but not the Molucca Passage), and Ausgroup
(Darwin area). In addition, there was a reconnaissance group which
was sub-divided into four groups and covered the whole area outside
Burma.

No sub-division of the ABDA area was made for purposes of naval
operations. The Chief of the Naval Staff, Admiral T. C. Hart,
United States Navy, with Rear-Admiral A. F. E. Palliser (Royal Navy)
as his deputy, commanded all Allied naval forces in the area
under the direction of the Supreme Commander. Normally the
naval forces operated under their own national commanders,
namely Vice-Admiral C. E. L. Helfrich, Royal Netherlands Navy,
Rear-Admiral W. A. Glassford,[2] United States Navy (Task Force
5) and Commodore J. A. Collins, Royal Australian Navy, whose
title from the 20th January 1942 was Commodore, Commanding
China Force. It was decided however that combined striking forces
should be formed from time to time for particular operations,
under a commander designated by Admiral Hart.

The functions of the American Task Force and of the China
Force were different. Admiral Hart had received instructions from
Washington that all available United States naval vessels were to be
used to close the passages in the eastern end of the Malay barrier,
and to support the defence of the Netherlands East Indies and
Australia. Admiral Glassford's task force had accordingly been based
at Sourabaya and Darwin, where it was held in readiness to cover
the occasional convoy proceeding through the Torres Strait to Darwin,
and to attack the enemy invasion forces east of Borneo as opportunity occurred.[3] The major pre-occupation of Commodore Collins'
China Force was the escort of convoys carrying reinforcements and
supplies from the Indian Ocean to Singapore. In this he had invaluable assistance from Dutch cruisers, destroyers and aircraft. The
employment of the ships on escort duty prevented in the first instance
their joining the Allied striking force.

General Wavell paid a second visit to Singapore on the 13th
January while his headquarters was being set up and saw both
Bennett and Heath, to whom the defence of Johore had been en-
trusted. He found that, although the plans he had outlined during

---

[1] Until Air Marshal Peirse arrived and assumed command on the 28th January 1942,
General Brereton held temporary command of all the Allied air forces.
[2] Promoted to Vice-Admiral on the 30th January 1942.
[3] See Strategic Map.

his previous visit had taken shape, the Japanese advance had been more rapid than he had expected and 9th and 11th Divisions had suffered further losses in the fighting north of Kuala Lumpur. Next day, when cabling the Chiefs of Staff, he said that the battle for Singapore would be a 'close-run thing'.

It was during this visit that he became involved in the question of the efficacy of the civil administration. On the 3rd January Mr. Duff Cooper had sent a cable to the Secretary of State for the Colonies in which he repeated the views expressed in his letter to the Prime Minister of the 18th December on the inadequacy of the arrangements for the civil defence of Singapore, and said that in his opinion the civil authorities had failed lamentably in making adequate preparations for war.[1] On the 11th January, just before leaving Singapore on the Prime Minister's instructions, he had again cabled saying that there existed a widespread and profound lack of confidence in the administration and that, as a breakdown might well paralyse the fighting services, changes were desirable. He had suggested that the simplest solution would be to declare a state of siege and appoint a military governor for the duration of the emergency. The Secretary of State for the Colonies had asked Wavell for his views. Having consulted General Pownall and Admiral Layton and learnt from Brigadier Simson of the difficulties which he was experiencing in carrying out his task, General Wavell replied that he considered it advisable that there should be certain changes in the senior personnel in the administration rather than the appointment of a military governor. His recommendation was acted on and the Governor was asked to ensure that members of the civil administration were those who enjoyed the confidence of the Services.

The strategical position in south-east Asia when Wavell took command was far from satisfactory. The Japanese had already captured the Allied advanced air bases in Celebes and Dutch Borneo, had occupied the whole of British Borneo and, in Malaya, were already in contact with the Australian and Indian formations in north-west Johore. He soon came to the conclusion that, with the resources available to him and with Menado and Tarakan in enemy hands, the only way he could support General MacArthur was by sending him ammunition by submarine and that, although there was no immediate threat to Sumatra or Java, further Japanese advances in Celebes and Borneo could shortly be expected, since their object would be to establish air bases nearer Java. He expected the enemy to make an early attempt to cut his vital air reinforcement route from Australia by occupying Amboina and Timor. He thought however

[1] See pages 233–234.

that there was a possibility that Johore could be held long enough to enable a counter-offensive to be launched, provided that the convoys bringing the promised reinforcements arrived safely and that fresh enemy landings on the east coast could be prevented.

Although the American and Dutch representatives on his staff urged the importance of reinforcing the forward air bases at Amboina, Kendari, Balikpapan and Sabang, Wavell thought that such dispersion of his limited resources could only end in piecemeal defeat. All he could hope to do was to check and hamper the enemy's advance in Borneo and further east, while he concentrated all his resources to hold the line of naval and air bases from Darwin, by way of Timor, Java and southern Sumatra, to Singapore. He decided therefore to send all land reinforcements as they arrived to Singapore, trusting that the outcome of the impending battle in Johore would be sufficiently favourable to enable them to restore the situation in Malaya. He realized that the security of the airfields in Sumatra, where he hoped to build up an air strength capable of securing local superiority, must be provided for as soon as possible.

His most difficult problem was that of delaying the advance on Java and Sumatra of an enemy enjoying all the advantages of command of the sea and air. The greater part of his slender Allied naval resources had to be employed in escorting the convoys bringing in reinforcements from the west, since on their safe arrival depended all his plans. He was thus left with only Admiral Glassford's weak task force and the submarines, with which to take offensive action and to interfere with enemy shipping routes. Since the Japanese moved neither their naval forces nor their convoys outside the range of their air cover, the opportunities for offensive action were limited. The best chance lay in using his ships for hit-and-run attacks by night. In the light of these grave deficiencies, Wavell informed the Chiefs of Staff that there would be better prospects of dealing the enemy a blow and of preventing him establishing himself between Australia and Java if more cruisers and destroyers could be sent to form a striking force; but no ships could be spared.

All available aircraft had to be employed in protecting the convoys, in watching the movement of enemy ships, in attacking enemy airfields and supporting the army in Malaya; this left very little with which to attack enemy shipping and to provide air cover for any naval striking force. The air forces earmarked for the ABDA area constituted, on paper, a formidable force. In addition to British air reinforcements the Americans had made arrangements for over 1,000 aircraft to arrive in the area during the next two months. With the prospect of these reinforcements in view, Wavell hoped to be able to replace air losses more quickly than the Japanese and so gradually build up air superiority.

The Japanese however had no intention of giving him time to do so. On the 20th January *56th Regimental Group*, leaving the *Kure 2nd Special Naval Landing Force* as a garrison, embarked at Tarakan for the capture of Balikpapan. The convoy was to have been covered by the *23rd Air Flotilla* from Tarakan, but bad weather made this impracticable. Before the convoy sailed, emissaries had been sent to Balikpapan to demand, under threat of reprisals, that the oil installations should be surrendered intact. The demand had however been treated by the Dutch with the contempt it deserved; the demolition scheme was at once carried out and, as at Tarakan, columns of smoke from the burning oilfields greeted the Japanese on their arrival. Fourteen transports anchored off Balikpapan in darkness on the 23rd and the troops at once began to disembark. A subsidiary landing was made from two transports twenty miles to the south, while Admiral Nishimura's destroyers carried out an anti-submarine patrol to the eastwards.

The southward movement of an enemy convoy in the Strait of Makassar had been reported on the 20th, and six American and two Dutch submarines had been sent from Sourabaya and the South China Sea to the Balikpapan area. On the afternoon of the 23rd Dutch aircraft from Samarinda II bombed and sank a transport, and on the following day a Dutch submarine sank another. Seeing an opportunity of striking the enemy a blow and thereby delaying his southward advance, ABDA Command had on the 20th ordered Admiral Glassford's task force, which was refuelling at Kupang Bay in Timor, to carry out a night attack on the convoy. As soon as fuelling had been completed, the Admiral, flying his flag in the *Boise* and accompanied by the *Marblehead* and four destroyers, weighed and set course for the Strait of Makassar.[1] When passing through the Sape Strait the *Boise* hit a rock and had to turn back. Sending his destroyers on ahead, the Admiral transferred his flag to the *Marblehead*, which owing to engine trouble could make only fifteen knots, and followed to a rendezvous position ninety miles south of Balikpapan, from where he could cover the destroyers' withdrawal after the attack. Leaving Makassar town well to starboard the destroyers made a feint to the eastwards. About an hour after sunset on the 23rd, they turned and set course for Balikpapan. During the night they were challenged by enemy patrols in the Strait but, leaving the challenge unanswered, passed them without being attacked. Shortly before 3 a.m. on the 24th they sighted the Japanese transports silhouetted against the light of the burning oilfields—a perfect target for destroyers. Transports were the principal targets and torpedoes the primary weapons. For nearly an hour the destroyers steamed

---

[1] Both American light cruisers. Armament: *Boise* fifteen 6-inch and eight 5-inch. *Marblehead* eight 6-inch.

between the enemy ships, using guns and torpedoes against ships now lit by the flames ashore and now hidden in clouds of oily smoke. At about 3.45 a.m. when all torpedoes had been fired the destroyers withdrew independently and, eluding the attempts by Admiral Nishimura to cut off their retreat, made for their rendezvous with the *Marblehead*. They sank or left sinking one old patrol boat and three transports. That the destruction was not greater must be attributed to the confusion inherent in a night action and, in particular, to the unnecessarily high speed of the attacking ships, the shortness of the range and the shallow water which prevented the torpedoes running true. Many of the torpedoes, as was only too common at that stage of the war, probably failed to explode. By the evening of the 24th the Japanese had occupied the town of Balikpapan, the Dutch garrison of one weak battalion having withdrawn inland after demolishing the oil refineries. Four days later aircraft of the *23rd Air Flotilla* were established on the adjacent airfields.

Admiral Takahashi's *Eastern Force*, which had captured Menado on the 11th January, had meanwhile been keeping step with the *Central Force*. Kendari was seized against slight opposition, on the very day that Balikpapan was occupied (24th), by the same forces as had been used at Menado. The Japanese immediately set to work to organize the air base, which they considered to be the best in the Netherlands East Indies, for use by bombers of the *21st Air Flotilla*. Thus in thirteen days the Japanese had gained possession of airfields within striking distance of the vital air reinforcement route from Australia and of the naval base at Sourabaya; and General Wavell had been powerless to delay them.

Constant air reconnaissance over the Anamba Islands and the South China Sea produced negative results, and this confirmed Wavell in his view that so long as he could hold Johore an enemy attack on southern Sumatra could be discounted.

Wavell had another important but distracting commitment which has not yet been mentioned—the defence of Burma. Although operations in this area had no effect on the defence of the Netherlands East Indies and on Malaya, he had the responsibility, thrust upon him much against his will, of providing land and air reinforcements for that theatre of war from those allotted to the ABDA area. Wavell found, as he had expected, that communications with Burma from ABDA Headquarters were most indifferent. He felt that a visit to Rangoon would have to be undertaken, even though it meant a journey of four thousand miles there and back which took him far from his more urgent responsibilities in the east. Towards the end of the third week in January news reached him that, despite their preoccupation with the Malayan campaign, the Japanese had invaded Tenasserim and had gained some easy success. He therefore flew from Java to Burma during the night of the 24th/25th January, spent the 25th at Rangoon with General Hutton, and flew back to Java that night. He found the atmosphere in the Burma theatre calmer and more confident than the telegrams he had received had led him to expect.

CHAPTER XIX

THE LOSS OF
NORTHERN JOHORE

See Maps 5, 18 and 20 and Sketches 6 and 7

TO REVERT to events in Malaya: on the 11th January, the day that his troops entered Kuala Lumpur, General Yamashita appreciated that the withdrawing British forces would defend northern Johore on the general line of the Sungei Muar, since this was in his opinion the last natural defensive position north of Singapore Island. He decided to rest the main body of *5th Division*, which had been marching and fighting for some thirty-five days, in the Seremban area while the *Imperial Guards Division* concentrated at Malacca.[1] He then planned to advance with *5th Division*, including its *21st Infantry Regiment* which was due to reach the forward area within the next few days, along the trunk road towards Segamat and Kluang, while the *Imperial Guards Division* moved down the west coast to force a crossing of the Sungei Muar and the Sungei Batu Pahat in order to threaten the communications of the British formations opposing *5th Division* on the trunk road. On the east coast he ordered *55th Infantry Regiment* (two battalions only) to relieve *56th Infantry Regiment* at Kuantan and then to advance southwards to occupy Endau and Mersing. The *56th Infantry Regiment* after relief was to reach Kuala Lumpur by the 24th January.

Southern Army had planned that the balance of *18th Division* should be landed at Endau.[2] However, in view of the fact that the British forces had withdrawn from Kuala Lumpur to northern Johore without offering any opposition, and that the air attacks on the 12th and following two days had failed to achieve a sufficient degree of air supremacy, *Southern Army* decided to cancel the proposed operation at Endau and arranged for the division to be landed at Singora on the 22nd and be moved to Johore by road. General Yamashita, finding that his tenuous lines of communication were overloaded, requested that certain auxiliary units together with stocks of petrol and bombs

---

[1] Consisting of *4th* and *5th Guards Infantry Regiments*.
[2] See page 286.

for use on the southern Johore airfields should be landed at Endau after its capture by *55th Infantry Regiment*. The *Southern Army* agreed to land the required units and stores there on the 26th at the same time as the Navy seized the Anambas.[1]

On the 14th January, while the main body of the Japanese *5th Division* rested, the *Mukaide Detachment*, consisting of a battalion of infantry mounted on bicycles, supported by a tank regiment and some artillery and engineer units, was sent forward to gain touch with the British forces.

General Bennett had disposed 'Westforce' so as to block the main communications from the north-west into Johore on the general line Batu Anam–Muar. He had placed 27th Australian Brigade (Brigadier Maxwell) astride the trunk road near Gemas, with its forward troops some seven miles further west; 9th Indian Division in rear of the Australians with 8th Brigade (Brigadier Lay) on the trunk road near Batu Anam, 22nd Brigade (Brigadier Painter) astride the Segamat–Malacca Road with its forward troops at Jementah and 2nd Loyals near Segamat.[2] They were supported by an anti-tank and four field artillery regiments (less one battery). The 45th Indian Brigade (Brigadier H. C. Duncan) supported by one field artillery battery was allotted to the coastal sector and given the dual role of defending the line of the Sungei Muar and guarding against possible further seaborne landings south of the river.[3]

Bennett had for long considered that the best way of inflicting a check on the Japanese was by means of ambushes. The trunk road west of Gemas provided suitable areas in which to put his idea into effect. He therefore selected a suitable position, covering seven hundred yards of the trunk road, immediately east of a bridge over a small river some three miles west of 2/30th Australian Battalion's position covering Gemas. One company of the battalion was concealed in the thick jungle on the side of the road east of the bridge, which had been prepared for demolition, and a field battery was disposed to cover the road west of it. At about 4 p.m. on the 14th the advanced guard of the *Mukaide Detachment* mounted on bicycles entered the ambush. About twenty minutes later, when a large number of Japanese had been allowed to pass over, the bridge was blown and fire was opened. Unfortunately the telephone link back to the gun positions, which had not been properly concealed, was cut and the artillery never

---

[1] See page 286.

[2] 2nd Loyals (less one company) were moved from Singapore to Segamat on the 12th January.

[3] 45th Indian Infantry Brigade consisted of: 7/6th Rajputana Rifles, 4/9th Jats, 5/18th Royal Garhwal Rifles.

came into action. Nevertheless it was estimated that large numbers of the enemy were killed or wounded. Having sprung the trap and inflicted as much damage as possible the company withdrew, not without difficulty, and rejoined its battalion.

On the morning of the 15th Gemas was heavily bombed, and at about 10 a.m. enemy troops made contact with 2/30th Battalion in position four miles west of the town. Fighting went on throughout the day in the course of which the battalion repulsed several attacks and threw the enemy into confusion by a well conducted counter-attack. The first encounter between the fresh Australian troops and the Japanese had been most encouraging; the Australians had destroyed several tanks and, in the ambush and fighting on the 15th, had caused the enemy considerable loss at the cost of some eighty casualties. It was clear however that the Japanese were being steadily reinforced, and that evening 2/30th Battalion was withdrawn to 27th Brigade's position covering Batu Anam. During the 16th there was little activity in front of Batu Anam, but on the afternoon of the 17th the enemy attacked the centre and left of 27th Australian Brigade, and despite being counter-attacked gained some ground. Maxwell then asked that 2/30th Battalion should be relieved because of the extreme fatigue of the troops, but, since he had sent the brigade's reserve battalion to Bakri, Bennett was unable to meet this request. On the 15th a small force of bombers, escorted by Buffalo fighters, successfully attacked Japanese motor transport on the Tampin–Gemas road, setting a number of vehicles on fire.

Because of the stiff resistance met with west of Gemas, *5th Division* took over control on the trunk road from the *Mukaide Detachment* on the evening of the 15th. General Matsui immediately ordered *9th Infantry Brigade* (*11th* and *41st Infantry Regiments*) to advance down the trunk road and overcome British resistance in front of Batu Anam, while *21st Infantry Brigade* (*21st* and *42nd Infantry Regiments*) moved on Segamat by the circuitous route through Ayer Kuning, the western side of Mount Ophir, and Jementah.

In the coastal area the *Imperial Guards Division* occupied Malacca on the 14th January and started its drive southwards in two columns, with *4th Guards Regiment* on the right and *5th Guards Regiment* on the left. General Nishimura realized that he might have considerable difficulty in crossing the Sungei Muar, particularly as he had not been allotted any landing craft, and air reconnaissance had shown that the British had removed nearly all local craft to the south bank. He decided therefore to contain the British forces holding Muar town with *4th Guards Regiment*, while *5th Guards Regiment* forced a crossing under cover of darkness further up stream and advanced on the town from the east. Once the river had been crossed, *4th Guards Regiment* was to move along the coast road towards Batu Pahat and *5th Guards*

Regiment along the inland road to Yong Peng. To assist *4th Guards Regiment* to capture Batu Pahat and prevent the British forces retreating down the coastal road, *1/4th Guards Battalion* was to move by sea and land south-west of the town. It was to conceal itself between Batu Pahat and Senggarang till the main body of the regiment attacked from the north and then close the southern escape route.

The defence of the Sungei Muar had been entrusted to the newly arrived and unblooded 45th Indian Brigade which, on the 11th, was in the Malacca area.[1] The brigade reached Muar on the 12th. Under instructions from Bennett, Brigadier Duncan deployed 7/6th Rajputana Rifles on the left from Muar to Jorak, a front of some nine miles, and 4/9th Jats on the right covering both the Grisek and Lenga crossings, a front of some fifteen miles, each battalion with two companies north of the river. He kept 5/18th Royal Garhwal Rifles in reserve near Bakri, with one company forward holding Simpang Jeram, and a small detachment watching the coast south of Parit Jawa. These dispersed dispositions were closely akin to those which contributed to the disaster at Jitra. General Bennett appears to have lost sight of the main reason for placing 45th Brigade in the Muar area—to protect the direct route from Muar to Yong Peng and so secure his line of communications—and to have attempted to cover all possible routes from the Sungei Muar towards Segamat and Labis as well as those southwards. The result was that when the enemy blow fell there was only one battalion to meet it and that was split into two by a river obstacle.

Every day from the 11th January onwards the town of Muar was constantly bombed, a sure indication of a coming offensive. On the morning of the 15th the enemy surprised and completely overran both forward companies of the Rajputana Rifles in the Kesang–Sungei Mati area. No news of this disaster reached battalion headquarters. At 11 a.m. the enemy appeared on the waterfront opposite Muar and was engaged by artillery fire. That afternoon boats were seen off the mouth of the Sungei Muar and small parties of infantry were reported landing on the coast between the river and Batu Pahat.

During the night of the 15th/16th, *III/5th Guards Battalion* moved south from Sungei Mati carrying a number of small boats taken from the rice-fields in that area. In these a few men crossed the river and collected the larger native craft moored on the south bank, in which they were able to bring over sufficient men to form a bridge-head. The crossing was effected before daylight, the only opposition being a brush with an Indian patrol which hastily withdrew and apparently failed to report the presence of Japanese on the south bank. At dawn the Japanese moved southwards and surprised a

---

[1] See Appendix 19.

company of 7/6th Rajputana Rifles—enemy accounts say with its arms piled—and routed it. They then moved towards Muar town and by 11 a.m. were attacking the advanced company of the Garhwalis at Simpang Jeram and the remaining company of the Rajputana Rifles which had been sent forward to protect Muar from the east. On being informed of the situation Duncan ordered a Garhwali company from his reserve battalion to reinforce the town. The company however lost its way and eventually returned to its battalion at Bakri. About the same time the officer commanding the Garhwalis, while carrying out a reconnaissance, encountered an enemy party and was killed.

The attacks at Simpang Jeram were at first held, but a counterattack launched at 1 p.m. to ease the pressure failed with heavy loss, and the Garhwalis, having suffered about a hundred casualties, withdrew during the afternoon to Bakri. At Muar *4th Guards Regiment* attempted to cross the river during the afternoon of the 16th, but 65th Australian Battery, firing over open sights, sank a number of the boats and the rest turned back. Later in the afternoon the enemy, attacking from the east, overwhelmed the remnants of the Rajputana Rifles defending the town and occupied their battalion headquarters. Both the commanding officer and the second in command of the battalion were killed. What was left of the garrison of the town then withdrew through Parit Jawa to Bakri. The main body of the enemy was thus freed to make its crossing of the river unopposed.[1]

In the meantime early on the 16th the Jats, dispersed in the Grisek–Panchor–Jorak area, had found an enemy road block at Bukit Pasir. Realizing that the enemy had crossed the river, they began to concentrate their scattered companies at Milestone 12 on the Muar–Lenga road. By the evening of the 16th, 45th Brigade, except for the Jats, had been forced off the river line and had fallen back to the vicinity of the Bakri road junction. In the course of the day's fighting the brigade had lost about one company and the commanding officer of the Garhwalis, and all but two officers and one hundred and twenty men of the Rajputana Rifles.

When the news that Muar was being attacked reached 'Westforce', Bennett, realizing that an enemy advance in that area would threaten the communications of his force at Gemas, decided to reinforce 45th Brigade with the reserve battalion (2/29th) of 27th Australian Brigade. He evidently had not at that time appreciated the Japanese strategy or grasped the full extent of the disaster at Muar, for he sent the battalion less a company and told its commanding officer that as the enemy strength was only about two hundred, he should have little difficulty in restoring the situation by counter-attack and should be able to return to Gemas within a few days.

---

[1] See Sketch 6.

Y

Reports reached Malaya Command during the day that enemy troops had been seen landing near the lighthouse five miles south-west of Batu Pahat town and moving inland.[1] Percival realized that the developments in the Muar area and the enemy landings on the coast, which without suitable naval craft and air cover could not be prevented, endangered 'Westforce's' communications. To meet this threat he adjusted the boundary between 'Westforce' and III Corps to make the protection of these communications General Heath's responsibility, and ordered 53rd British Infantry Brigade (Brigadier C. L. B. Duke), which had landed at Singapore only three days previously after eleven weeks in crowded troopships, to move immediately to Ayer Hitam where it was to come under command of III Corps.[2] It will be noted that this use of 53rd Brigade was not in accordance with Wavell's instructions given on the 8th January, but, in the changed circumstances, Percival considered that there was no time to carry out the proposed relief in the Mersing area.[3]

The 53rd Brigade reached Ayer Hitam at midday on the 17th January and Heath allotted it to General Key, now in command of 11th Division, with orders that it was to be used to strengthen the defences of the Batu Pahat–Yong Peng area.[4] Key ordered Duke to send a battalion to Batu Pahat to relieve the British Battalion, and, in order to protect Yong Peng, to send another battalion to hold the dangerous defile at Milestone $78\frac{1}{2}$ on the Yong Peng–Muar road.[5] Duke sent 2nd Cambridgeshire to Batu Pahat and 6th Norfolk to the defile.[6] The inexperienced Norfolks occupied Bukit Pelandok and Bukit Belah early on the 18th and sent two platoons forward, one to patrol the road to Parit Sulong and the other to guard the bridge there.

At a conference at 'Westforce' Rear Headquarters at noon on the 17th, attended by Bennett and Key, Percival, fearing that a withdrawal from Segamat area would be bad for morale, decided to make every effort to hold the Muar area. He therefore authorized the transfer to 45th Brigade of a battalion from 22nd Australian Brigade. This battalion (2/19th) was to move from Mersing on the 18th and be replaced at Jemaluang the same day by the remaining battalion (5th Norfolk) of 53rd Brigade.

Meanwhile on the east coast, patrols of 22nd Australian Brigade had made contact with the enemy north of Endau on the 14th

---

[1] The *1/4th Guards Battalion*, having made this landing, moved south-east and concealed themselves in a rubber estate some five miles south of Batu Pahat.

[2] See Appendix 21.

[3] See page 281.

[4] Key, who had been commanding 8th Brigade (9th Division), had relieved Paris when the 11th Division reached Johore. Paris then reverted to the command of 12th Brigade which had been sent to Singapore for reorganization.

[5] See Sketch 7.

[6] The garrison of Batu Pahat then consisted of: 2nd Cambridgeshire, one Squadron 3rd Cavalry, No. 1 Independent Company and one company 2nd Malay Battalion.

January. On the 16th and 17th both Endau and Mersing were bombed and the enemy appeared to be concentrating in strength on the coast. Having been ordered on the 17th to send 2/19th Battalion across to the west coast, Brigadier Taylor decided that the time had come to withdraw his brigade to the prepared defensive position at Mersing. Accordingly on the night of the 17th/18th the brigade retired behind the Sungei Mersing, having destroyed all the bridges and culverts on the Endau–Mersing road.[1] On the morning of the 18th, Heath visited Mersing and told Taylor that as from 6 a.m. on the 19th a new force, named 'Eastforce', would be formed under his command and that his task had been changed to that of protecting the Jemaluang–Kota Tinggi road instead of holding Mersing. 'Eastforce' would consist of 22nd Australian Brigade (less one battalion), 5th Norfolk and all other troops in the area.[2]

During the 17th January, General Bennett ordered Brigadier Duncan (45th Brigade), who had organized defensive positions near Milestone 103 on the Simpang Jeram road and one mile south of Bakri on the Parit Jawa road, to counter-attack and reoccupy Muar.[3] Duncan proposed to attack on the 18th on a three battalion front: 2/29th Australian Battalion (less one company) from Bakri, the Garhwalis along the coast road and the Jats from Bukit Pasir. During the afternoon the 2/29th and a troop of 2/4th Anti-Tank Regiment arrived and, in preparation for the contemplated attack, Duncan ordered it to leave a company to guard the road junction at Bakri and take over the position one mile west of Bakri from the Garhwalis, who were to move that night to Parit Jawa on the coastal road. The *4th Guards Regiment* had however crossed the river to Muar and occupied Parit Jawa. Thus, just as the Garhwalis reached the north-east of the village at 8 p.m., they were ambushed and suffered heavy casualties. Reduced to some four hundred, they straggled back to a position held by the remnants of the Rajputana Rifles one mile south of Bakri. With the enemy in complete control of the coastal road, Duncan at midnight cancelled the proposed counter-attack to retake Muar.

General Nishimura, having succeeded in crossing the Sungei Muar far more easily than he had expected, decided on the evening of 17th January that he would attempt to trap the British forces opposing him and annihilate them between the Sungei Muar and the

---

[1] See Sketch 8.

[2] The other troops in the area included the Jat/Punjab Battalion at Kahang, 2/17th Dogras at Kota Tinggi, two companies of the Johore Military Forces and the Johore Volunteer Engineers.

[3] See Sketch 6.

Sketch 6   BAKRI

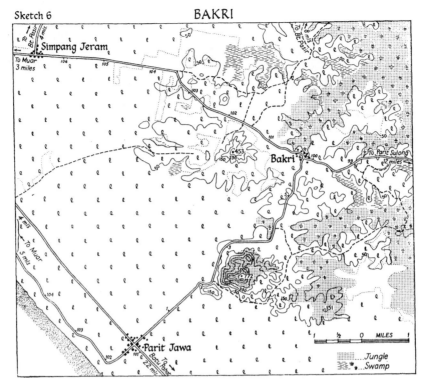

Sungei Batu Pahat. He therefore ordered *5th Guards Regiment* (consisting of *II/5th, III/5th* and *II/4th Battalions*) to attack the British forces holding Bakri and at the same time to move round their flank to cut the road immediately behind them, and *4th Guards Regiment* (consisting of *III/4th* and *I/5th Battalions*) to move along the coast road, cross the Sungei Batu Pahat north of the town and hold the stretch of road between Bukit Pelandok and Parit Sulong.

   At dawn on the 18th the Japanese launched an attack with light tanks unsupported by infantry along the Muar–Bakri road. The 2/29th Battalion drove it back, destroying eight tanks. Later in the day parties of Japanese infantry managed to cross the road between the battalion's position and the village, where they established a road block. When 2/19th Battalion (Lieut.-Colonel C. G. W. Anderson) arrived at Bakri about 10 a.m., Duncan ordered Anderson to occupy a position around Bakri covering both the Simpang Jeram and Parit Jawa roads and send back the company of 2/29th at Bakri to rejoin its battalion. Having broken through the road block with considerable difficulty the company eventually rejoined its battalion that evening. Meanwhile during the day Duncan had ordered the Jats to fall back on the 19th from the Bukit Pasir area to the 2/29th's position.

Percival received information on the 18th that the enemy formation which had attacked 45th Brigade was the *Imperial Guards Division*, and that *5th Division* was moving down the trunk road. He also heard that enemy patrols had been seen during the afternoon on the banks of the Sungei Batu Pahat some miles north of the town, that enemy aircraft had attacked 6th Norfolk near Bukit Pelandok and that 2nd Cambridgeshire had located enemy patrols south-west of Batu Pahat. He realized not only that there was every possibility of 45th Brigade being cut off, but that there was a growing threat to the communications of 'Westforce' and to the garrison of Batu Pahat. Thus, when Bennett proposed in the evening that 'Westforce' should be withdrawn without delay behind the Sungei Segamat as a preliminary to a further withdrawal, Percival agreed. To relieve Bennett of the responsibility for the Muar front at a time when he was likely to be fully occupied with the enemy on the trunk road, Percival had proposed on the 17th that its control should be transferred to III Corps, but Bennett, who felt he should keep a close eye on this threat to his rear, had requested that no change should be made. Percival now ordered the transfer to take place at 9.45 p.m. on the 18th.

Early on the 19th January, seeing that the threat to Batu Pahat was increasing, Key ordered 15th Brigade, commanded by Brigadier B. S. Challen, to undertake the defence of the town and reinforced the garrison with the British Battalion.[1] At the same time, expecting an enemy attack on the Bukit Pelandok defile, he moved 3/16th Punjab to reinforce 53rd Brigade (Brigadier Duke) which, because 2nd Cambridgeshire had been sent to Batu Pahat and 5th Norfolk to Jemaluang, consisted only of 6th Norfolk. He also obtained permission from III Corps to bring back 5th Norfolk from Jemaluang to Ayer Hitam. That afternoon, after a conference at Yong Peng at which Heath, Bennett, Key and Duke were present, Percival decided that 53rd Brigade should hold the Bukit Pelandok defile and should be further reinforced by 2nd Loyals from 9th Division, and that, by the 20th, 45th Brigade should be withdrawn through 53rd Brigade to a position west of Yong Peng, and 'Westforce' to Labis.

Unfortunately this decision to withdraw 45th Brigade was taken twenty-four hours too late. At about 1.30 p.m. on the 19th the advanced guard of *I/5th Battalion* surprised a company of 6th Norfolk holding Bukit Pelandok and forced it to retire. They then crossed the road and occupied the lower slopes of Bukit Belah, thus gaining control of the only road to Bakri. A company of the Norfolks

---

[1] Challen had taken over command of the brigade from Moorhead who at his own request had reverted to the command of his own battalion (3/16th Punjab).

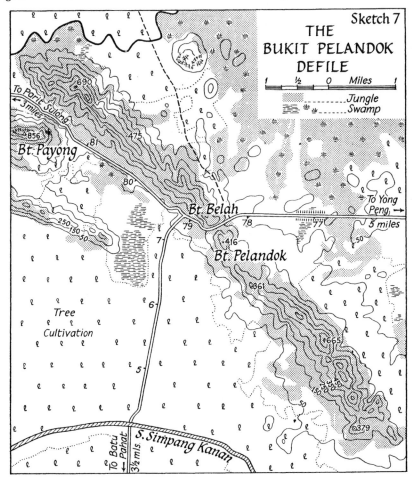

however managed to hold its position on the northern slopes of Bukit
Belah and later in the day, unknown to its battalion headquarters,
occupied the summit. The detached company of 2nd Loyals sent
forward from Singapore in lorries to rejoin its battalion arrived in
the area during the afternoon. It was immediately ordered to move
through the jungle south of the road, make its way to the top of the
ridge and attack Bukit Pelandok from the south. Completely strange
to the ground, the company cut its way through thick jungle and
after dark reached the crest of the ridge where it remained for the
night without food or water. At first light on the 20th it moved
towards its objective, only to find that the hill was being bombarded
by British artillery; thereupon it withdrew and that evening joined
its battalion west of the causeway.

Meanwhile Brigadier Duke had made plans to recapture the
defile. He had ordered 3/16th Punjab, which had arrived in the area

at 5 p.m. on the 19th, to occupy Bukit Belah and the ridge to its north by dawn on the 20th, and the Norfolks to attack Bukit Pelandok after daybreak assisted by fire from Bukit Belah. Moorhead (3/16th Punjab) launched his attack at 4 a.m. on the 20th. It was dogged by disaster. As the Punjabis reached the summit in the dark, they clashed with the Norfolks already established there. Despite this setback the whole feature was occupied, but before it could be organized for defence the enemy attacked and drove the British and Indian troops off it with heavy loss. Moorhead was killed. The attack on Bukit Pelandok also failed, and the enemy remained in possession of the defile. Duke then disposed the Norfolks and the Punjabis in defensive positions between the defile and the causeway and ordered 2nd Loyals (less its detached company), which had arrived that morning after a night move from Segamat, to take up a position in depth immediately east of the causeway and to patrol his exposed left flank.

Later on the 20th, Key ordered 53rd Brigade to attack again at dawn on the 21st to recapture the defile. Duke sent back a liaison officer to tell him that the brigade was not in a position to carry out this order, for both 6th Norfolk and 3/16th Punjab, after their attack that morning, were in no condition to be committed to any further attack for the time being, and the Loyals had arrived only that morning after a long and tiring night move. In the circumstances Key agreed that the attack might be deferred, but insisted that it had to take place at the earliest possible moment.

At 8 p.m. Percival, realizing that the enemy's hold on the Bukit Pelandok defile constituted a serious threat to the security of the line of communication to 'Westforce' on the trunk road, ordered Bennett to continue his withdrawal beyond Labis to the general line Paloh–the Sungei Gerchang bridge on the Labis road, sending one brigade as early as possible to hold the Yong Peng road junction.

During the 19th the situation of 45th Brigade had become increasingly critical. Duncan had ordered a company of 2/19th Battalion to pass through the 2/29th and counter-attack towards Simpang Jeram during the morning. At dawn however the 2/19th in Bakri village was heavily attacked from the south. The enemy (*II/4th Guards Battalion*) was repulsed with loss. Another attack by *II/5th Guards Battalion*, which was made simultaneously, overran the battalion transport lines and, although the drivers put up a heroic defence, succeeded in cutting the road to Yong Peng two miles east of Bakri. At 10 a.m. the building occupied by 45th Brigade Headquarters received a direct hit from a bomb and the entire signal section and some of the staff were killed. Brigadier Duncan and his brigade major however escaped serious injury, though Duncan was very badly shaken. In the circumstances Colonel Anderson of the 2/29th temporarily assumed command of the brigade.

In view of the isolated position of the 2/29th and the fact that the Japanese were between it and Bakri, Anderson decided that this battalion ought to be withdrawn to the village during the morning, but, since the Jats had not yet arrived, he was forced to leave it where it was. The Jats reached 2/29th's position at about 2 p.m. on the 19th, but without any transport, for owing to a failure in the transmission of an order it had been left behind. The two leading Jat companies then moved back without incident to Bakri but the remainder of the battalion was ambushed on its way. It suffered severe casualties and its commanding officer and adjutant were killed. The survivors made their way back to the 2/29th's position. Later in the afternoon the 2/29th came under heavy pressure which was relieved only by a spirited counter-attack. The 2/19th had repulsed a second heavy attack on Bakri village from the south during the afternoon, and this caused Anderson to order 2/29th Battalion to withdraw to the village at 6 p.m. The battalion, during its withdrawal, met strong opposition on the road. In the darkness and prevailing confusion the two leading companies, reduced to only seven officers and 190 other ranks, were able to fight their way through to the 2/19th's position, but the remainder of the battalion, with some of the Jats, was forced by enemy fire into the neighbouring swamps. Unable to break through to Bakri they tried to make their way across country towards Yong Peng and all were lost or captured.

Realizing that to remain at Bakri was to risk annihilation, Anderson decided to withdraw the whole force across the river at Parit Sulong, starting at dawn on the 20th. He believed that he could break through the enemy road blocks immediately east of Bakri, reach the edge of the jungle and rubber area at about Milestone 97 before dusk, and then cross the eight miles of open country to the shelter of the rubber estates near Parit Sulong during the night. 'Westforce', acting on behalf of III Corps, managed to establish wireless contact with 45th Brigade at about 8 p.m. and then sent orders for a withdrawal, which in effect confirmed the plan which Anderson had already prepared.

Anderson reorganized the depleted brigade into an Australian battalion of five companies and a composite Indian battalion made up from the remains of the three original Indian battalions. He placed three Australian companies at the head of the column, one as rearguard with the Indian troops, and retained one in reserve with the transport in the middle. About 8 a.m. on the 20th the withdrawing column was held up by a road block. Several attempts to break through failed. Eventually a bayonet charge led personally by Anderson cleared the block, but the delay of some two hours enabled enemy forces, which included light tanks, to catch up with the rearguard. In leading a counter-attack to ease this pressure Brigadier Duncan was killed. The column then ran into a group of three strong road blocks. A number of attempts to clear these failed, and it was not till late in the afternoon after a carefully co-ordinated attack, covered by every available supporting weapon, that Anderson eventually succeeded in breaking through and reached the edge of the jungle. After dark the column, encumbered with many casualties, crossed the open ground and at about midnight reached the rubber area two miles from Parit Sulong. Here it heard that the bridge was held by unknown troops.[1] Two despatch riders were sent to investigate and returned with the news that it was in enemy hands. The Japanese had seized this important bridge in the rear of 45th Brigade without opposition, for the two platoons of 6th Norfolk at Parit Sulong, who had been out of touch with their battalion since the morning of the 19th and without rations since the 18th, thinking they were cut off and isolated, had left their post on the morning of the 20th and moved across country to Batu Pahat.

In the meantime the destruction of the bridges over the Sungei Segamat and the Sungei Muar and the withdrawal of 'Westforce' from the Segamat area had proceeded according to plan, and by the morning of the 21st January 22nd Brigade was a few miles north of Labis, 8th Brigade some twelve miles further south and 27th Australian Brigade in a position covering the important road junction at Yong Peng. It was evident that the movements of 'Westforce' and those of 45th and 53rd Brigades now required most careful co-ordination. 'Westforce' already had a brigade in position covering Yong Peng, its wireless was the only means of communication with 45th Brigade and the shortening of communications had made it easier for it to assume complete control of both roads. Percival consequently decided at 8.30 a.m. on the 21st to transfer the command of all troops in the Muar–Yong Peng area back to 'Westforce' at noon that day and to hold a conference with his commanders at Yong Peng at 12.30 p.m.

The counter-attack by 53rd Brigade to recapture the Bukit Pelandok defile was destined never to take place. On his way to the conference at Yong Peng, Key, accompanied by a staff officer, visited the brigade at about 10.30 a.m. to find that, owing to the latter part of his instructions of the previous evening not having been transmitted to Duke, no attack had been arranged and the Loyals had been ordered to take up a defensive position at the eastern end of the causeway. He asked how soon an attack could·be organized, and

---

[1] These were from *III/4th Guards Battalion.*

was told by the brigade major, about 2 p.m.[1] He then issued the
following orders:

> 'At noon your brigade comes under the command of "West-
> force", but I am quite sure General Bennett will wish you to
> recapture the defile at the earliest possible moment. Make all
> arrangements for an attack at 2 p.m. and be prepared to send a
> carrier platoon through to Parit Sulong. I will ask "Westforce"
> to confirm these orders.'

No action however appears to have been taken within the brigade
pending the arrival of the confirmatory order.

At noon the staff officer whom Key had taken to Yong Peng
reached Duke's forward headquarters with 'Westforce's' confirmatory order for the attack to take place as soon as possible. Duke at
once sent for Lieut.-Colonel M. Elrington (Loyals), who arrived at
about 2 p.m. As the widely dispersed battalion had to be collected,
moved forward and given time to make its reconnaissance, the zero
hour was provisionally fixed for 5.30 p.m. Surprise was impossible,
for the enemy overlooked all the ground east of the ridge. Accurate
artillery support had therefore to be arranged. The artillery—and
only one battery could be used—had difficulty with its communications and could not be ready in time, while the Loyals, owing to the
difficulty of concentrating their scattered companies quickly and
delays in organizing transport, could not reach the start line by the
agreed hour. Consequently Duke first postponed the attack until
6 p.m., and later till the next morning, to give time for the artillery
to register properly and the Loyals to move over the exposed approach
into position under cover of darkness. While the conference at Yong
Peng was taking place Bennett was told that the attack would not
take place till about 5 p.m. He immediately sent his senior staff officer
to 53rd Brigade to order it to attack at 4 p.m. When this officer
reported back that 4 p.m. was impossible, he was sent a second time
to urge that the attack should go in as early as possible. Duke, owing
to the difficulties already described, was unable to comply.

Next morning the artillery registration took so long that Duke
ordered a further postponement until 9 a.m. The Loyals, who had
assembled under cover of darkness, were discovered by enemy aircraft during this final delay and heavily bombed and machine-
gunned. Surprise had been lost and Duke considered that the chances
of recapturing the defile, much less of holding it or being of assistance
to 45th Brigade, were remote. He therefore decided to call the attack
off and once again disposed his three battalions so as to hold the
causeway and the ground between it and the defile.

---

[1] Brigadier Duke was at the time absent on reconnaissance organizing the defensive
position.

Meanwhile at the Yong Peng conference Percival had stated that his intention was to fight the enemy north of the line Jemaluang–Kluang–Ayer Hitam–Batu Pahat. The conference agreed that the next stage of the battle resolved itself into two phases: the first, which was already taking place, was to withdraw 'Westforce' to the line Paloh–Yong Peng and 45th Brigade to safety; and the second to reorganize the available formations into three forces, each with its own line of communications to Singapore. These were to be: 'Eastforce' to hold Jemaluang with forward detachments in the Mersing area, covering the Kota Tinggi road; 'Westforce' (to which 2nd Loyals would revert) to hold the Yong Peng–Kluang–Ayer Hitam area covering the trunk road; and 11th Indian Division (to which 53rd Brigade would revert) to hold the Batu Pahat area and operate on the coastal road.

The position of 45th Brigade at Parit Sulong was by this time becoming desperate. An attempt on the morning of the 21st to capture the bridge failed. Later that morning enemy attacks with tank support on the rear of the column, though beaten off, created a serious situation. Fighting, in which the brigade suffered heavy loss, continued throughout the day; despite the loss of a number of tanks the Japanese, with the support of artillery and low-flying aircraft, had by nightfall forced the column into a very restricted area immediately west of the bridge.

Casualties had been heavy and many were dying for lack of attention. That evening Anderson sent two ambulances carrying the most seriously wounded forward to the bridge under a flag of truce with the request that they should be allowed to pass through to Bukit Pelandok. The reply was to demand the surrender of the column promising that, when resistance ceased, the wounded would be cared for. The ambulances were to remain on the approach to the bridge to act as a road block and would be fired on if they attempted to move. Anderson, still in the hope of relief, refused to consider these demands. After dark an officer and a driver, both of whom were wounded, released the brakes of the ambulances, allowing them to run silently backwards down the slope from the bridge and then, amidst the roar of the guns, started up their engines and drove them back to the position.

Early on the 22nd two aircraft from Singapore, in response to urgent requests, successfully dropped medical supplies and food on the beleaguered brigade. The restricted perimeter, under attack from all sides and containing an ever-growing number of wounded, has been described by a survivor as a 'pitiable inferno'. As a last bid Anderson ordered an Australian company to attack the enemy defences at the bridge. The attack failed and, seeing the position was hopeless, Anderson, anticipating an order that Bennett issued that morning, decided to extricate the brigade. He ordered the destruction of heavy arms and equipment, arranged for the many wounded to be left behind in charge of voluntary attendants and told the remnants of the brigade to make their way on foot through the jungle as best as they could to Yong Peng.[1] Eventually some 500 Australians, including some walking wounded,[2] and 400 Indian troops succeeded in doing so—but 45th Brigade now existed in name only. At Parit Sulong the triumphant Japanese troops, after treating the helpless wounded in the most inhuman fashion, massacred all but the few who, by feigning death, managed to survive. Japanese accounts state that during the fighting from the 16th to the 22nd January they lost a company of tanks and that their infantry casualties were equivalent to one battalion.

On the 19th January, having learnt from a liaison officer that no detailed scheme for a withdrawal to the island or for its defence had been issued, Wavell cabled to the Prime Minister drawing his attention to the weakness of the defences of Singapore Island against attack from the north and expressing his doubt whether it could hold out for long if Johore were lost. The same day he cabled Percival saying,

> '... You must think out problem of how to withdraw from mainland should withdrawal become necessary and how to prolong resistance on island ... Will it be any use holding troops on southern beaches if attack is coming from north. Let me have your plans as soon as possible. Your preparations must of course be kept *entirely secret*. Battle is to be fought out in Johore till reinforcements arrive and troops must not be allowed to look over [their] shoulders. Under cover of selecting positions for garrison of island to prevent infiltration of small parties you can work out scheme for large force and undertake some preparation such as obstacles or clearances but make it clear to everyone that battle is to be fought out in Johore without thought of retreat ...'

The following day Percival issued a secret and personal letter to Heath, Bennett and the Fortress Commander (Major-General F. Keith Simmons) which was to be shown only to senior staff officers

---

[1] Lieut.-Colonel Anderson was awarded the V.C. for his courage and fine leadership throughout this action.
[2] 2/19th—271, 2/29th—130 and 65th Battery—98.

and column commanders as they considered necessary. In this letter he reasserted his intention to hold the line Mersing–Kluang–Batu Pahat, and gave his outline plan for the conduct of operations, should events force a withdrawal to the island. This was that the three columns should fall back down the Mersing, Ayer Hitam and west coast roads respectively to Johore Bahru, their movements being co-ordinated by III Corps. A bridgehead covering Johore Bahru would be established through which the columns would pass; during the withdrawal selected positions on each road would be occupied and ambushes laid between them.

Perturbed by the course of events in Johore, Wavell paid another visit to Singapore on the 20th January. After discussions with Percival and Heath it became obvious to him that the British forces would shortly have to fall back on the line Mersing–Kluang–Batu Pahat and that there was every possibility of their being forced to withdraw into Singapore Island where, despite his instructions to prepare defences on the northern side given on his previous visit, he found that very little had been done.

That evening he told the Chiefs of Staff that the situation might now necessitate a general withdrawal towards Johore Bahru and eventually to Singapore Island, and that the successful defence of the island would depend on the numbers and state of the troops withdrawn from Johore, the arrival of reinforcements and the ability of the air force to maintain fighters on the island. Before returning to Java on the 21st, Wavell instructed Percival to continue the fight in Johore and to try to hold the Japanese there until further reinforcements arrived, but at the same time to make strenuous efforts to prepare the island for defence.

Meanwhile the Chiefs of Staff had been discussing the situation in Malaya and, on his return to Java, Wavell received a cable from them warning him to take account of the eventuality of the battle in Johore going against him, and telling him to make all preparations for the utmost possible defence of Singapore Island. They called his attention to a number of points on which action should be taken. These included: the use of the Fortress guns against a landward attack; the preparation of obstructions on the land approaches from the Johore Strait and of landing places and exits therefrom in the island; the diversion of some of the beach defences and machine-guns from the south to the north and west of the island; the control or destruction of all boats and small craft within reach of the island; the creation of self-contained defensive localities to cover the most dangerous avenues of approach; the preparation of switch lines to prevent exploitation of successful landings and the building-up of a system of mobile reserves to deliver rapid counter-attacks.

The Prime Minister too left Wavell in no doubt that he expected the island to be defended to the last. In a characteristic cable on the 20th he ended with the words:

> 'I want to make it absolutely clear that I expect every inch of ground to be defended, every scrap of material or defences to be blown to pieces to prevent capture by the enemy, and no question of surrender to be entertained until after protracted fighting among the ruins of Singapore city.'[1]

In reply to these communications Wavell said that all the points made by the Chiefs of Staff in connection with the defences of the island had been considered and action taken on them as far as possible.

The Chiefs of Staff also sent a personal message to Percival on the 21st calling his attention to the many failures to carry out demolitions according to plan ever since the war started, and expressing their anxiety that there should be no failure in Singapore if the worst came to the worst. They told him to ensure, in consultation with the Governor and Rear-Admiral, Malaya, that nothing which could possibly be of any use to the enemy was omitted from the general scorched earth scheme, and that responsibility was clearly defined in each case for ordering and seeing the demolitions carried out. On the same day the Admiralty requested Rear-Admiral, Malaya, to bear in mind the importance of the timely evacuation of the maximum number of trained naval and dockyard personnel, if Singapore Island were beleaguered.

Percival replied to the Chiefs of Staff that plans for denial of the property of the fighting services were being prepared. He pointed out that there was however already doubt in the minds of the Asian population as to the ability or even intention to hold Singapore. In the opinion of the Governor, Rear-Admiral, Malaya, and himself, any conspicuous measure of destruction or even preparations for destruction taken then, would be calculated to cause a land-slide in public morale which could never be stopped. In the circumstances he proposed to formulate plans for the denial of both military and civil installations and to make such preparations as were possible without attracting public attention. If and when the army was driven back to the island the preparations could be carried a stage further, but final destructions would take place only if there were danger of losing the island after seaborne or airborne landings. This proposal was accepted by the Chiefs of Staff.

During his visit to Singapore on the 20th Wavell had taken the opportunity of discussing with Percival the general dispositions for the defence of the island. He had suggested that 18th Division, as the freshest and strongest formation, should be placed in that part of the

---

[1] Churchill, Volume IV (Cassell, 1951), pages 46–47.

island most likely to be attacked, which he thought would be the north-west coast; 8th Australian Division in the next most dangerous sector—the north-east coast; and the remainder of the two Indian divisions, when re-formed, as a reserve behind them. Percival however had expressed the opinion that the main Japanese attack would be made down the Johore River and on the north-east of the island, and he therefore proposed to place 18th Division on the north-east and the Australians on the north-west. Finding that Percival, who had studied the problem for so long, seemed convinced of the probable direction of the enemy attack, Wavell allowed him to dispose the troops as he wished.

On his return to Java on the 21st January Wavell confirmed the outcome of his conversations with Percival by letter. Believing that decisions as to the dispositions should be made by the man on the spot he wrote to him saying:

> 'My idea of the best layout of the defences would be for the Australian Division and the 18th Division each to take one of the eastern or western sectors, and the present garrison the southern sector, with the Indians forming a central reserve strengthened possibly by the Gordons or some of the other British troops. . . . Please let me have your comments on this layout . . . '

Percival replied on the 24th that he proposed to divide the island into three sectors: Southern, Western and Northern, placing the Australians in the Western and 18th Division, provided that it arrived safely and was ready to take its place, in the Northern, in which case the Indian formations would be in Command Reserve. He had in fact issued orders on the 23rd for the defence of the island on these lines and instructed the fortress commander (Keith Simmons) to develop the plan assisted by a special staff under Brigadier Paris (12th Brigade, then re-forming on the island) and liaison officers from both III Corps and 8th Australian Division.

General Nishimura, having practically annihilated the British troops between Bakri and Parit Sulong, had to decide whether to direct his division on to Yong Peng or continue his drive southwards along the coast road. The *5th Division* on the trunk road had already reached Labis and, in view of its progress, he came to the conclusion that an advance on Yong Peng would be too late to trap the British forces further north. On the other hand his troops had already crossed the Sungei Simpang Kiri and, once across the Sungei Simpang Kanan, were in a position to isolate Batu Pahat. Further, a rapid drive southwards to the coast road not only would extricate *I/4th Guards Battalion* from its isolated position, but might well enable him to cut off the British garrison at Batu Pahat. He therefore ordered the *Guards Reconnaissance Battalion* to attack the town from the north-east and pin down its defenders, while *4th Guards Regiment* moved south to join its detached battalion near Senggarang, cut the coast road and encircle the garrison. The *5th Guards Regiment* was simultaneously to cross the Batu Pahat–Ayer Hitam road further east, move directly to Rengit, and thus prevent the British further south from coming to the rescue of their troops trapped at Batu Pahat.

At Batu Pahat a sweep around Bukit Banang on the 21st had met with considerable opposition, presumably from the unidentified Japanese unit which had landed in that vicinity on the 16th.[1] The same afternoon Heath and Key visited 15th Brigade in Batu Pahat. Brigadier Challen told them that the enemy was in a position to cut both the Ayer Hitam and Pontian Kechil roads and suggested a withdrawal from the line of the river to the road junction east of the town, the better to protect both roads. Heath did not agree. He ordered the town to be held and gave instructions that it should be stocked at once with ten days' supplies. He hoped that it would become a 'Tobruk', pinning down Japanese forces and disorganizing their planned advance down the trunk road. He made Challen responsible for the Pontian Kechil road as far back as the northern exits of Senggarang. By evening the Japanese had made contact with the brigade north-east of the town and had placed a road block on the Ayer Hitam road near Milestone 72.

At 6.30 a.m. on the 22nd, concerted action by 5th Norfolk from Ayer Hitam and the British Battalion from Batu Pahat reopened the road long enough for a supply convoy to be sent through into the town. The same day the enemy attacked a field battery on the Pontian Kechil road south of Batu Pahat, causing the loss of a number of lorries; this indicated that he would shortly be in a position to cut this road as well. Key, who considered that 15th Brigade would be unable to hold Batu Pahat with only two battalions, thereupon ordered 5th Norfolk to reopen the Ayer Hitam road in conjunction with 15th Brigade and move into the town early on the 23rd.[2] This attempt failed, for the Japanese had again placed strong road blocks near Milestone 72. Both the British Battalion and 5th Norfolk were recalled to Batu Pahat and Ayer Hitam respectively by noon on the 23rd.

At a conference at Rengam that morning Percival decided to fall back to a general line covering Kluang and Ayer Hitam, including the town of Batu Pahat. His plan was for 53rd Brigade to withdraw

---

[1] See page 306.
[2] Key could not use the battalion to reinforce Batu Pahat on the 22nd, for it was responsible for protection of the Ayer Hitam road junction till relieved by the Australians.

during the day, through 27th Australian Brigade at Yong Peng, to Ayer Hitam where on arrival it would, except for 2nd Loyals, revert to command of 11th Division; 2nd Loyals would come under command of 'Westforce'. During the night of the 23rd/24th 'Westforce' was to withdraw to positions covering Kluang and Ayer Hitam. On completion of these moves all mobile formations in southern Johore were to be organized into the three forces, as outlined at the conference on the 21st, all of which were to come under command of III Corps.

On receipt of these orders about noon on the 23rd, Key sent 5th Norfolk by bus to Pontian Kechil with the intention of moving the battalion, together with an ammunition convoy, to Batu Pahat early on the 24th. The 53rd Brigade started to disengage at Bukit Pelandok about midday, but during the process the enemy launched a heavy attack supported by tanks. This resulted in the bridges on the causeway having to be blown before all the troops were across. Great confusion followed, but eventually, having suffered severe casualties, the brigade got clear and by dawn on the 24th had reached Ayer Hitam, except for 2nd Loyals who joined 27th Australian Brigade. During the morning, 53rd Brigade (3/16th Punjab and 6th Norfolk only) moved by road to Skudai en route to Benut.

Meanwhile in Batu Pahat, Brigadier Challen was out of touch with 11th Division—his wireless having failed. The direct route to Ayer Hitam was closed, enemy strength north-east of the town was increasing, and there was the possibility that the coastal road might be cut at any moment. Feeling that his position resembled far too closely that of 45th Brigade at Bakri, he decided to evacuate Batu Pahat during the 23rd and take up a position clear of the town and in depth down the road to Senggarang. This movement was well under way when wireless communication with 11th Division was re-established and the fact that the withdrawal was taking place reported.

Key, who had specific instructions to hold Batu Pahat, immediately countermanded the withdrawal but, being extremely anxious as to the safety of 15th Brigade, informed III Corps of the situation. Heath held the view that a withdrawal from Batu Pahat meant the speedy crumbling of the Jemaluang–Kluang–Ayer Hitam line and the surrender to the enemy of the airfields at Kahang and Kluang which, in view of the imminent arrival of the convoys bringing large reinforcements, could not be allowed. Despite the risk to 15th Brigade Heath, after discussion with Percival, decided that Batu Pahat must be held and that Key's orders should stand. The town was reoccupied successfully against light opposition after nightfall on the 23rd.

From the 15th to 24th January the average Allied air strength was about 74 bombers and 28 fighters. Against this small force the
z

Japanese, using airfields in southern Siam and in Malaya, could bring some 250 bombers and 150 fighters. Under such conditions the Allied air effort had normally to be concentrated upon one task at a time. There were many calls for air support from 'Westforce' and III Corps, and every effort was made to meet them. Air Headquarters made use of every aircraft which could fly, including types which had long been obsolete, and, though priority had still to be given to ensuring the safe arrival of the convoys, frequent sweeps over the Segamat and Muar fronts, not always unopposed, were made by small formations of fighters—usually five or six Buffaloes.

During the same period a small scratch force of bombers (including six Dutch Glenn Martins), escorted by fighters from Singapore, was used to attack Japanese motor transport and troops on the main roads southwards from Muar and Gemas. Several attacks were made at night by Hudson, Blenheim and Vildebeeste bombers on the enemy-occupied airfields at Kuala Lumpur and Kuantan to destroy or damage as many enemy fighters on the ground as possible. That these attacks, weak though they were, achieved some success was disclosed by photographic reconnaissance and confirmed by the increased intensity of the anti-aircraft fire later met with at both airfields. A few heavy bombers of the United States Army Air Force based in Java also attacked enemy airfields in Malaya using Palembang as an advanced landing ground. One such raid was made by seven bombers against the airfield at Sungei Patani, a distance of 1,500 miles from their base in Java. In general however the scale of the Allied bomber effort at that time was so small that it had little effect on the course of operations.

When 'Westforce' began to withdraw from Segamat, Headquarters, Air Command, realized that the remaining airfields on the mainland would soon become untenable and, if they were not to fall intact into enemy hands, no time should be lost in preparing them for demolition. The small airfield near Batu Pahat had been put out of action as soon as the enemy reached Muar, and thus only the airfields at Kahang and Kluang were left to be dealt with. On the 21st January ground staff and technical equipment were withdrawn to Singapore from Kahang airfield. On the following day the buildings, installations, petrol and oil stocks were destroyed and the runways made unserviceable. Similar action was taken on the 23rd at Kluang and that night the denial scheme was completed.

Thereafter the Allied air forces in Malaya were confined to the four airfields on Singapore Island. It was obvious that these would be subjected to an ever-increasing scale of attack and that, because of the congestion of aircraft on the ground, serious losses would inevitably result. Dispersal beyond the limits of the island had therefore become imperative. This had been foreseen, and preparations had been made for bomber squadrons to be based on airfields in southern Sumatra.[1] On the 18th January, 223 Group had been established at Palembang for the control of the air operations from Sumatra, and a fighter group headquarters (226 Group) formed in Singapore to control the fighter squadrons which remained on the island for its defence.[2]

By agreement with the Netherlands Army Air Force, the Dutch squadrons were withdrawn between the 18th and 22nd and, on arrival in Java, reverted to Dutch control. Between the 23rd and 27th three Blenheim squadrons and the main parties of two Hudson squadrons were transferred, together with maintenance and administrative units. Although most of the ground staffs moved by sea, Dutch transport aircraft gave valuable assistance. On the 28th the flying-boat squadron flew to Java and by the end of the month the whole of the bomber force was based outside Malaya.

During the latter half of the month air attacks on Singapore increased in intensity. Raids by forces of twenty-seven or more bombers escorted by fighters became a daily occurrence, several raids often taking place on the same day. The main targets continued to be the airfields, the Naval Base and the docks; much of the bombing seemed however to be indiscriminate and the residential portion of the town sustained much damage.

These raids, besides destroying buildings, installations and grounded aircraft, had a serious effect on the civilian population, particularly as regards the maintenance of essential services, although the civil defence organization stood up well to the ordeal. Known civilian casualties during January were some 600 killed and 1,500 injured.

Strenuous efforts were made to reinforce the Buffalo fighter squadrons and to strengthen the air defence with the newly arrived Hurricanes. The first of these was flown within forty-eight hours of being landed; by the 20th January 232(F) Squadron was ready to play its part in the air defence with an initial establishment of eighteen aircraft. The squadron went into action for the first time that day when there were two raids on Singapore by ninety bombers with the usual fighter escorts. Three Hurricanes were shot down after being closely engaged with Japanese Zero fighters, and two pilots, one of whom was the squadron commander, were lost. On the following day, when the town was raided by about a hundred aircraft, two more were shot down. Enemy losses on these two days were assessed at the time as fourteen aircraft.

The air defence suffered heavier losses when on the 22nd two waves, each of twenty-seven naval bombers operating from bases

---

[1] See pages 239–240.
[2] 223 Group was shortly afterwards renumbered 225 Group.

in French Indo-China, bombed Singapore from a height of 22,000 feet. The raids were intercepted despite the short warning (approximately fifteen minutes), but five Hurricanes and four Buffaloes were lost and a number of aircraft were destroyed or damaged on the ground, as against an estimated enemy loss of six. By the end of the month the British losses in the air and on the ground in these operations were twenty-six aircraft destroyed and ten damaged. There is no official record of the Japanese losses, but at the time Air Command estimated them to be twenty-six aircraft destroyed, which seems not unreasonable.

There is no doubt that too much had been expected of the Hurricane fighters as a decisive factor in the air defence of Singapore, by both civilians and the Services. They proved superior in performance to the Japanese Zero fighters at altitudes of 20,000 feet and above, but at lower heights they were slower and less manœuvrable.[1] They were moreover invariably outnumbered by the enemy escorting fighters, so that the bombers themselves could seldom be attacked. Nevertheless in the short time during which it played its part in the defence 232(F) Squadron, in the face of overwhelming odds, achieved results which were greatly to its credit.

The greatest strain on the exiguous air resources developed between the 21st and the 30th January when the protection of convoys bringing reinforcements had to be given absolute priority. As a protection against surprise naval attack, patrols were flown from dawn to dusk as far out to sea as the Natuna Islands by eight Hudsons and Glenn Martins.[2] At the same time Catalina flying-boats undertook anti-submarine patrols south of Singapore, and during the final approach of the convoys a fighter escort of six Buffaloes was maintained over the ships. In addition a striking force of bombers and torpedo-bombers was held in constant readiness to meet a possible naval attack.

These convoys brought much-needed army reinforcements. On the 22nd January 44th Indian Infantry Brigade and 7,000 Indian reinforcements arrived;[3] on the 24th some 1,900 Australian reinforcements and 2/4th Australian Machine-Gun Battalion; and on the 29th the main body of 18th British Division.[4]

The 44th Brigade was no better trained than the ill-fated 45th, and on arrival was retained on the island for further training.[5] The 7,000 Indian reinforcements were made up largely of young and only partly trained recruits and there were few potential leaders among

---

[1] See Appendix 8.
[2] See Map 17.
[3] For composition of 44th Brigade see footnote, page 371.
[4] 18th Division Headquarters and 54th and 55th Infantry Brigades, See Appendix 21.
[5] See Appendix 19.

them; the great majority had therefore to be sent to reinforcement camps for further intensive training, instead of being drafted directly to the sorely pressed and depleted units in the field. Since the country in southern Johore was not suitable for its employment, the well-trained 2/4th Australian Machine-Gun Battalion was employed on preparing defensive positions on the north coast of the island. The fighting efficiency of the 1,900 Australian reinforcements was a grievous disappointment. Some of them had sailed within a fortnight of enlistment and had not even learnt how to handle their weapons, few of them had had time to assimilate even the rudiments of discipline or were in any sense trained.

The decision to select these untrained Australian reinforcements for Malaya was unfortunate. There were in mid-December some 16,600 reinforcements in the pool in the Middle East after all units had been brought up to strength, and an organization existed whereby recruits sent there could receive basic training under expert instructors. It would therefore have been possible to draw trained men from that source, replacing them by recruits. Alternatively there were 87,000 militiamen in Australia on full-time duty, many thousands of whom had already had months of training. Although soon after the war with Japan had broken out an order was issued debarring militiamen from enlisting in the A.I.F., some 12,500 of them had already done so. It should have been possible for the authorities to select 1,900 fairly well trained volunteers from that source for Malaya instead of the raw recruits that were sent.

That the reinforcements sent from India were only partly trained was unavoidable, for at the time nothing better was available. India had strained every nerve to expand her army quickly to meet the demand for field formations to provide garrisons for the Middle East, Iraq, Persia and Malaya. The country was drained of trained officers and men other than those required to staff the greatly enlarged instructional establishments and to provide cadres for the new formations to replace those sent overseas. To have despatched the few remaining fully-trained officers and men as reinforcements would have been a suicidal policy.

During January the provision of labour for the Services became a very serious problem. Shortly after the appointment of the Director General of Civil Defence, all demands from the three Services and the civil authorities were made through his office in order to avoid competition for labour. Although initially a substantial proportion of the demands were met, there was steadily increasing difficulty in meeting requirements for the more dangerous areas such as the airfields, the Naval Base and Keppel Harbour, all of which were regular targets for enemy bombers. In these areas men refused to work and could not be forced to do so. The result was a growing dislocation which forced the Services to rely more and more for labour on their own resources of manpower, and produced a tendency for individual bodies requiring labour to short-circuit the D.G.C.D.'s office, a procedure which only made the position more difficult.

The matter was discussed at frequent intervals by the War Council. Two points of view were put forward. The navy and air force advocated compulsion of labour, whereas the D.G.C.D. and the army considered that good treatment, such as protection while at work, the provision of meals, a high rate of wages and compensation in case of injury, would produce better results. It was finally decided in the War Council that a measure of compulsion would be necessary, but that, although conditions and terms of service would have to be made attractive, the payment of a special rate of wages for work in dangerous areas would be undesirable since it would lead to inflation. By the 21st January the Services and the D.G.C.D. had agreed in principle to conditions and terms of employment. It was not however till the 26th that these were fully accepted in detail by all concerned, but the Services did not have the authority to pay the agreed rates of wages and compensation. The Governor and the three Services therefore simultaneously cabled London to obtain carte-blanche to fix rates as necessary. On the 29th an emergency bill was passed and the agreed compulsory labour regulations were gazetted. But it was not till the 31st that London gave the local authorities a free hand to fix the rates of wages and compensation which the situation demanded. There is evidence that the labour situation then became more satisfactory and remained so until the Japanese landed on the island. This was partly due to this eleventh hour decision and partly to a falling-off in the demand for labour.

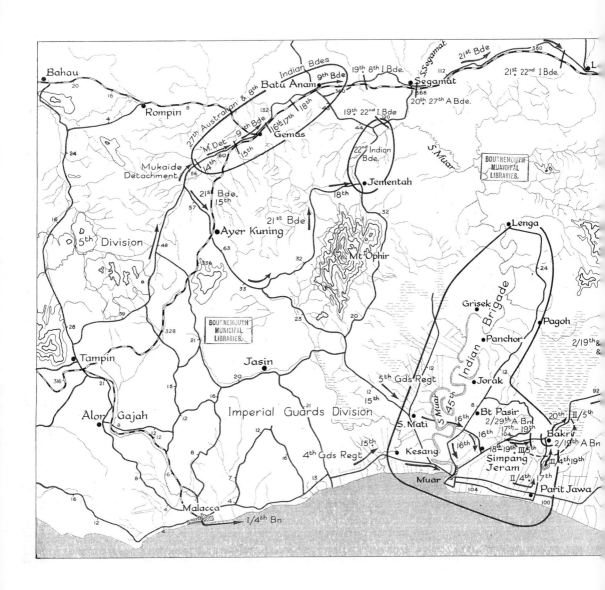

BOURNEMOUTH
MUNICIPAL
LIBRARIES.

BOURNEMOUTH
MUNICIPAL
LIBRARIES.

Bahau

Rompin

27th Australian & 8th Indian Bdes

Batu Anam

9th Bde

19th 8th I Bde.

21st Bde

21st 22nd I Bde.

Segamat

20th 27th A Bde.

19th 22nd I Bde.

132

16th 17th 18th

M. Det 9th Bde

Gemas

15th

14th

Mukaide
Detachment

22nd Indian
Bde.

S. Muar

21st Bde.
15th

18th

Jementah

5th Division

Ayer Kuning

21st Bde

Mt Ophir

Lenga

Grisek Brigade

Pagoh

2/19th &

Panchor

Tampin

Jasin

Jorak

45th Indian Brigade

S. Muar

Bt Pasir
2/29th A Bn
17th–19th

20th II/5th

Bakri
2/19th A Bn

Alor Gajah

Imperial Guards Division

5th Gds Regt

S. Mati

16th

16th

16th

18th 19th III/5th
Simpang
Jeram
II/4th 17th

II/4th 19th

4th Gds Regt

15th

Kesang

16th

Muar

Parit Jawa

Malacca

1/4th Bn

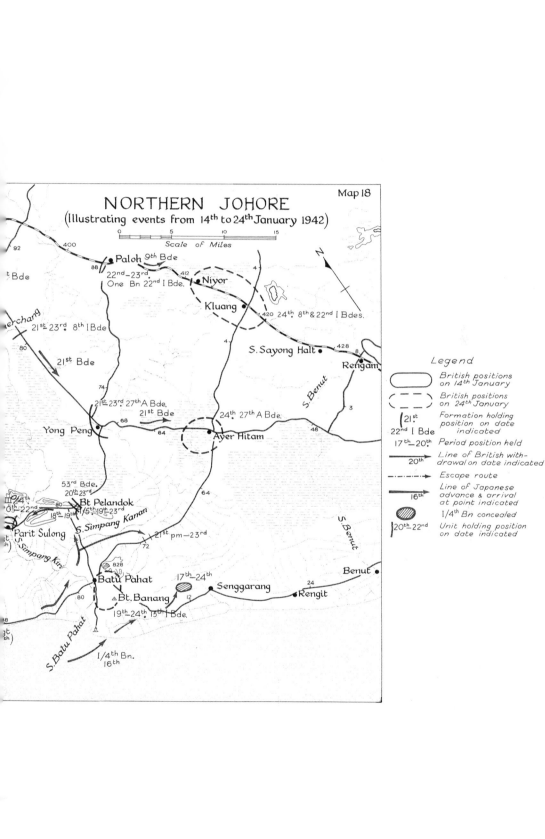

NORTHERN JOHORE
(Illustrating events from 14th to 24th January 1942)

Map 18

Scale of Miles

Paloh 9th Bde
22nd–23rd.
One Bn 22nd I Bde.
Niyor
Kluang
24th 8th & 22nd I Bdes.
S. Sayong Halt
Rengam
21st–23rd. 8th I Bde
21st Bde
21st–23rd. 27th A Bde.
21st Bde
24th 27th A Bde.
Yong Peng
Ayer Hitam
53rd Bde.
20th–23rd.
Bt Pelandok
18th–19th. 1/5th 19th–23rd
S. Simpang Kanan
Parit Sulong
21st pm—23rd
Batu Pahat
17th–24th
Senggarang
Rengit
Benut
Bt. Banang
19th–24th. 15th I Bde.
1/4th Bn.
16th

Legend

British positions on 14th January
British positions on 24th January
Formation holding position on date indicated
Period position held
Line of British withdrawal on date indicated
Escape route
Line of Japanese advance & arrival at point indicated
1/4th Bn concealed
Unit holding position on date indicated

CHAPTER XX

THE WITHDRAWAL TO
SINGAPORE ISLAND

See Maps 19 and 20 and Sketch 8

ON THE MORNING of the 24th January III Corps was disposed as follows: on the east coast 'Eastforce' was in contact with the enemy on the line of the Sungei Mersing.[1] On the trunk road 'Westforce', temporarily out of touch with the enemy, was disposed with 9th Division (8th and 22nd Indian Brigades) supported by 5th and 88th Field Regiments at Kluang, and 27th Australian Brigade supported by 2/15th Field Regiment and one battery of 155th Field Regiment at Ayer Hitam. On the west coast 11th Division, supported by 135th Field Regiment and one battery of 155th, was disposed with 15th Brigade at Batu Pahat in contact with the enemy, 28th Brigade at Pontian Kechil, and 53rd Brigade *en route* to Benut from Skudai.

Malaya Command believed on this date that the Japanese had the *Imperial Guards Division* and an unidentified division on the west coast, *5th Division* in the centre and probably *18th Division* on the east coast —a fairly accurate appreciation except that there was no unidentified division in the west. On the 24th General Percival issued an outline plan for a withdrawal to the island, should events make this necessary. This gave only an indication of the method to be adopted and included neither a timetable nor any allocation of troops other than to the bridgehead.

At Batu Pahat enemy pressure on 2nd Cambridgeshire, holding the north-eastern exits of the town, had increased during the night of the 23rd/24th, and at dawn enemy forces were seen crossing the Ayer Hitam road moving southwards. The 5th Norfolk, which, it will be remembered, had been sent from Ayer Hitam on the 23rd via Pontian Kechil to reinforce 15th Brigade, arrived at about 7 a.m. on the 24th, but without the expected ammunition convoy. Brigadier Challen immediately ordered it to take and hold two small hills about half a mile east of the junction of the Ayer Hitam and coast roads, so as to prevent the enemy moving round his right flank. The battalion, ill-supported by the artillery which was short of ammunition, failed

---

[1] See Sketch 8.

to reach its objectives. During the morning a staff officer from 11th Division visited 15th Brigade and Challen once again represented the danger of his position.[1] He was told that the intention was still to hold the line Mersing–Kluang–Batu Pahat and that 53rd Brigade which was moving forward would, from the morning of the 25th, be responsible for keeping the coast road open as far north as Senggarang.

The pressure north-east of the town increased during the night of the 24th/25th and, in the course of the morning of the 25th, Challen reported that the enemy appeared to be attempting to pin him down in Batu Pahat until arrangements for cutting the road behind him were complete. At noon, in a telephone conversation with Heath, Key emphasized the dangerous position of the brigade and asked to be allowed to withdraw it immediately if a general retirement from the line Mersing–Kluang–Batu Pahat were impending. He was told that a decision must await the result of a conference which Percival was holding that afternoon. Meanwhile an officer of 2nd Malay Battalion who, disguised as a coolie, had made a reconnaissance down the coast road reported that an enemy force of about battalion strength was concealed in a rubber plantation north of Senggarang. When this information was passed to Key, he realized that it was 'now or never' and he again approached III Corps for permission to withdraw the brigade, only to receive the same reply.

The same morning 53rd Brigade (by this time consisting of 6th Norfolk and 3/16th Punjab, each only two companies strong) reached Benut before dawn, where it took two squadrons of 3rd Cavalry and a field battery under command. Brigadier Duke immediately sent forward 6th Norfolk, supported by artillery and armoured cars, together with the ammunition convoy, with orders to leave a garrison of one company to hold Rengit and then to move on to Senggarang. The garrison was duly dropped at Rengit and the head of the column had just reached Senggarang at 8 a.m. when its tail was ambushed half a mile south of the village. It lost some vehicles and suffered casualties but the ammunition convoy got through. The enemy then established a road block at this point, and later in the day several others between Senggarang and Rengit.

At 3.15 p.m. on the 25th January Percival held his conference at 'Westforce' Headquarters. He was told of the dangerous position in the Batu Pahat area, and that on the central front spirited actions by 5/11th Sikhs of 22nd Indian Brigade at Niyor (near Kluang) and by 2/30th Australian Battalion and 2nd Loyals at Ayer Hitam had caused the enemy considerable loss and had temporarily relieved the

---

[1] See page 320.

pressure on 'Westforce'. He thereupon decided to pull back 15th Brigade at once to link up with 53rd Brigade at Senggarang; 'Westforce', during the night of the 25th/26th, to the line Sungei Sayong Halt–Milestone 48 on the trunk road; and 'Eastforce' to Jemaluang. This line was to be held at least till the night 27th/28th, and subsequent withdrawals were to be made to positions selected in advance, which would in turn be held for fixed periods, or longer if possible. III Corps was to ensure that the movements of 'Eastforce' and 11th Division conformed with 'Westforce'.

Heath, who had already prepared a tentative plan to meet such an eventuality, issued maps at the conference to both Bennett and Key, on which were marked a series of lines to be denied to the enemy with proposed timings, and that evening ordered 'Eastforce' to withdraw from Mersing to Jemaluang to conform with 'Westforce'. On his return to his headquarters Key ordered Challen to withdraw from Batu Pahat and reach Benut by the 27th, and Duke to open the road Rengit–Senggarang by dawn on the 26th. Challen was to take the troops at Senggarang and Rengit under his command on reaching these places. That evening 'Westforce' ordered 9th Division and 27th Australian Brigade to withdraw to the line Sungei Sayong Halt–Milestone 48.

Challen received his orders to withdraw at 5 p.m. He started to move at 8.30 p.m., the rearguard leaving the town at about 4 a.m. covered by fire from the gunboat *Dragonfly*. The brigade reached Senggarang early on the 26th, only to find that further movement southwards was prevented by the enemy road block just south of the village. The road, built on an embankment flanked by a wide expanse of close and swampy country which was impassable for wheels and extremely difficult for infantry, lent itself to effective blocking. In consequence three attempts by the brigade to break through to the south during the morning failed.

At about 10.30 a.m. at Benut, Duke learnt that the enemy had established road blocks north of Rengit. Before he could take any action, Key arrived at his headquarters and told him to organize a column to break through to 15th Brigade. From the exiguous resources remaining to the brigade Duke formed a column which included artillery, armoured cars, carriers, and a detachment of infantry in lorries under the command of Major C. F. W. Banham (135th Field Regiment). The column left Benut at 12.30 p.m. but ran into the road block north of Rengit. A scene of indescribable confusion ensued. Most of the vehicles were ditched or destroyed and, with the exception of the guns, the column as such ceased to exist. Banham's carrier however, driven by a junior Indian N.C.O. of 3/16th Punjab, drove through the road block and went on towards Senggarang. Shortly afterwards strong enemy forces placed road blocks south of Rengit, and later in the day assaulted the village and after heavy fighting captured it just before midnight.[1]

At about 2 p.m., just as Challen was about to launch an all-out attack to break through to the south, Banham's carrier suddenly appeared on top of the nearest road block. It balanced for a moment and then, lurching over, drove unscathed into safety. Hearing from Banham that his carrier had negotiated no less than six barriers during its hazardous journey, Challen came to the conclusion that he could not possibly get his guns and vehicles through to Rengit. He therefore destroyed them, left his wounded under the protection of the Red Cross and ordered his brigade to make its way across country to Benut.[2] Guided by an officer of the Malayan Police, one contingent of some 1,200 men, moving east of the coastal road, reached Benut in an exhausted condition on the afternoon of the 27th. The remainder of the brigade, moving west of the road, was halted by an unfordable river during the night of the 26th/27th. While reconnoitring to find a suitable route, Challen fell into enemy hands. Lieut.-Colonel C. E. Morrison then assumed command and, leading the column down the river, reached the coast some three miles west of Rengit about noon on the 27th. There he concealed his exhausted troops and sent his brigade major (Major F. E. K. Laman) by boat to Pontian Kechil to tell 11th Division of their plight.

Some warning of what had occurred had reached Heath during the day. An air reconnaissance, carried out by Squadron Leader H. Dane in an unarmed aircraft of the Malayan Volunteer Air Force, had disclosed that Senggarang was in enemy hands and that there were no signs of 15th Brigade. However, it was not until Laman reached Pontian Kechil late that night that the full extent of the disaster was known. Malaya Command immediately decided to evacuate the brigade by sea. This hazardous and difficult task was successfully accomplished by the gunboats *Dragonfly* and *Scorpion* helped by small craft from Singapore. To avoid detection the evacuation had to be carried out at night; there were no large scale charts and the coast was fringed by mangrove swamps and deep mud. The operation therefore took several nights. On the first night (28th/29th) some rations were got ashore and a few men embarked on a falling tide. On the next two nights better progress was made. By the 31st January more craft were available, the channel had been marked, and by dawn on the 1st February the evacuation had been completed. Some 2,700 ranks of the brigade reached safety and, although guns, vehicles and equipment were lost and the wounded abandoned, a

---

[1] This force was the advanced guard of *5th Guards Regiment* which had just arrived on the scene. See page 320.

[2] The 15th Brigade at this time included the British Battalion, 5th and 6th Norfolk and 2nd Cambridgeshire.

disaster comparable to that which befell 45th Brigade at Parit Sulong was averted.

Although there had been constant air attacks on Mersing, the Japanese had followed up 'Eastforce's' withdrawal from Endau very slowly. It was not until the 21st January that they had occupied the town, and the 22nd before their patrols had made contact with 2/20th Australian Battalion on the line of the Sungei Mersing.[1]

After the withdrawal from Kuantan, air reconnaissance had taken place daily between Endau and Redang Island to watch for enemy movement down the east coast and the expected landing at Endau.[2] These reconnaissance flights met fighter opposition for the first time on the 24th when two Hudsons were lost. At 7.45 a.m. on the 26th the long expected invasion force, reported as two cruisers, twelve destroyers and two transports, was sighted about twenty miles northeast of Endau.[3]

Jamming prevented the wireless signal reaching Air Headquarters, and it was not until the aircraft itself landed at Singapore at 9.20 a.m. that the report was received. The available striking force was only thirty-six aircraft, and of these the Vildebeestes of both 36 and 100 (T.B.) Squadrons had been operating during the previous night against enemy concentrations and motor transport in central Johore and had neither refuelled nor rearmed.

Air Headquarters instructed 225 Bomber Group in Sumatra to despatch all bombers to Endau, and ABDA Command was asked to send American bombers to attack the convoy. Orders were issued for the Vildebeestes of the striking force at Singapore to be rearmed with 250-lb. bombs, in place of their normal torpedoes, as it was reported that the enemy ships were lying in shallow water where the use of torpedoes would be impracticable.

Owing to the time required to rearm and refuel, it was not until the early afternoon that the first wave took off. It consisted of nine Hudsons and twelve Vildebeestes with an escort of fifteen Buffaloes and eight Hurricanes. The force flew up the coast at a height of 1,000 feet just below the clouds, the slow speed of the Vildebeestes proving difficult for the escorting fighters. The first attacks were delivered about 3 p.m. against heavy fighter opposition and anti-aircraft fire, despite which direct hits were made on the two transports

---

[1] See Sketch 8.
[2] See Map 5.
[3] The actual strength was four cruisers, one aircraft carrier, six destroyers, two transports and thirteen smaller craft.

and a cruiser. Troops in barges and on the beaches, and dumps of stores were also bombed. Five Vildebeestes were shot down.

Later that afternoon, a second wave of nine Vildebeestes, three Albacores and twelve fighters took off. On this occasion there was no cloud cover over the target area and, when the force went into the attack at about 5.30 p.m., it was met by large numbers of enemy fighters. The obsolete Vildebeestes were easy prey and five were shot down together with two Albacores and a fighter; even so, hits were made on one of the transports but the bombs failed to explode. Later that evening, five Hudsons from Sumatra attacked troops and barges in the Sungei Endau and returned to Singapore without loss.

In the course of the day, 36 and 100 (T.B.) Squadrons had lost more than half their aircraft: the commanding officers of both squadrons had been killed, and many of the remaining aircraft were badly damaged and their crews wounded. These two squadrons had been longer in Singapore than any other R.A.F. units, and had reached a high standard of efficiency in the technique of torpedo dropping. Yet when the opportunity came for them to go into action they had to be sent to attack the transports with bombs instead of torpedoes. It is only fair to add that the decision to substitute bombs for torpedoes was taken with great reluctance, after careful consideration by Air Marshal Pulford and with the agreement of both the squadron commanders.

At 4.30 p.m. the same day the destroyers *Vampire* and *Thanet* left Singapore to attack the enemy convoy. In the early hours of the 27th January these two old vessels met three powerful modern Japanese destroyers. The British ships carried only three torpedoes each and the *Vampire* had already fired two, without success, at an enemy vessel which had passed her a few minutes earlier. The remaining four torpedoes were then fired but all missed. The enemy concentrated on the *Thanet* which, hit in the engine room, began to sink. The *Vampire*, trying to cover her consort with smoke, became involved in a spirited engagement with two enemy destroyers on one side, and on the other with a third destroyer and a light cruiser which suddenly appeared on the scene. But in spite of these heavy odds she succeeded in escaping, and returned to Singapore. The enemy convoy had landed part of *96th Airfield Battalion* and its signal unit with stores, equipment, petrol and bombs needed for Kahang and Kluang airfields as soon as they had been occupied.

On the evening of the 25th January III Corps ordered 'Eastforce' to withdraw from Mersing to conform with the withdrawal of 'Westforce' and 11th Division. That night Brigadier Taylor, having prepared a 'box' ambush with 2/18th Battalion supported by two field batteries at a point on the road in the Nithsdale Estate some ten miles north of Jemaluang village, withdrew 2/20th Battalion to

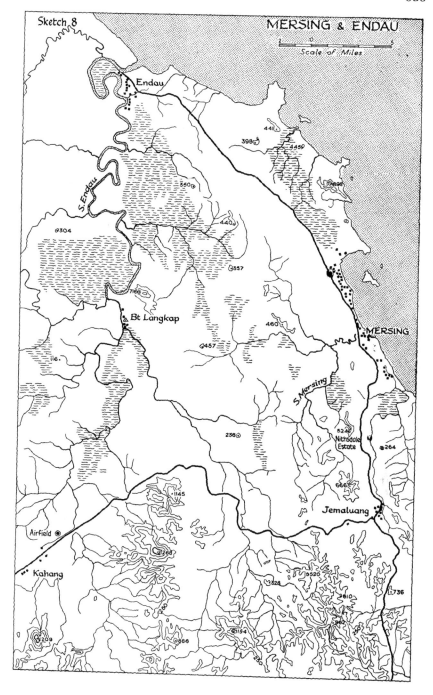

Sketch 8

MERSING & ENDAU

Scale of Miles

Endau

S. Endau

Bt Langkap

MERSING

S. Mersing

Nithsdale Estate

Jemaluang

Airfield

Kahang

Jemaluang. The Japanese at once followed up and at approximately midnight on the 26th/27th their leading battalion was allowed to enter the ambush.

As soon as the forward company of the 2/18th, forming the lid of the box, had taken up its position, the artillery opened on the enemy massed both inside and outside the box. Bitter fighting followed. At noon on the 27th the battalion withdrew in accordance with its time-table to Jemaluang, having suffered ninety-two casualties mainly to its forward company. The *55th Infantry Regiment* was so mauled that it withdrew towards Mersing and lost touch with 22nd Australian Brigade. Its reports on this action so alarmed *25th Army* that strong reinforcements were sent from Kluang to Jemaluang, where they arrived at dusk on the 28th.[1] The *55th Infantry Regiment*, instead of moving south in pursuit of the retreating British forces, was then ordered to move to Kluang where *18th Division* (*55th*, *56th* and *114th Infantry Regiments*) was to concentrate on the 31st January in preparation for the assault on Singapore Island.

During the afternoon of the 26th January Heath issued a timed programme for the withdrawal of III Corps to Singapore Island. The final evacuation of Johore was to take place on the night of the 31st January/1st February. Accordingly 'Eastforce' moved south from Jemaluang early on the 28th January. It was not followed up and reached Johore Bahru on the 30th. On the west coast 11th Division, less the isolated portion of 15th Brigade which was being evacuated by sea, was made responsible for securing the road junction at Skudai till 'Westforce' was clear, after which it was to withdraw through the bridgeheads. Key ordered the remnants of 53rd Brigade to move on the afternoon of the 28th from Benut to Milestone 22 on the Skudai road, and from there to withdraw on the night of the 29th/30th to the island, and 28th Brigade to hold Pontian Kechil till dusk on the 29th, after which it was to fall back to positions in depth along the Skudai road. Many attempts to outflank 28th Brigade during the 29th were frustrated, and it moved back to Milestone 27 on the Skudai road, where it remained unmolested until the final withdrawal to the island.

On the central front however the Japanese followed up closely and, as it was there that the final disaster in Johore occurred, resulting in the loss of 22nd Indian Brigade, the events on this front must be related in some detail. On the 26th January the dispositions of 'Westforce' were: 27th Australian Brigade on the trunk road with 2nd Gordons at Milestone 48 and 2/26th and 2/30th Australian

---

[1] These reinforcements consisted of: *5th Divisional Reconnaissance Regiment*, one battalion of infantry, one battery of field artillery, and an engineer company.

Battalions at Milestone 44½ and 41 respectively;[1] 9th Division on the railway with 8th Brigade at Sungei Sayong Halt and 22nd Brigade at Rengam.[2] In the afternoon 2nd Gordons, under heavy enemy pressure and short of ammunition, withdrew, with the Brigade Commander's permission, through 2/26th Battalion to Milestone 42½.

After the conference on the afternoon of the 25th, Bennett had issued orders for a gradual withdrawal southwards based on the lines and timings shown on Heath's map. On the 26th, on receipt of III Corps order giving the timed programme, these orders were cancelled and at 12.20 a.m. on the 27th Operation Instruction No. 4 was substituted.[3] This instruction laid down definite lines which were to be held until specific times. The 9th Division was to withdraw down the axis of the railway and 27th Australian Brigade down the trunk road. Since there was no road between Layang Layang and Kulai, the retirement down the railway entailed the withdrawal of all the guns and transport of 9th Division by the track leading from the railway south of Rengam through the Namazie Estate to the trunk road at Milestone 40½, while the track was still covered by 27th Australian Brigade. This meant that throughout its withdrawal 9th Division would have to depend on what could be carried on the men. Deprived of artillery and transport, it would have to rely for fire support on such mortars as could be carried, and on stretchers for the carriage of any wounded. Its only means of communication would be the railway telegraph line and its supplies would have to come up by rail.

Having first seen Bennett, Barstow held a conference on the morning of the 27th with his two brigadiers at Rengam and explained in detail the orders which he had received early that morning. He ordered them to start their withdrawal immediately, moving by successive bounds: 22nd Indian Brigade (Brigadier Painter) was to deny a line astride the railway at MS 437 till the night of the 28th/29th; 8th Brigade (Brigadier Lay) was to deny Sedenak till the night of the 30th/31st; and 22nd Brigade to deny Kulai till the night of the 31st January/1st February. The two brigadiers were to co-ordinate their movements by mutual agreement.[4]

Painter realized that the first line which he had been told to deny was almost impossible to defend, since it could easily be outflanked by the network of estate roads between Rengam and Layang Layang

[1] 2nd Gordons had been sent from Singapore to replace 2nd Loyals in 27th Australian Brigade.
[2] 8th Brigade at this time consisted of two battalions only: 1/13th Frontier Force Rifles and 2/10th Baluch plus one company of 3/17th Dogras. 22nd Brigade consisted of 5/11th Sikhs and an amalgamated battalion made up from one company of 2/12th Frontier Force Regiment and 2/18th Garhwalis.
[3] See Appendix 24 and Map 19.
[4] See Map 19.

and that, even with the closest co-operation between the two brigades, the enemy might interpose between them. He therefore asked
Barstow's permission to take up his initial position at Layang Layang.
He was told however that 'Westforce's' instructions were specific for,
in order to cover 27th Brigade's right flank, the cross track to the
trunk road at Milestone 40½ had to be covered till 4 p.m. on the
28th.

Barstow then returned to his headquarters at Sedenak. Later in the
day he went up the railway and personally selected a position on a
ridge astride the railway at MS 439½ covering the railway and road
bridge, with a good field of fire and some observation towards Layang
Layang station. He instructed Lay to occupy this position during the
evening. The 8th Brigade broke contact about midday and moved
back to the Layang Layang area, while 22nd Brigade took up its
position south of Rengam. During the afternoon all the transport
and guns were withdrawn from 9th Division by the track to Milestone 40½ on the trunk road. When at about 4.30 p.m. the enemy
made contact with 22nd Brigade, 5/11th Sikhs withdrew some three
miles, and by 7.30 p.m. the brigade held a position in depth close to
the railway between MS 434 and 437.

On the trunk road the foremost battalion (2/26th) of 27th Australian Brigade held off a number of enemy attacks at Milestone 44½ and
withdrew after dark on the 27th, not without some difficulty, to the
next position astride the road at Milestone 42 in the Namazie
Estate, which it had been ordered to occupy for forty-eight hours.
This position was held with 2nd Gordons at Milestone 42½, 2/26th
Battalion immediately north-east of the trunk road on the road leading to the railway in the Namazie Estate, and 2/30th Battalion in
reserve on the trunk road at Milestone 40. Neither Brigadier Maxwell
nor Lieut.-Colonel F. G. Galleghan (2/30th Battalion) was however
satisfied with this position. They felt the enemy might easily turn the
brigade's right flank through the rubber and cut them off by using
the tracks through the jungle which debouched on the trunk road
behind them. During the evening of the 27th Maxwell obtained
Bennett's permission to withdraw from the Namazie Estate position
twenty-four hours ahead of the scheduled time, if pressed too hard or
if his flanks were unduly threatened.

When 8th Brigade arrived at Layang Layang at about 10 p.m. Lay
told 22nd Indian Brigade on the telephone that he was moving south
of the village and would telephone again later. Two unfortunate
events then occurred. Firstly, at about midnight the railway bridge
across the stream at MS 439½ was blown up contrary to orders; this
not only destroyed the railway telegraph line which, since all wireless
sets had been sent back when the brigade transport had been withdrawn, was the only communication between the two brigades, but

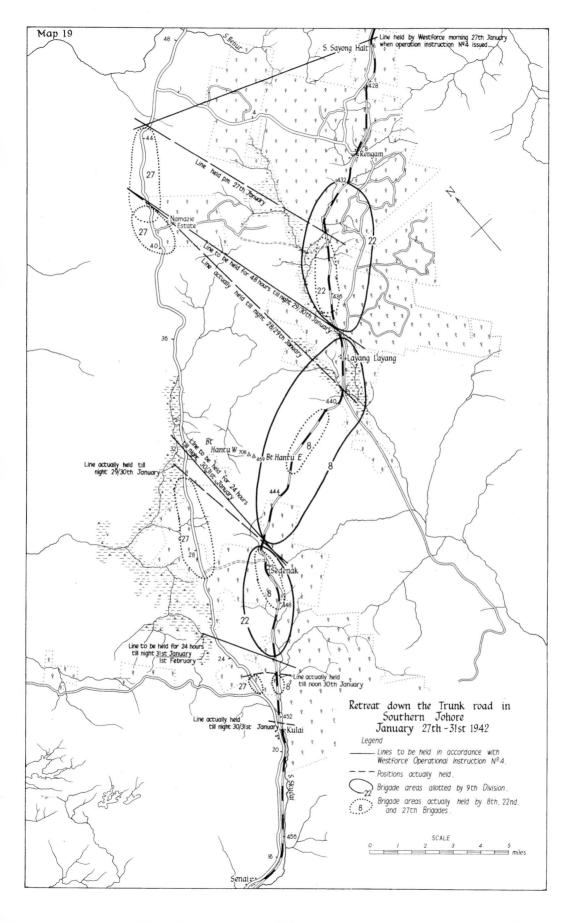

Map 19

Line held by Westforce morning 27th January
when operation instruction Nº 4 issued

S. Sayong Halt

S. Bekur

48

↑428

Rengam

↑432

Line held p.m. 27th January

↑27

↑44

Namazie
Estate

27

40

Line to be held for 48 hours till night 29/30th January

Line actually held till night 28/29th January

↑436

22

22

36

Layang Layang

↑440

Line to be held for 24 hours till night 30/31st January

Bt
Hantu W 708 △ △ 459 Bt Hantu E

8

8

Line actually held till
night 29/30th January

32

444

27

28

Sedenak

8

↑448

22

Line to be held for 24 hours
till night 31st January
1st February

24

Line actually held
till noon 30th January

27

8

Retreat down the Trunk road in
Southern Johore
January 27th–31st 1942

Legend

————— Lines to be held in accordance with
Westforce Operational Instruction Nº 4.

– – – – Positions actually held.

(22) Brigade areas allotted by 9th Division.

(8) Brigade areas actually held by 8th, 22nd,
and 27th Brigades.

Line actually held
till night 30/31st January

↑452

Kulai

20

S. Skudai

↑456

16

Senai

SCALE

0   1   2   3   4   5
▭▭▭▭▭▭ miles

also prevented rations and ammunition being sent forward. Secondly, 8th Brigade failed to occupy the position selected by Barstow and moved further south down the railway towards Sedenak, thus leaving a considerable gap between the two brigades. No attempt was made either to repair the telegraph line or inform 22nd Brigade that the bridge had been blown.

Brigadier Painter, acutely conscious of his danger, debated during the night whether he ought to withdraw without further delay to Layang Layang station. He had already queried his orders, but in view of their very definite nature he decided to hold the area allotted to him. During the early hours of the morning the rumble of transport on the estate roads on his right flank was heard and at dawn on the 28th he found that his worst fears had been realized: the enemy was on the railway line between him and 8th Brigade. Despite his instructions, he decided that an immediate withdrawal to regain contact with 8th Brigade had become inevitable and at 10.15 a.m. on the 28th he began to pull back, moving down the western side of the railway.

Meanwhile Barstow had made an adjustment to 9th Division's withdrawal programme which brought it in line with 'Westforce' operation instruction. In a message to both brigades, issued in the early hours of the 28th, he told them that, as 27th Australian Brigade was holding its Milestone 42 position until the night 29th/30th, 22nd Brigade was to deny Layang Layang until the same night, and 8th Brigade was to maintain its position during the 28th and 29th near the northern end of the area between MS 437 and Sedenak, and thereafter to deny Sedenak until the night of the 30th/31st as already ordered. This message did not reach 22nd Brigade.

Anxious about 22nd Brigade Barstow, with two staff officers, went forward up the railway in a trolley car shortly after daylight. He found 8th Brigade Headquarters about halfway between Layang Layang and Sedenak, and learnt for the first time from Lay that the railway bridge at MS 439½ had been prematurely demolished, and that his orders for the brigade to occupy the ridge covering this bridge had not been carried out. Annoyed and worried, for he realized the greatly increased danger to 22nd Brigade, he ordered Lay to send forward his leading battalion (2/10th Baluch) without delay to occupy the ridge position. He then continued up the line to see Painter.

He found 2/10th Baluch resting by the side of the line about one mile south of the bridge. He personally ordered the battalion forward and moved on with his staff officers as far as the demolished bridge, which was still passable on foot. They then walked along the railway embankment towards Layang Layang station. They had not gone far before they were challenged and fired on by an enemy party.

A2

All three jumped for cover. The general was last seen sliding down one side of the embankment. The two staff officers, having found each other on the other side of the embankment, tried to cross it but were driven back by fire which appeared to come from the south as well as the north. They decided to make their way back and, wading across the stream, climbed the ridge on which they expected to find 2/10th Baluch, only to discover to their dismay that it was held by the enemy. For the second time they managed to reach cover and by making a detour, eventually got back to the railway. There they met the vanguard of 2/10th Baluch moving forward and, while explaining the position to it, came under heavy fire from the ridge. Once again they escaped injury. The battalion attacked, but owing to the lack of any fire support failed to capture the ridge. General Barstow did not rejoin and it is now known that the Japanese found his body at the foot of the embankment.

There could by then have been no doubt in Lay's mind that the enemy had driven a wedge between the two brigades and that, unless he immediately attempted to join hands with Painter's brigade, it was likely to be cut off. Nevertheless he made no further efforts during the day to move up the railway.

The 27th Australian Brigade held its position in the Namazie Estate astride the trunk road throughout daylight on the 28th. During the morning, 2nd Gordons on the road, and 2/26th Battalion in the rubber on its right, withstood successive enemy attacks supported by mortar fire and by low-flying aircraft. At about 1 p.m. a staff officer from the brigade arrived at 2/30th Battalion Headquarters with the authority to order a withdrawal to Milestone 31 should the situation demand. During the afternoon a Japanese battalion attempted to move through the rubber round the right flank so as to reach the trunk road behind the brigade. The reserve battalion (2/30th) however detected this move and launched a counter-attack with the bayonet which caused the enemy considerable loss and forced him back in confusion. The Japanese covered their retreat by using smoke bombs; the irritant smoke was first thought to be gas and this caused some alarm. In view of the enemy's attempt to outflank the position and reach the defile behind the brigade, which he feared might be repeated during the night, Colonel Galleghan agreed that the withdrawal should take place shortly after dark.

'Westforce', informed of this decision but unaware of 22nd Brigade's plight (it had been told by 9th Division only that General Barstow was missing) ordered the division to conform by withdrawing that night to Sedenak. The division passed this order on to 8th Brigade. Lay, who received it at 9 p.m., promptly complied and withdrew to Sedenak. Neither formation protested against this order although they must have known that 22nd Brigade was isolated and that the only hope of rescuing it lay in 8th Brigade remaining as far forward as possible.

Meanwhile 22nd Brigade was moving down the railway in an effort to reach 8th Brigade. By midday on the 28th its advanced guard suffered some fifty casualites in trying to drive the enemy from Layang Layang station. Painter considered that he then had only two alternatives: either to deploy his maximum strength to break through, or to move across country to the west of the railway so as to gain touch with 8th Brigade. Unable, owing to lack of communications, to arrange for concerted action with that brigade, and influenced by the need to avoid further casualties, which could not be evacuated, and by the lack of fire support, he took the decision to move through the jungle. This had tragic results. Forcing its way through trackless forest, encumbered by its wounded, and having on one occasion to make a lengthy detour to avoid the enemy, 22nd Indian Brigade struggled on for four days and nights suffering great hardship. By that time the brigade had been reduced to headquarters and some 350 exhausted troops who were practically without ammunition. On the 1st February Painter, finding his way blocked by the Japanese and with no chance of breaking through, was forced to surrender. Only a few men, who had become separated from the main body, managed to reach the island.

Meanwhile, late on the 26th January, Percival had informed the Supreme Commander of his difficulties on the west coast and of the landing on the east coast, and said:

> 'Consider general situation becoming grave. With our depleted strength it is difficult to withstand enemy ground pressure combined with continuous and practically unopposed air activity. We are fighting all the way but may be driven back into the Island within a week.'

Twenty-four hours later, on the evening of the 27th, he had followed this up with a personal message to Wavell:

> 'Very critical situation has developed. The enemy has cut off and overrun majority of forces on west coast . . . Unless we can stop him it will be difficult to get our own columns on other roads back in time especially as they are both being pressed. In any case it looks as if we should not be able to hold Johore for more than another three or four days. We are going to be a bit thin on the Island unless we can get all remaining troops back. Our total fighter strength now reduced to nine and difficulty in keeping airfields in action.'

Wavell had replied immediately giving Percival discretion to withdraw into the island if he considered it advisable and continue the fight there, judging that it would be better to evacuate III Corps from the mainland rather than that it should be overwhelmed before the reinforcements landed.

A conference was held at Headquarters III Corps early on the 28th, attended by Percival, Heath and Bennett, to decide whether or not to withdraw to the island without further delay. Both Percival and Heath considered it unlikely that 11th Division could now hold the enemy's advance on the west coast and that, as there were no reserves available, any attempt to hold on in southern Johore for much longer would hazard the loss of the whole force. Percival thereupon decided that the withdrawal programme to which Heath had up to that time been working should be accelerated by twenty-four hours and the final stage carried out on the night of the 30th/31st January. This decision was the right one, for it is now known that the Japanese had high hopes of cutting off III Corps in Johore by a rapid advance inland from the west coast towards Skudai. They believed that without III Corps the small garrison left on the island would be forced to surrender, and they would thus avoid having to launch a costly assault across the strait.

Special precautions had been taken to protect the Causeway, which carried the only road and rail link between the mainland and the island. Anti-aircraft guns and searchlights from south Johore had been gradually withdrawn for use as a protection at likely bottlenecks and, in particular, to provide the maximum anti-aircraft defence for the Causeway. Its ground defence was to be provided by an outer and an inner bridgehead. The 22nd Australian Brigade, reinforced by 2nd Gordons and some artillery, was to hold the outer bridgehead. The inner bridgehead was to be held by 2nd Argylls (250 strong) on whom would devolve the responsibility for the final withdrawal and for the demolition of the Causeway.

After the conference Bennett, dissatisfied with the arrangements made by III Corps for the crossing of the Causeway, remained at Heath's headquarters to work out a revised plan. He then visited the Sultan of Johore to bid him farewell and it was not until after dark that he returned to 'Westforce' Headquarters. On arrival he ordered an acceleration of the withdrawal programme in accordance with the decision taken that morning. During the morning of the 29th, 'Westforce' ordered the withdrawal from the line Sedenak–Milestone 31 to Kulai to take place on the night of the 29th/30th instead of on the night of the 30th/31st.

Before the receipt of these orders, 9th Division, in a belated effort to rescue 22nd Brigade which it was believed might reach Sedenak that night, had early on the morning of the 29th ordered 8th Brigade to move forward should the tactical situation permit, and secure the railway as far as MS 440 and if necessary beyond. At 1.20 p.m. however, before this order could be acted on, the division, in compliance with the new time-table, ordered 8th Brigade to withdraw during the night of the 29th/30th to a position at MS 450½ some two and a half miles north of Kulai. This sealed the fate of 22nd Brigade.

Throughout the 29th January 27th Australian Brigade was repeatedly attacked in its Milestone 31 position on the trunk road.[1] The 2/26th Battalion however drove the enemy back at the point of the bayonet. The attacks ceased at dusk and the brigade withdrew during the night to Milestone 23, three miles west of Kulai. No attacks developed on the 30th and during the afternoon 27th Australian Brigade was withdrawn close to Kulai village at Milestone 21 and 8th Brigade into Kulai. During this move 8th Brigade Headquarters found Japanese cyclists in the village and drove them out. Here a final attempt to locate the lost 22nd Brigade and guide it to safety was organized. Officers of the Volunteer Forces who knew the country undertook to remain in Johore, and air reconnaissance and naval patrols in the Johore Strait were arranged. All these efforts proved fruitless, and only some sixty officers and men of 5/11th Sikh and some officers of 2/12th Frontier Force Regiment eventually found their way to the coast and thence to the island. After dark that night 'Westforce' withdrew to Senai, where it embussed and moved to the Causeway by the Tebrau loop road, thus leaving the main road clear for 11th Division.

By 5.30 a.m. on the 31st January, III Corps had crossed safely to the island. Excellent traffic control had been maintained, and the movement of the forces through the bottle-neck of Johore Bahru was completed without congestion on the roads. The enemy did not attempt to follow up closely and fortunately, despite a brilliant moon, there was little interference from the air.

Preparations had already been made to demolish the Causeway. This was one of the largest and perhaps the most important demolition in the campaign. The Causeway was about 1,100 yards long and some seventy feet wide. Its denial entailed the destruction of a steel road and railway bridge, a lock system at the north end and also the demolition of part of the Causeway itself to produce a water gap sixty yards wide.[2] The technical difficulties were considerable and involved the use of naval depth charges. British and Indian engineers, assisted by the Royal Navy, succeeded however in completing their preparations earlier than had been expected.

---

[1] 2/26th Battalion at Milestone 31, 2nd Gordons at Milestone 28½ and 2/30th at the road junction (Milestone 27).

[2] This gap was produced by the explosion of the demolition charges but did not provide the expected obstacle since it was not more than four feet deep at low tide and therefore fordable.

Shortly before 7 a.m. the troops of the outer bridgehead began to move on to the Causeway and, as they did so, the only two remaining pipers of the Argyll and Sutherland Highlanders played first the Australians and then the Gordons out of Johore. Heath then gave permission for the inner bridgehead to withdraw. The pipers played out the remnants of their own battalion and at 8.15 a.m. on the 31st January, when the last man had crossed the Causeway, the demolition charges were exploded.

Chapters XIX and XX cover the period from the 11th to the 31st January, the second and vital phase of the campaign. On his arrival at Singapore in January, General Wavell, realized that his original plan to hold the Japanese north of Johore was no longer feasible.[1] His only hope of gaining the time he required to build up his defences and prepare a counter-offensive was to hold northern Johore. The battle in northern Johore was the decisive battle for Singapore for, if the British forces were driven back into southern Johore, there would be neither the time nor the opportunity to stage a counter-offensive. A withdrawal to the island would then become inevitable and, since it had been prepared to withstand neither an assault from the north nor a siege and once invested could be neither relieved nor reinforced, this could end only in surrender. After consulting his commanders on the spot Wavell formed the opinion that by regrouping the forces and using some of the fresh troops that were available, there was a good chance of holding the Japanese advance in northern Johore long enough for the expected reinforcements, as they arrived, to be deployed and a counterstroke launched. How was it then that this period ended in a hasty withdrawal to the island with the loss of two brigades and much equipment and transport?

Wavell's plan for the defence of northern Johore differed from that which Percival had proposed in one respect only: the substitution of 'Westforce' under General Bennett's command for III Corps. Viewed in retrospect this plan had two important defects: it did not bring the greatest possible strength to bear on the decisive point, and it placed command of the critical battle in the hands of an officer who had had no first hand experience of Japanese methods and who had not an adequate staff to control a front which geographically was split into two parts.

The exact strength of the Japanese was not known, but it had been reasonably accurately assessed at two divisions with reserves behind them. To hold the vital area in northern Johore 'Westforce' had been given the equivalent of four brigades, two of which were tired

---

[1] See pages 283–284

and another partly trained. The untried though well trained and fresh 8th Australian Division was the best asset available to Malaya Command at this juncture. Earlier in the campaign Percival had rightly declined to take the risk of placing the defence of the Mersing area in the hands of troops who were not acquainted with it, for at that time a successful enemy landing there would have been a major disaster. But once the enemy's main forces had reached the borders of Johore they became the greatest danger and risks might justifiably have been taken both at Mersing and Singapore.

With the arrival of large reinforcements imminent, the Australian brigade defending Mersing might with advantage have been relieved by units from the Singapore garrison, all of which were trained in beach defence. Had this been done the whole of the Australian division could have been used at the decisive point. There would then have been a corps of three divisions to meet the main enemy threat, of which 9th Indian and 8th Australian Divisions, totalling five brigades, could have been deployed, with 53rd Brigade on arrival, and the remnants of the battle-weary 11th Division held in reserve. No such regrouping took place. In consequence the battle was fought by a force of only eleven battalions which was insufficient to cover the approaches into Johore adequately, while 8th Australian Division was used piecemeal on three separate fronts with only two-thirds of its strength fully engaged.

Once the enemy had reached the Tampin bottleneck there were two main routes to the south: the first, from Tampin either by way of Gemas or Jementah to Segamat, and then through Yong Peng to Ayer Hitam; the second, from Tampin either by way of Malacca along the coast or by the inland road to Muar, and then to Yong Peng or Batu Pahat. There was also the possibility that the enemy might land on the coast behind the defenders. There was thus a need for two separate forces in northern Johore co-ordinated by some higher formation; one for each of the two roads which were some forty miles apart with no lateral communication further north than the Batu Pahat–Yong Peng road. The III Corps with three divisions under its command could have afforded to allot one division to each line of approach and hold a reserve, which, however weak at the start of the battle, would have grown as reinforcements arrived.

But with the formation of 'Westforce' the conduct of the decisive battle and the control of these two widely separated fronts were taken from III Corps and given to 8th Australian Division, without additional staff and the communications necessary to control them. As a direct result of this change of control Percival was compelled to act as a corps commander himself and had to give most of his time to the detailed conduct of tactical operations, which distracted him from his main task as army commander. A further consequence was the

constant transfer of responsibility in the forward area from one commander to another, resulting in order and counter-order. This in
turn led to a considerable intermixture of units, and all troops, whatever their nationality, fight better under their own commanders and
in company with troops they know.

Let us now examine the dispositions which Bennett, with Percival's
agreement, made in northern Johore. It was probable that the
Japanese armour would use the inland route down the trunk road,
for on the coast road the unbridged Sungei Muar estuary presented a
formidable tank obstacle. The trunk road however had its tank obstacles in the jungle defile west of Gemas, the Sungei Muar and the
Sungei Segamat, all of which gave excellent opportunities for defence
against both infantry and armour; it was therefore by no means
certain that the enemy would make his main thrust along it. The
coast road was the shortest route to Yong Peng, the key point on the
line of communications of the forces guarding the trunk road, and
offered no serious difficulties other than the Sungei Muar estuary.
The Japanese had more than once outflanked strong defensive positions on the trunk road by advancing along the coast or by making
seaborne landings behind them. There was every reason to expect
them to repeat these tactics in an effort to reach Yong Peng or Ayer
Hitam which were both only some twenty miles inland.

Yet this probability was discounted and three of the four brigades
available were concentrated on the trunk road leaving only one—the
inexperienced 45th—to cover the coast road. The weakness on this
road was moreover aggravated by Bennett's orders to 45th Brigade
which forced it to take up positions covering a twenty-five mile front,
with its forward battalions astride an unbridged and unfordable
river. The brigade's weakness and its wide dispersion made the
defence of the coast road impossible. It is no wonder that the
Japanese forced the crossing of the Sungei Muar with such ease and
virtually destroyed the defending brigade. That the bulk of 'Westforce' was not then cut off and destroyed in northern Johore was due
to the prompt despatch of 2/19th and 2/29th Australian Battalions to
the coastal sector and the stubborn and gallant defence which they
put up at Bakri and Parit Sulong.

The loss of these battalions and the remnants of 45th Brigade at the
Parit Sulong bridge cannot be attributed to the failure of 53rd
Brigade to break through the seven-mile-long defile between Bukit
Pelandok and the bridge. The entrance to the defile at Bukit
Pelandok was seized by the Japanese when 53rd Brigade consisted
of one inexperienced battalion only. Thereafter the enemy held the
defile with *4th Guards Regiment* and had observation over the whole of
the area from which any counter-attack would have to be launched.
The 53rd Brigade, brought up to strength first by one battle-weary

battalion from 11th Division and then by a tired battalion hastily sent from Segamat, and without adequate artillery support, was never capable of capturing the entrance to the defile and forcing its way over the seven miles of difficult country to Parit Sulong.

The key to the whole defence of north-western Johore lay in holding the Muar–Batu Pahat–Yong Peng triangle, and the key to the latter's security lay in holding the area Muar–Bukit Pasir–Bakri–Parit Jawa. Once the enemy was across the Sungei Muar and had gained undisputed command of the coastal road, the only safe course of action was a speedy withdrawal of the reinforced 45th Brigade to the general line Parit Sulong–Bukit Pelandok–Batu Pahat, the remainder of 'Westforce' conforming. That this was not done was perhaps due to the justifiable anxiety of Malaya Command to retain ground in view of the Supreme Commander's orders that maximum delay should be imposed, and to the fear that morale would suffer severely if any further retirement were permitted. But the course taken resulted in 45th Brigade withdrawing too late, and entailed losses which gave the enemy an even greater superiority.

The delay in the decision to abandon Batu Pahat was no doubt due to the same causes. Although one of the two roads from Bukit Pelandok to Ayer Hitam passed through Batu Pahat, the retention of the town for the purpose of protecting the left flank of the Mersing–Kluang–Ayer Hitam line was of little value once the enemy had gained control of the Bukit Pelandok area and was therefore free to cross the Sungei Simpang Kanan and advance southwards. The country in the area bounded by Bukit Pelandok–Batu Pahat–Senggarang–Rengit and extending thence northwards to Milestone 64 on the Ayer Hitam–Batu Pahat road was intensively cultivated and numerous tracks ran from north to south. To the Japanese, who had in peacetime owned mines and rubber estates in the district and therefore knew the country intimately, and who were well able to operate without using the main roads, there was nothing in this stretch of country to prevent an advance either to Ayer Hitam or Senggarang and Rengit.

From the point of view of the defence, the narrow necks between the swamps on both the Yong Peng and Ayer Hitam roads, and the confined area between the coast and the swamp area east of Rengit offered positions with reasonably secure flanks which should have been capable of defence for some time by comparatively small forces. A withdrawal to these positions would not have been contrary to the spirit of the Supreme Commander's orders and would have protected the flank of the Mersing–Kluang–Ayer Hitam line much more effectively than the holding of Batu Pahat.

By this time commanders, even if they had not studied their potential enemy's methods before the war, must have realized his ability to move extremely quickly over all types of country, and that envelopment was the keynote of his tactics. Yet the plan adopted at this stage was to hold Batu Pahat at all costs, on the assumption that its retention secured the left flank of the whole line and, in order to keep the road open to it, to build up centres of resistance along the coastal road. All the troops of the weak 11th Division were thus locked up in the static defence of these widely separated points and there was no mobile reserve available to counter-attack. The Japanese were thus free to isolate each centre of resistance and deal with the division piecemeal. Even when it became clear that the town was about to be surrounded, the idea that Batu Pahat protected the left flank of the general defence line persisted, and the withdrawal of the garrison was delayed, with the result that 15th Brigade (by then three and a half British battalions) was cut off. The 11th Division, then reduced to a veritable skeleton, was no longer in a position to hold the coastal road and it became necessary to accelerate the withdrawal to the island if 'Westforce' were to be saved from encirclement.

The battle for Johore was lost, and with it the Malay peninsula. The Naval Base, for which the campaign in Malaya was being fought, had become useless, and it was now a question of holding on to Singapore Island in order to deny it to the Japanese and contain their divisions in Malaya for as long as possible.

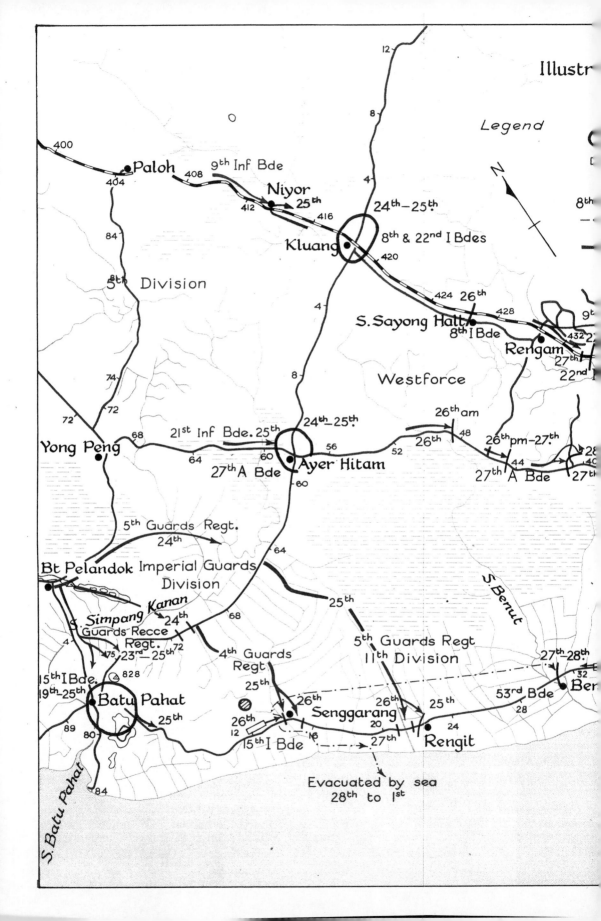

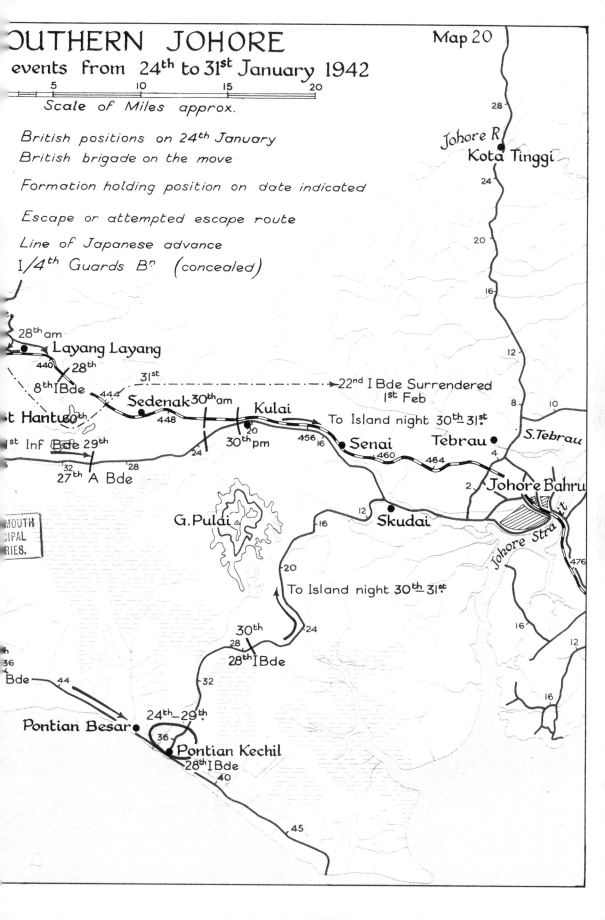

OUTHERN JOHORE
events from 24th to 31st January 1942

Map 20

5 10 15 20
Scale of Miles approx.

British positions on 24th January
British brigade on the move

Formation holding position on date indicated

Escape or attempted escape route

Line of Japanese advance

I/4th Guards Bn (concealed)

Johore R
Kota Tinggi

28
24
20
16
12
8   10

28th am
Layang Layang
440   28th
8th I Bde   444
31st

Sedenak 30th am   Kulai
448   30th pm
t Hantu 30th   24
20
456 16

Senai
460   464

Tebrau   S. Tebrau
4

22nd I Bde Surrendered
1st Feb

To Island night 30th 31st

2   Johore Bahru
476

st Inf Bde 29th
32   28
27th A Bde

G. Pulai

12
Skudai

16
20

To Island night 30th 31st

16
12

16

30th
28
28th I Bde

24

32

36
Bde   44

24th–29th
36
Pontian Besar
Pontian Kechil
28th I Bde
40

45

CHAPTER XXI

THE GROWING THREAT TO
JAVA AND SUMATRA

See Maps 17 and 26 and Sketch 9

THE LOSS of the air base at Kendari on the 24th January increased the threat not only to Java but to the island of Timor.[1] This island was part Dutch and part Portuguese. Before the outbreak of war a Japanese consul had been appointed to Dili, the capital of Portuguese Timor, and a Japanese air service had been established between there and Palau. The British Government, suspicious of Japanese intentions, had made their old allies, the Portuguese, an offer of assistance in the event of a Japanese attack. The Portuguese Government had accepted this offer on the 12th December 1941, and had agreed that there should be staff conversations at Singapore to work out details. Meanwhile Australian and Dutch reinforcements had been sent to reinforce Dutch Timor.[2] On the 15th December the Dutch authorities, in agreement with the Australian Government, decided that in view of the activities of the Japanese in that area it was essential to send troops immediately to Portuguese Timor and, on the 17th December, Dutch and Australian troops landed at Dili.[3] The Portuguese reaction was violent and unfavourable. They had apparently interpreted the agreement to mean that an Allied force would be provided only when an attack actually developed, and not when it threatened. Discussions went on for some time and it was eventually agreed that the Allied garrison would be withdrawn when an adequate garrison of Portuguese troops from East Africa had arrived. Before this agreement could be fulfilled however the island had been captured by the Japanese.

General Wavell had realized that, if he were to halt the Japanese advance, he must gain local air superiority. This meant bringing into the ABDA area sufficient fighter aircraft not only to replace wastage but to build up a force of adequate strength. The airfield at Kupang, at the south-west corner of Timor, provided an essential staging point for short-range aircraft on the air reinforcement route from

---

[1] See page 298.
[2] 2/40th Australian Battalion, 2/2nd Independent Company, a battery of Australian coast artillery, 2 (Hudson) Squadron R.A.A.F., and 400 Dutch troops.
[3] 2/2nd Independent Company and 250 Dutch troops.

Australia, but the small Australian and Dutch garrison was quite inadequate to repel an invasion in force. In these circumstances Wavell reluctantly decided to depart from his principle that outlying garrisons should not be reinforced. On the 27th January he asked Lieut.-General V. A. H. Sturdee, the Australian Chief of the General Staff, to send an Australian battalion from Darwin to Timor and to agree to the despatch of an American artillery regiment (less one battalion), to which the Americans had already given their consent. Sturdee, concerned at Japanese attacks on Rabaul and the weakness of the Darwin garrison, replied the following day regretting his inability to find an Australian battalion and urging that the American artillery regiment should not be moved. He expressed the opinion that the reinforcement proposed would have little effect in preventing the loss of Kupang.

Wavell returned to the charge on the 31st January and again on the 4th February, urging the despatch of the reinforcements, and at the same time saying that he was himself sending to Timor some light anti-aircraft guns from Java. He proposed that six American air squadrons (three fighter and three dive-bomber) which were assembling in Australia for use by ABDA Command should be allotted to Java, Timor and Darwin as they became available, one fighter and one dive-bomber squadron to each of the three places in that order. After some hesitation, natural in view of the weakness of the garrison at Darwin, the Australian Government agreed on the 7th February to despatch the Australian and American reinforcing units. Arrangements were immediately put in hand for their embarkation about the middle of February.

The loss of Kendari had increased the threat to Amboina. The Australians, in accordance with an agreement with the Dutch reached in February 1941, had reinforced the small Dutch garrison of that island (some 2,600 N.E.I. troops) during December with 2/21st Australian Infantry Battalion and 13 (Hudson) Squadron R.A.A.F. The Japanese, in order to protect the eastern flank of their southward advance and to eliminate any Allied air threat from the air base in Amboina, had planned to invade the island as soon as they had captured Kendari. The date of the attack was fixed for the 31st January. The assault was to be undertaken by *228th Infantry Regiment*, part of *38th Division*, which had been transferred to Davao from Hong Kong on the 18th January, and by the *Kure 1st Special Naval Landing Force*. Two fleet carriers of the *2nd Carrier Squadron*, which had taken part in the raid on Pearl Harbour and had later proceeded to Palau, were allotted to Admiral Takahashi for preparatory attacks on the island defences and to provide air cover for the landing.

The convoy carrying the invasion forces left Davao on the 27th under strong naval escort, and anchored off Amboina during the

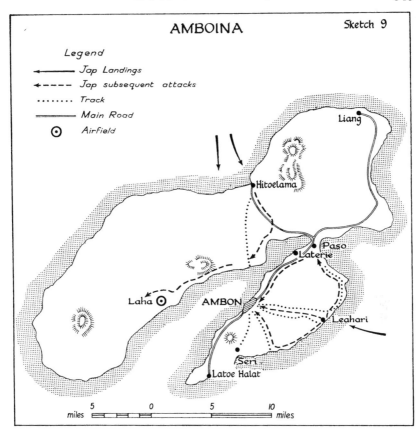

AMBOINA   Sketch 9

Legend
→ Jap Landings
←---- Jap subsequent attacks
········ Track
═══ Main Road
⊙ Airfield

night of the 30th/31st.[1] Shortly after the fall of Menado all Allied aircraft had been withdrawn from the island to replace losses elsewhere, and thus the enemy met no air opposition. Pre-dawn landings were made by the naval landing force at Hitoelama on the north coast and by *228th Infantry Regiment* near Leahari on the south-east coast. The Dutch holding a position at Paso, threatened from the north and attacked from the south, surrendered on the night of the 31st. The Australians holding Laha airfield held out till the 2nd, while a mixed Australian and Dutch force covering Ambon resisted till the 3rd. By the 4th the Japanese were in complete control of the island and its airfield.

The prospect which faced General Wavell at the beginning of February was a gloomy one. With the very small naval and air forces

---

[1] See Appendix 22.

at his disposal he had been powerless to stop the southward drive of the Japanese in the Molucca Passage and the Strait of Makassar, though some damage had been inflicted on their convoys and air forces, especially at Balikpapan. Kendari and Amboina had fallen. There was a large Japanese convoy anchored off Balikpapan which might at any moment move to either Bandjermasin or Makassar—both air bases within range of Java. There were also reports of a Japanese airborne division concentrating at Camranh Bay for an attack on southern Sumatra. In Malaya the British forces had been forced to withdraw into Singapore Island. In Burma the enemy had captured Moulmein and the threat to Rangoon had increased.[1]

To stem the tide of the Japanese advance on Java and Sumatra Wavell had at that time no naval striking force, for Admiral Glassford's ships were undergoing repairs or re-fitting and all other naval units were fully engaged on escort duties. His air striking force had been reduced to a daily average of seven American heavy bombers; his fighters and light bombers were fully occupied in protecting convoys and in the defence of Singapore, leaving no aircraft for the defence of the airfields in Java.

The arrival on the 27th January of forty-eight Hurricane fighters flown off the aircraft carrier *Indomitable* did not actually provide an accretion of strength, for they were barely sufficient to replace wastage.[2] To make matters worse the Australian Government were pressing for the American aircraft, already allotted to ABDA Command and now being assembled near Brisbane, to be used for the defence of Australia. The only redeeming feature was that all but a few units of 18th Division had arrived safely at Singapore. General Wavell considered at the time that its arrival gave General Percival sufficient troops to enable him, by active defence, to hold the island for some months. No further military reinforcements were however in sight until the expected arrival at the end of February and early March of 7th Armoured Brigade in Malaya, the Australian corps in the Netherlands East Indies and the Indian brigade groups in Burma.

Wavell's problem was how to slow down the Japanese advance until military and air reinforcements reached the ABDA area. The key points which he felt must be held were Singapore Island, the air bases in central and southern Sumatra, the naval base at Sourabaya and the airfield at Kupang. Meanwhile there was little he could do but try to form a naval striking force as soon as possible and continue, with the few aircraft available, to attack Japanese convoys as weather permitted and opportunity offered.

Accordingly he ordered repeated air attacks to be made on the enemy convoy off Balikpapan. These however achieved only

[1] See Volume II, Chapter II.
[2] See page 257.

moderate results, mainly because of bad weather. He sent anti-aircraft guns, as they became available, to Palembang and to Batavia for the defence of the airfields at Sourabaya, and Malang, where the American fighters from Australia were to be based. He requested the Chiefs of Staff to allot an aircraft carrier to bring to Java fifty American fighter aircraft which were expected to be available in Brisbane by the 15th February, for he considered it more than probable that the reinforcement route via Timor would be closed before these aircraft could make use of it.

But before the air defences of Java could be strengthened the Japanese struck. On the 3rd and 5th February, fighters from Balik-papan and bombers from Kendari carried out what the Japanese described as 'an air annihilation operation', concentrating their attacks on the airfields in eastern Java and on the naval base at Sourabaya. Meeting with practically no fighter or anti-aircraft defence, they were able to fly low and pin-point their targets almost unmolested, and destroyed a number of American heavy bombers which were under repair and so could not be moved.

By the 2nd February Admiral Hart had at last been able to form a combined American-Dutch naval striking force. He placed Admiral Doorman in command and instructed him to carry out a second night attack on the Balikpapan convoy.[1] The striking force sailed from Boender Roads[2] on the night of the 3rd/4th. Admiral Doorman, flying his flag in the *De Ruyter*, was accompanied by the Dutch cruiser *Tromp*, the American cruisers *Houston* and *Marblehead* and three Dutch and four American destroyers.

Fate seemed always against Admiral Doorman. Enemy aircraft approaching Sourabaya on the 3rd had sighted the Allied striking force as it left Boender Roads and shortly before 10 a.m. on the following day, when the force was north of Bali, some sixty enemy bombers from Kendari launched an attack. The ships had no radar and thus the warning of attack was extremely short. Waves of bombers came in from a high level and, attacking unopposed in V formation, dropped their bombs in salvos from fourteen thousand feet.

The *Marblehead* was severely damaged. The *Houston's* after triple 8-inch turret received a direct hit and was rendered useless for the remaining weeks of the ship's life. The *De Ruyter* had her anti-aircraft control put out of action. The Japanese claimed to have sunk two cruisers and damaged two more, but all these ships though badly scarred were able to make port in safety. The Admiral withdrew his force to Tjilatjap on the south coast of Java, where he hoped to be more secure from air attack. The damage to the *Marblehead* was such that she had to be sent to the United States after temporary repairs.

---

[1] See page 297.
[2] Sixty miles east of Sourabaya.

This disaster was not the only one which the Allied forces suffered during the first week of February: a ship carrying sixteen badly needed anti-aircraft guns was sunk off Banka Island on its way to Palembang; a train accident in Java resulted in the loss of irreplaceable anti-aircraft personnel; and a flight of the much needed American fighters was lost in an air attack on the airfield at Bali, while it was refuelling on its way to Java. On the 6th February however the first ten American fighter aircraft arrived at Sourabaya.

The Japanese convoy lying off Balikpapan did not carry out the expected move further south. The enemy had decided, owing to his losses in ships during the invasion of Balikpapan, to make an overland advance on Bandjermasin supported by a subsidiary force moving by sea, instead of a seaborne landing as originally planned. On the 31st January a battalion from *56th Regimental Group* left Balikpapan in small craft under cover of darkness and, disembarking at a point some sixty miles further down the coast, made its way through the mountainous jungle to Bandjermasin. An infantry company left on the same evening in landing craft and, moving only by night, occupied Laut Island off the south-east corner of Borneo and later went on to join the battalion at Bandjermasin. The town and airfield were occupied against slight opposition on the 10th February, and by the 25th, the *23rd Air Flotilla* was using the airfield as an intermediate base. Small Japanese detachments then moved west along the coast, and it was these that met the survivors of 2/15th Punjab on their arrival at Sampit after their arduous march from Kuching.[1]

Meanwhile the Japanese *Eastern Force* was still keeping in step; the co-ordination of the two advances was remarkable. On the 6th February the *Sasebo Special Landing Force* which had captured Kendari sailed for Makassar. The convoy was sighted by Allied aircraft when off the south-east coast of Celebes and Admiral Doorman, then at Tjilatjap, was ordered to attack; but before his ships had even left harbour the enemy was already landing. The Japanese convoy, which had been joined by five destroyers from Balikpapan to give additional support during the landing,[2] anchored off Makassar during the night 8th/9th and the assault force landed at dawn the next morning. During the approach an American submarine torpedoed and sank one of the Japanese escorting destroyers. As elsewhere, the small garrison of two companies was able to put up little opposition and by nightfall the town and airfield had been surrendered to the enemy. Thus by the beginning of the second week in February Amboina and the key points in Celebes and Borneo were all in enemy hands. The net had begun to tighten round the eastern end of Java.

---

[1] See page 226.
[2] See Appendix 22.

With the enemy in control of the Malay peninsula and thus of the Strait of Malacca, General Wavell realized that the ability of the Allies to hold Singapore and Java depended largely on the successful defence of Sumatra. The strategic importance of Sumatra had always been recognized, and before the war airfields had been partly developed in the north as advanced landing grounds for operations against the flank of a possible Japanese advance. But within a few days of the outbreak of war these were dominated by Japanese squadrons based on the newly-captured airfields in Malaya, and the strategic centre of Sumatra shifted to its southern half, for it was from this area that the air defence of Singapore and of the line of communications northwards from the Sunda Strait had now to be conducted.

On the 30th January, while the withdrawal of the army from the mainland was in progress, General Wavell, accompanied by Air Marshal Peirse, again visited Singapore to discuss with Air Vice-Marshal Pulford the situation in general and, in particular, the effect of the withdrawal on the air defence of Singapore.

All four main airfields on the island were being subjected to constant bombing and great difficulty was being experienced in maintaining serviceable landing strips on them. Three of them—Tengah, Sembawang and Seletar—were near the northern coastline and were soon likely to be exposed to observed artillery fire at close ranges from Johore, which would make it impracticable to operate aircraft from them.[1] The fourth airfield at Kallang (the original civil airport) on the south coast was rapidly becoming of limited use, for the surface had been laid on a salt marsh at sea level which made it most difficult to fill in the bomb craters with which it was becoming pitted.

Towards the end of December 1941 a number of special landing strips had been constructed to relieve the congestion that would obviously arise in the event of a withdrawal to the island, and to provide dispersion for the Hurricane fighters. The plan had been to construct two strips in southern Johore and five on Singapore Island. Priority for labour had been given to Air Headquarters for this purpose, but the constant air raids caused the civilian labourers to desert. By the end of January only two strips had been completed though others were in course of preparation. Their existence, whether completed or not, provided the enemy with possible landing grounds for airborne troops—a threat which could have been countered only by detailing special detachments to guard them. Since no troops could be spared for this purpose all five strips on the island had to be made unfit for use. In addition all other open spaces which might possibly be used as temporary landing grounds were covered by obstructions.

---

[1] See Map 21.

General Wavell approved the transfer of all remaining aircraft from Singapore to bases in southern Sumatra, except a small token force of two flights, one of eight Hurricanes and one of eight Buffaloes. This decision was, as he well knew, open to criticism since it deprived the land forces of protection against air attack at a crucial time. Nevertheless it was in his opinion inevitable, for the loss of Crete had shown that it was impossible to maintain a weak air force within close range of a stronger enemy one, and that the sacrifice of aircraft entailed by the attempt brought no relief to the land forces in the long run.

As can well be imagined, the withdrawal caused considerable alarm in London and the Prime Minister asked for an explanation, since it seemed to imply despair of defending Singapore. General Wavell explained that the airfields on Singapore Island were exposed to artillery fire as well as to bombing, and that to leave fighter aircraft on them after the army had left the mainland would invite their destruction within a few days. He pointed out that the loss of Malaya made the maintenance of airfields in southern Sumatra of vital importance, for it was only from those airfields that operations to reduce the scale of attacks on Singapore could be carried out. The provision of fighter defence for them was thus essential. He added that he was making every effort to maintain the fighter defence of Singapore by retaining the equivalent of one squadron at Kallang, and by using other airfields on the island as circumstances permitted for refuelling fighters from Sumatra. He felt that these arrangements offered the best prospects for the air defence of Singapore, which there was 'every intention and hope of holding'.

The island of Sumatra—bisected by the equator—is just over a thousand miles long and its area is six times that of Holland. Its northern half runs parallel to the Malay peninsula and is separated from it by the Strait of Malacca. Its southern tip is divided from Java by the Sunda Strait. A chain of mountains runs down the west coast throughout the whole length of the island. The remainder of the island, with the exception of the foothills, is low-lying and consists mainly of jungle and swamp, intersected by many rivers flowing generally west to east. The climate is similar to that of Malaya.[1]

Much of the island in 1942 was uncultivated and undeveloped. Communications were poor. Roads were few and, although there were single line railway systems radiating from Medan in the north and Palembang in the south, these served very limited areas and did

---

[1] See page 154.

not connect. The only through road from the north lay along the western side of the island. The country therefore was divided strategically into two parts: the north served by the port of Medan and smaller ports on the Strait of Malacca, and the south by the ports of Palembang and Oosthaven. Ports on the west coast had little strategical importance.

The island possessed no trunk telephone system and communication between the principal towns was by radio telephone with an external connection to Java. This system from a military point of view was far too insecure to be of much value.

The chief economic importance of Sumatra lay in the south in the oilfields and refineries near Palembang.[1] The town of Palembang lies fifty miles up the Moesi River, which divides below the town into a number of channels flowing through mangrove and swamp into the Banka Strait. The main channel is navigable by sea-going vessels. The principal oilfields were in the area surrounding the town and at Djambi, one hundred miles to the north. The oil from these fields was pumped to two refineries at Pladjoe and Soengi Gerong, situated about five miles east of the town on the opposite side of the Moesi River. Roads connected Palembang with the principal towns, and a single track railway ran south to the port of Oosthaven.

There were two airfields at Palembang known as P.1 and P.2. P.1 was the Dutch civil airfield and was, in 1942, a large L-shaped field, with two all-weather runways. It had reasonable dispersal facilities, but there was no accommodation for personnel nearer than the town eight miles to the south. P.2, the other airfield, forty miles to the south-west, was a huge grass field with a perimeter of about ten miles which had good natural cover for aircraft. It could not be seen from the road. Several similar clearings in the area made it difficult to find from the air, even by crews who knew it well. Great care had been taken to preserve its secrecy and the Japanese never discovered it although they frequently flew over it both by day and night, and though at one time more than a hundred aircraft were based on it. The roads between the two airfields were poor; there were no bridges over the Moesi River, to the north of which lay Palembang town and P.1 airfield, and the river crossing had to be made by a ferry which could carry only about half-a-dozen vehicles at a time.

Neither airfield had a radar warning system, and both were dependent on the Dutch Civil Observer Corps stationed at points on concentric circles round the town with radii of 50–100 kilometres. This volunteer observer corps was full of enthusiasm but lacked experience, and warnings were consequently erratic. As soon as the

[1] See Map 26.

British bomber group headquarters had been established,[1] steps had been taken with the willing and energetic help of the Dutch to improve the warning system; but events moved too quickly and the original system was the only one available during the critical period.

The Dutch garrison in Sumatra, mainly composed of East Indian militia, was concentrated for the defence of the airfields and oilfield areas. The Dutch were reluctant to withdraw troops from their already inadequate forces in Java to reinforce the garrison, and from the first it had been clear that reinforcements must come from British sources. At the end of December, General Pownall (Commander-in-Chief, Far East) had told the Chiefs of Staff that he hoped, as soon as 18th Division had arrived, to send an Indian brigade group to strengthen the garrison in Sumatra. But the unexpected speed of the Japanese advance and the increasing threat to Singapore made this impossible.

On the 9th January, two days after his arrival in Singapore on his way to assume command of the ABDA area, General Wavell had reluctantly to inform General ter Poorten that the Indian brigade group would be required in Malaya, and that no infantry could be spared at that time for Sumatra. He added however that he hoped to send two batteries (one light and one heavy) of anti-aircraft artillery for the protection of the airfields in southern Sumatra which were fast becoming the centre from which the air defence of both Singapore and Sumatra itself would have to be carried out.

Later, when it became obvious that Singapore Island would be invaded and that reinforcements arriving in February and March could not be landed there, Wavell decided that the first Australian division to arrive (due at the end of February) would be used in Sumatra, and the second division and 7th Armoured Brigade (due in March) in Java. He realized that everything turned on holding the Palembang area till the arrival of the Australians, for if the enemy succeeded in occupying southern Sumatra it would be unprofitable to send reinforcements to Java since they would then inevitably be lost.

After the transfer from Singapore, all aircraft in Sumatra were based on the two Palembang airfields (P. 1 and P. 2). The combined strength of the British and Dutch aircraft towards the end of January was the equivalent of three light bomber and three fighter squadrons. The crews were given no respite. On the 27th January, owing to the removal of the Dutch Buffalo fighter squadron to Java, Blenheim bombers had to act as fighter escort to the convoy carrying 18th Division during its passage through the Banka Strait, while the remainder of the bombers stood by in case of attack by surface

---

[1] See page 323.

forces. During the first week in February repeated attacks were made on airfields in Malaya and Penang, and even as far north as the docks at Singora. The strikes were of necessity pitiably small and seldom consisted of more than half a dozen bombers without fighter escort. They operated under appalling difficulties. Strikes had to be made by night, for the first disastrous two days of the war had taught that to send the obsolete British bombers against the Japanese Zeros without fighter escort was little short of suicide. Air navigation in the inky blackness of a moonless tropical night, when thunderstorms of great violence and magnitude were frequent, was hardly less hazardous. To reach their targets in Malaya the bombers had to fly long distances over mountainous jungle without the aid of radar and with the primitive equipment of 1942. The strain on the bomber crews was heavy. They more often than not failed to hit their targets, but they did well to achieve such modest success as they did.

Signs that the enemy was preparing to launch an attack on southern Sumatra had become evident by the end of January. Japanese aircraft began to make daily reconnaissance flights over Palembang and Banka Island, Allied convoys were attacked in the Banka Strait and the scale and intensity of bombing attacks on the airfield at Palembang steadily increased.

Japanese bombers made P.1 airfield their principal target and took a heavy toll of the already overworked and depleted British squadrons, for the anti-aircraft defences were inadequate and the warning system ineffective. P.2 airfield however remained unmolested. The attacks on P.1 were made, with typical Japanese inflexibility, only between the hours of 8.30 a.m. and 5.30 p.m. Immunity could be relied upon at other times of the day and advantage was quickly taken of this to fly aircraft from P.1 to P.2. Nevertheless, during the second week in February sixteen Hurricanes and five Blenheims were destroyed in the air or on the ground. The arrival of thirty-nine Hurricanes in the *Athene* at Batavia on the 6th February enabled the wastage to be covered but did not increase the air strength in the island.

Meanwhile intelligence had been received at ABDA Headquarters early in February giving more definite indications of a Japanese plan to attack Palembang. On the 4th February the *Hobart* from Batavia and two destroyers, withdrawn from the escort of a convoy nearing Singapore, joined the *Exeter* and made a search for enemy forces north of Banka Island. The ships were attacked by waves of bombers on the 5th, but escaped damage. No enemy ships were sighted and the force returned to Batavia. Dutch submarines were sent to patrol the waters north of the island.

Indications which had already been received that an attack on southern Sumatra was imminent were strengthened by the receipt of information on the 4th February that an enemy convoy from Saigon had been ordered to rendezvous at the Anamba Islands on the 5th February, and by increased air activity over Banka and Billiton. General Wavell therefore asked General ter Poorten on the 5th February to send two battalions from Java to strengthen the garrison of southern Sumatra. One of these was sent to Palembang and the other provided garrisons for the islands of Banka and Billiton. Some airmen, especially trained for action against parachute troops, and two anti-aircraft batteries reached Palembang early in the month (though some of the guns and ammunition were lost through enemy action on the way). On the 6th a reconnaissance aircraft from Palembang reported a cruiser, two or possibly four destroyers and four merchant ships at anchor off these islands. There was the possibility that this force might be used for a seaborne attack on Singapore Island. But on the 10th intelligence was received at ABDA Command Headquarters that the Japanese were using the Anambas as the base for a force which had been ordered to be north of Banka and Billiton on the 13th. By the 11th reconnaissance showed that the size of the force had considerably increased and included fourteen warships as well as a number of small craft. There were also indications of a concentration of Japanese air strength in Borneo, which would be well placed for support of operations in the Palembang area. Since it was now clear that an attack on Palembang was likely to take place within a very few days, Wavell gave orders that all shipping was to be cleared from the Moesi River, and that a naval striking force, under command of Admiral Doorman, was to assemble at the western end of Java in readiness to attack the convoy from the Anambas as soon as it moved southwards.

On the night of the 11th/12th a force of twenty-one Hudson and Blenheim bombers was ordered to attack the convoy. It met with nothing but misfortune. Three aircraft crashed on taking off from P.2 airfield; the pilot of a fourth returned to make a hazardous landing in a thunderstorm, with all blind-flying instruments unserviceable and only the flashes from the lightning to guide him. Owing to the bad weather only five aircraft reached the Anambas. Four dropped their bombs in the target area which was obscured by low cloud, and the fifth jettisoned its load. On the evening of the 13th a single aircraft was sent to investigate. It reported that the enemy ships had left the Anambas, and that a large number of Japanese transports under a strong naval escort had been sighted north of Banka Island moving towards the Strait. The invasion of southern Sumatra had begun.

CHAPTER XXII

PRELUDE TO THE ASSAULT
ON SINGAPORE ISLAND

See Map 21

T HE ISLAND OF SINGAPORE, connected to the mainland across the Johore Strait by a causeway, is about the size of the Isle of Wight which in shape it somewhat resembles. It has a maximum length from east to west of about twenty-seven miles and a maximum width from north to south of thirteen miles. The Strait varies in width from about six hundred to five thousand yards, and is about its narrowest at the Causeway. At high water it is navigable by small vessels from the western entrance by a difficult and narrow channel, but from the eastern entrance it can be used by the largest ships as far as the Naval Base.

The surface of the island is generally undulating. The only features of importance are the group of hills in the centre—including Bukit Timah and Bukit Mandai—which rise to some 600 feet. From these an extensive view can be obtained over the greater part of the island and the Strait. In the south the Pasir Panjang ridge, some four miles in length, overlooks the western approaches to Singapore. Although in 1942 there were considerable areas of derelict land covered with secondary jungle, there were also many large rubber and other plantations, orchards and small market gardens. The town of Singapore is at the southern point of the island, and in 1942, with the commercial port stretched for about six miles along the water front. On the north side of the town is the large residential area covering several square miles.

The coastline, except on the south-east, is broken by many small rivers and creeks flanked by mangrove swamps; at high tide the higher ground between these swamps becomes a series of islands. There are a number of good roads, most of which converge on Singapore.

The bulk of the population of the island was concentrated in or near the town, the total of whose peacetime inhabitants (about 550,000) had by the end of January 1942 been nearly doubled by the influx of refugees. Over the rest of the island the population was fairly evenly distributed. There were few large villages and these were usually at important road junctions.

The pre-war daily consumption of water on the island averaged about twenty-four million gallons, of which seventeen million came from three reservoirs in a municipal catchment area in the centre of the island, consisting of primary jungle traversed by few tracks. Ten million gallons were supplied daily from a reservoir on the mainland by a pipeline carried over the Causeway. By mid-January 1942, despite the increased population, the consumption had been reduced by rigid economies to fifteen million gallons a day; an amount which could be supplied indefinitely from the reservoirs on the island so long as there was no wastage.

The plan for the defence of the island had of necessity to be based on the organization that existed at the outbreak of war. The permanent fixed defences, built up over a period of nearly twenty years, were designed primarily to ensure the security of the Naval Base against attack from seaward. The north coast of the island was without permanent beach defences and was vulnerable to attack from the mainland. This was not however due to any oversight. In 1938 General Dobbie had begun to construct defences in Johore to cover the Base against attacks from the north; these defences, had they been completed, would have been useful as a line to fall back on, but they would not by themselves have sufficed. When the Japanese entered Indo-China in 1940 the defence of the Base necessitated holding the whole of the Malay peninsula by land and air forces, with a forward line of defences on the southern frontier of Siam.

A general reconnaissance of the northern shores of the island had been ordered on the 23rd December 1941, but nothing further appears to have been done till the 9th January, after General Wavell's first visit, when 1st and 2nd Malaya Brigades were instructed to reconnoitre specific sectors of the north coast.[1] Despite considerable pressure from Wavell little more was done until the 23rd when an outline plan for the defence of the island was issued, followed by a more detailed one on the 28th.[2] By that time it was too late, for civil labour was no longer available. Labour recruited by the Director General of Civil Defence had been allotted to the preparation of fighter strips and to the docks, both of which were obvious targets for the Japanese bombers. Labour exposed to frequent air raids quickly scattered, and hesitated to come forward again. As a result very little construction had been started by the end of the month.

Before the withdrawal from the mainland, the defence of the island had been organized as the Singapore Fortress Command, under General Keith Simmons. The Fortress comprised the island of

---

[1] See page 285.
[2] See page 340.

Singapore with its adjacent islands, the island of Tekong Besar and also Pengerang on the south-east coast of Johore. It was not a fortress in the strict sense of the word, but was so named for the sake of convenience.

The defences were divided into three: the fixed (coastal) defences, the beach defences and the anti-aircraft defences. The first two were under command of the Fortress Commander, but the last came directly under Headquarters, Malaya Command, to enable the gun and fighter defence of the island to be co-ordinated.

The fixed defences comprised the Changi Fire Command, which covered the eastern approaches to the Naval Base, and the Faber Fire Command covering the approaches to Keppel Harbour and the western channel of the Johore Strait. The rapid progress of the Japanese advance southwards emphasized the need for the fixed defences to be ready to meet a landward attack as well as an attack from seawards, for which they had been sited. This raised many difficulties for not all the guns could be brought to bear to the north, and their ammunition was armour-piercing for use against ships. The 9·2-inch guns had however a limited amount of high explosive ammunition suitable for use against land targets.[1] Observation of fire was difficult, the field of view inland was limited, there were no communications and, in the face of Japanese superiority, air observation was out of the question. Nevertheless a temporary counter-bombardment organization was evolved.

The beach defences had been designed to cover that part of the south coast of the island which appeared suitable for enemy landings. They extended along the beaches for some twenty miles from Changi and consisted of concrete pill-boxes at intervals of about 600 yards, anti-tank and anti-boat obstacles made of wood, 18-pounder field guns, land mines and barbed wire. Two positions had been selected to protect the centre of the island in case of enemy landings on the east or west coasts. The position on the east—known as the Serangoon Line—was sited between the airfield at Kallang and Paya Lebar some four miles to the north; while that on the west—known as the Jurong Line—covered the narrow stretch of land between the sources of the Sungei Kranji flowing northwards and the Sungei Jurong flowing southwards. These had been reconnoitred before the outbreak of war and a layout of the defences prepared, but no works had been constructed or trenches dug. During January, on the Jurong Line an anti-tank ditch had been partially dug, a few section posts had been constructed and some clearing had been undertaken to provide a field of fire, but no other preparations had been made by the time the troops were withdrawn from Johore.

---

[1] Thirty rounds per gun.

At the end of January the anti-aircraft defences, after all guns and searchlights from Johore had been withdrawn to the island, consisted of four heavy anti-aircraft regiments (plus one battery), two light anti-aircraft regiments (less one battery), a total of about one hundred and fifty guns, and one searchlight regiment. These were sited to cover the airfields, Keppel Harbour and other vulnerable points. Their efficiency however was much reduced, as the evacuation of the mainland had resulted in the loss of the greater part of the warning system.

After the withdrawal had been completed on the 31st January, General Percival assumed operational command of all troops on the island. The strength of the garrison was approximately 85,000 men, but this included some 15,000 base, administrative and non-combatant troops. The infantry consisted of thirteen British, six Australian, seventeen Indian, and two Malay battalions, the equivalent of the infantry of about four and a third divisions. In addition there were three machine-gun battalions (two British and one Australian), one reconnaissance battalion, three Straits Settlements Volunteer battalions and four Indian State Force battalions organized for airfield defence only. On paper this appeared to be a formidable force, but it was far from being so. Of the British units, six infantry battalions (54th and 55th Brigades of 18th Division) had only recently landed; one machine-gun battalion and the reconnaissance unit were due to disembark on the 5th February and the remaining seven battalions were all much under strength. Of the Australian units only 2/4th Machine-Gun Battalion was complete. The remainder had been brought up to strength with untrained reinforcements. Two battalions, 2/19th with 370 and 2/29th with 500 reinforcements, had as a result a greatly reduced fighting value. To increase the Australian strength General Bennett had used the spare infantry reinforcements to add a platoon to each company of his six battalions, and had formed a Special Reserve Battalion (440 strong) of three companies from men of the Australian Army Service Corps and the reinforcements for 2/4th Machine-Gun Battalion. Of the Indian battalions, only 2/17th Dogras—a pre-war regular battalion which had not seen action on the mainland—was up to strength; three battalions (44th Brigade) had recently arrived from India and were semi-trained; nine battalions, having been hastily reorganized, included a high percentage of young recruits and were very short of officers; four battalions were in process of being re-formed and could not be considered fit for action. The two Malay battalions had not seen active service and their value was unknown, and, with the exception of their European companies, the three Volunteer battalions were fit only for static defence.

Many units, particularly those which had taken part in the long retreat on the mainland, were short of weapons. Their morale, lowered by their experiences, suffered further when they realized that the air forces were being withdrawn from Singapore and that the Naval Base had been evacuated. Yet it was on these men that the defence of the island depended.

General Percival estimated at the time that the Japanese would use three divisions for their attack on the island—the *Imperial Guards Division, 5th Division* and one division presumed to have landed at Endau but not yet identified. He thought that they had other divisions in local reserve in Malaya and a general reserve in Indo-China. He knew that they had strong armoured forces and might have some airborne troops, and he expected them to lose no time in launching their offensive. He estimated that they would require approximately one week for preparation. He thought that their main assault might be launched either on the north-west coast of the island or, by way of the Johore River from Kota Tinggi, on the north-east coast.[1] He felt he could not discount a direct seaborne attack on the south-east coast, launched from the Anambas, or a subsidiary seaborne attack on the south-west coast of the island by way of the Strait of Malacca. Airborne attacks on the airfields were also probable. He decided therefore that he would have to guard against all these and defend the whole seventy miles of coastline.

He considered two possible alternative plans—the first, to prevent the Japanese landing or, if they succeeded in doing so, to stop them near the beaches and destroy them or drive them out by counterattack; the second, to hold the coastline thinly, retaining large reserves with a view to fighting a battle inland. The first alternative had the disadvantage that it was not possible with the available forces to build up a really strong coastal defence all round the island. Further, the coastline was too intersected with creeks and mangrove for any normal form of beach defence. The defences would therefore have to take the form of defended localities to cover the lines of approach afforded by rivers, creeks and roads leading inland, supported by mobile reserves. The lack of depth in which to fight a defensive battle in front of the vital areas, which included the greater part of the centre of the island, was, he considered, the main disadvantage of the second alternative. Bearing in mind the close nature of the country, which would favour the enemy, and also the demoralizing effect which a successful landing would have both on the troops and on the civil population, Percival decided to adopt the first alternative despite its inherent defects. Since in his opinion the terrain was unsuitable for the handling of large forces, he decided to leave the

[1] See Map 5.

control of the battle in the hands of his subordinate commanders and from time to time supply them with such resources and give them such instructions as he thought necessary.

Accordingly he organized the defence of the island in the way he had outlined to General Wavell on the 24th January, dividing it into three areas—Northern, Southern and Western, which together included the entire coastline of the island. Northern Area extended from Changi to the Causeway; III Corps, consisting of 11th Indian and 18th British Divisions, was made responsible for it.[1] Southern Area extended from Changi along the south coast to the Sungei Jurong and was held by the 1st and 2nd Malaya and the Straits Settlements Volunteer Infantry Brigades under Fortress Command. Western Area extended from the Sungei Jurong round the west coast to the Causeway. General Bennett was made responsible for this area and given 8th Australian Division and 44th Indian Infantry Brigade. Each area was to find its own reserves; 12th Indian Infantry Brigade (Brigadier Paris) was to form the Command Reserve.[2] The 11th Indian, 18th British and 8th Australian Divisions were each left with their normal quota of field artillery. Of the two field regiments thrown up when 9th Indian Division was disbanded, one was allotted to Western Area to cover 44th Brigade and the other to Southern Area. As a result Northern Area had five field artillery regiments and three batteries (two of which were equipped with 75-mm. field guns), two anti-tank and one mountain regiment; Western Area three field artillery regiments and three anti-tank batteries; and Southern Area one field regiment and one anti-tank battery.

The outlying defences in some of the adjoining islands were to be given weak garrisons, which were all that could be spared. In addition a small force of irregulars, recruited from Chinese of all classes and political opinions, which had been operating on the mainland, was expanded and became known as 'Dalforce'.[3] It was only partly armed and trained, but detachments were placed under orders of the area commanders to assist in patrolling the mangrove swamps, where landings might take place, and to work with fighting patrols on the mainland.

All administrative units which were an integral part of III Corps and 8th Australian Division, other than hospitals, were located in the areas allotted to the formations to which they belonged; thus many of them were within range of the enemy artillery and suffered

---

[1] 9th Division, after the loss of 22nd Indian Infantry Brigade, had been reduced to one weak infantry brigade. It was therefore broken up, 8th Brigade being absorbed into 11th Division.

[2] This brigade had two battalions only: 2nd Argyll and Sutherland Highlanders which then consisted of 250 Argylls and 150 Marines, and 4/19th Hyderabad some 500 strong, of which the majority were semi-trained recruits. The 5/2nd Punjab has not yet fit fit in active.

[3] Locally enlisted Chinese under British officers. The force was to have an initial strength of 2,000.

accordingly. Administrative units which had arms were made responsible for their own local defence. Although a number of corps and line of communication units were by that time surplus to requirements, no steps were taken to use the manpower thus freed to form infantry units until well after the enemy was established on the island. Stragglers' posts in brigade and divisional areas were not organized nor were any steps taken to tighten up security arrangements. On the 4th February civilians were evacuated from a belt one mile deep along the north coast, a difficult task owing to the numbers and the different nationalities involved. Enemy agents were active and the Japanese commanders were well supplied with intelligence regarding the British dispositions. As an example of this, a broadcast on the Tokyo radio was picked up one morning. It said, ' . . . Australian General Hospital move from . . . today.' That afternoon a salvo of shell fell in the hospital grounds, presumably as a notice to quit. The unit was moved before nightfall and after dark the building was badly damaged by a heavy bombardment.

Owing to the shortage of civilian labourers, who continued to disappear daily, work on the defences had to be undertaken almost entirely by the troops who were to occupy them. Since digging was usually impossible near the beaches, these defences normally consisted of breastworks protected by double-apron barbed-wire fences and anti-tank mines. Defended localities and gun positions were prepared for all-round defence. Forward and support lines were hurriedly erected, and ten days' reserves of ammunition and supplies dumped in forward zones. To avoid air observation most of this work in both Northern and Western Areas had to be done at night.

The III Corps, in whose area the Naval Base lay, had taken over responsibility for its defence and the elaborate denial scheme (known as Scheme 'Q'), which was to have been carried out by the dockyard staff, was handed over to the C.R.E. of 11th Division. When on the 28th the withdrawal to the island had been ordered, Admiral Spooner, in view of the Admiralty's reminder of the timely evacuation of skilled personnel,[1] had transferred the whole of the European naval and civilian dockyard staff to Singapore, and on the 31st had sent the greater part to Ceylon, retaining only a small nucleus in the town to maintain local defence facilities and to give technical advice to the army in the work of demolition.

No doubt the Admiral wished to seize the opportunity of evacuating valuable technicians while shipping was still available but the hurried evacuation of the Base left an unfortunate impression in the minds of many soldiers who did not know that the Admiral, although perhaps precipitately, was acting under instructions. Neither Headquarters, Malaya Command, nor III Corps appears to have

---

[1] See page 318.

been informed that Scheme 'Q' had been handed over and that 11th Division was taking over the work of demolition, nor did the Admiral discuss this important decision with General Percival. The last minute transfer of responsibility and the lack of co-ordination on the proper level led to somewhat haphazard denial, which was further complicated by the decision to delay final destruction, not only in the dockyard but throughout Singapore, until the last possible moment.

On the 2nd February General Percival told the Chiefs of Staff that plans for denial of material and equipment likely to be of use to the enemy had been prepared and the responsibility for carrying it out defined. He pointed out however that he had been given two objects: to hold Singapore to the last and to ensure that in the last resort a complete scorched earth policy was carried out. He could not, he said, do both. He was convinced that to carry out complete denial immediately would so undermine the morale of both troops and public as to prejudice seriously his ability to hold Singapore. The Chiefs of Staff replied on the 6th that the docks and workshops in the Naval Base should be given priority and that all fortress guns should be destroyed and, as the sites of these were in forbidden areas, these important demolitions could be made forthwith.

A start had in fact already been made in the Naval Base. The large floating dock had been scuttled to clear the line of fire across the Strait; all navigable ships and boats as well as the smaller floating dock had been sailed to Keppel Harbour and the remainder destroyed. A search had been made on both sides of the Strait to collect and destroy small craft but many of these had been hidden by their owners and escaped destruction. The pumping machinery of the King George V graving dock had been destroyed and on the 5th the caisson had been wrecked. Meanwhile the removal of valuable stores and equipment was being carried out by small parties from the dockyard staff left at Singapore and by the army. Work was hampered by a shortage of labour and transport and by the fact that after the 3rd February the Naval Base was under fire and work could be carried out only at night.

Military establishments and depots had been made responsible for the preparation and execution of their own denial schemes, which were to be carried out only on the orders of the General Officer Commanding, Malaya. In the event of it not being possible for him to issue such orders, commanders on the spot were to take the initiative themselves. Similar arrangements, particularly for the destruction of petrol and oil stocks, had been made by the Rear-Admiral, Malaya, and the Air Officer Commanding, Far East.

The destruction of the ammunition in the main magazines on the island (near Alexandra) presented a difficult problem, for it could not be done without causing widespread damage over an area which contained a number of hospitals.[1] Since in his opinion this ammunition would be of no use to the enemy, Percival told the Chiefs of Staff that he proposed to exempt it from the denial plans. The Chiefs of Staff however ruled that, should the worst appear imminent and inevitable, as much ammunition as possible should be fired off at the enemy, and the balance, together with the magazines themselves, should then be destroyed or otherwise prevented from falling into Japanese hands. As the defences had been sited to meet a seaborne attack, some magazines had been constructed on the northern side of the island. One of the largest of these was near Kranji and there were others at Nee Soon and Seletar, areas likely to be overrun if the enemy succeeded in obtaining a foothold on the island. The removal of ammunition from these magazines was of considerable importance, for the total stocks on the island were small, but, owing to shortage of labour and interference by shelling, little was accomplished, and as a result, much of the reserves of field-gun ammunition was captured by the Japanese early in the battle.

It is of interest that the Japanese felt some anxiety lest the British should make use of the millions of gallons of oil and petrol stored on the island, much of it near the northern coastline, to create a barrier of fire along the coast in those areas in which attack was probable. No such steps were however taken and petrol, especially from airfield stocks, was run to waste into rivers and the Strait before the enemy attacked. Some ingenious booby traps designed to spread small quantities of burning oil on the water were constructed and placed in creeks on the north-east coast but, as the enemy did not attack in this area, they were never used.

The Director General of Civil Defence was given the responsibility for the destruction of civil installations, plant and machinery, railway locomotives, stocks of rubber and tin, the docks and the liquor in bonded warehouses and in hotels. Since this involved the destruction, when the need arose, of private property and affected many vested interests, much of the preparatory work had to be carried out in secrecy. The Governor, with the concurrence of the War Council, ruled that Public Services such as water, gas, electricity and sewerage were to be left intact.

In spite of precautions to avoid alarming the population, the work on the defences and the preparations for the denial scheme had a disturbing effect which was aggravated as reports spread of the withdrawal of the air forces. Rumours soon began to circulate that Singapore was not to be defended—a possibility especially alarming to the large Chinese community which had more reason than most to fear the arrival of a triumphant Japanese army. In an endeavour to restore confidence, General Percival published a statement in the

---

[1] See Map 25.

Singapore newspapers in which he explained the need to gain time so as to enable Allied forces to concentrate in the Far East. The task was, he said, to hold the Fortress (sic) until help arrived. He also held a press conference on the 5th February and, later the same day, received a deputation of the unofficial leaders of the European community. At both of these meetings he explained the reason for the withdrawal of the air forces, emphasized the strategic importance of Singapore and made it clear that the island would be defended.

During the night of the 4th/5th February the last of the convoys bringing reinforcements approached Singapore. It consisted of four ships carrying the remaining units of 18th British Division, together with some Indian troops and vehicles. At about 11 a.m. on the 5th the convoy was attacked by bombers, and the *Empress of Asia* which had dropped astern, received several direct hits, caught fire and had to be abandoned. Most of the troops were rescued by H.M.A.S. *Yarra*. Nearly all the weapons and equipment on board, which included the guns of 125th Anti-Tank Regiment, were lost and the ship itself became a total wreck. This was the only vessel in any of the convoys which brought reinforcements to Malaya to be lost through air attack.

Throughout this period the Japanese bombed the dock area on an ever-increasing scale destroying some seventy per cent of the warehouse accommodation, and the loading of stores and equipment for transfer to Sumatra and Java became very difficult. Owing to the frequency of air raids ships had to be dispersed and, while some were loaded direct from the quayside, others had to be loaded at their moorings from lighters. To add to the difficulties, most of the civil dock labour disappeared and had to be replaced by any troops—mostly airmen—who could be spared, but these naturally lacked the skill of professional stevedores. It is not surprising that in such conditions the planned embarkation of men and stores became disorganized. Units inevitably got split up, the men in many instances becoming separated from their equipment. Much of the equipment urgently required by the bomber force in Sumatra could not be loaded at all, while sometimes because of air attacks ships were obliged to sail partly loaded. Bombing of ships during the voyage from Singapore also caused heavy loss, and considerable quantities of technical stores and motor vehicles—all of which were badly needed in Sumatra and Java—were lost at sea.

During the first week of February, 225 Bomber Group based in Sumatra, with an average operational strength of about twenty Hudsons and fifteen Blenheims, was very active. Whenever aircraft could be spared from protecting convoys, attacks were made on enemy-held airfields in Malaya, on Penang harbour and installations at Singora and elsewhere. But the scale of attack was so small that it caused little interference with Japanese preparations for the assault on the island.[1]

Meanwhile the air defence of Singapore was being precariously maintained by the token force left on the island, supported whenever possible by fighters from Sumatra. These fighters were however becoming more and more involved with the defence of the airfields at Palembang.[2] Air raids on Singapore became almost continuous at this stage, and the air defence organization was severely tested by having little or no warning. The force of defending fighters— the flight of Buffaloes soon wasted away and was replaced by Hurricanes—was too small to affect materially the scale of enemy attack. Throughout the first ten days of February the Hurricanes were almost constantly airborne during the hours of daylight, but their task of interception became increasingly difficult. The Japanese, who frequently varied their tactics from low-level attacks against villages and other targets on the island to high-level attacks on the docks, were able to drop their bombs and withdraw before the defending fighters could reach them. Unchallenged therefore, enemy formations of from eighteen to twenty-seven aircraft bombed the town and the harbour and made frequent dive-bombing attacks on the troops in the northern part of the island. The air defence was further handicapped, as had been foreseen, when on the 4th and 5th February the airfields at Seletar, Sembawang and Tengah came under observed artillery fire from the mainland and all operations had to be carried out from the only remaining airfield at Kallang. The Japanese then concentrated their bombing attacks on that airfield, which was soon so badly cratered that, by the 6th, fighter pilots experienced great difficulty in taking off and landing.

The three Area Commanders had meanwhile disposed their forces as follows:[3]

Northern Area: Heath had allotted 18th Division to hold the seven mile line from Changi to the Sungei Seletar with its two brigades (54th and 55th) in the line. The 11th Division held the remaining seven miles from the Sungei Seletar to the Causeway with two brigades (53rd and 28th) forward and one (8th) in reserve. The 15th

---

[1] Order of Battle 225 (B) Group:

1 Squadron R.A.A.F.:	16 Hudson II	
8 Squadron ,,	6 Hudson III	
34 Squadron R.A.F.:	6 Blenheim IV	
62 Squadron ,,	10 Hudson III and 5 Blenheim I	
27 Squadron ,,	3 Blenheim I	
84 Squadron ,,	10 Blenheim IV ⎱ Recently arrived by air	
211 Squadron ,,	4 Blenheim IV ⎰ from the Middle East.	

[2] See Chapter XXI.

[3] For order of battle on the 8th February see Appendix 21.

brigade which had been reconstituted since its rescue from the west coast, became III Corps Reserve.

Southern Area: Keith Simmons had allotted 2nd Malaya Brigade and the S.S.V.F. Brigade to hold the beaches from Changi to Keppel Harbour, 1st Malaya Brigade those west of Singapore to the Sungei Jurong and 2/17th Dogras to hold Pulau Tekong Besar.

Western Area: Since it was here that the Japanese made their first landings, the problem of its defence merits careful examination. The Sungei Kranji and the Sungei Berih divided the area into three unequal parts: the sector from the Causeway to the Sungei Kranji with one and a half miles of coastline facing north; the eight mile sector between the two rivers facing north-west and the ten mile sector at the south-west corner of the island. The first two of these contained the most likely points of attack. Difficulties of communications and control prevented any of the three brigades being placed astride the rivers. In the outline plan for the defence of the island, issued on the 28th January, a brigade had therefore been allotted to each sector.

The inexperienced 44th Indian Brigade had been given the south-west sector—the least likely to be attacked—before the withdrawal from Johore, and Bennett had selected his strongest brigade (22nd) for the extensive north-western sector and 27th Brigade, which had borne the brunt of the retreat from Gemas, for the shorter Causeway sector. Because of the comparatively narrow frontage to be held by the last named, he had placed one of its battalions in area reserve.[1] The 2/29th Battalion which at this time was fit only for a static role, for after the Bakri–Parit Sulong action it had been entirely reconstituted (largely from untrained recruits) and lacked its proper quotas of N.C.Os. and specialists, was selected as the reserve. Bennett was precluded from holding a brigade in reserve for a deliberate counter-attack role by the lack of troops and Percival's instructions that the whole coastline had to be defended on the beaches.

The 27th Australian Brigade had been disposed with 2/30th Battalion from Woodlands to the Sungei Mandai and 2/26th in depth from Kranji southwards. One company of 2/4th Machine-Gun Battalion covered the coastline. The 2/10th Field Regiment (less one battery) and 13th Anti-Tank Battery were in support.

The defence of the long front allotted to 22nd Australian Brigade had presented Brigadier Taylor with a difficult problem. His sector included the whole of a large peninsula connected to the rest of the island by the narrow neck of land between Ama Keng village and the Sungei Berih. Moreover the coast was intersected by many creeks and inlets fringed by mangrove swamps which made the siting of the defences difficult, and afforded the enemy opportunities for infiltration. Because of the extent of this front, Taylor was unable to

---

[1] See Map 22.

hold it with two battalions and keep one in reserve. He had therefore decided to use all three battalions in defended localities on or
near the coast, each with local reserves. The 2/20th Battalion with a
company of 'Dalforce' was placed on the right—the most easily
defended part of the brigade area—with a front of some 7,000 yards
between the Sungei Kranji and the Sungei Sarimbun; 2/18th
Battalion in the centre on a 3,500 yards front between the Sungei
Sarimbun and Tanjong Murai; and the reconstituted 2/19th
Battalion on the left with a front of 3,500 yards from Tanjong Murai
to the Sungei Berih. Each battalion had three companies forward and
one in local reserve sited to protect as far as possible the short neck of
land between Ama Keng and Sungei Berih. A company of 2/4th
Machine-Gun Battalion was distributed along the whole front;
2/15th Field Regiment and 15th Anti-Tank Battery were in support.
The Jind Infantry Battalion, responsible for the local defence of
Tengah airfields, had been placed under Taylor's command.

When training, 22nd Australian Brigade had been taught that
when holding a defensive position the forward troops, if surrounded
and in danger of being overwhelmed, should fight their way back to
their respective company headquarters and there form defensive
perimeters. If these in turn were overrun, the companies were to fall
back to previously selected areas and establish battalion perimeters
which, loosely linked together, would form a final defensive zone. In
this instance the final line was to be the Ama Keng neck. This
unorthodox method of conducting a defensive action was fraught
with danger even with trained troops, but, with one of the battalions
concerned containing a high percentage of untrained men, the danger
was even greater.

The 44th Indian Brigade (Brigadier G. C. Ballentine) had two and
a half battalions on the coast and two companies in reserve.[1] It was
supported by 5th Field Regiment, 16th Anti-Tank Battery and one
company of 2/4th Machine-Gun Battalion. In all three sectors of
Western Area beach searchlights, manned by 5th Searchlight
Regiment and supplemented by headlights removed from cars, were
sited to illuminate those areas in which it was thought landings might
be attempted.

No consideration appears to have been given by Bennett to the
preparation of a defensive position across the Ama Keng neck or to
the incorporation of the Jurong Line in the defensive plan, although
the danger of infiltration between the widely dispersed forward units
should have been evident. The staff of Western Area, on their own
initiative however, sent divisional liaison officers, together with artillery and signal representatives, to reconnoitre the Jurong Line.

44th Indian Infantry Brigade consisted of: 6/1st Punjab, 7/8th Punjab, 6/14th Punjab.

When studying the problem of the assault on Singapore Island before the outbreak of war the Japanese had come to the conclusion that the most favourable line of attack would be across the narrow portion of the Johore Strait on the north-west coast of the island. The Johore coast opposite this area was intersected by a number of rivers and had many roads so that, provided they had air superiority, they could make their preparations for the assault in comparative secrecy. They had appreciated that the British defence would be based on holding initially the line Changi–the northern shore to the Causeway–and thence the line of the Sungei Kranji and Sungei Jurong, with only outposts to the west of these two rivers.

On reaching the south coast of Johore on the 31st January, General Yamashita concentrated *5th* and *18th Divisions* in the Sungei Skudai area and the *Imperial Guards Division* in the Sungei Tebrau area. His intelligence reports indicated that the British expected the main attack to be launched against the Naval Base area and that the defences were stronger there than elsewhere. He therefore decided to adhere to the pre-war plan and mount his main attack against the north-west coast of the island between Tanjong Buloh and Tanjong Murai, with *18th Division* on the right and *5th Division* on the left. A subsidiary attack by the *Imperial Guards Division* immediately west of the Causeway was to take place shortly after the main attack had been launched.

The *18th Division* was to attack with two regiments and a battalion forward and one regiment, less one battalion, in reserve. The *5th Division* was to deploy greater strength with three regiments in the line and one in reserve. The main attack involved a total of sixteen battalions, with a further five in reserve, on a front of four and a half miles—a very considerable concentration of force. The *1st Tank Regiment* was attached to *5th Division*. The main attack was to be launched between 8 p.m. and midnight on the 8th/9th February. The first objective was Tengah airfield, to be reached by the morning of the 9th, and the second the general line Point 138–Bukit Panjang Village.

The *Imperial Guards Division*, consisting at this time of two regiments plus one battalion, was given the task, aided by deceptive artillery concentrations, of diverting the attention of the defenders to the east of the Causeway. With this object dummy camps were erected east of the Sungei Tebrau; convoys of lorries moving eastwards were organized and a landing on Pulau Ubin was to be staged on the night of the 7th/8th. Twenty-four hours after the main attack the division was to cross the Strait immediately west of the Causeway and, having landed, swing east towards the Sungei Seletar and then south to interpose itself between Singapore and Changi, in order to prevent the British withdrawing into the Changi area. This attack was to be carried out by one regiment and a battalion, while the other regiment was kept in reserve. The *14th Tank Regiment* was attached to this division.[1]

The divisions were not to move forward from their concentration areas to the northern shores of the Strait until the day before the main assault. The artillery preparation was to continue for a period of several days while the arrangements for the attack were being completed, and was to be directed against the forward defences, communications, the airfield, the Naval Base and battery positions in the northern part of the island. In addition to the normal allotment of divisional artillery, two medium field regiments and one heavy artillery regiment were to be deployed in the vicinity of Johore Bahru directly under the command of *25th Army*—a concentration of 168 guns.

On the 1st February, from positions on high ground behind Johore Bahru and with the aid of an observation balloon, the Japanese opened harassing fire against targets on the island, but it was not until the 5th that they brought the full weight of their artillery to bear. Fire was then directed on the three northern airfields, the Naval Base and key points on the main roads. The British artillery, using roving sections to avoid giving away its permanent positions, replied with counter-bombardment and harrassing fire against enemy observation posts on the mainland. It was however limited in these tasks to an average expenditure of only twenty rounds a gun a day since ammunition stocks, especially for the 25-pounder guns, were low and Percival was planning for a three months' siege. Thus the enemy was allowed to make his preparations with negligible interference, while his aircraft, practically unmolested, were able to pinpoint the defences.

Arrangements do not appear to have been made before the withdrawal from Johore to leave behind small parties drawn from local forces and equipped with wireless to provide information of enemy movements. Thus, in the absence of air reconnaissance, reliance had to be placed on information supplied by patrols sent across the Strait. On the 5th and 6th February, Japanese artillery fire was directed mainly on the north-eastern coast of the island and the area around the southern end of the Causeway, whereas on the north-western front enemy artillery confined its activities to intermittent harassing fire. This seemed to indicate that the enemy intended an assault on either III Corps or 27th Australian Brigade front. No patrols from 22nd Australian Brigade front had crossed to the Johore shore, but nightly patrols across the Strait east of the Causeway reported no enemy concentrations.

---

[1] See Appendix 25 for detailed Japanese order of battle.

By the 6th, Malaya Command intelligence staff had come to the conclusion that all indications pointed to an assault being launched on the north-western corner of the island within the next few days. Accordingly Western Area was ordered to send over patrols that night to search for enemy concentrations, and to ascertain the cause of the sounds of chopping and hammering which had been heard in the area.

During the night of the 7th/8th a boat, carrying some thirty Japanese approaching the island just west of the Causeway, was destroyed and its occupants killed by machine-gun fire; a small party of enemy troops landed on Pulau Ubin and occupied that island, patrols from 4th Norfolk withdrawing to Changi. The two patrols from 22nd Australian Brigade, which had made a reconnaissance of the coast between the Sungei Malayu and the Sungei Pendas to a depth of about one and a half miles, returned and reported that large enemy forces were concentrating in the rubber plantations and around the river estuaries and that there was much movement of motor transport on the roads in that area. They also brought back information of the location of some Japanese units and their headquarters. They had not seen any landing craft, for they had not penetrated as far as the Sungei Skudai or to the upper reaches of the Sungei Malayu, the only areas where these craft could be launched.[1] These reports clearly confirmed the views of the intelligence staff that the assault was likely to be launched against Western Area, but gave no definite indication of the date of attack. They were not however passed to Malaya Command until about 3.30 p.m. on the afternoon of the 8th. Bennett then asked for a reconnaissance aircraft to check their accuracy and to observe for his artillery. No aircraft was available so, late that afternoon, Western Area artillery put down unobserved harassing fire on the areas indicated by the patrols' reports. It should now have been clear to all concerned that the stage had been set and that the curtain was about to rise.

---

[1] See Appendix 26.

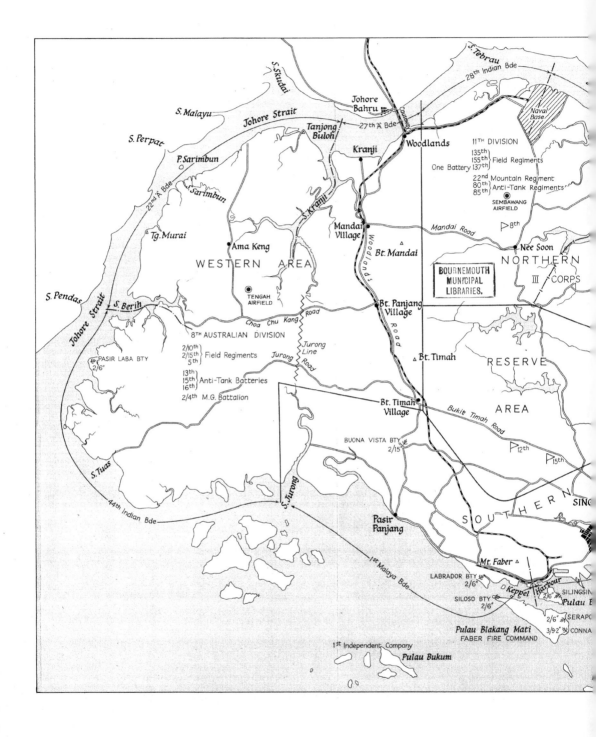

S. Tebrau

28th Indian Bde

Naval Base

S. Skudai

S. Malayu

Johore Strait

Johore Bahru

Tanjong Buloh

27th "A" Bde

Causeway

S. Perpat

P. Sarimbun

Kranji

Woodlands

11TH DIVISION

135th
155th Field Regiments
137th

One Battery

S. Sarimbun

22nd Mountain Regiment
80th Anti-Tank Regiments
85th

SEMBAWANG
AIRFIELD

22nd "A" Bde

S. Kranji

Mandai
Village

Mandai Road

▷ 8th

Tg. Murai

Ama Keng

WESTERN   AREA

Woodlands Road

Bt. Mandai

Nee Soon

NORTHERN

BOURNEMOUTH
MUNICIPAL
LIBRARIES.

III ─ CORPS

S. Pendas

Johore Strait

S. Berih

TENGAH
AIRFIELD

Choa Chu Kang Road

Bt. Panjang
Village

Road

Bt. Timah

RESERVE

8TH AUSTRALIAN DIVISION

Jurong
Line

2/10th
2/15th Field Regiments
5th

Jurong Road

AREA

PASIR LABA BTY
2/6"

13th
15th Anti-Tank Batteries
16th

2/4th M.G. Battalion

Bt. Timah
Village

Bukit Timah Road

△ Bt. Timah

S. Tuas

BUONA VISTA BTY
2/15"

▷ 12th   ▷ 15th

44th Indian Bde

S. Jurong

1st Malaya Bde

Pasir
Panjang

S O U T H E R N   SING

Mt. Faber △

LABRADOR BTY
2/6"

Keppel Harbour

2/6" SILINGSI

SILOSO BTY
2/6"

Pulau B

2/6" SERAPO

3/92" CONNA

Pulau Blakang Mati
FABER FIRE COMMAND

1st Independent Company

Pulau Bukum

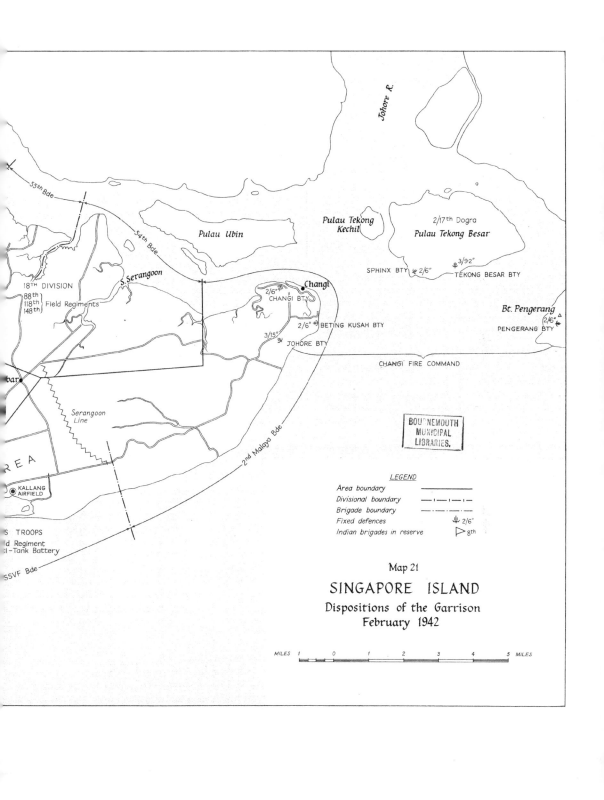

Johore R.

55th Bde

54th Bde

Pulau Ubin

Pulau Tekong
Kechil

2/17th Dogra
Pulau Tekong Besar

SPHINX BTY ⚓ 2/6″   3/92″
                        TEKONG BESAR BTY

18TH DIVISION
88th ⎫
118th ⎬ Field Regiments
148th ⎭

S. Serangoon

Changi
2/6″
CHANGI BTY

2/6″ BETING KUSAH BTY

3/15″
JOHORE BTY

Bt. Pengerang
2/6″ △
PENGERANG BTY

CHANGI FIRE COMMAND

bar

Serangoon
Line

2nd Malaya Bde

BOURNEMOUTH
MUNICIPAL
LIBRARIES.

REA

KALLANG
AIRFIELD

S TROOPS
d Regiment
i-Tank Battery

SSVF Bde

LEGEND

Area boundary	————
Divisional boundary	—·—·—·—
Brigade boundary	—··—··—
Fixed defences	⚓ 2/6″
Indian brigades in reserve	▷ 8th

Map 21

SINGAPORE ISLAND
Dispositions of the Garrison
February 1942

MILES 1   0   1   2   3   4   5 MILES

CHAPTER XXIII

THE BATTLE FOR
SINGAPORE ISLAND

See Maps 22, 23, 24 and 25

AT DAWN on the 8th February enemy air activity increased, and bombing and machine-gun attacks were made on the forward defences in 22nd Australian Brigade's sector. These were followed by an artillery bombardment which by 1.30 p.m. became heavy, the forward defences, headquarters and communications receiving special attention. After a lull at sunset, by which time all telephone lines had been cut, the enemy bombardment was renewed and greatly intensified. Neither Malaya Command nor Western Area Headquarters was however seriously perturbed by this, each apparently thinking either that it was the first of a number of days of softening up, or that the enemy would switch the bombardment back next day to the Causeway and north-eastern shores of the island. As a result no orders were given during the evening for artillery fire to be brought down on the probable enemy forming-up places. At about 10.30 p.m. landing craft were seen approaching the north-west coast, and soon the whole of the front between Tanjong Buloh and Tanjong Murai was being attacked.[1] The assault was supported by mortars from the Johore side of the Strait, from Pulau Sarimbun which the enemy's leading troops had occupied, and from moored landing craft, as well as by heavy artillery concentrations.

Strict instructions had been given by Brigadier Taylor that beach lights were not to be exposed except on the specific instructions of unit commanders, since it was thought that once located they would inevitably be destroyed. With communications severed, such lights as survived the bombardment were never exposed. Neither did the planned defensive artillery fire open immediately, since calls for such fire never reached the batteries. It was not until the S.O.S. light signals sent up by the infantry were seen that the guns opened. The artillery was moreover quite inadequate to meet the demands for defensive fire on the whole brigade front and in some areas, particularly on the front of 2/18th and 2/19th Battalions, the infantry was left almost without artillery support.

---

[1] See Map 22.

Machine-guns however, aided by light from a burning landing craft, took a heavy toll of the first flight and remained in action till their ammunition was exhausted. Some landings were successful only on the second or third attempt, but the weight of the assault was so great that the Japanese were soon able to get a footing ashore along the whole front. Once ashore they quickly made their way inland between the widely separated defended localities, and the Australians, who fought gallantly, found themselves attacked from all sides. The heaviest assaults were delivered on the coast to the north of Pulau Sarimbun and astride the Sungei Murai. Enemy parties, amongst which were men with compasses strapped on to their wrists, began at once to advance through the gaps in the defences towards Ama Keng to cut off the defenders in the forward areas. Five enemy craft which attempted to enter the Sungei Berih estuary were quickly sunk and their occupants killed.

It was not till nearly midnight that Brigadier Taylor was able to give Western Area Headquarters any clear picture of events on his front. He then emphasized his lack of reserves and the need for fresh troops to counter-attack at dawn. Shortly after midnight, as a first move to restoring the situation, General Bennett placed 2/29th Battalion under the command of 22nd Brigade and instructed it to move immediately to Tengah airfield, gave instructions that 2/10th Field Regiment was to bring down fire on the Johore coastline at the mouth of the Sungei Skudai, and asked Malaya Command for maximum air support from first light over the area of the enemy landings. At 3 a.m. on the 9th he ordered the Special Reserve Battalion and the reserve company of 2/4th Machine-Gun Battalion to 'stand to'.[1] At 4.45 a.m. he placed both these units under command of 22nd Brigade, and ordered them forward to Tengah airfield.

To comply with Bennett's request, all aircraft on the island (ten Hurricanes and four obsolete Swordfish) were ordered to be at readiness from 6 a.m. The Hurricanes took off at dawn and successfully intercepted a force of no less than eighty-four aircraft approaching from Johore. After making their first attacks, in which one fighter was lost, they landed at Kallang and by hurriedly refuelling and re-arming were able to make a second attack against the same force. In these two engagements despite the overwhelming odds the Hurricanes destroyed several aircraft.

At about 8.30 a.m., after receiving the morning situation report which indicated that all was quiet in Northern Area, General Percival ordered his only reserve—the weak 12th Indian Brigade—to move at once to Keat Hong, where it was to come under command of Western Area.[2]

---

[1] The formation of the Special Reserve Battalion was completed on the 8th February.

[2] *A.O.O. 9/Sel. Fwsng.*

23. The Bukit Pelandok defile looking west.

24. 5th Japanese Division's point of attack on Singapore Island.

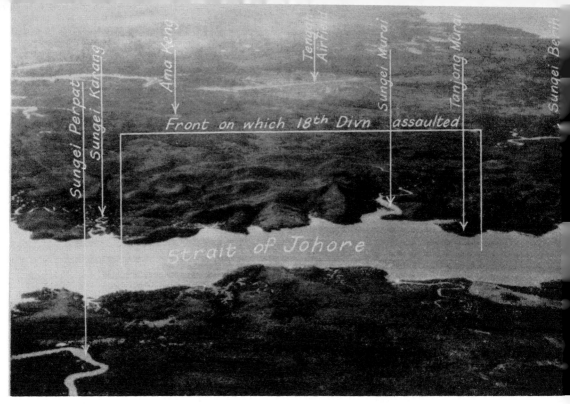

25. *18th Japanese Division*'s point of attack on Singapore Island.

26. *Imperial Guards Division*'s point of attack on Singapore Island.

Meanwhile between 1 a.m. and 3 a.m. the forward troops of all three battalions of 22nd Australian Brigade had been ordered by their commanders to make their way back as best they could to their previously selected battalion perimeters. Engaged at close quarters with the enemy, they found this movement extremely difficult in darkness and over intricate country. Three companies of 2/20th Battalion succeeded by dawn in concentrating in the Namazie Estate about two miles north of Ama Keng but the fourth, as no orders reached it, remained in position; only about half the men of the 2/18th managed to get to their battalion perimeter near this village; the 2/19th, with the exception of its company at Choa Chu Kang which remained in position unmolested, fought its way back to its position with great difficulty. The withdrawal disorganized the whole brigade area. Small parties became separated from their units or lost direction as they moved inland and, missing the battalion perimeters, straggled vaguely onwards. Some were collected later as far back as Bukit Timah, while others eventually reached Singapore where they were reorganized and sent back to their units.

Shortly after dawn, the remnants of 2/18th Battalion were attacked near Ama Keng. Fierce fighting ensued. The battalion, assisted by 2/10th Field Company, counter-attacked and managed to retain its position for some time, but eventually, finding the enemy moving round its southern flank, was forced to withdraw to Tengah airfield which was reached about 9.30 a.m. Further north, when the 2/20th tried to move south at 7.30 a.m. to link up with the 2/18th, it found the enemy in strength astride the road. In attempting to break through, the battalion became split up and only isolated parties, by crossing the Sungei Kranji, reached brigade headquarters at Bulim. Further south, the remnants of the 2/19th, finding themselves surrounded, attempted to cut their way out. They lost heavily in the process and it was only scattered parties that eventually reached Tengah airfield at about 10 a.m. The 22nd Australian Brigade was for the time being no longer a cohesive fighting formation.

There had been considerable delay in collecting the 2/29th which was widely dispersed, for part of it was employed in a defensive role and part was undergoing training; consequently it did not arrive at the airfield until 6 a.m. on the 9th. Taylor then organized a position from the northern end of the airfield to link up with the company of the 2/19th at Choa Chu Kang. He placed the Jind Battalion on the right and the 2/29th on the left and retained the Special Reserve Battalion, which arrived at 7.45 a.m., in reserve at the airfield. Behind this position he then set to work to reorganize what was left of his original three battalions. At about 9.30 a.m. Bennett ordered him to use 2/29th Battalion to recapture the general line Ama Keng–Sungei Berih. Artillery support was organized and zero hour fixed for 1 p.m. During the morning however the enemy worked around his right flank, and Taylor found himself obliged to cancel his orders for the attack.

When at about 10.15 a.m. Brigadier Paris (12th Brigade) reported at Western Area Headquarters, Bennett ordered him to move his brigade forward to gain touch with 22nd Australian Brigade and assist Taylor in preventing enemy infiltration around the headwaters of the Sungei Kranji. The brigade reached Keat Hong at about noon. At about 1.30 p.m., after a discussion between the two brigadiers, 12th Brigade took up a position astride the Choa Chu Kang Road at Milestone 12½ on the northern end of the Jurong Line,[1] with the Argylls on the right and 4/19th Hyderabad on the left.

Taylor feared that his brigade could not hold for long the position he had organized, because the wide frontage and the open nature of the country made it very vulnerable to infiltration during darkness. He had been out of touch with his divisional headquarters since about 10 a.m., and had no knowledge of Bennett's plans or of the situation in 44th Brigade area. He considered the success of the defence now rested on holding the Jurong Line. He realized that if the enemy reached Bulim during the night his brigade would be isolated and an enemy attack might force 12th Brigade out of the Jurong Line. In these circumstances he decided, on his own initiative, to withdraw to a new position facing west from Bulim southwards to the Jurong Road. He placed the Johore Volunteer Engineers to the north of the Choa Chu Kang Road, 2/18th Battalion (then about 400 strong) astride the road, and 2/29th Battalion with the survivors of 2/10th Field Company extending the position along a track to the south-west nearly as far as Milestone 12½ on the Jurong Road. A company of 2/4th Machine-Gun Battalion was in support and the remnants of 2/19th and 2/20th Battalions, each about one company strong, in reserve. At the same time he ordered the Special Reserve Battalion to occupy Point 117 in the Jurong Line, thus prolonging 12th Brigade's position to the south. Meanwhile 2/15th Field Regiment, which had lost eight guns during the night, moved back to previously selected positions south of Bukit Panjang Village, from which it could support the troops holding the Jurong Line.

The Bulim position which Taylor had selected happened to coincide with the outposts of the previously reconnoitred Jurong Line. A divisional liaison officer who had taken part in its reconnaissance had fortunately been sent forward to Bulim and was thus able to direct the troops into their positions. The move was completed by 3 p.m. without interference from the enemy, except for dive-bombing and low-flying attacks which continued throughout the day. Since the

---

[1] See Map 21.

rearward movement uncovered 44th Brigade's right flank, Taylor sent a staff officer to inform Brigadier Ballentine of his intentions.

At about 2.30 p.m. it was suggested to Bennett by his staff that it might be wise to withdraw both 22nd and 44th Brigade into the Jurong Line before dark. This he refused to do. Shortly afterwards telephone communications between 22nd Brigade and Western Area were re-established and Taylor told Bennett that his troops were in the process of withdrawing to the Bulim position. Still an advocate of taking the offensive, Bennett expressed strong disapproval and told Taylor that he had acted wrongly and without orders.

Later that afternoon, Percival visited Headquarters, Western Area. He discussed with Bennett the possibility of using 44th Brigade to counter-attack the enemy's right flank, but dismissed it as impracticable. He then decided that 27th Australian Brigade was to continue to hold the Causeway sector; 44th Brigade was to withdraw from its position on the coast and occupy the southern part of the Jurong Line at Milestone 12 on the Jurong Road; 12th Brigade and the reinforced 22nd Australian Brigade were to occupy the northern part of the Jurong Line in contact with 44th Brigade. He had already ordered III Corps to place 15th Brigade in Command Reserve at one hour's notice to move. He now ordered this brigade to move without delay to a rendezvous near the Racecourse on the Bukit Timah Road, where it was to come under orders of Western Area, to be used to guard against an enemy break-through into the Bukit Timah area where there were large food, petrol, ammunition and supply depots.[1] He ordered the destruction of the oil depots at Kranji and Woodlands that night and directed III Corps to assist the navy in destroying the stores and equipment remaining at the Naval Base.

The 44th Indian Brigade, in its position covering the south-west coast of the island, had not been actively engaged during the day, but it had been shelled and the 6-inch coast defence battery at Pasir Laba had been put out of action by air attack. The Japanese penetration into 22nd Brigade sector, however, threatened to isolate 44th Brigade in the area between the Sungei Jurong and the coast and during the morning Ballentine moved his reserve (two companies) to a position one mile south of Choa Chu Kang to protect his right flank. About noon he was warned by Western Area that in all probability he would have to withdraw to the Jurong Line. He at once concentrated his beach defence guns and some of his scattered machine-gun posts, and thus on receipt of the order at about 4.30 p.m. he was able to move without much delay. By 10 p.m. the brigade, without any serious interference by the enemy, was in its new position. During

---

[1] See Map 23.

the afternoon, a Western Area liaison officer was fired on near 44th Brigade Headquarters. His report of the incident on his arrival at his own headquarters gave Western Area the impression that the brigade would have difficulty in fighting its way back. This was to have serious consequences.

By nightfall it appeared that Western Area would be able temporarily to stabilize the position. With the Jurong Line occupied by the weak 12th Brigade on the right, the Special Reserve Battalion in the centre, 44th Brigade on the left, the reinforced 22nd Australian Brigade in a covering position at Bulim and 15th Brigade in reserve, the situation though far from satisfactory was by no means hopeless. The Japanese *18th* and *5th Divisions* however had captured their first objective, were firmly established on the island and were engaged in bringing over their reserves, transport and tanks as quickly as their resources in landing craft permitted.

After his visit to Western Area on the afternoon of the 9th February, Percival prepared a plan to meet the situation which would arise should the enemy break through and advance down the Bukit Timah Road, thus forcing him to concentrate his forces for the defence of part of the island. He considered two alternatives: either to fall back on the eastern end of the island or to concentrate on Singapore town. The position of the main dumps, depots and hospitals, and the main reservoirs supplying the town with water, led him to adopt the latter alternative. He decided that, should it become necessary, the troops were to fall back on to a perimeter round the town which would include Kallang airfield, the MacRitchie and Pierce Reservoirs, Point 581 and the hills immediately west of Bukit Timah, and would then run due south to Pasir Panjang.[1] The sector of this line allotted to Western Area extended from the Pipe Line just east of Point 581 to Raja Road.

During the evening Percival outlined this plan verbally to Heath and Keith Simmons. Shortly after midnight on the 9th/10th he issued it in writing as a secret and personal instruction for the information of his three senior commanders and senior members of his own staff.[2] Western Area however issued a normal operation order based on it to the brigades under its command, allotting them their positions in the perimeter. This had, as will be seen, a far-reaching effect on future operations.

That evening three armed patrol boats raided the western channel of the Johore Strait with the object of disrupting the enemy communications and sinking landing craft. Under heavy fire from both

---

[1] See Maps 23 and 25.
[2] See Appendix 27.

sides of the Strait they forced their way almost to the Causeway, sinking the few enemy craft that they sighted. They then withdrew safely to Singapore.

The dwindling force of Hurricanes continued in action throughout the hours of daylight on the 9th. Four of them concluded this eventful day by responding to an urgent call for air support and, under cover of the smoke from burning oil tanks, succeeded in driving off bombers which were harassing the troops. With only Kallang airfield available the hopelessness of the air situation was only too evident. With Percival's consent Pulford withdrew what was left of the Hurricane squadron to Sumatra, and from then onwards used Kallang as an advanced landing ground only.

In the Causeway sector, events were occurring which were to have a considerable influence on the battle for the island. The news that the enemy had landed in 22nd Brigade area had reached Brigadier Maxwell, whose headquarters were at Dairy Farm six miles south of the Causeway, early on the 9th. Apprehensive that the enemy might cross the Sungei Peng Siang, now uncovered by the removal of 2/29th Battalion, and thus outflank his brigade, he asked permission at 11 a.m. to withdraw 2/26th Battalion from Kranji and swing back his left flank to face north-west. Bennett refused this request, but authorized him to use the reserve company of 2/26th Battalion and a composite company formed from the other three companies to cover the right bank of the Sungei Peng Siang. At about 1.30 p.m. Oakes (2/26th), Galleghan (2/30th) and an intelligence officer from each battalion were called to a conference at Headquarters 27th Brigade.[1] Maxwell told Oakes to make arrangements to cover his left flank as authorized by Western Area, and warned him that, in order to close the gap between 27th and 12th Brigades, both battalions might later be withdrawn from the Causeway area to a position from the junction of the Kranji and Woodlands Roads to approximately Milestone 12 on the Woodlands Road. He said that this withdrawal, if authorized, was not to begin until the oil tanks at Woodlands had been destroyed, and that Oakes was to co-ordinate the movement of both battalions to their new positions. Oakes returned to his battalion about 5.30 p.m., but during the afternoon Maxwell sent Galleghan to hospital and ordered his second-in-command (Major G. E. Ramsay) to take his place in command of 2/30th Battalion. This resulted in both battalions suffering a change of command at this critical moment, and in Ramsay, who had not

---

[1] Major R. F. Oakes from 2/29th Battalion relieved Lieut.-Colonel A. H. Boyes as commanding officer of 2/26th Battalion on the 9th February. Boyes assumed command of 'X' Battalion forming in Singapore from disbanded administrative units.

been at headquarters during the afternoon, receiving his orders at second hand from the battalion intelligence officer.

During the day the Japanese intensified their artillery fire on the sector held by 27th Australian Brigade. By 6 p.m. most of the telephone cables in the forward areas had been cut and the defences near Kranji Pier had been almost completely destroyed. At about 8.30 p.m. the bombardment lifted and half an hour later a battalion of *4th Guards Regiment*, which had embarked in the Sungei Skudai, began its assault. Some of the landing craft lost their way and found themselves in the mangrove swamps at the mouth of the Sungei Kranji, some landed the assault troops on the Kranji peninsula and others entered the Sungei Mandai and the Sungei Mandai Kechil. A number were sunk by machine-gun and mortar fire.

The 27th Brigade front was covered by two batteries of 2/10th Field Regiment. Owing to the presumed danger to the left flank one of these, sited west of the trunk road, had been ordered to move after dark to the Mandai Road area and thus was not available when the attack started. Only one battery, the one allotted to cover the front of 2/30th Battalion, answered the calls for defensive fire. Nevertheless the Japanese at first made but little progress against stiff resistance. Some were cut off on the swampy shore by the rising tide and many fell to the cross-fire from machine-guns, but, as further landing craft arrived, many succeeded in gaining a footing. By midnight the three forward companies of the 2/26th, much reduced in numbers, had been forced back and were concentrated in a strong position across the neck of the Kranji peninsula some 500 yards from the shore. There they repelled all attempts to dislodge them.

Brigadier Maxwell has since affirmed that he was eventually given permission by Western Area to withdraw his brigade to the new positions facing west as he had planned. Accordingly at midnight, when communications between his headquarters and 2/26th Battalion had been temporarily re-established, he told Oakes that, as soon as the oil tanks had been destroyed, he was to carry out the plan which had been discussed during the afternoon, but added the proviso that if the plan were upset by enemy action he was to move both battalions as he thought fit. He also ordered 2/10th Field Regiment to withdraw to the Racecourse.

The Australian engineer officer in charge of the demolition of the oil tanks met with a disaster when the truck containing his explosives was destroyed by shell fire. Undeterred he opened the valves so that the oil would run to waste. The oil caught fire and flowing into the Strait was carried up the river and into the swamps by the incoming tide, causing the enemy considerable loss. He then went back, collected a new supply of explosives and on his return at 2 a.m. informed Oakes that the demolition would be completed by 4 a.m.

Doubtful if his depleted forward companies could hold the enemy for much longer, Oakes ordered both the 2/30th and his own battalion to withdraw at 4 a.m. to the new positions. These were: 2/30th Battalion astride the Mandai Road at Milestone 14 facing west, and 2/26th Battalion, also facing west, on the eastern side of the road from Point 422 through Point 290 to the hills north of Bukit Panjang Village. The Causeway was thus abandoned, the trunk road uncovered, the enemy allowed to consolidate his landings unopposed and a gap of some 4,000 yards left undefended between 27th Brigade and the flank of 11th Division.

It is interesting at this point to view the scene through Japanese eyes. General Nishimura judged, from reports which reached him during the night, that the situation of his troops was extremely serious. He therefore sought permission of *25th Army Headquarters* to call off his attack and to land his division on the island next day in rear of *5th Division*. Before agreeing, General Yamashita demanded a further report on the situation at Kranji. A senior staff officer from *Army Headquarters*, after a personal reconnaissance, reported about 4.30 a.m. that the fierce resistance which the division had encountered had suddenly slackened and that it had become possible to proceed with the original plan.

Meanwhile at Western Area Headquarters the staff were unaware of events in the Causeway sector. At 3.10 a.m. on the 10th they told Malaya Command Headquarters that all was quiet in the sector. It was not known till about 5 a.m. that the enemy had succeeded in landing at Kranji and not till about 5.10 a.m. that 27th Brigade had withdrawn. By 5.30 a.m. this information had been passed to Malaya Command for transmission to III Corps and 11th Division whose left flank had been completely exposed. About 6 a.m. Western Area reported that 2/30th Battalion was taking up a position at Milestone 14 on the Mandai Road.

The information that the Australians had withdrawn reached 11th Division about 6.30 a.m.[1] As soon as General Key received the news he telephoned Western Area asking for the immediate reoccupation of the Causeway area. He was told that there were insufficient Australian troops to do this. To secure his flank he ordered his divisional reserve (8th Brigade) to counter-attack and occupy the high ground from Point 95 through Point 120 to Point 168 bordering the trunk road south-west of Woodlands. At 8 a.m. he sent a message to Maxwell telling him what he was doing, and urging him to cover the trunk road by the occupation of Mandai Village as soon as possible.

---

[1] At about the same time the left forward battalion of 28th Brigade received a message by runner from 2/30th Battalion informing it of the withdrawal.

During the evening of the 9th Bennett, whose intention at this time was to hold the Jurong Line against all attacks, had ordered 22nd Australian Brigade to hold Bulim till 6 a.m. on the 10th and then to move back and take over the central sector in the Jurong Line between 12th and 44th Brigades. At about 9 a.m., being uncertain whether 44th Brigade would be able to make its way back from the south-west coast successfully, he ordered 15th Brigade (Brigadier J. B. Coates)—his only remaining reserve—to take up a position by dawn on the 10th on the left of 22nd Australian Brigade between Point 117 and the Jurong Road. At the same time he altered 44th Brigade's original orders and instructed it to occupy a position from the Jurong Road southwards, with its left in touch with 1st Malaya Brigade at Kampong Jawa. Brigadier Ballentine received this order at about 10 p.m. just as his brigade was settling into the positions originally allotted to it. It had therefore to move for the second time that day to new and unreconnoitred positions, but this time in the dark.

Taylor issued orders at 4.15 a.m. that his sector of the Jurong Line was to be held by 2/29th Battalion on the right in contact with 12th Brigade, the Special Reserve Battalion on the left at Point 117 in contact with 15th Brigade, and the remnants of his original three battalions in reserve near Keat Hong. Shortly before dawn on the 10th, 22nd Australian Brigade began its withdrawal from the Bulim position. At daybreak the carriers of 2/18th Battalion, covering the withdrawal down the main road, saw two companies of enemy infantry advancing eastwards in close formation. They opened fire from concealed positions and created such havoc that the subsequent withdrawal proceeded with little interference.

It was at this point that the confusion began which led to the Jurong Line being abandoned. At about 9 a.m. Taylor received a copy of Western Area's orders based on Percival's secret instructions. Taylor and his staff took these to be an order to the brigade to occupy at once its position in the Reformatory Road–Ulu Pandan area in the proposed perimeter. He therefore ordered all the units under his command, except 2/29th and Special Reserve Battalions then in position in the Jurong Line, to occupy a line immediately west of that road. At the same time he asked 2/15th Field Regiment to move to an area from which it could cover the brigade in its new line. He then set out to reconnoitre the new position and on the way reported at Western Area Headquarters. When told of Taylor's action Bennett expressed his extreme displeasure; nevertheless he allowed the orders to stand. The 2/18th Battalion and 'Merrett's Force' (formed from the remnants of the 2/19th and 2/20th) moved during the morning from Keat Hong to Reformatory Road where they were joined by 'X' Battalion.

As the 2/29th Battalion moved back to its allotted position, it

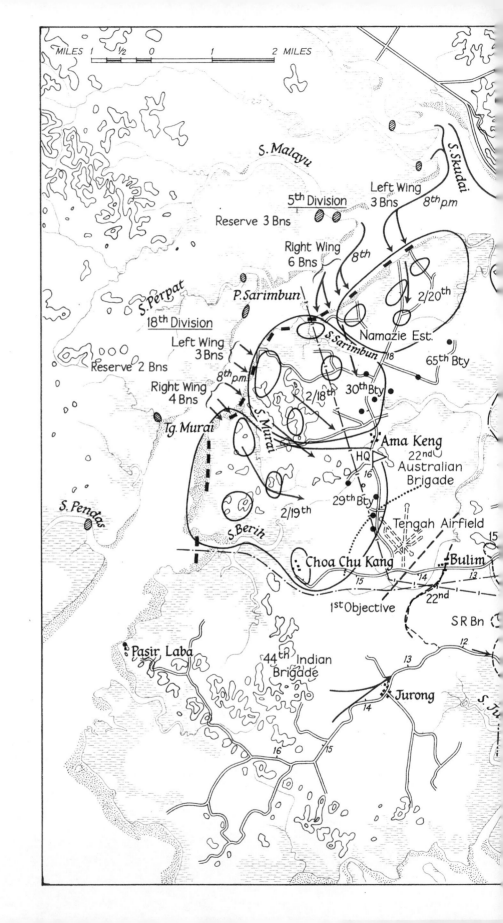

MILES 1   1/2   0   1   2 MILES

S. Malayu

5th Division

Reserve 3 Bns

Left Wing
3 Bns   8th p.m

S. Skudai

Right Wing
6 Bns   8th

2/20th

S. Perpat

18th Division

P. Sarimbun

Namazie Est.

Left Wing
3 Bns

S. Sarimbun   18

65th Bty

Reserve 2 Bns

8th p.m.

30th Bty

Right Wing
4 Bns

S. Murai

2/18th

Tg. Murai

Ama Keng

HQ   22nd
16   Australian
Brigade

29th Bty

2/19th

S. Pendas

S. Berih

Tengah Airfield

15

Choa Chu Kang   14   Bulim

15   14   13

1st Objective   22nd

S R Bn

12

Pasir Laba

44th Indian
Brigade

13

Jurong   S. Ju

14

16   15

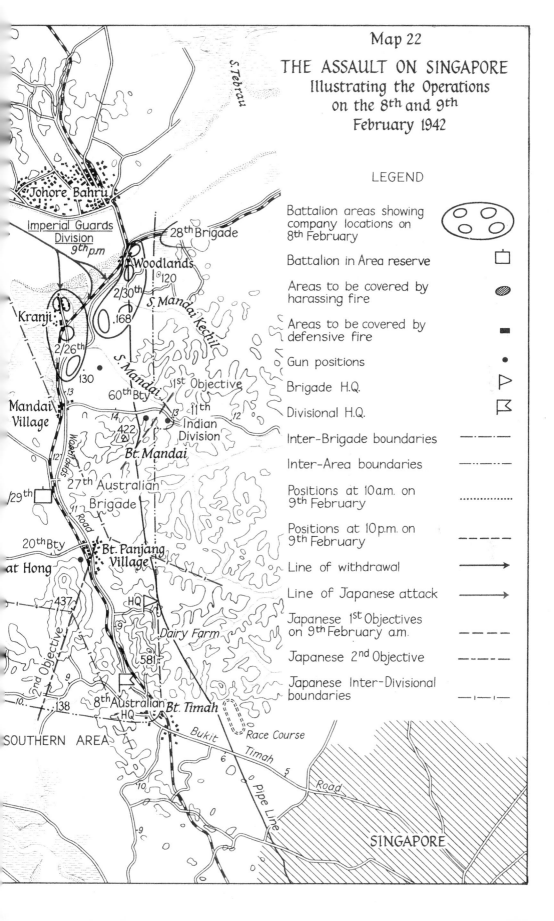

Map 22

THE ASSAULT ON SINGAPORE
Illustrating the Operations
on the 8th and 9th
February 1942

LEGEND

Battalion areas showing company locations on 8th February	
Battalion in Area reserve	
Areas to be covered by harassing fire	
Areas to be covered by defensive fire	
Gun positions	
Brigade H.Q.	
Divisional H.Q.	
Inter-Brigade boundaries	————
Inter-Area boundaries	————
Positions at 10a.m. on 9th February	....
Positions at 10p.m. on 9th February	————
Line of withdrawal	⟶
Line of Japanese attack	⟶
Japanese 1st Objectives on 9th February a.m.	————
Japanese 2nd Objective	———
Japanese Inter-Divisional boundaries	—·—·—

Johore Bahru

Imperial Guards
Division
9th p.m.

28th Brigade

Woodlands
120

2/30th
.168

Kranji

S. Mandai Kechil
S. Mandai

2/26th
130

Mandai
Village

13

60th Bty
14
422

1st Objective
13
11th
Indian
Division
12

Bt. Mandai

27th Australian
Brigade

/29th
11
Woodlands Road

20th Bty
Bt. Panjang
Village

at Hong

437

HQ

9

Dairy Farm

581

8th Australian
HQ

Bt. Timah

SOUTHERN AREA

138

Bukit
Timah
6

Race Course

5

Road

10

Pipe Line

SINGAPORE

became split up, three companies, under command of Major F. Hore, moving back along the Choa Chu Kang Road, while the headquarters and one company moved across country and reached the southern end of Point 117 at about 7.30 a.m. Later in the morning Lieut.-Colonel S. A. F. Pond, unable to locate the rest of his battalion, went back to 22nd Brigade Headquarters leaving the company in position. During the day it withdrew without orders to Racecourse Village.

On the Choa Chu Kang Road the Argylls were in position at Point 156 with 4/19th Hyderabad in depth behind them at Milestone 11. The three companies of 2/29th by agreement with Stewart prolonged the Argylls' left towards Point 110. By 8 a.m. the Japanese, despite the check they had received at Bulim, began to subject the Argylls to mortar and machine-gun fire and to move round their right flank. Stewart then got Paris' permission to withdraw the Argylls and the 2/29th to a position on the high ground at Milestone 12 behind the Sungei Peng Siang. By 9.30 a.m. the 2/29th was astride the road at this point with the Argylls behind it. This move further widened the gap which already existed in the Jurong Line. The enemy followed up slowly and began to probe for the flanks, but did not attack.

Paris had in the meantime sent patrols to make contact with 27th Australian Brigade on his right. They reported that they could not find any Australians and that the trunk road as far as the Kranji road junction (held by the enemy) was unprotected. Realizing that the Japanese at Kranji might well move straight down the trunk road to Bukit Timah, Paris, out of touch with Western Area Headquarters, decided on his own initiative to withdraw his brigade to defend the Bukit Panjang Village road junction. He ordered 4/19th Hyderabad to remain astride the road at Milestone 11 west of the village; the three companies of 2/29th Battalion, which he had taken under his command, to move into the village to cover the road junction itself; the Argylls to be in reserve at Milestone 9 further south, and the Jind Battalion to occupy Point 437. By early afternoon 12th Brigade was in its new position. Its withdrawal had completely uncovered the right flank of the Special Reserve Battalion on Point 117 and 15th and 44th Brigades further south. The northern half of the Jurong Line had been abandoned.

Meanwhile 15th Brigade, which had reached Milestone 11 on the Jurong Road at 5 a.m. on the 10th, found 44th Brigade on the move. By early morning both brigades were in position. The 44th Brigade had disposed 6/1st Punjab with its right on the Jurong Road, 6/14th Punjab further south behind the Sungei Jurong, and 7/8th Punjab in reserve at Milestone 10. The 15th Brigade held a line running northeast from Milestone 11½ with the British Battalion immediately north

D2

of the road, 3/16th Punjab echeloned behind its right, and 2/9th Jats in reserve. The troops of both brigades were very tired, especially those of 44th Brigade (Ballentine) which had been on the move for twelve hours.

At about 10.30 a.m. a copy of the order based on Percival's secret instruction reached Ballentine who told Coates (15th Brigade) of its contents and gave his battalion commanders the routes to be used if they were ordered to withdraw to Pasir Panjang. During the morning enemy aircraft bombed and machine-gunned 15th and 44th Brigades' positions, and about 1.30 p.m. an infantry attack compelled the right company of 6/1st Punjab, in position astride the road, to withdraw to Milestone 11. At 1.45 p.m., unable to contact the Australians on his right and with his left flank under attack, Coates ordered his brigade to withdraw to Milestone 9. When he heard firing in 6/14th Punjab's sector and observed that 15th Brigade was pulling back, Ballentine, fearing his forward battalions might be out-flanked, ordered them to withdraw, apparently intending them to readjust their positions to conform with 15th Brigade. Having given the order to 6/1st Punjab at about 2.30 p.m. over the only existing tele-phone line, he moved his headquarters to Reformatory Road. The 6/1st Punjab sent liaison officers to give the order to 6/14th Punjab and to its own right company and then withdrew to Pasir Panjang, taking with it 7/8th Punjab less two companies. Neither liaison officer reached his destination, but the 6/14th, becoming aware about 3 p.m. that the 6/1st had gone, also withdrew to Pasir Panjang. The commanding officers of both battalions had come, quite inde-pendently, to the conclusion that they were to move to the area given in the warning order of that morning and had acted accordingly. The right company of the 6/1st and two companies of the 7/8th joined up with 15th Brigade.

Meanwhile the Special Reserve Battalion, finding itself entirely isolated, had also withdrawn and, having made contact with 15th Brigade at Milestone 9, took up a position on its left. To the south in the coastal sector Brigadier G. G. R. Williams (1st Malaya Brigade), seeing the withdrawal of 6/14th Punjab taking place, con-formed with it by moving 2nd Malay Battalion from the Sungei Jurong to Pasir Panjang, leaving outposts on the Sungei Pandan. That evening, on orders from Southern Area, 44th Brigade moved to the junction of Reformatory and Ulu Pandan Roads.

Thus by dusk on the 10th February the partly reconnoitred and prepared Jurong Line, on whose retention the success of the defence rested, had been abandoned and Western Area's brigades were widely dispersed. By the late afternoon of the 10th the Japanese had succeeded in concentrating three infantry regiments of *5th Division*, supported by tanks, in the vicinity of Tengah airfield and three regiments of *18th Division* at about Milestone 13 on the Jurong Road.

They were then ready to continue their advance eastwards along two roads towards their second objective.

Early on the 10th February, General Wavell had arrived at Singapore on what was to be his last visit. Accompanied by Percival, he drove straight to Headquarters, Western Area, at Holland Road. A few minutes after his arrival the headquarters was heavily bombed. The building was straddled; one bomb made a direct hit but fortunately failed to explode, and the three Generals escaped with a shaking. Wavell was told of the events of the 9th and of the plans for holding the Jurong Line. It was evident to the Supreme Commander that the battle was not going well. Bennett however had little information at that time of the course of events in the Causeway sector except that 27th Australian Brigade had withdrawn. It was not therefore until Wavell, having seen Heath on the way, reached Headquarters, 11th Division, that he and Percival learnt from Key of 27th Brigade's dispositions in the Bukit Mandai area and of the danger to the division's left flank.

Realizing that the trunk road was uncovered, Percival saw the need for a reserve in the Bukit Timah area, the retention of which he considered to be vital. He accordingly ordered III Corps to form a force of three battalions and move it to a rendezvous near the Racecourse, where it was to come under the orders of Western Area. This force, drawn from different brigades of 18th British Division and commanded by Lieut.-Colonel L. C. Thomas, became known as 'Tomforce'.[1] It began to arrive at rendezvous at 5 p.m. on the 10th. Realizing also that the security of 11th Division now largely depended on the co-ordination of its movements with those of 27th Brigade, Percival decided to place the latter under Key's command. Pending the actual transfer, which he felt could not take place till he had seen Bennett, he sent a personal message by despatch rider to 27th Brigade instructing Maxwell to reoccupy Mandai Village, at the junction of the Mandai and Woodlands Roads.

The two Generals paid a second visit to Western Area Headquarters at about 2.30 p.m. There they were told by Bennett that during the morning his line had been forced back to between Milestone 11 on the Choa Chu Kang Road and Point 138 on the Jurong

---

[1] 'Tomforce' was composed of:
   18th Battalion Reconnaissance Corps
   4th Norfolk (from 54th Brigade)
   1/5th Sherwood Foresters (from 55th Brigade)
   One battery 85th Anti-Tank Regiment
   The staff, signals and transport for the force were found by 18th Division. One battery of 5th Field Regiment supported the force from the 11th February.

Road, and that the Jurong Line had been lost. Wavell urged that a counter-attack should immediately be organized to recapture this line; he considered its retention vital to the defence since it alone safe-guarded the Bukit Timah area against attack from the west of the island, where the Japanese had by now firmly established them-selves. Percival thereupon ordered Bennett to launch a counter-attack, at the same time informing him that 27th Australian Brigade would be placed under command of 11th Division from 5 p.m. that day.

That evening Wavell ordered the immediate transfer of the remaining air force officers and men to the Netherlands East Indies, and placed Air Vice-Marshal P. C. Maltby in command of all the British and Commonwealth air forces in Java and Sumatra, under the general direction of Air Headquarters.[1] Before leaving for Java the Supreme Commander told Percival that there was to be no thought or question of surrender, that every unit was to fight it out to the end and that a counter-offensive should be launched on the western front with all the troops that could be made available.

On his return to Java he telegraphed the Prime Minister:

> 'Battle for Singapore is not going well. Japanese with their usual infiltration tactics are getting on much more rapidly than they should in the west of Island. I ordered Percival to stage counter-attack with all troops possible on that front. Morale of some troops is not good and none is as high as I should like to see . . . The chief troubles are lack of sufficient training in some of reinforcing troops and an inferiority complex which bold and skilful Japanese tactics and their command of the air have caused. Everything possible is being done to produce more offensive spirit and optimistic outlook. But I cannot pretend that these efforts have been entirely successful up to date. I have given the most categorical orders that there is to be no thought of surrender and that all troops are to continue fighting to the end . . .'

In Northern Area, General Key went forward early on the afternoon of the 10th to see for himself the progress of the counter-attack he had ordered that morning. He found that after fierce fighting 8th Brigade (Brigadier W. A. Trott), had succeeded in securing Point 95

---

[1] Air Vice-Marshal Maltby had arrived at Singapore from the United Kingdom on the 4th January 1942 as Chief of Staff designate to General Pownall, the new Commander-in-Chief, Far East. On the formation of ABDA Command shortly afterwards, the appointment lapsed, but he remained at Singapore and acted as Assistant Air Officer Commanding at Air Headquarters.

and Point 120, but had failed to capture Point 168, and that the Garh-walis had suffered severe casualties in hand-to-hand fighting. Key thereupon instructed Trott that 2/10th Baluch was to occupy Point 130 at dawn on the 11th February so as to fill the gap between the Garhwalis and 27th Australian Brigade. Meeting Major Ramsay, whose battalion (2/30th) was still holding a position astride the Mandai Road at Milestone 14, he urged him to send forward troops to the road junction at Mandai Village. Ramsay, who had been instructed by Maxwell to retain his existing position and did not know that 27th Australian Brigade was being placed under the command of 11th Division, declined, and asked that the matter be referred to his Brigadier. On his return to his headquarters at 2.30 p.m. Key sent Maxwell a message informing him of the situation north of the Mandai Road and of the proposed action by 2/10th Baluch next morning, and asking him to occupy Mandai Village without delay. Meanwhile Maxwell, having received his copy of Western Area's order based on Percival's secret and personal instruction, had at 2 p.m. sent his two battalions instructions that, in the event of their being unable to hold the enemy in their new positions near Bukit Mandai, they were to withdraw down the Pipe Line to a rendezvous in the vicinity of the Racecourse. These orders reached 2/26th Battalion at 4 p.m. but failed to reach the 2/30th.

At about 3 p.m. Maxwell, who on instructions from Western Area had moved his headquarters back to Holland Road during the previous night, received the order placing his brigade and 2/10th Field Regiment under the command of 11th Division. He also received at least one of the messages from Percival and Key urging him to occupy Mandai Village, and accordingly ordered 2/30th Battalion to move forward. At about 6.30 p.m. he reported at 11th Divisional Headquarters and was once again told by Key to ensure that Mandai Village was occupied. At 7 p.m. he informed Key that the 2/30th had in fact occupied the village. This information was passed to Trott, who thereupon arranged that the start line for the 2/10th Baluch attack on Point 130 next morning should be the Mandai Road.

The 2/30th Battalion had received Maxwell's orders to move forward about 5 p.m. Ramsay had thereupon ordered three companies to advance at 9 p.m. to the high ground south of the road immediately east of the village, and his fourth company to remain on the road astride the Pipe Line to guard against any enemy move from the north, for he knew that until the arrival of 2/10th Baluch there would be a gap between him and the Garhwalis further north. Since the area occupied by the battalion that night did not include the road junction and village, Key's orders were not in fact carried out. Meanwhile 2/26th Battalion had shortened its position, and by nightfall was holding a line some 2,000 yards in length on the western slopes of Point 290 and the hills to the south.

We must now revert to what was happening in Western Area. At about 3 p.m. on the 10th, after Wavell and Percival had left him, Bennett considered how best he could comply with the instructions which he had received. He could not have been fully aware of the ~~disaster which had overtaken 44th Brigade or of 15th Brigade's plight) but, basing his plans on such information as he had, he~~ *[handwritten: withdrawal of 15th, 44th and 1st Malay Brigades. (in the Jurong Line but, basing his plans on such information as he had, he]* decided to organize a counter-attack with 12th Brigade on the right, 15th Brigade in the centre, 22nd Australian Brigade on the left, and 44th Brigade in reserve. This attack was to be carried out in three stages. The first was to be the occupation, by 6 p.m. on the 10th, of the line Milestone 11 on the Choa Chu Kang Road–Milestone 9 on the Jurong Road–Point 138; the second, to be completed by 9 a.m. on the 11th, was to be the occupation of a line approximately 1,200 yards west of the first stage; and the third, to be completed by 6 p.m. on the 11th, was to be the reoccupation of the Jurong Line. The 2/15th Field Regiment was to support 12th Brigade, and 5th Field Regiment 15th and 22nd Brigades.

At 4.45 p.m. on the 10th February, Western Area Headquarters issued the necessary orders through liaison officers to all the brigades concerned. It will be seen that these bore little relation to the facts. At the time they were being thought out 44th Brigade was retreating to Pasir Panjang; 15th Brigade, because of its isolation, was withdrawing to Milestone 9 on the Jurong Road; and the Special Reserve Battalion was moving back to join 15th Brigade. Nevertheless, as events turned out, all four brigades were near their allotted positions for the first stage by the time that the orders reached them; but none of them was in a fit state to carry out the movements ordered.[1] Actually a counter-attack would have been feasible only if fresh troops had been provided for the purpose. The attempt to launch such an attack with the troops available resulted, as the reader will see, in making confusion worse confounded.

The 5th Field Regiment, located near Racecourse Village, was in a position to cover the left of the proposed attack, but 2/15th Field Regiment, which had moved back to Farrer Road to cover 22nd Brigade in its Reformatory Road position, was out of range and had to move forward. It did not receive its orders until night was falling

---

[1] The strengths of the brigades at this time were:
  12th Brigade (including 2/29th) approximately 1,300
  22nd Brigade (2/18th, 'X' Battalion and 'Merrett's Force') approximately 1,100
and 15th Brigade approximately 1,500.

so could not possibly have been ready to support 12th Brigade's second stage attack at dawn the next day. Nevertheless its reconnaissance parties gained touch with Brigadier Paris late that evening, and the gunners moved forward to take up new positions in the Bukit Timah area; but, as will be seen, the Japanese forestalled them. In consequence 2/15th Field Regiment spent most of the night in trying to avoid capture, and by dawn, weary and exhausted, found itself back in the Farrer Road area.

Brigadier Taylor, who had visited Western Area Headquarters during the afternoon and had protested in vain against Bennett's plan for the counter-attack, ordered 'X' Battalion to occupy Point 138, 'Merrett's Force' Point 85, and retained the weak 2/18th Battalion and two platoons of 2/4th Machine-Gun Battalion in reserve at Reformatory Road. He realized that he had set his battalions an extremely difficult task, for they would have to occupy their first stage positions in darkness and in strange country and would have no opportunity of reconnoitring for their subsequent advance.

On receiving his orders at about 5.30 p.m., Brigadier Coates (15th Brigade) also took steps to occupy his first stage position which was just in front of the line he was then holding, and made his preparations to move forward at first light on the 11th on the second stage of the counter-attack. He moved 3/16th Punjab to the ridge immediately north of the road, placed the Jats on its right, with instructions to contact 12th Brigade, and kept the British Battalion in its existing position astride the road at Milestone 9. All these units had completed their moves by 11 p.m. The Jats on the right reported—somewhat naturally—that they were unable to make contact with 12th Brigade. The Special Reserve Battalion, which had received no orders of any kind from its brigade since the afternoon of the 9th, remained in its position prolonging the British Battalion's left to the south of the road.

Before describing the fate of the two brigades which were endeavouring to carry out their orders for the counter-attack, we must turn to events on the Choa Chu Kang Road. Shortly after dusk, enemy infantry attacked 12th Brigade. The 4/19th Hyderabad at Milestone 11 disintegrated and came back through the 2/29th with the enemy in pursuit. The Australians stopped the enemy advance, but shortly afterwards a column of medium tanks drove down the road. Three tanks were destroyed, but the remainder broke through and turned south towards Bukit Timah. Later, being heavily attacked by Japanese infantry, the 2/29th was forced into the hills on its eastern side. At 10.30 p.m., seeing that Bukit Timah was in flames and that

the enemy was moving southwards in large numbers, the remnants
of the 2/29th withdrew along the Pipe Line to the Racecourse. There
they were reunited with their battalion headquarters and the fourth
company from which they had become separated that morning.[1]
Pond then reconstituted his unit, and on the following morning
crossed the Bukit Timah Road and moved into a position on the
left of 'Tomforce'.

The Argylls, who now stood alone between the advancing
Japanese and the vital Bukit Timah depots, hurriedly improvised two
road blocks, using all the vehicles and the few anti-tank mines that
they had. When the leading tanks reached these at about 10.30 p.m.
one was knocked out, but the column of about fifty tanks supported
by infantry broke through, forcing the Argylls and Headquarters,
12th Brigade, to withdraw to the east of the road and Dairy Farm
respectively. Just before the break-through however a staff officer
had been sent back to Bukit Timah by Brigadier Paris to warn the
troops in rear of the danger of tank attack. There he met an Australian
liaison officer who organized another road block covered by Australian anti-tank guns some three hundred yards south of the Bukit
Timah road junction.

A few enemy tanks and some infantry reached the road junction
at Bukit Timah about midnight on the 10th/11th, thus gaining
control of the eastern end of the Jurong Road and cutting direct
communications with both 15th Brigade and the advanced elements
of 22nd Brigade. The main column of tanks however made no
attempt to penetrate southwards and halted in line ahead on the
road with infantry on either side to protect them. Enemy fighting
patrols, moving south towards the Buona Vista 15-inch Battery and
into the Sleepy Valley area,[2] very nearly overran Western Area
Headquarters at Holland Road.

At about 2.15 a.m. this headquarters, having heard that there
was a gap in the defences near Bukit Panjang Village, ordered
'Tomforce' to send a battalion to the village to support 12th Brigade.
The 18th Reconnaissance Battalion was ordered forward, but, before
it could move, it was learnt that the enemy had captured Bukit
Timah; the order was promptly countermanded and the battalion
disposed astride the road, in support of the road block. Meanwhile
the Argylls had concentrated near the Dairy Farm in order to
attack the enemy in flank at dawn, but reconnaissance at first light
showed that, owing to the enemy's strength, any such plan was
impracticable. On Paris's orders, Headquarters, 12th Brigade,

---

[1] See page 385.
[2] See Map 21.

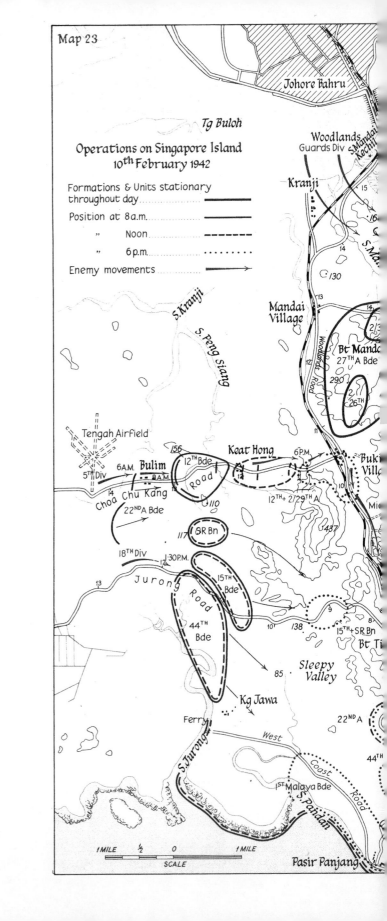

Map 23

Operations on Singapore Island
10th February 1942

Formations & Units stationary
throughout day ....
Position at 8 a.m. ....
  "   Noon ....
  "   6 p.m. ....
Enemy movements ....

Tg Buloh

Johore Bahru

Woodlands Guards Div

S. Mandai Kechil

Kranji

15

16

S. Mandai

14

130

13

Mandai Village

14

2/3

Bt Mandai
27TH A Bde

12

290

2/
26TH

11

S. Kranji

S. Peng Siang

Tengah Airfield

6 A.M. Bulim
5TH Div 8 A.M.
14
Choa Chu Kang
22ND A Bde

156

12TH Bde

Keat Hong

6 P.M.

Buki
Vill

Road

110

14

12TH + 2/29TH A

10T

Mic

437

SR Bn
117

18TH Div 1.30 P.M.

13

Jurong Road

15TH
Bde

44TH
Bde

10T 138

9

8T

15TH + SR Bn
Bt Ti

Sleepy
Valley

22ND A

Kg Jawa

85

Ferry

West

S. Jurong

Coast Road

1ST Malaya Bde

44TH

S. Pandan

1 MILE ½ 0 1 MILE
SCALE

Pasir Panjang

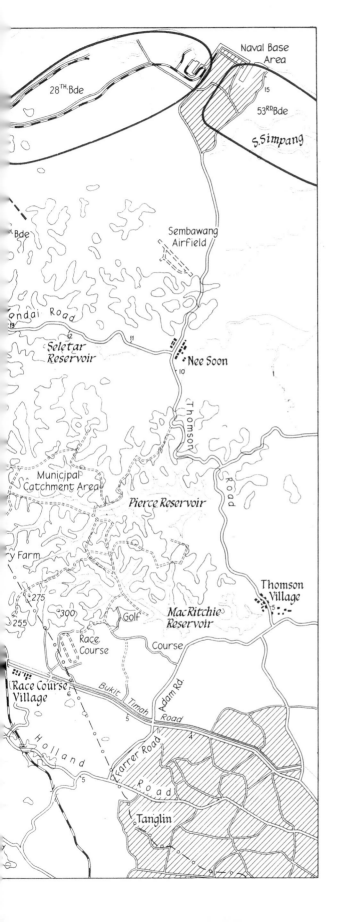

and the Argylls then withdrew along the Pipe Line to the Golf Course and eventually to Tanglin.

While these disasters were occurring on the right flank, 22nd Brigade was attempting to move into its position on the left of 15th Brigade for the counter-attack. At 11 p.m. 'X' Battalion reached the position held by 15th Brigade. After reconnaissance carried out in pitch darkness this inexperienced unit moved forward and by 2.30 a.m. had occupied Point 138, 500 yards west of the Special Reserve Battalion's position. Further south 'Merrett's Force', unable in the darkness to locate Point 85, halted and formed a defensive perimeter in Sleepy Valley where it waited for daylight.

At 3 a.m. on the 11th the Japanese *18th Division* attacked down the Jurong Road.[1] 'X' Battalion had only just reached its position; assaulted from the front and the flanks and silhouetted against the flare of a burning petrol dump set alight by a mortar bomb, it was overwhelmed, and Colonel Boyes was killed. Only a few survivors succeeded in finding their way back to Reformatory Road. The 15th Brigade, which had had the advantage of seeing its position in daylight, was more fortunate and the enemy attack was held. Later both the British and the Special Reserve Battalions were withdrawn to better positions. At about 2.30 a.m. Brigadier Coates, hearing the sound of firing behind him, made an attempt to report his position to Western Area Headquarters and to find out what was happening in the Bukit Timah area. His liaison officer managed to get through after his car had been fired on by enemy tanks near the Bukit Timah road junction, but all communications to the rear were severed and Coates realized that he was isolated. At 5.30 a.m. he decided to cancel the counter-attack. An effort to contact 2/9th Jats, which had already started to move to its second objective, failed and the battalion was never seen again. Half an hour later brigade headquarters, one mile north-west of Bukit Timah, was attacked from the east and Coates was forced to take refuge with the British Battalion.

At 7.30 a.m. the enemy again attacked astride the Jurong Road. A spirited counter-attack with the bayonet at 9 a.m. by a company of the British Battalion and by the Special Reserve Battalion drove the enemy back and gave Coates the opportunity to disengage. A withdrawal down the Jurong Road being impossible, he split his force into three columns (one British, one Australian and one Indian) and at about 9.30 a.m. set off on a compass bearing in a south-easterly direction towards Reformatory Road. While crossing Sleepy Valley the columns came under heavy fire and suffered severe casualties. All cohesion was lost and eventually at about 1 p.m. some 400

---

[1] See Map 24.

survivors—all that was left of a brigade some 1,500 strong—reached 22nd Australian Brigade's positions.

Meanwhile 'Merrett's Force', realizing from the sound of firing to the east that it was in danger of being cut off, had started just before day-break to make its way back to its brigade. It too was ambushed and lost heavily before it managed to break through to Reformatory Road. Even Taylor's reserve units and his brigade headquarters became involved in the early morning fighting, for enemy patrols, which had pushed south from Bukit Timah during the night, attacked them at daybreak and were driven back only after hand-to-hand fighting. By 7 a.m. this attack had been broken and the enemy had withdrawn. The presence of enemy patrols in this area during the night led to orders being issued to blow up the 15-inch battery at Buona Vista. This was done just before dawn. Thus ended a night of disaster. Singapore was saved from occupation that morning only by the failure of the enemy's tanks to advance south of Bukit Timah. The Japanese in their accounts give as a reason for this that their troops had reached their allotted objectives and, being short of artillery and ammunition owing to the difficulties of getting them over the Strait quickly enough, were not expected to be able to resume their advance till early on the 13th.

The extent of the disaster to 12th Brigade was not fully realized at Western Area Headquarters till the early hours of the 11th February. To restore the situation, Bennett ordered 'Tomforce' to attack astride the trunk road, firstly to retake Bukit Timah and the vital food and petrol dumps in its vicinity, and secondly, to occupy Bukit Panjang Village. 'Tomforce' attacked with 4th Norfolk on the right, 18th Reconnaissance Battalion astride the road in the centre and the Sherwood Foresters on the left. The 4th Norfolk captured Points 255 and 275 but, unable to make further progress, was eventually driven off both these hills. The centre of the attack was pinned down by heavy enemy fire on the line of the railway. The left, moving across country, reached Milestone 8 on the Jurong Road but, becoming involved in the retreat of 15th Brigade, withdrew. By 1 p.m. Thomas had to admit failure and reported that his force was being dive-bombed and subjected to heavy machine-gun, mortar and artillery fire. It is not to be wondered at that this attack failed since, by the time it was launched, both the enemy *18th Division* and *5th Division* were in the Point 581–Point 225–Bukit Timah area, each division with two regiments forward. Japanese accounts of this action all report heavy fighting and admit severe casualties.

At 7 a.m. that morning Percival had realized that a dangerous gap existed west of MacRitchie Reservoir, and, as a temporary measure, had formed a composite infantry unit of seven companies from the reinforcement camps, which he had sent to hold the eastern end of the Golf Course. At the same time he had placed 2nd Gordons from Changi under the orders of Western Area. He had also altered the boundaries between Northern and Western Areas so as to make the former responsible for all ground east of the Racecourse.

On hearing of the change of boundaries, Heath held a conference at 9 a.m. to consider the effect of the serious position which had developed in Western Area. With Bukit Timah in the enemy's hands and the left flank of 11th Division exposed, there was a danger that the enemy would infiltrate towards the reservoirs from the north, and between them from the west. To counter this he felt he would have to withdraw further troops from 18th Division's front. He there-fore instructed Major-General M. B. Beckwith-Smith (18th Division) to form immediately a second composite force of brigade strength under command of Brigadier T. H. Massy-Beresford, to be known as 'Massy Force'.[2] This force, under the direct command of III Corps, was given as a primary task the blocking of the enemy's approach to Thomson Village from the north and the protection of the pumping station at Woodleigh.[3] Its secondary task was to fill the gap between the right of 'Tomforce' and the reservoirs. It was to assemble during the afternoon at the eastern end of MacRitchie Reservoir.

During the morning of the 11th events went from bad to worse in the 11th Divisional area. At about 7.30 a.m. Maxwell informed Key that 27th Australian Brigade was being removed from his command. Later he told Key that he had been ordered to occupy and hold Bukit Panjang Village. The origin of this order is obscure. It seems probable that it originated in Western Area, for it was known during the night at that headquarters that a counter-attack to regain Bukit Panjang Village was to be made from the north-east as well as by 'Tomforce', and Maxwell told both Key and his senior staff officer in the morning that the order was sent to him by Bennett. Percival's subsequent actions and an order issued by him at 8 p.m. that evening, part of which read '27th Brigade will revert to the command of the A.I.F. when it can be released by III Corps', show that he himself could not have issued it.

At about 7.30 a.m. Maxwell sent a warning order to his two battalions and, at approximately 8.40 a.m., followed it up with his

---

[2] 'Massy Force' consisted of:
    1st Cambridgeshire from 55th Brigade
    4th Suffolk from 54th Brigade
    5/11th Sikh from Southern Area
    A detachment 3rd Cavalry
    342nd Field Battery.
  In addition there was a detachment of 100th Light Tank Squadron from 11th Division equipped with eighteen light tanks of obsolescent type.

[3] See Map 25.

THIS FORCE INCLUDED THE WEAK 5/2ND PUNJAB

attack orders. He fixed 10.30 a.m. as zero hour and tried to arrange for some covering fire, but, owing to the lack of communications and the position of 2/10th Field Regiment, was unable to do so. The 2/30th Battalion received the warning order at about 8 a.m. and the orders for the attack about an hour later. The three forward companies, who were in contact with the enemy, immediately disengaged and moved south towards the rendezvous with the 2/26th. At about 10 a.m., just as the company on the Mandai Road, the last to leave, was about to move, it was attacked by strong forces from the north and west. After a sharp action at close range, it too managed to disengage and, fighting a skilful rearguard action against greatly superior numbers, succeeded with difficulty in rejoining the rest of its battalion.

Having become aware of the break through to Bukit Timah during the night of the 10th/11th, Oakes had decided to withdraw 2/26th Battalion to the rendezvous near the Racecourse given by 27th Brigade the previous day. The battalion moved off at first light along the Pipe Line with the result that the warning order for the counter-attack only reached its rearguard just as it was about to move, too late to be acted on. On reaching Dairy Farm the advanced guard found the area occupied by very large numbers of the enemy. Feeling that he was much too weak to attack, Oakes made a detour eastwards through the difficult jungle country. After a brush between patrols, the battalion, except for one company which became separated and was forced to move north-east, reached the Golf Course safely and then moved to Tanglin.

When Ramsay reached the rendezvous he learnt that the 2/26th had moved south earlier in the morning. Knowing that the enemy was advancing in force in his rear, he decided that the projected attack was no longer feasible and that he ought to rejoin his brigade headquarters. He therefore moved 2/30th Battalion eastwards along a track through the Municipal Catchment Area. On the way he was joined by the detached company of the 2/26th. The column then met the brigade's signal officer laying a telephone cable to the rendezvous and Ramsay was able for the first time for some days to speak to his brigadier. Maxwell ordered him to move to Milestone 9 on Thomson Road where he was to organize a position to prevent the enemy from using the same track and threatening the communications of 11th Division.

The unexpected move by the Australians described above exposed Key's left flank and compelled him to alter his plans. He ordered Trott (8th Brigade) to cancel the proposed attack by 2/10th Baluch and to arrange for the battalion to take up a defensive position astride the Mandai Road at about Milestone 13. Lieut.-Colonel P. W. Parker (2/10th Baluch), while making a reconnaissance for his attack, had however already learnt from 2/30th Battalion that a move was pending and had anticipated the order.

As soon as he realized that 27th Brigade could no longer be counted upon to protect his left flank, Heath decided that the moment to abandon the Naval Base had arrived and ordered the final demolitions to be carried out. By 6 p.m. on the 11th the Base had been evacuated; 53rd Brigade had swung its left flank back and taken up a position from the Sungei Simpang facing north-west, covering the Sembawang airfield; 8th Brigade had withdrawn to a line just west of Nee Soon road junction and 28th Brigade had been placed in divisional reserve south of it. The 18th Division, almost entirely denuded of infantry by the creation of 'Tomforce' and 'Massy Force', remained holding its sector.

During the afternoon of the 11th, Percival had visited Massy-Beresford. He considered that the second objective given to 'Massy Force' had by that time become the more urgent, and directed him, with Heath's agreement, to capture Point 300 and make contact with 'Tomforce', leaving small detachments to guard Thomson Village and the Woodleigh pumping station. By the time however that 'Massy Force' had assembled and was ready to attack, the hill had been occupied by the Japanese and the attack was called off.

Meanwhile General Beckwith-Smith (18th Division) had visited 'Tomforce' and 'Massy Force' and had come to the conclusion that the former could make no further progress and that the position it had reached was unsuitable for defence. With Heath's agreement he therefore ordered both forces to take up a defensive position by nightfall on the general line MacRitchie Reservoir–Racecourse–Racecourse Village. During the evening 'Tomforce' withdrew to the new line in touch with 'Massy Force' on its right and with 2nd Gordons, who were being moved up to fill the gap between 'Tomforce' and 22nd Australian Brigade, on its left.

The Australian brigade, strengthened by organized reinforcements[1] and by stragglers rejoining their units, held a position on an arc from the junction of the railway and Holland Road through Point 200 to the junction of Reformatory and Ulu Pandan Roads. Throughout the afternoon the centre of this position was incessantly attacked but, although they had little artillery support and were constantly harried by low-flying aircraft, the Australians put up a stout defence and conceded no ground. The Japanese records show that these attacks were made by *56th* and *114th Regiments* of *18th Division*; they admit heavy casualties.

The 44th Brigade extended the line along the western side of Reformatory Road southwards to its junction with Raja Road; from

---

[1] 2/4th Machine-Gun Battalion, equipped as infantry.

there 1st Malaya Brigade, reinforced by 5th Bedfordshire and Hertfordshire (less two companies) from 18th Division, and an engineer battalion formed from British and Indian engineer units, continued the line to the coast at Pasir Panjang. Neither of these brigades was attacked that day. During the afternoon the artillery,[1] having recovered from the confusion of the previous day, reorganized and with its communications re-established, was once again able to support the infantry. This resulted in a relaxation of enemy pressure, and the front from 22nd Australian Brigade to the coast had a comparatively quiet night.

At about 8 p.m. on the 11th Percival again changed the boundaries between formations. At midnight III Corps was to take control of all troops as far west as the Bukit Timah road (near Racecourse Village); 8th Australian Division, from there to the Ulu Pandan Road; and Southern Area, the remainder of the front as far as the coast. 'Tomforce' was to be transferred from Bennett's command to III Corps and combined with 'Massy Force'.

It was on this day that General Yamashita dropped a letter by air calling for the surrender of the fortress. In a message to General Wavell informing him of the incident Percival said that he had no similar means of replying, but made it clear that his answer would have been in the negative. That night he issued an instruction on measures to be taken to prevent valuable military material falling into enemy hands.

Early on the 12th the cruiser *Durban*,[2] two destroyers and an armed patrol vessel left Singapore, escorting the *Empire Star* and another merchant ship carrying the greater part of the shore-based naval personnel, the remainder of the air force ground staff and a number of military staff officers and technicians. The ships were heavily attacked on passage by aircraft, the *Durban* being hit once and the *Empire Star* three times, but reached Batavia with surprisingly few casualties.

The same day the Japanese attacked 'Massy Force' astride the Bukit Timah Road and, by 8.30 a.m. their tanks had reached Racecourse Village.[3] Here they were brought to a standstill by the fire of a troop of 45th Anti-Tank Battery. By noon enemy infiltration had become so serious that Massy-Beresford, who had already reconnoitred and begun to prepare a defensive position on the easily discernible line Adam Road–Farrer Road, ordered his force to withdraw to it. The withdrawal was covered by fire from the fixed coast

[1] 2/15th Australian Field Regiment and 5th Field Regiment.
[2] A light cruiser which had been on escort duty.
[3] See Map 25.

defence batteries and, despite constant low-level bombing and machine-gun attacks, was successfully accomplished during the late afternoon. The new position was held by 'Massy Force' (which now included 'Tomforce') reinforced by 3/17th Dogras.

In Northern Area, the Japanese began to press 8th Brigade shortly after dawn. This brigade held a position one mile west of Nee Soon with 2/10th Baluch astride the Mandai Road and 1/8th Punjab on its right. The Punjab battalion, which after it had been re-formed consisted almost entirely of untrained reinforcements, began to disintegrate. Since enemy penetration in this area would have isolated 53rd Brigade, Key brought up 2/9th Gurkhas and 499th Field Battery from 28th Brigade (then in reserve). The 1/8th Punjab's position was reoccupied and the situation restored.

Meanwhile Percival had visited the headquarters of Western Area, 'Massy Force' and III Corps and, after discussion with the commanders concerned, had come to the conclusion that there was a very real danger of the enemy breaking through on the axis of the Bukit Timah Road and reaching Singapore. He decided that the time had come to organize a close perimeter defence round the town itself—which involved the withdrawal of all troops from the beach defences on the north-east and south-east coasts of the island and from the Changi areas, with the consequent loss of the Changi fixed defences. He then went to see Sir Shenton Thomas at Government House and explained the dangerous situation which had arisen on the Bukit Timah Road. The Governor, in view of the proximity of the enemy, ordered the destruction of the Singapore Broadcasting Station, and arranged for the greater part of the stock of currency notes held by the Treasury to be burnt.

Percival gave orders that a perimeter was to be established during the night 12th/13th on the general line Kallang airfield–Paya Lebar airstrip–Woodleigh crossroads–Thomson Village–Adam Road–Farrer Road–Tanglin Halt and thence, via The Gap, to the sea west of Buona Vista village.

At noon on the 12th, Heath began to withdraw 11th and 18th Divisions to their sectors in the perimeter. At 3 p.m., while 53rd Brigade, under whose orders 2/30th Battalion had been placed,[1] was moving back to a position immediately south of Nee Soon, the Japanese, using tanks, made a determined attempt to capture the road junction. After a sharp action, they were repulsed by 2/10th Baluch supported by a troop of 273rd Anti-Tank Battery and 499th Battery of 135th Field Regiment; three tanks were knocked out. The 53rd Brigade reached its allotted position intact. The 8th and 28th Brigades were in turn withdrawn without incident, passing through

---

[1] 27th Australian Brigade Headquarters, now redundant, rejoined 8th Australian Division that day.

Map 24

Operations on Singapore Island
11th February 1942

Position at 3 a.m. ————————
  "   during morning – – – – – –
  "   at 6 p.m. · · · · · · · · · ·
Movements during morning ———→
Enemy movements ═══⟹

Johore Bahru

Tg Buloh

Woodlands

Kranji

Mandai
Village

Bt Ma

2/3

27TH

290

26TH

130

S.Kranji

S. Peng Siang

Tengah Airfield

Keat Hong

5TH Div

Bulim

Choa Chu Kang Road

110

117

437

Jurong Road

15TH Bde
&SR
Bn

18TH Div

18TH Div
P.M.

3 A.M. 'X' Bn

138

Bt

Sleepy
Valley

Merretts
Force

Kg Jawa

22ND Bde

Ferry

West Coast Road

44TH
Bde

S. Jurong

S. Pandan

Pasir Panjang

1 MILE ½ 0 1 MILE
SCALE

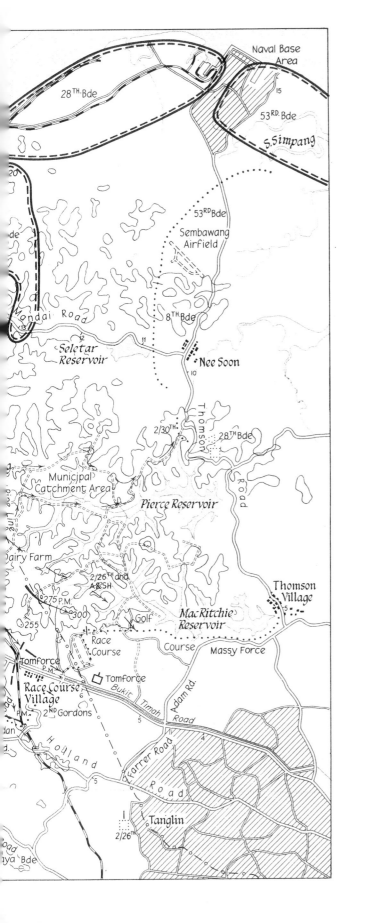

53rd Brigade which remained immediately south of Nee Soon to cover the evacuation of stores and the destruction of the magazines at Seletar rifle range. The withdrawal of the residue of 18th Division from the coast to join 'Massy Force' was carried out without interruption. The troops in Southern Area, having demolished the Changi defences, also fell back during the night to their sector in the perimeter.

Throughout the day the Japanese *18th Division*, now supported by artillery, attacked both flanks of the area held by 22nd Australian Brigade.[1] Although it penetrated the position in several places it was forced back at the point of the bayonet, and the line held till dusk. After dark however further enemy attacks pierced the centre and enveloped the left flank. In view of the danger of encirclement Brigadier A. L. Varley, who had succeeded Brigadier Taylor, obtained permission to move back to the perimeter. This was successfully accomplished. Nearer the coast, on the front of 44th Indian and 1st Malaya Brigades, there had been little enemy activity during the day, but to conform with the Australians both brigades withdrew after dark.

By the morning of the 13th, the occupation of the twenty-eight mile perimeter covering Singapore was complete, except that part of 53rd Brigade remained south of Nee Soon till noon, and 1st Malaya Brigade remained in occupation of the western end of the Pasir Panjang ridge. The 2nd Malaya Brigade held from Kallang airfield to Paya Lebar airstrip and 11th Division from there to a point on Braddell Road one mile west of Woodleigh. The 18th Division continued the line: 53rd Brigade, now under its orders, held the Chinese Cemetery area north of Braddell Road; 55th Brigade absorbed 'Massy Force' and held a sector from Thomson Road to Adam Park; and 54th Brigade (Brigadier E. H. W. Backhouse) took over the remnants of the original 'Tomforce' astride the Bukit Timah Road. The 2nd Gordons remained in the Farrer Road sector and the Australians held a sector from the junction of Farrer Road and Holland Road to the railway north of Tanglin Halt.[2] The 44th Brigade was astride the Buona Vista Road west of Tanglin Halt,[3] and 1st Malaya Brigade held Point 125 (near the Buona Vista Road), Point 270, Point 125 (on Reformatory Road) and Pasir Panjang.[4] Bennett ordered all Australian troops (except some medical units)

---

[1] The strength of 22nd Australian Brigade had, by the morning of the 12th, been reduced to 800 all ranks. Attached to the brigade were about 200 survivors of 15th Brigade and also 100 men of 1/5th Sherwood Foresters, who had been isolated from 'Tomforce'. The 2/26th Battalion was placed under command of 22nd Brigade during the afternoon.

[2] 2/30th Battalion rejoined 8th Australian Division on the 13th.

[3] The strength of 44th Brigade was approximately 1,200 all ranks at this time.

[4] 1st Malaya Brigade consisted of 2nd Loyals (less one company), 1st and 2nd Malay Battalions, 5th Beds and Herts (less two companies) and the composite Royal Engineer Battalion.

when falling back to the perimeter, to move into an area with Tanglin Barracks as its centre; there, if necessary, they were to fight to a finish.

The withdrawal of 11th Division had been carried out none too soon, for, after the failure of *4th Guards Regiment* to break through at Nee Soon, General Nishimura decided to contain the British forces at that point while he sent two battalions south through the catchment area to cut Thomson Road behind the defenders. These enemy battalions reached their objective on the 13th, just after 53rd Brigade had been withdrawn.

By this time some of the troops forming the garrison had begun to lose confidence in their leaders, and their morale, already low, had started to crack. Reports had come into Malaya Command that sullen, armed deserters, in greater numbers than could be controlled by the Military Police, were skulking in the town and hiding in bomb-proof buildings or engaged in looting. Some of them were also seizing small boats in which to escape from the island, while others were forcibly boarding ships leaving for Java and Sumatra. Most of these were deserters from administrative units, and men who had recently arrived in Malaya as reinforcements, inadequately trained and disciplined.[1]

---

[1] See page 325.

E2

CHAPTER XXIV

THE SURRENDER OF
SINGAPORE

See Maps 21 and 25

BY THE morning of the 13th February the battle for Singapore Island was irretrievably lost and it was only a question of time before capitulation would become inevitable. It may therefore be appropriate to consider how it was that, as General Wavell reported to the Prime Minister, 'the Japanese with their usual infiltration tactics are getting on much more rapidly than they should on the west of the island', and why he recorded in his despatch, 'I left Singapore on the morning of the 11th February without much confidence in any prolonged resistance'.

Two months of continuous retreat on the mainland and the destruction of the Naval Base, which it was their task to defend, had undoubtedly lowered the morale of the troops. Many of them, officers and men alike, had developed a withdrawal complex and some, perhaps with the evacuation of Dunkirk in their minds, were beginning to look over their shoulders with the idea of escape to the south. Many of the Australian and Indian units had been brought up to strength with large numbers of partly trained reinforcements. For three of the infantry brigades the fighting on the island was their first experience of war. These factors reduced the fighting value of the garrison as a whole. They could not however have been responsible for the complete failure of the defence on the 9th and 10th February, for there is clear evidence that the majority of the men of 22nd Australian Brigade, outnumbered by some five to one, fought gallantly in their forward positions till ordered to withdraw, as did 2/26th Battalion at Kranji. The courageous stand by 22nd Australian Brigade near Holland Road and the stubborn fighting by 11th Division in the Causeway area on the 10th and 11th, by 18th Division on the Bukit Timah Road and by 1st Malaya Brigade on the Pasir Panjang ridge, showed conclusively that there was little wrong with the fighting spirit of many of the troops when given the opportunity of meeting the enemy on reasonably equal terms.

The defence of an island always presents a difficult problem for the soldier. The first aim of the defence is to prevent the enemy from landing by hitting him when he is most vulnerable—on the water. Should he succeed in gaining a foothold, the object must be to prevent him establishing a bridgehead which would enable him to bring in his reinforcements, tanks and artillery. This can be achieved only if there are prepared positions at points of tactical importance to halt the enemy and if formed bodies of troops are in reserve ready to launch counter-attacks. In the case of Singapore the problem was more than usually difficult. The enemy had complete control of both the sea and air and was thus able to attack at any point. The island had some seventy miles of indented coastline much of which was difficult to defend, and it was therefore probable that the enemy would succeed in landing somewhere. Moreover the country inland did not lend itself to defensive action. Much therefore depended on the initial dispositions.

General Percival decided to base his plan of defence on preventing the Japanese from landing on the beaches and, if they managed to gain a footing, to drive them out by counter-attack. Since the enemy could be expected to concentrate his maximum strength for an assault on a selected narrow front, making feint or subsidiary assaults elsewhere, the problem was to decide on the most likely points of attack and then to concentrate on their defence, retaining in reserve the greatest possible strength.

General Wavell and Brigadier Paris had come to the conclusion that the Japanese would attack on the north-west coast of the island, for the lay-out of the roads and rivers in Johore made it possible for them to mount an attack in that area comparatively quickly and, since they had command of the air, their preparations could be carried out in secrecy. No other line of attack offered such advantages. Yet Percival, possibly influenced by the trend of pre-war planning which had envisaged a landing at Mersing followed by an advance to Kota Tinggi and thence down the Johore River, was not prepared to accept the north-west coast as the most probable line of assault. He decided to defend the whole seventy miles of coastline and disposed his forces in such a way that the density of the defence, both in infantry and artillery, was less in the north-west of the island than in the Causeway area or in the north-east. Practically the whole of the garrison was committed to static defence. This inevitably resulted in there being inadequate forces everywhere, and no reserves available for the all-important immediate counter-attack role.

It was thus that, at the point where the Japanese made their assault, defended posts were widely separated and commanders were unable to keep in hand sufficient local reserves for immediate counter-attack; there was not enough artillery to provide either adequate harassing fire to interfere with the enemy's embarkation arrangements, or general defensive fire on more than one-third of the front to be covered, and there were no general reserves readily available for deliberate counter-attack. The 22nd Australian Brigade, entrusted with the defence of the front where the landing took place, was given an impossible task. That this brigade was overrun during the night of the 8th/9th February and that the enemy reached Tengah airfield by the afternoon of the 9th, was due far more to the way the defence had been planned than to any failure on the part of the formation itself.

Once it was clear that the enemy was committed to the assault, the object of the defence should have been to bring him to a halt as near the coast as possible and counter-attack before he could recover from the confusion inherent in an assault landing. There was thus every reason for hurrying all available reserves to the area in which the landing had taken place. Western Area reacted slowly and it was not till between 6 a.m. and 7.45 a.m. that exiguous reserves (the re-formed 2/29th Battalion and the newly-raised Special Reserve Battalion, neither fit for anything but static defence) reached Tengah airfield. Malaya Command, thinking that the assault might be a feint which would be followed by an attack on the north-east coast, did not send forward 12th Brigade, the only Command Reserve, till after the receipt of the morning situation report indicating that all was quiet on III Corps front. This brigade did not therefore reach the threatened area till about midday. The fleeting opportunity to launch a counter-attack to hold the vital Ama Keng neck and confine the enemy to the north-west corner of the island was lost.

By the afternoon of the 9th, the Japanese had occupied their first objective—Tengah airfield—and, as they then had sufficient depth to land artillery and tanks, the battle for the island entered its second phase. All now depended on the ability of the defence to hold the Jurong Line and launch from it a deliberate counter-offensive with the greatest possible strength. But to prevent this line being turned it was essential that the Kranji–Woodlands coastline should be retained. Since by that time it was abundantly clear that the enemy's attack on the north-west coast was in great strength and the increased artillery fire in the Kranji–Woodlands area indicated that he might shortly make an attempt to widen his bridgehead, there was on the evening of the 9th an immediate need to strengthen the defences near the Causeway, and to create a powerful mobile reserve in the Bukit Timah area for the all-important counter-offensive. The only way such a reserve could have been found was to leave the north-eastern coastline defended by a skeleton garrison with a high proportion of machine-guns, and to withdraw 18th Division, concentrating it on the Bukit Timah road by the morning of the 10th ready for any eventuality. The risk was not great; the threat of a landing on the north-eastern sector had receded and a seaborne landing on the south-east coast could by that time have been almost entirely discounted.

General Percival has since stated that he estimated the strength of the landing in the north-west as at least one division out of the three available and that, Pulau Ubin being in enemy hands, it would have been possible for the Japanese, who had drawn the defence to the west of the island, to throw one division against the north-eastern coast. He therefore felt that he could not weaken his defences in the latter area. His decision on the afternoon of the 9th to base the defence on holding the Jurong Line and the Causeway sector and to despatch his last reserve (15th Brigade) to reinforce Western Area was however of little value unless at the same time he took steps to create a fresh general reserve. But for the reasons given above he did not re-create a reserve on the 9th and thus lost the only chance he had of regaining the initiative.

The retention of the coastline in the Causeway area was of such importance that Percival would have been wise to relieve Bennett of the responsibility for it and thus free him to give his full attention to the critical battle on the Jurong Line. The 11th Division had a brigade in reserve in close proximity to the Causeway and it should have been possible to transfer the control of this vital area to III Corps, and allot 27th Australian Brigade to 11th Division, even though Bennett might have opposed the transfer of an Australian formation to the control of others.

The reasons for the withdrawal of 27th Brigade from the coast-line are obscure. Because of the fear that the enemy might cross the Sungei Peng Siang and attack his brigade from the rear, Brigadier Maxwell sought permission throughout the 9th to withdraw 27th Australian Brigade from the Kranji–Woodlands area and re-adjust his line to face west. Such a threat did exist, but it was scarcely likely that the Japanese, with two good roads leading straight to the heart of the island, would trouble to cross this mangrove-fringed river in any strength unless they were unable to make progress by the more direct route. Bennett quite rightly refused to agree to Maxwell's request and told him to make his own arrangements to watch the river line. He could indeed hardly have done otherwise in view of Percival's orders for the conduct of the defence. It is quite clear from the evidence available that neither he nor his staff knew anything of the events at the Causeway during the night of the 9th/10th and were as surprised as 11th Division was when, in the early hours of the morning, they learnt that 27th Brigade had withdrawn during the night. It must be assumed that Maxwell acted under a misapprehension of Bennett's intentions.

The position in the Causeway sector might have been retrieved if, when he learnt that the enemy had made a landing and had been checked, Maxwell had cancelled his withdrawal orders of the afternoon, told his battalion commanders to hold on and asked Bennett to provide him with the means to counter-attack at dawn. But he allowed his orders to stand and the vital sector was abandoned at the very moment that the Japanese assault had been brought to a standstill.

The result of the various errors of judgement committed on the 9th was that by dawn on the critical 10th February the pivot position at Kranji had been abandoned; the two battalions of 27th Australian Brigade, out of touch with their brigadier, had taken up positions which gave protection to neither the right flank of the Jurong Line nor the left flank of III Corps. Bennett had committed his last reserve formation to the static defence of part of the Jurong Line and Percival had no other reserve immediately to hand. But this was not all. Western Area had issued to the commanders of its subordinate formations an order to be acted on in certain circumstances, based on Percival's secret and personal instructions to his senior commanders regarding the occupation of a perimeter position around Singapore town. To these weary and distracted officers, sorely in need of reinforcements and encouragement to fight on despite their difficulties, the receipt of such an order was tantamount to an admission that the higher command regarded the situation as hopeless. The psychological effect of this order undoubtedly had a considerable bearing on their actions during the 10th.

A study of the events on that day shows clearly that throughout it Western Area failed to co-ordinate the actions of its subordinate formations. Paris, finding that 27th Australian Brigade had left the Causeway sector, withdrew his brigade on his own initiative from the Jurong Line to the Bukit Panjang Village area to guard against any enemy attempt to strike through to the Bukit Timah area. The other brigade commanders, influenced either by what they knew of the situation or by their interpretation of the orders relating to the occupation of a perimeter position around Singapore, all acted independently. Thus, despite the fact that the enemy during the day had done nothing more than probe the defences with his advanced troops, the Jurong Line was abandoned. Further north it was left to Heath and Key to do their best to retrieve the desperate situation created by the withdrawal of 27th Australian Brigade.

The order given to Western Area to counter-attack and regain the Jurong Line was impossible to carry out. Such a counter-attack might have been successful during the day had a fresh formation been available and had a stable base from which to launch it existed. But no fresh reserve had been created; the front in Western Area was utterly disorganized and no steps had been taken to ensure that the Kranji pivot was firmly held. In the conditions which existed no counter-attack could have succeeded. But Bennett had to attempt to carry out Percival's order given on the Supreme Commander's instructions. He could not use 'Tomforce' for the purpose, since it had been hurriedly improvised during the 10th and was not due to assemble in the Racecourse area till the evening.[1] He was left therefore to organize the counter-attack with the formations already under his command. These were by this time quite unfit to undertake co-ordinated offensive action and the front was already crumbling. The counter-attack ordered had no hope of success, and the attempt to launch it resulted only in further confusion and in the destruction in detail of the forces involved.

As soon as it became known on the 9th February that the enemy had landed on the island, last minute efforts were made to complete the demolitions in the Naval Base. The power station, most of the cranes and much valuable machinery and plant were destroyed. The large floating crane and the smaller floating dock which had been towed to Keppel Harbour were both sunk at their moorings. Tanks in fuel depots which had not already been destroyed were holed or fired. It was inevitable however that some plant and machinery were left intact. In the circumstances it is perhaps surprising how much was accomplished.

The execution of the civil denial scheme had also been ordered by the Governor on the 9th. Teams drawn from the Public Works Department and the Royal Engineers, aided by Excise and Customs Officers and volunteers from the Observer Corps and the Chinese and Indian population, worked round the clock to complete their task. They succeeded in destroying the stocks of rubber, the tin smelting plants on Pulau Brani and a number of factories. They also disposed of some one and a half million bottles of spirits and 60,000 gallons of Samsu (Chinese spirit)—a precaution which undoubtedly saved the town from excesses both before and after the capitulation.

They were however greatly handicapped, when they began the denial of plant and machinery, by the fact that some persons with vested interests did their utmost to delay the destruction of their property by lodging appeals with local authorities. Some firms, whose head offices were in Britain, Australia or India, even appealed to their home Governments. Some went so far as to obstruct the work of the denial teams. The withdrawal of all European supervisory staff from the Singapore Harbour Board installations on the 10th, by orders of the Governor, also hampered the work.

---

[1] See page 387.

Furthermore some officials and other civilians in key positions left the island without authority on the 9th and 10th February, and again on the 13th. Nevertheless with certain exceptions the work was completed by the day of surrender. The exceptions were the installations captured by the enemy before they could be destroyed and those exempted by the Government on the plea of the effect of the denial operations on morale. The latter included the installations of some forty Chinese firms and the workshops and vehicles of two large motor dealers and their subsidiaries. This resulted in the enemy receiving a welcome present of new vehicles and well-equipped workshops.

The denial scheme was carried out under great difficulties, for there was much to be done and little time in which to do it. Enemy bombardment and the disorganization of those last few hectic days added to the difficulties. As General Percival pointed out, a last ditch stand and complete denial were incompatible. A retreating army can scorch the earth behind it, but an army defending a fortress cannot fight to the last man and burn the ground on which it stands.

By the 13th the administrative situation in Singapore had begun to cause considerable anxiety. Owing to the influx of refugees, the civil population within a three-mile radius of the waterfront had increased to about a million. The withdrawal to the perimeter defence line had brought about a concentration of military transport and equipment within the town so that there was hardly any part of it which was not a fair military target. The enemy bombed and shelled the town throughout the day causing severe damage to the water mains, which soon made the water supply precarious. The loss of the Bukit Timah depots had reduced the military food reserves, apart from those held by units and by the civil authorities, to seven days. Reserves of ammunition were still reasonably good but petrol was becoming very short.

The same day Rear-Admiral, Malaya, who was personally responsible for the denial of all naval stores, asked for and was given authority to destroy the large oil supplies on Pulau Bukum.[1] Demolitions were carried out that afternoon, but were not entirely successful.

At 2 p.m. Percival held a conference in Fort Canning which was attended by all area and divisional commanders and by the principal staff officers of Headquarters, Malaya Command. The future conduct of operations was discussed, and in particular the possibility of organizing a counterstroke. In the opinion of all formation commanders the exhaustion of the troops was such that a major counter-attack would have little chance of success. Heath and Bennett

---

[1] See Map 21.

advocated capitulation. Percival however believed that the situation, though undoubtedly grave, was not hopeless and gave orders that the defence of the town was to continue.

The conference also discussed arrangements for the evacuation of women and the military nursing services, and of selected staff officers and technicians. Since Rear-Admiral, Malaya, had earlier decided that all the remaining ships and sea-going craft, including some naval patrol vessels, would have to sail on the night of the 13th/14th February, this was the last opportunity for any organized parties to leave Singapore. The ships had accommodation for 3,000 in addition to the crews, and this was apportioned to the Services and the Civil Government.

That night the flotilla of small ships sailed from Singapore in an attempt to reach Sumatra and Java. Rear-Admiral Spooner, in a naval motor launch, sailed with them. He was accompanied, at Percival's instigation, by Air Vice-Marshal Pulford who had declined to leave until all air force officers and men who could be spared had been evacuated. When the flotilla sailed no one was aware that the Japanese Fleet had interposed itself between Singapore and its destination.

Percival reported the situation fully and candidly to Wavell during the day and indicated that it was unlikely that resistance could last more than a day or two. He said that there must come a stage when, in the interest of the troops and the civil population, further blood-shed would serve no useful purpose and asked that he might be given wider discretionary powers. Wavell in reply said:

> 'You must continue to inflict maximum damage on enemy for as long as possible by house-to-house fighting if necessary. Your action in tying down enemy and inflicting casualties may have vital influence in other theatres. Fully appreciate your situation but continued action essential.'

There was no serious enemy pressure during the 13th in the sectors held by 2nd Malaya Brigade, 11th Division, 18th Division and the Australians. On the western flank of the perimeter the Japanese *18th Division*, having found on the 12th that the Australians were too hard a nut to crack, decided to transfer their efforts further south along the Pasir Panjang ridge and astride the Raja Road. The *56th Infantry Regiment*, supported by a considerable force of artillery, attacked the ridge during the morning. Fighting continued all day, but despite determined resistance by the units of 1st Malaya Brigade, who fought most gallantly, and covering fire from the heavy guns of the fixed defences, the enemy succeeded late in the evening in capturing The Gap. This penetration led to the withdrawal after dark of both 44th Indian and 1st Malaya Brigades to the general line Mount Echo–junction of the Raja and Depot Roads–Buona Vista village, some three miles from the centre of the town and immediately west of the main ordnance and ammunition depots and the Alexandra British military hospital. During the day, 27th Australian Brigade was re-formed with its original battalions and 2nd Gordons, and given a sector within the Australian perimeter.

Early on the 14th Percival received a report from the Director General of Civil Defence saying that a complete failure of the water supply was imminent. At about 10 a.m. he held a conference at the Municipal Offices at which the Chairman of the Municipality and the Director General of Civil Defence were present. The Municipal Water Engineer reported that, owing to breaks in the water mains caused by the bombing and shelling, more than half the supply from the reservoirs was being lost. He estimated that the supply might last for forty-eight hours at the most, and perhaps for not more than twenty-four hours.

Percival thereupon arranged for about one hundred men of the Royal Engineers, then fighting as infantry in the south-western sector, to be withdrawn to assist in the work of repairs. About 10.30 a.m. he saw Sir Shenton Thomas who emphasized the danger from epidemic that would arise if the large population in Singapore were suddenly deprived of water. Percival told him that, although the shortage at the time was serious, it did not in his opinion make the further defence of Singapore impossible and that he intended to continue fighting. The situation was reported by Sir Shenton to the Colonial Office and by Percival to Wavell who replied that the fighting must go on wherever there was sufficient water for the troops. He added in a later message, 'Your gallant stand is serving a purpose and must be continued to the limit of endurance'.

On the 14th in the western sector the enemy again launched a heavy attack at 8.30 a.m., supported by intense mortar and artillery fire, on the front held by 1st Malaya Brigade. This and a number of other attacks were beaten off after bitter hand-to-hand fighting, with severe losses on both sides. At 4 p.m. an attack supported by tanks eventually succeeded in penetrating the left, and the defenders on this flank were forced back to a line from the junction of the Raja and Depot Roads through the Brick Works and along the canal to Bukit Chermin. As on the preceding day the Australians were undisturbed except for occasional heavy shelling. Bennett had given orders during the morning that, because of the shortage of ammunition, the Australian artillery was to fire only in defence of the Australian perimeter or on observed targets. Although there was excellent observation over the area further south in which the enemy was advancing, the guns remained silent. Eye witnesses from 2/4th Machine-Gun Battalion say that throughout the day they saw enemy columns moving west but, as they had been rearmed as infantry, they could take no useful action.

East of the reservoir the enemy attacked down Thomson Road and captured Point 105, thereby causing a gap to develop between 53rd and 55th Brigades. A battalion from 11th Division was sent to fill the gap. North of the Bukit Timah Road the enemy heavily bombarded the positions held by 55th and 54th Brigades, throughout the morning. In the afternoon an attack down Sime Road led by medium tanks broke through, some tanks reaching the edge of the residential district at Mount Pleasant before they could be brought to a standstill. A counter-attack was organized but failed to develop. By nightfall a line had been established from the Pier on MacRitchie Reservoir southwards to Mount Pleasant Road and thence westwards south of Bukit Brown to the original line west of Adam Road.

On the eastern side of the perimeter the enemy attacked about midday immediately south of the satellite strip for fighter aircraft at Paya Lebar. The front of 2nd Malaya Brigade was penetrated and 11th Division had to form a defensive flank along the southern boundary of the air strip. By dusk however the position was stabilized.

In addition to the continuous shelling, there were a number of air attacks on Singapore which caused heavy casualties among the civilian population; nevertheless, the civil defence organization continued to function despite almost overwhelming difficulties. Streets were blocked by the wreckage of bombed buildings, many of which still smouldered, and by broken telegraph poles and tangled wires. Civil labour had disappeared and little could be done to clear the wreckage or even to bury the dead. The civil hospitals were crowded with injured, and the ground floors of several of the largest hotels and buildings, in use as temporary hospitals and aid posts, were full of casualties.

About 5 p.m., on the 14th, after visiting formation headquarters in Northern Area, Percival held a second conference at the Municipal Offices, the same officials being present. The Municipal Water Engineer reported that the position had slightly improved. Percival thereupon asked the Director General of Civil Defence for an accurate forecast of the situation at 7 a.m. next morning.

During the night of the 14th/15th February there was little enemy activity on the Singapore perimeter as a whole. Some infiltration on 18th Division front caused the withdrawal of units in forward positions, and 2nd Malaya Brigade was forced to give ground south of the defensive flank held by 11th Division. But the general line still held at daybreak on the 15th.

That morning the report from the Director General of Civil

Defence showed a serious deterioration in the state of the water supply. Though the enemy had captured all the reservoirs by mid-day on the 13th, the flow of water to the pumping stations at Woodleigh, and thus to the mains serving the town, had not been interfered with. The rate of breakage of the main and subsidiary pipelines from bombs and shell fire had however steadily increased and the proportion between used and wasted water had risen from about one to three on the 12th/13th to about one to six on the 15th. Because of the shortage of labour and the difficulty of moving pipes and other material through streets blocked by debris, repairs could not keep pace with the breakages so that most of the water ran to waste, and it was only the buildings in the low-lying parts of the town that got any.

At 9.30 a.m. Percival held a conference at Fort Canning. The commanders of Northern, Western and Southern Areas and the anti-aircraft defences were present, together with some staff officers. The Director General of Civil Defence and the Inspector General of Police, Straits Settlements, also attended. After the formation com-manders had reported on the tactical situation in their respective sectors, the Director General explained that the water supply was unlikely to last for more than about twenty-four hours and that, in the event of total failure, several days would elapse before it could be restored.[1]

Percival then gave a summary of the administrative situation as known that morning. The military food reserves were reduced to a few days, but there were still fairly large civil stocks. There were adequate reserves of small arms ammunition, but ammunition for field guns was very short and the reserves of light anti-aircraft shell were almost exhausted. Apart from what vehicles had in their tanks there was hardly any petrol left.

The conference discussed possible measures for improving the general administrative situation, in which the imminent failure of the water supply was the greatest danger. In Percival's opinion there was nothing to be gained by remaining on the defensive since, apart from the need to ease the administrative difficulties, there was every chance that a determined enemy attack might break through into the crowded town, with disastrous consequences for the civil population. He told the conference that there seemed to him to be only two alternatives: either to counter-attack at once in an effort to regain control of the reservoirs and of the military food depots in the Bukit

---

[1] This proved to be an underestimate, for the Royal Engineer working parties and the Municipal Staff who after the capitulation continued to repair the mains, under Japanese supervision, repaired some two hundred bomb or shell breaks in the first eleven days. It was five and a half days before supplies reached the first floors of buildings in the lower-lying areas of the town, ten days before all buildings obtained supplies and some six weeks before pressure became normal.

Timah area, or to capitulate immediately. The formation commanders were still unanimously of the opinion that, in the circumstances, a counter-attack was impracticable. Confronted with this, and with no immediate solution for the critical water problem, Percival decided to capitulate. The conference concurred in his decision.

In the course of the morning General Percival received a telegram from General Wavell which again said that time gained and damage caused to the enemy were of vital importance in the existing crisis, and that, so long as he was able to inflict damage and loss to the enemy, and his troops were physically capable of doing so, he must fight on. When however he was fully satisfied that this was no longer possible he was given discretion to cease resistance.

About 11.30 a.m. a joint military and civil deputation, consisting of a senior staff officer, the Colonial Secretary and an interpreter, drove in a motor car bearing a flag of truce along the Bukit Timah Road towards the Japanese lines. The deputation had instructions to propose to the Japanese a cessation of hostilities from 4 p.m. on the 15th February and to invite the Japanese to send representatives to Singapore to discuss terms.

Meanwhile 53rd Brigade had been forced by the threat to their left flank to withdraw behind Braddell Road. In the south-west sector of the perimeter, 1st Malaya Brigade, owing to the failure of units on both its flanks to hold their ground, withdrew at 2.30 p.m. to the general line Mount Echo–railway crossing on Depot Road–the western slopes of Mount Faber–Bukit Chermin. The Alexandra depot area with the remaining reserves of ammunition and stores was thus lost. The Japanese entered the Alexandra Military Hospital where, on the excuse that the hospital had been used as an artillery position, they killed some of the staff and shot all the walking wounded in cold blood. Elsewhere, apart from some infiltration on the 18th Division front, enemy activity throughout the morning and afternoon was chiefly confined to the shelling of selected localities.

About 1 p.m. the joint deputation returned from the enemy lines with instructions that the commander of the British forces was to go personally with his staff to meet the Japanese representatives at the Ford Factory at Bukit Timah. At 5.15 p.m. General Percival, accompanied by his chief staff officer, was received by the commander of the Japanese *25th Army*, General Yamashita, who demanded the unconditional surrender of the British garrison. After a discussion lasting fifty-five minutes Percival agreed, and at 6.10 p.m. signed the terms of surrender. These read:

(a) The British Army shall cease hostilities at 8.30 p.m.
(b) The British Army shall disarm themselves in the positions they occupy on the cease fire by 9.30 p.m., with the exception of 1,000 men who

will be allowed to carry arms in order to maintain peace and order in Singapore until further notice.

Before signing, Percival asked that the Japanese Imperial Forces would protect British civilians, men, women and children. General Yamashita undertook to do this.

On his return to his headquarters Percival issued the orders necessary to implement these terms. All fighting ceased at 8.30 p.m. and quiet descended on the bomb-scarred burning town. Thus ended a disastrous campaign of seventy days—thirty days less than the Japanese had allowed for in their original plan. That evening a message from General Percival was received at Headquarters, ABDA Command. It read:

'Owing to losses from enemy action, water, petrol, food and ammunition practically finished. Unable therefore to continue the fight any longer. All ranks have done their best and grateful for your help.'

Thereafter all communication with Singapore ceased.

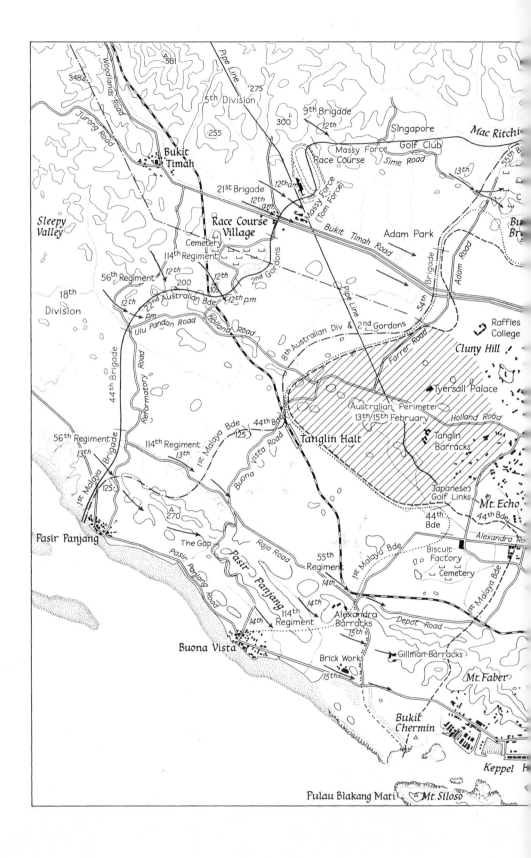

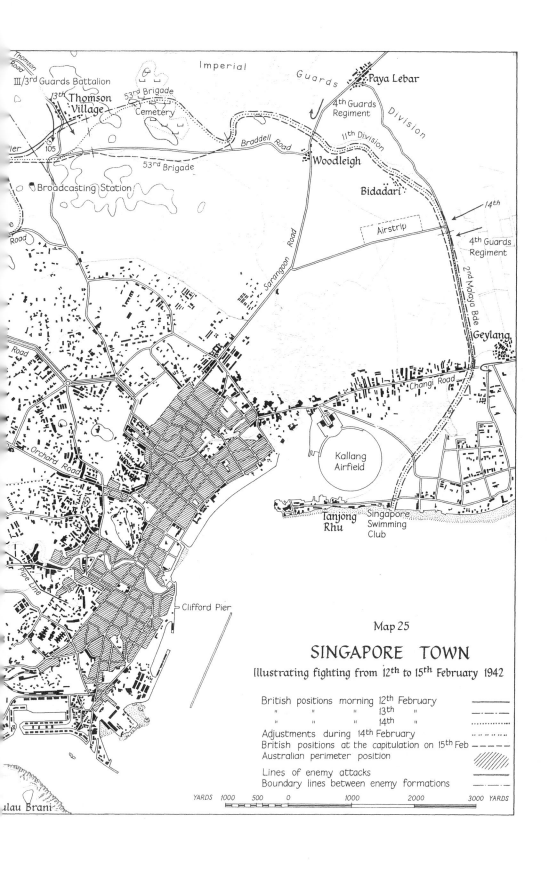

III/3rd Guards Battalion
Thomson Road
13th
Thomson Village
53rd Brigade
Cemetery
105
Pier
Broadcasting Station
Road
Braddell Road
53rd Brigade
Imperial
Guards
Division
Paya Lebar
4th Guards Regiment
11th Division
Woodleigh
Bidadari
14th
Airstrip
4th Guards Regiment
2nd Malaya Bde.
Serangoon Road
Geylang
Changi Road
Orchard Road
Kallang Airfield
Pipe Line
Tanjong Rhu
Singapore Swimming Club
Clifford Pier
Pulau Brani

Map 25

SINGAPORE TOWN

Illustrating fighting from 12th to 15th February 1942

British positions morning 12th February	
" " " 13th "	
" " " 14th "	
Adjustments during 14th February	
British positions at the capitulation on 15th Feb	
Australian perimeter position	
Lines of enemy attacks	
Boundary lines between enemy formations	

YARDS 1000   500   0   1000   2000   3000 YARDS

CHAPTER XXV

THE INVASION OF SOUTHERN SUMATRA AND THE LOSS OF BALI AND TIMOR

See Maps 17 and 26

THE JAPANESE did not wait for the fall of Singapore before launching the western arm of their three-pronged attack on Java.[1] By the end of January preparations for their next step were well advanced. The *229th Infantry Regiment* and one battalion of *230th Infantry Regiment* of *38th Division* had been moved on the 20th January from Hong Kong to Camranh Bay. As soon as the fall of Singapore was assured, Lieut.-General Sano, commanding the division, was instructed to proceed with the plan for the occupation of southern Sumatra. The first objectives were to be the airfield and oil refineries at Palembang and the oilfields in the surrounding area.

On the 9th February part of *229th Infantry Regiment* (commanded by Colonel Tanaka) left Camranh Bay under naval escort. Two days later it was followed by the remainder of the regiment in fourteen small transports. Vice-Admiral Ozawa, flying his flag in the cruiser *Chokai*, with the *7th Cruiser Squadron* and the light carrier *Ryujo* screened by a division of destroyers, sailed on the 10th February to act as cover to the convoys.[2] When the first convoy entered the Banka Strait Admiral Ozawa spread his covering force across the approaches, while aircraft from the *Ryujo* carried out a search of the waters to the north.

For some days previously a stream of ships and small craft had been flowing southward from Singapore. Many of these had sailed under official auspices (such as the convoy of the 12th February and the flotilla of small ships on the night of the 13th/14th February), but among them were small craft carrying soldiers who had been cut off on the mainland and were trying to escape. Others carried deserters who had managed to obtain yachts or native craft and had slipped away secretly at night. Some of the bigger ships also carried deserters who had forced their way on board at the point of the pistol.

---

[1] See page 291.
[2] See Appendix 22.

Few of those outside the official parties had any plans. Their one idea was to put the blazing town of Singapore and the nightmare of the last few days as far astern of them as possible. The elements, if not the enemy, were kind to them. The sea was calm. The waters to the south of Singapore are dotted with innumerable small islands between which, during the north-east monsoon, the currents run strongly to the south-west. Thus those of the small boats which escaped the enemy, despite the lack of knowledge of navigation of their occupants, reached the shores of Sumatra.

For most of those who sailed after the 12th it was their last voyage. The larger ships were routed to Java by way of the Banka Strait. Most of those who survived the constant bombing ran straight into the guns of Admiral Ozawa's squadron. His cruisers, destroyers and aircraft struck at the defenceless and crowded ships, and massacre resulted. In the space of two or three days some forty ships, both large and small, were sunk by bomb or gunfire.

Many of those which escaped were wrecked and their occupants marooned on the islands. The naval motor launch carrying Rear-Admiral Spooner, Air Vice-Marshal Pulford and a small party of officers and men, was bombed and beached on a small island twenty miles north of Banka. There was little food in the island, which was malarial and unhealthy. It was over two months before the party was able to cross to Sumatra in a native boat, where it surrendered to the Japanese. By then eighteen of its number had died including the Admiral and the Air Marshal.

There were many deeds of heroism and self-sacrifice during this last exodus from Singapore. Among these shines the epic of the *Li Wo*. This small auxiliary patrol vessel left Singapore on the morning of the 13th February and, although repeatedly attacked by aircraft, was only slightly damaged. On the afternoon of the 14th she sighted a Japanese convoy escorted by a cruiser and a destroyer. Lieutenant T. Wilkinson, R.N.R., her commanding officer, at once decided to attack and, altering course towards the enemy, opened fire on the transports with his one old 4-inch gun. The convoy was masking the fire of the warships and by a miracle the *Li Wo*, although hard hit by the guns of the transports, remained afloat. Knowing that it could be only a matter of minutes before his ship was blown out of the water by the warships, Wilkinson resolved to sell his life and his ship dearly. Putting his engines at full speed he turned to ram the nearest transport and hit her amidships. A few minutes later his ship was sunk at point blank range by the cruiser, taking her gallant captain and crew with her. It was not until the end of the war that this story came to light: Lieutenant Wilkinson was then posthumously awarded the Victoria Cross.

The full story of the adventures of many who escaped from

Singapore makes thrilling reading, but lack of space debars its inclusion in this history. Some of those who survived the sea passage reached Java; others landed on the east coast of Sumatra, from where they made their way across the island by river, road and rail. Three escape routes were organized by officers who had formed part of the official evacuation party from Singapore, all of which led to Padang on the west coast. The Dutch gave the most willing and generous help. Their efficiency and hospitality evoked the admiration and gratitude of the many hundreds whom they helped to escape to freedom.

Parties left from Padang as soon as shipping could be found to take them. Two small ships left the port on the 26th February. One ship reached Ceylon safely; the other, in which Brigadier Paris was a passenger, was torpedoed and sunk by a Japanese submarine when half-way to Colombo. A single lifeboat escaped filled to the gunwales with eighty persons, including the Brigadier, with some fifty more in the water clinging to her sides. For twenty-six days the boat drifted under a tropical sun until it reached a lonely island about sixty miles west of Sumatra. Of the 135 who left the sinking ship in the lifeboat only four survived—a Scottish soldier, a Chinese woman and two Javanese sailors.

A large party of some 800 left Sumatra on the 1st March in the three cruisers and two destroyers of the Western Striking Force which called at Padang on their way to Colombo.[1] In all about 1,600 officers and men from Padang reached India and Ceylon; a small number reached Java and some even Australia. At least 800 are known to have been left behind in Sumatra and were taken prisoner when the Japanese completed their occupation of that island in March.

During the night of the 13th/14th February the leading Japanese convoy, which had already been sighted,[2] was attacked by all available bombers but, owing to stormy weather, it escaped almost unscathed. The following morning air reconnaissance reported that the convoy had entered the Banka Strait and once again all the bombers, escorted by any Hurricanes which could still fly, took off to repeat the attack. In spite of strong fighter defence and heavy anti-aircraft fire from the Japanese naval escort, the bombers dived to drop their bombs. Weather conditions were better and several ships were hit and some set on fire, but only one was sunk.

The Japanese had decided that to achieve surprise and capture the airfields intact they would use parachute troops as the spearhead of their attack. They had therefore concentrated about 460 of these troops at airfields in southern Malaya. At dawn on the 14th February

---

[1] See page 437
[2] See page 358.

transport aircraft carrying 360 of them, escorted by fighters and a strong force of bombers, set course for the mouth of the Moesi River. Smoke from burning oil tanks hung over Singapore and stretched as far south as Palembang, making navigation difficult but increasing the chances of surprise. The formation reached the mouth of the river without having been sighted, and, dividing into two parts, approached its objectives using the river as a guide.

On the day of the enemy attack mixed detachments, formed from the R.A.F., men from British anti-aircraft units and Dutch troops, were holding P.1 airfield and Palembang town. At each of the oil refineries there were two Dutch infantry platoons, and three companies were in reserve at P.2 airfield. The air striking force had just left to attack the enemy convoy in the Banka Strait, when the Observer Corps reported the approach of a large force of enemy aircraft making for Palembang. Attempts to divert the Hurricanes to intercept were unsuccessful. A few minutes later P.1 airfield was heavily bombed and aircraft on the ground were machine-gunned by the large fighter escort. Shortly afterwards about 260 parachute troops were dropped in the scrub surrounding the airfield, and a further 100 near the two refineries a few miles away at Pladjoe and Soengi Gerong. The drops were not carried out without loss, for anti-aircraft fire brought down one troop carrier and forced another to make an emergency landing.

The first attempt by the paratroops to rush the airfield was driven back. This gave time for the aircraft which had escaped damage to take off for P.2 airfield, and for all unarmed ground staff to leave for Palembang. The Japanese however formed a road block between P.1 airfield and the town. Efforts to reinforce the airfield were made twice during the day but only a few men succeeded in reaching it. Meanwhile hand-to-hand fighting was going on. The anti-aircraft gunners, firing over open sights, were repeatedly attacked by the paratroops, who used small arms and hand grenades, and both sides suffered heavy casualties. In the middle of the battle Hurricanes were reported returning to the airfield from the raid on enemy shipping in the Banka Strait. They were diverted to P.2 airfield, but some which failed to receive the order landed at P.1 where they quickly refuelled under fire before taking off again for P.2. Towards the end of the afternoon the Allied defenders began to run short of ammunition. Reports from the oil refineries were bad, there were rumours that Palembang town was cut off from the south and fresh Japanese reinforcements were known to be off the mouth of the Moesi River. There seemed therefore little hope of a prolonged defence and later in the evening, when it was found that the road to the town was open, all the unserviceable aircraft and equipment remaining were destroyed and the ground forces withdrawn to P.2 airfield.

At Pladjoe the garrison had been taken by surprise. The Japanese quickly gained possession of the refinery and entrenched themselves in the oil yards where they beat off all counter-attacks. Reserves were called up from P.2 and were joined by British anti-aircraft crews. With these reinforcements, supported by mortar fire, the enemy was dislodged after some fierce fighting. The surviving paratroops fled to the mangrove swamps nearby leaving behind them nearly half their number dead or wounded. The recapture of the refinery was however of little value to the Allies, since fires which had broken out in the buildings and in the yards during the fighting prevented the demolition scheme from being put into effect. All that could be done was to increase the number of fires. This achieved no permanent result, and the Japanese claim to have been able to resume full production within a very short time. At the other refinery at Soengi Gerong the defence was more successful and the enemy attack was held until demolitions had been completed.

By the night of the 14th the Dutch were still in possession of Pladjoe, and a mixed force held a position on the road between the airfield and the town. The Dutch commander was confident that the airfield could be recaptured next morning. In all probability the heterogeneous Allied force could have disposed of the remaining Japanese paratroops, but on the morning of the 15th a further 100 paratroops were dropped on P.1 airfield and, when reports were received that Japanese reinforcements were on their way up the river, the proposed counter-attack was called off. The Dutch commander, on his own initiative, then withdrew to the south-west. In face of the strength of the enemy invasion forces at Palembang and with Singapore in enemy hands, General Wavell realized that there was no hope of holding southern Sumatra. He therefore ordered all British units in Sumatra to withdraw to Java.

The Japanese had planned that Colonel Tanaka's advanced force should arrive at Palembang on the day following the parachute landing. Its arrival was however delayed, possibly by the Allied bombing attack on the 14th, and it was thirty-six hours before the hard-pressed paratroops were relieved. On the evening of the 14th the convoy anchored at Muntok in Banka Island, opposite the Moesi delta. Two companies were landed on the island and, meeting only token resistance, soon occupied it. Leaving one company as garrison, the remainder of the force transhipped to landing craft during the night and, at dawn on the 15th, entered the Moesi River.

The landing craft were reported by a dawn reconnaissance from P.2 where a striking force of thirty-eight bombers and twenty-two Hurricanes, all the operational aircraft that remained in Sumatra, were awaiting orders to attack. At 6.30 a.m. the first flight of six Blenheims, escorted by Hurricanes, took off and, despite strong fighter opposition, pressed home its attack. From then on, a constant stream of aircraft struck at the transports at anchor and at the barges in the river. The number of sorties was limited only by the speed with which they could refuel and rearm. The Japanese fighter opposition ceased soon after the first attack, and the Hurricanes were thus free to use their machine-guns; the Blenheims joined them when their bombs were expended. At first there was heavy but inaccurate anti-aircraft fire, but this ceased about midday. Attacks were continued until late afternoon, by which time all movement on the river had stopped, and the barges had pulled in under the shelter of the undergrowth on the river bank. There is no accurate record of the result of these attacks but there is no doubt that many casualties were inflicted. One transport was sunk by bombing and many of the barges destroyed. But although the approach of Tanaka's force had been checked it had not been stopped, and during the night of the 15th/16th the leading Japanese troops reached the outskirts of Palembang and joined up with the paratroops.

It may well be wondered how the convoy carrying the Japanese advanced force had been able to reach Muntok without encountering the striking force which Wavell had ordered Admiral Doorman to assemble west of Java.[1] When Doorman received his orders his ships were to the south of Bali over 800 miles from Banka Island, where he had been sent by Admiral Hart to be out of range of enemy air attacks. The other ships of the striking force were employed in escorting convoys. Thus, with the inevitable delays due to refuelling and the distances involved, he was unable to collect his force until the 14th February.

Doorman sailed at dusk that day from a rendezvous north of the Sunda Strait with the three Dutch cruisers *De Ruyter*, *Java* and *Tromp*, and the *Hobart* and *Exeter*, screened by four Dutch and six American destroyers. His shortest route, and that which gave the best chance of meeting the enemy, was through the Banka Strait. Without air cover the passage of the narrow strait, where there was no room to manœuvre and where there was the risk of enemy mines, had been adjudged too hazardous and he had been ordered to take the longer route through the Gaspar Strait, attack from the north of Banka Island (from where there was always the possibility of taking the enemy in the rear) and return, if practicable, through the Banka Strait. Fate was once again against him from the start. That night one of the Dutch destroyers struck a reef east of Banka and became a total loss. When he arrived north of the island, the Japanese convoy carrying the advanced force was already anchored in Muntok harbour, and the convoy with the main force was still 120 miles to the northward.

---

[1] See page 358.

Vice-Admiral Ozawa received news of the approach of the Allied striking force soon after daylight on the 15th. He at once ordered the convoy, already at Muntok, to move into the mouth of the Moesi River, turned the main convoy which was then east of Lingga Island back to the northward and gathered his forces for a surface attack. Meanwhile he ordered aircraft from the *Ryujo* and naval land-based aircraft from western Borneo to attack the Allied striking force.

Throughout the day Doorman's force was attacked by successive waves of bombers. Fortunately all bombing was from a high level, no torpedo-bombers were used and the only damage sustained was from two near misses to two of the American destroyers. Nevertheless the Admiral felt that to risk an encounter with a possibly superior force and without fighter protection was to court disaster, and that afternoon, abandoning his projected thrust into the Banka Strait, he turned his force to the southward and withdrew through the Gaspar Strait.

With the threat of surface attack to his convoys removed, Ozawa ordered the main force to resume its southerly course. The second convoy thus reached the mouth of the Moesi River on the evening of the 16th and, crossing the bar at high water, went up river on the following day to Palembang, where the troops disembarked and joined Tanaka's force which, by that time, had occupied the town.

By the evening of the 15th February the Dutch and British forces had left Palembang by road and rail for Oosthaven, from where they were to cross the Sunda Strait to Java. All aircraft from P.2 still able to fly had flown to Java with the exception of a few bombers which had been operating until dark, by which time it was too late to take off; these left early on the 16th heavily overloaded with as many of the ground crews as they could take. There was much confusion during the hurried retreat to Oosthaven. Many of the bridges on the route had been built with wooden roofs. These were too low to allow the passage of some of the guns and tractors and had to be sawn off before they could pass. Owing to misunderstandings some of the bridges were prematurely blown up by the Dutch. The suddenness of the move and the lack of a proper movement control staff caused delay and disorder at the docks where much equipment, which would have been invaluable in Java, was needlessly left behind. To add to the confusion the two leading ships bringing the advanced parties of the Australian corps, as well as a squadron of light tanks (3rd Hussars) which was to have reinforced the garrison at Palembang, had just arrived.[1] Some of these troops had already disembarked and were used to cover the embarkation, but no attack developed. By the 17th all Allied forces from Palembang had left for Java.

---

[1] These ships carried 2/3rd Australian Machine-Gun Battalion and 2/2nd Pioneer Battalion. See page 350.

Two days later, as Oosthaven was reported to be still clear of the enemy, a party of some fifty R.A.F. volunteers left Batavia in H.M.A.S. *Ballarat* for that port, where they loaded the ship to the gunwales with air force equipment and stores;[1] having destroyed as much of the harbour and railway works as they could, they returned without interference from the enemy. There is no doubt that the evacuation of both Palembang and Oosthaven was premature. The Japanese advanced force had received a severe hammering in the passage up the river and needed time to re-equip and reorganize. It was not until the 17th that the enemy's advance was resumed. Detachments then thrust south to Oosthaven, west to Benkoelan and northwest to Djambi and Padang, meeting only slight resistance from the scattered Dutch troops at some of the towns.

With Singapore, southern Sumatra, Borneo and Celebes in enemy possession, General Wavell knew that the Japanese invasion of Java would probably take place before the end of February. He saw little prospect of preventing landings or repelling the invaders with the naval, land and air forces at his disposal, or likely to be available in the immediate future. His problem was whether to attempt to bring part or the whole of the Australian corps, then on its way east, into Java or to recommend its diversion elsewhere. In view of the time factor (the leading division could not be fully ready for action until 21st March), and the fact that the enemy possessed both naval and air superiority and would be able to bring the available disembarkation ports under heavy air attack, he considered that the former course would be unjustified. On the 16th February Wavell informed the Chiefs of Staff of his views and recommended that, as the defence of both Burma and Australia was vital to the successful prosecution of the war against Japan, the Australian corps should be used for this purpose. He proposed that at least one division, and if possible the whole corps, should be diverted to Burma, where also a heavy bomber force should be built up as rapidly as possible. Two days later, after discussion with the commanders concerned, he reported that the successful defence of Java with the resources available and in sight was extremely doubtful and he again repeated his recommendations as to the disposal of the Australian corps.

There were soon to be further signs that the Japanese intended to invade Java without delay, for the loss of southern Sumatra was quickly followed by the invasion of both Bali and Timor. On the 15th February, escorted by the American cruiser *Houston*, the destroyer *Peary* and two Australian sloops the *Swan* and *Warrego*, a convoy of two American and two Australian transports carrying 49th

---

[1] The party was drawn from 605 (County of Warwick) Squadron Royal Auxiliary Air Force and led by Group Captain G. E. Nicholetts.

Battalion of 148th U.S. Field Artillery Regiment and 2/4th Australian Pioneer Battalion left Darwin under cover of darkness to reinforce the garrison in Timor.[1] They had not been long under way before they were sighted and shadowed by an enemy seaplane. The next morning the convoy was attacked by some thirty-five Japanese bombers from Kendari. The ships suffered only minor damage from near misses, but further attacks were inevitable; enemy aircraft carriers were known to be in the vicinity—one had been sighted and attacked by Allied aircraft on the 4th February—and there were rumours of warships near Timor. In these circumstances Wavell considered the risk to the convoy was too great and ordered it to return to Darwin, where it arrived on the 18th February.

The *Houston*, after refuelling, left to rejoin the striking force at Tjilatjap. It was lucky for her that she did, for the day after she sailed Darwin received a devastating bombardment from the air. The attack was made by aircraft from Vice-Admiral Nagumo's four fleet carriers and from the *21st Air Flotilla*. The carriers were escorted from Staring Bay (south of Kendari) by two heavy cruisers and a flotilla of destroyers. They made the passage of the Banda Sea under cover of darkness and at dawn on the 19th February reached the flying-off position in the Timor Sea, where the carriers turned into the wind and flew off their aircraft—152 bombers and torpedo-bombers and 36 fighters. Aircraft of the *21st Air Flotilla* from Kendari followed two hours later.

Ten American fighters had left Darwin for Java at 9.15 a.m. that morning but had been forced back by adverse weather. Five of them had landed at 9.40 a.m. to refuel while the remainder were circling the harbour as top cover. It was at this moment that Nagumo's aircraft arrived without warning. They shot down four of the American aircraft, destroyed those on the airfield and then attacked the harbour, the docks, the oil installations and the town.

The harbour was unusually crowded that morning for the *Houston*'s convoy had just returned. Fire from the shore anti-aircraft batteries and from the ships' guns was unable to break up the attack, and almost the whole of the convoy was lost. Two transports, one tanker and three supply ships were sunk; two transports and a supply ship had to be beached and another, unloading ammunition, blew up; a transport, a supply ship and a hospital ship were hit and damaged. The American destroyer *Peary*, which should have sailed with the *Houston* but had been delayed by a fruitless search for a submarine outside Darwin and had returned to refuel, received several hits and sank. The American seaplane tender *William B. Preston* and the Australian sloop *Swan* were damaged. When their bombs were expended the aircraft flew over the harbour, machine-gunning the

---

[1] See page 348.

men in the water as they escaped from the sinking and burning ships. The town, attacked from a low level, also suffered severe damage.

Just before midday, with rescue and salvage operations proceeding, the aircraft of the *21st Air Flotilla* arrived on the scene and bombed the airfield, completing the task of destruction begun by those from the carriers. The attack was a severe blow to Darwin: eleven ships were lost, twenty-three aircraft destroyed and two damaged, and valuable stores and airport buildings demolished. Casualties were some 240 killed and 300 injured, mainly among ships' crews and civilians. The enemy lost five aircraft. The second attack, so soon after the first, was thought to be a pre-invasion bombardment and, with the exception of the army units and the naval men ashore, the town was evacuated by nightfall.

Further west, and concurrently with this attack, the enemy invaded Bali. Its capture had not been included in the original Japanese plan, but, finding towards the end of January that their operations from the newly-captured airfields in Celebes and Borneo were greatly hampered by the weather, they decided to seize the island with its important airfield for use as an advanced air base for the invasion of Java. One infantry battalion from the Japanese *48th Division* was taken from Luzon, where it had participated in the landing at Lingayen, and was sent to Makassar in preparation for the attack. The advanced invasion force left the port in two transports escorted by four destroyers on the 18th February, and landed unopposed that night on the south-east coast of the island.

There had been indications early in February of the enemy's intention to attack the island and General Wavell had intended that Admiral Doorman should meet the invasion force in superior strength, but the approach of Admiral Ozawa's expedition for the capture of Palembang had made him send Doorman to the westward. Thus on the 17th February, when the Bali invasion force was reported to be on the point of leaving Makassar, the striking force was scattered and Doorman was unable to collect his ships until after the landing had been completed. The Admiral himself with the *De Ruyter* and *Java* and two Dutch and two American destroyers was at Tjilatjap; the *Tromp* was at Sourabaya and four American destroyers were refuelling in the Sunda Strait. Admiral Helfrich realized that if Doorman were to strike he had to do so at once. He ordered him therefore to attack on the night of the 19th February without previous concentration. The ships from Tjilatjap were to attack from the southward at 11 p.m. The *Tromp* and the four destroyers from the Sunda Strait were to sail by way of the Madoera and Bali Straits and attack three hours later. Finally, after an interval of at least one hour, four or five Dutch motor torpedo-boats were to be sent in to take advantage of what he hoped would be a scene of confusion.

Flying his flag in the *De Ruyter* followed by the *Java* and the four Dutch and American destroyers, Doorman left Tjilatjap on the evening of the 18th February. Ill luck again dogged him. As the ships were leaving, one of the Dutch destroyers, the *Kortenaer*, ran aground in the narrow entrance to the harbour and had to be left behind. As it grew dusk on the following evening the destroyers took station three miles astern of the cruisers. A few hours later the squadron reached the southern end of Bali. By this time the two Japanese transports had landed their troops and one of them, escorted by two destroyers, was on her way back to Makassar; the other transport was just getting under way with the two remaining destroyers standing by. The *Java* was the first to sight the enemy and at 10.25 p.m. opened fire. In the brief action which followed, a Dutch destroyer was hit in the boiler room and sunk. The enemy transport was damaged by gunfire and received at least one hit from a torpedo. The Dutch ships left the island on a northerly course while the two American destroyers returned to Tjilatjap.

The *Tromp* and her four American destroyers came in about three hours afterwards as planned, and also made their attack from the southward. This time the destroyers were ahead, with the *Tromp* about five miles astern. The ships had been unable to establish communications with Admiral Doorman and had no knowledge of how he had fared. The position of the enemy ships was first disclosed by their signal lights. The destroyers went in to attack at high speed and fired salvoes of torpedoes, none of which hit, at a target dimly outlined in the darkness. Shortly afterward the two Japanese destroyers were sighted. In the gun duel which followed, one of the American destroyers was hit before contact with the enemy was lost. Behind the destroyers came the *Tromp* which, in her turn, engaged the enemy destroyers; she scored a hit on one of them but herself received a hit forward of the bridge, which killed several men.

Hearing of the first attack at 10.30 p.m., Rear-Admiral Kubo in the *Nagara* turned south with his three destroyers from his supporting position north of the island.[1] Unable himself to reach the scene of action in time, he sent the two destroyers, then escorting one of the transports back to Makassar, to the help of their sister ships. They met the Allied force at 2.20 a.m. in Lombok Strait. Both sides fired torpedoes and opened up with gun fire. A Japanese destroyer was severely damaged and half her crew killed; she eventually had to be towed back to Makassar. When the *Tromp* arrived she received the concentrated fire of the enemy, and was so hard hit that she had subsequently to be sent to Australia for repairs. By 3 a.m. all Allied ships were clear of Bali and on their way back to Sourabaya. When

---

[1] See Appendix 22.

the motor torpedo-boats came in about an hour later, they found the anchorage deserted.

Enemy fighter aircraft occupied the airfield on Bali on the 20th February, and four days later the main invasion force landed unopposed from six transports. The loss of the airfield was a serious blow to the Allied chances of holding Java. With the airfields in southern Sumatra, in Borneo and Celebes and now Bali in the hands of greatly superior enemy air forces, it was obvious that the Allied air forces, almost entirely cut off from reinforcement by air, would be overwhelmed within a comparatively short time. Wavell told the Chiefs of Staff on the 19th February that the Allied fighter force, then consisting of some eighty-five aircraft, could not remain effective for more than two weeks.

On the following day (20th) the expected attack on Timor took place. Leaving the naval detachment as garrison, *228th Infantry Regiment* left Amboina on the 17th, escorted by the *2nd Destroyer Flotilla*, and arrived off Timor during the night of the 19th/20th. A force of two battalions with some light tanks was landed at a point some sixteen miles south-east of Kupang in the early hours of the 20th and advanced in two columns towards the town, which was heavily bombed. At about 10 a.m. the same day, three hundred naval parachute troops of the *Yokosuka 3rd Special Naval Landing Force* were dropped by aircraft of the *21st Air Flotilla* from Kendari in the vicinity of the airfield, which lay on the main road to the interior some fifteen miles east of Kupang. Faced with this encircling attack the Allied force evacuated Kupang during the 20th and moved eastwards along the road in the hope of reaching the interior. That evening they found the Japanese forces firmly established astride the road to the east of the airfield and attacks both on the 21st and 22nd failed to break through. By the morning of the 23rd the force found itself surrounded and at 10 a.m. was forced to surrender, only a few escaping to the hills.

Simultaneously with the attack on Kupang Japanese troops went ashore at Dili under cover of naval bombardment and, meeting only slight resistance from the small Allied garrison, soon captured the airfield and by 1 p.m. were in occupation of the town. The Australian and Dutch detachment withdrew southwards towards the centre of the island where they were joined some time later by those who had managed to make their escape from Kupang. From there they waged guerrilla warfare. From bits and pieces they built a wireless set with which they managed to get in contact with Australia, where they had been posted as 'missing believed killed'. Aided by the native population they then directed air attacks, laid ambushes and made frequent raids on the Japanese garrison, even venturing as far as Dili itself. After regaining contact with Australia, they were supplied with essentials by air from Darwin and by light surface craft, although for the most part they lived off the country. They remained a thorn in the Japanese side until they were finally withdrawn to Australia in December 1942.

On the 20th February the Chiefs of Staff told General Wavell that, since every day gained was of importance, Java should be defended with the utmost resolution by all the combatant troops for whom arms were available. They gave him liberty to augment the defences of the island with any available naval forces in the ABDA area and with the American aircraft already allotted to him which were being assembled in Australia. On the 21st they told him that Burma would be removed from his command and once again placed under the control of India, and that all land reinforcements from the west were being diverted elsewhere.

On the same day he received instructions from the Combined Chiefs of Staff in Washington that his headquarters were to be withdrawn in such a manner, at such time and to such place within or without the ABDA area as he might decide. Wavell recommended that his headquarters should be not withdrawn but dissolved. He pointed out that since the control of Burma had reverted to India there was practically nothing left to command in the ABDA area. He believed that the local defence of Java could be better exercised under the original Dutch organization. He stressed however that it should be made quite clear that the dissolution of ABDA Headquarters did not mean the stoppage of warlike supplies to Java. Next day the Combined Chiefs of Staff cabled accepting these views, whereupon Wavell decided to dissolve his command at 9 a.m. on the 25th February, just six weeks after its formation, and hand over the command of all forces in the Netherlands East Indies to the Dutch Governor-General, Jonkheer Dr. van Starkenborgh Stachouwer.

Under this arrangement the British forces in Java were to be placed under the orders of the Dutch Commanders-in-Chief: Admiral Helfrich,[1] General ter Poorten, and Major-General Van Oyen (the Dutch Air Officer Commanding). Admiral Palliser was to remain as Senior British Naval Officer; Admiral Glassford remained in command of the United States naval forces under Admiral Helfrich's direction; Commodore Collins, R.A.N., with the title of Commodore Commanding, China Force, was to be in command of the British naval forces, Major-General H. D. W. Sitwell of the British army forces still in Java, and Air Vice-Marshal Maltby of the British air forces.

---

[1] Vice-Admiral Helfrich succeeded Admiral Hart who resigned his command of the Allied naval forces on the 14th February.

With the loss of Timor and the consequent severance of the air reinforcement route from Australia, the loss of ten American fighter aircraft destined for Java but destroyed in the air raid on Darwin, and the heavy losses in air combat and on the ground in Java which had reduced his fighter strength to some forty aircraft, Wavell revised the estimate which he had given to the Chiefs of Staff; on the 21st February he informed them that the Allied air forces could remain effective for only one more week—a forecast which proved correct.

The American seaplane tender *Langley*, with thirty-two assembled American fighter aircraft on deck and with pilots and ground personnel on board, and the cargo vessel *Seawitch*, with twenty-seven crated fighters in her hold, were at that date with a convoy on passage from Australia to Ceylon. The need for more fighter aircraft being vital for the defence of Java, Wavell, using the authority given him by the Chiefs of Staff, gave orders that these two ships were to be diverted to Java. The *Langley* left the convoy several hours before the *Seawitch* and sailed at best speed, without escort, for Tjilatjap.

This last attempt to bring air reinforcements to the island was however doomed to disaster. On the morning of the 27th February, when within a hundred miles of her destination, the *Langley* was sighted by a Japanese air patrol and was attacked an hour or two later by nine enemy bombers. Her flight deck was too small to fly off any of the fighters she carried, and no help could be sent since the few fighters left in Java were already committed. On the enemy's third and last bombing run the *Langley* received five direct hits and was set on fire. She had later to be sunk by the American destroyers sent to meet her. The *Seawitch* arrived at Tjilatjap on the 28th but, as events turned out, there was no time to erect the crated planes before the arrival of the Japanese invading forces and they were destroyed when the port was abandoned.

General Wavell left Java on the 25th February to resume his appointment as Commander-in-Chief, India. He left instructions with the British commanders to go on fighting as long as the Dutch continued effective resistance and, when that ended, to extricate from Java such men and materials as they could. He warned them that no further help could be expected for some time. General Sitwell's comment on receiving these instructions was that big game shooting in Java had always been one of his ambitions in life.

PALEMBANG

Map 26

5 0 5 10 15 20
Scale of Miles

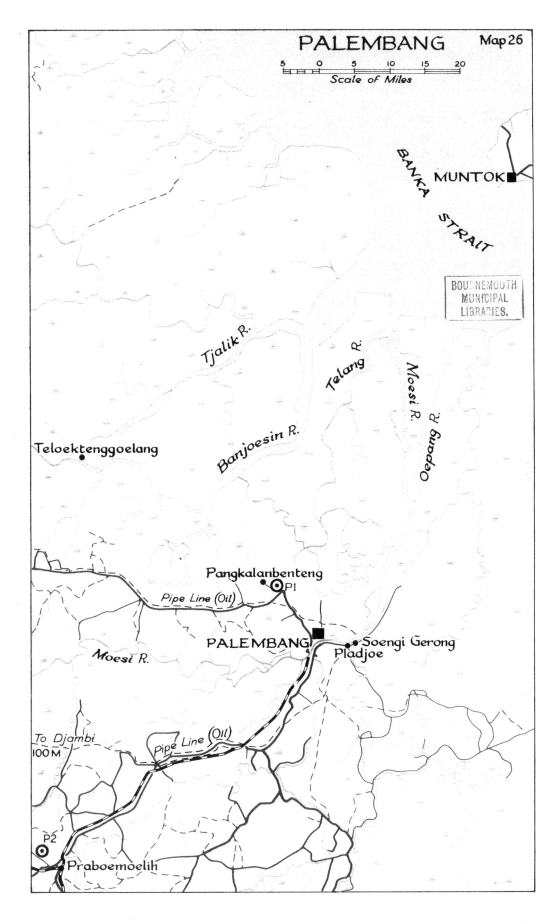

BANKA STRAIT

MUNTOK■

BOURNEMOUTH
MUNICIPAL
LIBRARIES.

Tjalik R.

Telang R.

Moesi R.

Oepang R.

Banjoesin R.

Teloektenggoelang

Pangkalanbenteng
◉P1

Pipe Line (Oil)

PALEMBANG■   ●Soengi Gerong
●Pladjoe

Moesi R.

Pipe Line (Oil)

To Djambi
100 M

P2
◉
Praboemoelih

CHAPTER XXVI

THE FALL OF JAVA

See Maps 17, 27 and 28

THE CAPTURE of Palembang and the occupation by the Japanese of southern Sumatra had destroyed the last hope of a prolonged defence of Java. Invasion was expected in a matter of days and the stream of civilian evacuees which had been debouching from Sourabaya and Batavia had swelled to a flood. At Tanjong Priok, the port of Batavia, this outflow of evacuees met the inflow of soldiers, airmen and refugees from Singapore and Sumatra, with the result that the harbour and the roadstead became congested with shipping, and unloading took place as best it could. The quays, the sheds and the roads leading from them became blocked with an inextricable confusion of equipment, motor transport, abandoned cars and goods of every description. The town became crowded with refugees and newly-arrived soldiers and airmen, in addition to the Dutch troops mobilized for the defence of the area.

Confusion was worse confounded by the arrival of about 10,000 air force reinforcements and evacuees from Singapore and Sumatra, mostly between the 12th and 18th February. Those from Singapore had embarked under heavy air attack with large numbers of civilian refugees; units had become separated and much of their equipment had been left behind or lost through enemy action. Those from Sumatra had also lost most of their equipment during the hasty withdrawal from the airfields at Palembang and the confusion of the embarkation at Oosthaven.

Although an appreciable number of aircraft had reached airfields in West Java, the R.A.F. and Commonwealth air strength, after losses suffered in the defence of Palembang, had been reduced to about twenty-six reconnaissance aircraft, twenty-six bombers, nine torpedo-bombers and twenty-five fighters, and of these only eighteen of the fighters and less than one third of the others were fit for operations.

Air Vice-Marshal Maltby with a nucleus staff had arrived in West Java on the 14th February and had set up his headquarters at Soekaboemi, some fifty miles west of Bandoeng. He at once began to reorganize his battered air force and build up an air defence for Java from the handful of worn-out aircraft and the disorganized and

431

tired body of men at his disposal. Twelve days were destined to be all the time given him. Aircraft were concentrated by types into squadrons and were allocated to the airfields in West Java at Tjilili-tan near Batavia, Semplak near Buitenzorg, and at Tjikampek and Kalidjati north of Bandoeng.[1] Fighter and bomber group head-quarters were improvised to assist in re-establishing these squadrons. Efficient operation and filter rooms were quickly connected to the Dutch Observer Corps, the fighter airfields, the anti-aircraft defences of Batavia and the air operations room in Bandoeng. Two radar sets were erected in the Batavia district. The Dutch did every-thing they could to help and even staffed the filter and operation rooms with volunteer youths and women whose alertness and enthu-siasm, said Maltby, could hardly have been better.

The number of airmen who had arrived in Java was far more than was necessary for the maintenance of the depleted squadrons, and arrangements were therefore put in hand for the evacuation from the island of some 6,000 men who were unarmed and surplus to requirements. This number tended to increase as the British squadrons dwindled away.

The rest of the Allied air force was in little better shape. The Dutch had about five bomber, three fighter and two observation squadrons in Java, all of which had played their full part in action against the enemy in Malaya, Sumatra or the outlying islands since the outbreak of war, and were in consequence much under strength. All that was left of the American squadrons were some twenty heavy bombers and about twenty-four fighters, many of which were unserviceable.

The Dutch regular army in Java consisted of about 25,000 men, made up of four infantry regiments each of three battalions, with artillery, ancillary troops and garrison units. They had very few tanks and armoured cars and other up-to-date weapons, for the Allies had been unable to supply them. In addition to the regular troops there was a Home Guard of about 40,000 men of doubtful value. Though they were well armed with rifles and tommy-guns, their training had of necessity been very limited and they had little experience in the tactical use of their weapons.

The British army was little more than a token force consisting of 'B' Squadron 3rd Hussars with twenty-five light tanks, and the two well trained Australian battalions of 1st Australian Corps which, it will be recalled, had arrived from the Middle East after fighting throughout the Syrian campaign. In addition there were two heavy and three light regiments of anti-aircraft artillery which had been sent to Java for the defence of the airfields. Most of their equipment

---

[1] See Map 28.

had however been lost through enemy action or other causes. There was also one American field artillery regiment.

The Allied naval forces were greatly reduced in numbers from those which had started the war ten weeks earlier. The services of no less than sixteen ships had been lost through enemy action or misadventure, and Admiral Helfrich was left with eight cruisers, twelve destroyers, thirty-two submarines fit to operate and a number of auxiliary craft.

Such were the Allied naval, army and air forces available for the defence of Java. Against them the Japanese could bring overwhelming strength. In comparison with those of the Allies their naval resources were practically unlimited; it was estimated that they could deploy up to six divisions as an invasion force, and put in the air 400–500 fighters and 300–400 bombers.

Japanese aircraft had not been used against Java until the airfields in southern Celebes and Borneo had been captured and the first attacks did not take place therefore until the 3rd February. From then on the ports and airfields received almost daily attacks. The naval base at Sourabaya was one of the most frequent targets, but surprisingly enough the crowded port of Batavia received comparatively little attention until the last few days before the invasion. There was a short lull during the Japanese preparation for the capture of Palembang, but attacks were resumed on the 19th February and, with the airfields in southern Sumatra and Bali in enemy hands, increased in strength and frequency as the day of invasion approached.

The ground defences were pitiably weak and fighter aircraft too few to make any serious challenge to Japanese attacks. Normal odds met in air fighting were about ten to one. Warnings of approach of enemy aircraft were erratic and in consequence many aircraft were destroyed on the ground. Nevertheless the dwindling Allied squadrons continued to strike at enemy shipping and airfields when and where they could, but the scale of attack was of necessity ludicrously light and strikes, for the most part of about half a dozen bombers, could do little to hamper the enemy's plans.

The navy, too, was doing what it could in the face of appalling difficulties. The oil supplies of Borneo and Sumatra, on which the mobility of the fleet depended, were lost, and lack of fuel was threatening to restrict movement. The supply of torpedoes for the American destroyers was running short; many of the ships had been damaged in action and most were badly in need of refit. At sea the ships, without reconnaissance aircraft, were working blind against superior surface forces, and were constantly exposed to air attack without the hope of fighter support. Even in harbour there was no rest for the tired ships' companies, for the Japanese bombers kept them constantly on the alert.

G2

After the Japanese occupation of southern Sumatra, Admiral Helfrich had sent minesweepers to patrol the Sunda Strait and to deal with the possibility of Japanese attempts to infiltrate across to Java. He ordered the bulk of his submarines to concentrate in the eastern part of the Java Sea, where they could cover the exit from the Strait of Makassar and the line Makassar–Bali. The American submarines were widely dispersed and only six were able to join the five Dutch submarines operating in the area. As the enemy convoys converged on Java, Admiral Helfrich brought the submarines closer in to cover the expected landing places, but there were too few to have any decisive effect on the progress of the invasion.

Since he could obtain no definite indication of the scale and direction of the Japanese movements towards Java, Helfrich decided on the 21st February to form a striking force at each end of the island. He was influenced by the fact that his scanty stocks of fuel were divided between Sourabaya and Batavia and he could not rely on using tankers to replenish his ships. Part of the striking force formed by his predecessor, Admiral Hart, was already at Sourabaya and consisted of the two Dutch cruisers *De Ruyter* and *Java*, three American and three Dutch destroyers.[1] This became the Eastern Striking Force. It was joined three days later by the American cruiser *Houston* from Darwin and two destroyers from Tjilatjap. Most of his remaining ships were based on Batavia and were still engaged in escorting convoys, and the Western Striking Force could not therefore be assembled until the 26th February. By that time he had formed the Combined Striking Force and little more than a token force (the light cruisers *Dragon* and *Danae*, the Australian cruiser *Hobart* and two destroyers) was left at Batavia.

On the 20th February Admiral Helfrich represented to General Wavell the impossibility of defending Java with the forces at his disposal and proposed that, if reinforcements could not be sent, the Anzac Force from the south-west Pacific and the Eastern Fleet from the Indian Ocean should carry out raids or demonstrations into or towards the Java and China Seas to divert Japanese strength. Wavell however felt unable to approve this proposal on the grounds that these moves would be ineffectual unless the ships actually entered the Banda or Java Seas and there, without the protection of fighter aircraft, they would be exposed to an unacceptable scale of air attack.

For the invasion of Java the Japanese reorganized their forces into two, an *Eastern* and *Western*, both under Vice-Admiral Takahashi

---

[1] The *Tromp* had been damaged during the action off Bali and had left for Australia on the 19th February. One Dutch destroyer was bombed and put out of action on the 25th.

with his flag in the cruiser *Ashigara*. On the 19th February *48th Division*, which had been withdrawn from the Philippines at the end of January and concentrated at Jolo in the Sulu Sea, sailed in forty-one transports escorted by Rear-Admiral Nishimura, in the light cruiser *Naka*, with six destroyers.[1] The convoy, having called at Balikpapan to embark *56th Regimental Group* (less the detachment which had captured Bandjermasin), left there on the 23rd February. At the southern end of the Strait of Makassar Rear-Admiral Takagi's force of two heavy cruisers and the *2nd Destroyer Flotilla* took station well ahead of the convoy to cover its approach to the landing points in Eastern Java.

On the 18th February the *Western Invasion Force*—fifty-six transports carrying *Headquarters 16th Army*, *2nd Division* and *230th Infantry Regiment* of *38th Division*—left Camranh Bay escorted by the *5th Destroyer Flotilla*. On the 26th it was joined by the *7th Cruiser Squadron*, one light carrier and the *3rd Destroyer Flotilla*, under the command of Rear-Admiral Kurita.

Vice-Admiral Nagumo's powerful force of two battleships, four carriers, two heavy cruisers and a flotilla of destroyers had returned to Kendari after its attack on Darwin. It was joined there a few days later by Vice-Admiral Kondo's force of two battleships, three heavy cruisers and three destroyers. Both forces sailed on the 25th February for the Indian Ocean in order to cut off the Allied escape route south of Java.

Within a few days of the capture of Palembang signs of the expected invasion became evident. On the 20th February about ninety ships were reported at Jolo and forces were believed to be gathering at Muntok for the final assault. The first definite indication that invasion was imminent was a report, received on the 24th February, of a large fleet of enemy transports with a strong escort, heading southward in the Strait of Makassar. It was calculated that this convoy could reach Java by dawn on the 27th February.

The Dutch High Command expected the Japanese to attack at both ends of the island, near Sourabaya in the east and in the Sunda Strait in the west. A landing in Middle Java was considered possible but unlikely. The Dutch defence plan had been laid accordingly. Such bombers as were left were to attack enemy transports as far out to sea as possible. A naval striking force was to engage the main invasion convoy when it appeared. The bulk of the Dutch forces was to be concentrated in West Java in which were the principal port of Batavia and the seat of government at Bandoeng. Middle Java was to be held by a few territorial units only, while in East Java the main

---

[1] Forming the *Eastern Force*. See Appendix 22.

concentration was to be at Sourabaya for the defence of the naval base. The Home Guard, which was insufficiently trained to be capable of manœuvre, was to be used for static defence of vital points. Should the Japanese succeed in landing they were to be resisted; if necessary the troops were to fall back on to previously prepared positions covered by large scale demolitions of bridges: in the east from Sourabaya to the Malang plateau, and in the west on the two roads leading to Batavia and later to Bandoeng where the final stand would be made.

In deciding how the British contingent could best be employed, General Sitwell was influenced by three considerations: firstly, the necessity to delay the enemy for as long as possible; secondly, that, as there was no time for training, troops should be used in roles for which they had already been trained; and thirdly, that, as he had no signal organization available for his headquarters, his force in the early stages would have to be controlled by Dutch commanders. Holding the view that the main British weapon of attack, reduced in numbers though it was, was the air force, he concentrated all anti-aircraft units for the defence of airfields, except 77th Heavy Anti-Aircraft Regiment, which was retained for the defence of Batavia. The 6th Heavy Anti-Aircraft Regiment, which had lost most of its guns at sea or in southern Sumatra, was equipped as an infantry unit to deal with possible parachute attacks and sent to Tjililitan airfield on the 26th February. The two Australian battalions and a hastily formed composite Australian battalion, together with 'B' Squadron of 3rd Hussars, an Australian engineer unit and a British signal section, were formed into a mobile striking force under the command of Brigadier A. S. Blackburn, v.c.[1]—to be known as 'Blackforce'. An improvised field ambulance, the American artillery and about 500 airmen who had been equipped as infantry were added later. The force was ready for action by the 28th February. General Sitwell proposed that 'Blackforce' should be kept under his own hand in the Bandoeng area. General ter Poorten however preferred the Buitenzorg area, since it was more suitable for mechanized warfare and provided good cover in the many rubber plantations, and placed 'Blackforce' under the orders of Major-General W. Schilling, commander of the forces in West Java.

On the 25th February Admiral Nishimura's destroyers landed a small force on Bawean Island, eighty-five miles north of Sourabaya, and set up a wireless station. At 11.25 a.m. that day Admiral Helfrich ordered all available cruisers and destroyers to join Admiral Doorman's Eastern Striking Force at Sourabaya. Commodore Collins accordingly despatched the cruisers *Exeter* and *Perth* with the

---

[1] An Australian officer.

destroyers *Jupiter, Electra* and *Encounter* from Batavia to Sourabaya.[1] The Australian cruiser *Hobart* remained in harbour. She was short of fuel and could not be replenished in time to sail, for the only oiler in port had been damaged in an air raid that morning.

Without waiting for the arrival of the British reinforcements, Admiral Doorman sailed with his three cruisers and seven destroyers from Sourabaya at dusk that evening (25th February). He carried out a sweep to the eastward along the coast of Madoera in the hope of intercepting the transports reported near Bawean Island. No contact was made however and the Allied force returned the next morning to Sourabaya, where it was joined by the *Exeter*'s detachment from Batavia. From then onwards the Eastern Striking Force became known as the Combined Striking Force, under the command of Admiral Doorman.

On the 26th February further reports confirmed the presence of large numbers of transports, escorted by warships, in the eastern end of the Java Sea steering south-south-west. Less definite information was received that the enemy transports off Muntok were expected to sail that day. It was clear that the invasion was about to begin.

The *Hobart, Dragon* and *Danae* sailed from Batavia at 10 p.m. on the 26th with orders to seek out and attack the Muntok convoy, but returned at 1 p.m. the next day without having sighted the enemy. After refuelling, they left harbour again shortly after midnight accompanied by a Dutch destroyer to sweep north from Batavia with orders, if contact were not made by 4.30 a.m. on the 28th, to abandon the search and proceed to Trincomalee via the Sunda Strait. The sweep was really no more than a demonstration, since to keep the small and hopelessly outnumbered force in the west Java Sea would have been suicidal. No enemy was encountered by the time laid down, and the force withdrew as ordered and finally arrived at Colombo on the 5th March.

Meanwhile at Sourabaya on the 26th February, Admiral Doorman's Combined Striking Force was refuelling in preparation for the next move.[2] At 4.15 p.m. he received orders from Admiral Helfrich to carry out a night attack on thirty Japanese transports, escorted by two cruisers and five destroyers, which had been sighted shortly before noon that day about two hundred miles to the north-north-east heading west by south at ten knots. After the attack had been carried out Doorman was to proceed to Batavia. He accordingly weighed and left harbour with his entire force at 6.30 p.m. on the

---

[1] *Exeter* and *Perth* had both recently arrived at Batavia from escort duties.
[2] The Combined Striking Force consisted of:
    8-inch cruisers: *Exeter* (British) and *Houston* (American).
    6-inch cruisers: *Perth* (Australian), *De Ruyter* and *Java* (Dutch).
    Destroyers: *Electra, Encounter* and *Jupiter* (British). *Witte de With* and *Kortenaer* (Dutch). *John D. Edwards, Alden, Ford* and *Paul Jones* (American).

26th, flying his flag in the *De Ruyter*, and set course to the eastward
so as to sweep along the north coast of Madoera where a landing
was thought possible. If no enemy were sighted he intended to sweep
back to the west and search the Bight of Toeban. He had originally
considered a sweep to the north and north-east, but had decided that,
without reconnaissance aircraft, there was a better chance of intercepting the enemy by crossing his line of advance close to his probable
landing points.

As the Combined Striking Force was leaving Sourabaya, American
bombers found and attacked a Japanese convoy about twenty-five
miles north-east of Bawean Island. No report of this sighting was
however made direct to Doorman and the information was not
passed to him by the commander of the naval base at Sourabaya
till 10.20 p.m. The exact time he received it is not known, but at
10.35 p.m. it was repeated by Admiral Helfrich, to whom the report
was originally made. This signal was received by Commodore Collins
at 2.25 a.m. on the 27th. It was probably received by Doorman at
the same time, eight hours after the attack had been made by the
American bombers and too late to be of value. He decided however
to keep to his intention of covering the expected landing places, and
did not go after the convoy which lay to the northward.

At dawn he was about ten miles north-west of the entrance to
Sourabaya and had seen no sign of the enemy. Just before 9 a.m. the
drone of aircraft was heard overhead and shortly afterwards a few
bombs were dropped near the *Jupiter*. From then on the ships were
shadowed by aircraft, and it was obvious that further attacks were to
be expected. At 9.30 a.m. Doorman turned the striking force
towards Sourabaya.

As the force was entering harbour at about 2.30 p.m., a report was
received of two enemy convoys escorted by warships sighted less than
an hour previously; here at last was definite and timely news of the
enemy. Anticipating Admiral Helfrich's orders, Admiral Doorman
immediately turned his force 180 degrees and set course to intercept
the nearest convoy which was reported to be twenty miles west of
Bawean Island.

The convoys were the advanced portion of the enemy's *Eastern
Invasion Force*. Reconnaissance aircraft had reported the movements
of the Allied striking force and at noon Admiral Nishimura had
turned the leading convoy to a safe course, with an escort of two
destroyers, while Admiral Takagi's two 8-inch cruisers, the *Nachi*
and *Haguro*, and the 5·5-inch cruisers, the *Jintsu* and *Naka*, leading
the *2nd* and *4th Destroyer Flotillas* respectively—fourteen destroyers in
all—held their course.[1]

_____

[1] See Map 27.

On paper there was little to choose between this force and Admiral Doorman's force of five cruisers (two 8-inch) and nine destroyers. But in reality the Allied squadron was no match for the Japanese ships, all of which had been modernized. It was a heterogeneous collection of ships of three nationalities deprived of a secure base, hastily assembled without any previous combined training and without time to establish a co-ordinated system of unified command. Most of the ships were in need of refit, and the *Houston*'s after triple turret had been out of action for the past three weeks. The ships' companies had been working for a long time under constant strain against an enemy with a seemingly inexhaustible supply of ships, men and aircraft, and were very tired. A few hours before the start of the last tragic sea battle of the campaign Admiral Doorman reported that the men had reached the limit of their endurance.

The combined Striking Force had hardly cleared the minefields before enemy aircraft appeared and dropped a few bombs. The *Houston* opened fire and the ships scattered, but by 3.50 p.m. they had re-formed and resumed their north-westerly course. The cruisers were in line ahead with the British destroyers forming a screen, the American destroyers astern of the cruisers and the two Dutch destroyers on the port quarter.

At 4.0 p.m. aircraft were sighted to the northward and a minute or two later smoke was seen on the horizon. At 4.10 p.m. the *Electra* sighted the enemy force, which was soon accurately identified, on a course which would bring it across the Allied line of advance.

At 4.16 p.m. the Japanese 8-inch cruisers opened fire at a range of 28,000 yards and the *Exeter* and *Houston* replied. Admiral Doorman was in a difficult position. His fire power was superior if he could get his 6-inch cruisers within range, which he could do most quickly by holding to his course. If however he did this, the Japanese would cross his 'T' which would enable them to bring all their guns to bear while only the foremost guns of the Allied ships could reply. He compromised. He altered twenty degrees to port to a course parallel to that of the enemy which brought his full 8-inch broadsides to bear but left the 6-inch cruisers out of range.

About 4.30 p.m. the Japanese flotillas attacked with torpedoes at long range. They were engaged by the 6-inch cruisers as they came in and one destroyer was hit by the *Perth*'s second salvo, upon which the flotilla turned away behind smoke. Meanwhile the enemy cruisers were still out of range of the Allied 6-inch guns. The Captain of the *Perth* in his report says, 'I found a long period of being Aunty Sally very trying without being able to return the fire'.

Shortly after 5.0 p.m. the Japanese made a second torpedo attack, again at long range, in which the two heavy cruisers and the second destroyer flotilla, led by the *Jintsu*, fired no less than sixty-eight torpedoes. Almost simultaneously the *Exeter* was hit in one boiler room by an 8-inch shell and hauled out to port with her speed reduced to fifteen knots.

The handicap imposed by lack of combined communications and training now revealed itself. The *De Ruyter* held her course but the remainder, instead of following in her wake, altered to port with the *Exeter* and the force was thrown into considerable disorder. To make matters worse it was at about this time that the torpedoes fired in the second Japanese attack reached the Allied cruiser line, but only one found a target—the Dutch destroyer *Kortenaer*. She was hit in the engine-room and immediately blew up and broke in two.

The disablement of the *Exeter* and the loss of the *Kortenaer* were heavy blows to the Allied fleet, which up till then had held its own in the long-range engagement. The destroyers were quick to lay a smoke screen round the *Exeter* which thus escaped further damage but, with her reduced speed, she could only have been a liability to Admiral Doorman and he ordered her to proceed to Sourabaya escorted by the *Witte de With*.

By 5.25 p.m. the Allied cruiser line had re-formed and was led by the *De Ruyter* in a wide arc between the *Exeter* and the enemy. Doorman now ordered the British destroyers to attack. The *Electra*, *Encounter* and *Jupiter* were widely separated and proceeded to do so independently. Conditions were difficult, for the smoke made by the destroyers to screen the *Exeter* was very thick. The *Electra*, emerging from the smoke, met three enemy destroyers at almost point blank range and, although she claimed hits on the leading destroyer, she was herself repeatedly hit and her guns silenced one by one. At about 6 p.m., when only one gun remained in action, the order was given to abandon ship. The *Jupiter* and *Encounter* both had short and inconclusive engagements with the enemy destroyers before rejoining the cruisers.

From 5.30 to 5.45 p.m. the cruiser forces were screened from each other by smoke, and here the Japanese had the advantage for, with the help of their spotting aircraft, they were able to maintain accurate fire. The action for the next hour was confused. Ships on both sides were emerging from or disappearing into smoke-screens and the light was beginning to fail. At a few minutes before 6.0 p.m. the Japanese *4th Flotilla* made another torpedo attack, the third in the action, but missed with all twenty-four torpedoes fired. About the same time Doorman ordered the four American destroyers to counter-attack, but almost immediately cancelled the order and told them to make smoke. Under cover of this, he turned his cruisers on to an easterly course which placed the destroyers between them and the enemy. On being ordered to cover the cruisers' retirement, the destroyers closed to 14,000 yards of the enemy heavy cruisers, fired their starboard tubes and then turning 180 degrees fired their port tubes. The enemy cruisers altered course to the northward making smoke, and the *De Ruyter* wore round gradually to a similar course, signalling to the destroyers to follow her.

The sun set at 6.21 p.m. In the gathering darkness the *De Ruyter* continued to lead the cruisers in a northerly direction, in an attempt to work round the enemy forces and reach the convoy. At 7.27 p.m., by the light of the full moon, the *Jintsu* and three destroyers were sighted on the port beam and engaged for a few minutes at a range of 9,000 yards. At the same time enemy aircraft dropped flares silhouetting the Allied ships and the *Jintsu* fired a salvo of torpedoes. But the *Perth*, seeing the flashes of discharge, turned away followed by all ships, and the attack was avoided.

After re-forming in line ahead, the Allied cruisers turned to the eastward and contact with the enemy was lost. At 7.45 p.m. Doorman altered course to the southward. Why he did this is not clear. It must be borne in mind that he did not know where the convoy was. He had to depend on information relayed through the circuitous channels of communication from Sourabaya or Batavia, which never reached him in time. The enemy on the other hand could watch his every movement with shadowing aircraft. It is probable that the Admiral decided that in these conditions it was impracticable to circumvent the enemy and reach the convoy, and that it would be better to interpose his force between it and the Java coast.

At about 9 p.m. the *De Ruyter*, followed by the *Perth, Houston, Java* and *Jupiter*, turned to the westward, keeping about four miles from the coast. The four American destroyers broke off and returned to Sourabya to replenish with torpedoes and refuel. At about 9.25 p.m. the *Jupiter*, which had been following the *Java's* gentle zigzag, suddenly blew up. It was thought at the time that she had been torpedoed by a submarine, but it is possible that she may have struck a stray mine, for the position was only three miles north of a minefield laid that day by the Dutch off Toeban.

Shortly after the *Jupiter* sank, Admiral Doorman turned his cruisers to the northward in one last attempt to reach the convoy. It was a forlorn hope, for flares were dropped by the Japanese at each alteration of course, and it was obvious that they were well informed of his movements. At about 10 p.m. the fleet passed the survivors of the *Kortenaer* standing on or clinging to their rafts. They were rescued by the *Encounter* and taken to Sourabaya.

At 10.30 p.m. two cruisers were sighted in the moonlight on the port beam at a range of eight miles. These were the *Nachi* and *Haguro* which had not been seen since 6.30 p.m. All ships opened fire, and within a few minutes the *De Ruyter* and *Java* were both struck by torpedoes. It was obvious that the ships were doomed, and the order was given in each to abandon ship. They sank soon after. The gallant Admiral Doorman went down with his flagship.

Lacking destroyers and with the *Houston* short of ammunition, Captain H. M. L. Waller, R.A.N., commanding the *Perth*, decided that further attempts to attack the convoy were hopeless and, in accordance with previous orders not to stand by damaged ships, he withdrew in company with the *Houston*.

The two ships reached Batavia at 2.0 p.m. on the 28th. The port had been under frequent air attack and all shipping was being cleared. After refuelling they left harbour at 7.30 p.m. intending to pass through the Sunda Strait to Tjilatjap. Unknown to the Allied ships, part of the Japanese *Western Invasion Force* was that very night being landed in Bantam Bay, forty miles west of Batavia. Shortly after 11 p.m. the two ships, rounding a headland, suddenly saw ahead of them a line of transports at anchor. They opened fire at point blank range; so short was the range that the cruisers used their machine-guns to sweep the decks of the enemy ships. Two transports were sunk and others damaged before part of Admiral Kurita's covering force of three cruisers and nine destroyers arrived on the scene. A grim but hopeless fight ensued under the full moon until, with their guns silenced, and their sides holed by torpedoes—no less than eighty-five were fired at them—the Australian and American ships went down.

An hour or two later the Dutch destroyer *Evertsen*, which was to have accompanied the *Perth* and *Houston* but had been delayed, ran into two enemy cruisers and, after a brief encounter, beached herself in a sinking condition on an island off the coast of Sumatra.

Meanwhile on the 28th the damaged *Exeter* had refuelled and carried out emergency repairs to her boiler rooms at Sourabaya; having buried her dead, she left harbour that evening in company with the *Encounter* and *Pope* with orders to proceed by way of the Sunda Strait to Colombo. The problem of the *Exeter*'s route had been carefully considered. She could not use the eastern channel from Sourabaya owing to her draught. To make her escape to the eastward she would have had to use the western channel and come north around the island of Madoera, which would have brought her within close range of Bali airfield by daylight. Rear-Admiral Palliser therefore decided to send her west. She was ordered to go east of Bawean Island, skirt the south coast of Borneo in daylight, and then run south for the Sunda Strait the following night. But these ships, too, were doomed. Soon after leaving Sourabaya they were sighted by enemy aircraft and were intercepted at 10.0 a.m. the next morning (1st March) by four heavy cruisers and three destroyers. There could be only one result. For an hour and a half the *Exeter* survived the concentrated fire of the four cruisers until a torpedo from one of the Japanese destroyers delivered the *coup de grace*. By this time the *Encounter* had been sunk, and shortly after the *Pope* followed her. Two damaged Dutch destroyers, the *Witte de With* and the *Bankert*, remained at Sourabaya. Both were bombed and put out of action in an air attack a few days later.

Of all the Allied ships which took part in the Battle of the Java Sea only four survived—the four American destroyers which had been detached to Sourabaya and ordered to rearm in Australia. They sailed under cover of darkness on the night of the 28th, passed through Bali Strait and, except for a short skirmish with three Japanese destroyers south of the island, arrived in Fremantle in Western Australia on the 4th March without incident.

On the 1st March all ships in Tjilatjap harbour were instructed to disperse to safety. Some escaped to Ceylon and Australia but others were intercepted and sunk by forces under Admirals Kondo and Nagumo south of Java. Among the latter were the British destroyer *Stronghold*, the Australian sloop *Yarra*, two American destroyers and a few auxiliaries. With nothing left to him but his submarines, even the indomitable Admiral Helfrich realized that continued naval defence of Java was impossible. He accordingly asked the Governor-General to relieve him of the command of the Allied naval forces and on the 2nd left with his staff in four Dutch Catalina flying-boats for Colombo, where he set up his new headquarters. The British and American naval forces then reverted to the respective commands of Commodore Collins and Vice-Admiral Glassford. The former hoisted his broad pennant in H.M.A.S. *Burnie* the same day and sailed from Tjilatjap for Fremantle while the latter, accompanied by Admiral Palliser, flew to Australia. Three days later Japanese warships bombarded the port.

The Battle of the Java Sea, despite the sacrifice of ships and men, delayed the invasion of Java by but twenty-four hours. The convoys, which had been turned back at the beginning of the action, resumed their southerly course when the battle was over and simultaneous landings were made on the night of the 28th February/1st March in Eastern and Western Java by the two invasion forces.

The convoy carrying the *Eastern Force*, in the pursuit of which Admiral Doorman had lost his fleet, anchored off Kragan, about 100 miles west of Sourabaya, at 12.20 a.m. on the 1st March. The disembarkation began almost at once. The night was ideal for a landing. There was a light off-shore wind, and the moon was one day past full. There was no opposition on the beaches, but Allied aircraft made repeated attacks on the transports, causing some casualties and damage to two of them.

The enemy, brushing aside a company of Dutch regular troops, the only defence forces in the area, advanced rapidly thirty-five miles southwards and occupied the oilfields and the railway junction at Tjepoe. The main body of *48th Division* then advanced on Sourabaya by the Ngawi–Ngandjoek–Djombang road, with a flank guard of one regiment moving over the northern and coastal roads through Bodjonegoro and Toeban.

Major-General G. A. Ilgen, the commander of the Dutch forces in East Java, was unable to concentrate his forces in time to check the enemy's advance, and could attempt only minor delaying actions. By the evening of the 7th the Japanese, having approached from the west and from the south, were in the outskirts of Sourabaya. When demolitions in the town had been effected, the Dutch commander withdrew the garrison to the island of Madoera and left the Home Guard to defend the town. The remainder of the Dutch forces in East Java were withdrawn to the Loemadjang district. On the 8th, Japanese troops occupied both Sourabaya and Malang. The *56th Regimental Group* in the meantime had advanced diagonally across the island to the south-west. It met with little opposition from the few Dutch troops in Middle Java and on the afternoon of the 7th entered Tjilatjap.

The convoy carrying the *Western Force* divided on reaching the Java Sea. The larger portion, carrying *2nd Division*, proceeded to its anchorages on either side of the peninsula dividing Merak from Bantam Bay; the smaller portion, carrying *230th Infantry Regiment* of *38th Division*, went on to Eretenwetan 150 miles to the eastward.

Allied bombers from Kalidjati attacked the smaller convoy during the night when it was fifty miles from the coast, but the scale of attack was too light to do any serious damage. The Japanese began to disembark at Eretenwetan about 2 a.m. on 1st March. Once again there was no opposition on the beaches, but in the air twelve Hurricanes, pressing home their attacks to low heights despite intense anti-aircraft fire, caused casualties among Japanese troops in landing craft, at least six of which were set on fire. By 8 a.m. the enemy had begun to advance inland in two columns, each of battalion strength; one column was directed on Soebang with the airfield at Kalidjati as its objective, and the other on Tjikampek to cut the northern railway between Bandoeng and Batavia. The first column, moving in lorries accompanied by a number of light tanks, entered Soebang and within two hours pressed on westwards to the airfield.

The airfield defence party—a combination of soldiers and airmen —was taken by surprise, but fought gallantly and gave time for an Australian squadron of Hudsons to fly off their aircraft to Andir airfield, near Bandoeng; a British Blenheim squadron however, which was on the airfield dispersal area, was overrun. The Japanese gave no quarter and by 12.30 p.m. on the 1st practically the whole of the defence party was wiped out and the airfield was in their hands. In less than two days aircraft of *3rd Air Division* were using it in support of the army. Although the British bombers had been overrun at Kalidjati, fighters continued their attacks with some success against troops and vehicles which had landed at Eretenwetan.

The following morning the Dutch, supported by tanks from Bandoeng, counter-attacked Soebang. The tanks reached the centre of the town, but the infantry were unable to support them and the whole force had to withdraw. The Dutch planned to use a reserve regiment which had been withdrawn from Buitenzorg for a second attack on the 3rd, but when it was about twenty miles short of its objective it was heavily attacked by aircraft from Kalidjati airfield. Caught in the open, with no air support and practically no anti-aircraft artillery, it was completely scattered.

The advance of the second enemy column was delayed by low-flying attacks by the only remaining British fighter squadron from Tjililitan, which was also engaged in repelling air attacks on the airfield.[1] By midday on the 3rd the column had reached Djatisari, some eight miles short of Tjikampek; here it was brought to a halt, for the Dutch had destroyed the bridges over the river.

Meanwhile the column which had captured the airfield, having sent a detachment to occupy Poerwakerta on the 4th, concentrated at Soebang where it was joined by the remainder of *230th Infantry Regiment*. The advance on Bandoeng began on the 5th and by the 7th had reached the suburbs of Lembang, only seven miles north of the capital.

The enemy landings at Merak and in Bantam Bay were also successfully carried out before dawn on the 1st March. At Merak the Dutch offered some opposition, and in Bantam Bay the brief attack by the *Perth* and *Houston* and bombing by the few remaining Allied aircraft caused some confusion. The Dutch fell back on prepared positions but were unable to check the enemy's advance, and by the afternoon the road junction at Serang was in enemy hands.

The Japanese *2nd Division* then advanced eastwards in two columns, with its main body on the direct or northern road to Batavia and one regiment on the more southerly road through Rangkasbitoeng to Buitenzorg and Bandoeng. The main body was however so delayed by the destruction of bridges that on the 3rd a

---

[1] 232(F) Squadron reduced to ten Hurricanes, all of which received damage in varying degrees from anti-aircraft fire in these low-flying attacks. At noon on the 3rd March the squadron was withdrawn to Andir, destroying *en route* several enemy aircraft on the airfield at Kalidjati.

regiment was diverted to the Buitenzorg road, thus making the southerly column the stronger. The northern column eventually occupied Batavia on the 5th after the Dutch garrison had withdrawn.

On the night of the landings 'Blackforce' was concentrated at a tea plantation eight miles west of Buitenzorg. Its orders were to move with a regiment of Dutch infantry at dawn to Leuwiliang (four miles further west), and thence to operate offensively on the southern road west of the river on which the town stood. Late that night however orders were received from Bandoeng that the Dutch regiment taking part in the attack was to be withdrawn and used to stop the advance of the Japanese who had landed at Eretenwetan and were threatening Bandoeng. After some hesitation General Schilling decided that 'Blackforce' would have to conduct the defence of the southern road alone. 'Blackforce' reached Leuwiliang at daybreak on the 2nd, only to find that the withdrawing Dutch infantry, in ignorance of the latest orders, had blown up the bridge across the river which flows through the town. As its destruction prevented any effective offensive action to the west Brigadier Blackburn disposed his force for the defence of the river crossing.

On the afternoon of the 2nd 'Blackforce' was ordered to leave a detachment to hold the river line at Leuwiliang, and move to the east to take part in the counter-attack on Soebang at dawn the following morning in co-operation with the main Dutch forces. This would have meant a move of 125 miles followed by an unprepared attack over unreconnoitred country unknown to the commander or any of the officers of 'Blackforce'. Not only would such an attack have had little chance of success, but it would have left the defence of Leuwiliang seriously weakened at a moment when a heavy attack by the enemy was expected. Blackburn, supported by Sitwell, protested strongly and the proposed move was cancelled.

During the morning of the 2nd, advanced units of the enemy's southern column reached the west bank of the river at Leuwiliang. Repeated attempts to cross the river both during the afternoon and during the night of the 2nd/3rd were repelled. From daylight on the 3rd, enemy pressure increased and the American artillery was brought into action for the first time with good effect. Throughout the day and the night of the 3rd/4th all attempts by the enemy to cross the river were frustrated.

Meanwhile the Dutch counter-attack on Soebang had failed, and the Japanese were moving southwards on Bandoeng. Faced with this situation, the Commander-in-Chief (General ter Poorten) decided on the 4th to withdraw his forces from Batavia and Buitenzorg to reinforce the defence of the capital. Since the direct road and railway from Batavia to Bandoeng had already been cut by the enemy, the garrison of Batavia had to be withdrawn through Buitenzorg. 'Black-force' was given the task of keeping this route open until demolitions at Batavia had been completed and the garrison withdrawn. On receipt of these orders Blackburn decided to withdraw from the river line and hold a rearguard position on a much narrower front nearer to Buitenzorg, protected by the destruction of bridges.

During the afternoon of the 4th, a strong enemy force succeeded in crossing the river some miles south of Leuwiliang, and Blackburn sent a company of 2/2nd Pioneer Battalion to hold it while he disengaged. The Australians attacked and, having driven the Japanese back some distance, held them off while 'Blackforce' withdrew under cover of darkness. The rearguard (one battalion and 'B' Squadron 3rd Hussars) occupied a position four miles west of Buitenzorg, while the main body withdrew to Soekaboemi which it held without difficulty until 3.15 p.m. on the 5th, when the Dutch staff reported that the withdrawal from Batavia had been completed. They then withdrew to rejoin the main body. The Japanese entered Buitenzorg the same evening, and on the following day 'Blackforce' fell back on the 'stronghold' of Bandoeng. At the cost of 150 casualties it had delayed the enemy advance for four days and enabled the garrison of Batavia to be withdrawn safely.

At a conference at his headquarters on the 5th General ter Poorten pointed out the gravity of the situation, and told the British commanders that the capital could not hold out for long. As it was full of refugees, he proposed to declare it an open town as soon as the enemy penetrated the outer defences. He said that no guerilla warfare would be attempted by the Dutch because of the uncertain attitude of the local population towards the Europeans; and that, owing to difficulties of communication, Dutch General Headquarters could operate only from Bandoeng and therefore would not move elsewhere. Nevertheless resistance was to be carried on under the direction of local commanders. He then added an unexpected rider that he had instructed his troops to disregard any order he might subsequently issue to them to cease fighting: they were to disobey it and go on fighting.

Sitwell assured ter Poorten that the British would fight as long as resistance was continued by the Dutch, and asked that an area in the hills where they could concentrate for a last stand should be allotted to them. The area suggested by the Commander-in-Chief, in the hills south of Bandoeng, was reconnoitred by the British commanders on the 6th, but proved unsuitable for protracted defence and, on the suggestion of General Schilling, another area further to the east was chosen.

There were at that time about 2,500 airmen awaiting evacuation at Poerwokerta some thirty miles north of Tjilatjap. They were without arms, and were therefore ordered to place themselves under the orders of the local Dutch commander and surrender when called upon to do so. The remainder, which included the ground staffs at Andir airfield (Bandoeng) and those awaiting evacuation at Tasik-malaja (about 1,750 all told, all of whom were armed), were ordered to join 'Blackforce' in the concentration area on the 8th. The combined force was about 8,000 strong.

By the 7th the Japanese had occupied Tjilatjap; Sourabaya was being evacuated in the face of strong enemy forces; Batavia had been lost, and the Japanese were converging on Bandoeng from both west and north. Further resistance appeared useless, and at 9 a.m. on the 8th the Commander-in-Chief broadcast a proclamation to the effect that organized resistance by the Royal Netherlands East Indian Army in Java would end. The Governor-General and General ter Poorten met the Japanese Commander-in-Chief at Kalidjati that afternoon and agreed to the capitulation of all the troops in the Netherlands East Indies.

The proclamation, as broadcast, was telephoned to the British Headquarters shortly after 10 a.m. on the 8th, while troops were still arriving in the concentration area, with the addition of a message that ter Poorten expected all Allied forces in the Netherlands East Indies to lay down their arms. The Allied forces possessed small arms and ammunition and a few Bofors guns but no mortars, heavy anti-aircraft guns or artillery. Most of the troops were entirely untrained in the type of fighting which lay before them, namely as infantry in the jungles and mountains. Rations were down to three or four days supply, transport was scarce and petrol limited to the amount vehicles had in their tanks. The combined British-Australian field hospital in Bandoeng was already overcrowded with patients and could not be moved to the hills. Thus medical facilities were reduced to those carried by units and were little more than first-aid outfits, and a high rate of sickness was expected during the rainy season in the hills.

All these difficulties might have been overcome given local help and time, but there was no prospect of either. As regards the former, not only was the local population uncertain but practically no help was forthcoming from the Dutch: their liaison detachments with the British had been withdrawn at a moment when they were vitally necessary, and they withheld all but a fraction of the supplies and other assistance which was sought. Moreover the Dutch had ceased fighting everywhere at the express orders of their Commander-in-Chief, whose staff had informed the British commanders that he expected the British to obey his order to surrender.

All this was weighed in the minds of the British commanders before coming to a decision whether to comply with the terms of the

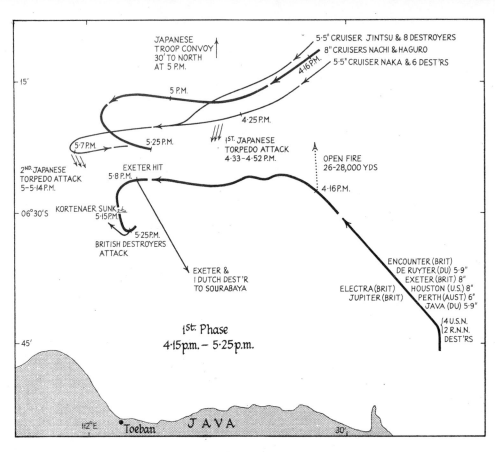

JAPANESE
TROOP CONVOY
30' TO NORTH
AT 5 P.M.

5·5" CRUISER JINTSU & 8 DESTROYERS
8" CRUISERS NACHI & HAGURO
5·5" CRUISER NAKA & 6 DEST'RS

4·16 P.M.

5 P.M.

4·25 P.M.

5·7 P.M.

5·25 P.M.

1ST JAPANESE
TORPEDO ATTACK
4·33 – 4·52 P.M.

OPEN FIRE
26-28,000 YDS

4·16 P.M.

2ND JAPANESE
TORPEDO ATTACK
5 – 5·14 P.M.

EXETER HIT
5·8 P.M.

KORTENAER SUNK
5·15 P.M.

5·25 P.M.

BRITISH DESTROYERS
ATTACK

EXETER &
I DUTCH DEST'R
TO SOURABAYA

ENCOUNTER (BRIT)
DE RUYTER (DU) 5·9"
EXETER (BRIT) 8"
ELECTRA (BRIT)   HOUSTON (U.S.) 8"
JUPITER (BRIT)   PERTH (AUST) 6"
                              JAVA (DU) 5·9"

4 U.S.N.
2 R.N.N.
DEST'RS

1st. Phase
4·15 p.m. – 5·25 p.m.

112°E   •Toeban   J A V A   30'

—15'

—06°30'S

—45'

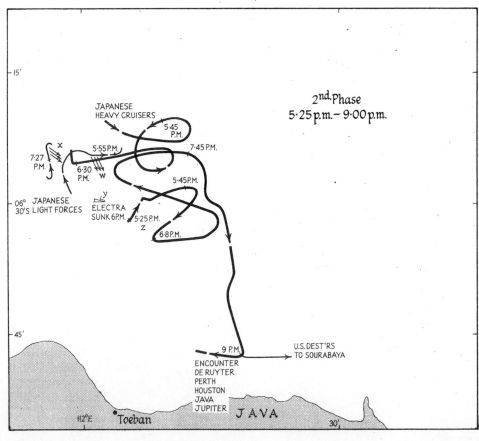

—15'

2nd. Phase
5·25 p.m. – 9·00 p.m.

JAPANESE
HEAVY CRUISERS

5·45
P.M.

7·45 P.M.

x

7·27
P.M.

5·55 P.M.

6·30
P.M.

w

5·45 P.M.

06°
30'S

JAPANESE
LIGHT FORCES

y

ELECTRA
SUNK 6 P.M.

5·25 P.M.

z

6·8 P.M.

—45'

9 P.M.

U.S. DEST'RS
TO SOURABAYA

ENCOUNTER
DE RUYTER
PERTH
HOUSTON
JAVA
JUPITER

112°E   •Toeban   J A V A   30'

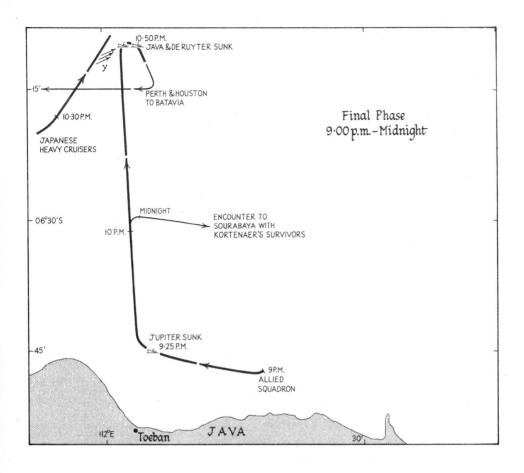

10·50 P.M.
JAVA & DE RUYTER SUNK

y

PERTH & HOUSTON
TO BATAVIA

Final Phase
9·00 p.m. – Midnight

15'

10·30 P.M.

JAPANESE
HEAVY CRUISERS

MIDNIGHT

ENCOUNTER TO
SOURABAYA WITH
KORTENAER'S SURVIVORS

06°30'S

10 P.M.

JUPITER SUNK
9·25 P.M.

45'

9 P.M.
ALLIED
SQUADRON

112°E
•Toeban   JAVA   30'

Map 27.

The Battle of the Java Sea
27th. Feb. 1942

ALLIED SQUADRON...................
DETACHED ALLIED FORCES........
JAPANESE HEAVY CRUISERS......
JAPANESE LIGHT FORCES...........

In 1st. Phase
1ST. & 2ND. JAPANESE TORPEDO ATTACKS.......................

In 2nd. Phase
3RD. JAPANESE TORPEDO ATTACK (5·38–5·55 P.M.)........ W
4TH.   „   „   „   (7·36 P.M.)................ X
ELECTRA SUNK 6 P.M. IN BRITISH DESTROYER ATTACK.......... y
U.S.N. DESTROYER ATTACK (6·14 P.M.)............................ z

In Final Phase
5TH. JAPANESE TORPEDO ATTACK (10·45 P.M.).............. y

JAPANESE TRACKS ESTIMATED

10,000
YDS.   0   5   10   MILES
            SCALE

broadcast or to fight on. They had become aware of the fact that the Japanese, whose troops could quickly reach the concentration area along good motorable roads, already knew of their exact position and that it had been their intention to fight on. What turned the scale was the possible implication in the broadcast that resistance by the Allied as well as the Dutch forces had ceased. The two commanders considered that continued resistance by the British forces in possession of arms would place them outside international law and render them liable to summary execution if captured. Added to this there was the fear of reprisals on their unarmed comrades who had no alternative but to obey the broadcast.

Maltby and Sitwell realized that in the circumstances they had no prospect of organizing anything effective, and regretfully decided that they had no alternative but to obey General ter Poorten's order to surrender. At 2.30 p.m. on the 8th March all British, Australian and American units were ordered to lay down their arms, and on the 12th their commanders were summoned to Bandoeng where the formal instrument of surrender was signed in the presence of the Japanese commander in the Bandoeng area, Lieut.-General Maruyama, who promised them the rights of the Geneva Convention for the protection of prisoners of war.

That same day the *Imperial Guards Division* sailed from Singapore and landed, without opposition, at a number of points in northern Sumatra. No naval escort was used, except for the landings at Sabang and Keotaradja in the extreme north-west. Air support was provided for these two landings only, though it was available elsewhere if called for. The Japanese met little opposition and by the 28th March had occupied the whole island.

The Malay barrier was thus shattered and the gateway to the Indian Ocean open. The Allied fleet in the Far East had been destroyed. In three months the Japanese had completed the conquest of Malaya and the Netherlands East Indies and had gained possession of all the resources of that rich southern area for which they had gone to war.

H2

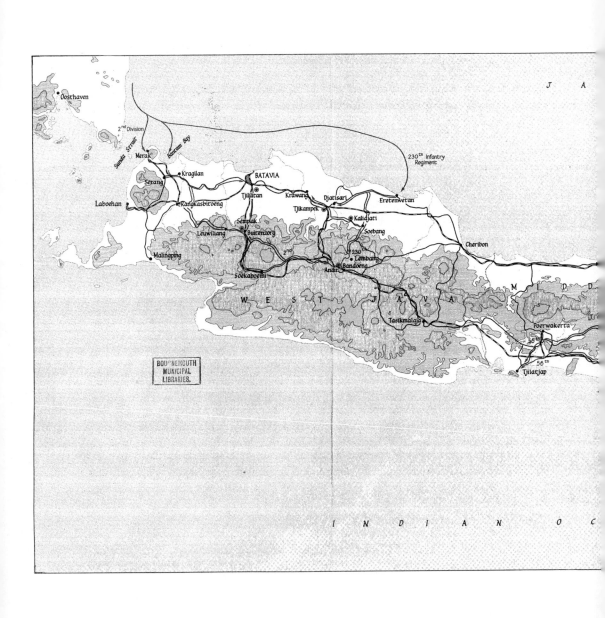

BOURNEMOUTH
MUNICIPAL
LIBRARIES.

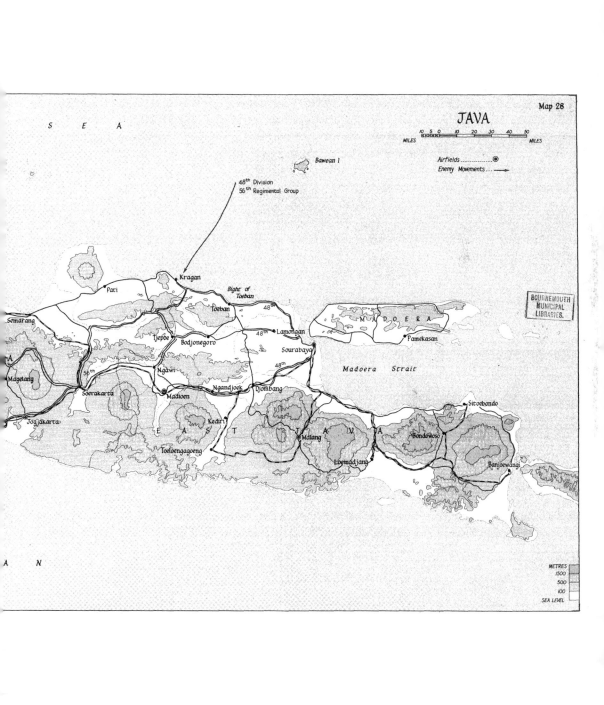

Map 28

JAVA

MILES   10 5 0   10   20   30   40   50   MILES

Airfields .... ⊚
Enemy Movements .... ⟶

S E A

Bawean I

48ᵗʰ Division
56ᵗʰ Regimental Group

BOURNEMOUTH
MUNICIPAL
LIBRARIES.

Kragan

Pati

Bight of
Toeban

Toeban   48ᵗʰ

Semarang   48ᵗʰ Lamongan   M A D O E R A

Tjepoe   Pamekasan
          Bodjonegoro   Sourabaya

A   Ngawi   48ᵗʰ   Madoera   Strait

Magelang   56ᵗʰ

Soerakarta   Madioen   Ngandjoek Djombang

Jogjakarta   Sitoebondo
                        Kediri
                                          Mdlang   Bondowoso
          E A S T   J A V A
                                                                          Banjoewangi
          Toeloengagoeng   Loemadjang

A   N

METRES
1500
500
100
SEA LEVEL

CHAPTER XXVII

RETROSPECT

AT THE END of the First World War the victors reigned supreme. By the Treaty of Versailles Germany's armies had been disbanded and her air force abolished. Her fleet lay at the bottom of Scapa Flow. Britain and the British Commonwealth, whose safety depended on sea power, were left with no major naval rival in Europe. Japan was their ally and the eastern horizon was clear. There seemed no danger in sight. Yet, within less than a generation, Britain was on the verge of defeat by a new and more powerful Germany and had lost her Far Eastern possessions to Japan.

How was it that British strength had been so reduced in the intervening years that Japan was able so swiftly to overrun the vast southern areas from the Philippines to the borders of India and wrest from Britain, Hong Kong, Borneo, Malaya and Burma?[1] This is a military and not a political history and comment on the conduct of British foreign policy does not lie within its scope. Nevertheless, since the disasters which befell the British Commonwealth forces in the Far East had their origin in events which took place between the First and Second World Wars, it is necessary to examine this period before considering the Far Eastern scene.

By 1919 Great Britain was exhausted both physically and economically. For four and a half years she had poured out her gold and given the lives of her young men to free the world from the threat of German military domination. She needed time to recuperate. There was a general outcry for disarmament. Faith was placed in the League of Nations as an instrument for the organization of peace by means of collective security. With no major war foreseeable for at least ten years the British Army was reduced to little more than an Imperial police force, and the Royal Air Force to a nucleus. The Royal Navy, which for a hundred years had had sufficient strength to give the world the *Pax Britannica*, was so reduced that Britain could maintain only a single main fleet, stationed in home waters and the Mediterranean, which might be sent to any threatened point when required. Work on the construction and defence of the Naval Base at Singapore then began, for there was no suitable base in the Far East from which this centrally-held fleet could operate.[2]

The abrogation of the Anglo-Japanese Alliance and the signature

---

[1] The loss of Burma is described in Volume II.
[2] See pages 2–3.

of the Washington and Nine-Power Treaties in 1922 had ushered in a new order of sea power. Although Britain retained superiority over Japan in capital ships, the ratio of five to three was out of all proportion to her larger responsibilities.[1] Parity with America however gave an Anglo-American preponderance of some three to one. Had the two navies been allowed to work together in pursuit of common policies they could have exercised that command of the Seven Seas which in the nineteenth century the Royal Navy had held alone. But the policies of the two countries diverged as the United States withdrew into isolation. Thus when in 1931 Japan invaded Manchuria and the international situation began to deteriorate, neither country was able by itself to take the necessary steps to halt aggression.[2]

The assumption that no major war was likely for ten years, made in 1919 and given the force of a rule in 1928 (the year of the Kellogg Pact), gravely affected Britain's security.[3] It virtually placed the Services at ten years' notice for war and had a far-reaching effect on Britain's ability to rearm should the necessity arise. The rule was used as a means to cut the Service estimates to the bone. Many of the great industrial firms, on which the country depended in time of emergency for weapons of war, were forced to turn over to the production of goods for civil consumption. Highly trained skilled labour was lost and valuable plant scrapped, which, when the emergency did arise, took years to replace.

The Services, faced with extreme financial stringency and conscious of their growing weakness, lacked an incentive to pull together. They began to contend with each other over the allocation of funds and the control and development of weapons. The air force, young and enthusiastic but not fully fledged, overstating the potentialities of air power at that time, claimed that it could fulfill the functions of the older Services of providing a sure defence of overseas bases. The navy and army rejected these claims and controversy ensued.[4]

It was not till 1932 at the time of the Shanghai Incident, when it became clear that Britain might find herself at war with Japan, not in ten years but in ten days, that the rule was at last set aside.[5] Little however could be done at that time to increase the strength of the Services, for the economic crisis which had engulfed the world was at its height. The nations were preparing for a world disarmament conference. When in 1933 Hitler, within a few months of assuming office as Chancellor, withdrew Germany from the conference and from the League of Nations, a committee was set up to prepare a programme for making good the worst deficiencies in the British

[1] See page 3.
[2] See pages 9–11.
[3] See page 8.
[4] See pages 7–8 and 11–12.
[5] See page 11.

defences, but it was not till the middle of 1934 that the Cabinet made its final decision on the Committee's report.

With that decision Britain began to rearm but it was some time before she could get into her stride, and the aggressors both in Europe and the Far East gained a flying start. Financial considerations were allowed to overrule the recommendations of the Chiefs of Staff who advised the rearmament of the three fighting Services as a balanced force. They were told by the Government that the financial danger to the country was greater than the military one: 'We must aim at securing our Service needs without interference with, or reduction of, production for civil and export trade'. Within the limits thus imposed, priority had to be given to the creation of a powerful air force to maintain air parity with Germany. The traditional reluctance to be drawn into war on the Continent helped to justify a reduction in the army's requirements. The naval programme, recommended by the committee set up to study defence requirements, was reduced in the hope that some agreement with Germany on the limitation of armament would be reached at the proposed naval conference in London in 1935.

Rearmament had begun, but it was too late and too slow. Thus, when war did break out in Europe, Britain found herself with a serious deficiency in ships, aircraft and all types of military weapons and equipment, and the demands of her expanding forces could not be met. Her resources in manpower were in any case inadequate to meet the combination of two major Powers in Europe and at the same time wage a war in the Far East, but the deficiencies in material rendered it impossible to make full use of such manpower as she had.

The inactivity during the first eight months of the war in Europe gave a welcome breathing space, but the disasters culminating in the Dunkirk evacuation resulted in the loss of most of the equipment of the British Expeditionary Force, and its replacement left the storehouses empty. Every effort was made to expand production in Britain and throughout the Commonwealth. The United States inaugurated the Lend Lease programme, but it was to be some years before the supply of arms and equipment could fully meet the demand. During the intervening period those forces which were defending vital areas or actively engaged with the enemy had first claim on what was available. Naturally the defence of Britain, the Middle East, the vital sea communications in the Atlantic and the Mediterranean—all within the active theatres of war—and the minimum training needs of the expanding forces took precedence over the Far East, where war was a threat and not a reality.

Thus, throughout the period dealt with in this volume, so great was the shortage of naval vessels of every kind that the Royal Navy was unable to send a fleet to the Far East and at the same time safeguard the sea communications on which the existence of Britain depended; army formations received their weapons and equipment just before they were called upon to go into action, too late for them to become proficient in their use; air squadrons gallantly took the skies in inadequate strength and in obsolete aircraft; and reserves of arms and equipment to replace battle losses in all three Services were lacking.

The Services have the same three basic requirements: up-to-date weapons and equipment; men well trained in their use; men who have the will to fight and win. As the first was missing, the second could not be attained. Thus, whatever the spirit of the troops, commanders entrusted with the defence of British possessions in the Far East had perforce to meet attack by a fully-prepared enemy with naval, army and air forces insufficient for the task. This was the fundamental cause of the disasters described in this volume.

The factors which hindered Britain's rearmament during the inter-war years had their counterpart in Malaya during the years 1934 to 1939. War demands the fullest co-operation not only between the fighting Services, but between them and the civil administration. But in Malaya willing co-operation was not always forthcoming. Before the outbreak of war in Europe the Government in Singapore, intent on the orderly administration of a prosperous country and on trade, either treated with indifference or at times even opposed the demands the Services made on them as a result of the defence measures being taken. In adopting this attitude they appear to have overlooked the danger to the British Commonwealth of inadequate defence of the Naval Base and the fact that, if weakly defended, it might prove an irresistible attraction to a Japan bent on expansion. Although after September 1939 much was done to develop a civil defence organization, full co-operation with the Services had not been reached by the time that France fell in the summer of 1940.[1]

The Services themselves were not in complete harmony, for the army and the air force held divergent views on the measures necessary for the defence of Malaya. The former, involved in the construction of the authorized fixed defences designed to secure the Base against a seaborne attack, was more interested in Singapore Island and southern Johore than in northern Malaya. The latter, seeking to increase the range of its aircraft to seawards and thus more concerned with the Malay peninsula, had between 1936 and 1939 constructed airfields on the east coast. But these new airfields had been sited without proper consultation between the Services in Singapore and without

---

[1] See pages 157–159.

due regard to the possibility of their defence against enemy forces which might succeed in landing.[1]

The fall of France and the entry of Italy into the war in the summer of 1940 entirely altered the situation in the Far East. The removal of the barrier hitherto provided by Indo-China opened the way for Japan's further expansion southwards and increased her temptation to strike while Britain was engaged unaided with two powerful enemies in the West. Without allies, and unable to send the fleet to Singapore, which had been the basis of her Far East strategy for nearly twenty years, Britain had now to face the growing danger of a war with Japan at a time when her resources were already strained to the utmost.[2]

Victory, or at least security, in Europe had clearly to be achieved first, even at the risk of the loss of some or all of the British possessions in the Far East, for defeat in Europe spelt utter disaster. Therefore, if war with Japan could not be avoided, it had to be postponed for as long as possible in the hope that a measure of victory in Europe would allow forces, particularly naval and air, to be released for the Far East. Since Japan would obviously hesitate before embarking on a war with both the United States and Britain, a united front in the Far East was clearly the best guarantee of peace in the Pacific.

With these objects in view the British Government tried to persuade the Government of the United States, whose interests in the Far East were equally threatened, to combine with them and the Dutch Government in the face of the common danger and to issue a joint declaration that any further act of aggression by Japan would mean war with all three. They hoped that, if they succeeded, Japan would consider it expedient to abandon her southward drive. Should they fail, they hoped at least to persuade the Americans and Dutch to pool their resources and join in building up the defence of the whole area from the Philippines to Burma. The reader will have seen in Chapter III how these efforts came to nought. Although by December 1940 the President of the United States and his advisers had seen clearly that their country must sooner or later be drawn into the war, they could not act so far in advance of public opinion. For twenty years the American people had been allowed to believe that they could remain in isolation and that no Power would dare to attack or threaten them. The President could lead only as fast as Congress would go. The Dutch with their homeland in German hands were well nigh powerless. Nevertheless they put up

---

[1] See pages 14–15.
[2] See pages 33–35.

a courageous stand against all Japanese attempts to absorb them into the Greater East Asia Co-prosperity Sphere.

The Services of each of the three countries were however permitted to start work on combined plans to meet the possibility of a Japanese attack on the territories of any one of them. This led to a number of conferences in Washington and Singapore from which an Anglo-Dutch plan emerged—and in the event was acted upon—but the Americans would not agree to a joint plan on the ground of British naval weakness in the Far East.[1] Thus the attempt to arrange for concerted action by the three Powers failed.

Meanwhile, realizing that she could not send a fleet of sufficient strength to ensure command of the sea in the Far East, Britain had to do her best to provide army and air forces to protect the Naval Base against any attacks launched from Indo-China and Siam. This meant holding the whole of Malaya—a fact which had been pointed out by General Dobbie as far back as 1937.[2] In the absence of a fleet the Chiefs of Staff decided that reliance would have to be placed primarily on an air force capable of preventing the enemy from either gaining air superiority or effecting a landing in strength. This air force would have to be backed by sufficient land forces to secure the airfields and destroy any enemy troops which succeeded in gaining a footing ashore.[3] The problem was to find these forces. The strength needed was assessed and, as the reader has seen, reviewed from time to time.[4]

Despite the fact that the Commonwealth was at that time fighting single-handed against Germany and Italy, much had been done by the end of July 1941 to strengthen Malaya. The garrison had been brought up to a strength equivalent to approximately three divisions with a reasonable quota of administrative units; a number of additional airfields had been made, existing airfields improved and air-force maintenance organizations built up. Some additional squadrons had been sent out, but such was the shortage of aircraft, especially of fighters, that the strength of the air forces in Malaya still remained at one-third of that judged necessary.

But had the best use been made of the men and material provided? The official view held in the Far East, based on those held in London, was that war with Japan, though possible, was improbable. This was understandable, but there was little excuse for the false estimate of Japanese military prowess. Reports of the inefficiency of Japanese soldiers and airmen, emanating from China, were accepted at their

---

[1] See Chapter III and page 86.
[2] See page 15.
[3] See page 35.
[4] See pages 35; 48–49 and 54.

face value in Singapore, while the accurate reports received from the attachés in Tokyo were disbelieved or ignored.[1] Indeed those who told the truth were often regarded as pro-Japanese and defeatists. Whatever the reasons, the opinion was general throughout the Far East that war was unlikely and that, even if it came, there was little to fear from the Japanese armed forces. But to make matters worse the army and air force, at least till the arrival of the Commander-in-Chief, Far East, at the end of 1940, continued to hold different views as to the employment of the forces available for the defence of Malaya.

Thus, although defensive plans and preparations had been speeded up, they had failed to produce the best results. The appointment of a Commander-in-Chief, Far East, although intended to co-ordinate defence throughout the Far East, to overcome the difference of opinion between the army and the air force and to ensure thorough preparation for war, was subject to too many limitations to be effective.[2] In retrospect one can see that only by the appointment of one man with supreme authority, to whose direction all Service and civil authorities, including the Governor and the civil administration, were subject, could real co-ordination of effort have been achieved.

It was perhaps because of these factors that very little effort had been made by headquarters staffs from 1939 onwards to study either enemy methods or the art of war in jungle and close country, and that the training carried out had been very similar in both tempo and type to that carried out by British troops in other theatres of war, although the circumstances in Malaya demanded different methods.[3]

The belief that war was unlikely also had its effect on the preparations made in Malaya. Although much was done to improve the civil defence organization and plans were made to build up reserves of essential commodities, it does not seem that sufficient effort was made to foresee and provide for the abnormal situations which were bound to arise in war. The problem of the administration of their own territory after it had been invaded by an enemy was a novel one for British administrators and there was little precedent to guide them. Committees were appointed to consider certain aspects of this problem, but by the time war broke out no comprehensive plans had been evolved.

At the end of July 1941 the situation took a sharp turn for the worse. The Japanese occupation of southern Indo-China, with its ports and

---

[1] See page 166.
[2] See pages 50–51.
[3] See pages 165–169.

air bases within striking range of Malaya and Borneo, vastly increased the threat to the British, American and Dutch possessions in the Far East. When the Japanese refused to consider the American proposal to neutralize Indo-China and allow Japan full access to its resources, it became clear that they were bent on aggression. The United States therefore decided, as a deterrent, to use the weapon of economic sanctions. Despite the danger inherent in this course of action, both the British and Dutch agreed to do likewise.[1]

The sanctions imposed cut off Japan from nearly all her supplies of raw material and oil. Since nine-tenths of her oil supplies were imported, she was forced immediately to draw on the reserves which she had accumulated over many years in case of war. In August her leaders realized that Japan had either to abandon her designs in south-east Asia, or go to war and capture the oilfields in the Netherlands East Indies which alone could meet her full requirements. A decision had to be taken quickly since, in the event of the second course being selected, no appreciable delay could be accepted, as the already diminishing reserves would suffice for only about two years of war, and time would inevitably elapse before the Dutch oilfields, after capture, could be restored to full production. The Japanese Navy, which had always opposed war with Britain and the United States simultaneously, found itself obliged to change its views and for the first time come into line with the Army, eager for the southern adventure. With the leadership of Japan in the hands of the expansionist military clique there could be only one answer. In September 1941 Japan began to make final preparations for war, and had decided on a date by which diplomatic efforts to find a solution in keeping with her national dignity, if still unsuccessful, would be replaced by military action.[2]

That this decision was taken was naturally not known to either the British or American Governments. Although it was evident, if only from the repeated Japanese attempts to obtain large quantities of oil from the Netherlands East Indies, that oil was vital to Japan and that the cutting off of supplies would place her under great temptation to go to war as soon as her forces were ready,[3] the view prevailed in both London and Washington that a major war in the Pacific was not likely to break out till Russia was clearly faced with defeat or, at the earliest, in the spring of 1942.

At the end of September 1941 the Commander-in-Chief, Far East, (Air Chief-Marshal Sir Robert Brooke-Popham) estimated the Far Eastern situation thus:

---

[1] See page 70.
[2] See pages 73–74 and 83–84.
[3] It was estimated in London that the Japanese oil stocks were sufficient only for twelve months requirements on a war basis.

'Taking into account (a) [Japan's] uncertainty whether or not Germany is going to bring Russia to terms before the winter; (b) the time that would elapse before the Japanese could disengage from the north, even if Russia collapsed; (c) the bad weather in the South China Sea area between November and January inclusive, it is [I think] highly improbable Japan can be contemplating war in the south for some months.'

In the middle of October, when visiting Australia, he told the Advisory War Council in Melbourne that, in the air, Japan had superiority in numbers but not in quality, and that all indications were that, as Russia's preoccupation in the war with Germany presented an opportunity for Japan to rid herself of the Russian threat from Vladivostok, she had temporarily diverted her attention from the south to the north. He said that it would take her some time to concentrate for a move southwards, and that for the next three months she would not be able to undertake a large scale attack in the south; the Allies would thus be given time to complete their defences and to perfect their plans.[1]

On the 26th October Mr. Churchill telegraphed to the Australian Prime Minister expressing the view that Japan would not run into war unless or until Russia was decisively broken. He added that the Russians were still resisting strongly, the winter was near and, even if Russia were broken, Japan might wait for the promised invasion of Britain in the spring of 1942 before attacking. He went on to say that, in order to deter Japan, Britain's newest battleship the *Prince of Wales*, with the *Repulse*, was being moved to eastern waters.[2] Thus, while Japan was secretly completing her preparations for an early war, Britain was waiting on events in the Far East.

At that time, despite the fact that the air force was to be the primary weapon of defence and the airfields it required had been constructed, its strength in Malaya was not only well below the minimum which had been considered necessary, but many of its aircraft were obsolescent and there was a deplorable lack of reserves. The army, dispersed for the defence of airfields which could not be left unprotected, was short, on the basis of General Percival's appreciation, of nearly two divisions, two armoured regiments, a considerable amount of anti-aircraft artillery as well as large quantities of equipment, and moreover it was without a pool of reinforcements to replace battle casualties.[3] The strength of the defence forces in Malaya was entirely inadequate.

Why, one asks, did not Britain at this eleventh hour send at least sufficient aircraft to ensure that a balanced force was available in

---

[1] Hasluck, *Australia in the War of 1939–1945: The Government and the People, 1939–1941* (Canberra, 1952) page 537.
[2] *Churchill*, Volume III (Cassell, 1950), page 525.
[3] See page 77.

Malaya even if she could not have sent all the army formations required? The primary reason was the failure to foresee an early Japanese resort to force as a result of the application of sanctions. With their heavy commitments in Europe and the Middle East, the War Cabinet were not prepared to lock up more of Britain's slender resources to meet a threat which it was hoped might never materialize. The attempt to strengthen the Far East after the war had started came too late, and the reinforcements eventually sent merely swelled the numbers destined to languish in captivity under appalling conditions for over three years.

In writing of the defence of naval bases, Admiral Mahan has said: 'In places which justify fortification both the works and the garrison must be adequate to all probable exigencies'.[1] General Sir Ian Hamilton, knowing only too well his countrymen's tendency to underrate their enemies and to indulge in wishful thinking, wrote in 1924 about Singapore: 'I have no fears, unless we ourselves fit out a half-way house and then—half garrisoning it, as is our wont—make a present of it to the wrong people'.[2] It was the failure to heed warnings such as these which made defeat at Singapore inevitable and gave the commanders entrusted with its defence an impossible task. The Naval Base at the western gateway to the Pacific, the keystone of British strategy in the Far East, was doomed before the war started. The Japanese, in whose hands the initiative lay, knew the weakness and calculated that they could capture it in one hundred days. They beat their own estimate by some thirty days. We must therefore examine the conduct of the campaign and see how it was that the defence was overrun so much more quickly than even the enemy expected.

The Japanese looked upon Singapore as the main strategic point in that Southern Area for the control of which they went to war. They had an excellent intelligence service and were well aware of the strength of the British garrison and had correctly assessed its fighting value. They selected as the spearhead of their attack well trained troops who had seen active service in China, and gave them training suited to the terrain which they would meet in Malaya. These troops had a fanatical belief in their cause. Brought up in the spirit of 'Bushido'—the way of the warrior—every officer and man counted it a privilege to die for his country. They were backed by an air force equipped with first class aircraft and enjoying a four to one numerical superiority over the defenders. Adequate naval cover was provided to protect their communications against any interference by the

[1] Mahan, *Naval Strategy* (London, 1911), page 194.
[2] Letter to Editor of *The Times* dated 25th March 1924.

Prince of Wales and *Repulse*. The initiative lay in their hands and thus they were free to select their point of attack.

The plan for the defence of Malaya had been based on the presence of an air force capable of maintaining air superiority over Malaya and the area round it, and thus of preventing the Japanese from making a landing in any appreciable strength. But such an air force did not exist in the Far East. There was no strong bomber force with which to attack the Japanese air bases in Indo-China or approaching convoys; the inadequate fighter force was equipped with inferior aircraft and the few torpedo-bombers were obsolete. The onus of defending Malaya therefore fell on an army intended for a secondary role and dispersed to protect airfields.

The state of the garrison in the summer of 1941 has already been described.[1] General Percival, assisted by General Heath, had during the short period between assuming command and the outbreak of war raised the tempo of training and of preparations for war, had nearly finished work on a defensive position at Jitra and had planned to construct a second position at Gurun. He was unable to overcome the effects of years of inadequate preparation and the long-standing lack of close co-operation in Malaya between all concerned in its defence. Shackled by the accepted view that war with Japan was unlikely and with his hands tied by the retention of control of major expenditure in London, no commander could have accomplished much in this period.

The start of the campaign was disastrous, not only in the air but on land and sea. The weak air force, thrown on the defensive, was virtually destroyed within the first twenty-four hours and thereafter the Japanese had all the advantages of complete air superiority. But the decision, following the losses in aircraft incurred in the first two days, to give priority over all other tasks to the defence of the Naval Base itself and to the protection of convoys bringing reinforcements, seems to have been made earlier than was required. It was known that the first convoys could not possibly reach Singapore before the beginning of January. The adoption of this policy at this early stage, in an endeavour to conserve the air force for the principal tasks, inevitably left the army with little support throughout the fighting in northern and central Malaya.

On land 'Matador' was an important contributory cause of the initial disaster. The idea of an advance into Siam to forestall the Japanese at Singora originated in the Far East Command.[2] Had it been successfully carried out, 'Matador' would have prevented the

---

[1] See pages 164–169.
[2] See page 76.

Japanese using Singora and the adjacent airfields and given additional depth to the defence, but it had certain inherent defects. The operation depended for its success on correct timing, since it had to be undertaken early enough to give the troops sufficient time firmly to establish themselves after reaching Singora, but late enough to disrupt the enemy plans. The timing however was bound up with political and diplomatic considerations which lay outside the competence of the military commanders in the Far East and led to hesitation at the moment when clear-cut and instant decisions were essential. Moreover, the complexity of the administrative problem and the speed at which the troops would have to move along the poor road and single line railway into Siam was such that the normal organization of the formations taking part had to be broken up. This naturally would make it difficult for them rapidly to adjust themselves to the alternative defensive plan and, in the conditions envisaged, it was more than an even chance that the alternative plan would have to be adopted. The effect on the morale of the troops of a change from the offensive to the defensive at the start of a campaign appears to have been overlooked. In the circumstances the plan was fundamentally impracticable and should never have been accepted.

As it happened, a declaration of American policy in the event of a Japanese attack on Siam, Malaya or on both was ultimately obtained on the 4th December. The following day, only some twenty-four hours before the Japanese convoys were sighted, the responsibility for the decision to launch the operation was delegated to the Commander-in-Chief, Far East.[1] Uncertain of the enemy's intentions, and conscious that on his shoulders rested the responsibility for a decision which might involve his country in an unwanted war, he hesitated to launch 'Matador' when the convoys were first sighted, and thus the only possible opportunity to forestall the Japanese at Singora was lost.[2]

The news of the next sightings reached his headquarters some thirty-four hours later and again he was faced with a difficult decision. Influenced by the passionate appeal from the British Minister in Bangkok not to be the first to violate Siamese territory and realizing that it was probably then too late to forestall the Japanese and that to move into Siam would be to risk an encounter battle near Singora for which 'Matador' was not designed, the Commander-in-Chief, after consultation with his naval colleagues, rightly decided not to order the operation. It was at this point however that, swayed perhaps by the information received on the 2nd December of the attitude of the Siamese and the thought that, if

[1] See page 175.
[2] See pages 179–181.

the Japanese convoys were not directed on Singora, it might still be advisable to move into Siam, instead of cancelling the operation he made the mistake of keeping III Corps ready to carry it out at dawn on the 8th, in the hope that by then he might have received further news of the destination of the convoys.[1]

Information of events at Singora should have been obtained by agents and immediately passed to Singapore. Had this been done the necessity for this decision would have been avoided. As it was, the delay, together with the loss of time in passing orders, resulted in III Corps not being told to adopt the alternative defensive plan until 1.30 p.m. on the 8th. The enemy was thus given the inestimable advantage of ten hours start over the defence.[2] The adoption of the alternative plan at the last moment and the loss of these precious hours threw the defence into confusion, and set in motion a train of events which led to the initial disasters on the northern frontier and the defeat of 11th Division at Jitra.[3]

The causes of the defeat at sea are more easily discernible. The despatch of the *Prince of Wales* and the *Repulse* was a political move accepted reluctantly by the Admiralty, who would have preferred to wait until the early part of 1942 when a more balanced force could have been assembled.[4] It was hoped that the presence of the two ships would act as a deterrent to Japanese aggression. It was a bluff and the bluff was called.

When the Japanese struck, it soon became clear that they had succeeded in landing and that things were not going well. To Admiral Phillips it was unthinkable that the Navy should do nothing while British territory was being invaded within easy striking distance of his force; he felt that it was his duty to make an attack on the Japanese transports and endeavour to disrupt their sea communications. His decision to make the attempt was based on his appreciation that, given fighter support and surprise, he would have a good chance of success. It was taken before he knew the full extent of the disaster to the British air forces in northern Malaya. It was endorsed by all his senior staff officers and by the Captains of the two capital ships. When he sailed he knew that it was doubtful if he would have fighter cover over Singora and yet he decided to accept the risk involved.[5] Was the risk justifiable?

For the two years of the war in Europe the Admiral had been Vice-Chief of the Naval Staff. He had studied all the reports from Norway and Crete, and the lessons they had taught must have been fresh in his memory. He well knew the danger of taking his ships

[1] See page 182.
[2] See pages 185–186.
[3] See pages 210–211.
[4] See pages 75–76 and 84–85.
[5] See pages 193–199.

within range of shore-based aircraft without fighter cover. Phillips went down with his ship and no one will ever know all that was in his mind. It is reasonable to suppose however that he took into account the fact that, up to that time, attacks by heavy or torpedo-bombers against ships had not been made at long range. It is probable, too, that he was influenced by the generally held belief that the Japanese made poor airmen and that they would be incapable of delivering an attack with the boldness and skill which they did display. Taking into consideration all the circumstances he could hardly have acted otherwise. When however he was informed shortly after midnight on the 8th December that he would certainly be without fighter cover in the Gulf of Siam, he must have realized that one of the main factors on which his plan had been based had gone. The wisdom of his decision to go on with his plan, provided he was not sighted by aircraft during the 9th, is therefore open to question.

What would have happened if he had turned back earlier or had not acted on the false report of a landing at Kuantan, and what he would have done had he escaped the Japanese bombers on that fateful 10th December, can only be matters for conjecture. His force could not have remained at the Naval Base, nor could it have played any useful part in the defence of Malaya, for after the loss of the northern airfields fighter cover in the Gulf of Siam was impossible. On the other hand his two powerful ships could have formed the nucleus of a strong Allied striking force in the south-west Pacific, which could have been organized before the Japanese had established air bases in Borneo and Celebes. Such a force would undoubtedly have been a grave menace to the invasion convoys destined for the Netherlands East Indies, would certainly have interfered with the Japanese plans and might have delayed their advance into that area, with inestimable advantage to the defenders whose problem was always that of time. But, trusting to surprise alone, he went on into the net which the Japanese had spread for him. It was a courageous decision, but as a result he lost not only his ships and his life but the only means whereby the command of the sea in eastern waters could have been disputed.

By the morning of the 13th December, without control of the sea or air in the Far East and with the garrison reeling from a severe blow, Malaya already faced defeat. The problem was whether the enemy could be held long enough in northern Malaya to enable hastily assembled reinforcements to arrive, be disembarked and be organized to launch a counter-offensive while there was still sufficient room to manœuvre. Could reinforcements reach Singapore when the enemy had control of the sea and air around Malaya? Could they arrive in Singapore in time for the invader to be driven back, and if so was the reinforcement of Malaya the best possible strategy? Such was the strategical and political importance of the Naval Base that it was decided to make the attempt. It then became a race against time, with the odds on the Japanese.

General Percival's problem was to hold the enemy in northern Malaya for at least two months. The enemy's mastery of the sea and air had brought about strategical paralysis. That mastery prevented Percival from concentrating his widely dispersed forces to meet the threat from the north, without uncovering the flanks and rear of III Corps and opening wide the direct approaches through Johore to Singapore. It also conferred on the enemy the hardly less important tactical advantage of being able to use the Strait of Malacca to outflank the defence on the west coast. He had no alternative but to order General Heath to delay the enemy's advance along the trunk road for as long as possible while giving up as little ground as he could. Since III Corps could not be reinforced by 9th Division, the mauled 11th Division, reinforced by 12th Brigade, had to fight a long delaying action on the western side of the peninsula with a vulnerable flank and with no hope of reinforcement or relief.

To assist it in carrying out this task, the corps required every artificial device which the ingenuity of military and civil engineers could devise: prepared positions where the enemy could be held and behind which its battered brigades could rest and reorganize, or from which a counterstroke could be launched; tank obstacles at frequent intervals in all the defiles, of which there were quite a number; and inundations where possible. The opportunity to provide these in the months before the war had not been taken, and it is surprising that, when time was all important, little was done after the true situation had become apparent on the 13th December.

General Heath, knowing that the elimination of 11th Division in northern Malaya would open the road to Singapore and result in the defeat in detail of the rest of the garrison, could afford to take no risks. The division had somehow to be preserved as an effective fighting formation. He could have stood and fought to the last man and the last round in a number of positions, and might have temporarily stopped the Japanese, but they had fresh formations to call on while he had none. Such action would have been spectacular but suicidal. He was thus forced to continue the withdrawal, gaining such time as he could.

The Japanese however gave him no respite. They were able to maintain the momentum of their offensive by leap-frogging fresh units through those which were becoming exhausted. They made full use of bicycles, of which there were many in the towns and villages, to save their troops both time and fatigue. They used their engineers in strength well forward and, although the engineer units with the

12

defence successfully destroyed most of the bridges on the trunk road and railway, the Japanese succeeded with remarkable rapidity in crossing obstacles which the defence confidently expected would impose considerable delay. In this they were helped by the speed of the advance which prevented the defenders from destroying bridging material, and were aided by a complete knowledge of the bridging problems that would face them, supplied by their intelligence services before the outbreak of war.[1] They had a great advantage too over the defenders in that they could be ruthless in their dealings with the civilian population. Finally, when they were likely to be held up on the main axis of their advance, they were able to manœuvre the defence out of position by landings from the sea.

In the circumstances the battle could but develop into an almost continuous retreat. With no opportunity to rest and reorganize and no prepared positions to fall back on, the endurance of the troops was gradually undermined, and it was exhaustion which was partly responsible for the disaster to 11th Division at the Slim River. The fact that the morale of the troops, at a low ebb after Jitra and Gurun, recovered sufficiently to enable them to put up a stubborn resistance whenever called upon to stand and fight, says much for the disciplined stoicism and intrinsic fighting qualities of both the British and the Indian soldier.

The plans to reinforce Malaya made after the outbreak of war were based on the assumption that III Corps could hold the Japanese in northern Malaya for some two months so as to allow the reinforcing formations to be brought into action on arrival. But by the time the decision was taken to send reinforcements the assumption was no longer justified. The fact that III Corps was forced back some 300 miles to Kuala Lumpur in approximately five weeks was not surprising. The further withdrawal to Johore was unavoidable, and by the middle of January a decisive battle had to be fought in northern Johore, long before sufficient reinforcements could arrive to tip the balance in favour of the defence.

Immediately war broke out army formations and aircraft to meet the known deficiencies were despatched on their long journey from distant bases, and the storehouses of equipment were opened; but by then it was too late. The reinforcing formations could not arrive in time to change the course of events, and much of the equipment so badly needed was still in the holds of ships in the Indian Ocean when Singapore fell.

The organization of the air reinforcement route to the Far East proved to be inadequate, and there were no transport aircraft in which ground staffs could accompany operational aircraft. Only a

---

[1] Quantities of cut timber had been dumped near the major bridges before the war so that they could quickly be repaired should they be damaged by Japanese bombing.

few of the large number of bombers which started to fly to Malaya ever got there, and those which succeeded were not only in bad condition when they arrived but were without the essential technicians and equipment required to service them. The enemy, by capturing Victoria Point, had effectively prevented the short-range fighters, so vitally necessary to the defence, from using the route, with the result that they had either to be shipped in cases by the slow sea route or flown off aircraft carriers, which could ill be spared for the purpose.

Writing to the Chief of the Imperial General Staff shortly after Singapore surrendered, General Wavell said he had realized from the first that the campaign was a race against time. He felt confident that, if Malaya and Singapore could have held out long enough for a strong air force to be built up in the Netherlands East Indies, air superiority could have been regained, in which event the Japanese ships and convoys could have been kept from approaching Java or Sumatra or other parts of the island barrier from Malaya to Australia. After that the enemy could have been gradually pushed back again. He considered that the race was lost by a month.

By the time Wavell arrived everything turned on bringing the Japanese offensive to a halt on the northern borders of Johore. The failure to concentrate the maximum strength for the decisive battle, and the wisdom of the decision to form 'Westforce' and place it in charge of that battle, have already been discussed in Chapter XX. Whatever the reasons, the dispositions then made led to disaster. During this period of eight days, from the 16th to 24th January, the Japanese out-generalled, out-manœuvred and decisively defeated the British forces in the Muar–Yong Peng–Batu Pahat triangle and won the battle for Johore. Speaking of these days, Wavell has said that he could never find the means to establish a solid defence and that, whatever he did, the front seemed to crumble. The reasons for this are obvious.

The end was now in sight. One is bound to ask at this point whether early in January, when the time factor was so greatly in favour of the enemy and when the chances of retrieving the situation appeared to be so slight, it might not have been better, for military reasons, to cut the losses at Singapore and to concentrate on holding Burma and the road to China. The diversion to Burma of the balance of 18th Division, and any other reinforcements which could have reached Singapore in time, was contemplated, but, as the abandonment of Singapore was impracticable both for political reasons and in the interests of Commonwealth relations, such a course was ruled out.[1]

We thus come to the final act of the tragedy. By the time the battle for Singapore Island began the Naval Base was no longer of any

---

[1] *Churchill*, Volume IV (Cassell, 1951), pages 51–52.

value. It was now a question of holding on to the island for as long as possible in order to prevent the enemy from using the Base, and to tie down his forces in southern Malaya so as to prevent their being used on the Burma front or elsewhere. These objects would have been well worth fighting for, even though the garrison would eventually have had to capitulate, since, after the loss of southern Sumatra in mid-February, it could not have been relieved. The feeling that nothing could be gained by continuing the struggle had however become general and, as has been shown in Chapter XXIV, there was a lack of inspired leadership. The combination of these two factors resulted in the island capitulating after a struggle lasting only seven days.

Two days after the capitulation General Wavell wrote:

> 'The trouble goes a long way back: climate, the atmosphere of the country (the whole of Malaya has been asleep for at least 200 years), lack of vigour in our peace-time training, the cumbrousness of our tactics and equipment, and the real difficulty of finding an answer to the very skilful and bold tactics of the Japanese in this jungle fighting.'

He added that, looking back, he saw only two ways by which he might have gained the additional month he so greatly needed. The first would have been to launch a determined counter-offensive with the Australians and the fresh Indian brigade, instead of the active defence which he had ordered. This, he felt, might have thrown the Japanese off their balance for the necessary period of time. The second would have been to appoint some really vigorous ruthless man to organize the defence of the island, to make people work and to inspire belief in the possibility of protracted defence. In retrospect one can see that a counter-offensive could have had no chance of success in the circumstances, nor could any one man in the short space of six weeks have been able to rectify the failures of the previous twenty years. It was already too late when Wavell took control.

The reader will have noticed how the foundations on which the security of Malaya and the Far East should have rested were in some cases never even provided or were removed stone by stone or gave way, until eventually the whole edifice crashed. There is one factor however which appears to run like a thread through the whole of the many tragic blunders which were made in the twenty years from 1921 onwards—the lack of unity. Had there been unity of purpose between the Western Powers, Japan would never have been able to encroach southwards until she directly menaced British, American, Dutch and French interests. On more than one occasion concerted action on the part of these Powers might well have prevented the war. The story is one of 'might have beens'. But it was not only on the international level that this lack of unity showed itself. It existed between the various authorities within the British colonies, between the Services themselves and between the Malays and Chinese in Malaya.

In the event of war with Japan the isolated outpost of Hong Kong was always doomed to fall. It could have been demilitarized in the early 1930's without loss of face, but such a course was not thought to be politically advisable.[1] The Colony had no strategical importance, and the few extra days of resistance which were gained by the presence of the two reinforcing battalions sent at the eleventh hour could not, and did not, have any effect on the course of events. The despatch of these reinforcements proved to be a lamentable waste of valuable manpower. The same criticism applies to the breaking up of the third brigade of 8th Australian Division and its use to provide entirely inadequate garrisons in Amboina and Timor.

The defence of the Netherlands East Indies was essentially a naval and air problem. The main strength of the small Dutch army was in Java, and its forward bases in Borneo and Celebes could only be weakly garrisoned. The only hope of holding these bases therefore lay in destroying the enemy before he landed.

Even with the *Prince of Wales* and *Repulse* the Allied forces available in the Far East at the outbreak of war could not in the long run have prevented the invasion of the Dutch islands whatever temporary success they might have had. The Japanese could always have brought overwhelming force to bear. The lack of an agreed naval plan and the diverse interests of the Allies made even temporary success almost impossible. The main British aim was the security of Singapore; the American aim soon became the protection of the supply routes to Australasia and the build-up of forces for the counter-offensive. Until the beginning of 1942 all British cruisers and destroyers as well as many of the Dutch naval vessels were employed in escorting convoys carrying reinforcements to Singapore. Admiral Glassford's task force which had come south from Manila was operating at the eastern end of the Malay Barrier escorting convoys through the Torres Strait and acting as the only striking force. A Dutch-American striking force was formed on the 2nd February but it was not until the fall of Singapore that the British ships were able to join it. By that time two of Glassford's cruisers had been damaged by air attack and the third had been sent home after grounding. The combined fleet of ships of three nationalities, hastily assembled and

---

[1] See page 17.

without a common doctrine, was annihilated in its first encounter with the enemy at the Battle of the Java Sea.

Japanese mastery in the air was a dominating factor throughout the campaign. Reduction of Allied air strength by the systematic bombing of airfields was the preliminary to every Japanese seaborne attack, and the capture and rapid development of these airfields for their own use their invariable practice. Each airfield extended the range of Admiral Tsukahara's air flotillas further south to cover the next forward movement of the invasion forces. Convoys never moved outside the range of fighter cover and any attempt by the Allied striking force to intercept them invited heavy and dangerous air attack.

On paper an Allied air force, of sufficient strength to have at least a fair chance of gaining air superiority, was due to be assembled in Java by February or March. In practice the reinforcements which arrived barely sufficed to meet wastage. Only a small proportion of the aircraft promised ever set out for the Netherlands East Indies, and of those that did nearly half failed to arrive. The sources of supply were too remote, the air route too long and hazardous and the sea route too slow. The airfields in southern Sumatra and Java were only partially developed, the warning system was ineffective and the anti-aircraft defence inadequate. From early February onwards the airfields were constantly under air attack and many aircraft were destroyed on the ground. All these factors militated against the build-up of the Allied air strength which had been hoped for. Instead of increasing, it diminished with growing rapidity until it was at last completely destroyed.

The widely separated channels of the Japanese southern advance increased the difficulty of the naval problem. If the striking force were divided, its parts would be too weak to meet any Japanese force. If it were kept concentrated, it was unlikely to be at the right place at the right time. Owing to lack of reconnaissance aircraft, accurate reports of enemy movements were infrequent. When reports were sent they were often passed through the scanty and congested communications of ABDA Command before reaching the striking force commander. Again and again the striking force arrived too late or failed to sail until the enemy had landed. Luck may not always have been with the Allies but, when it appeared to be on the side of the Japanese, it was, more often than not, earned by their superior mobility and careful planning.

Better use might have been made of the submarines. Dutch submarines did gallant work and sank a number of transports and supply ships but were too few to have any decisive effect. The twenty-nine submarines of the United States Asiatic Fleet should have been a formidable force. They, too, had some success against enemy shipping but on the whole their performance was disappointing. They were hampered by orders not to operate in water of a depth less than fifty fathoms. Japanese transports were small and used their light draught to keep whenever possible in shallow water, which reduced the number of targets. The tonnage sunk was further reduced by the frequent failure of American torpedoes to explode owing to a faulty design of firing pistol. Better results might have been obtained had Admiral Hart concentrated his submarines at focal points instead of dispersing them as he did. So wide was this dispersion that, when Admiral Helfrich took over command of the Allied naval forces on the 14th February and was forced to bring his submarines in to form a defensive screen, he was unable to assemble more than six American submarines in the Java Sea to take part in the final defence of Java.

The main reason for the failure in this area was the same as that in Malaya. The Japanese multiple attack in December 1941 found the Allies unprepared. The speed with which their enemy moved never gave them time to collect the forces necessary to remedy their initial weakness and to stage an effective counter-attack. ABDA Command was given an impossible task. Formed when the structure of the Allied defence was already crumbling, it did not have a chance in the six hectic weeks of its existence to weld the Allied forces of four nationalities into an effective whole. Before its forces had had time for combined training or to learn a common doctrine they were in action against a ruthless and efficient enemy, fully prepared for the task in hand.

The battle for the Netherlands East Indies is a melancholy chapter in the history of the war, but not one of which the Allies need be ashamed. They fought on against heavy odds until hardly a ship or an aircraft remained, and it was only when Java was overrun and their military forces were surrounded and without hope of reinforcements that they laid down their arms.

The loss of Malaya and the Singapore Naval Base was a disaster of the first magnitude. Never before in the course of British history had such a large force capitulated, and the fall of Singapore came as a terrible shock to the British Commonwealth and to all who had the cause of the Allies at heart. The man in the street had been led to believe that Singapore was an impregnable fortress upon which the safety of Australia, New Zealand and India depended. This belief had been rudely shattered. The effects of the loss of the Naval Base— the keystone of British strategy in the Far East—were far-reaching.

Most serious of all was, of course, the effect on British sea power, for there was now no base for operations in the Pacific nearer than Ceylon or Australia. Ceylon itself was threatened and the British

Eastern Fleet which was forming in the Indian Ocean was, for a period in 1942, forced back to the east coast of Africa.[1] Japanese naval and air power dominated the Bay of Bengal, which meant that—again for a period—not only was the great port of Calcutta closed to shipping, but the eastern coast of India was open to invasion.

The conquest of Malaya and Singapore greatly facilitated Japanese operations against Burma: their southern flank was now secure, large air and land forces were freed to reinforce their western front if required, and the main obstacle blocking the sea route to Rangoon was removed.

The effect of the catastrophe on Australia and New Zealand, themselves not immune from invasion, hardly needs to be stressed. In 1937, when Australia's anxieties for her safety were growing, both Governments had been assured that the whole British policy in the Far East was directed to ensuring that Singapore would not be allowed to fall, and that no consideration for the security of British interests in the Mediterranean would be allowed to interfere with the despatch of the Fleet to the Far East.[2] In June 1939 Australia was assured that a fleet, capable of containing the Japanese Fleet to a degree sufficient to prevent a major act of aggression against her and to ensure that Singapore would not fall, would be sent, although reservations were made as to the size of this fleet.[3] In November 1939 both Australia and New Zealand were told that Britain would never allow Singapore to fall nor permit a serious attack on either country and that, if it came to a choice, the Mediterranean would take second place to their security.[4] In these circumstances both Governments were entitled to assume that Singapore would be provided with defences which would enable the 'fortress' to hold out till the arrival of a fleet in eastern waters, and that they could continue to base their defence plans on this supposition.

The entry of Italy into the war and the fall of France, on whose navy Britain had relied to maintain control of the Western Mediterranean, altered the whole naval strategical situation. The despatch of a fleet of sufficient strength to the Far East had become impossible. Nevertheless the intention remained that Singapore should not be allowed to fall. The garrison was reinforced and the view freely expressed, till a few weeks before war broke out, that not only was Japan unlikely to go to war with Britain and America, but that the 'fortress', if attacked, could hold out. It was thus no wonder that the fall of Singapore, after a campaign lasting only ten short weeks, came as a shock to both Australia and New Zealand. The bastion

---

[1] See Volume II.
[2] See page 17.
[3] See page 20.
[4] See page 24.

on which they had depended was no more, and they were exposed to attack from a Power with command of the sea and supremacy in the air.

It was not only India, Burma, Australia and New Zealand, that were vitally affected by the Japanese victory: reports of the British Ambassador to China all indicated that the fall of Singapore and the Malay barrier, coupled with the loss of the Philippines, came as a tremendous shock to China. The entry of Britain and America into the war against Japan had afforded great encouragement to the Chinese nation and Government, and had given hope that the hated invader who had laid waste their land for four and a half long years must in the end be driven from their shores. It is therefore little to be wondered at that the unbroken series of military disasters in the early months of 1942, resulting as they did in the loss of all British, American and Dutch possessions in the Far East and the virtual isolation of China, caused bitter disappointment and had a most disheartening effect on the Chinese people and their Government. Inevitably comparisons were drawn between China's ability to resist the invader for nearly five years and the swift collapse of the British in Malaya.

The economic consequences of the loss of Malaya and the Netherlands East Indies were hardly less important than the strategical and political repercussions. The rubber, tin and oil which were so badly needed for the Allied war effort passed to the enemy. It was largely for these strategic raw materials, especially oil, that Japan had gone to war and her acquisition of them enormously increased her ability to prolong the struggle.

To the strategic and economic effects of the disasters must be added, of course, the tragic loss of manpower, a tragedy heightened by the barbarous treatment to which many prisoners of war were later subjected by their captors. The total battle casualties—officers and other ranks—sustained by the British and Commonwealth military forces in the Malayan Campaign were: British 38,496, Australian 18,490, Indian 67,340, and local Volunteer troops 14,382, giving a grand total of 138,708 of which more than 130,000 were prisoners of war. Against this, the final figure of Japanese battle casualties as given in their official records was only 9,824. These figures serve to underline what an appalling disaster the Malayan Campaign was to the British Commonwealth. The losses at Hong Kong amounted to 11,848 all ranks. In addition there were the naval and air force losses between the 8th December 1941 and the 8th March 1942 and the Australian losses in the Netherlands East Indies which together totalled 15,958. The total loss of manpower to the British Commonwealth was approximately 166,500. The comparable Japanese casualties during the period, killed and wounded, were approximately 15,000.

The material effects have already been shown. The demoralizing effects were equally great. On the 10th December 1941 the Japanese had scored a resounding success at sea by sinking the *Prince of Wales* and the *Repulse*. In ten weeks they had crowned their brilliant land campaign by capturing the western gateway to the Pacific and forcing the surrender of a very large army; in three months they had captured the Malay barrier and reached their appointed goal. The moral effect was so marked that in the eastern countries, which hitherto had believed in the might of the British 'Raj', it gave birth to the myth of Japanese invincibility—a belief which was not to be eradicated from the oriental mind till the Japanese, in their turn, were forced to surrender some four years later.

Appendices

APPENDIX I

Tables showing the economic importance of Malaya and the Netherlands East Indies to the Allied War Effort

A. RUBBER

1. Percentage of World Production

	World Production in Long Tons	Percentage produced in Malaya	Percentage produced in Netherlands East Indies	Total
1940	1,417,500	38%	41%	79%
1941	1,200,000 (estimate 9 months)	37%	41%	78%

2. Exports in Long Tons

	1940	1941
Malaya	538,448	435,181 (8 months only)
N.E.I.	536,734	470,449 (9 months only)
	1,075,182	905,630

3. Percentage of Malaya's Exports to Canada and U.S.A.

1940	$63\frac{1}{2}\%$
1941	$74\frac{1}{2}\%$

B. TIN

1. Percentage of World Production

	World Production in Long Tons	Percentage produced in Malaya	Percentage produced in Netherlands East Indies	Total
1940	225,900	56%	9%	65%
1941	162,000 (9 months)	58%	9%	67%

2. Exports in Long Tons

	1940	1941
Malaya	129,450	98,163 (9 months)
N.E.I.	22,035	15,704 (9 months)
	151,485	113,867

477

3. Percentage of Malaya's Exports to Canada and U.S.A.

1940	82%
1941	90%

C. OIL

1. Production of crude oil in Netherlands East Indies and British Borneo in 1940 (million statute tons)

	Dutch Borneo	Java	Sumatra	British Borneo (Brunei and Sarawak)	Total
1940	1·86	0·82	5·13	1·06	8·87

2. Exports of crude oil and refined products from Netherlands East Indies to Japan (statute tons)

1940	534,308
1941	358,058

3. Exports of bunker fuel oil from Sarawak to Japan (statute tons)

1940	68,000
1941	33,000

Note: The exports of crude oil and refined products from U.S.A. to Japan in similar periods were (statute tons)

1940	3,069,700
1941	1,618,100

APPENDIX 2

The system of Government in Tokyo during the years preceding the outbreak of war

The Japanese Constitution, enacted in the latter years of the 19th century, was based on the Prussian system and provided for an Imperial House, Diet and Cabinet, the members of the last named holding responsibility to the Emperor and not to the Diet. In theory, the Emperor was the head of the State and was assisted by State Ministers who were the members of the Cabinet headed by the Prime Minister, but it was laid down that responsibility for results remained with these Ministers and did not reflect on the Emperor.

In declaring that the Emperor held the Supreme Command of the Army and Navy, the Constitution laid down that the Chiefs of the Army and Naval General Staffs would be responsible to the Emperor for the command of the armed forces and would constitute the 'Supreme Command', and the division of responsibility between the Chiefs of Staff and the Army and Navy Ministers was detailed in regulations implementing the Constitution.

The responsibility of the Supreme Command was entirely outside the administrative authority of Cabinet Ministers, including the Army and Navy Ministers. The Army and Navy Chiefs of Staff acted for the Emperor in all matters concerning military strategy and operations, and possessed the right of direct access to the Emperor without going through Cabinet channels. Thus the Supreme Command was completely independent. Matters regarding military and naval operations were decided by them alone and not disclosed to anyone, not even Cabinet Ministers, unless and until they thought fit to do so.

The Army and Navy named their own Cabinet Ministers. Since the Government could not continue to function if one of these Ministers resigned, it could carry on only as long as it was able to absorb or modify the views and policies of the Army and Navy. The Services had thus the power to force any Government to resign. This power was frequently used. Since, during the period with which this history deals, senior Military and Naval officers were often influenced by the fanaticism of many Army officers and the younger Naval officers, this power was not at times used in the best interests of the nation.

In November 1937, Imperial General Headquarters was created to co-ordinate operations resulting from the China Incident, and consisted of the Emperor and the Chiefs of the Army and Naval General Staffs.

The principal organs of government in Tokyo were therefore:

> The Emperor, with the Lord Privy Seal as his chief political secretary and advisor.

The Cabinet, chiefly the Prime Minister, Foreign Minister, Army
    Minister and Navy Minister.
Imperial General Headquarters.
The Diet, whose parties were later merged into the Imperial Rule
    Assistance Association.

In theory each had a certain role to play, either advisory or executive.
In practice, however, some of them, for example the Emperor and the
Diet, had little or no executive responsibility or power to influence policy
or decisions.

After 1937 a Liaison Conference System between Imperial General
Headquarters and the Cabinet was developed to co-ordinate matters of
joint importance to both organs. This system, which at various times was
known as The Round Table Liaison Conference, Supreme War Direction
Conference, etc., was maintained continuously until the end of the war.
The members of the Conference were the Prime Minister, Foreign
Minister, Army Minister and Navy Minister on behalf of the Government
and the Chiefs of the Army and Naval General Staffs for the Imperial
General Headquarters. Other Cabinet members were called as needed.
The decisions at these Conferences were reached by mutual agreement.
They received the full support of both the Supreme Command and of the
Government.

Imperial Conferences were meetings held in the presence of the
Emperor to confirm important national policies which had already been
decided on, and were held merely to give added weight and prestige to the
decision. The Emperor was accompanied by the Lord Privy Seal and
normally remained silent throughout the proceedings.

The executive action to put into effect the decisions reached at these
high level conferences was taken by the responsible Ministers through
their departments and, in the case of decisions having strategical or operational effect, by the Chiefs of the Army and Naval General Staffs.

The machinery of government in Tokyo in the period under review was,
therefore, that there was a Cabinet responsible for home and foreign policy
without any control over, or even at times knowledge of, the activities of
the armed forces, whilst the leaders of the latter were independent and
entirely free from any form of government or civilian control. Though
nominally staff officers of the Emperor—the titular head of the forces—
they were in fact in supreme control, and had the power to act how and
when they wished.

APPENDIX 3

The Japanese Oil Position

1. Japan's home production of crude oil represented 0·1 per cent of the world's total production and provided some 10 per cent of her annual requirements. The remainder had to be found from overseas sources.

2. Japan's normal annual imports were obtained from the United States (80 per cent) the Netherlands East Indies (10 per cent) and the remainder from various sources.

3. Realizing that the position was a source of great weakness in war the Japanese Government passed, in 1934, the Petroleum Industry Law which provided government assistance to, and a measure of compulsion for, both importers and refiners in an endeavour to increase storage and refining capacity in the country. As a result, by 1941 there were bulk storage facilities for 60 million barrels and refinery capacity for ~~⊘~~ *32* million barrels per annum and the latter figure was planned nearly to double in the following four years. Both these steps were taken as part of the Japanese war planning: the increased storage to enable her to carry over the period of conquest and exploitation of the oil resources captured, and the increased refining capacity to handle the flow from the captured oilfields.

4. At the same time plans were made to increase home production, with very little success as will be seen from Table 'A' below, and to set up a large synthetic oil production industry with a ceiling production of some 14 million barrels per annum in 1943. Actually, owing to lack of technical knowledge and the inability to import the necessary equipment or fabricate it locally, the production never reached more than 10 per cent of the target.

5. During the years 1934 to 1940, as the storage facilities increased, Japan purchased larger quantities of oil from overseas and gradually built up her reserves from some 30 million barrels in 1934 to just over 51 million barrels in 1939 and 48 million barrels on the outbreak of war.

6. The position over the years 1934–1942 is given in tabular form below (all figures in millions of United States barrels).

Table A

Year	Imported	Home Crude Production	Home Synthetic Production	Stocks	Refining Capacity
1934	29·1	1·8	—	30·6	37·2 *13.4*
1935	33·5	2·2	—	32·7	39·1 *14.0*
1936	34·7	2·4	—	36·1	45·8 *16.5*
1937	36·8	2·5	0·03	43·1	54·8 *19.5*
1938	32·4	2·5	0·07	44·4	57·3 *20.5*
1939	30·7	2·3	0·13	51·4	63·2 *22.7*
1940	37·2	2·0	0·15	49·6	66·0 *23.7*
1941	8·4	1·9	1·20	48·9	88·1 *31.6*
1942	—	1·7	1·5	42·7	88·1 *31.6*

K2

7. The Japanese estimated their annual requirements in war as under (all figures in millions of United States barrels).

Table B

User	1942	1943	1944
Army	5·7	6·3	7·6
Navy	17·6	15·7	15·7
Civilian	12·6	12·6	12·6
Total	35·9	34·6	35·9

8. They estimated that their home crude and synthetic production would be as in Table 'C', leaving deficits as shown.

Table C

	1942	1943	1944
Home Crude	1·6	1·9	2·2
Synthetic	1·6	1·9	3·1
Total	3·2	3·8	5·3
Deficit	32·7	30·8	30·6

9. This deficit had to be met from the stock held for that purpose, and from imports from the oilfields in the Netherlands East Indies, which were to be captured and to form part of the Greater East Asia Co-prosperity Sphere. The production for this area in 1940 was (all figures in millions of United States barrels).

Table D

	Borneo	Java	Sumatra	Total
1940	19·0	6·1	40·0	65·1

The Japanese planners realized that this production would meet all their estimated requirements, provided that it could be obtained and transported. They also realized that the Dutch would take denial action in the oilfields if attacked. They therefore planned to forestall such action, if possible, and their invading forces took with them technicians to restore production rapidly. They estimated that they could obtain and transport the following quantities from the Dutch oilfields.

1942	1·9 million United States barrels
1943	12·6 million United States barrels
1944	28·5 million United States barrels

Their estimate therefore worked out as follows (figures in millions of United States barrels).

Table E

	1942	1943	1944
Home production	3·2	3·8	5·3
Imported from N.E.I.	1·9	12·6	28·5
Taken from stock	30·8*	18·2*	2·1*
Total	35·9	34·6	35·9

* Total from stock 51·1. Stock available in January 1942 42·7.

It was clear that Japan could not therefore stand a long war, and that oil might well be the bottleneck. The Japanese planners had not, however, reckoned on either the heavy losses in tankers that occurred, or the bombing of their homeland which destroyed stocks, refineries and synthetic plant; on the other hand they underestimated the production from the Dutch oilfields which was restored more rapidly than they had anticipated.

APPENDIX 4

A

The Directive to the Commander-in-Chief, Far East, dated 22nd October 1940

1. You are appointed Commander-in-Chief, Far East.

2. You will be responsible to the Chiefs of Staff for the operational control and general direction of training of all British land and air forces in Malaya,[1] Burma and Hong Kong and for the co-ordination of plans for the defence of these territories.

You will also be responsible for the operational control and general direction of training of British Air Forces in Ceylon and of the general reconnaissance squadrons of the Royal Air Force which it is proposed to station in the Indian Ocean and Bay of Bengal for ocean reconnaissance in those areas.

3. For these purposes, the following will be under your command:
>   General Officer Commanding, Malaya
>   General Officer Commanding, Burma
>   General Officer Commanding, Hong Kong
>   Air Officer Commanding, Far East

4. It is intended that you should deal primarily with matters of major military policy and strategy. It is not the intention that you should assume administrative or financial responsibilities or the normal day to day functions at present exercised by the General Officers Commanding and Air Officer Commanding.

These officers will continue to correspond as at present with the War Office, Air Ministry, Colonial Office and Burma Office, on all matters on which they have hitherto dealt with these departments, to the fullest extent possible consistent with the exercise of your command; keeping you informed as and when you wish.

5. Your staff will consist of the following only, and no expansion of this staff is contemplated:
>   A Chief of Staff (an army officer of the rank of Major-General)
>   A senior Royal Air Force Staff Officer
>   A Naval Liaison Officer
>   An Army Officer of the rank of General Staff Officer 1st Grade
>   An officer from each Service of the equivalent rank of General Staff Officer 2nd Grade

together with the necessary clerical and cypher staff.

---

[1] Including the Straits Settlements, the Federated and Unfederated Malay States, Brunei, Sarawak and North Borneo.

6. You will, where appropriate, consult and co-operate with the Commander-in-Chief, China, the Commander-in-Chief, East Indies, and the Commander-in-Chief in India. You will also communicate direct with the Defence Departments of the Governments of the Commonwealth of Australia and New Zealand on all routine matters of interest to them, but on matters of major policy you will communicate to these Dominion Governments through the appropriate Service Department of His Majesty's Government.

7. You will keep the Governor of the Straits Settlements and High Commissioner for the Malay States, the Governor of Burma and the Governor of Hong Kong closely and constantly informed and will consult them as appropriate.

8. The General and Air Officers mentioned in paragraph 3 above remain, subject to your general direction and supervision, in touch with the Governor of the Straits Settlements and High Commissioner for the Malay States, the Governor of Burma and the Governor of Hong Kong. In the case of Burma you will ensure that the constitutional relations between the Governor and the General Officer Commanding are not affected. This is of particular importance with regard to any movement of troops which might affect internal security.

9. You will, where appropriate, maintain touch with His Majesty's representatives in Japan, China, the United States of America and Thailand, and with His Majesty's Consuls-General in the Netherlands East Indies and Indo-China. The maintenance of touch with His Majesty's representatives and Consuls-General in these countries will rest with you exclusively and not with the General and Air Officers referred to in paragraph 3.

10. The Far East Combined Intelligence Bureau, in addition to keeping you informed of current intelligence, will be charged with the duty of collecting such special intelligence as you may require. The Bureau will remain under the control of the Admiralty.

11. You will normally communicate as necessary with the Chiefs of Staff, the Air Ministry being used as a channel of communication for telegrams and letters being addressed to the Secretary, Chiefs of Staff Committee; but you have the right to correspond direct with an individual Chief of Staff on matters particularly affecting his Service.

B

The Revised Directive to the Commander-in-Chief, Far East, dated 2nd December 1941

1. You are appointed Commander-in-Chief, Far East. You will be jointly responsible with Commander-in-Chief, Eastern Fleet to H.M. Government for the conduct of our strategy in the Far East, and for the co-ordination of plans with our allies and potential allies in accordance with instructions issued to you from time to time.

2. You will be responsible to H.M. Government for the strategic control of all British land and air forces in Malaya,[1] Burma and Hong Kong and for the co-ordination of plans for the defence of these territories.

You will also be responsible for the strategic control of British Air Forces in Ceylon and of the general reconnaissance squadrons of the Royal Air Force which it is proposed to station in the Indian Ocean and Bay of Bengal for ocean reconnaissance in those areas.

3. For these purposes, the following will be under your command:

> General Officer Commanding, Hong Kong
> General Officer Commanding, Malaya
> General Officer Commanding, Burma
> Air Officer Commanding, Far East.

4. It is intended that you should deal primarily with matters of major military policy and strategy. It is not the intention that you should assume operational control, or the administrative and financial responsibilities and the normal day to day functions now exercised by the General Officers Commanding and Air Officer Commanding.

These Officers will continue to correspond as at present with the War Office, Air Ministry, Colonial Office and Burma Office, on all matters on which they have hitherto dealt with these departments, to the fullest extent possible consistent with the exercise of your command, keeping you informed as and when you wish.

5. You will, where appropriate, consult and co-operate with the Commander-in-Chief, East Indies, and the Commander-in-Chief in India.

You will also communicate direct with the Defence Departments of the Governments of the Dominions on all routine matters of interest to them, but on matters of major policy you will communicate with Dominion Governments through H.M. Government.

6. You will, in close collaboration with the Commander-in-Chief, Eastern Fleet:

> (a) Keep the Governor of the Straits Settlements and High Commissioner for the Malay States, the Governor of Burma and the Governor of Hong Kong closely and constantly informed and consult them as appropriate.
>
> (b) Where appropriate, maintain touch with His Majesty's representatives in Japan, China, the United States of America and Thailand and with His Majesty's Consuls-General in the Netherlands East Indies and Philippines and Indo-China.

7. The General and Air Officers mentioned in paragraph 3 above remain, subject to your general direction and supervision, in touch with the Governor of the Straits Settlements and High Commissioner for the Malay States, the Governor of Burma and the Governor of Hong Kong, as appropriate. In the case of Burma you will ensure that the constitutional relations between the Governor and the General Officer Commanding are not affected. This is of particular importance with regard to any movement of troops which might affect internal security.

---

[1] Including the Straits Settlements, the Federated and Unfederated Malay States, Brunei, Sarawak and North Borneo.

8. The Far East Combined Intelligence Bureau, in addition to keeping you informed of current intelligence, will be charged with the duty of collecting such special intelligence as you may require. The Bureau will remain under the control of the Admiralty.

9. You will normally communicate as necessary with the Chiefs of Staff, the War Office being used as your channel of communication; but you have the right to correspond direct with a Service Department on matters particularly affecting one service. Communications from the Chiefs of Staff dealing with matters affecting the joint responsibility of Commander-in-Chief, Far East, and Commander-in-Chief, Eastern Fleet, will be sent through the War Office or the Admiralty as from the Chiefs of Staff.

10. A copy of the Directive to the Commander-in-Chief, Eastern Fleet, and of the instructions which have been issued to him by the Admiralty, are attached for your information.

C

The Directive to the Commander-in-Chief, Eastern Fleet, dated 2nd December 1941

1. On assumption of your duties as Commander-in-Chief, Eastern Fleet, you will become jointly responsible with the Commander-in-Chief, Far East, to H.M. Government for the conduct of our strategy in the Far East, and for the co-ordination of plans with our allies and potential allies in accordance with instructions issued to you from time to time.

2. You are to communicate direct with the Defence Departments of the Dominions on all routine matters of interest to them, but on matters of major policy you are to communicate with the Dominion Governments through H.M. Government.

3. In close collaboration with the Commander-in-Chief, Far East, you are to:

(a) Keep the Governor of the Straits Settlements and High Commissioner for the Malay States, the Governor of Burma and the Governor of Hong Kong closely and constantly informed and consult them as appropriate.

(b) Maintain touch, where appropriate, with His Majesty's Representatives in Japan, China, United States of America and Thailand, and with His Majesty's Consuls-General in the Netherlands East Indies, the Philippine Islands and Indo-China.

4. You are to communicate as necessary with the Chiefs of Staff through the Admiralty. Communications from the Chiefs of Staff dealing with matters affecting the joint responsibility of Commander-in-Chief, Far East, and Commander-in-Chief, Eastern Fleet, will be sent through the War Office or the Admiralty as from the Chiefs of Staff.

5. A copy of the Directive to the Commander-in-Chief, Far East, is attached for your information.

D

Admiralty Instructions to the Commander-in-Chief, Eastern Fleet, dated 2nd December 1941

A. It has been decided to replace the appointment of C.-in-C. China by a new appointment styled C.-in-C. Eastern Fleet.

B. While Japan remains neutral the duties of C.-in-C. Eastern Fleet will be:

  (1) The Command and the administration of the Eastern Fleet (see paragraph F below) and of naval forces and establishments on the China Station at present carried out by C.-in-C. China.

  (2) The preparation of plans and war orders for the whole Eastern Theatre in collaboration with C.-in-C., Far East, C.-in-C., East Indies, A.C.N.B., N.Z.N.B., and U.S. and Dutch authorities. The Eastern Theatre is defined in paragraph H below.

C. On the outbreak of war with Japan, or when directed by the Admiralty, C.-in-C., Eastern Fleet will, in addition to the above duties, assume the strategic control of all British and Dutch Naval Forces, with the exception of Local Defence Forces, in the Eastern Theatre subject to the following:

  (1) While the distribution and general plan of employment of naval forces throughout the Eastern Theatre is the responsibility of C.-in-C. Eastern Fleet, Cs.-in-C. of each Station will retain operational control of the Naval Forces other than the Eastern Fleet operating on their station.

  (2) Dominions and Associated Powers have the right to withdraw or withhold forces from the strategic control of C.-in-C. Eastern Fleet provided prior information is given to the latter.

D. The degree of strategic control exercised by C.-in-C. Eastern Fleet over the Naval Forces of the U.S.A. should the latter be a belligerent will be governed by such agreement as may be in force at the time between the U.S. and Great Britain.

E. In order that C.-in-C. Eastern Fleet may fly his flag afloat he will be provided with a Chief of Staff and a Chief Staff Officer. The former will deputize for C.-in-C. Eastern Fleet at Singapore in his absence; the latter will remain afloat.

F. It is possible that a part of the Eastern Fleet may be assembled in the Eastern Theatre before the outbreak of war with Japan. The disposition of any such units within the Eastern Theatre will be the responsibility of C.-in-C. Eastern Fleet who will delegate operational control of them while employed on stations other than the China Station as he considers necessary. Units which are to be considered as forming the Eastern Fleet will be promulgated by the Admiralty in due course.

G. The above arrangements will come into force when ordered by the Admiralty.

H. The Eastern Theatre comprises:

(1) While the U.S. are non-belligerent, the existing East Indies, China, Australian and New Zealand Naval Stations.

(2) If the U.S. are belligerent the existing East Indies, China, Australian and New Zealand Naval Stations bounded on the north and east by the following line:

> The parallel of 30 degrees N. from the coast of China to meridian 140 deg. E. down the latter to the Equator, along the Equator to 180th Meridian and down the latter. The Pacific Ocean to the east of this line will be an area of U.S. strategic responsibility.

APPENDIX 5

The Organization of the Japanese Navy, Army and Air Forces

A. THE JAPANESE NAVAL ORGANIZATION

When, on the 15th January, 1936, Japan withdrew from the negotiations arising out of the second London Naval Conference she was free of the limitations on warship tonnage which she had agreed to under the Washington Treaty. She at once embarked on an intensive building programme. In five years she added four aircraft carriers, six cruisers and a number of destroyers and submarines to her fleet. By 1941 her existing battleships had been modernized and three new gigantic battleships were building—the result of a directive to her constructors to build the largest and most powerful warships in the world. The keel of the first of them, the *Yamato*, was laid in 1937. She was completed and placed in commission within a few days of the outbreak of the war. Her standard displacement was about 64,000 tons, her overall length 863 feet and her main armament nine 18·1-inch guns. The *Musashi* followed her a year later. Construction of the third ship of the class, the *Shinano*, began in 1940 but after the loss of four carriers at the Battle of Midway, her design was altered and she was completed as a carrier. The giant carrier was never commissioned. In November 1944, when almost ready for service, she was torpedoed and sunk by an American submarine when moving from Tokyo Bay to the Inland Sea to escape the threat of American bombers.

There was no radical difference between Japanese, British and American warship design. As regards their cruisers however, the Japanese tended to put heavier armaments into smaller hulls at the expense of armoured protection, but their ships could and did take comparable punishment, probably owing to greater subdivision of hulls. Heavy cruisers normally carried float aircraft for tactical reconnaissance. Destroyers were fast and well armed and their torpedoes were more reliable, in the early days of the war, than those of the Americans. Submarines ranged in size from the twenty ton midget to the submersible transport of some 3,500 tons.

Fleet carriers normally carried about sixty-three aircraft, of which twenty-seven were fighters and the remainder torpedo-bombers or bombers. The light fleet carrier's complement was about twenty-four aircraft, of which half or more were fighters. There were two seaplane carrier squadrons capable of carrying in all some seventy seaplanes (an additional thirty-five with wings folded). Land-based aircraft were an integral part of the naval establishment, and close co-operation between these and carrier-borne aircraft played an important part in the early successes of the Japanese. The bulk of the combat strength of the shore based naval air force was contained in 11th Air Fleet.

Ships' companies were larger than in western navies and living conditions on board were spartan by British standards. Their training was rigorous in the extreme.

Japanese squadrons usually consisted of from two to four ships commanded by a Rear-Admiral. The normal strength of their destroyer flotillas was two or four divisions of four vessels each, with a light cruiser as flotilla leader flying the flag of a Rear-Admiral.

During the nineteen years following the Washington Treaty of 1922, the Japanese nearly doubled the tonnage of their Navy and at the outbreak of war their fleet was more powerful than the combined Allied fleets in the Pacific. On the 8th December, 1941 its main units consisted of:

> Ten battleships (two 16-inch, eight 14-inch)
> Six fleet carriers
> Four light fleet carriers
> Eighteen heavy cruisers
> Twenty light cruisers
> One hundred and twelve destroyers (fleet type)
> Sixty-five submarines.

These (except for the naval forces in China) formed the Combined Fleet. The two 16-inch battleships and later the *Yamato* came directly under the Commander-in-Chief, Combined Fleet. All other ships were organized for administrative purposes in six fleets and an air fleet, viz. 1st Fleet (Battle Fleet), 2nd Fleet (Scouting Force), 3rd Fleet (Blockade and Transport Force), 4th Fleet (Mandates Fleet), 5th Fleet (Northern Fleet), 6th Fleet (Submarine Fleet) and 1st Air Fleet (Carrier Fleet). From these administrative fleets the High Command formed task forces to implement the war plan. The two principal forces were the Striking Force (fast carrier force) which attacked Pearl Harbour, and the Southern Force which was used for the conquest of the Philippines, Malaya and the Netherlands East Indies.

Task Forces

C.-in-C., Combined Fleet, Admiral Yamamoto

Main Body (Admiral Yamamoto)
> 1st Battle Squadron (two 16-inch battleships and later the *Yamato*)
> 2nd Battle Squadron (four 14-inch battleships)
> 9th Cruiser Squadron (two light cruisers)
> Eight destroyers

Striking Force (Vice-Admiral Nagumo)
> 3rd Battle Squadron, 1st Division (two 14-inch battleships)
> 1st Carrier Squadron (two fleet carriers)
> 2nd Carrier Squadron (two fleet carriers)
> 5th Carrier Squadron (two fleet carriers)
> 8th Cruiser Squadron (two 8-inch cruisers)
> 1st Destroyer Flotilla (one light cruiser, sixteen destroyers)

Southern Force (Vice-Admiral Kondo)

     3rd Battle Squadron, 2nd Division (two 14-inch battleships)
     4th Carrier Squadron (two light fleet carriers)
     4th Cruiser Squadron (four 8-inch cruisers)
     5th Cruiser Squadron (two 8-inch cruisers)
     7th Cruiser Squadron (four 8-inch cruisers)
     16th Cruiser Squadron (one 8-inch and three light cruisers)
     2nd Destroyer Flotilla (one light cruiser, twelve destroyers)
     3rd Destroyer Flotilla (one light cruiser, sixteen destroyers)
     4th Destroyer Flotilla (one light cruiser, twelve destroyers)
     5th Destroyer Flotilla (one light cruiser, twelve destroyers)
     4th, 5th and 6th Submarine Flotillas (eighteen submarines)

South Sea Force (Vice-Admiral Inoue)

     One light cruiser
     6th Cruiser Squadron (four 8-inch cruisers)
     18th Cruiser Squadron (two light cruisers)
     6th Destroyer Flotilla (one light cruiser and twelve destroyers)
     7th Submarine Flotilla (one light cruiser and nine submarines)

Northern Force (Vice-Admiral Hosokaya)

     21st Cruiser Squadron (two light cruisers), one seaplane tender and
     two destroyers

Submarine Fleet (Vice-Admiral Shimizu)

     One light cruiser
     1st, 2nd and 3rd Submarine Flotillas (thirty submarines)

Training Squadron

     3rd Carrier Squadron (two light fleet carriers)

B. THE JAPANESE ARMY ORGANIZATION

1. Strength of the Japanese Army

(a) The pre-1937 Japanese Army was organized into seventeen divisions, which were stationed in Japan (11), Korea (2) and Manchuria (4). There were no cavalry, armoured, airborne, or divisions of other categories. The strength of a division in Japan was approximately 10,000 and in Manchuria 18,000.

(b) In 1941, when the decision to go to war was taken, the number of divisions available was fifty-one, plus one cavalry group. These were disposed in December 1941 as under:

Japan (5 divisions)	Nos. 7, 52, 53, 54, 56
Korea (2 divisions)	Nos. 19, 20
Manchuria (13 divisions)	Nos. 1, 8, 9, 10, 11, 12, 14, 23, 24, 25, 28, 29, 57
North China (10 divisions)	Nos. 17, 21, 26, 27, 32, 35, 36, 37, 41,

Central China, including Shanghai (11 divisions)	Nos. 3, 4, 6, 13, 15, 22, 33, 34, 39, 40, 116
South China (4 divisions)	Nos. 18, 38, 51, 104
French Indo-China (2 divisions)	No. 55, Guards
Formosa and Okinawa (3 divisions)	Nos. 2, 16, 48
Hainan Island (1 division)	No. 5
Mongolian Garrison Army	One cavalry group

In Japan there were, in addition to the five divisions, ten depot divisions which were used to train reinforcements for divisions overseas.

In addition to the above formations, there were twenty-two independent mixed brigades, and thirty-seven other formations of approximately brigade size, i.e. South Sea detachment, border garrison forces and railway guard units.

2. Divisional Organization

In 1937 each division was composed of two infantry brigades com-manded by Major-Generals. Each infantry brigade was composed of two infantry regiments commanded by Colonels, and organized into three infantry battalions and a regimental gun unit. Each battalion consisted of three infantry companies, one machine-gun company and one battalion gun unit. On mobilization, a fourth infantry company was added to each infantry battalion.

From 1937 onwards the infantry element in the division was gradually changed from a 'square' organization of two infantry brigades of two infantry regiments each, to a 'triangular' organization of one infantry group headquarters and three infantry regiments. The infantry group commander was a Major-General. The divisions which were left on the 'square' organization were designed primarily for garrison duties. The situation in December 1941 was that most divisions had been changed to the 'triangular' organization of three infantry regiments, but a few were still on the 'square' organization.

Each infantry division usually had in addition to its infantry element the following divisional troops:

    One field artillery regiment
    One engineer regiment
    One transport regiment
    One signal unit
    One medical unit

Japanese records show, however, that there was no standard in this respect but that each division was organized with a view to its operational use and the availability of men and material.

3. Organization of Japanese Artillery and Engineers

The Japanese field artillery was organized into regiments, one regiment being within the organization of each division. A few divisions had a mountain artillery regiment in place of a field artillery regiment.

The field artillery regiment was commanded by a Colonel and normally organized into two field-gun battalions and one howitzer battalion. A field-gun battalion was organized into three batteries each of three sections and armed with two 75-mm. field-guns in each section. The howitzer battalion was organized into four batteries each of two sections with two 105-mm. field howitzers per section.

Mountain artillery regiments were normally organized into three battalions each of three batteries. Each battery consisted of two sections, each section armed with two 75-mm. mountain guns. In some cases regiments were on a two battalion basis.

Heavy field artillery regiments were organized into heavy field artillery brigades which were army troops. Some regiments were equipped with 105-mm. guns and some with 105-mm. howitzers. The normal organization of the regiment was two battalions each of three batteries. Each battery was equipped with four guns or howitzers.

Japanese field engineer units were organized into divisional engineer regiments and independent engineer regiments. The divisional engineer regiment, of which there was one in each division, was normally organized into two field companies and one bridging company. Independent engineer regiments were army troops and of no fixed organization though often on a similar basis to that of the divisional engineer regiments.

4. Higher Formations

Divisions overseas were grouped into Armies. An Army consisted of from two to five divisions with attached army troops. Armies were grouped into area armies known either by a proper name, e.g. Burma Area Army, or by a number, e.g. No. 7 Area Army.

The British corps organization did not exist in the Japanese army either in peace or war.

Area armies were in most cases grouped into a higher formation, the nomenclature of which was not fixed. For example, the official title of Field-Marshal Count Terauchi who commanded all land forces in Burma, Malaya, Borneo, French Indo-China, Siam, and the Netherlands East Indies was 'Supreme Commander-in-Chief, Japanese Forces, Southern Region'. On the other hand the official title of the Commander-in-Chief of the Japanese forces in Manchuria, who commanded two field armies and various lower formations, was 'Kwantung Army Commander'.

C. THE JAPANESE AIR FORCE ORGANIZATION

1. The Japanese Air Force was not a separate service, but consisted of two supporting forces for the Army and Navy functioning on strictly independent lines. The Army Air Force was primarily responsible for giving support to the land forces, whilst the Naval Air Force supported the

surface fleets and was responsible for coastal defence, sea and anti-submarine patrols and convoy protection. This policy of divided responsibility proved satisfactory only while the Japanese were able to fight the war according to their own preconceived plan.

In the early stages of the development of her air forces, Japan was influenced by western methods and design. From 1937 the influence of Germany, both in organization and equipment, became predominant.

On the outbreak of war the Japanese air forces had a combined numerical strength of about 4,300 first-line aircraft with adequate reserves to meet immediate requirements. The capacity of the aircraft industry in Japan to provide a continuous flow of new aircraft to replace wastage and at the same time maintain adequate stocks of reserves was however unequal to the strain. As the war progressed Japan was compelled to make greater and greater efforts to increase the rate of aircraft production and to expand the training organization for the air forces. Her resources, particularly of raw materials for the aircraft industry, were insufficient for the task. Thus it was that in December 1941 the two air forces were prepared only for a swift, short and conclusive war.

2. Army Air Force

At the start of the war the highest formation was an air division, commanded by a Lieutenant-General. The numerical strength of an air division varied from 275 to 350 first-line aircraft. At that time there were five air divisions of which two, the 3rd and 5th, took part in the operations described in this volume. The former gave air support to the forces which landed in Malaya, Sumatra and Java; the latter after co-operating in the occupation of the Philippines was responsible for supporting the invasion of Burma. Of the remaining three air divisions, the 1st never moved from Japan and the 2nd and the 4th did not move south until 1944.

An air division was composed of two or three air brigades each commanded by a Major-General. An air brigade usually consisted of three or four air regiments—not necessarily all of the same kind—equipped with between twenty-seven and forty-eight aircraft each, the actual number depending partly on the type of aircraft and partly on the location of the regiment.

The air regiments were normally divided into three squadrons—fighter squadrons with sixteen aircraft and bomber squadrons with nine or twelve aircraft each.

The air division included an indefinite number of airfield battalions, which provided the ground staffs for operational airfields and the maintenance crews for servicing aircraft. The establishment of airfield battalions usually totalled about 600 officers and men. They were more or less permanently located on airfields for which they were responsible, while the air regiments made only temporary use of them according to operational requirements. By this means a high degree of mobility was achieved. Airfield battalions were responsible for the defence of their airfields and anti-aircraft sections armed with automatic cannons and machine-guns formed part of the organization. They also held considerable supplies of fuel, bombs and ammunition.

By the summer of 1942 three air army headquarters had been formed: the 1st in Japan, the 2nd in Manchuria and the 3rd in Singapore. The 4th was formed at Rabaul in August 1943 for the south-east front and the 5th in February 1944 for the China theatre.

An air army, commanded by a Lieutenant-General, contained flying and ground units of various kinds. It was planned that an air army should consist of two air divisions but, in practice, the number varied to meet operational requirements.

With the formation of the five air armies completed, the total numerical strength of the Army Air Force was about 2,000 first-line aircraft.

3. *Naval Air Force*

The basic formation was an air group—a self-contained, tactical and administrative formation normally equipped with aircraft of one type. The air groups each consisted of a flying unit, with complementary ground staffs adequate in strength both for maintenance of the flying unit and to administer an airfield—or if the air group were not land-based, to provide similar services on board a carrier. Air groups varied in size, according to their role and equipment, from 18 aircraft in a small reconnaissance group to 84 in a large medium bomber group, having an establishment of over 2,000 officers and men.

Two or more air groups were usually organized into an air flotilla under the command of a Rear-Admiral. The numerical strength of an air flotilla varied, according to the tasks it was planned to undertake, from about 60 to 150 first-line aircraft. Two or more air flotillas under a headquarters formed an air fleet, commanded by a Vice-Admiral. On the outbreak of war there were two air fleets in being—the 1st and the 11th.

The 1st Air Fleet was the carrier fleet, the bulk of which undertook the attacks on Pearl Harbour. It contained the 1st, 2nd and 5th Carrier Squadrons, each with two fleet carriers, and the 3rd and 4th Carrier Squadrons each with two light fleet carriers. The total number of aircraft carried by the 1st Air Fleet was about 490. The carrier pilots were the cream of the naval air force. Many of them had gained experience in China and all had been well trained and flew their aircraft with skill and daring.

The 11th Air Fleet, which was land-based, was the expeditionary naval air force which moved from Japan with the navy in the invasion of French Indo-China, Malaya and the Netherlands East Indies. It consisted of the 21st and 23rd Air Flotillas based in Formosa and the 22nd Air Flotilla based in southern Indo-China. The 21st and 23rd Air Flotillas each consisted of three air groups and the 22nd of two air groups. Some flying-boats were included in each group. The 11th Air Fleet had a total strength of about 500 first-line aircraft.

Until April 1942, the only other operational flotilla was the 24th Air Flotilla which was under control of the 4th Fleet in the Mandated Islands. It consisted of two air groups with a total of about sixty first-line aircraft.

The Naval Air Force included a force for use with various classes of ships such as converted cruisers and seaplane tenders, which had a total first-line strength of about 200 aircraft. There was also a reconnaissance force totalling some 130 seaplanes and 65 flying-boats.

Some air units were stationed in the Mandated Islands, but their combined total first-line strength did not exceed fifty aircraft.

In Japan there were Homeland Defence Forces which consisted of air groups not specifically allocated for operations overseas. Excluding training types, these forces had a first-line strength of about 650 aircraft.

According to Japanese sources, the total operational strength of the Naval Air Force on the outbreak of war was about 3,300 aircraft. This figure however includes some reserves, estimated to have amounted to a tenth of the total.

L2

APPENDIX 6

Japanese Order of Battle and plan of attack against Hong Kong

Lieut.-General T. Sakai commanding 23rd Army in South China was ordered to take Hong Kong.[1] The task was entrusted to 38th Division (Lieut.-General T. Sano) with certain additional units under command. The force included the following:

Infantry (Major-General T. Ito):

    38th Infantry Group: 228th, 229th and 230th Regiments, each of three battalions.

    66th Infantry Regiment and attached troops[2] (for protection against Chinese interference).

Artillery:

    38th Mountain Artillery Regiment (three battalions).

    2nd and 5th Independent Anti-Tank Artillery Battalions.

    One independent mountain artillery regiment.

    One heavy field artillery regiment (plus one battalion).

    21st Mortar Battalion.

Siege Artillery:

    One heavy artillery regiment (24-cm. howitzers).

    One heavy artillery battalion (15-cm. guns).

    One independent mortar battalion.

Engineers:

    38th Engineer Regiment.

    One independent engineer regiment (two field engineer units, one landing craft unit).

Army Air Units:

    45th Air Regiment (light bomber).

    One reconnaissance squadron.

    One fighter squadron.

    Detachment of 5th Air Division (eighteen heavy bombers) [from 16th December onwards].

    47th Airfield Battalion.

    67th Airfield Company.

---

[1] The South China 2nd Expeditionary Fleet supplied a small force to blockade the Colony and prevent either reinforcement or evacuation by sea. The plan provided for the employment of naval air forces from the 21st and 23rd Flotillas of 11th Air Fleet in Formosa to carry out raids on Hong Kong and cover the landing operations.

[2] This was known as the Araki Detachment, and was stationed about 40 miles north-east of Hong Kong. According to the Japanese, a Chinese column, estimated at one and a half divisions, advanced on this detachment after the attack on Hong Kong had started but took no offensive action.

Imperial General Headquarters' Operational Plan (summarized)

1. Object of the Operation: To capture Hong Kong by destroying the enemy forces.

2. Policy: 38th Division and attached units from 23rd Army will attack Kowloon Peninsula and Hong Kong Island from the mainland, in co-operation with the Navy.

3. Strength: (as in foregoing Order of Battle).

4. Strategy:
    (a) The Attack Group of 23rd Army will assemble in strict secrecy in the Canton area. [Note: all moves were made by night.]
    (b) The operation will begin directly the operation against Malaya is known to have started.
    (c) As soon as the invasion starts, air units will strike Hong Kong. They will neutralize the enemy air power, and destroy all vessels in the harbour as well as important military installations.
    (d) The Invasion Group will break across the frontier near Sham Chun Hu, and after firmly occupying Tai Mo Shan will press forward to the line running east and west beyond the hill.
    (e) The Invasion Group will then prepare for a major attack, overwhelm and smash the enemy positions aligned from east to west near the reservoir, and drive down to the southern tip of the Kowloon peninsula. Landings from the sea may be necessary, depending upon battle exigencies.
    (f) Upon completion of the capture of Kowloon, immediate preparations to attack Hong Kong will be made, but enemy military installations on the small islands must first be destroyed.
    (g) In attacking Hong Kong, troops will land on its northern beach and from there enlarge their gains.
    The Navy will stage a demonstration to lead the enemy to believe that landings on the southern beach are intended.

38th Division's Invasion Plan (summarized)

1st Phase: The advance across the frontier at Sham Chun Hu to be in two groups:

Right Wing Unit (under Major-General Ito):
     228th Infantry Regiment (less III/228th Battalion in reserve).
     230th Infantry Regiment (less III/230th Battalion in reserve).
     One mountain artillery battalion.
     One anti-tank gun battalion.
     One engineer battalion.
     In support: 38th Mountain Artillery Regiment (less one battalion).

Left Wing Unit:
     229th Infantry Regiment (less I/229th Battalion).
     Small artillery and engineer detachments.
     In support: One mountain artillery regiment.
         One independent artillery battalion.
         One mortar battalion.

Reserve: I/229th Battalion.

Orders: Contact to be gained with the main British position, which is to be attacked in strength within a week from the commencement of operations. The main strength of the attack to be delivered on the right flank, i.e. south-west of Jubilee Reservoir.

Note: The Right Wing was to advance via Shui Tau across country south-west of Tai Mo Shan, with a right flank-guard on the Brothers Point circular road.

The Left Wing was directed on to Tai Mo Shan and Tai Po.

2nd Phase: Consolidation of the mainland and preparation for the assault on the island.

Note: This phase included the capture of Green Island and Stonecutters Island.

3rd Phase: Capture of Hong Kong Island, 38th Division to land on the north of the island, combined with feints by the Navy of landings on the south coast.

Plan: The three infantry regiments (less one battalion each) were to land simultaneously between Pak Sha Wan and North Point. Once the troops were established ashore, an advance was to be made westward towards Victoria: 230th Regiment on the right, the 228th in the centre, and the 229th on the left.

By daylight on the 19th it was expected that two regiments would be in position immediately east of The Peak isolating the city.

III/228th and I/230th Battalions were left to guard Kowloon. These with I/229th Battalion constituted the divisional reserve which was brought across to the island later.

APPENDIX 7

The Organization of the British Navy, Army and Air Force in 1941
with particular reference to the Far East

THE ROYAL NAVY

The word FLEET is a loose term, officially defined as meaning a number of vessels working in company. When reference is made to a specific fleet, such as the Eastern Fleet, it includes all H.M. ships and vessels operating in the area denoted—under the command of the Commander-in-Chief.

Ships and vessels of His Majesty's Fleets were organized in SQUADRONS for cruisers and above, and FLOTILLAS for destroyers and below. Unlike the First World War when the Grand Fleet was composed of numerous battle squadrons, there was normally only one battle squadron with each of the main fleets during the Second World War. Squadrons and flotillas, if numbers permitted, were further subdivided into two DIVISIONS and four SUBDIVISIONS. The term BATTLEFLEET included not only the battle squadron, but also those ships screening it and manœuvring with it.

Squadrons of battleships, aircraft carriers, and cruisers consisted of two or more ships, each squadron being under the command of a Flag Officer.

A flotilla of destroyers consisted of not more than eight vessels—as far as possible of the same class—under the command of a Captain (D). Whereas divisions of battleships and cruisers were numbered as integral parts of the squadron to which they belonged, e.g. Second Division of the 3rd Battle Squadron, Second Division of the 4th Cruiser Squadron, destroyer divisions were not. Thus, the Sixteenth Division of Destroyers might on one occasion form part of the Eleventh Flotilla, and on another of the Seventh Flotilla.

Any number of submarines formed a flotilla for administrative purposes, but as the boats operated independently they were not organized into divisions like destroyers. Flotillas were normally administered and operated by a Captain (S) who commanded the depot ship or shore establishment which happened to be their operational base.

Squadrons of the Fleet Air Arm were organized on similar lines to those of the Royal Air Force, but they were usually smaller. Twelve aircraft (without reserves) was the normal complement of a squadron, which was divided into flights and sub-flights. Carriers of the *Indomitable* class could carry in their hangars about forty-five aircraft, the *Formidable* thirty-three and the old and much smaller *Hermes* about twelve. Deck loads of aircraft were however sometimes carried for specific tasks which could increase the complement of aircraft by as much as fifty per cent. The type of aircraft embarked varied according to the tasks and the aircraft available.

The endurance of ships at sea depended on the amount of fuel carried, the age of their machinery, the speed at which they were operating, the state of their bottoms and the weather. The old 'R' class battleships had an endurance of about 2,500 miles at 20 knots in calm weather. The modernized *Warspite*, on the other hand, had almost twice the endurance of the *Royal Sovereign*. Destroyers were often fuelled from larger warships at sea but in 1942 fuelling at sea was not the commonplace that it later became.

Operational endurance depended also on the supply of ammunition, and particularly anti-aircraft ammunition. The ammunitioning of ships at sea was not developed until the later stages of the war.

The supply services in the Navy, unlike those in the Army and the Royal Air Force, were largely run by civilians.

THE ARMY

1. The organization of the British Army was centred round the DIVISION, in which the basic arm was the infantry.

The Division

2. The division was the smallest formation to contain, as an integral part, a proportion of all arms.

The unit of infantry was the BATTALION. An INFANTRY BRIGADE was a permanent grouping of three battalions, together with a headquarters through which the Brigadier exercised control.

The division, commanded by a Major-General, consisted of a headquarters, three infantry brigades, and certain units of other arms collectively known as the DIVISIONAL TROOPS: e.g. three field regiments and an anti-tank regiment of artillery; three field companies and a field park company of engineers; divisional signals, a machine-gun battalion and a battalion of the Reconnaissance Corps; and so on.

Occasionally a portion of the divisional troops would be attached temporarily to an infantry brigade for some special purpose; this improvised formation was known as a BRIGADE GROUP.

Non-Divisional Units

Many types of fighting units existed (mostly on paper) which did not form part of a division; such as medium, heavy, and anti-aircraft artillery, machine-gun battalions, and various engineer, signal, and infantry tank units. These NON-DIVISIONAL UNITS were intended for allotment to formations as the situation might demand. Thus, if two or more divisions were grouped for purposes of command into a CORPS, a proportion of non-divisional units would become the CORPS TROOPS. Similarly, if two or more corps were grouped as an ARMY, there would be an appropriate allotment of ARMY TROOPS. It will be seen, therefore, that an increase in the total strength of a force implied a decrease in the proportion of infantry to the whole. As the war progressed it became increasingly necessary to apply the bulk of the corps troops, and even army troops, to support first one and then another of the divisions.

Many other types of non-divisional units were required for administrative and maintenance purposes, principally at the base and on the lines of communication. Their activities covered a very wide range, and the more undeveloped the country the more varied was the work to be done.

Armoured Formations

3. No armour other than carriers and some armoured cars took part in the fighting against the Japanese in either Hong Kong or Malaya. The first British armoured formation to go into action was 7th Armoured Brigade, consisting of two regiments of cruiser tanks, which arrived in Burma just before the fall of Rangoon. By the end of 1943 Indian armoured brigades were becoming available and three, armed mainly with medium tanks, took part in the 1944 and 1945 fighting under command of corps but never as a division.

Dominion Forces

4. The Dominions had decided to organize any forces they might raise on the same lines as the British, with only minor differences; and to equip and train them similarly.

The Indian Army

5. The Indian Army, as it played such a major part in the war against Japan, requires special mention. The pre-war Indian Army was a standing regular army of long-service volunteers, organized and trained on the same lines as the British Army. There was no difficulty in keeping units up to strength and in 1941 many of them had had recent experience of active service on the North-West Frontier. Its officers were British and Indian, the former predominating in most units. Commanders and staffs of formations were appointed from either the Indian or British Army. Most Indian infantry brigades contained one British battalion, but never more than one. The proportion of artillery to infantry was comparatively low. It was mostly British and had not yet been fully rearmed with the latest weapons. There was little anti-aircraft artillery, but a big expansion was about to be carried out as the necessary weapons became available. There was a general shortage of anti-tank guns, light machine-guns, mortars and carriers except in the Western Desert. Indian Cavalry was in process of conversion to armour but as yet had no tanks. It was equipped with trucks, carriers and armoured cars in various proportions, 'soft' vehicles being replaced by armoured ones as they became available.

Strengths

6. Even without comparing particulars of weapons—which is of course a matter of fundamental importance—it will be seen that the counting of heads in any theatre of war can by itself give only a very rough and possibly quite erroneous picture of the fighting power of a force. But in order to give an idea of the size of formations and units of British, Dominion or Indian forces, approximate strength in men, guns and tanks are shown below. The actual strengths in the Far East, particularly in 1941, were often well below these figures—for instance some field artillery regiments had sixteen guns only. Details of transport and weapons, other than guns, are omitted.

Formation or unit	Officers and men	Guns		Tanks
Infantry division	13,700	Field Anti-tank Anti-aircraft	72 48 48	
Infantry brigade	2,500			
Infantry battalion	800			
Infantry company	127			
Field artillery regiment	670	25		
Field artillery battery	200	8		
Anti-tank battery	160	12		
Anti-aircraft battery	170	12		
Field engineer company	240			
Divisional signals	490			
R.A.C. regiment or tank battalion	650			78
Armoured squadron (three per regiment)				19
Armoured troop (five per squadron)				3

The supply and ordnance services of a division were approximately 1,300 strong.

THE ROYAL AIR FORCE

Headquarters Royal Air Force, Far East, was formed in 1933 to control and administer the air force stations and units in Ceylon, Burma, Malaya and at Hong Kong. At that time and for several years thereafter, the strength was such that there was no need for any subordinate formation in the organization and Air Headquarters exercised direct command.

In 1941 however a degree of decentralization was achieved when the first group (221 Group) was formed for the command of air force units in Burma. The same year further groups were formed to control flying-boat operations based on Ceylon (222 Group) and for air defence at Singapore (224 Group). Shortly before the outbreak of war with Japan, Norgroup was formed for the command of air force units that might be placed under it in northern Malaya and to control air support for the Army.

The number of stations or units directly under Air Headquarters (or under a group headquarters) varied according to operational requirements from time to time. Later, when additional groups were formed, each was composed of units of the same type, e.g.: 225 (Bomber) Group, 226 (Fighter) Group.

Under these formations were the fighting units—the SQUADRONS, the maintenance units responsible for the maintenance and supply of all equipment, signals and radar units and training units for both air and ground crews. There was also an air/sea rescue service and a bomb disposal unit was formed to serve all Services including civil defence.

When a number of units were located together, which was generally the case in the Far East, they were described as a STATION and came under the control of the station commander.

Squadrons were armed with fighter, bomber, torpedo-bomber or reconnaissance types of aircraft—the latter including flying-boats. Their operational role, to which they were normally restricted, could be defined by
those general classifications of types.

Squadrons were subdivided into two or three flying FLIGHTS and a headquarters flight. The latter usually included engine and aircraft repair
sections, signals, armament, photographic, transport and administrative
sections.

The first line strength of a squadron consisted of a number of initial
equipment (I.E.) aircraft. These were backed by an immediate reserve
(I.R.) of up to fifty per cent. of the I.E. which might be held by each
squadron. In practice in the Far East, so as to make the best use of the
inadequate stocks, the I.R. aircraft were usually held centrally for allocation to squadrons as directed by Air Headquarters.

The following are some examples of the established strengths of
squadrons in the Far East in 1941–42.

Role of Squadron	Type of Aircraft	I.E.	I.R.	Approximate strength Officers and Airmen
Fighter	Buffalo	16	8	250
	Hurricane	16	8	250
Bomber	Blenheim	16	8	400
Torpedo-bomber	Vildebeeste	12	6	330
General reconnaissance	Hudson	12	6	330
	Catalina	6	2	250

With a few exceptions all the airmen of a squadron or a technical unit
were tradesmen. For example in a Blenheim bomber squadron there were
electricians, fitters, instrument makers, wireless and electrical mechanics,
fabric and metal workers, photographers, armourers and so on. To
reach the required standard of skill in the majority of those trades much
training and experience were required, so that the expansion of the air
force was not only a matter of numbers of aircraft and airmen and of
flying training.

The state of the air force in the Far East on the outbreak of war with
Japan, is referred to in Chapter X. Some particulars of the types of aircraft with which squadrons were equipped, their functions and performance are given in Appendix 8.

There was always difficulty in maintaining the serviceability of aircraft
in the Far East due generally to the acute shortage of spares and tools. This
was further aggravated when squadrons moved to advanced airfields, as
for instance in northern Malaya, where the facilities for servicing aircraft
in the open were often improvised and usually quite inadequate.

APPENDIX 8

Some particulars of British and Japanese aircraft in use in the Far East Theatre during the period of this volume

The figures in these tables are no more than a general guide to the characteristics and capabilities of each type of aircraft. The performance was affected by the climate, the skill of the pilot, the accuracy of navigation and by the uncertainties of flying in the presence of the enemy. For those reasons the operational range—not to be confused with the radius of action—was always much less than the still air range. Broadly speaking, after allowing for the running of the engines on the ground and for the climb to the height quoted, the still air range was the distance that could be flown in still air until the tanks were empty.

Notes: (i) The most economical cruising speed was the speed at which the greatest range was achieved.
(ii) The height given in column iv was the optimum height for the maximum speed.

FIGHTER AIRCRAFT
BRITISH

Aircraft	Fuel and Still Air Range at Most Economical Cruising Speed		Most Economical Cruising Speed in Miles Per Hour	Maximum Speed in Miles Per Hour	Gun Armament	Remarks
	Gals.	Miles				
Buffalo Single engine monoplane Crew 1	133	759	180 at 15,000 ft.	295 at 18,500 ft.*	4 × ·50 in.	American design and manufacture first received in Far East from U.S.A., February 1941
Hurricane Mk. II Single engine monoplane Crew 1	97 183 (2 × 43)	480 970	200 at 15,000 ft.	342 at 22,000 ft.†	12 × ·303 in. or 4 × 20 mm	

* (i) Actual experience in Malaya showed that the speed of 295 m.p.h. for the Buffalo could not be obtained. It is not possible to say whether that was due to the aircraft, to the climate or to the pilots.
(ii) The Buffalo was less manoeuvrable and much inferior to the Japanese Naval Zero at heights of 10,000 ft. and above; also it had a relatively poor rate of climb—6·1 minutes to 13,000 ft. compared with 4·3 minutes for the Zero.
† The Hurricane was less manoeuvrable than the Naval Zero below 10,000 ft., but at medium heights and above 20,000 ft. the Hurricane proved superior.

BOMBER AIRCRAFT
(*including torpedo-bomber and bomber reconnaissance*)

BRITISH

Aircraft	Still Air Range with Associated Bomb-load — Miles	Still Air Range with Associated Bomb-load — Bomb-load	Most Economical Cruising Speed in Miles Per Hour	Maximum Speed in Miles Per Hour	Gun Armament	Remarks
Albacore Single engine biplane Crew 2 or 3	521	1 torpedo or 1,500 lb	105 at 6,000 ft.	163 at 4,800 ft.	2 × ·303 in.	Figures relate to use as torpedo-bomber.
Blenheim Mk. I Twin engine monoplane Crew 3	920	1,000 lb	165 at 15,000 ft.	265 at 15,000 ft.	2 × ·303 in.	Specially modified was used as a night fighter.
Blenheim Mk. IV Twin engine monoplane Crew 3	1,457	1,000 lb	170 at 15,000 ft.	266 at 11,800 ft.	5 × ·303 in.	
Glenn Martin Twin engine monoplane Crew 3	1,210 1,080	1,500 lb 2,000 lb	176 at 15,000 ft.	278 at 11,800 ft.	8 × ·303 in.	American design and manufacture. Used by the Dutch Army Air Service.
Shark Mk. II Single engine biplane Crew 2	572	1 torpedo or 1,500 lb	108 at 5,000 ft.	149 at 5,000 ft.	2 × ·303 in.	Figures relate to use as torpedo-bomber.

BOMBER AIRCRAFT
(including torpedo-bomber and bomber reconnaissance)

BRITISH

Aircraft	Still Air Range with Associated Bomb-load		Most Economical Cruising Speed in Miles Per Hour	Maximum Speed in Miles Per Hour	Gun Armament	Remarks
	Miles	Bomb-load				
Swordfish Single engine biplane Crew 2	528	1 torpedo or 1,500 lb	103 at 5,000 ft.	139 at 5,000 ft.	2 × ·303 in.	Figures relate to use as torpedo-bomber.
Vildebeeste Mk. III Single engine biplane Crew 2 or 3	970	1 torpedo or 1,870 lb	99 at 5,000 ft.	137 at 5,000 ft.	2 × ·303 in.	Figures relate to use as torpedo-bomber.
Hudson Mk. II Twin engine monoplane Crew 4	1,540	950 lb	195 at 10,000 ft.	225 at 7,900 ft.	4 Browning 3 × ·303 in.	American design and manufacture.
Singapore Mk. III Four engine flying-boat Crew 7	1,340	2,200 lb	104 at 5,000 ft.	136 at 5,000 ft.	3 × ·303 in.	
Catalina Twin engine flying-boat Crew 9	1,395 2,950	2,000 lb Nil	123 at 5,000 ft.	177 at 5,000 ft.	2 × ·303 in. 2 × ·500 in.	American design and manufacture.
Walrus Single engine amphibian Crew 2 or 3	428	500 lb	118 at 5,000 ft.	135 at 5,000 ft.	2 × ·303 in.	

FIGHTER AIRCRAFT

JAPANESE

Aircraft	Fuel and Still Air Range at Most Economical Cruising Speed — Gals.	Miles	Most Economical Cruising Speed in Miles Per Hour	Maximum Speed in Miles Per Hour	Gun Armament	Allied Code Name
Army 97 Single engine monoplane Crew 1	70	540	135 at 13,000 ft.	250 at 13,000 ft.	2 × 7·7 mm or 1 × 7·7 mm plus 1 × 12·7 mm	'NATE'
Army 1 Mk. II Single engine monoplane Crew 1	126	950	155 at 18,000 ft.	325 at 18,500 ft.	2 × 12·7 mm	'OSCAR 2'
Navy Zero Mk. II Single engine monoplane Crew 1	112	885	160 at 18,000 ft.	335 at 18,500 ft.	2 × 7·7 mm plus 2 × 20 mm	'ZEKE 2'

BOMBER AIRCRAFT

(including bomber reconnaissance and torpedo-bomber)

JAPANESE

Aircraft	Still Air Range with Associated Bomb-load — Miles	Bomb-load	Most Economical Cruising Speed in Miles Per Hour	Maximum Speed in Miles Per Hour	Gun Armament	Allied Code Name
Army 98 (Kawasaki) Single engine monoplane Crew 2	665	660 lb	130 at 12,000 ft.	225 at 12,000 ft.	3×7·7 mm	'MARY'
Navy 98 Single engine monoplane Crew 2	590	330 lb	140 at 13,000 ft.	225 at 13,000 ft.	3×7·7 mm	'BABS'
Army 97 Mk. III Twin engine monoplane Crew 7	1,635	2,200 lb	150 at 13,000 ft.	294 at 15,500 ft.	6×7·7 mm or 5×7·7 mm plus 1×12·7 mm plus 1×20 mm	'SALLY 2'
Navy 96 Twin engine monoplane Crew 7	2,125	1,100 lb	157 at 19,000 ft.	270 at 19,600 ft.	4×7·7 mm 1×20 mm	'NELL'
Navy I Twin engine monoplane Crew 7	3,075	2,200 lb	145 at 15,000 ft.	283 at 13,800 ft.	5×7·7 mm 2×20 mm	'BETTY'

NOTE: The Japanese system of numbering each type of aircraft was related to the last one or two digits of the year of issue. Type numbers correspond to the year of issue according to the Japanese calendar, by which the year 1940 was the Japanese year 2600. Thus the aircraft brought into service in 1939 were designated 'Type 99' and those issued in 1940 were 'Type 0'.

To simplify reference to particular types and to avoid possible confusion, the Allies allotted a code name to each type.

APPENDIX 9

Strength and Dispositions of Squadrons in Malaya, 7th December 1941

Airfield	Squadron No.	Type	Strength in Aircraft
Alor Star	62	Blenheim I (B)	11
Sungei Patani	21 (R.A.A.F.)	Buffalo	12
Sungei Patani	27	Blenheim I (N.F)	12
Kota Bharu	1 (R.A.A.F.)	Hudson II	12
Kota Bharu	36	Vildebeeste	6
Gong Kedah	100	Vildebeeste	6
Kuantan	60 (a)	Blenheim I (B)	8
Kuantan	8 (R.A.A.F.)	Hudson II	8
Kuantan	36	Vildebeeste	6
Tengah	34	Blenheim IV	16
Kallang	243 and 488 (R.N.Z.A.F.)	Buffalo	32
Sembawang	8 (R.A.A.F.)	Hudson II	4
Sembawang	453 (R.A.A.F.)	Buffalo	16
Seletar	100	Vildebeeste	6
Seletar	205	Catalina	3
		Total	158

(a) No. 60 Squadron had arrived from Burma for bombing practice, and was retained in Malaya on the start of the war with Japan. About the middle of December the personnel were sent back to Burma by sea, the aircraft being retained in Malaya to replace wastage in other squadrons.

There were two maintenance units, No. 151 at Seletar and No. 153 at Kuala Lumpur.

Reserve Aircraft in Malaya

Blenheim I and IV	15
Buffalo	52(b)
Hudson	7
Vildebeeste	12
Catalina	2
Total	88

(b) Of these, twenty-one were temporarily out of action owing to trouble with the engine valve gear on a new type of engine.

Sketch 4 is complementary to this appendix. It shows the positions of air force units after several moves had taken place early in the morning of the 8th December. It therefore differs in certain respects from the appendix.

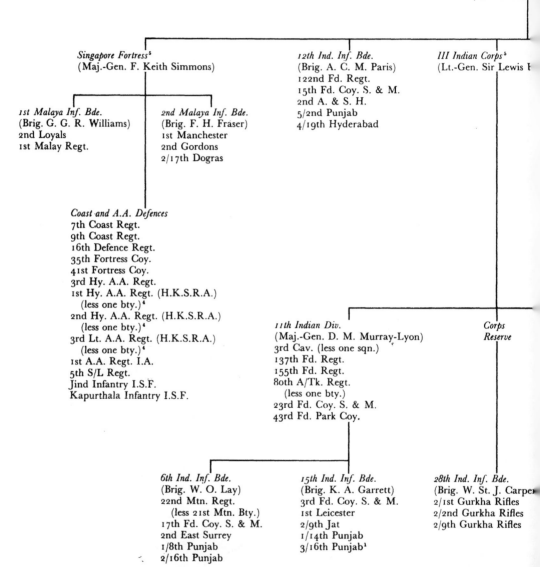

H.Q. MALAY*
(Lt.-Gen. A.

Singapore Fortress[5]
(Maj.-Gen. F. Keith Simmons)

12th Ind. Inf. Bde.
(Brig. A. C. M. Paris)
122nd Fd. Regt.
15th Fd. Coy. S. & M.
2nd A. & S. H.
5/2nd Punjab
4/19th Hyderabad

III Indian Corps[5]
(Lt.-Gen. Sir Lewis F

1st Malaya Inf. Bde.
(Brig. G. G. R. Williams)
2nd Loyals
1st Malay Regt.

2nd Malaya Inf. Bde.
(Brig. F. H. Fraser)
1st Manchester
2nd Gordons
2/17th Dogras

Coast and A.A. Defences
7th Coast Regt.
9th Coast Regt.
16th Defence Regt.
35th Fortress Coy.
41st Fortress Coy.
3rd Hy. A.A. Regt.
1st Hy. A.A. Regt. (H.K.S.R.A.)
  (less one bty.)[4]
2nd Hy. A.A. Regt. (H.K.S.R.A.)
  (less one bty.)[4]
3rd Lt. A.A. Regt. (H.K.S.R.A.)
  (less one bty.)[4]
1st A.A. Regt. I.A.
5th S/L Regt.
Jind Infantry I.S.F.
Kapurthala Infantry I.S.F.

11th Indian Div.
(Maj.-Gen. D. M. Murray-Lyon)
3rd Cav. (less one sqn.)
137th Fd. Regt.
155th Fd. Regt.
80th A/Tk. Regt.
  (less one bty.)
23rd Fd. Coy. S. & M.
43rd Fd. Park Coy.

*Corps
Reserve*

6th Ind. Inf. Bde.
(Brig. W. O. Lay)
22nd Mtn. Regt.
  (less 21st Mtn. Bty.)
17th Fd. Coy. S. & M.
2nd East Surrey
1/8th Punjab
2/16th Punjab

15th Ind. Inf. Bde.
(Brig. K. A. Garrett)
3rd Fd. Coy. S. & M.
1st Leicester
2/9th Jat
1/14th Punjab
3/16th Punjab[1]

28th Ind. Inf. Bde.
(Brig. W. St. J. Carpei
2/1st Gurkha Rifles
2/2nd Gurkha Rifles
2/9th Gurkha Rifles

NOTES: (1) Allotted for d
(2) In reserve for
(3) Temporarily a
(4) The missing b
(5) For Volunteer

8th Aus. Div.
(Maj.-Gen. H. G. Bennett)
2/10th Fd. Regt.
2/15th Fd. Regt.
4th A/Tk. Regt.
  (less one bty.)
2/10th Fd. Coy.
2/12th Fd. Coy.
2/6th Fd. Park Coy.

O.C. Troops
Sarawak & Brunei
(Lt.-Col. C. M. Lane)
2/15th Punjab
Detachment H.K.S.R.A.
  (two 6-in. guns)
Detachment 35th
  Fortress Coy.

O.C. Troops Christmas Is.
Detachment H.K.S.R.A.
  (one 6-in. gun).

us. Inf. Bde.
H. B. Taylor)
Bn.
Bn.
Bn.

27th Aus. Inf. Bde.
(Brig. D. S. Maxwell)
2/26th Bn.
2/29th Bn.
2/30th Bn.

f C. Area
G. Moir)
M.S.V.F.

Penang Fortress
(Brig. C. A. Lyon)
11th Coast Regt.
36th Fortress Coy.
5/14th Punjab[2]

9th Indian Div.
(Maj.-Gen. A. E. Barstow)
5th Fd. Regt.
88th Fd. Regt.
1st Bty. 80th A/Tk. Regt.
42nd Fd. Park Coy. S. & M.

Airfield Defence
Troops
1st Bahawalpur Infantry I.S.F.
1st Hyderabad Infantry I.S.F.
1st Mysore Infantry I.S.F.

8th Ind. Inf. Bde.
(Brig. B. W. Key)
21st Mtn. Bty.
  (less one section)
19th Fd. Coy. S. & M.
2/10th Baluch
3/17th Dogras
1/13th F.F. Rifles

22nd Ind. Inf. Bde.
(Brig. G. W. A. Painter)
One Sec. 21st Mtn. Bty.
22nd Fd. Coy. S. & M.
5/11th Sikhs
2/18th R. Garhwal Rifles
2/12th F.F. Regt.[3]

roh road.
Kroh road.
8th Ind. Inf. Bde.
attached to III Corps.
e Appendix 13.

APPENDIX 11

Notes on the Indian Army

The reader who is unacquainted with the Indian Army may find it difficult to reconcile the sometimes rather disappointing performance of the Indian formations in Malaya in 1941–42 with the distinguished part played by 4th and 5th Indian Divisions in the Middle East in 1940–41 and the overwhelming defeat which the Fourteenth Army, composed very largely of Indian troops, inflicted on the Japanese armies in Burma later in the war.

The explanation is simple. The units which went to the Middle East had not been denuded of experienced officers, non-commissioned officers and men to anything like the same extent as those which were serving in Malaya. Moreover after their arrival they had been afforded the opportunity of undergoing brigade and divisional training before being subjected to the shock of war. The victories gained by the Fourteenth Army were won, after the ill effects of expansion had been overcome, by troops who had been fully trained in jungle warfare, who were led by experienced officers, and who had been welded together in brigades and divisions. On the other hand the units sent to Malaya before December 1941 had been severely 'milked' and, as shown in Chapter X, this had seriously affected their training and consequently their efficiency. They had had little or no opportunity to carry out that higher training above battalion level without which a brigade and a division cannot be expected to operate as a team. Furthermore the two reinforcing brigades received from India after the outbreak of war contained only one pre-war battalion and had been hurriedly sent overseas while they were still formations in name only. These troops in Malaya were thrown into battle against what were at that time some of the finest infantry in the world. To employ a cricket analogy, it was as if a county second eleven had been pitted against a Test Match side.

It may be argued that it was not only the Indian Army which, at this time, had rapidly to be expanded and that newly raised British and Commonwealth forces usually reached an adequate standard of efficiency in less time. To understand why it was more difficult to accelerate the training of Indian troops in the face of sudden and rapid expansion, one must understand something of the background and organization of the Indian Army. This army was originally a small professional force designed primarily for a special task: the defence of the North-West Frontier. Many of its units had been raised by individual officers and until the First World War it was almost feudal in character: for instance it was not unusual for men of substance to join up with their own following, while cavalrymen brought their own horses with them on enlistment. The hereditary principle was firmly established: both officers and men often had family ties binding them to their regiments. Thus there sprang up a strong tradition of personal loyalties despite the very marked differences of religion and caste.

This system, while excellent for the purposes of a small professional army with a definite role, did not lend itself to expansion. Consequently in 1921, as a result of lessons learnt in the First World War, a major reorganization took place under which four or five active battalions were grouped into regiments with a training battalion which provided the regimental depot, and fixed terms of colour and reserve service were introduced.[1] Under this reorganization provision was made for each regiment to double itself in the event of a major war, but it depended on two factors for its success: that expansion should be limited, and that a reasonable period of time should be allowed before newly raised units were sent into action. The Indian military machine was thus geared to meet the requirements of a war in the west and, so long as these two conditions were fulfilled, India was able to meet, and indeed exceed, her commitments.

There is a great difference between raising new formations in countries possessing a homogeneous and educated population like Britain, Australia and Canada, and raising large forces, on a purely voluntary enlistment basis, in a country which was a subcontinent comprising a multitude of different races, castes, creeds and languages. The attempt to keep to the time-honoured composition of regiments which, like most Punjabi and Frontier Force regiments, contained men of different religion, customs and even language enormously complicated the problems of expansion, for it was a case of providing the right proportion of Viceroy's Commissioned Officers, Non-Commissioned Officers and men of the various classes and of bringing each of these classes up to the requisite strength.

What mechanization meant to the Indian Army will be apparent when it is realized that the first thing many a recruit had to do was to discard his mother tongue or provincial dialect and learn Urdu—the language in which all instruction was imparted. Then, after basic training, he had to become proficient in a number of new and complicated weapons. To teach all this to a man who on joining was often completely illiterate, and then expect him in addition to learn to drive and maintain a heavy mechanical vehicle was asking a lot.

Not only did the Army have to expand rapidly but the increase demanded was out of all proportion to the resources available. This was particularly the case in regard to technical arms and artillery. Mechanization of the Indian Army had only just begun and technical corps were therefore in their infancy. Even the twelve year old Signal Corps was unable to cope with the great expansion of wireless technicians required for the conversion of cavalry to armour. The Indian Artillery consisted of six Mountain and one Field Regiment;[2] there was therefore only a small pool of trained artillerymen on which to draw for the nuclei of new regiments. In consequence the main source of supply was the regular

---

[1] This reorganization did not apply to Gurkhas until the outbreak of war with Japan, for, under the terms of the treaty with Nepal, Gurkha Regiments were limited to two battalions, each of which was limited to only 100 reservists.

[2] The Field Regiment was formed in 1935 and from that date Indian cadets from the Military Academy were gazetted direct to artillery.

infantry regiments, normally consisting of four to six battalions, which were called upon not only to double and even treble themselves, but, in addition, to provide officers and men for new artillery and signal units, technical corps, schools of instruction and parachute battalions. This resulted in the regular units themselves being left with only a handful of experienced leaders and specialists, and sometimes in formations, which had been hurriedly put together, being disrupted just as they were beginning to function.

Another and most serious problem was the shortage of officers. The number of reserve officers was far too small to meet the demand and it took time to collect and train the splendid material coming forward from the tea gardens, the business community, the civil services and the rising generation of young Indians. In the meantime young officers who could not even speak the language had to be recruited from Britain and elsewhere.

To sum up, the whole difficulty lay not in the fact that the Indian Army had to be expanded, but that, despite all the circumstances peculiar to India, an almost unlimited expansion had to be undertaken and, moreover, undertaken at a speed which had never been envisaged. There were not enough regular officers and men to leaven the whole. The flood of raw human material which had to be absorbed knew nothing of the old loyalties, and consequently the mutual confidence and genuine deep-rooted friendship that had existed between officers and men, and between men of different creeds within the unit, were temporarily lost. It takes time to lay what may be called the spiritual foundation on which a good unit depends; to train junior leaders and build up that confidence which good leadership, combined with skill in the use of weapons, alone can give. What is surprising is not that new units in the early stages of the Japanese war failed to stem the enemy's advance, but that they fought as well as they did. By the end of 1943 the whole structure of the Indian Army had been rebuilt, and in 1944 the young Indian troops in Burma were fighting like veterans to turn disaster into triumph.

---

[1] Between February and September 1942, 2,000 officers were sent out from the United Kingdom for the Indian Army.

APPENDIX 12

Notes on the Australian Imperial Forces

The Australian Army in peacetime consisted of a regular staff corps and a number of militia divisions in cadre form in which nearly all the commands were held by militia officers, while officers of the staff corps held nearly all the staff appointments. On the outbreak of war the Australian Government decided to form a second Imperial Force (A.I.F.) from volunteers and the regular staff corps, militiamen being permitted to volunteer. The 6th and 7th Australian Divisions were formed in this manner and sent to the Middle East. The 8th Division was composed mainly of men who had volunteered after the fall of France. Its units had been formed between July and October 1940, and on the outbreak of war with Japan had been training in Australia or Malaya for from 14 to 17 months. On an average its units had been training a little longer than had those of the 6th, 9th and 7th Divisions when they first went into action in North Africa and Syria in 1940 and 1941.

Lieut.-General V. A. H. Sturdee was originally appointed to command this division, but when he became Chief of the General Staff in Australia he was replaced by Major-General H. Gordon Bennett, an officer who had earned a considerable reputation as a young battalion and brigade commander in the 1914–18 war and had commanded a militia division from 1926 to 1931.

The terms of General Bennett's appointment provided that his force on arrival in Malaya would come under the operational control of the General Officer Commanding, Malaya, (General Percival) subject to the following reservations:

(a) The force was to retain its identity as an Australian force.

(b) No part of the force was to be employed apart from the whole without Bennett's consent.

(c) Should the G.O.C., Malaya, in certain circumstances of emergency insist on an extensive operational dispersal of the Australian forces, Bennett, after registering such protest as he might deem essential, was to comply with the order of the G.O.C., Malaya, and immediately report the full circumstances to Army H.Q., Australia.

General Bennett was to have the right of direct communication with Army Headquarters, Australia, as necessary in respect of matters of pay, promotion, establishments and discipline. At a later stage Bennett was requested by the Minister for the Army to report direct to him. Thereafter when, in his opinion the occasion required, he did so.

This directive was normal practice for any Australian force sent to fight alongside other British Commonwealth forces outside Australia. Nevertheless, it made it highly desirable that an Australian commander should be sufficiently flexible in his attitude to make adequate allowance for the difference in background and viewpoint between his force and those drawn from other parts of the Commonwealth, and of course that this attitude should be reciprocated.

APPENDIX 13

Notes on Local Forces in Malaya

The majority of the States maintained their own defence forces—primarily for internal security duties within their respective territories.

The Government of the Federated Malay States maintained and financed a regular Malay infantry battalion, composed of British and Malay officers and Malay other ranks, on the pattern of an Indian Army battalion. The raising of a second battalion of the Malay Regiment had been started on 1st December 1941. In addition, the Volunteer Forces comprised four Federated Malay States Volunteer infantry battalions, plus certain ancillary units, raised locally within the separate Federated States. Their combined establishment was 194 officers and 4,328 other ranks, about one-third of whom were Europeans and Eurasians, and the rest Malays and Chinese.

The Government of the Straits Settlements maintained and financed four Straits Settlements Volunteer infantry battalions, with associated supporting formations. Their employment within the Straits Settlements was intended primarily to reinforce the defences of the Singapore Base but they had one detached battalion, raised from and based in the Penang area.

The State of Johore maintained its own regular and volunteer military forces, composed of British and Malay personnel, but they too amounted to little more than an infantry battalion, with some light artillery in support,, and a field company Royal Engineers. Others of the Unfederated States had volunteer forces of their own but they were generally small and, in practice, represented the equivalent of an infantry company or at most a weak infantry battalion.

Finally, Malaya had a Royal Naval Volunteer Reserve formed from European officers and Malay ratings, and the Malay Volunteer Air Force, formed from British civilians resident in the country. Both were small, but keen and enthusiastic; indeed the latter was formed from the local civil flying clubs, using their light training and communication aircraft.

The volunteer units which were mobilized consisted of:

1st, 2nd, 3rd and 4th Battalions, Straits Settlements Volunteer Force.
1st, 2nd, 3rd and 4th Battalions, Federated Malay States Volunteer Force.
Armoured car company, Singapore Volunteer Force.
Singapore Royal Artillery Volunteers.
Armoured car company, Federated Malay States Volunteer Force.
Light artillery battery, Federated Malay States Volunteer Force.
Kelantan Volunteer Force.
Kedah Volunteer Force.
Perak River Platoon.
Sultan Idris Company.
Johore Infantry.
Johore Volunteer Engineers.

APPENDIX 14

Disposition of Allied Naval Forces in the Eastern Theatre on 8th December 1941

1. British Forces

A. EASTERN FLEET

Commander-in-Chief, Admiral Sir Tom Phillips
(succeeded by Vice-Admiral Sir Geoffrey Layton, 10/12/41)

	Singapore	Hong Kong	Shanghai
Battleship	*Prince of Wales* (ten 14-inch guns)		
Battlecruiser	*Repulse* (six 15-inch guns)		
Cruisers	*Danae* (six 6-inch guns) *Dragon* (six 6-inch guns) *Durban* (six 6-inch guns)		
Destroyers	*Electra* *Express* *Tenedos* *Vampire* (R.A.N.)	*Scout** *Thanet** } Sailed for Singapore 8/12/41	
Gunboats	*Dragonfly** *Grasshopper** *Scorpion**	*Tern** *Cicala** *Robin**	*Peterel** (sunk 8/12/41)
Armed Merchant Cruisers	*Manoora* (R.A.N.) *Kanimbla* (R.N.Z.N.) (Penang)		
Motor Torpedo-boats		Eight*	

REFITTING OR UNDER REPAIR

	Singapore	Hong Kong	Shanghai
Cruisers	*Mauritius* (East Indies Squadron)		
Destroyers	*Encounter* *Jupiter* *Stronghold** *Vendetta* (R.A.N.) *Isis* (Mediterranean Fleet)	*Thracian**	
Gunboat		*Moth**	
Submarine	*Rover*		

* Local naval defence.

B. EAST INDIES SQUADRON BASED ON CEYLON

Commander-in-Chief, Vice-Admiral G. S. Arbuthnot

Battleship	*Revenge*
Cruisers	*Exeter* (six 8-inch guns). Arrived Singapore 10/12/41
Armed Merchant Cruisers .	*Corfu, Ranchi*

REFITTING
Aircraft Carrier . .	*Hermes* (at Durban)
Cruiser	*Enterprise* (six 6-inch guns)

C. AUSTRALIAN AND NEW ZEALAND SQUADRONS

Cruisers	*Canberra* (eight 8-inch guns)
	Adelaide (eight 6-inch guns)
	Perth (eight 6-inch guns)
	Achilles (eight 6-inch guns)
	Leander (eight 6-inch guns)
Armed Merchant Cruiser .	*Westralia*
Destroyer (*torpilleur*) . .	*Le Triomphant* (Free French)
Sloops	*Swan*
	Warrego
	Chevreuil (Free French)

REFITTING
Armed Merchant Cruiser.	*Monowai*
Destroyers	*Stuart*
	Voyager

2. *Netherlands East Indies Forces*

Commander-in-Chief, Vice-Admiral C. E. L. Helfrich, R.N.N.

Cruisers	*De Ruyter* (seven 5·9-inch guns)
	Rear-Admiral K. W. F. M. Doorman
	Java (ten 5·9-inch guns)
	Tromp (six 5·9-inch guns)
Destroyers	*Van Nes*
	Bankert
	Witte de With
	Kortenaer
	Piet Hein
	Evertsen
	Van Ghent
Submarines	Thirteen

REFITTING
Submarine . . .	One

OUT OF COMMISSION
Cruiser . . .	*Sumatra*
Submarines . . .	Two

3. United States Asiatic Fleet
Commander-in-Chief, Admiral T. C. Hart

	Philippines	Borneo
Cruisers	*Houston* (nine 8-inch and eight 5-inch guns) Rear Admiral W. A. Glassford *Boise* (fifteen 6-inch and eight 5-inch guns)	*Marblehead* (eight 6-inch guns)
Destroyers	*Pope* *John D. Ford*	*Paul Jones* *Stewart* *Bulmer* *Barker* *Parrott* *Whipple* ⎫ On *Alden* ⎬ passage *John D. Edwards* ⎨ to *Edsall* ⎭ Singapore
Seaplane Tenders	*Langley* *Childs*	
Gunboats	Six (one on passage from Hong Kong)	
Submarines	Twenty-five	
REFITTING		
Destroyers	*Peary* *Pillsbury*	
Submarines	Four	

APPENDIX 15

Order of Battle of Japanese 25th Army on the 8th December 1941

A

25th Army Headquarters (Lieut.-General T. Yamashita).
Imperial Guards Division (Lieut.-General T. Nishimura).
5th Division (Lieut.-General T. Matsui).
18th Division (Lieut.-General R. Mutaguchi).
1st Independent Anti-Tank Battalion.
Eight independent anti-tank companies.
3rd Tank Group (four tank regiments: 1st, 2nd and 6th [medium] and
   14th [light] Regiments and ancillary units).
3rd Independent Mountain Artillery Regiment.
3rd and 18th Heavy Field Artillery Regiments.
21st Heavy Field Artillery Battalion.
3rd and 5th Trench Mortar Battalions (horsed).
14th Independent Mortar Battalion.
17th Field Air Defence Unit (four field anti-aircraft battalions).
Three independent field anti-aircraft companies.
1st Balloon Company.
4th, 15th and 23rd Independent Engineer Regiments.
5th Independent Heavy Bridging Company.
21st, 22nd and 27th Bridging Material Companies (two horsed, one
   mechanized).
10th and 15th River Crossing Material Companies (one horsed, one
   mechanized).
21st River Crossing Company (horsed).
2nd Field Military Police Unit.
2nd Railway Unit (two railway regiments, one railway material depot,
   two railway station office and two special railway operating units).
25th Army Signal Unit (one telegraph regiment [horsed], one independent wire company [mechanized], three independent wireless platoons
   [two mechanized, one horsed] and five stationary wireless units).

B

Line of Communication Headquarters and Units. These included four
   line of communication sector units, eight independent motor transport
   battalions, twelve independent motor transport companies, two horse
   transport units, ten land service companies, five construction service
   companies, also survey, water, road, construction, ordnance and
   medical units.

521

Notes

		Men	Vehicles	Horses
1.	A. totalled	88,689	4,325	10,442
	B. totalled	36,719	2,995	1,074
	Total	125,408	7,320	11,516

The numbers landed in Malaya however fell far short of these figures.

2. The 56th Division was originally allotted to 25th Army but as it did not join has been excluded from the order of battle.

3. The 2nd Tank Regiment (less its light tank company) was transferred from 25th to 16th Army on the 29th January 1942. The organization of 3rd Tank Group at the end of January 1942 was therefore:

	Medium Tanks	Light Tanks	Vehicles
1st Tank Regiment	37	20	91
6th Tank Regiment	37	20	91
14th Tank Regiment	—	45	48
One light tank company	—	10	8
3rd Tank Group H.Q.	5	5	several
	79	100	238 at least

4. The 1st Tank Regiment was organized into regimental headquarters (two medium tanks and one light tank), three medium tank companies and one light tank company, plus the regimental munition train (five medium and three light tanks). A medium tank company was equipped with ten medium and two light tanks; a light tank company with ten light tanks.

A medium tank (sixteen tons) was armed with one 57-mm. tank gun and two 7·7-mm. machine-guns, and a light tank (eight tons) with one 37-mm. tank gun and one 7·7-mm. machine-gun.

Order of Battle of Japanese Divisions

5th Division (Mechanized)

Divisional Headquarters (Lieut.-General T. Matsui)
9th Infantry Brigade Headquarters (Major-General S. Kawamura)
11th Infantry Regiment (Colonel Watanabe)
41st Infantry Regiment (Colonel Okabe)
21st Infantry Brigade Headquarters (Major-General E. Sugiura)
21st Infantry Regiment (Colonel Harada)
42nd Infantry Regiment (Colonel Ando)
5th Reconnaissance Regiment
5th Field Artillery Regiment
5th Engineer Regiment

Divisional signal unit
5th Transport Regiment
Ordnance service unit
Divisional medical unit
Two field hospitals
Total: Men, 15,342; Vehicles, 1,008; Horses, Nil.

Imperial Guards Division (Mechanized)

Divisional Headquarters (Lieut.-General T. Nishimura)
    Guards Infantry Group Headquarters
        3rd Guards Regiment
        4th Guards Regiment (Colonel Kunishi)
        5th Guards Regiment (Colonel Iwaguro)
    Reconnaissance regiment
    Field artillery regiment
    Engineer regiment
    Divisional signal unit
    Transport regiment
    Ordnance service unit
    Medical unit
    Two field hospitals
    Total: Men, 12,649; Vehicles, 914; Horses, Nil.

18th Division (Horse transport)

Divisional Headquarters (Lieut.-General R. Mutaguchi)
  35th Infantry Brigade Headquarters (Major-General K. Kawaguchi)
        114th Infantry Regiment
        124th Infantry Regiment
  23rd Infantry Brigade Headquarters (Major-General H. Takumi)
        55th Infantry Regiment (Colonel Koba)
        56th Infantry Regiment (Colonel Nasu)
    22nd Cavalry Battalion
    18th Mountain Artillery Regiment
    12th Engineer Regiment
    Divisional signal unit
    12th Transport Regiment
    Ordnance service unit
    Medical unit
    Three field hospitals
    Veterinary hospital
    Total: Men, 22,206; Vehicles, 33; Horses, 5,707.

Note

1. An infantry regiment consisted of three battalions. The strength of an infantry regiment was:

5th Division (mechanized)	2,600
Imperial Guards Division (mechanized)	2,600
18th Division (horsed)	3,525

APPENDIX 16

Order of Battle of Japanese 3rd Air Division and Naval Air Forces supporting 25th Army

A. 3rd Air Division

Headquarters	
3rd Air Brigade	one fighter and three light bomber regiments
7th Air Brigade	one fighter and three heavy bomber regiments
12th Air Brigade	two fighter regiments
15th Independent Air Regiment	two reconnaissance squadrons
81st Reconnaissance Regiment	one reconnaissance squadron
Maximum operational strength:	146 fighters (of which 56 were Zero types) 172 bombers 36 reconnaissance

Total	354 aircraft

B. Naval Air Forces supporting the Malayan Operation

(i) The 22nd Air Flotilla, consisting of the Mihoro and Genzan Air Groups each with forty-eight light bombers. In addition a detachment of forty-two light bombers from the Kanoya Air Group (21st Air Flotilla) was specially allotted for the operation and these, with thirty-six fighters and six reconnaissance aircraft attached to 22nd Air Flotilla Headquarters, provided a maximum operational strength of 180 aircraft.

(ii) Seaplane Tenders

Kimikawa Maru	14 seaplanes
Sanyo Maru	8 seaplanes
Sagara Maru	8 seaplanes

C

The combined maximum operational strength of the Japanese air forces supporting 25th Army thus amounted to about 560 aircraft, of which some 180 were fighters.

APPENDIX 17

Order of the Day issued on
the 8th December 1941

Japan's action today gives the signal for the Empire Naval, Army and Air Forces, and those of their Allies, to go into action with a common aim and common ideals.

We are ready. We have had plenty of warning and our preparations are made and tested. We do not forget at this moment the years of patience and forbearance in which we have borne, with dignity and discipline, the petty insults and insolences inflicted on us by the Japanese in the Far East. We know that those things were only done because Japan thought she could take advantage of our supposed weakness. Now, when Japan herself has decided to put the matter to a sterner test, she will find out that she has made a grievous mistake.

We are confident. Our defences are strong and our weapons efficient. Whatever our race, and whether we are now in our native land or have come thousands of miles, we have one aim and one only. It is to defend these shores, to destroy such of our enemies as may set foot on our soil, and then, finally, to cripple the power of the enemy to endanger our ideals, our possessions and our peace.

What of the enemy? We see before us a Japan drained for years by the exhausting claims of her wanton onslaught on China. We see a Japan whose trade and industry have been so dislocated by these years of reckless adventure that, in a mood of desperation, her Government has flung her into war under the delusion that, by stabbing a friendly nation in the back, she can gain her end. Let her look at Italy and what has happened since that nation tried a similar base action.

Let us all remember that we here in the Far East form part of the great campaign for the preservation in the world of truth and justice and freedom; confidence, resolution, enterprise and devotion to the cause must and will inspire every one of us in the fighting services, while from the civilian population, Malay, Chinese, Indian, or Burmese, we expect that patience, endurance and serenity which is the great virtue of the East and which will go far to assist the fighting men to gain final and complete victory.

R. BROOKE-POPHAM,
Air Chief Marshal
Commander-in-Chief, Far East.

G. LAYTON,
Vice-Admiral,
Commander-in-Chief, China.

APPENDIX 18

Details of Japanese First Flights landed at Singora, Patani and Kota Bharu

A. Singora

25th Army Headquarters (forward operational headquarters)
5th Division (excluding the Patani detachment, 21st Infantry Brigade
    Headquarters and 21st Infantry Regiment).
1st Tank Regiment (less one light tank company).
Three independent anti-tank companies.
One battalion 3rd Heavy Field Artillery Regiment.
Headquarters 17th Field Air Defence Unit and 34th Anti-Aircraft Artillery
    Battalion.
One independent field anti-aircraft company.
Elements of 1st Telegraph Regiment.
One stationary wireless unit.
One bridge material company.
Two companies 9th Railway Regiment.
Airfield battalion.
Proportion of line of communication troops.

B. Patani

42nd Infantry Regiment.
One battalion 5th Field Artillery Regiment.
One company 5th Engineer Regiment.
One light tank company 5th Reconnaissance Regiment.
One light tank company 1st Tank Regiment.
Elements of divisional signals, transport and medical units.
One independent anti-tank company.
One bridge material company.
One airfield company.

C. Kota Bharu

23rd Infantry Brigade Headquarters⎫ From 18th Division directly under
56th Infantry Regiment.   ⎬   command of 25th Army.
One company 18th Mountain Artillery Regiment.
One company 12th Engineer Regiment.
One independent field anti-aircraft company.
Two independent anti-tank companies.
Approximately one-third of 18th Divisional signal and medical units.
One independent wireless platoon.
One airfield company.

Notes

1. The 21st Infantry Brigade Headquarters and 21st Infantry Regiment landed at Singora with the third flight on 27th December and did not take part in the operations till the 20th January in Johore.

2. The approximate number of men landed in first flight were:

Singora	13,500
Patani	7,550
Kota Bharu	5,590

26,640 (of which 17,230 were combat troops)

3. The approximate Japanese strength in Malaya on the 8th February 1942 was:

Combat troops	67,660
Service troops	33,000
Air and air service troops	10,000
Total	110,660
Artillery	168 pieces
Tanks	150

APPENDIX 19

State of Training of Reinforcing Formations from India

Brigadier Ballentine, who commanded 44th Indian Infantry Brigade, gave the following estimate of the state of training of his brigade when it embarked for Malaya. The state of affairs disclosed also applied to 45th Indian Infantry Brigade, which had already been sent to Malaya, and to 46th Indian Infantry Brigade, which was sent to Burma:

'The battalions were raised in the autumn of 1940, and the brigade was formed in Poona in July 1941. All battalions arrived in Poona under strength, consisting of equal proportions of trained regular soldiers, reservists and drafts straight from the Regimental Training Centres. 6/1st Punjab was minus one company which did not rejoin until November. The various ancillary units of the brigade group were raised from scratch in the autumn of 1941, except the signal section which was not complete until immediately before the brigade sailed for Malaya. The bulk of transport, equipment and weapons came in steadily, and the only serious shortages on departure were in Bren guns and anti-tank weapons.

Excellent progress in all branches of training, designed solely for Middle East conditions, was made in Poona, but this was largely negatived by the appalling milking inherent in the large-scale Indian Army expansion. During the six months July to December 1941, each battalion threw off some 250 men, culminating in their sending, on the point of departure for Malaya, 45 V.C.Os., N.C.Os. and potential N.C.Os. to form their respective training companies at the training centres. During the last month in India, each battalion took in some 250 recruits to replace wastage, many of whom had only 4 or 5 months service and were under 18 years of age. Thus the battalions were very largely composed of recruits who had been less than three months with them, some of whom joined during the journey to the port of embarkation; and the numbers of experienced V.C.Os. and N.C.Os., few to begin with, had been gravely reduced. In common with all Indian Army units, British Officers averaged rather less than three regulars per battalion, the remainder being E.C.Os. (Emergency Commissioned Officers) drawn from outside India with, at the most, twelve months experience of Indian troops, their ways and their language.'

APPENDIX 20

Directive to the Supreme Commander, ABDA Area
dated 3rd January 1942

By agreement among the Governments of Australia, Netherlands, United Kingdom and United States, hereinafter referred to as the ABDA Governments.

AREA

1. A strategic area has been constituted, to comprise initially all land and sea areas, including general regions of Burma–Malaya–Netherlands East Indies and Philippine Islands: more precisely defined in Annex 1. This area will be known as ABDA area.

FORCES

2. You have been designated as Supreme Commander of ABDA area and of all armed forces, afloat, ashore and in the air, of ABDA Governments, which are, or will be (a) stationed in area; (b) located in Australian territory when such forces have been allotted by respective Governments for services in or in support of the ABDA area. You are not authorized to transfer from territories of any ABDA Government land forces of that Government without consent of local Commander or his Government.

3. The Deputy Supreme Commander and, if required, a Commander of the Combined Naval Forces and the Commander of Combined Air Forces will be jointly designated by the ABDA Governments.

4. No Government will materially reduce its armed forces assigned to your area nor any commitment made by it for reinforcing its forces in your area except after giving to other Governments, and to you, timely information pertaining thereto.

STRATEGIC CONCEPT AND POLICY

5. The basic Strategic Concept of the ABDA Governments for conduct of war in your area is not only in immediate future to maintain as many key positions as possible, but to take offensive at the earliest opportunity and ultimately to conduct an all-out offensive against Japan. The first essential is to gain general air superiority at the earliest moment, through employment of concentrated air power. The piece-meal employment of Air Forces should be minimized. Your operations should be so conducted as to further preparations for the offensive.

6. General Strategical policy will be, therefore:
   (a) To hold Malay barrier, defined as line Malay Peninsula, Sumatra, Java, North Australia, as basic defensive position of ABDA area and to operate sea, land and air forces in as great depth as possible forward of Barrier in order to oppose Japanese southward advance.
   (b) To hold Burma and Australia as essential support positions for the area and Burma as essential to support of China, and to defence of India.

2N

(c) To re-establish communications through Dutch East Indies with Luzon and to support Philippine Islands garrison.
(d) To maintain essential communications within the area.

DUTIES, RESPONSIBILITIES AND AUTHORITIES OF
SUPREME COMMANDER

7. You will co-ordinate in ABDA area strategical operations of all armed forces of ABDA Governments; where desirable to arrange formation of task forces, whether national or international, for executing specific operations; and appointing any officers irrespective of seniority or nationality to command such task forces.

8. While you have no responsibilities in respect of the internal administration of the respective forces under your command, you are authorized to direct and co-ordinate the creation and development of administrative facilities and the broad allocation of war materials.

9. You will dispose of reinforcements which from time to time may be despatched to the area by ABDA Governments.

10. You are authorized to require from Commanders of the armed forces under your command such reports as you deem necessary in discharging your responsibilities as Supreme Commander.

11. You are authorized to control the issue of all Communiqués concerning the forces under your command.

12. Through channels specified in paragraph 18, you may submit recommendations to the ABDA Governments on any matters pertaining to the furthering of your mission.

LIMITATIONS

13. Your authority and control with respect to the various positions of ABDA area and to forces assigned thereto will normally be exercised through Commanders duly appointed by their respective Governments. Interference is to be avoided in administrative processes of armed forces of any of the ABDA Governments, including free communication between them and their respective Governments. No alterations or revision is to be made in basic tactical organizations of such forces, and each national component of a task force will normally operate under its own Commander and will not be sub-divided into small units for attachment to other national components of task forces, except in cases of urgent necessity. In general, your instructions and orders will be limited to those necessary for effective co-ordination of forces in execution of your mission.

RELATIONS WITH ABDA GOVERNMENTS

14. The ABDA Governments will jointly and severally support you in the execution of duties and responsibilities as herein defined, and in the exercising of authority herein delegated and limited. Commanders of all sea, land, and air forces within your area will be immediately informed by their respective Governments that, from a date to be notified, all orders and instructions issued by you in conformity with the provision of this directive will be considered by such Commanders as emanating from their respective Governments.

15. In the unlikely event that any of your immediate subordinates, **after** making due representation to you, still considers obedience to your orders would jeopardize national interests of his country to an extent unjustified by the general situation in ABDA area, he has the right, subject to your being immediately notified of such intention, to appeal direct to his own Government before carrying out orders. Such appeals will be made by most expeditious methods, and copies of appeals will be communicated simultaneously to you.

STAFF AND ASSUMPTION OF COMMAND

16. Your staff will include officers of each of ABDA Powers. You are empowered to communicate immediately with national Commanders in area with view to obtaining staff officers essential your earliest possible assumption of Command. Your additional staff requirements will be communicated as soon as possible to ABDA Governments through channels of communication described in paragraph 18.

17. You will report when you are in position effectively to carry out essential functions of Supreme Command, so that your assumption of Command may be promulgated to all concerned.

SUPERIOR AUTHORITY

18. As Supreme Commander of ABDA area you will be directly responsible to ABDA Governments through agency defined in ANNEX II.

ANNEX I. BOUNDARIES OF ABDA AREA

The ABDA area is bounded as follows:

On the North. By boundary between India and Burma, thence eastward along Chinese frontier and coastline to latitude 030 degrees North, thence along parallel 030 degrees North to meridian 140 degrees East.
(Note: Indo-China and Thailand are not included in this area.)
On the East. By meridian 140 degrees East from 030 degrees, to the Equator, thence east to longitude 141 degrees East, thence south to the boundary of Dutch New Guinea Coast on south coast, thence east along southern New Guinea Coast to meridian 143 degrees East, then south down this meridian to the coast of Australia.
On the South. By the northern coast of Australia from meridian 143 degrees East westward to meridian 114 degrees East, thence north-westward to latitude 015 degrees South, longitude 092 degrees East.
On the West. By meridian 092 degrees East.

2. Forces assigned to ABDA and adjacent areas are authorized to extend their operations into other areas as may be required.

ANNEX II

1. On all important military matters, not within the jurisdiction of Supreme Commander of ABDA area, United States Chiefs of Staff and representatives in Washington of British Chiefs of Staff will constitute agency for developing and submitting recommendations for decisions by

President of United States and by British Prime Minister and Minister of Defence. Among chief matters on which decisions will be required are:

(a) Provision of reinforcements.

(b) Major change in policy.

(c) Departures from Supreme Commander's Directive.

2. This agency will function as follows:

(a) Any proposals coming either from Supreme Commander or from any of the ABDA Governments will be transmitted to Chiefs of Staff Committee both in Washington and in London.

(b) The Chiefs of Staff Committee in London will immediately telegraph to their representatives in Washington to say whether or not they will be telegraphing any opinion.

(c) On receipt of these opinions the United States Chiefs of Staff and representatives in Washington of British Chiefs of Staff will develop and submit their recommendations to President, and by telegraphing to Prime Minister and Minister of Defence. Prime Minister will then inform the President whether he is in agreement with these recommendations.

3. Since London has machinery for consulting Dominion Governments, and since Dutch Government is in London, the British Government will be responsible for obtaining their views and agreement and for including these in the final telegrams to Washington.

4. Agreement having been reached between President and Prime Minister and Minister of Defence the orders to Supreme Commander will be despatched from Washington in the name of both of them.

Addition to Supreme Commander's Directive dated 12th January 1942

1. The inclusion of Burma in the ABDA area requires a definition of the respective responsibilities of the Supreme Commander and Commander-in-Chief, India, *vis-à-vis* Burma.

2. Accordingly, the following Directive has been drawn up in consultation with our Delegation in Washington:

(1) The Supreme Commander in the South-West Pacific, in view of his responsibility for all operations in the ABDA area (which includes Burma), is responsible for issuing all operational instructions to Burma.

(2) At the same time, India is necessarily closely concerned with the defence of Burma as part of the defence of India itself, and must play a large part in the provision and administration of the forces in Burma. Consequently, Commander-in-Chief, India, must be kept in the closest touch with the events in and requirements of Burma, and Supreme Commander will give Commander-in-Chief, India, earliest possible information of the demands likely to be made on India.

(3) The Supreme Commander in the South-West Pacific will in any case repeat to Commander-in-Chief, India, direct, and to the War Office, all instructions (including administrative), whether for land or air operations, issued to Burma. Commander-in-Chief, India, will comment, if he so desires, on any instructions which affect him, repeating such comments to the War Office. Burma will repeat to Commander-in-Chief, India, any demands made to the Supreme Commander or War Office for personnel and material.

(4) Should conflict of views arise between the Supreme Commander in the South-West Pacific and the Commander-in-Chief, India, matter will be referred to His Majesty's Government for decision.

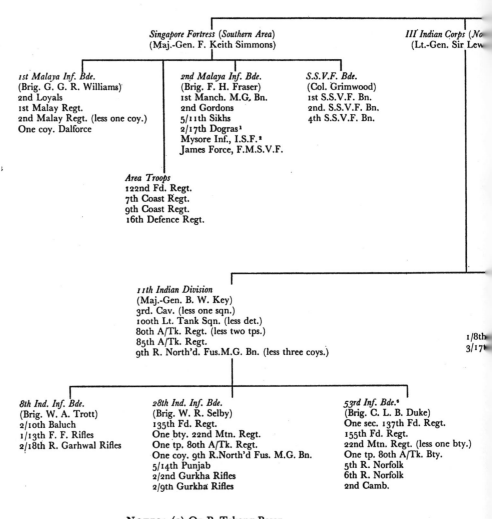

Singapore Fortress (Southern Area)
(Maj.-Gen. F. Keith Simmons)

III Indian Corps (No
(Lt.-Gen. Sir Lew

1st Malaya Inf. Bde.
(Brig. G. G. R. Williams)
2nd Loyals
1st Malay Regt.
2nd Malay Regt. (less one coy.)
One coy. Dalforce

2nd Malaya Inf. Bde.
(Brig. F. H. Fraser)
1st Manch. M.G. Bn.
2nd Gordons
5/11th Sikhs
2/17th Dogras[1]
Mysore Inf., I.S.F.[2]
James Force, F.M.S.V.F.

S.S.V.F. Bde.
(Col. Grimwood)
1st S.S.V.F. Bn.
2nd. S.S.V.F. Bn.
4th S.S.V.F. Bn.

Area Troops
122nd Fd. Regt.
7th Coast Regt.
9th Coast Regt.
16th Defence Regt.

11th Indian Division
(Maj.-Gen. B. W. Key)
3rd. Cav. (less one sqn.)
100th Lt. Tank Sqn. (less det.)
80th A/Tk. Regt. (less two tps.)
85th A/Tk. Regt.
9th R. North'd. Fus.M.G. Bn. (less three coys.)

1/8th
3/17

8th Ind. Inf. Bde.
(Brig. W. A. Trott)
2/10th Baluch
1/13th F. F. Rifles
2/18th R. Garhwal Rifles

28th Ind. Inf. Bde.
(Brig. W. R. Selby)
135th Fd. Regt.
One bty. 22nd Mtn. Regt.
One tp. 80th A/Tk. Regt.
One coy. 9th R.North'd Fus. M.G. Bn.
5/14th Punjab
2/2nd Gurkha Rifles
2/9th Gurkha Rifles

53rd Inf. Bde.[6]
(Brig. C. L. B. Duke)
One sec. 137th Fd. Regt.
155th Fd. Regt.
22nd Mtn. Regt. (less one bty.)
One tp. 80th A/Tk. Bty.
5th R. Norfolk
6th R. Norfolk
2nd Camb.

NOTES: (1) On P. Tekong Besar.
(2) On Pengerang.
(3) These battalions were being reformed at the beginning of Februar
(4) Transferred to Command Reserve on 9/2/42.
(5) Two batteries had been lost in the Slim River disaster, see page 2
(6) From 18th Division.
(7) Northern Area had, in addition, two field batteries, one equipped
(8) Four battalions I.S.F. were employed as follows: Jind Infantry
Kapurthala In
Hyderabad In
Bahawalpur In

MMAND
ercival)

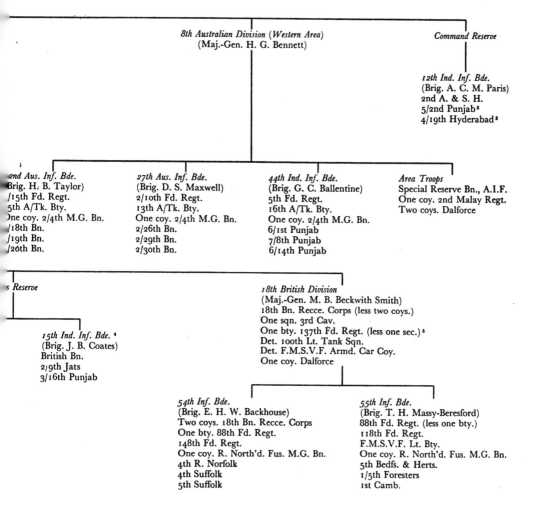

8th Australian Division (Western Area)
(Maj.-Gen. H. G. Bennett)

Command Reserve

12th Ind. Inf. Bde.
(Brig. A. C. M. Paris)
2nd A. & S. H.
5/2nd Punjab[3]
4/19th Hyderabad[3]

2nd Aus. Inf. Bde.
(Brig. H. B. Taylor)
/15th Fd. Regt.
5th A/Tk. Bty.
One coy. 2/4th M.G. Bn.
/18th Bn.
/19th Bn.
/26th Bn.

27th Aus. Inf. Bde.
(Brig. D. S. Maxwell)
2/10th Fd. Regt.
13th A/Tk. Bty.
One coy. 2/4th M.G. Bn.
2/26th Bn.
2/29th Bn.
2/30th Bn.

44th Ind. Inf. Bde.
(Brig. G. C. Ballentine)
5th Fd. Regt.
16th A/Tk. Bty.
One coy. 2/4th M.G. Bn.
6/1st Punjab
7/8th Punjab
6/14th Punjab

Area Troops
Special Reserve Bn., A.I.F.
One coy. 2nd Malay Regt.
Two coys. Dalforce

s Reserve

15th Ind. Inf. Bde. [4]
(Brig. J. B. Coates)
British Bn.
2/9th Jats
3/16th Punjab

18th British Division
(Maj.-Gen. M. B. Beckwith Smith)
18th Bn. Recce. Corps (less two coys.)
One sqn. 3rd Cav.
One bty. 137th Fd. Regt. (less one sec.) [5]
Det. 100th Lt. Tank Sqn.
Det. F.M.S.V.F. Armd. Car Coy.
One coy. Dalforce

54th Inf. Bde.
(Brig. E. H. W. Backhouse)
Two coys. 18th Bn. Recce. Corps
One bty. 88th Fd. Regt.
148th Fd. Regt.
One coy. R. North'd. Fus. M.G. Bn.
4th R. Norfolk
4th Suffolk
5th Suffolk

55th Inf. Bde.
(Brig. T. H. Massy-Beresford)
88th Fd. Regt. (less one bty.)
118th Fd. Regt.
F.M.S.V.F. Lt. Bty.
One coy. R. North'd. Fus. M.G. Bn.
5th Bedfs. & Herts.
1/5th Foresters
1st Camb.

half-trained recruits, and were not then considered fit for action.

guns.

ld protection.

ction of vital points.

APPENDIX 22

Japanese Naval Forces for the invasion of the Netherlands East Indies

1. Vice-Admiral Kondo (in command of all Naval Southern Operations)
   3rd Battle Squadron, 2nd Division, *Kongo, Haruna*
   4th Cruiser Squadron (part), *Atago, Takao*
   Ten destroyers

2. Vice-Admiral Takahashi (in command of Eastern and Central Forces)

A. EASTERN FORCE

(A) MENADO, KENDARI AND AMBOINA

Troop Convoys

Menado:	Six transports carrying Sasebo Combined Special Naval Landing Force.
	Transport aircraft carrying paratroop units of the 1st Yokosuka Special Naval Landing Force.
Kendari:	Six transports carrying Sasebo Combined Special Naval Landing Force.
Amboina:	Transports carrying Kure 1st Special Naval Landing Force and 228th Infantry Regiment.
Escort:	Rear-Admiral Tanaka in *Jintsu* (5·5-inch cruiser) and destroyers of 2nd Flotilla.
Covering Force:	Rear-Admiral Takagi.
	5th Cruiser Squadron (8-inch cruisers)—*Nachi, Haguro, Myoko* and two destroyers.
Air Group:	Rear-Admiral Fujita.
	Seaplane tenders *Chitose, Mizuho*.
Base Force:	Rear-Admiral Kubo in *Nagara* (5·5-inch cruiser) and some light craft of 1st Base Force.

Minesweepers and anti-submarine vessels.

Note: (1) In the Kendari operation Rear-Admiral Kubo relieved Rear-Admiral Tanaka as escort commander and the *Jintsu* and the two destroyers did not participate.

(2) In the Amboina operation two fleet carriers of the 2nd Carrier Squadron, *Hiryu* and *Soryu* took part.

(B) MAKASSAR TOWN

Troop Convoy:	Six transports carrying Sasebo Combined Special Naval Landing Force.
Escort:	Rear-Admiral Kubo in *Nagara*.
	Destroyers of 2nd Flotilla and some light craft of 1st Base Force.

535

Close Support:	Rear-Admiral Hirose with five destroyers of 4th Flotilla from Balikpapan.
Covering Force:	Rear-Admiral Takagi.
	5th Cruiser Squadron—*Nachi, Haguro* and two destroyers.
Air group:	Rear-Admiral Fujita.
	Seaplane tenders *Chitose, Mizuho* and *Sanuki Maru.*

Minesweepers and anti-submarine vessels.

(c) TIMOR

Troop Convoys:	Nine transports carrying 228th Infantry Regiment, transport aircraft carrying paratroops of 3rd Yokosuka Special Naval Landing Force.
Escort:	Rear-Admiral Tanaka in *Jintsu* and destroyers of 2nd Flotilla.
Covering Force:	Rear-Admiral Takagi with 5th Cruiser Squadron—*Nachi, Haguro* and four destroyers.
Air Group:	Seaplane tender *Mizuho.*

Minesweepers and anti-submarine vessels.

(d) BALI

Troop Convoy:	Two transports carrying an infantry battalion of 48th Division.
Escort:	Destroyers of 2nd Flotilla.
Covering Force:	Rear-Admiral Kubo in *Nagara* and three destroyers.

B. CENTRAL FORCE

(a) TARAKAN

Troop Convoy:	Sixteen transports carrying 56th Regimental Group and Kure 2nd Special Naval Landing Force.
Escort:	Rear-Admiral Nishimura in *Naka* (5·5-inch cruiser) and destroyers of 4th Flotilla.
Base Force:	Rear-Admiral Hirose and 2nd Base Force (small craft).

Minesweepers and anti-submarine vessels.

Air Group:	Seaplane tenders *Sanyo Maru* and *Sanuki Maru.*

(b) BALIKPAPAN

Troop Convoy:	Sixteen transports carrying 56th Regimental Group.
Escort:	Rear-Admiral Nishimura in *Naka* and destroyers of 4th Flotilla.
Air Group:	Seaplane tenders *Sanyo Maru* and *Sanuki Maru.*

Minesweepers and anti-submarine vessels.

(c) BANDJERMASIN

One battalion of 56th Regimental Group moved overland, less one company which went by sea.

APPENDIX 22

537

C. WESTERN FORCE

3. Vice-Admiral Ozawa

PALEMBANG

Advanced Troop Convoy:	Eight transports carrying advanced force of 229th Infantry Regiment.
Escort:	*Sendai* (5·5-inch cruiser) and four destroyers.
Main Troop Convoy:	Fourteen transports carrying main body of 229th Infantry Regiment and one battalion 230th Infantry Regiment.
Escort:	*Kashii* (5·5-inch cruiser) and four destroyers.
Covering Force:	Vice-Admiral Ozawa in *Chokai* with 7th Cruiser Squadron (8-inch cruisers)—*Mogami, Mikuma, Suzuya* and *Kumano*. Light fleet carrier *Ryujo*, *Yura* (5·5-inch cruiser) and three destroyers.

COMBINED FORCE FOR INVASION OF JAVA

4. Vice-Admiral Takahashi (8-inch cruisers *Ashigara* [fleet flagship], *Myoko* and two destroyers).

(A) WESTERN FORCE (MERAK, BANTAM BAY AND ERETENWETAN)

Troop Convoys:	Fifty-six transports carrying HQ 16 Army, 2nd Division and 230th Infantry Regiment.
Escorts:	Rear-Admiral Hara. *Yura* and *Natori* (5·5-inch cruisers) and 3rd and 5th Destroyer Flotillas (thirteen destroyers).
Covering Force:	Rear-Admiral Kurita. 7th Cruiser Squadron—*Mikuma, Mogami, Suzuya, Kumano* and three destroyers.
Air Group:	Rear-Admiral Kakuta. Light fleet carrier *Ryujo* and one destroyer.
Base Force:	Rear-Admiral Hirose and 2nd Base Force.

(B) EASTERN FORCE (KRAGAN)

Troop Convoys:	Forty-one transports carrying 48th Division and 56th Regimental Group.
Escorts:	Rear-Admiral Nishimura in *Naka* with *Jintsu* and 2nd and 4th Destroyer Flotillas (thirteen destroyers).
Covering Force:	Rear-Admiral Takagi. 5th Cruiser Squadron—*Nachi, Haguro*.

Minesweepers and anti-submarine vessels.

Air Group:	Seaplane tenders *Mizuho, Sanyo Maru* and *Sanuki Maru*.

NAVAL FORCES OPERATING SOUTH OF JAVA IN SUPPORT
OF THE INVASION

5. Vice-Admiral Kondo (in command)
 3rd Battle Squadron, 2nd Division, *Kongo, Haruna.*
 4th Cruiser Squadron (part), *Atago, Takao, Maya.*
 Three destroyers.

Vice-Admiral Nagumo (1st Air Fleet)
 1st Carrier Squadron, *Akagi, Kaga.*
 2nd Carrier Squadron, *Soryu, Hiryu.*
 3rd Battle Squadron, 1st Division, *Hiei, Kirishima.*
 8th Cruiser Squadron, 1st Division, *Tone, Chikuma.*
 Abukuma (light cruiser) and eight destroyers.

NAVAL AIR FORCES FOR THE INVASION OF
THE NETHERLANDS EAST INDIES

6. Vice-Admiral N. Tsukahara (in command of 11th Air Fleet)
 21st and 23rd Air Flotillas (each about 150 aircraft).

APPENDIX 23

Skeleton Order of Battle of Japanese 16th Army

1. 2nd Division
   Employed for invasion of West Java.
2. 38th Division (after fall of Hong Kong)
   228th Infantry Regiment employed for the invasion of (1) Amboina, (2) Timor.
   229th Infantry Regiment employed to make initial attack on Palembang in Southern Sumatra;
   230th Infantry Regiment accompanied 2nd Division for the invasion of West Java.
3. 48th Division (after being used under 14th Army in the invasion of the Philippines)
   Employed for the invasion of East Java (a small detachment occupied Bali).
4. 56th Regimental Group (Sakaguchi Detachment)
   Employed for capture of (1) Tarakan, (2) Balikpapan, (3) invasion of East Java.

Attached Naval Units
1. Kure 1st Special Naval Landing Force
   Employed for the capture of Amboina.
2. Kure 2nd Special Naval Landing Force
   Employed for the capture of Tarakan.
3. Sasebo Combined Special Landing Force
   Employed for the capture of (1) Menado, (2) Kendari.
4. Yokosuka 1st Special Naval Landing Force
   Employed for the capture of Menado.
5. Yokosuka 2nd Special Naval Landing Force
   Employed for the capture of Miri and Kuching.
6. Yokosuka 3rd Special Naval Landing Force
   Employed for the capture of Timor.

Attached Air Units

3rd Air Division (about 150 aircraft)

Notes

56th Regimental Group consisted of:
   56th Regimental Group Headquarters
   146th Infantry Regiment
   Armoured vehicle unit
   I/56th Field Artillery Regiment
   1st Company 56th Engineer Regiment
   2nd Company 56th Transport Regiment
   Medical unit
   1st Field Hospital 56th Division

Kure 1st Special Naval Landing Force consisted of three rifle companies and one machine-gun company—strength 820.

Kure 2nd Special Naval Landing Force consisted of three rifle companies, one machine-gun company, and one anti-aircraft battery—strength 1,000.

Sasebo Combined Special Landing Force consisted of two units, 1st and 2nd, each of three rifle companies and one machine-gun company. Strength of each unit—800. Total strength—1,600.

Yokosuka 1st Special Naval Landing Force. A paratroop unit organized as battalion headquarters and three companies totalling 519 paratroops, which provided the initial landing force of 334 paratroops, and a second landing force of 185 paratroops. In addition there was a rear force consisting of a light machine-gun unit, a medical unit and paymaster unit.

Yokosuka 2nd Special Naval Landing Force. An amphibious unit organized as battalion headquarters, three rifle companies and one machine-gun company, with a strength of 28 officers and about 1,150 other ranks.

Yokosuka 3rd Special Naval Landing Force. An airborne unit consisting of battalion headquarters and three rifle companies, with a strength of approximately 1,000.

APPENDIX 24

Westforce Operation Instruction No. 4

Most Secret
Copy No. 1
27 January 1942

1. It has been decided that tps. in Johore will be withdrawn by gradual stages on Singapore Island.

2. (i) Westforce is believed to be opposed by Japanese 5 Div advancing down rail and central rd.
   (ii) 11 Ind. Div. is opposed by Jap Guards Div.
   (iii) Eastforce up to night 25/26 Jan. has been opposed by only 300 in the Mersing area. At 0700 hrs. on 26 Jan. a convoy was reported off Endau, which will permit an enemy force of about two regts. being landed in that area unless our air action should prove highly successful.

3. *Our present dispositions*
   (i) Eastforce, morning 26 Jan:
      one bn. North of Jemaluang
      one bn. South of Jemaluang
      one bn. 35 MS area with one coy. Sedili Boom
      one bn. moving to Kota Tinggi
      one bn. South of Kota Tinggi
   (ii) Westforce. On general line Rengam–S. Rengam.
   (iii) 11 Ind Div. 15 Ind Inf Bde reported 0910 hrs. 26 Jan. from Sengarang and is to continue to withdraw and link with 53 Bde. in the Sengarang area and then withdraw South.

4. Westforce will withdraw to Singapore according to the following programme. This MUST NOT be departed from. Appendix A shows the stages co-ordinated with Eastforce and 11 Ind Div.
      Night 26/27 Jan.: hold present posns.
      Night 27/28 Jan.: withdraw to line Rail Mile 440
                                               Road Mile 44
      Night 29/30 Jan.: withdraw to line Sedenak
                                               Road Mile 32
      Night 30/31 Jan.: withdraw to line Rail Mile 450
                                               Road Mile 25
      Night 31/1 Feb.: on to Island
   Suitable delaying posns. giving depth will be recced in these immediate areas forthwith.

5. To cover the final withdrawal two bridgeheads, an inner and an outer, will be established covering the Causeway.

The details of command, dispositions and co-ordination will be issued separately.

6. Route of final withdrawal on the Island:

By Senai estate rd. leaving main rd. about 610445 crossing ry. about 615451 and joining Tebrau loop rd. about 733381.

Thence (a) A.I.F. via rd. passing new J.M.F. Barracks (7533) thence keeping West of ry. past old HQs. (Bukit Semyum) to level crossing (750294) thence if passable by rail route over causeway to rail and rd. junc. (732222).

(b) 9 Ind. Div. units by rd. going West from rd. junc. 741366 over rail br. thence South from 710358 to sea front at 741289 thence to Causeway.

7. Westforce will be liable to a certain degree of infiltration from the West, especially:

(a) via S. Pontian when uncovered by 11 Ind. Div.

(b) via rd. and track leading to Ayer Hitam rd. from coast via North of Pulai.

27 Aust. Inf. Bde. will secure the western flank against such possible threats North of Pulai.

8. Fd. arty. 9 Ind. Div. will return by 0700 hrs. 29 Jan. one 25 pr. bty. to Johore Bahru to operate subsequently with 155 Fd. Regt. Gp. for support of bridgehead. C.R.A. 3 Corps for instructions. Any surplus A. tk. guns will be also returned to this quarter.

9. All surplus tpt. and equipment will be returned to the Island now.

As the force moves South the front narrows and as far as is consistent with security units, particularly of supporting arms, will be returned. The minimum number of carriers only will be retained.

27 Bde. A.I.F. will send three armd. cars to 2/19 Bn. (G.B.D.) on 30 Jan.

All 3rd Line tpt. with columns except that which is required for tp. carrying will be sent to the Island, into dispersal areas, by 0730 hrs. 29 Jan. All 2nd line tpt. will be sent back to dispersal areas on Island by 0730 hrs. 30 Jan.

ACK.

Sd./   xxx   xxx   xxx
Col.
GSO I WESTFORCE

Signed at 0020 hrs.
Issued by safe hand.

Distribution	*Copy No.*
9 Ind. Div.	1
27 Aust. Inf. Bde.	2
22 Aust. Inf. Bde.	3
File	4
Spare	5

Note: In view of the need for utmost secrecy only five copies are produced. This must not be duplicated or reproduced in any way and must not be taken forward of HQs.

APPENDIX A

	11 Ind. Div.	Westforce	Eastforce
Night 26/27	15 Ind. Inf. Bde. Sengerang Rengit	Rail Mile 432 S. Benut	Jemaluang
27/28	Benut	Rail Mile 437 Road Mile 42	North of Ulu Sedili Sedili Boom
28/29	M.S. 45 Kg. Pulai Sebatang		Mawai–S. Dohol
29/30	P. Besar P. Kechil	Sedenak Road Mile 32	North of Hajimod Jambi–Limbong
30/31	Area West of M.S.25 (Kg. Peng Raja)	Rail Mile 450 Road Mile 25	Kota Tinggi
31/1st	Rear parties withdrawn Singapore	Rear parties from M.S.20 to Singapore via Estate Road East of Ry. from Senai	Rear parties from North of Ulu Tiram

APPENDIX 25

Order of Battle of Japanese 25th Army for the attack on Singapore Island

Main attack on the night of 8th/9th February 1942

(a) 18th Division

Right Wing: 23rd Infantry Brigade (less Regimental Headquarters and II and III/56th Battalions).
Element 1st Independent Anti-Tank Battalion.
Attached engineer and medical units.

Left Wing: 114th Infantry Regiment (less one company).
Element 1st Independent Anti-Tank Battalion.
Attached engineer and medical units.

Artillery: 18th Mountain Artillery Regiment (less one battery).
21st Heavy Field Artillery Battalion.

Engineers: 12th Engineer Regiment (less element attached to the infantry wings).
Engineer unit of 21st Independent Brigade.

23rd Independent Engineer Regiment   }   For
15th River Crossing Material Company   } crossing the
22nd Bridge Building Material Company }   Strait

Reserve: 56th Infantry Regiment (less one battalion).

Divisional Units: One battery 18th Mountain Artillery Regiment
Ordnance unit.
3rd Field Hospital.
Element 28th Water Purification Unit.

(b) 5th Division

Right Wing: 21st Infantry Brigade.
2nd Independent Anti-Tank Company.
One medium tank company.
III/5th Field Artillery Regiment (less one battery).
5th Engineer Regiment (less one company).
Medical units.

Left Wing: 9th Infantry Brigade (less 41st Infantry Regiment).
1st Independent Anti-Tank Company.
One battery III/5th Field Artillery Battalion.
One company 5th Engineer Regiment.
Medical units.

Artillery: 5th Field Artillery Regiment (less one battalion).

Engineers: 15th Independent Engineer Regiment

Element engineer unit 3rd Tank Group

5th Independent Engineer Company   For

One company 26th Independent Engineer   crossing
   Regiment   the

21st River Crossing Material Company   Strait

27th Bridge Building Material Company

One platoon 58th Construction Duty
   Company

Reserve: 41st Infantry Regiment.

5th Reconnaissance Regiment.

14th Independent Mortar Battalion.

Divisional Units: 1st Tank Regiment (less one medium company).

Ordnance unit.

2nd Field Hospital.

4th Field Hospital.

2nd Water Purification Unit.

Salvage unit.

(c) Imperial Guards Division

Assault Group: Infantry Group Headquarters.

4th Guards Infantry Regiment.

III/3rd Guards Battalion.

Half Regimental gun and anti-tank companies of
   3rd Guards Infantry Regiment.

Two companies 1st Independent Anti-Tank Battalion.

One company Guards Engineer Regiment.

Medical unit.

Left Flank   II/5th Guards Battalion.
  Guard: Half Regimental gun company 5th Guards Infantry
                   Regiment.

Anti-tank company 5th Guards Infantry Regiment.

One platoon No. 1 Company Guards Engineer
   Regiment.

Medical unit.

Artillery: Guards Artillery Regiment (less two batteries).

One battery formed from captured equipment.

Engineers: Guards Engineer Regiment (less detachments with
   assault group and left flank guard).

20th Independent Engineer Regiment   For

One company 26th Independent   crossing the
   Engineer Regiment   Strait

Reserve: 5th Guards Infantry Regiment (less one battalion).

Half Regimental gun and anti-tank companies.

20

Divisional Units: 14th Tank Regiment plus two companies of Guards
    Reconnaissance Regiment.
    Ordnance unit.
    No. 1 Field Hospital.
    No. 4 Field Hospital.
    12th Water Purification unit.

Note. All three divisions had their normal allotment of signal and transport units.

APPENDIX 26

Japanese Military Landing Craft used in Malaya: 8th December 1941–15th February 1942

1. Japanese military landing craft were manned entirely by army personnel, who belonged to the shipping branch of the engineer arm of the Service. This branch was a separate command, having been formed at the time of the Russo-Japanese war in 1904–05, and was commanded by a Lieutenant-General with headquarters at Hiroshima, the chief military embarkation port in Japan.

Before the 8th December 1941 landing craft had been extensively used in China both on the coast and inland, and as a result a high standard of efficiency in their employment had been reached both by the crews and by the other arms of the Service. This particularly applied to 5th and 18th Divisions.

2. *Types of Craft*

The craft consisted of several types, four of which were chiefly used in the Malaya campaign, as under:

(*a*) *Collapsible Boats*. These were made of plywood with rubber folding joints in a standard size of 15 ft. length, 5 ft. beam and 3 ft. draught, and could be assembled by one man in two minutes. Speed 8 knots, driven by an outboard motor.

One boat could carry twelve fully equipped men, or an infantry or mountain artillery gun with a crew of four. On land it was usually carried by lorry but could be manhandled by fourteen men. It was part of the equipment of 23rd Independent Engineer Regiment and 15th and 21st River Crossing Material Companies.

(*b*) *Small Landing Craft*. Made of steel, size 33 ft. by 8 ft. with a weight of $3\frac{3}{4}$ tons. Speed 10 knots, driven by 60 horse-power inboard diesel engine. This craft could carry thirty-five fully equipped soldiers with a crew of six. It was included in the equipment of 26th Independent Engineer Regiment, and on land was moved by rail.

(*c*) *Pontoons*. Made of steel and driven by an outboard motor. Size: 22 ft. length, $3\frac{1}{2}$ ft. beam and $2\frac{1}{2}$ ft. draught. Each pontoon consisted of four sections bolted together. In addition to use as bridge pontoons, they were used as landing craft and were capable of carrying twenty fully equipped soldiers. On land they were carried on lorries or manhandled by fifteen men.

They were included in the equipment of 22nd and 27th Bridge Material Companies.

(*d*) *Heavy Pontoons*. These were similar in construction to (*c*), but larger and stronger. Each pontoon consisted of three or more parts joined together so as to carry heavy field vehicles, or tanks up to 16 tons. Carried by rail or on lorries. They formed part of the equipment of the engineer unit of a tank group.

3. *Strait of Malacca Boat Column*

This column consisted of military landing craft which had been used at the initial landings at Singora, and which were carried from that port to Alor Star by rail, road and manhandling. They were launched at Alor Star and assembled at Port Weld for the embarkation of the infantry. In addition to the military landing craft, about twenty civilian boats which had been captured at Penang were also used.

4. *Crossing of Strait of Johore*

(a) The 23rd Independent Engineer Regiment tested landing craft on the Sungei Muar from the 1st to 3rd February 1942. The 5th and 18th Divisions practised carrying collapsible boats and boarding on the 4th February 1942 on the Sungei Muar. As both these divisions had had considerable experience in river crossing operations and, as 5th Division had received specialist training in amphibious operations prior to the 8th December 1941, extensive rehearsal was not considered necessary. The Guards Division practised boarding landing craft on the 8th February 1942 in an area near its embarkation point. The craft used for the actual crossing of the Strait of Johore were manhandled to the launching points in order to ensure secrecy.

(b) The planned allotment of craft for the crossing was:

Guards Division:	30 collapsible boats[1]
5th Division	30 collapsible boats
	30 small landing craft
	30 pontoons
	7 heavy pontoons
18th Division:	140 collapsible boats
	30 pontoons

The actual number used was slightly less as losses prior to the crossing were about 10 per cent.

---

[1] This number was increased by craft taken from the *5th* and *18th Divisions* allotment after their successful landing.

APPENDIX 27

Malaya Command Operation Instruction No. 40

Secret and Personal

O425

Ref Map Johore and
Singapore 1/25,000

1. Enemy attacked Western Area in strength 9 February and succeeded in penetrating to the East of Tengah aerodrome. A party of the enemy is reported to have blocked the rd Hong Kah Village 6917–rd junc 6313 in rear of 44 Ind Inf Bde.

2. A.I.F. Malaya have been ordered to withdraw to and hold the line S. Kranji–Bulim Village 6919–S. Jurong. 6/15 Bde has been placed under comd of A.I.F. Malaya.

3. Should it be impossible to hold the enemy on the line mentioned in para 2 above, G.O.C. Malaya intends to withdraw to an inner posn on which the final battle for Singapore will be fought.

4. General line of this inner posn will be:
   West Bank of Kallang River in 8711–thence West of the inundated area in 8611, 8612, and 8712 to Mt. Vernon 8814–North of Peirce Reservoir 8118–Hill 581 in 7616–West of Bukit Timah Village 7515–pt 105 in 7412 –Pasir Panjang Village 7409–thence along the South coast of Singapore Island to West Bank of Rochore River in 8710. Pulau Blakang Mati, Pulau Brani, Pulau Tekong and the defended perimeter of Pengerang will also be held.

5. This posn will be divided into three areas:

   Northern Area: Comd—Comd 3 Ind Corps.
   Tps—3 Ind Corps of 11 Ind Div and 18 Div.

   Southern Area: Comd—Comd Southern Area (Major-Gen Keith Simmons).
   Tps—existing garrison of Southern Area.

   Western Area: Comd—Comd A.I.F. Malaya.

   Note: Allocation of 12 Ind Inf Bde and 44 Ind Inf Bde will be decided later. At least one of these formations will be in Comd Reserve.

6. *Boundaries*
   The defended area defined in para 4 above will be divided into sectors by boundaries as follows:

   Between 3 Ind Corps and A.I.F. Incl A.I.F. Electric Transmission Line 7716 –incl Swiss Rifle Club 7715–incl rd junc 780143–incl Bukit Timah Rd–rd junc 838117.

   Between 3 Ind Corps and Southern Area. Incl 3 Ind Corps Macpherson Rd– Serangoon Rd–excl Farrer Park–rd junc 838117.

Between A.I.F. and Southern Area. Incl Southern Area track 750107–Ayer Raja Rd–Alexandra Rd–rd junc 809092–incl rd junc 812102–Grange Rd–incl rd junc 827102–excl rd junc 829108–excl rd junc 838117.

Comd Southern Area will be responsible for defence of Pulau Blakang Mati, Pulau Brani, Pulau Tekong and Pengerang.

7. Recces of Areas will be carried out at once and the plans for the movement of formations into the areas allotted to them will be prepared. Formations will arrange to move back and locate in their new areas units located in their present areas which are under comd of H.Q. Malaya Comd.

8. C.A.A.D. will remain responsible to G.O.C. Malaya for A.A. Defences.

9. H.Q. of G.O.C. Malaya will be located at Fort Canning (Battle H.Q.) together with H.Q. Southern Area.

10. Administrative adjustments which can be made now to fit in with the above organization will be put in hand immediately.

11. ACK.

Sd.   xxx   xxx   xxx
Lt. Col.
for Brigadier,
General Staff, Malaya Command.

Adv H.Q.M.C.

10 Feb 42.

T.O.O. . . . .

Distribution:	*Copy No.*
Lt. Gen. Sir Lewis M. Heath	1
Maj. Gen. H. Gordon Bennett	2
Maj. Gen. F. Keith Simmons	3
Brig. A. W. G. Wildey	4
Brig. H. F. Lucas	5
Brig. T. K. Newbigging	6
Brig. Goodman	7
Col. H. A. Urquhart	8
Col. G. L. Giblin	9
War Diary	10–12
File	13
Copy No. 14	Rear Adm. Spooner
„ „ 15	A. V. M. Pulford

Index

INDEX

Note: Formations and units of the British, Commonwealth, and Indian Armies and of the Colonial forces are indexed under 'Army'. British infantry battalions are in order of regimental seniority.

A.B.C.1 War Plan: 58
ABDA Command: need for, 263–4; discussions on, 264–7; Wavell's appointment, 264, 265, 267; area of Command defined, 265, 266, 267; defects of, 268; significance of, 268; Wavell's strategy for, 283, 296; H.Q. established, 293; sub-areas and commanders, 293–4; control of air operations, 293–4; naval Commands, 294; inferiority at sea and in air, 296–7; difficulties of air reinforcement, 347; faces threat to Java and Sumatra, 357–8; dissolved, 429; *see also* Wavell
A.D.A. Agreement: 55–6; criticisms of, 56
A.D.B. Agreement: 62–3; criticisms of, 63
A.D.B.2 Agreement: 76; U.S. objections to, 86
Admiralty: recommend site for Singapore Naval Base, 6; favour fixed defences, 7, 12; on fleet available for Far East, 20; withdraw units from China Squadron, 21, 24; plan for an Eastern Fleet, 75–6, 85; order co-ordination of plans for Allied naval forces, 173; on evacuation of dockyard and naval personnel from Singapore, 318
Air Ministry: favour air defence of Singapore Naval Base, 7, 11; consult with Dutch on defence in Far East, 14; policy for new airfields in Malaya, 14, 15, 31; in relation to A.O.C. Far East, 51
Air raid precautions: *see* Civil defence
Air reinforcement route to Far East: 253 fn. 4; cut by Japanese, 254; diversion made, 254; fighter reinforcement delays, 261–2
Alden, U.S. destroyer: 437 fn. 2, 443
Amboina, loss of: 348–9
Anderson, Lieut.-Colonel C. G. W., V.C.: at Muar, 308, 311, 312; retreats from Bakri, 312–3; at Parit Sulong, 315–6; 316 fn.
Anglo-Japanese Alliance: 1; abrogated, 4, 5
'Anzac area' (Pacific) created: 266
'Arcadia' Conference: 263–7
Armoured cars in Malaya: 213, 217 fn., 230, 277, 329
Armoured train in Malaya: 188, 214, 229 fn.
Army:
  7th Armoured Brigade: 258 fn. 1; ordered to N.E.I., 260, 261, 356
  100th Light Tank Squadron, 395 fn. 1
  Artillery:
    73rd Field Battery R.A.: at Kota Bharu, 189, 190; on Selangor coast, 272, 273 fn. 1; in withdrawal to Johore, 288
    342nd Field Battery R.A.: in battle for Singapore, 395 fn. 1
    350th Field Battery R.A.: at Slim River, 280

Army—*cont.*
  Artillery—*cont.*
    499th Field Battery R.A.: in battle for Singapore, 399
    2nd Anti-Tank Battery R.A.: in covering force, 188 fn. 2; at Jitra, 204, 205; in retreat to Kampar, 244
    45th Anti-Tank Battery R.A.: in battle for Singapore, 398
    215th Anti-Tank Battery R.A.: at Kampar, 246; at Slim River, 274
    272nd Anti-Tank Battery R.A.: on Selangor coast, 273 fn. 1
    273rd Anti-Tank Battery R.A.: in 'Krohcol', 186 fn. 4; in covering force, 187 fn. 2, 188 fn. 2; at Kampar, 246; in battle for Singapore, 399
    65th Field Battery R.A.A.: at Muar, 305; 316 fn. 2
    13th Anti-Tank Battery R.A.A.: in Singapore defences, 370
    15th Anti-Tank Battery R.A.A.: in Singapore defences, 371
    16th Anti-Tank Battery R.A.A.: in Singapore defences, 371
    4th Mountain Battery (Indian): in covering force, 188 fn. 1; at Jitra, 204 fn. 3
    7th Mountain Battery (Indian): in covering force, 188 fn. 2
    10th Mountain Battery (Indian): in 'Krohcol', 186 fn. 4, 187; in withdrawal to Krian River, 229
    21st Mountain Battery (Indian): at Kota Bharu, 189
    16th Light Anti-Aircraft Battery Hong Kong & Singapore R.A.: at Slim River, 279
    8th Coast Regt. R.A.: at Hong Kong, 109 fn. 3
    12th Coast Regt. R.A.: at Hong Kong, 109 fn. 3
    5th Field Regt. R.A.: 80 fn. 4; at Kuantan, 269; in Johore, 327; in Singapore defences, 371; in battle for Singapore, 387 fn., 390, 398 fn. 1
    88th Field Regt. R.A.: 80 fn. 4; at Gurun, 215; in withdrawal to Krian River, 229; at Kampar, 246; at Kuantan, 269; on Selangor coast, 273 fn. 1; in Johore, 327
    137th Field Regt. R.A.: 80 fn. 4; in withdrawal to Krian River, 229 fn.; in retreat to Kampar, 243; at Kampar, 246, 247; at Slim River, 274, 275, 279, 280; in Johore, 327

553

Army—*cont.*
  Artillery—*cont.*
    155th Field Regt. R.A.: at Jitra, 204
      at Kampar, 246; at Slim River, 274,
      279; in Johore, 327
    80th Anti-Tank Regt. R.A.: 80 fn. 4; at
      Jitra, 204; in withdrawal to Krian
      River, 229 fn.; at Slim River, 274
    82nd Anti-Tank Regt. R.A.: 253 fn. 1
    85th Anti-Tank Regt. R.A.: 253 fn. 2;
      arrives Singapore, 287; in battle for
      Singapore, 387 fn.
    125th Anti-Tank Regt. R.A.: 368
    6th Heavy Anti-Aircraft Regt. R.A.:
      253 fn. 2; arrives Singapore, 287;
      in Java, 436
    77th Heavy Anti-Aircraft Regt. R.A.:
      258 fn. 2; in Java, 436
    21st Light Anti-Aircraft Regt. R.A.: 258
      fn. 2
    35th Light Anti-Aircraft Regt. R.A.:
      253 fn. 2; arrives Singapore, 287
    5th Searchlight Regt. R.A.: in Singa-
      pore defences, 371
    2/10th Field Regt. R.A.A.: in Singapore
      defences, 370; in battle for Singa-
      pore, 376, 382, 389, 396
    2/15th Field Regt. R.A.A.: in Singapore
      defences, 371; in battle for Singa-
      pore, 378, 384, 390, 391, 398 fn. 1
    2/4th Anti-Tank Regt. R.A.A.: at
      Muar, 307
    22nd Mountain Regt. (Indian): 21; at
      Jitra, 204; in withdrawal to Krian
      River, 229 fn.
    Hong Kong & Singapore R.A.: at
      Hong Kong, 113
  Cavalry:
    3rd Hussars, 'B' Squadron: 257; arrives
      Sumatra, 423; in Java, 432, 436,
      447
    3rd Cavalry (Indian): 80 fn. 3; 217; in
      withdrawal to Krian River, 229 fn.;
      on Grik road, 236; at Kampar, 246,
      247, 248; on Selangor coast, 272,
      273 and fn. 1; in withdrawal to
      Johore, 288; in Johore, 328; in
      battle for Singapore, 395 fn. 1
  Corps, I Australian: 260, 261, 356;
    destination in doubt, 424
  Corps, III Indian: formed in Malaya, 57;
    164, 166; dispositions, N. Malaya,
    169–71; 174; on defensive, 185, 186;
    operations N. Malaya, 203–19, 229–33,
    235–8, 242–9; operations central
    Malaya, 269–81; rôle in defence of
    Johore, 282, 285; withdraws to Johore,
    288–9; operations Johore, 306, 309,
    313, 320, 321; withdrawal to Island,
    327–30, 332–9, 340–1, 342; in Singa-
    pore defences, 364, 369–70; in battle
    for Singapore, 383, 395, 398
  Divisions:
    18th (British): availability for Malaya,
      253, 254, 256, 258, 259; ordered to
      Malaya, 260, 261; 318, 319; arrives
      Singapore, 324; in Singapore de-

Army—*cont.*
  Divisions—*cont.*
      fences, 364, 369; in battle for Singa-
      pore 397, 399, 400, 403, 412, 414
    8th Australian: 57, 163, 168, 169; rôle
      in defence of Johore, 282; as 'West-
      force', 285, 319; in Singapore de-
      fences, 364; *see also* 'Westforce'
      (Johore) *and* Western Area Com-
      mand (Singapore)
    9th Indian: 39; in Malaya, 57; 163,
      169; in N.E. Malaya, 170; opera-
      tions, 182, 188–91; withdraws
      from Kelantan, 217; Kuantan
      operations, 269–72; 285; in with-
      drawal to Johore, 289; joins 'West-
      force', 289; in Johore, 302; in with-
      drawal to Island, 327, 335, 336, 337,
      338, 340; disbanded, 364 and fn. 1
    11th Indian: to Malaya, 47; 163, 169;
      in N.W. Malaya, 170; frontier
      operations, 186–8; at Jitra, 203–13;
      withdraws to Gurun, 214–15; at
      Gurun, 215, 216; withdraws to
      Muda River, 216–17; withdraws to
      Krian River, 229–30; on Grik
      road, 235–6; retreats to Kampar,
      243–4; at Kampar, 245–8; at Slim
      River, 274–81; 285; withdraws to
      Johore, 288–9; in Johore, 306, 315,
      321; in withdrawal to Island, 327–
      30, 334; in Singapore defences, 364,
      369; in battle for Singapore, 383,
      388–9, 395, 396, 399, 400, 401, 403,
      406, 412
  Engineers:
    2/10th Field Company, R.A.E.: in
      battle for Singapore, 377, 378
    3rd Field Company, King George V's
      Own Bengal Sappers & Miners:
      188 fn. 2; in retreat to Kampar,
      244; at Slim River, 274, 280
    17th Field Company, Royal Bombay
      Sappers & Miners: 187 fn. 2
    23rd Field Company, Royal Bombay
      Sappers & Miners: 188 fn. 1; in
      retreat to Kampar, 244; at Slim
      River, 274
  Infantry Battalions:
    2nd Royal Scots: at Hong Kong, 113,
      115; in Mainland operations, 120,
      121, 122, 123, 124; in defence of
      Island, 128, 134, 135, 137, 139, 140,
      142, 143, 144
    4th Royal Norfolk Regt.: in battle for
      Singapore, 374, 387 fn., 394
    5th Royal Norfolk Regt.: in Johore,
      306, 307, 309, 320, 321; in with-
      drawal to Island, 327, 330 fn. 2
    6th Royal Norfolk Regt.: at Batu Pahat,
      306, 309–10, 311, 313, 321; in with-
      drawal to Island, 328, 330 fn. 2
    4th Suffolk Regt.: in battle for Singa-
      pore, 395 fn. 1
    5th Bedfordshire & Hertfordshire Regt.:
      in battle for Singapore, 398, 400
      fn. 4

Army—*cont.*
Infantry Battalions—*cont.*
1st Leicestershire Regt.: at Jitra, 204, 206, 207, 208, 209, 210 fn.; in withdrawal to Krian River, 229 fn.; 242 fn. 4; *see also* British Battalion
2nd East Surrey Regt.: at Jitra, 204, 208; 214 fn.; at Gurun, 216; 242 fn. 4; *see also* British Battalion
1/5th Sherwood Foresters: in battle for Singapore, 387 fn., 394, 400 fn. 1
2nd Loyal Regt.: in Johore, 285, 302, 309, 310, 311, 313, 314, 321; in withdrawal to Island, 328; in battle for Singapore, 400 fn. 4
2nd Gordon Highlanders: in withdrawal to Island, 334, 335 and fn. 1; 336, 338, 341 fn. 1; in battle for Singapore, 395, 397, 400, 411
2nd Argyll & Sutherland Highlanders: 168, 213, 214; on Grik road, 230 and fn., 235, 236; in retreat to Kampar, 244, 248; at Kampar, 248; at Slim River, 275, 277, 278, 281 fn.; in Causeway bridgehead, 340, 342; in Singapore defences, 364; in battle for Singapore, 378, 385, 392, 393
1st Cambridgeshire Regt.: in battle for Singapore, 395 fn.
2nd Cambridgeshire Regt.: in Johore, 306, 309, 327; in withdrawal to Island, 330 fn. 2
British Battalion: 242 fn. 4; at Kampar, 246–7, 248; on Selangor coast, 273 fn. 2; in Johore, 306, 309, 320, 321; in withdrawal to Island, 330 fn. 2; in battle for Singapore, 385, 386, 391, 393
2/18th Australian: in withdrawal to Island, 332, 334; in Singapore defences, 371; in battle for Singapore, 375, 377, 378, 384, 390 fn. 2, 391
2/19th Australian: in Johore, 306, 308, 311, 312, 316 fn. 2; in Singapore defences, 362; in battle for Singapore, 375, 377, 378, 384
2/20th Australian: in withdrawal to Island, 331, 332; in Singapore defences, 371; in battle for Singapore, 377, 378, 384
2/21st Australian: in Amboina, 348, 349
2/26th Australian: in withdrawal to Island, 334, 335, 336, 338, 341 and fn. 1; in Singapore defences, 370; in battle for Singapore, 381 and fn. 1, 382, 383, 389, 396, 400 fn. 1, 403
2/29th Australian: in Johore, 305, 307, 308, 311, 312, 316 fn. 2; 362; in Singapore defences, 370; in battle for Singapore, 376, 377, 378, 381 and fn. 1, 384, 385, 391, 392, 405
2/30th Australian: in Johore, 302–3, 328; in withdrawal to Island, 334, 336, 338, 341 fn. 1; in Singapore

Army—*cont.*
Infantry Battalions—*cont.*
defences, 370; in battle for Singapore, 381, 382, 383, 389, 396, 399, 400 fn. 2
2/40th Australian: in Timor, 347 fn. 2
Special (Australian) Reserve: 362; in battle for Singapore, 376 and fn., 377, 378, 384, 386, 390, 391, 393, 405
Royal Rifles of Canada: to Hong Kong, 82, 113–14, 115; in defence of Island, 127–8, 131, 135, 136, 137 fn., 138, 139, 140, 141, 142–3, 143–4
Winnipeg Grenadiers: to Hong Kong, 82, 113–14, 115; on Mainland, 123–4; in defence of Island, 128, 131, 132, 133–4, 135, 136, 137, 138–9, 140, 141 and fn., 142, 143, 144
6/1st Punjab Regt.: in Singapore defences, 371 fn.; in battle for Singapore, 385, 386
5/2nd Punjab Regt.: 213, 214; in withdrawal to Krian River, 229, 230; on Grik road, 235, 236; in retreat to Kampar, 244; at Slim River, 275–6, 276–7, 281 fn.
7/6th Rajputana Rifles: in Johore, 302 fn. 3, 304, 305, 307
5/7th Rajput Regt.: at Hong Kong, 113, 115; in Mainland operations, 120, 122, 124, 125; in defence of Island, 127 fn. 1, 130–1, 132, 134, 135, 140, 141, 142, 143
1/8th Punjab Regt.: 187 fn. 2; at Jitra, 206, 207; in withdrawal to Gurun, 215; at Gurun, 215, 216; in battle for Singapore, 399; *see also* Jat/Punjab Battalion
7/8th Punjab Regt.: in Singapore defences, 371 fn.; in battle for Singapore, 385, 386
2/9th Jat Regt.: at Jitra, 204, 206, 207, 208, 209, 210 fn.; in battle for Singapore, 386, 391, 393; *see also* Jat/Punjab Battalion
4/9th Jat Regt.: in Johore, 302 fn. 3, 304, 305, 307, 308, 312
2/10th Baluch Regt.: in withdrawal to Island, 335 fn. 2, 337, 338; in battle for Singapore, 389, 396, 399, 400
5/11th Sikh Regt.: at Kuantan, 269; in withdrawal to Johore, 288; in Johore, 328; in withdrawal to Island, 335 fn. 2, 336, 341; in battle for Singapore, 395 fn. 1
2/12th Frontier Force Regt.: at Kota Bharu, 189; at Kuantan, 269, 271, 272; in withdrawal to Island, 335 fn. 2, 341
1/13th Frontier Force Rifles: at Kota Bharu, 189; in withdrawal to Island, 335 fn. 2
1/14th Punjab Regt.: 188; at Jitra, 204, 205; 242 fn. 4; on Selangor coast, 273 fn. 2; in withdrawal to Johore, 288 fn.

Army—*cont.*
Infantry Battalions—*cont.*
2/14th Punjab Regt.: at Hong Kong, 113, 115; in Mainland operations, 124; in defence of Island, 128, 131, 132, 133, 134, 135, 136, 137, 139, 140, 141, 142
5/14th Punjab Regt.: in 'Krohcol', 186 fn. 4, 187, 213; in withdrawal to Krian River, 229; at Kampar, 246; at Slim River, 274, 275, 277, 278, 281 fn.
6/14th Punjab Regt.: in Singapore defences, 371 fn.; in battle for Singapore, 385-6
2/15th Punjab Regt.: in Borneo, 222, 223, 224, 225, 226, 227
2/16th Punjab Regt.: 188 fn. 2; at Jitra, 204, 206, 209; 242 fn. 4; on Selangor coast, 263 fn. 2; in withdrawal to Johore, 287
3/16th Punjab Regt.: in 'Krohcol', 186 fn. 4, 187, 209, 213; in withdrawal to Krian River, 229; on Grik road, 235; 242 fn. 4; on Selangor coast, 273 fn. 2; in Johore, 309, 310, 311, 321, 328; in battle for Singapore, 386, 391
2/17th Dogra Regt.: in Johore, 307 fn. 2; 362; in Singapore defences, 370
3/17th Dogra Regt.: at Kota Bharu, 188, 189; on Selangor coast, 272, 273 fn. 1, 274; in withdrawal to Johore, 288 and fn.; in withdrawal to Island, 335 fn. 2; in battle for Singapore, 399
2/18th Royal Garhwal Rifles: at Kuantan, 193, 269, 270-1; in withdrawal to Island, 335 fn. 2; in battle for Singapore, 389
5/18th Royal Garhwal Rifles: in Johore, 302 fn. 3, 304, 305, 307
4/19th Hyderabad Regt.: at Kota Bharu, 189, 190; 217; on Grik road, 236; in retreat to Kampar, 243; at Slim River, 275, 276, 277, 278, 280, 281 fn.; in Singapore defences, 364; in battle for Singapore, 378, 385, 391
2/1st Gurkha Rifles: at Jitra, 204, 205, 206, 210 and fn.; in withdrawal to Perak River, 236; at Kampar, 246 and fn.; at Slim River, 279, 280, 281 fn.
2/2nd Gurkha Rifles: at Jitra, 206, 208, 210; in retreat to Kampar, 244 fn.; at Kampar, 247; at Slim River, 279, 280, 281 fn.
2/9th Gurkha Rifles: at Jitra, 210; in withdrawal to Gurun, 214; in retreat to Kampar, 244 fn.; at Kampar, 246; at Slim River, 279, 280, 281 fn.; in battle for Singapore, 399
Jat/Punjab: 242 fn. 4; at Kampar, 248; on Selangor coast, 273 and

Army—*cont.*
Infantry Battalions—*cont.*
fn. 1; in withdrawal to Johore, 288; in Johore, 307, fn. 2
Jind (Indian State Forces): in Singapore defences, 371; in battle for Singapore, 377, 385
1st Malay: 16; in battle for Singapore, 400 fn. 4
2nd Malay: in battle for Singapore, 386, 400 fn. 4
Infantry Brigades:
53rd (British): to Malaya, 256, 260, 283; arrives Singapore, 287; in Johore, 306, 309, 311, 313, 320, 321; in withdrawal to Island, 327, 328, 334; in Singapore defences, 369; in battle for Singapore, 395, 399, 400, 401, 412, 414
54th (British): arrives Singapore, 324 fn. 4; 362; in Singapore defences, 369; in battle for Singapore, 400, 412
55th (British): arrives Singapore, 324 fn. 4; 362; in Singapore defences, 369; in battle for Singapore, 400, 412
22nd Australian: arrives Malaya, 75 fn. 1; 168, 285; in Johore operations, 306-7, 332; in Causeway bridgehead, 340; in Singapore defences, 370, 371; in battle for Singapore, 375, 376, 377, 378, 379, 380, 384, 390 and fn. 2, 392, 393, 397, 398, 400 and fn. 1, 403, 405
27th Australian: arrives Malaya, 80 fn. 2; 168, 283; in Johore operations, 302, 303, 313, 321; in withdrawal to Island, 327, 334, 335, 336, 337, 338, 341; in Singapore defences, 370; in battle for Singapore, 379, 382, 383, 389, 396, 406, 407, 411
6th Indian: arrives Malaya, 47 fn. 2; 170; at Jitra, 204, 205, 206, 207, 210; in withdrawal to Gurun, 214-15 at Gurun, 215, 216; in withdrawal to Muda River, 217; in withdrawal to Krian River, 229; absorbed in 15th Indian Brigade, 233
8th Indian: arrives Malaya, 47 fn. 2; 170; at Kota Bharu, 182, 185, 189, 190-1; withdraws from Kelantan, 217; in Johore, 302, 313; in withdrawal to Island, 335, 336, 337, 338, 339, 340-1; to 11th Indian Division, 364 fn. 1; in Singapore defences, 369; in battle for Singapore, 383, 388-9, 397, 399
12th Indian: arrives Malaya, 21, 38; 169, 213; in withdrawal to Krian River, 229-30; on Grik road, 231, 235-6; 242; in retreat to Kampar, 243, 244; condition of troops, 243; at Kampar, 246, 247, 248; at Slim River, 274, 275-8, 281; 285; in withdrawal to Johore, 287, 288; in

Army—*cont.*
  Infantry Brigades—*cont.*
    Singapore defences, 364; in battle for Singapore, 376, 378, 379, 380, 385–6, 390 and fn. 2, 391, 392, 405
  13th Indian: to Burma, 39
  15th Indian: arrives Malaya, 57 fn. 2; 170; at Jitra, 204, 205, 206, 207, 208, 210; in withdrawal to Gurun, 214; at Gurun, 215, 216; in withdrawal to Muda River, 216–17; in withdrawal to Krian River, 229; absorbs 6th Indian Brigade, 233; at Kampar, 242 and fn. 4, 246, 248; on Selangor coast, 273, 287; 285; in withdrawal to Johore, 288; in Johore, 309, 320, 321, 327–30; evacuated by sea, 330–1; in Singapore defences, 369; in battle for Singapore, 379, 380, 385, 386, 390 and fn. 2, 392, 393, 400 fn. 1; 406
  16th Indian: to Burma, 39
  22nd Indian: arrives Malaya, 57 fn. 2; at Kuantan, 170, 193; action at airfield, 269–72; in Johore, 302, 306, 313; in withdrawal to Island, 334, 335, 336, 337, 338, 339; disaster to, 339, 341
  28th Indian: arrives Malaya, 28 fn. 2; 169, 170, 185; at Jitra, 204, 206, 207, 210; in withdrawal to Gurun, 214; at Gurun, 215, 216; in withdrawal to Muda River, 217; in withdrawal to Krian River, 229; 236, 242; in retreat to Kampar, 244; at Kampar, 246; at Slim River, 274, 275, 278, 279, 280, 281, 285; in withdrawal to Johore, 287, 288; in withdrawal to Island, 327, 334; in Singapore defences, 369; in battle for Singapore, 383 fn., 397
  44th Indian: for Malaya, 260, 261; arrives Singapore, 324; 362; in Singapore defences, 364, 370, 371; in battle for Singapore, 379, 380, 384, 386, 390, 398, 400 and fn. 3, 411
  45th Indian: arrives Malaya, 249, 260; 261; in Johore, 285, 302, 304, 305 309, 311–12, 312–13, 315–16
  1st Malaya: in Singapore defences, 364, 370; in battle for Singapore, 386, 398, 400 and fn. 4, 403, 410, 411, 414
  2nd Malaya: in Singapore defences, 364, 370; in battle for Singapore, 400, 412
  East (Hong Kong): in defence of Island, 127–8, 130–1, 132–3, 135–6, 138–9, 140, 142, 143, 143–4, 145
  Island (Hong Kong): 115
  Mainland (Hong Kong): 114–5; operations, 120–5
  West (Hong Kong): in defence of Island, 128, 131, 133–5, 136, 137, 139, 140–1, 142, 143, 144

Army—*cont.*
  Infantry Brigades—*cont.*
    Straits Settlements Volunteer: in Singapore defences, 364, 370
  Machine-Gun Battalions:
    1st Middlesex: at Hong Kong, 113, 115; in defence of Island, 127 fn. 2, 128, 132, 133, 135, 137 fn., 140, 141, 142, 143
    2/3rd Australian: arrives Sumatra, 423 fn.; in Java, 432, 436
    2/4th Australian: 260; arrives Singapore, 324; 325; in Singapore defences, 362, 371; in battle for Singapore, 376, 378, 391, 397 fn. 3, 412
  Pioneer Battalions:
    2/2nd Australian: arrives Sumatra, 423 fn.; in Java, 432, 436, 447
    2/4th Australian: 425
  Reconnaissance Corps:
    18th Battalion: in battle for Singapore, 387 fn., 392, 394

  1st Independent Company: at Gurun, 217; in withdrawal to Krian River, 229 fn.; on Grik road, 231, 235; at Kampar, 246, 247, 248; on Selangor coast, 273 and fn. 1

  2/2nd Australian Independent Company: in Timor, 347, fns. 2 and 3

  Federated Malay States Volunteer Force: 21, 273 fn. 1
  Hong Kong Volunteer Defence Corps: on Mainland, 118, 123; in defence of Island, 128, 132, 133, 135, 137 and fn., 140, 142, 143, 150
  Johore State Forces: 21, 307 fn. 2
  Johore Volunteer Engineers: 307 fn. 2; in battle for Singapore, 378
  Sarawak Rangers: 222, 224
  Sarawak State Forces: 222, 225
  Straits Settlements Volunteers: 219

Ashigara, Jap. cruiser: 435
Athene, H.M.S.: 254 and fn. 1, 357
Atlantic Conference: 72; Churchill's proposal at, 72; U.S. attitude at, 72
Auchinleck, General Sir C.: 252, 257
Australia: enquires about fleet for Singapore, 20; criticizes A.D.A. Agreement, 56; to reinforce N.E.I., 62; air reinforcements from, 253; offers more troops for Malaya, 256–7; on limitation of ABDA area, 266; reluctance to spare forces for ABDA Command, 348, 350

Babington, Air Vice-Marshal J. T.: advocates air defence of Malaya, 26; 31, 32, 48, 49, 57
Backhouse, Brigadier E. H. W., in battle for Singapore: 400
Baldwin Sub-Committee on Singapore Base: 11, 12
Bali, invasion of: 426; Allied naval action, 426–8; landings unopposed, 426, 428
Ballarat, H.M.A.S.: 424

Ballentine, Brigadier G. C.: 370; in battle for Singapore, 379, 384, 386

Banham, Major C. F. W.: 329, 330

Bankert, Dutch destroyer: 443

Barstow, Major-General A. E.: 57 fn. 2, 189; at Kuantan, 270, 271; in withdrawal from Johore, 335, 336, 337; killed 338

Batu Pahat area, operations in: 306, 309–11, 313–14, 315–16, 319–21, 327–30

Beckwith-Smith, Major-General M. B.: in battle for Singapore, 395, 397

Bell, Captain L. H., R.N., 193

Bennett, Major-General H. G.: 57 fn. 1, 203; on need for another Australian division, 258; 282; criticizes III Corps, 283; 285 fn.; in Johore, 302, 303, 304, 305, 306, 307, 309, 314, 316; in withdrawal to Island, 335, 336, 340; 362; commands Western Area (Singapore), 364; his dispositions, 370–1; in battle for Singapore, 376, 377, 378, 379, 381, 384, 387, 390, 394, 400, 406, 407, 408; advocates capitulation, 409–10; 411

Bismarck, Ger. battleship: 85

Blackburn, Brigadier A. S., V.C.: in Java, 436, 446, 447

'Blackforce' (Java): 436, 446, 447, 448

Blake, Major-General D. V. J.: 293

Blamey, General Sir T.: 263 fn. 2

Boise, U.S. cruiser: 297 and fn.

Bond, Major (Lieut.)-General L. V.: urges compulsory service for Malaya, 25; his defence appreciation, 28–30; 31–2, 48, 49, 57; presses for organized military labour, 161

Borneo: Allied air and naval operations, 223, 224, 225

Borneo, British North: not to be defended, 35, 221; 222; occupied by Japanese, 223

Borneo, Dutch: Allied surrender in S.W., 226–7; loss of Balikpapan, 297; loss of Bandjermasin, 352

Bowden, Mr. V. G. (Australia): 203; on urgent need of reinforcement of Malaya, 258

Boyes, Lieut.-Colonel A. H.: 381 fn; killed, 393

Brereton, Major-General L. H. (U.S.): 293, 294 fn. 1

Brooke, General Sir A., 263 fn. 1

Brooke-Popham, Air Chief Marshal Sir R.: appointed C.-in-C. Far East, 50; his directive, 51; his first appreciation, 53; advocates reinforcement of Hong Kong, 56, 57; his 'Matador' plan, 76–7; supports plea for reinforcement of Malaya, 77–8; 80, 82; on forces required to defend Hong Kong, 115; his view of Japanese intentions (Oct.–Nov. 1941), 172–3; raises 'Matador' question, 173, 174–5; asks U.S. to undertake naval and air reconnaissance, 173–4; his authority to launch 'Matador', 175; delays, then cancels, 'Matador', 180, 181–2, 185–6; his Order of the Day, 183–4; urges reinforcement, 192, 255–6; approves withdrawal from Kelantan, 217; hands over command, 241; 458–9

Brunei: 221; not to be defended, 222; occupied by Japanese, 223

Buffalo fighter, performance of: 240, 241, 286

Burma: in Far East Command, 50; difficulty of reinforcing, 54; Japanese intention to invade, 91; transferred to India Command, 253, 254; reinforcements for, 255; Wavell on state of communications in, 255; diversion of forces from, 256; lack of resources for, 260; place in ABDA Command, 265; returned to India Command, 429

Burma Road: closed on demand of Japan, 45–6; reopened, 48

Burnie, H.M.A.S.: 443

Canada agrees to send troops to Hong Kong: 82

Carpendale, Brigadier W. St. J.: 80 fn. 2; at Jitra, 206, 207, 208; 215 fn. 2; at Gurun, 216

Casualties: at Pearl Harbour, 99; Hong Kong (British), 150; Hong Kong (Japanese), 150; in loss of *Prince of Wales* and *Repulse*, 198; 8th Indian Brigade in Kelantan, 217; totals in S.E. Asia area, 473

Causeway (Singapore): bridgehead at, 340; demolition of, 341, 342

Celebes: loss of airfields in, 292–3, 298, 352

Central Provision Office (India): 42

Challen, Brigadier B. S.: in Johore, 309 and fn. 1, 320, 321, 327, 328, 329; captured, 330

Chamberlain, Rt. Hon. N. (Prime Minister): 19; to Australia on fleet for Singapore, 20

Chan Chak, Admiral: 112, 137; escapes from Hong Kong, 145

Chatfield Commission (India): 37, 38

Chiang Kai-shek: British support of, 53; British mission to, 53; receives aid from U.S.A. and Great Britain, 58; anxious that Hong Kong should be defended, 112; promises assistance to Hong Kong, 120; Allied links with, 266–7; Supreme Commander, China theatre, 267–8

Chiefs of Staff Committee: differ on character of Singapore Base defences, 7; discount prospect of landward attack on Singapore, 8; urge abandonment of 'no major war for ten years' assumption, 11; urge increase in defence estimates, 12; review Imperial defence problems, 17; on Hong Kong, 17, 18, 34; consider despatch of fleet to Far East, 19, 34; advise withdrawal of British garrisons in China, 23–4, 34; inform Australia and New Zealand of effect of fall of France, 33; forecast Japanese reaction, 33–4; suggest a settlement with Japan, 34, 45; recommend reinforcement of, and defence preparations in, Malaya, 35–6; propose Singapore conversations with Dutch, 46; promise air and land reinforcements for Malaya, 54; criticize A.D.A. Agreement, 56; refuse reinforcement of Hong Kong, 57; criticize A.D.B. Agreement, 63; their plan for an Eastern fleet, 75; discuss 'Matador', 78; views on Command in Far East, 80; approve reinforcement of Hong Kong, 81; in final discussions on 'Matador', 173, 174, 175; on type of

Chiefs of Staff Committee—*cont.*
  fighter for Far East, 240 fn. 3; policy on naval reinforcement of Far East (Dec. 1941), 252; on military reinforcement, 253; action on air reinforcement, 253, 254; action on military reinforcement, 256; to Wavell on weakening his resources, 259; final decisions on reinforcement of Far East, 259–60; at 'Arcadia' conference, 263, 264, 265, 266; to Wavell on defence of Singapore Island, 317; to Percival on importance of demolitions, 318; urge utmost resistance in Java, 429; return Burma to India Command, 429
China: Japanese demands on, 1; subject of Nine-Power Treaty, 4; protests against Japan's invasion of Manchuria, 10; the 'Shanghai incident', 10; at war with Japan, 18; situation (Sept. 1939), 23; British gunboats withdrawn from, 23; British garrisons withdrawn from, 46, 47; British aid for, 53–4; promises support at Hong Kong and in Burma, 54; her theatre of war defined, 265–6; Allied links with, 266–7
China Squadron reduced in strength: 21, 24
Chinese Army, fire power of division: 120 fn. 1
Chokai, Jap. cruiser: 179, 417
Churchill, Rt. Hon. W. S. (First Lord): on despatch of fleet to Far East, 24
Churchill, Rt. Hon. W. S. (Prime Minister and Minister of Defence): disapproves of large air reinforcement of Far East, 55; his views on Hong Kong, 56; at Atlantic Conference, 72; differs from Admiralty on Eastern Fleet plan, 75–6, 84–5; agrees to reinforcement of Hong Kong, 81; on defence of Hong Kong, 151; to Wavell on reinforcements for Far East, 254–5; asks Middle East to reinforce Malaya, 257; at 'Arcadia' Conference, 263, 264, 265; on defence of Singapore, 318; 459
Cicala, H.M. gunboat: 122, 129, 136; sunk, 139
Civil Defence: Hong Kong, 111; Malaya and Singapore, 25, 158–9, 183, 233–5
Clark-Kerr, Sir A.: 78
Coates, Brigadier J. B.: in battle for Singapore, 384, 386, 391, 393
Collins, Commodore J. A., R.A.N.: 294, 429 436, 438, 443
Collinson, Commodore A. C.: at Hong Kong, 109, 122, 131, 133, 144; 171
Colonial Office: on defence of Malaya, 36; in relation to civil authorities in Far East, 51; on civil defence in Malaya, 159
Colorado, U.S. battleship: 99
Combined Chiefs of Staff: 265, 267; accept dissolution of ABDA Command, 429
Combined Intelligence Bureau (Far East): 51, 240
Committee of Imperial Defence: select Singapore for naval base, 2–3; their view on nature of defences, 7–8; endorse 'no major war' assumption, 8; abandon same, 11; on co-operation with Dutch, 14; 15–16; on prospects of despatch of Fleet to Far

Committee of Imperial Defence—*cont.*
  East (May 1939), 19; raise 'period before relief' of Singapore, 21
Conferences:
  A.D.A. (Singapore): 55–6
  A.D.B. (Singapore): 61–3
  Allied (Singapore): 233
  Anglo-Dutch (Singapore): 51–2, 63
  Anglo-French (Singapore): 20
  'Arcadia': 263–7
  Atlantic: 72
  Defence (Singapore): 49–50
  Duff Cooper (Singapore): 79
  Imperial: (1921), 3; (1923), 6; (1930), 9; (1937), 18; (1939), 24
Craigie, Sir R. 45
Cumming, Lieut.-Colonel A. E., V.C.: 272 and fn. 1
Curzon Committee on Singapore Base: 6–7

'Dalforce': in Singapore defences, 364, 371
Danae, H.M. cruiser: 434, 437
Dane, Squadron Leader H.: 330
Darwin: weakness of garrison, 348; air raids on, 425–6
Deakin, Lieut.-Colonel C. C.: 244, 275–6, 277
Defence Committee (Malaya): 157
Defence Council (Hong Kong): 144
Denial schemes: Kowloon, 124; Penang, 219; N. Borneo, 222, 223; Kuala Lumpur and Port Swettenham, 289; Tarakan, 292; Balikpapan, 297, 298; Singapore, 365–7, 382, 397, 399, 408–9; Palembang, 421
Dennys, Major-General L. E.: 53, 120
De Ruyter, Dutch cruiser: 351, 422, 426, 427, 434, 437 fn. 2, 438, 440, 441; sunk, 442
Dill, Field Marshal Sir J.: 263 fn. 1
Dobbie, Major-General W. G. S.: reports on defence requirements for Malaya, 15–16; 57 fn. 3; 456
Dockyard Defence Corps (Hong Kong): 141 fn. 2
Doi, Colonel: 121–2, 137
Doorman, Rear-Admiral K. W. F. M. (R.N.N.): 351, 352, 422, 426, 427, 437, 438, 439, 440, 441; lost in his flagship, 442
Dragon, H.M. cruiser: 434, 437
Dragonfly, H.M. gunboat, 329, 330
Duff Cooper, Mr.: his conference at Singapore, 79; his report, 79–80; on Command in Far East, 80; his broadcast on loss of two capital ships, 199; appointed Resident Minister for Far East, 202; his terms of reference, 202–3; presides over Allied conference, 233; to Prime Minister on civil defence in Singapore, 233–4; to War Council on same, 234; to Colonial Secretary on same, 295
Duke, Brigadier C. L. B.: in Batu Pahat operations, 306, 309, 310, 311, 313–14, 328, 329
Duke of York, H.M. battleship: 263
Duncan, Brigadier H. C.: at Muar, 302, 304, 305, 307, 308, 311; killed 313
Durban, H.M. cruiser: 398

'Eastforce' (Johore): formed, 307; 315; in withdrawal to Island, 327, 332–4

Eastern Fleet: necessity for despatch, 17, 19, 20; difficulty of providing, 34; long-term plan for, 75, 252; diverse views on composition of, 75–6, 85; rôle in defence of Malay Barrier, 171; absorbs China Squadron, 172; loss in action of capital ships, 193–9; *see also* Z, Force

Eastern Group Supply Council: 42

Economic warfare complications with Japan: 23

Electra, H.M. destroyer: 194, 198, 437 and fn. 2, 439; lost 440

Elrington, Lieut.-Colonel M.: 314

Empire Star, s.s.: 398

Encounter, H.M. destroyer: 437 and fn. 2, 440, 441, 442; sunk, 443

Endau, enemy landing at: 331–2

Enterprise, U.S. aircraft carrier: 99

Evertsen, Dutch destroyer: lost, 442

Exeter, H.M. cruiser: 357, 422, 436, 437 fns. 1 and 2, 439, 440, 442; sunk 443

Express, H.M. destroyer, 194, 196

Far East, Commander-in-Chief: *see* Brooke-Popham

Flame throwers, Japanese: 143

Ford, U.S. destroyer: 437 fn. 2, 443

Fortress Command (Singapore): 360–1; in Singapore defences (Southern Area), 364, 370

Galleghan, Lieut.-Colonel F. G.: 336, 338, 381

Garrett, Brigadier K. A.: 57 fn. 2; at Jitra, 204, 205; missing, 206; 215 fn. 2

Gemas, action at: 302–3

Geneva Disarmament Conference: 12

Germany: leaves League of Nations, 12; invades Rhineland, 16; enters Czechoslovakia, 19; denounces London Naval Treaty, 19; starts war in Europe, 21, 23; invades Russia, 65

Gillman Committee on Singapore Base: 8

Gindrinkers Line (Hong Kong): as defensive position, 114; Japanese advance to, 120; action on, 121–4; withdrawal from, 124–5

Glassford, Rear (Vice) - Admiral W. A. (U.S.N.): 233, 294; conducts raid on Balikpapan, 297–8; 429, 443

Gneisenau, Ger. battle cruiser: 85

Grasett, Major-General A. E.: advocates reinforcement of Hong Kong, 81; 112, 113

Greater East Asia Co-Prosperity Sphere: 44, 63, 69

Gurun position: withdrawal to, 214–15; state of, 215; dispositions, 215; attacks on, 215, 216; withdrawal from, 216–17

Haguro, Jap. cruiser: 438, 441

Harrison, Colonel A. M. L.: 280

Hart, Admiral T. C. (U.S.N.): 86, 171, 180 fn. 3, 294, 351, 422, 429 fn., 434, 471

Haruna, Jap. battleship: 195

Hata, General: 113

Heath, Lieut.-General Sir L., 57: his dispositions in N. Malaya, 169–70; 180, 185; favours withdrawal on east coast, 191; 207; orders delaying action from Jitra, 209; 209 fn.; takes over 'Krohcol', 213; urges withdrawal from Gurun, 216; orders evacuation of Penang, 219; withdraws to Krian River, 229; 236; withdraws from Perak River, 238; selects rear positions, 242; 247; orders abandonment of Kuantan airfield, 270, 271; 273; plans defence of Kuala Lumpur, 272–3; reinforces coastal flank, 273; at Slim River, 280; 282; orders withdrawal to Johore, 282, 287–8; in Johore, 306, 307, 309, 316, 320, 321; in withdrawal to Island, 328, 329, 330, 334, 340, 342; commands Northern Area (Singapore), 369; in battle for Singapore, 380, 387, 395, 397, 399, 407; advises capitulation, 409–10; 461, 465

Helfrich, Vice-Admiral C. E. L. (R.N.N.): 171, 294, 426, 429 and fns., 434, 436, 437, 438; leaves N.E.I., 443; 471

Hermes, H.M. aircraft carrier: 252

Hobart, H.M.A. cruiser: 357, 422, 434, 437

Holme, Lieut.-Colonel: 229

Homma, Lieut.-General: 100

Hong Kong: unsuitable as naval base, 2, 18; an 'outpost', 17, 18, 34–5; isolated by Japanese forces, 19; situation (Sept. 1939), 21–2; question of reinforcing, 56–7; reinforcement approved, 81; Canadian troops sent, 82, 113–14; extent of colony, 107; the Island, 107; the Leased Territories, 107–8; the inhabitants, 108; climate, 108; water supply, 108–9, 111; defence scheme, 109; coastal armament, 109; naval forces, 109; beach defences, 110, 111; air forces, 110; security measures, 110; air raid precautions, 111; food reserves, 111; isolation and threatened attack, 111–2; women and children evacuated, 112; the Chinese mission, 112; Japanese provocative actions 112, 117; garrison and expected reinforcements, 113–14; defence scheme revised, 114–15; combatant strength of garrison, 115; two disabilities, 116; naval responsibilities, 116; reports and intelligence concerning Japanese, 116, 117; precautionary measures, 117, 118; enemy dispositions prior to attack, 118

Hong Kong, invasion and loss of: frontier demolitions, 119; air raid on Kai Tak, 119; Japanese advance, 119–20; removal of naval stores, 120; threats from seaward, 120, 129; action on Gindrinkers Line, 121–4; evacuation of airfield, 123; plan for withdrawal from Mainland, 124; Kowloon denial scheme, 124; withdrawal to Island, 124–5, 126; fifth-column activities, 126, 127, 130, 131; the dynamite 'incident', 126; surrender refused, 127, 128–9; Island defence plan and dispositions, 127–8; first landing attempt, 128; enemy plan of attack, 130; the landings, 130, 133; loss of Lye Mun peninsula, 131; the fight for Wong Nei Chong Gap, 131, 132, 133–5,

Hong Kong, invasion and loss of—*cont.*
137–8, 139, 141; withdrawal in East, 132; MTB attack in harbour, 133; resistance on north shore, 133, 140, 142, 143; counter-attack along Repulse Bay, 135–6; counter-attacks in Aberdeen area, 136, 139; loss of Mount Nicholson, 137; report of Chinese assistance, 137; counter-attack towards Tai Tam Gap, 137–8; defence of Stanley peninsula, 140, 141, 142, 143, 144; the Wan Chai Gap area, 140, 141, 142, 143, 144; surrender of Colony, 145; retrospect, 145–51; casualties, 150
Hore, Major F.: 385
Houston, U.S. cruiser: 351, 424, 425, 434, 437 fn. 2, 439, 441; sunk, 442; 445
Hughes, Colonel A. W.: 133
'Hughesiliers': 133
Hurricanes: arrive Singapore, 287; in action, 323–4; performance of, 324
Hutton, Lieut.-General T. J. (Burma), 293, 299

Ilgen, Major-General G. A.: 444
Imamura, Lieut.-General: 291
India: her responsibilities in war, 36–7; modernization of Army and R.A.F., 37–8; first troops sent overseas, 38; expansion of Army, 38–9; deficiencies and handicaps of forces, 39–40; re-equipment and state of R.A.F., 40, 41; production of war material, 41; as source of supplies for Far East, 41–2; drain on Army, 251; her part in reinforcement of Malaya, 253, 254, 255–6, 259, 260, 261
Indian Ocean: strategic importance of, 251
Indo-China: entered by Japanese forces, 44; British negotiations with, 45; dominated by Japan, 61; occupation by Japan completed, 70
Indomitable, H.M. aircraft carrier: 85, 252, 257, 350
Infiltration tactics of Japanese: Malaya, 214, 216, 271; Singapore, 376, 388, 399, 412, 414
Inouye, Vice-Admiral: 103, 105
Italy: aligned with Germany, 16; invades Albania, 19; her pact with Germany, 19
Ito, Major-General: 119, 139

Japan: in First World War, 1–2; her demands on China, 1; her mandates in Pacific, 2, 4, 5; signatory to Four and Nine-Power Treaties, 4–5; her Alliance with Great Britain abrogated, 5; her 'Liberal' Government, 5–6; change to aggressive policy, 9; occupies Manchuria, 10; creates Manchukuo state, 10; the Shanghai 'incident', 10; leaves League of Nations, 12; invades N. China, 12; denounces Washington Naval Treaty, 13; enters into Anti-Comintern Pact, 16; contravenes Nine-Power Treaty, 18; at war with China, 18; requests withdrawal of foreign garrisons and gunboats from China, 23; demand on

Japan—*cont.*
N.E.I. for raw materials, 43, 46–7, 60; 65; change of Government (July 1940), 43–4; her new policy, 44; enters Indo-China, 44; secures closure of Burma Road, 45–6; signs Tripartite Pact, 46; signs neutrality pact with Russia, 59–60; gains control over Indo-China and Siam, 60–1; negotiations with U.S.A., 64–5, 72, 73–4, 82–4, 86–8; her policy (April 1941), 63–4; her policy which led to war (June 1941), 66–7; occupies S. Indo-China, 70; embargo on her trade, 70–1; warned by U.S.A. and Great Britain, 73; committed to war, 74; decides date for opening hostilities, 88
Japanese Army:
Southern Army: 93, 94, 95, 96, 221, 286, 301
14th Army: 93, 95; invades Philippines: 100
15th Army: for invasion of Siam and Burma, 93, 95, 178
16th Army: 93, 95; invades N.E.I., 291
25th Army: 93, 95; invades Malaya, 177–8, 230, 334; at Singapore, 373, 383, 414
96th Airfield Battalion: in Malaya, 332
Guards Reconnaissance Battalion: in Malaya, 320
Brigades:
9th Infantry: in Malaya, 177, 203, 207, 246, 303
21st Infantry: in Malaya, 303
65th Independent: 93, 94
Divisions:
3rd Air: 93, 95; in Malaya, 179, 191, 201; in N.E.I., 444
5th Air: 93, 95; in Philippines, 101
Imperial Guards: 93, 95; in Malaya, 177, 178, 301, 303, 327; at Singapore, 372, 383; to Sumatra, 449
2nd Infantry: 93, 95; in Java, 435, 444, 445
5th Infantry: 93, 95; in Malaya, 177, 178, 179, 180 fn. 2, 203, 204 fn. 2, 210, 238, 243, 244, 273, 301, 302, 303, 319, 327; at Singapore, 372, 380, 394
16th Infantry: 93, 94; in Philippines, 100, 101
18th Infantry: 93, 95, 116; in Malaya, 177, 178, 301, 327, 334; at Singapore, 372, 380, 393, 394, 397, 400, 410
38th Infantry: 93, 94, 95, 116, 118; at Hong Kong, 119, 130, 146; in Sumatra, 417
48th Infantry: 93, 95; in Philippines, 100, 101; in Java, 435, 444
51st Infantry: 116, 120 fn. 2
56th Infantry: 93, 95, 178
104th Infantry: 116, 120 fn. 2
Mukaide Detachment in Malaya: 302, 303
55th Regimental Group: 94
56th Regimental Group: 93, 95; in N.E.I., 292, 297, 352, 435, 444
Regiments:
4th Guards: in Malaya, 178, 238, 243, 248, 273, 288, 303, 304, 305, 307,

Japanese Army—*cont.*
  Regiments—*cont.*
    308, 311, 319, 320; at Singapore, 382, 401
    5th Guards: in Malaya, 285, 303, 304, 308, 309, 311, 320, 330 fn 1.
    11th Infantry: in Malaya, 177, 203, 207, 273
    21st Infantry: 177 and fn. 2; in Malaya, 285, 301
    41st Infantry: in Malaya, 177, 203, 204 fn. 2, 207, 246, 273
    42nd Infantry: in Malaya, 177, 203, 230, 246, 273, 281
    55th Infantry: in Malaya, 269, 301, 334
    56th Infantry: in Malaya, 177, 178, 269, 301; at Singapore, 397, 410
    114th Infantry: in Malaya, 286; at Singapore, 397
    124th Infantry: 178; in Borneo, 223
    143rd Infantry: 178, 179, 180 fn. 1
    144th Infantry: 94
    228th Infantry: at Hong Kong, 119, 121, 130, 131, 134, 137, 139, 141, 143; casualties, 150; in Amboina, 348, 349; in Timor, 428
    229th Infantry: at Hong Kong, 119, 130, 131, 132–3, 138, 139, 142, 143, 144; casualties, 150; in Sumatra, 417
    230th Infantry: at Hong Kong, 119, 130, 131, 134, 137, 138, 139, 142, 143; casualties, 150; in Sumatra, 417; in Java, 435, 444, 445
    5th Reconnaissance: in Malaya, 204 fn. 2, 334 fn.
    1st Tank: at Singapore: 372
    14th Tank: at Singapore, 373
  South Sea Detachment, 94; in Pacific, 103, 105
Japanese Navy:
  1st Air Fleet: at Pearl Harbour, 98; in Pacific, 104, 105
  11th Air Fleet: organized, 64; 90, 94, 95; in Malaya, 179; in N.E.I., 291
  China Area Fleet: 94
  2nd Fleet: in Philippines, 100; in N.E.I., 291
  3rd Fleet: in Philippines, 100
  4th Fleet: in Pacific, 103, 105
  6th Fleet: at Pearl Harbour, 98
  Southern Force: 94, 95; at Malaya, 179
  South Sea Force (Pacific): 94
  Striking Force (Pacific): 94
  21st Air Flotilla: in Philippines, 100, 103; in N.E.I., 291, 292, 293, 298, 425; attacks Darwin, 426; 428
  22nd Air Flotilla: 95; sinks *Prince of Wales* and *Repulse*, 195–8
  23rd Air Flotilla: in Philippines, 100, 103; in N.E.I., 291, 292, 297, 298, 352
  24th Air Flotilla: 94; in Pacific, 103
  2nd Destroyer Flotilla: 95; in N.E.I., 428, 435, 438
  3rd Destroyer Flotilla: 95; in N.E.I., 435
  4th Destroyer Flotilla: 95; in N.E.I., 438, 440

Japanese Navy—*cont.*
  5th Destroyer Flotilla: 95; in N.E.I., 435
  3rd Battle Squadron (2nd Division): 94
  2nd Carrier Squadron: in N.E.I., 348
  4th Carrier Squadron: 94
  4th Cruiser Squadron: 94
  5th Cruiser Squadron: 94
  7th Cruiser Squadron: 94; at Malaya, 179, 195; in N.E.I., 417, 435
  8th Cruiser Squadron: at Pearl Harbour, 98
  16th Cruiser Squadron: 94
  Kure 1st Special Naval Landing Force: in N.E.I., 348, 349
  Kure 2nd Special Naval Landing Force: in N.E.I., 292, 297
  Sasebo Special Naval Landing Force: in N.E.I., 352
  Yokosuka 1st Special Naval Landing Force: in N.E.I., 292
  Yokosuka 2nd Special Naval Landing Force: in Borneo, 223
  Yokosuka 3rd Special Naval Landing Force: in N.E.I., 428
Japanese strategy: economic influence on, 89–90; influence of weather, 90; land and air forces available, 90; sequence of major offensives, 90–1; the three periods, 91–2; three phases of opening operations, 92–3; deployment and tasks of naval and military forces, 93–5; timetable of initial attacks, 96
Java, Dutch cruiser: 192, 422, 426, 427, 434, 437 fn. 2, 441; sunk, 442
Java, invasion and loss of: situation in, 431; Allied air strength, 431–2; military forces, 432–3; naval forces, 433; air attacks on Island, 433; Allied naval dispositions, 434; enemy forces, 434–5; signs of invasion, 435; defence plan, 435–6; Java Sea battle, 437–43; enemy landings, 443, 444, 445; Allied air attacks, 443, 444, 445; Japanese progress, 444, 445, 446, 447; occupation of Sourabaya, 444; occupation of Batavia, 446; attitude of local population, 447, 448; Allied capitulation, 448–9
Java Sea, Battle of the: 437–42, 443
Jintsu, Jap. cruiser: 438, 439, 441
Jitra: position occupied, 203; state of defences, 204; dispositions, 204; the covering forces, 204–6; Japanese attacks, 206–8; withdrawal from, 209–10; retrospect, 210–13
John D. Edwards, U.S. destroyer: 437 fn. 2; 443
Johore: defence forces for, 21, 169; defence plans, 282, 284–5; withdrawal to, 288–9; operations in, 301–16, 319–21, 331–9; plans for withdrawal from, 316–17, 334, 340; airfields abandoned, 322; withdrawal to island, 340–2; restrospect, 342–6
Jupiter, H.M. destroyer: 437 and fn. 2, 438, 440; sunk, 441

Kampar: retreat to, 243–5; dispositions at, 245–6; action at, 246–8; withdrawal from, 248
Kashii, Jap. light cruiser: 179
Kawamura, Major-General: 207

Keith Simmons, Major-General F.: 316, 319, 361; commands Southern Area (Singapore), 370; in battle for Singapore, 380
Kelantan: withdrawal from, 217
Kellogg-Briand Pact: 8, 10
Key, Brigadier B. W.: 47 fn. 2; at Kota Bharu, 182, 188–9, 190; conducts withdrawal from Kelantan, 217; in Johore, 306, 309, 311, 313–14, 320 and fn. 2, 321; in withdrawal to Island, 328, 329, 334; in battle for Singapore, 383, 387, 388–9, 395, 396, 399, 407
King, Admiral (U.S.N.): 266
Kondo, Vice-Admiral: 94, 100, 179, 195, 291, 435, 443
Kongo, Jap. battleship: 195
Kortenaer, Dutch destroyer: 427, 437 fn. 2; sunk, 440
Kota Bharu: landings near, 182, 188, 189; air attacks on Japanese, 182, and fn. 2, 189; airfields abandoned, 189–90; withdrawal southward from, 190
'Krohcol' (Malaya): 170; start delayed, 184–5, 186; operations, 186–7, 207, 209, 212; withdrawal of, 213–14; disbanded, 229
Kuala Lumpur: occupied by Japanese, 289; denial scheme, 289
Kuantan: losses on airfield at, 192–3; false alarm at, 193; attacks at, 269, 270, 271, 272; airfield abandoned, 271–2
Kubo, Rear-Admiral: 427
Kuching (Sarawak): defence of airfield, 222; air attack on town, 223; airfield abandoned, 224–5
Kudat, H.M.S.: sunk, 245
Kurita, Rear-Admiral: 179, 195, 435

Labuan Island: 221; occupied by Japanese, 223
Laman, Major F. E. K.: 330
Landings, Assault, by Japanese: Hong Kong, 130; Kota Bharu, 182, 188, 189; Borneo, 224; Utan Melintang, 247, 248; Kuala Selangor attempt, 273; Endau, 331–2; Singapore, 375–6, 382; Palembang, 421–2
Lane, Lieut.-Colonel C. M.: 222, 224, 225
Langley, U.S. seaplane tender: sunk, 430
Lawson, Brigadier J. K.: 113; commands Island Brigade (Hong Kong), 114; commands West Brigade, 128; 131, 132; killed, 134
Lay, Brigadier W. O.: 47 fn. 2; at Jitra, 206, 207; at Gurun, 215, 216; in Johore, 302; in withdrawal to Island, 335, 336, 337, 338
Layton, Vice-Admiral Sir G.: 48, 49; produces 'Plenaps' plan, 86; 171, 173–4, 180; to command Eastern Fleet, 199; his view on naval strategy, 252; 295
Leach, Captain, J. C., R.N.: 193; lost in *Prince of Wales*, 198
League of Nations: 2, 4, 8, 10, 11; withdrawal of Germany and Japan, 12
Ledge, The (Siam): 170, 184, 185, 186, 187
Lexington, U.S. aircraft carrier: 99
Li Wo, H.M. patrol vessel: 418
Lyon, Brigadier: at Penang, 218, 219

Lyons, Rt. Hon. J. A. (P.M. Australia): seeks assurance on despatch of fleet to Singapore, 20

MacArthur, Lieut.-General D. (U.S.): 70 fn. 2, 103, 263 fn. 2, 293
Malaya: new airfields for, 14; involved in defence of Singapore Naval Base, 15, 26; development of defence policy, 15–16, 25–30, 35–6, 48–50, 52–3; 54–5, 77–8; defence situation (Sept. 1939), 21; economic v. defence interests, 24, 25; civil defence and Volunteer Force difficulties, 25; Service differences, 31–3; Colonial Office orders state of readiness, 36; pre-War reinforcement of, 39, 41, 47, 57, 80; 'Matador' plan, 76–7; terrain and climate, 153–4; railways and roads, 154–5; the variety of peoples, 155–6; constitution of Government, 157; defence administration, 157–8; air raid precautions, 158; observer system, 158–9; civil defence, 159; food reserves, 159–60; labour supply and control, 160–2; air forces at outbreak of War, 162–3; land forces, 163; characteristics of jungle warfare, 164; quality of the troops, 164–5; efficiency of staffs, 165–6; training difficulties, 166, 167, 168; under-estimation of enemy, 166–7; shortage of equipment, 168; the Volunteer forces, 168–9; the defence scheme, 169–71; defensive positions, 170–1; doubt as to Japanese intentions, 172–3; 'Matador' in question, 173, 174–5; Allied naval and air reconnaissance, 173–4
Malaya, invasion and loss of: Japanese plans, 177–9; Allied reconnaissance, 179–80, 181; 'Matador', 180, 181–2, 184, 185, 186; landings at Kota Bharu, 182, 188, 189; R.A.F. in action, 182, 191–2, 193, 202; air attacks on northern airfields, 184, 192, 201; operations of 'Krohcol', 186–8, 207, 209, 212; advance into Siam from northwest, 188; withdrawal from Kota Bharu, 188, 189, 190; R.A.F. losses, 192, 193, 201 false alarm at Kuantan, 193; invasion in north-west, 203, 204–6; Jitra, 203–4, 206–13; Gurun, 214–16; withdrawal from Kelantan, 217; Penang, 218–19; R.A.F. success at Butterworth, 218; withdrawal continued in west, 229–30; 230–1; 235–8; air situation, 232; evacuation of northern airfields, 238–40; R.A.F. reconnaissance and attacks continued, 241, 248; Kampar, 243–8; Kuantan, 269–72; Selangor coast operations, 272, 273–4; Slim River, 274–81; plans for defence of Johore, 282, 284–5; reorganization of forces, 285; air operations, 286–7; withdrawal to Johore, 288–9; the losing battle in Johore, 301–16, 319–21; plans for withdrawal to Island, 316–17, 334, 340; Allied air operations, 322, 323–4; Johore airfields abandoned, 322; air bases moved to N.E.I., 323; air protection of convoys, 324; arrival of reinforcements, 324; quality of same, 325; air and naval attacks on Endau convoy, 331–2; enemy

Malay, invasion and loss of—*cont.*
landing at Endau, 331–2; withdrawal from Johore to Island, 334–9, 340–2; Johore retrospect, 342–6
Malaya: States and Territories of, 157
Malay Barrier: naval forces for defence of, 171, 252; no combined defence plan, 172; importance of, 263; shattered, 449
Maltby, Air Vice-Marshal P. C.: 388 and fn. 1; in Java, 429, 431, 449
Maltby, Major-General C. M.: 81, 112; reviews Hong Kong defence scheme, 113–15; his intelligence reports, 116–17, 118; 120, 122; orders abandonment of Kai Tak airfield, 123; orders withdrawal from Mainland, 124; his defence plan for Island, 127–8; 131, 132, 134, 136, 138, 139, 141; his decision to surrender, 144; 149 fns. 1 and 2
Manila occupied by Japanese: 103
Manners, Major C. M.: 144
Marblehead, U.S. cruiser: 297 and fn., 298, 351
Marshall, General G. C. (U.S.): at 'Arcadia' Conference, 264, 266
Maruyama, Lieut.-General: 449
Massy-Beresford, Brigadier T. H.: in battle for Singapore, 395, 397, 399
'Massy Force': in battle for Singapore, 395, 397, 398, 399, 400
'Matador' operation: plan for, 76–7; discussed, 78; difficulties of, 170; final discussions on, 173, 174–5; authority to launch, 175; reasons for delay, 180–2; abandoned, 184–5, 185; 186
Matsui, General: 303
Maxwell, Brigadier D. S.: 80 fn. 2; at Gemas, 303; in withdrawal to Island, 336; in battle for Singapore, 381, 382, 389, 395–6, 406, 407
'Merrett's Force': in battle for Singapore, 384, 390 fn. 2, 391, 393, 394
Mines, anti-tank: in Malaya, 275 fn., 276, 277, 281; in battle for Singapore, 392
Moir, Brigadier R. G.: in Malaya, 272, 273, 288
Moorhead, Lieut.-Colonel H. D.: commands 'Krohcol', 186, 187, 235; commands 15th Indian Brigade, 242 fn. 2; at Kampar, 248; on Selangor coast, 273–4; to battalion command, 309 fn.; killed, 311
Morrison, Lieut.-Colonel C. E.: 248, 330
Motor Torpedo Boat Flotilla, 2nd: at Hong Kong, 110, 125, 128, 129, 133, 145–6
Muar area: dispositions in, 302; operations, 303–5, 307–8, 311–12
Murray-Lyon, Major-General D. M.: 47 fn. 2, 170; at Jitra, 204, 205, 206, 207, 208, 209, 211, 212–13; in withdrawal to Gurun, 214; at Gurun, 215–16; orders withdrawal, 216; in withdrawal behind Perak River, 236; 242

Nachi, Jap. cruiser: 438, 441
Nagumo, Vice-Admiral: 94, 98, 99, 425, 435, 443
Naka, Jap. cruiser: 438
Natori, Jap. cruiser: 60

Naval detachments at Hong Kong: 131, 134, 139
Netherlands East Indies: defence of, discussed, 14; question of co-operation with, 34; strength of air force, 35 fn. 1; Japan's demands on, for raw materials, 43, 46–7, 60, 65; staff conferences and conversations with, 51–2, 55–6, 61–3, 63; her embargo on Japanese trade, 70, 71; naval and air forces reinforce British, 192; to be reinforced from Middle East, 260, 261; in ABDA Command, 267
Netherlands East Indies, invasion and loss of: Japanese plan, 291–2; Allied air and naval operations, 292, 297–8; loss of Tarakan, 292; loss of Menado airfield, 292–3; loss of Balikpapan, 297, 298; naval action at Balikpapan, 297–8; loss of Kendari airfield, 298; threat to Timor, 347; loss of Amboina, 348–9; air attacks on Java, 351; air attacks on Allied naval forces, 351; loss of Bandjermasin and Makassar, 352; Sumatra as air base, 355, 356–7; threat to Sumatra, 357–8; occupation of Sumatra, 417, 419–22, 423–4; Allied naval action, 422–3, 426–8; loss of Bali, 426; loss of Timor, 428; dissolution of ABDA Command, 429; conditions in Java, 431–3; defence dispositions, 434–6; Java Sea battle, 437–43; enemy landings in Java, 443, 444, 445; land operations, 444, 445, 446, 447; Allied capitulation, 448–9; occupation of Sumatra completed, 499
New Zealand presses for fleet in Far East: 18
Nicholetts, Group Captain G. E.: 424 fn.
Niimi, Vice-Admiral: 128, 129
Nishimura, General: 303, 307, 319, 383, 401
Nishimura, Rear-Admiral: 297, 298, 435, 438
Noble, Admiral Sir P.: 45, 48 fn. 1
Noble, Wing Commander: 182
Northcote, Sir G.: 113
Northern Area Command (Singapore): 369; in battle for Singapore, 383, 387, 389–90, 395, 396–7, 398, 399–400, 401

Oakes, Major R. F.: 381 and fn., 382, 383, 396
Osborn, C. S.-M. J. R., V.C.: 133–4
Oversea Defence Committee: composition of, 27; views on defence of Singapore and Malaya, 27–8; favour compulsory service, 30
Ozawa, Vice-Admiral: 179, 291, 417, 423

Pacific Islands, Japanese conquest of: 103–5
Painter, Brigadier G. W. A.: 57 fn. 2; at Kuantan, 193, 270, 271; in Johore, 302; in withdrawal to Island, 335–6, 337; forced to surrender, 339
Palembang (Sumatra) evacuated: 421, 424
Palliser, Admiral A. F. E.: 180; his signals to Force 'Z', 194, 195; 294, 429, 442, 443
Paratroops, Japanese, in N.E.I.: 292–3, 419–20, 421, 428
Paris, Brigadier A. C. M.: 213–14; in withdrawal to Krian River, 229, 230; on Grik

Paris, Brigadier A.C.M.—*cont.*
  road, 235, 236; commands 11th Indian
  Division, 242; in Kampar operations, 242,
  243–4, 247, 248; at Slim River, 274, 275,
  276, 278, 280; in withdrawal to Johore,
  288; commands 12th Indian Brigade, 306
  fn. 4; in Singapore defences, 364; in battle
  for Singapore, 378, 384, 392, 407; fate of,
  419
Parker, Lieut.-Colonel P. W.: 396
Paul Jones, U.S. destroyer: 437 fn. 2., 443
Pearl Harbour: Japanese plan of attack, 64,
  97–8; the attack, 99; U.S. losses, 99
Peary, U.S. destroyer: 424; sunk, 425
Peirse, Air Marshal Sir R.: 293, 294 fn. 1, 353
Penang: garrison, 21; threat to, 218; air raids
  on, 218; evacuation accepted, 218; plight
  of the Island, 219; evacuation ordered, 219;
  the denial scheme, 219
Perak Flotilla: 233; first action, 245; heavy
  losses from air attack, 245; state of, 274
Percival, Lieut.-General A. E.: 57; his estimate of Malaya's defence needs, 77; presses
  for organized military labour, 161; his
  defence dispositions, 169; 180, 185, 190,
  207, 209, 213, 216, 217; his orders for
  Borneo, 224; on 2/15th Punjab Regt., 227;
  decides to withdraw behind Perak River,
  231–3; his action to provide labour for
  field defences, 242; agrees to Kampar withdrawal, 247; his request for 53rd Brigade,
  256; his policy for Kuantan airfield, 270
  fn.; on defence of Kuala Lumpur, 272;
  plans defence of Johore, 282; his future
  plans, 282–3; reorganizes forces, 285; 293;
  his control of Johore operations, 306, 309,
  311, 313, 315, 320, 321, 328–9, 330; his
  plan for withdrawal to Island, 316–17; on
  difficulties of Singapore denial scheme, 318;
  his defence plan for Island, 319; to Wavell
  on crisis in Johore, 339; decides on immediate withdrawal, 340; 362; his appreciation and fresh Singapore defence plan,
  363–4; to Chiefs of Staff on denial scheme,
  366; his reassurances to civil population,
  367–8; controls battle for Singapore, 376,
  379, 380, 387, 394, 395, 397, 398; to
  Wavell on enemy summons to surrender,
  398; orders perimeter defence, 399; defects
  of his defence plan, 404–5; resolves to continue resistance, 410; reports to Wavell,
  410, 411; his action on water supply, 411;
  his decision to capitulate, 412–13; agrees to
  unconditional surrender, 414–15; 415; his
  last message to ABDA Command, 415;
  461, 465
Perlis: evacuated, 205; protest by Sultan,
  205
Perth, H.M.A. cruiser: 436, 437 fns. 1 and 2,
  439, 441; sunk, 442; 445
Philippines: Japanese plan of invasion, 100;
  attacks launched, 101; Manila occupied,
  103; conquest completed, 103
Phillips, Admiral Sir Tom: commands Eastern
  Fleet, 85, 86, 171; 172, 173, 180 fn. 3, 181;
  his plea for air reinforcements, 192; his
  plan for naval intervention, 193–4; his

Phillips, Admiral Sir Tom—*cont.*
  handling of Force 'Z', 194–5, 196; lost
  with his flagship, 198; 463–4
Playfair, Major-General I. S.O.: 293
'Plenaps' plan: 86
Pond, Lieut.-Colonel S. A. F.: 385, 392
Poorten, General H. ter: 52 fn.; 293, 356, 358,
  429, 436, 446, 447; capitulates in Java, 448
Pope, U.S. destroyer: 442; sunk, 443
Portugal: attitude over Timor, 347
Pownall, Lieut.-General Sir H.: 80; his directive as C.-in-C. Far East, 241–2; 253, 263
  fn. 2; Chief of Staff ABDA Command, 267;
  293, 295, 356, 388 fn. 1
Prince of Wales, H.M. battleship: 85, 171, 173,
  193; in Force 'Z', 194, 195, 196, 197;
  sunk, 198; casualties, 198
Pulford, Air Vice-Marshal C. W. H.: 57; his
  Air Command, 162; 182, 184; orders withdrawal from Kota Bharu airfield, 189;
  orders bomber attacks, 191; 192–3; on
  reconnaissance and protection for Force
  'Z', 194; 202, 203, 239, 332, 353; withdraws fighters to Sumatra, 381; leaves
  Singapore, 410; fate of, 418

'Q' Denial Scheme (Singapore): 365

Ramsay, Major G. E.: 381, 389, 396
Repulse, H.M. battle cruiser: 85, 171; in Force
  'Z', 194, 195, 196; sunk, 197–8; casualties,
  198
Retrospect, General: state of Great Britain
  (1919), 451; new order of sea power, 451–2;
  economy to detriment of Services, 452,
  453; re-armament too slow, 453; Second
  World War—military weakness in Far
  East, 453–4; unprepared Malaya, 454–5;
  Japan a growing menace, 455; lack of
  Allied unity, 455–6, 469–70; Malaya's
  defence problem, 456, 459; over-optimism
  as regards Japan, 456–7, 458–9; effect of
  sanctions on Japan, 458; weakness of
  Singapore Naval Base, 460; initiative held
  by Japan, 460–1; Malaya's defence plan,
  461; the initial disasters, 461–4; the race
  against time, 464; troubles of the
  Malayan campaign, 465–6, 467; the reinforcement problem, 466–7; battle for
  Singapore, 467–8; Wavell's verdict, 468;
  the case of Hong Kong, 469; naval and
  air weakness in N.E.I., 469–71; effects of
  loss of Malaya and Singapore, 471–3; comparison of casualties in S.E. Asia area, 473;
  moral effect of Japanese victories, 474
Robin, H.M. gunboat, 129, 139, 144
Roosevelt, Mr. F. D. (President U.S.A.): to
  Japan on Indo-China, 70; at Atlantic
  Conference, 72; his warning to Japan, 73;
  his plea to Emperor of Japan, 118; at
  'Arcadia' Conference, 264
Rose, Colonel H. B.: 136, 137, 141
'Roseforce' (Malaya): 233 and fn.; in coastal
  raid, 245; on Selangor coast, 273 and fn. 1

Royal Air Force:
  223 (225) Bomber Group: 323; at Endau, 331; 368–9
  226 (Fighter) Group: 323
  1 (General Reconnaissance) Squadron: 180
  8 (General Reconnaissance) Squadron: 193
  11 (Bomber) Squadron: 21 fn. 2
  27 (Bomber) Squadron: 41, 369 fn.
  34 (Bomber) Squadron: 21 fn. 2, 191, 224, 241, 369 fn.
  36 (Torpedo Bomber) Squadron: 21 fn. 2; at Endau, 331, 332
  39 (Bomber) Squadron: 21 fn. 2
  60 (Bomber) Squadron: to Burma, 41
  62 (Bomber) Squadron: 21 fn. 2, 191, 369 fn.
  84 (Bomber) Squadron: 369 fn.
  100 (Torpedo Bomber) Squadron: 21 fn. 2; at Endau, 331, 332
  205 (Flying Boat) Squadron: 21 fn. 2
  211 (Bomber) Squadron: 369 fn.
  230 (Flying Boat) Squadron: 21 fn. 2
  232 (Fighter) Squadron: at Singapore, 323, 324; in Java, 445
  453 (Fighter) Squadron: 202; action at Penang, 218; 239
  605 (County of Warwick) Squadron, R. Auxiliary Air Force: 424 fn.
Royal Australian Air Force:
  2 (Bomber) Squadron at Timor: 347 fn. 2
  13 (Bomber) Squadron at Amboina: 348
Royal Marines: at Hong Kong, 142; at Singapore, 364 fn. 2
R.N.V.R. at Hong Kong: 133 fn.
Rubber production in Malaya: 24 and fn. 4
Russia: *see* U.S.S.R.
Ryujo, Jap. aircraft carrier: 101, 291, 417, 423

Sakai, Lieut.-General T.: 127, 128–9, 144
Sano, Lieut.-General: 130, 417
Sansom, Sir G.: 203
Saratoga, U.S. aircraft carrier: 99, 104
Sarawak: 221; the oilfields, 222–3; evacuated, 225; *see also* Kuching
'Sarfor' (Borneo): formed, 222; disbanded, 225
Scarf, Squadron Leader A. S. K., V.C.: 191
Scharnhorst, Ger. battle-cruiser: 85
Schilling, Major-General W.: 436, 446, 447
Scorpion, H.M. gunboat: 330
Scout, H.M. destroyer: 109, 233
Seawitch s.s.: 430
Selangor coast operations: 272, 273–4
Selby, Lieut.-Colonel: 242 fn. 2; commands 28th Indian Brigade at Kampar, 246; at Slim River, 278, 280
Sendai, Jap. light cruiser: 178
Shanghai 'incident': 10
Shields, Mr. A. H. L.: 144
Shing Mun Redoubt (Hong Kong): 121
Siam: 20; advance into, suggested, 48; Japan's relations with, 60–1; Japan's plan to invade, 177–8; Japanese landings in, 183, 203; British advances into, 186, 188
Simson, Brigadier I. (D.G.C.D. Singapore): 234–5, 295

Singapore: airfield and seaplane base approved, 7; pre-War garrison of, 21, 169; first air attack on, 183; defences of north shore, 285, 317, 360; ineffective A.A. defence, 286–7; civil defence, 295; difficulties of denial scheme, 318; defence plan, 318–19; increased air raids on, 323, 324; British air losses, 324; provision of labour, 325–6; state of airfields, 353; aircraft based on Sumatra, 354; town and coast line, 359; roads, 359; population, 359; water supply, 360; fixed defences, 360, 361; labour difficulties, 360, 365; beach defences, 361; A.A. defences, 362; strength of garrison, 362; condition of troops, 362–3; defence areas and dispositions, 364–5, 369–71; enemy agents, 365; denial schemes, 365–7; arrival of last convoy, 368; air attacks on dock area, 368; air defence, 369
Singapore, loss of: Japanese plan, 372–3; bombardment, 373; indications of attack, 373–4; the landings, 375–6, 382; air operations, 376, 381; withdrawal to Jurong Line, 377–80, 384; raid in Johore Strait, 380–1; withdrawal in Causeway sector, 382, 383; Jurong Line abandoned, 384–6; counter-attack in Causeway sector, 383, 389; counter-attack towards Jurong Line prepared, 390–1; Bukit Timah, 391–3, 394; the Jurong road, 393–4; 395–7; evacuation and demolition of naval base, 397; summons to surrender, 398; evacuation by sea, 398, 410; coastal batteries in action, 399, 410; withdrawal to perimeter, 399–401; morale of troops, 401, 403; capitulation inevitable, 403; problems of the defence, 403–4; defects of the defence plan, 404–5; conduct of the battle, 405–6; the subordinate commanders, 406–8; denial schemes, 408–9; water supply, 409, 411, 412, 412–13, 413 fn.; food and ammunition reserves, 409, 412; question of capitulation, 409–10; attacks on the perimeter, 410–11, 411–12; plight of the town, 412–13; surrender, 414–15; perils of flight by sea, 417–19
Singapore Naval Base: site approved, 2–3; Commonwealth views on, 6, 9; delays in construction, 6, 7, 8, 9, 11; fixed defences v. air defence, 7, 8, 11–12; attack from Mainland discounted, 7, 8, 15; inter-Service defence plan approved, 12; dependence on arrival of Fleet, 13, 15, 17, 21; period before relief, 17, 21, 28; state of defences (Sept. 1939), 21; departure of Force 'Z', 194; denial scheme, 365; evacuation of naval and dockyard personnel, 365; scale of destruction, 366; evacuation and final demolitions, 397, 408
Singkawang II airfield (Dutch Borneo): importance of, 222; air raid on, 223–4; ground defence of, 225–6; supplied by air, 225; evacuated, 226
Singora (Siam): Japanese landings at, 183, 203; British air attacks on, 191–2
Sitwell, Major-General H. D. W.: in Java, 429, 430, 436, 446, 447, 449

Slim River: dispositions, 274–5; action at, 276–81; causes of disaster, 281
Southern Area Command (Singapore): 370; in battle for Singapore, 398, 400
Spooner, Rear-Admiral E. J.: 171, 365, 409; leaves Singapore, 410; fate of, 418
Stachouwer, Jhr. Dr. A. W. L. T. van S.: 263 fn. 2, 429
Steedman, Lieut.-Colonel J. F. D.: 214
Stewart, Lieut.-Colonel I. McA.: 213, 235; commands 12th Indian Brigade, 242 fn. 2; in retreat to Kampar, 243; at Slim River, 275, 276, 277, 278; commands battalion in battle for Singapore, 385
Stilwell, Major-General J. W. (U.S.): 267
Straits Settlements' view on costs of Singapore Base: 8
Stronghold, H.M. destroyer: sunk, 443
Sturdee, Lieut.-General V. A. H.: 348
Sugawara, Lieut.-General: 179
Sumatra: strategic importance of, 353; terrain and climate, 354; roads, railways and communications, 354–5; economic importance, 355; Palembang airfields, 355–6; garrison, 356; reinforcements expected, 356; Allied air strength, 356; air strikes against Malaya, 356–7; enemy air attacks, 357; naval and air reconnaissance from, 357–8; invasion convoy located, 358; failure of British air attack, 358; invasion convoy sails, 417; Allied air attacks, 419, 420, 421–2; Allied forces in Palembang area, 420; paratroop landings, 420, 421; loss of Palembang and airfields, 420–2; Allied naval action, 422–3; Allied forces leave for Java, 423; Japanese occupation continued, 424; occupation completed, 449
Suzuki, Colonel: 110–1
Swan, H.M.A. sloop: 424, 425

Takagi, Rear-Admiral: 435, 438
Takahashi, Vice-Admiral: 100, 292, 298, 348, 434
Tanaka, Colonel: 132, 138, 417
Tanaka, Rear-Admiral: 428
Tanks, Allied, in Java: 445
Tanks, Japanese: in advance from Siam, 187, 188; in advance to Jitra, 205; at Jitra, 206, 211, 212; at Gurun, 215; 230; in advance to Kampar, 244; at Slim River, 273, 276, 277, 278, 279, 280, 281; in Johore, 303, 308, 315, 316, 321; in battle for Singapore, 387, 391, 392, 393, 394, 398, 399, 400, 405, 411, 412; in Java, 444
Taylor, Brigadier H. B.: 57 and fn. 1; in Johore, 307; in withdrawal to Island, 332; 370; in battle for Singapore, 376, 377, 378, 379, 384, 390, 391, 394; 400
Templer, Major C. R.: 138
Tenedos, H.M. destroyer: 194, 196 and fn. 1, 198
Tennant, Captain W. G., R.N.: 193, 197, 198
Terauchi, General Count: 94
Tern, H.M. gunboat: 122
Tester, Lieut.-Colonel C. K.: 288

Thanet, H.M. destroyer: 109; sunk, 332
Thomas, Lieut.-Colonel L. C.: 387, 394
Thomas, Sir Shenton: opposes conscription in Malaya, 25; advocates air and naval defence, 26; his memorandum on civilian manpower, 28; accepts offer of Chinese population, 155; orders destruction of broadcasting station and currency in Singapore, 399; orders completion of civil defence denial schemes, 408; to Colonial Office on situation, 411
Thracian, H.M. destroyer: 109, 125, 128, 140
Timor (Dutch): reinforced, 347; importance of Kupang airfield, 347; invasion, and capture of Kupang, 428; Australian guerrilla warfare in, 428
Timor (Portuguese): Allied troops land in, 347; captured by Japanese, 428
Tin production in Malaya: 24
Tirpitz, Ger. battleship: 85
'Tomforce' in battle for Singapore: 387, 394, 397, 398, 399, 408
Transport aircraft, lack of: 262
Treaties:
  Anglo-German (Naval): 13; consequences of, 13; denounced by Hitler, 19
  Four-Power: 4
  London (Naval): 9
  Nine-Power: 4; contravened by Japan, 18
  Washington Naval: 3–4; denounced by Japan, 13
Tripartite Pact: 46
Tromp, Dutch cruiser: 351, 422, 426, 427, 434 fn.
Trott, Brigadier W. A.: in battle for Singapore, 388, 396
Tsukahara, Vice-Admiral; 291

Under-estimation of Japanese: 116–17, 147, 166, 195, 240 and fn. 3
U.S.A.: part in Washington Naval Treaty, 3–4; in Four-Power and Nine-Power Treaties, 4; in London Naval Treaty, 9; her reaction to Tripartite Pact, 46, 47; her possible actions to deter Japan, 58; in Allied discussions on Far East defence, 58, 61–2, 63, 76, 86, 233; gives assistance to Chiang Kai-shek, 58; her negotiations with Japan, 64–5, 72, 73–4, 82–4, 86–8; puts embargo on Japanese trade, 70; warns Japan, 73; her attitude on eve of war, 172, 175; her part in formation of ABDA Command, 264–7
U.S. forces:
  Asiatic Fleet: 62, 86, 100, 171, 172
  Far Eastern Air Force: 100–1
  Pacific Fleet: 96, 97–100
  Task Force (N.E.I.): 233
  49th Battalion, 148th Field Artillery Regiment: 424–5
U.S.S.R. signs neutrality pact with Japan: 59–60; invaded by Germany, 65

Vampire, H.M.A. destroyer: 194, 198, 332
Van Oyen, Major-General: 429

Varley, Brigadier A. L.: in battle for Singapore, 400
Vested interests in Singapore: 408

Waller, Captain H. M. L., R.A.N.: 442
Wallis, Brigadier C.: commands Mainland Brigade (Hong Kong), 114, 120, 121, 122, 123, 125; commands East Brigade (Island), 127, 129, 131, 132, 135–6, 137, 138, 140, 142, 143; surrenders at Stanley, 145; 149 fn. 1
War Committee (Malaya): 157
War Council (Malaya): composition of, 203; agrees on no retreat from Jitra, 207; accepts evacuation of Penang, 218; their decision on civil defence, 234; decides on no compulsion of labour, 236
War Office: advocate fixed defences for Singapore Base, 7, 12; accept Dobbie's proposals for Malaya, 16; on Far East situation, 27; concentrate on defence of Singapore Base, 31; in relation to military Commands, 51
Warrego, H.M.A. sloop: 424
Wavell, General Sir A.: on lack of labour in Malaya, 162; his proposals for defence of Burma, 255; on need of air reinforcements for Malaya, 255; offers troops for Malaya, 255, 256; protests at weakening of his forces, 259; his lack of troops for Burma, 260; 263 fn. 2; appointed to ABDA Command, 264, 265, 267; first visit to Malaya, 283–4; his ABDA strategy, 283, 296; his plan for defence of S. Malaya, 284–5; on Japanese ineffective use of air superiority, 286; 293–4; second visit to Malaya, 294–5; on civil defence in Singapore, 295; his problem in S.E. Asia, 295–7; visits Burma, 299; on Johore and defence of Singapore, 316; third visit to Malaya, 317; his suggestions for defence of Island, 318–19; approves evacuation of Mainland, 340; his efforts to reinforce Kupang, 348; strengthens air defences of Java and Sumatra, 350–1; visits Singapore, 353; approves transfer of air bases to Sumatra, 354; tries to reinforce Sumatra, 356, 358; orders naval concentration off Java, 358; his last visit to Singapore, 387, 388; orders final transfer of R.A.F. to N.E.I., 388; reports to Churchill, 388, 403; to Percival

Wavell, General Sir A.—*cont.*
on continued resistance, 410, 411; last message to Percival, 414; has no hope of holding Java, 424; suggests diverting I Australian Corps to Burma, 424; orders convoy from Darwin to return, 425; to Chiefs of Staff on weakness of air forces in Java, 428, 430; recommends dissolution of ABDA Command, 429; leaves to resume India Command, 430; his orders to British forces in Java, 430; rules out naval demonstration towards Java and China seas, 434; 467, 468
Western Area Command (Singapore): 370–1; in battle for Singapore, 375–80; 381–3, 384–7, 388, 390–4, 395–6, 397–8, 398–9, 399 fn., 400–1, 405–8
'Westforce' (Johore): formed, 285, 289; in Johore operations, 302–6, 307–9, 311, 313, 314, 315, 321; in withdrawal to Island, 327, 329, 334–9, 340
Wilkinson, Lieut. T., R.N.R., V.C.: 418
William B. Preston, U.S. seaplane tender: 425
Williams, Brigadier G. G. R.: in battle for Singapore, 386
Witte de With, Dutch destroyer: 437 fn. 2, 440; lost 443

X Battalion in battle for Singapore: 381 fn., 390 fn. 2, 391, 393

Yamamoto, Admiral: 64, 94
Yamashita, Lieut.-General: 177, 238, 243, 269, 273, 301, 372, 383; summons Singapore to surrender, 398
Yangtze 'incident': 18
Yarra, H.M.A. sloop: 368; sunk, 443
Young, Sir Mark: 112; refuses to surrender Hong Kong, 128–9; surrenders, 144; 151

Zero fighter, superiority of: 240 and fn. 3, 286, 324
'Z' Force (Hong Kong): 150
'Z', Force (Eastern Fleet): its objective, 193–4; leaves Singapore, 194; air reconnaissance and fighter cover, 194; withdrawal, 194–5; course for Kuantan, 195; 196; enemy naval and air movements, 195–6; loss of two capital ships, 197–9

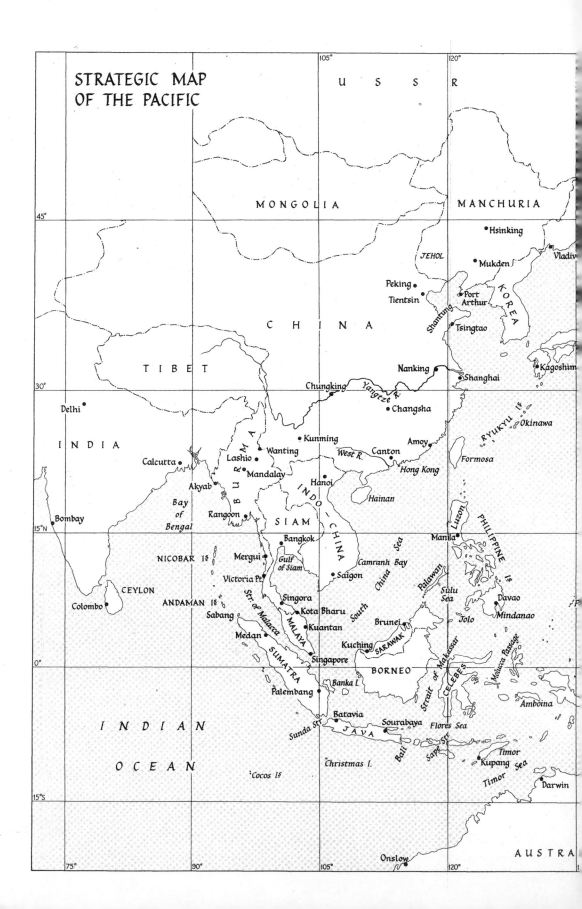

STRATEGIC MAP
OF THE PACIFIC

U   S   S   R

MONGOLIA

MANCHURIA

•Hsinking

•Mukden

Vladiv

JEHOL

Peking•
Tientsin

•Port
Arthur

Tsingtao

KOREA

Shantung

CHINA

Nanking

•Shanghai

Kagoshim

Delhi•

TIBET

Chungking

Yangtze R.

Changsha

RYUKYU Is

•Okinawa

INDIA

Kunming

Wanting

West R.

Canton

Amoy

Formosa

Calcutta•

Lashio•

Mandalay

Hanoi

Hong Kong

Hainan

Akyab

BURMA

Bay
of
Bengal

Rangoon•

SIAM

INDO-CHINA

Luzon

Manila•

PHILIPPINE Is

Bombay•

Bangkok

NICOBAR Is

Mergui•

Gulf
of Siam

Camranh Bay

Palawan

Sulu
Sea

Davao

Victoria Pt•

Saigon

South China Sea

Jolo

Mindanao

CEYLON

ANDAMAN Is

Singora

Kota Bharu

Brunei

Molucca Passage

Colombo•

Sabang•

Str. of Malacca

Kuantan

MALAYA

Kuching

SARAWAK

CELEBES

Medan•

SUMATRA

Singapore

BORNEO

Strait of Makassar

Palembang•

Banka I.

INDIAN

Batavia

Sourabaya

Flores Sea

Amboina

OCEAN

Sunda Str.

JAVA

Bali

Sape Str.

Timor
Kupang

Timor
Sea

Christmas I.

•Cocos Is

Darwin

Onslow

AUSTRA

45°

105°

120°

30°

15°N

0°

15°S

75°

90°

105°

120°

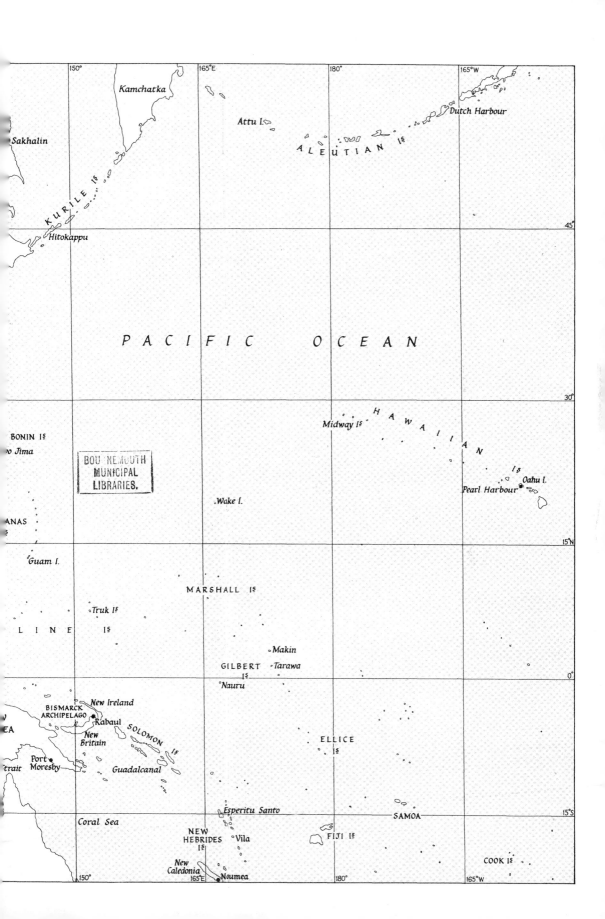

150°

Kamchatka

165°E

Attu I.

180°

165°W

Dutch Harbour

Sakhalin

A L E U T I A N   I^S

K U R I L E   I^S

Hitokappu

45°

P A C I F I C   O C E A N

30°

BONIN I^S

o Jima

BOU NEMOUTH
MUNICIPAL
LIBRARIES.

Midway I^S

H A W A I I A N

I^S

Oahu I.

Pearl Harbour

Wake I.

15°N

ANAS

Guam I.

MARSHALL I^S

Truk I^S

L I N E   I^S

Makin

GILBERT   Tarawa
I^S

0°

Nauru

New Ireland

BISMARCK
ARCHIPELAGO   Rabaul

EA

New
Britain

SOLOMON   I^S

Port
Moresby

Guadalcanal

ELLICE
I^S

trait

Esperitu Santo

Coral Sea

SAMOA

15°S

NEW
HEBRIDES   Vila
I^S

FIJI I^S

New
Caledonia
165°E   Noumea

COOK I^S

150°

180°

165°W

HISTORY OF
THE SECOND WORLD WAR
UNITED KINGDOM MILITARY SERIES

Reprinted by the Naval & Military Press in twenty two volumes with the permission of the Controller of HMSO and Queen's Printer for Scotland.

THE DEFENCE OF THE UNITED KINGDOM

Basil Collier

Official history of Britain's home front in the Second World War, from the Phoney War, through the Battle of Britain and the Blitz to victory in Europe.
ISBN: 1845740556
Price £22.00

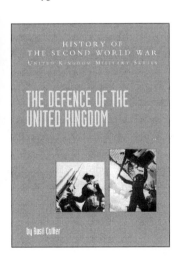

THE CAMPAIGN IN NORWAY

T. H. Derry

The catastrophic 1940 campaign which caused the downfall of Neville Chamberlain and brought Winston Churchill to power.
ISBN: 1845740572
Price: £22.00

THE WAR IN FRANCE AND FLANDERS 1939-1940

Major L. F. Ellis

The role of the BEF in the fall of France and the retreat to Dunkirk.
ISBN: 1845740564
Price £22.00

VICTORY IN THE WEST
Volume I: The Battle of Normandy

Major L. F. Ellis

The build-up, execution and consequences of D-Day in 1944.
ISBN: 1845740580
Price: £22.00

Volume II: The Defeat of Germany

Major L. F. Ellis

The final stages of the liberation of western Europe in 1944-45.
ISBN: 1845740599
Price £22.00

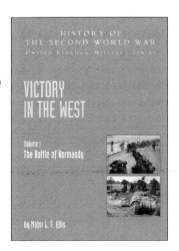

THE MEDITERRANEAN AND MIDDLE EAST

Volume I: The Early Successes against Italy (to May 1941)

Major-General I. S. O. Playfair

Britain defeats Italy on land and sea in Africa and the Mediterranean in 1940.
ISBN: 1845740653
Price: £22.00

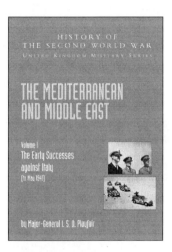

Volume II: The Germans Come to the Help of their Ally (1941)

Major-General I. S. O. Playfair

Rommel rides to Italy's rescue, Malta is bombarded, Yugoslavia, Greece and Crete are lost, and Iraq and Syria are secured for the Allies.
ISBN: 1845740661
Price: £22.00

Volume III: (September 1941 to September 1942) British Fortunes reach their Lowest Ebb

Major-General I. S. O. Playfair

Britain's darkest hour in North Africa and the Mediterranean, 1941-42.
ISBN: 184574067X
Price: £22.00

Volume IV: The Destruction of the Axis Forces in Africa

Major-General I. S. O. Playfair

The battle of El Alamein and 'Operation Torch' bring the Allies victory in North Africa, 1942-43.
ISBN: 1845740688
Price: £22.00

Volume V: The Campaign in Sicily 1943 and the Campaign in Italy — 3rd Sepember 1943 to 31st March 1944

Major-General I. S. O. Playfair

The Allies invade Sicily and Italy, but encounter determined German defence in 1943-44.
ISBN: 1845740696
Price: £22.00

Volume VI: Victory in the Mediterranean Part I: 1st April to 4th June 1944

Brigadier C. J. C. Molony

The Allies breach the Gustav, Hitler and Caesar Lines and occupy Rome.
ISBN: 184574070X
Price: £22.00

Volume VI: Victory in the Mediterranean Part II: June to October 1944

General Sir William Jackson

The 1944 Italian summer campaign breaches the Gothic Line but then bogs down again.
ISBN: 1845740718
Price: £22.00

Volume VI: Victory in the Mediterranean Part III: November 1944 to May 1945

General Sir William Jackson

The messy end of the war in Italy, Greece, and Yugoslavia.
ISBN: 1845740726
Price: £22.00

THE WAR AGAINST JAPAN

Volume I: The Loss of Singapore

Major-General S. Woodburn Kirby

The fall of Hong Kong, Malaya and Singapore in 1941–42.
ISBN: 1845740602
Price: £22.00

Volume II: India's Most Dangerous Hour

Major-General S. Woodburn Kirby

The loss of Burma and Japan's threat to India in 1941–42.
ISBN: 1845740610
Price: £22.00

Volume III: The Decisive Battles

Major-General S. Woodburn Kirby

Turning the tide in the war against Japan at the battles of Kohima, Imphal and the Chindit campaigns.
ISBN: 1845740629
Price: £22.00

Volume IV: The Reconquest of Burma

Major-General S. Woodburn Kirby

The reconquest of Burma by Bill Slim's 'forgotten' 14th Army.
ISBN: 1845740637
Price: £22.00

Volume V: The Surrender of Japan

Major-General S. Woodburn Kirby

Victory in South-East Asia in 1945 – from Rangoon to Nagasaki.
ISBN: 1845740645
Price: £22.00

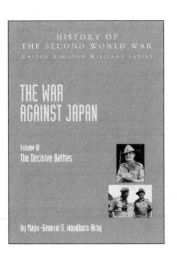

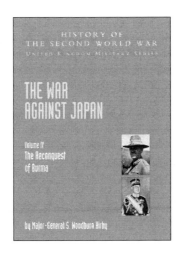

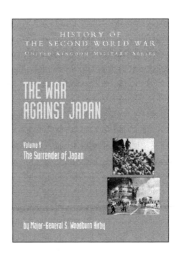

THE WAR AT SEA - 1939—1945

Captain Roskill has long been recognised as the leading authority on The Royal Navy's part in the Second World War. His official History is unlikely ever to be superceded. His narrative is highly readable and the analysis is clear. Roskill describes sea battles, convoy actions and the contribution made by technology in the shape of Asdic & Radar.

Volume I: The Defensive

Captain S. W. Roskill, D.S.C., R.N.

2004 N&MP reprint (original pub 1954).
SB. xxii + 664pp with 43 maps and numerous contemporary photos.
ISBN: 1843428032
Price: £32.00

Volume II: The Period of Balance

Captain S. W. Roskill, D.S.C., R.N.

2004 N&MP reprint (original pub 1956).
SB. xvi + 523pp with 42 maps and numerous contemporary photos.
ISBN: 1843428040
Price: £32.00

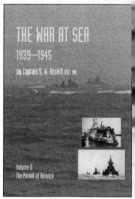

Volume III: Part I The Offensive
1st June 1943-31 May 1944

Captain S. W. Roskill, D.S.C., R.N.

2004 N&MP reprint (original pub 1960).
SB. xv + 413pp with 21 maps and numerous contemporary photos.
ISBN: 1843428059
Price: £32.00

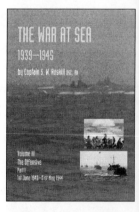

Volume III: Part 2 The Offensive
1st June 1944-14th August 1945

Captain S. W. Roskill, D.S.C., R.N.

2004 N&MP reprint (original pub 1961).
SB. xvi + 502pp with 46 maps and numerous contemporary photos.
ISBN: 1843428067
Price: £32.00

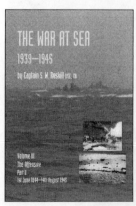